Fodor's 2003

London

The Guide
for All Budgets

Completely
Updated

Where to Stay, Eat,
and Explore

On and Off
the Beaten Path

When to Go,
What to Pack

Maps, Travel Tips,
and Web Sites

Fodor's Travel Publications • New York, Toronto, London, Sydney, Auckland
www.fodors.com

Fodor's London 2003

EDITOR: Diane Mehta

Editorial Contributors: Stephanie Adler, Catherine Belonogoff, Jacqueline Brown, Heather Elton, Julius Honnor, Alex Wijeratna
Editorial Production: Ira-Neil Dittersdorf
Maps: David Lindroth, *cartographer*; Rebecca Baer and Bob Blake, *map editors*
Design: Fabrizio La Rocca, *creative director*; Guido Caroti, *art director*; Jolie Novak, *senior picture editor*; Melanie Marin, *photo editor*
Cover Design: Pentagram
Production/Manufacturing: Robert B. Shields
Cover Photograph: Jodi Cobb/National Geographic *(Regent's Park)*

Copyright

ISBN 1-4000-1033-0

ISSN 0149-631X

Important Tip

Although all prices, opening times, and other details in this book are based on information supplied to us at press time, changes occur all the time in the travel world, and Fodor's cannot accept responsibility for facts that become outdated or for inadvertent errors or omissions. So **always confirm information when it matters,** especially if you're making a detour to visit a specific place.

Special Sales

Fodor's Travel Publications are available at special discounts for bulk purchases for sales promotions or premiums. Special editions, including personalized covers, excerpts of existing guides, and corporate imprints, can be created in large quantities for special needs. For more information, contact your local bookseller or write to Special Markets, Fodor's Travel Publications, 280 Park Avenue, New York, NY 10017. Inquiries from Canada should be directed to your local Canadian bookseller or sent to Random House of Canada, Ltd., Marketing Department, 2775 Matheson Boulevard East, Mississauga, Ontario L4W 4P7. Inquiries from the United Kingdom should be sent to Fodor's Travel Publications, 20 Vauxhall Bridge Road, London SW1V 2SA, England.

PRINTED IN THE UNITED STATES OF AMERICA

10 9 8 7 6 5 4 3 2 1

CONTENTS

Maps

ON THE ROAD WITH FODOR'S

THE MORE YOU KNOW before you go, the better your trip will be. London's most fascinating small museum or its most delightful pub could be just around the corner from your hotel, but if you don't know it's there, it might as well be on the other side of the globe. That's where this book comes in. It's a great step toward making sure your next trip lives up to your expectations. As you plan, check out the Web as well. Guidebooks have been helping smart travelers find the special places for years; the Web is one more tool. Whatever reference you consult, be savvy about what you read, and always consider the source. Images and language can be massaged to make places appear better than they are. And one traveler's quaint is another's grimy. Here at Fodor's, and at our on-line arm, Fodors.com, our focus is on providing you with information that's not only useful but accurate and on target. Every day Fodor's editors put enormous effort into getting things right, beginning with the search for the right contributors—people who have objective judgment, broad travel experience, and the writing ability to put their insights into words. There's no substitute for advice from a like-minded friend who has just come back from where you're going, but our writers, having seen all corners of London, are the next best thing. They're the kind of people you'd poll for tips yourself if you knew them.

Stephanie Adler worked for three years as an editor at Fodor's before donning wellies and heading into the English countryside. While updating the Side Trips chapter this year, she took particular pleasure in playing the old-fashioned slot machines on Brighton Pier and following Harry Potter's footsteps around Oxford.

Born and raised in San Francisco, **Catherine Belonogoff** started travel writing during her college days when she wrote part of the *Fodor's UpClose Los Angeles* guide. After graduating from UC Berkeley, she roamed the globe from Moscow to Cape Town, staying three years in Vilnius, Lithuania, where among other things she updated the Baltic States chapter for *Fodor's Europe*. She currently resides in north London and updated the London Lodging and Smart Travel Tips chapters.

No matter how many historical and cultured cities she has explored across Europe, writer and editor **Jacqueline Brown** declares there are equal treasures not far from her own doorstep. A London resident for more than 20 years, she has found both the best and the quirkiest places, as her recent *Fodor's Around London with Kids* testifies. Jacqueline has updated the Exploring and Shopping sections of this book.

Born in Calgary, Alberta Canada, freelance writer and photographer **Heather Elton** now lives in London. She founded two Canadian art magazines, *Last Issue* and *Dance Connection,* and has written extensively about the arts and contemporary dance. She also wrote *Banff's Best Dayhikes,* a hiking guide in the Canadian Rockies. When not in the theatre or gallery, she can be found visiting ancient stone circles, ski touring on glaciers in the Canadian Rockies or the Alps, or practicing yoga (in a performance context). She is co-director of Vanguard Arts Association, a UK organization dedicated to performance and training in movement disciplines. For this edition she updated the Nightlife and the Arts chapter.

Julius Honnor, our Outdoor Activities and Sports updater, has traveled widely but now lives in London. He currently works for a company that makes tailored travel books. He enjoys playing sports in his free time and is a keen viewer of all things sports-related.

Londoner born and bred, **Alex Wijeratna** is a stalwart of Notting Hill. With English/Sri Lankan roots, Alex is well aware that London's true flavor lies in its ethnic diversity. He has written mainly for newspapers, including the *Times*. And he's chuffed that London has emerged as a top-notch foodie city. For this edition, he updated the Dining chapter.

Don't Forget to Write

Your experiences—positive and negative—matter to us. If we have missed or misstated something, we want to hear about it. We follow up on all suggestions. Contact the London editor at editors@fodors.com or c/o Fodor's, 280 Park Avenue, New York, New York 10017. And have a fabulous trip!

Karen Cure
Editorial Director

ESSENTIAL INFORMATION

ADDRESSES

Central London and its surrounding districts are divided into 32 boroughs—33, counting the City of London. More useful for finding your way around, however, are the subdivisions of London into postal districts. Throughout the guide we've given the full postal code for most listings. The first one or two letters give the location: N means north, NW means northwest, etc. Don't expect the numbering to be logical, however. You won't, for example, find W2 next to W3. The general rule is that the lower numbers, such as W1 or SW1, are closest to the city center. Post codes are also added to streets to differentiate one Main St. from another Main St. in a different borough.

AIR TRAVEL TO AND FROM LONDON

BOOKING

When you book **look for nonstop flights** and **remember that "direct" flights stop at least once.** Try to avoid connecting flights, which require a change of plane. Two airlines may operate a connecting flight jointly, so ask if your airline operates every segment of the trip; you may find that the carrier you prefer flies you only part of the way. For more booking tips and to check prices and make on-line flight reservations, log on to www.fodors.com.

CARRIERS

British Airways is the national flag carrier and offers mostly nonstop flights from 18 U.S. cities to Heathrow and Gatwick airports, along with flights to Manchester, Birmingham, and Glasgow. As the leading British carrier, it has a vast program of discount airfare–hotel packages.

➤ TO AND FROM LONDON: **American Airlines and TWA** (☏ 800/433–7300; 020/8572–5555 in London, WEB www.aa.com, WEB www.twa.com) to Heathrow, Gatwick, and Glasgow. **British Airways** (☏ 800/247–9297; 0845/773–3377 in London, WEB www.britishairways.com) to Heathrow, Gatwick. **Continental** (☏ 800/231–0856; 0800/776464 in London, WEB www.continentalairlines.com) to Heathrow, Gatwick, and Glasgow. **Delta** (☏ 800/241–4141; 0800/414767 in London, WEB www.delta.com) to Gatwick. **Northwest Airlines** (☏ 800/447–4747; 0870/507–4074 in London, WEB www.nwa.com) to Gatwick. **United** (☏ 800/241–6522; 0845/844–4777 in London, WEB www.ual.com) to Heathrow. **US Airways** (☏ 800/622–1015; 0845/600–3300 in London, WEB www.usairways.com) to Gatwick. **Virgin Atlantic** (☏ 800/862–8621; 01293/747747 in London, WEB www.virgin-atlantic.com) to Heathrow, Gatwick, and Glasgow.

➤ WITHIN EUROPE: **British Airways** (☏ 800/247–9297; 0845/773–3377 in London, WEB www.britishairways.com). **British Midland** (☏ 800/788–0555; 020/8745–7321 in London, WEB www.flybmi.com). **Buzz** (☏ 0870/240–7070 in London, WEB www.buzzaway.com). **Easyjet** (☏ 0870/600–0000 in London, WEB www.easyjet.com). **Go** (☏ 0870/607–6543 in London, WEB www.gofly.com). **Ryanair** (☏ 0870/156–9569 in London, WEB www.ryanair.com). **Virgin Atlantic** (☏ 800/862–8621; 01293/747747 in London, WEB www.virgin-atlantic.com).

CHECK-IN & BOARDING

Check-in at least three hours in advance for trans-Atlantic flights and at least two hours in advance for European or domestic flights in order to have enough time to pass security control and board your flight.

Assuming that not everyone with a ticket will show up, airlines routinely overbook planes. When everyone does, airlines ask for volunteers to give up their seats. In return, these volunteers usually get a certificate for a free flight and are rebooked on the next flight out. If there are not enough volunteers, the airline must choose who will be denied boarding. The first to get bumped are passengers who checked in late and those flying on discounted tickets, so get to the gate and **check in as early as possible,** especially during peak periods.

Always **bring a government-issued photo I.D. to the airport;** even when it's not required, a passport is best.

CUTTING COSTS

The least expensive airfares to London are priced for round-trip travel and must usually be purchased in advance. Airlines generally allow you to change your return date for a fee; most-low fare tickets, however, are nonrefundable. It's smart to **call a number of airlines,** and when you are quoted a good price, **book it on the spot**—the same fare may not be available the next day. Always **check different routings** and look into using alternate airports. Also, price off-peak flights, which may be significantly less expensive than others. Travel agents, especially low-fare specialists (☞ Discounts & Deals), are helpful.

Consolidators are another good source. They buy tickets for scheduled international flights at reduced rates from the airlines, then sell them at prices that beat the best fare available directly from the airlines. Sometimes you can even get your money back if you need to return the ticket. Carefully read the fine print detailing penalties for changes and cancellations, purchase the ticket with a credit card, and **confirm your consolidator reservation with the airline.**

When you **fly as a courier,** you trade your checked-luggage space for a ticket deeply subsidized by a courier service. There are restrictions on when you can book and how long you can stay. Some courier companies list with membership organizations, such as the Air Courier Association and the International Association of Air Travel Couriers; these require you to become a member before you can book a flight.

In Britain, the best place to search for consolidator, or so-called bucket shop, tickets is through www.cheapflights.com, a Web site that pools together all flights available and then directs you to either a phone number or Web site to purchase tickets.

Some airlines offer discount passes, which you must purchase before you leave home. The Discover Europe Airpass from British Midland is available on all of the airline's British and European flights. The pass is valid for up to 90 days and starts at $109 for shorter routes and $159 for longer flights. The Europe pass from British Airways offers travelers a way to choose from the airline and their partner's network in Great Britain and Europe. Prices vary according to how many stops you make.

➤ CONSOLIDATORS: **Cheap Tickets** (☎ 800/377–1000, WEB www.cheaptickets.com). **DER Travel Services** (✉ 9501 W. Devon Ave., Rosemont, IL 60018, ☎ 800/782–2424, FAX 800/282–7474 for information; 800/860–9944 for brochures, WEB www.der.com). **Discount Airline Ticket Service** (☎ 800/576–1600). **Unitravel** (☎ 800/325–2222, WEB www.unitravel.com). **Up & Away Travel** (☎ 212/889–2345). **World Travel Network** (☎ 800/409–6753).

➤ DISCOUNT AIR PASSES: **British Airways** (☎ 877/428–2228, WEB www.britishairways.com). **British Midland** (☎ 800/788–0555, WEB www.flybmi.com).

➤ COURIER RESOURCES: **Air Courier Association** (☎ 800/282–1202, WEB www.aircourier.org). **International Association of Air Travel Couriers** (☎ 352/475–1584, WEB www.courier.org).

ENJOYING THE FLIGHT

State your seat preference when purchasing your ticket, and then repeat it when you confirm and when you check in. For more legroom, you can request one of the few emergency-aisle seats at check-in, if you are capable of lifting at least 50 pounds—a Federal Aviation Administration requirement of passengers in these seats. Seats behind a bulkhead also offer more legroom, but they don't have under-seat storage. Don't sit in the row in front of the emergency aisle or in front of a bulkhead, where seats may not recline.

If you have dietary concerns, **ask for special meals when booking.** These can be vegetarian, low-cholesterol, or kosher, for example. It's a good idea to pack some healthy snacks and a small bottle (plastic) of water in your carry-on bag. On long flights, try to maintain a normal routine, to help fight jet lag. At night, **get some sleep.** By day, **eat light meals, drink water** (not alcohol), and **move around the cabin** to stretch your legs. For additional jet-lag tips consult *Fodor's FYI: Travel Fit & Healthy* (available at bookstores everywhere).

Smoking policies vary from carrier to carrier. Many airlines prohibit smoking on all of their international flights; others allow smoking only on certain routes or certain departures. Ask your carrier about its policy.

FLYING TIMES

Flying time to London is about 6½ hours from New York, 7½ hours from Chicago, 9 hours from Houston, 11 hours from San Francisco, and 21½ hours from Sydney.

HOW TO COMPLAIN

If your baggage goes astray or your flight goes awry, complain right away. Most carriers require that you **file a claim immediately.** The Aviation Consumer Protection Division of the Department of Transportation publishes *Fly-Rights*, which discusses airlines and consumer issues and is available on-line. At PassengerRights.com, a Web site, you can compose a letter of complaint and distribute it electronically.

➤ AIRLINE COMPLAINTS: U.S. Department of Transportation **Aviation Consumer Protection Division** (✉ C-75, Room 4107, Washington, DC 20590, ☎ 202/366–2220, WEB www.dot.gov/airconsumer). **Federal Aviation Administration Consumer Hotline** (☎ 800/322–7873).

RECONFIRMING

Check the status of your flight before you leave for the airport. You can do this on your carrier's Web site, by linking to a flight-status checker (many Web booking services offer these), or by calling your carrier or travel agent.

Always confirm at least 72 hours ahead of the scheduled departure time for both international and domestic flights. Not all airlines require a reconfirmation; check with your carrier when you purchase your ticket.

AIRPORTS & TRANSFERS

International flights to London arrive at either Heathrow Airport (LHR), 15 mi west of London, or at Gatwick Airport (LGW), 27 mi south of the capital. Most flights from the United States go to Heathrow, which is the busiest and is divided into four terminals, with Terminals 3 and 4 handling transatlantic flights (British Airways uses Terminal 4). Gatwick is London's second gateway. It has grown from a European airport into an airport that serves 21 scheduled U.S. destinations. A third, newer airport, Stansted (STN), is 35 mi east of the city. It handles mainly European and domestic traffic, although there is also scheduled service from New York. Luton airport (LLA), just 30 mi north of the city, serves British and European destinations. Luton is the hub for the low-cost Easyjet airline. London City Airport is the smallest of the London airports and is just 9 mi east of the city. The airport is used mainly for private jets and helicopters as well as a few domestic flights and short European flights. The cost of hotels and car rentals varies little between Heathrow and Gatwick.

➤ AIRPORT INFORMATION: **Gatwick Airport** (☎ 01293/535–353). **Heathrow Airport** (☎ 0870/000–0123). **London City Airport** (☎ 0207/646–000, WEB www.londoncityairport.com). **Luton Airport** (☎ 01582/405–100, WEB www.london-luton.co.uk). **Stansted Airport** (☎ 0870/000–0303).

AIRPORT TRANSFERS

London has excellent bus and train connections between its airports and downtown. If you're arriving at Heathrow, you can pick up a map and fare schedule at a London Transport (LT) Information Centre (in Terminals 1 and 2). Train service is direct and there are multistop train routes; the downside to this mode of transport is having to move around on escalators and connecting subways with luggage. Airport link buses may ease the luggage factor and drop you closer to central hotels, but they are subject to London traffic, which can be horrendous. Taxis can be more convenient, but beware that prices can go through the roof. Airport Travel Line has transfer information and takes advance booking for transfers between airports and into London.

Heathrow by Taxi: A taxi from Heathrow can take more than an hour and can cost about £90. Add a tip of 10% to 15% to the basic fare. The best way by car is to reserve Hotelink before you arrive by fax or on-line. Someone will meet you at Heathrow airport and drive you into London for about £14 each way. Try to avoid rush hour if you want to get into London in less than an hour.

Heathrow by Bus: Airbus A2 takes about 90 minutes to two hours to Victoria Coach Station and costs £8 one-way and £10 round-trip. It leaves for King's Cross and Euston, with stops at Marble Arch and Russell Square, every 30 minutes 5:30 AM–9:45 PM, but there are around 14 stops along the route, so it can be tedious. For the same price, National Express buses leave every 55 minutes to Victoria Coach Station direct from 5:40 AM–9:30 PM.

Heathrow by Train: The cheap, direct route into London is via the Piccadilly line of the Underground (London's extensive subway system, or "tube"). Trains run every four to eight minutes from all four terminals from 5 AM until 11:45 PM Mon.–Sat. and 6 AM–11 PM on Sunday; the 50-minute trip costs £3.60 one-way and connects with other central tube lines. The Heathrow Express provides more comfort and speeds into London Paddington in 15 minutes, but is more expensive. Standard one-way tickets cost £12 (£22 round-trip) or £11 or £20 if you book over the Internet in advance. Service is daily, from 5:10 AM to 11:40 PM, with departures every 15 minutes.

Gatwick by Taxi: The taxi fare is at least £70. Add a tip of 10% to 15% to the basic fare. The best way by car is to reserve Hotelink before you arrive by fax or on-line. Someone will meet you at Gatwick airport and drive you into London for about £20 each way. Try to avoid rush hour if you want to get into London in less than an hour.

Gatwick by Train: Fast, nonstop Gatwick Express leaves for Victoria Station every 15 minutes 5:50 AM–midnight, then hourly 12:35 AM–5:20 AM. The 30-minute trip costs £10.20 one-way, £11.70 for a same-day round-trip (after 9:30 AM), and £20.40 for a round-trip valid for 30 days. Connex South Central also has a frequent local train from Victoria that runs every 15 minutes during the day and every hour between 1 and 4 AM. It takes about 40 minutes and costs £8.20 one-way, £8.30 for a same-day round-trip (after 9:30 AM), and £16.40 for a round-trip valid for 30 days. Thameslink runs trains from King's Cross or Euston (they're adjacent to each other). Check with Thameslink for frequency and trip lengths. Tickets cost £9.80 one-way and £19.60 round-trip.

London City Airport by Bus: The blue and white Shuttlebus runs every 10 minutes from 6:50 AM–9:10 PM Mon.–Fri., 6:50 AM–10 PM Sat., 11 AM–10 PM Sun. The 30-minute journey costs £5 one-way to Liverpool Street Station and £2 one-way to Canary Wharf.

London City Airport by Taxi: It costs just £20 for the 30-minute ride.

Luton by Train: The Luton Airport Parkway station is just a short shuttle bus ride from the airport. From King's Cross station in London, Thameslink runs every five to ten minutes and takes about 40 minutes. Tickets cost £9.50 one-way, £19 round-trip. Contact Thameslink for a schedule.

Luton by Bus: The Green Line 757 bus runs from Victoria Coach Station to Luton in about 90 minutes three times every hour. Tickets cost £7.50 one-way, £12 round-trip.

Luton by Taxi: Taxis take at least an hour and cost about £65.

Stansted by Taxi: The fare is about £80. Add a tip of 10% to 15% to the basic fare. The best way by car is to reserve Hotelink before you arrive by fax or on-line. Someone will meet you at Stansted airport and drive you into London for about £20 each way. Try to avoid rush hour if you want to get into London in less than an hour.

Stansted by Bus: Hourly bus service on Jetlink 777 (12:30 AM–11:30 PM) to Victoria Coach Station with stops at Hendon Central, Finchley Road Tube and Marble Arch, costs £8 one-way, £10 round-trip and takes about 1 hour and 40 minutes.

Stansted by Train: The Stansted Skytrain to Liverpool Street Station runs every half hour, takes about 45 minutes, and costs £12 one-way, £22 round-trip.

➤ TAXIS & SHUTTLES: **Airbus A2** (☎ 0870/574–7777). **Connex South Central** (☎ 08457/484–950, WEB www.connex.co.uk). **Gatwick Express** (☎ 099/030–1530, WEB www.gatwickexpress.co.uk). **Green Line 757** (☎ 0870/608–7261, WEB www.greenline.co.uk). **Hotelink** (☎ 01293/532–244, FAX 01293/531–131, WEB www.hotelink.co.uk). (☎ 0845/600–1515, WEB www.heathrowexpress.co.uk). **Jetlink 777** (☎ 0870/574–7777). **National Express** (☎ 0870/580–8080). **Shuttlebus** (☎ 0207/646–0088). **Stansted Skytrain** (☎ 0845/748–4950). **Thameslink** (☎ 0845/748–4950, WEB www.thameslink.co.uk).

➤ TRANSFER INFORMATION: **Airport Travel Line** (☎ 0870/574–7777).

DUTY-FREE SHOPPING

Heathrow, Gatwick, and Stansted have an overwhelming selection of duty-free shops, but the tax-free advantages are for travelers departing the United Kingdom for a country outside the European Union. For travel outside these countries, duty-free shopping is business as usual. For allowances, *see* Customs & Duties.

BIKE TRAVEL

Bikes are banned from motorways and most dual carriageways or main trunk roads, but on side roads and roads with bike lanes, a bike is a great way to explore London. The ambitious National Cycle Network project covers about 6,000 mi of cycling routes with some of that in London. **Sustrans** and **CTC** can provide route guides and information on cycling in London. A range of bikes, from racing to mountain, are usually available for rental, and prices vary, anywhere from £3–£5 an hour, to £7–£20 for a full day. A deposit of £25 or more is often required. For night cycling, the law requires a full set of reflectors on the wheels and pedals, and lights at the back and front.

For maps, the Landranger by Ordnance Survey series costs £5.50 a map and covers the country in scale 1:50,000 in more than 30 editions. Stanfords bookshop boasts the world's largest selection of maps and has a telephone and Internet ordering service.

➤ BIKE ROUTE INFORMATION: **CTC** (✉ Cotterell House, 69 Meadrow, Godalming GU7 3HS, ☎ 01483/417217, WEB www.ctc.org.uk). For information about the National Cycle Network, call **Sustrans** (☎ 0117/929–0888, WEB www.sustrans.org.uk).

➤ BIKE MAPS: **Landranger** by Ordnance Survey (✉ Order Processing, Romsey Rd., Southampton SO16 4GU, ☎ 02380/792439, WEB www.ordnancesurvey.co.uk). **Stanfords** (✉ 12–14 Long Acre, London WC2E 9LP, ☎ 020/7836–1321, WEB www.stanfords.co.uk).

➤ BIKE RENTALS: **Britain Visitor Centre** (✉ 1 Regent St., London SW1Y 4NX, ☎ no phone, WEB www.visitbritain.com). **Yellow Pages** (WEB www.yell.co.uk).

BIKES IN FLIGHT

Most airlines accommodate bikes as luggage, provided they are dismantled and boxed. Airlines sell bike boxes, which are often free at bike shops, for about $5 (it's at least

$100 for bike bags). International travelers can sometimes substitute a bike for a piece of checked luggage at no charge; otherwise, the cost is about $100. Domestic and Canadian airlines charge $25–$50.

BIKES BY RAIL

Most train services allow bicycles on board for free or for up to £3 per journey. Bicycles are generally not allowed during commute times when the trains are full. Folding bicycles are almost always allowed. Always check with the railway before bringing your bike on board.

BOAT & FERRY TRAVEL

Ferries, hovercraft, and seacats travel regular routes to France, Spain, Ireland, and Scandinavia. There are also numerous canal ways through the countryside and to the coast.

Hoverspeed provides fast travel to France and Belgium. P&O runs major ferry routes between Belgium, Great Britain, Ireland, France, Holland, and Spain. DFDS Seaways covers Denmark, Holland, Germany, Norway, Poland, and Sweden. Stena Line covers routes to Ireland and Holland.

FARES & SCHEDULES

➤ BOAT & FERRY INFORMATION: **Hoverspeed** (☎ 0870/524–0241, WEB www.hoverspeed.com). **P&O Stena Line** (☎ 0870/600–0600, WEB www.posl.com). **P&O Portsmouth** (☎ 0870/242–4999, WEB www.poportsmouth.com). **P&O** Ireland and Holland (☎ 0870/570–7070). **P&O Irish Sea** (☎ 0870/242–4666, WEB www.poirishsea.com). **P&O North Sea** (☎ 0870/129–6002, WEB www.ponsf.com). **DFDS Seaways** (☎ 01255/240240, WEB www.dfdsseaways.co.uk). **Stena Line** (☎ 0870/570–7070, WEB www.stenaline.co.uk).

BUSINESS HOURS

Generally, businesses are closed on Sundays and national (bank) holidays (☞ Holidays). New Year's Day is a national holiday, but many major stores are open for the annual sales reductions. Many restaurants are closed over the Christmas period.

BANKS & OFFICES

Banks are open weekdays 9:30–4:30; offices, 9:30–5:30.

GAS STATIONS

Most gas stations in central London are open seven days, 24 hours. As you get farther out of town, and off trunk/major roads, hours vary considerably depending on the gas company, but are usually 8 AM–8 PM.

MUSEUMS & SIGHTS

The major national museums and galleries are open daily, with shorter hours on weekends than weekdays. But there is a trend toward longer hours, such as one late-night opening a week.

PHARMACIES

Pharmacies are called chemists and are open, for the most part, Monday–Saturday 9:30 AM–5:30 PM. The leading chain drugstore, Boots, is open until 6 PM (the Oxford Street and Piccadilly Circus branches are also open Sunday and until 8 PM Thursday).

SHOPS

Shops and offices in central London tend to keep longer hours than those in the surrounding districts. Usual business hours are Monday–Saturday 9–5:30. In the main shopping streets of Oxford Street, Kensington High Street, and Knightsbridge, hours are 9:30 AM–6 PM, with late-night opening in Oxford Street on Thursday until 7:30–8 PM, and in the latter areas, on Wednesday. Many small general stores and newsagents stay open on Sunday; some chain and fashion stores in the tourist areas of Oxford Street and Piccadilly (and out-of-town shopping malls) also remain open.

BUS TRAVEL TO AND FROM LONDON

National Express is the largest British coach operator and the nearest equivalent to Greyhound. It is fast (particularly its Rapide services, which do not detour to make pick-ups and have steward service for refreshments) and comfortable (all coaches have washroom facilities on board). Services depart mainly from Victoria Coach Station, a well-signposted short walk behind Victoria mainline rail station. The departures and main information point is situated on the corner of Buckingham Palace Road, while the arrivals point is opposite at Elizabeth Bridge. It's wise to arrive at least 30 minutes before departure so as to locate the correct exit gate (it's an extremely busy place at peak holiday and weekends). Smoking is not permitted on board.

For some, the benefits of traveling by bus outweigh the negatives. Bus tickets can be up to half the price of a train ticket and buses are just as comfortable as trains. However, most bus services are double the traveling time of trains. Nearly all bus services have a no-smoking policy and both National Express and Scottish Citylink offer onboard light refreshments and toilets.

Green Line serves the counties surrounding London, as well as airports. Bus stops (there is no garage) are on Buckingham Palace Road, between Victoria mainline station and Victoria Coach Station.

FARES & SCHEDULES

Tickets can be bought from the Victoria, Heathrow, or Gatwick coach stations by phone with a credit card, via the National Express Web site, or from travel agencies. Apex tickets save money on standard fares, and traveling midweek is cheaper than over weekends and at holiday periods. National Express's Tourist Trail Passes, sold by British Travel International in the United States, make for great savings if you plan to tour Britain, and they can be bought in advance. Prices run from £49 for two days of travel within a three-day period; £85 for five days of travel within 30 days; £135 for eight travel days within 30 days; £190 for 15 travel days within 30 days; and £205 for 15 travel days within 60 days. A Discount Coach Card for students 16–25 years old, and for those over 50, costs £9 and is good for one year. It qualifies you for 20%–30% discounts off many standard fares. You can buy your National Express Tourist Trail Pass in advance from U.S.-based British Travel International travel agency.

RESERVATIONS

➤ BUS INFORMATION: **British Travel International** (✉ Box 299, Elkton, VA 22827, ☏ 800/327–6097, WEB www.britishtravel.com).

Green Line (✉ Green Line Travel Office, 4a Fountain Sq., 123-151 Buckingham Palace Rd., London, SW1, ☏ 0870 /608–7261, WEB www.greenline.co.uk). **National Express** (☏ 0870/580–8080, WEB www.gobycoach.com). **Scottish Citylink** (☏ 0870/550–5050, WEB www.citylink.co.uk). **Victoria Coach Station** (✉ Buckingham Palace Rd., London SW1W 9TP, ☏ 020/7730–3466, WEB www.btinternet.com/~victoriacoachstation).

BUS TRAVEL AROUND LONDON

The red London Transport (LT) buses, which travel all over town, have been joined by the bright colors of other private bus companies that cover the suburbs. Bus stops are clearly indicated; the main stops have a red LT symbol on a plain white background. When the word "Request" is written across the sign, you must flag the bus down. Each numbered route is listed on the main stop, and buses have a large number on the front with their end destination. Not all buses run the full route at all times; check with the driver or conductor. If you want to decipher the numbers, pick up a free bus guide at an LT Travel Information Centre (at Euston, Hammersmith, King's Cross, Oxford Circus, Piccadilly Circus, St. James's Park, Victoria tube stations, and at Heathrow). Buses are a good way of seeing the town, particularly if you plan to hop on and off to cover many sights, but **don't take a bus if you are in a hurry.** To get off, pull the cord running above the windows on old buses, or press the button by the exit. Expect to get a little squashed during rush hours, from 8 AM to 9:30 AM and 4:30 PM to 6:30 PM.

Night Buses, denoted by the prefix "N" to their route numbers, run from 11 PM to 5 AM on a more restricted route than day buses. Avoid sitting alone on the top deck of a Night Bus; it gives a mugger an ideal opportunity.

There is a no-smoking policy on all buses.

FARES & SCHEDULES

All journeys within the central zone are £1, and all others outside are 70p. Travel from the outer to the central zone costs £1. If you plan to make a number of journeys in one day, consider buying a discount pass (☞ Underground Tube Travel) good for both tube and bus travel. Traveling without a valid ticket makes you liable for a fine (£10 at press time). Buses are supposed to swing by every five or six minutes, but, in reality, you may wait 15 minutes or more.

➤ BUS INFORMATION: **LT Travel Information** (☎ 020/7222–1234).

PAYING

Payment is made to the driver as you enter (exact change is best so as to avoid incurring the driver's wrath). On some of the old buses where you enter the bus from the rear, take a seat and a conductor will come to you and issue you a ticket from a grinder-like contraption strapped to his or her front.

CAMERAS & PHOTOGRAPHY

Don't be surprised if you are asked not to take pictures during theater, ballet, or opera productions, and in galleries, museums, and stately homes. Locals are generally happy to feature in your photos, but it's polite to ask if they mind before fixing the lens. There are many must-take sights in London, but guards on horseback in Whitehall and Big Ben are top of the list.

The *Kodak Guide to Shooting Great Travel Pictures* (available at bookstores everywhere) is loaded with tips.

➤ PHOTO HELP: **Kodak Information Center** (☎ 800/242–2424, WEB www.kodak.com).

EQUIPMENT PRECAUTIONS

Don't pack film and equipment in checked luggage, where it is much more susceptible to damage due to high-intensity X-ray machines that are used to view checked luggage and are likely to ruin unprocessed film and single-use cameras. Random checks at security points at airports may now include putting carry-on luggage through checked-luggage scanners so you should always **pack your film in clear plastic or mesh bags** for easy inspection and **ask for hand inspection whenever possible.** Remember that if carry-on baggage scanners are marked "film safe" then it's ok to put your film through. **Be prepared to turn on your camera or camcorder** to prove to security personnel that the device is real. **Keep videotapes away from metal detectors.** Always **keep film and tape out of the sun** and carry an extra supply of batteries.

FILM & DEVELOPING

Film is available from pharmacies, newsagents, and supermarkets, as well as photographic stores. Kodak and Agfa are the most common brands, and prices range from £2–£4 for a roll of 36-exposure color print film. Larger drugstore branches and photographic stores stock the Advantix line. These stores provide 24-hour film developing services.

VIDEOS

Videos from the United States are not compatible with British and European models. If you're bringing your own video-camcorder, bring a supply of cassettes as well.

CAR RENTAL

Rental rates vary widely but are generally expensive, beginning at £50 ($80) a day and £200 ($320) a week for a small economy car, usually with manual transmission. Air-conditioning and unlimited mileage generally come with larger automatic transmission cars. The one exception to the rule is Easy Car, who rent stick-shift Mercedes A-class minivans for as little as £9 ($12) a day. To take advantage of the low prices, you must book early and via the Web site. Phoning them costs a hefty 60p ($1) per minute. Costs are also kept low by not offering any extras such as children's car seats, by using their vehicles as advertising boards, and only renting out of London.

➤ MAJOR AGENCIES: **Alamo** (☎ 800/462–5266 in the U.S.; 514/875–9988 in Canada; 020/7408–1255 in the U.K., WEB www.alamo.com). **Avis** (☎ 800/230–4898 in the U.S.; 800/272–5871 in Canada; 02/9353–9000 or 02/9136–333 in Australia; 080/

065–5111 in New Zealand; 0870/606–0100 in the U.K., WEB www.avis.com). **Budget** (☎ 800/527–0700 in the U.S.; 800/268–8900 in Canada; 0144/228–0181 in the U.K., WEB www.budget.com). **Dollar** (☎ 800/800–6000 in the U.S.; 514/828–9494 in Canada; 020/7582–1769 in the U.K., where it's affiliated with Sixt; 02/9223–1444 in Australia, www.dollar.com; WEB www.sixt-europe.com). **Easy Car** (☎ 0906/333–3333 (60p/minute only within the U.K.); WEB www.easycar.com). **Hertz** (☎ 800/654–3001 in the U.S.; 800/263–0600 in Canada; 0870/848–4848 in the U.K.; 03/9698–2555 in Australia; 0800/654–321 in New Zealand, WEB www.hertz.com). **National Car Rental** (☎ 800/227–7368 in the U.S.; 418/871–1224 in Canada; 020/750–2800 in the U.K., WEB www.nationalcar.com).

CUTTING COSTS

For a good deal, **book through a travel agent who will shop around.** Do **look into wholesalers,** companies that do not own fleets but rent in bulk from those that do and often offer better rates than traditional car-rental operations. Prices are best during off-peak periods. Rentals booked through wholesalers often must be paid for before you leave home.

➤ LOCAL AGENCIES: **Dimple Car Hire** (✉ 19 Varley Parade, London NW9 6RR, ☎ 020/8205–1200, FAX 020/7243–4408). **Enterprise** (✉ 466–480 Edgeware Rd., London W2 1EL, ☎ 020/7723–4800, FAX 020/7723–4368). **Europcar** (✉ 30 Woburn Pl., London WC1H 0JR, ☎ 020/7255–2339, FAX 020/7255–2347; WEB www.europcar.com).

➤ WHOLESALERS: **Auto Europe** (☎ 0207/842–2000 in London or 888/223–5555 in the U.S., FAX 0207/842–2222, WEB www.autoeurope.com). **Europe by Car** (☎ 212/581–3040 or 800/223–1516 in the U.S., FAX 212/246–1458, WEB www.europebycar.com). **DER Travel Services** (✉ 9501 W. Devon Ave., Rosemont, IL 60018, ☎ 800/782–2424, FAX 800/282–7474 for information; 800/860–9944 for brochures, WEB www.der.com). **Kemwel Holiday Autos** (☎ 800/576–1590, FAX 207/842–2286, WEB www.kemwel.com).

INSURANCE

When driving a rented car you are generally responsible for any damage to or loss of the vehicle. Collision policies that car-rental companies sell for European rentals typically do not cover stolen vehicles. Before you rent—and purchase collision or theft coverage—see what coverage you already have under the terms of your personal auto-insurance policy and credit cards.

REQUIREMENTS & RESTRICTIONS

In London your own driver's license is acceptable (as long as you are over 23 years old, with no endorsements or driving convictions). An International Driver's Permit is a good idea; it's available from the American or Canadian Automobile Association and, in the United Kingdom, from the Automobile Association or Royal Automobile Club. International permits are universally recognized, and having one may save you a problem with the local authorities. Companies frequently restrict rentals to people over age 23 or under age 75. Children must be in car seats and must be in the back of the car.

SURCHARGES

Before you pick up a car in one city and leave it in another, **ask about drop-off charges or one-way service fees,** which can be substantial. Note, too, that some rental agencies charge extra if you return the car before the time specified in your contract. To avoid a hefty refueling fee, **fill the tank just before you turn in the car,** but be aware that gas stations near the rental outlet may overcharge. It's almost never a deal to buy the tank of gas in the car when you rent it; the understanding is that you'll return it empty, but some fuel usually remains. Car seats usually cost about £20 extra. Adding one extra driver is usually included in the original rental price.

CAR TRAVEL

The best advice on driving in London is: don't. London's streets are a winding mass of chaos, aggravated by one-way streets. Parking is also restrictive and expensive, and traffic is tediously slow at most times of the day; during rush hours—from 8 AM to 9:30 AM and 4:30 PM to 6:30 PM—it often grinds to a standstill, particularly on Friday, when everyone wants to leave town. The center shopping areas are to be avoided. Watch out also for cyclists and motorcycle couriers.

Starting Feb. 17, 2003, the city will impose £5 "congestion charge" to all vehicles entering central London (bounded by the Inner Ring Road) on weekdays from 7 to 6:30, excluding bank holidays. Pay in advance or on that day until 10 PM if you're entering the central zone. You can pay by phone, post, Internet, or at retail outlets. If you don't pay and you're caught on camera, it will cost you £80.

Remember that Britain drives on the left, and the rest of Europe on the right. Therefore, you may want to leave your rented car in Britain and pick up a left-side drive if you cross the Channel (☞ The Channel Tunnel).

EMERGENCY SERVICES

The general procedure for a breakdown is the following: position the red hazard triangle (which should be in the trunk of the car) a few paces away from the rear of the car. Leave the hazard warning lights on. If you are on a highway (motorway), emergency roadside telephone booths are positioned at intervals within walking distance. Contact the car-rental company, or an auto club. The main automobile help groups in the United Kingdom are the Automobile Association (A.A.) and the Royal Automobile Club (R.A.C.) If you are a member of the American Automobile Association (A.A.A.) check your membership details before you depart for Britain as, under a reciprocal agreement, roadside assistance in the United Kingdom should cost you nothing. You can join and receive roadside assistance from the A.A. on the spot, but the charge is higher—around £75—than a simple membership fee.

➤ IN THE U.K.: **Automobile Association** (☎ 0870/550–0600, WEB www.theaa.co.uk). **Royal Automobile Club** (☎ 0870/572–2722, WEB www.rac.co.uk).

➤ CONTACTS: **Australian Automobile Association** (☎ 02/6247–7311 in Australia, WEB www.aaa.asn.au). **Canadian Automobile Association** (☎ 613/247–0117 in Canada, WEB www.caa.ca). **New Zealand Automobile Association** (☎ 09/377–4660 in New Zealand, WEB www.nzaa.co.nz). **American Automobile Association** (☎ 800/564–6222 in the U.S., WEB www.aaa.com).

GASOLINE

Gasoline (petrol) is sold in liters and is increasingly expensive (73p per liter at press time). Unleaded petrol is predominant, denoted by green pump lines. Premium and Super Premium are the two varieties, and most cars run on regular premium. Supermarket pumps usually offer the best value, although they are often on the edge of town. You won't find too many service stations in the center of town; these are generally on main, multi-carriageway trunk roads out of the center. Service is self-serve, except in small villages, and these gas stations are likely to be closed on Sundays and late evening. Most accept major credit cards.

PARKING

During the day—and probably at all times—it is safest to believe that you can park nowhere except at a meter, in a garage, or where you are sure there are no lines or signs; otherwise, you run the risk of a towing cost of about £100 or a wheel clamp, which costs about the same. Restrictions are indicated by the NO WAITING parking signpost on the sidewalk, and restricted areas include single yellow lines or double yellow lines. Parking at a bus stop or in a red-lined bus lane is also restricted. It is illegal to park on the sidewalk, across entrances, or on white zigzag lines approaching a pedestrian crossing.

Meters have an insatiable hunger in the inner city—a 20p piece buys just six minutes—and some will only permit a two-hour stay, with no return to top up. Meters take 10p, 20p, 50p, and £1 coins. In the evening, after restrictions end, meter bays are free. Daytime, take advantage of the many N.C.P. parking lots in the center of town, which are often a better value (about £2.50–£3 per hour, up to 8 hours). A London street map should have the parking lots marked. The ***London Parking Guide*** (£4.99, Two Heads Publishing) provides indispensable advice.

ROAD MAPS

Good planning maps are available from the Automobile Association and the Royal Automobile Club (☞ Car Travel). Or choose from the excellent Ordnance Survey or Collins road maps, available from newsagents and bookstores; prices run from about £3.95 for a paper fold-out to £6.99 for a spiral-bound paperback.

RULES OF THE ROAD

If you must risk life and limb and drive in London, note that the speed limit is 30 mph in the royal parks, as well as on all streets—unless you see the large 40 mph signs (and small repeater signs attached to lampposts) found only in the suburbs. Other basic rules: pedestrians have right-of-way on "zebra" crossings (black and white stripes that stretch across the street between two Belisha beacons—orange-flashing globe lights on posts) and it is illegal to pass another vehicle at a zebra crossing. At other crossings pedestrians must yield to traffic, but they do have right-of-way over traffic turning left at controlled crossings—if they have the nerve.

Traffic lights sometimes have arrows directing left or right turns; try to catch a glimpse of the road markings in time, and don't get into the turn lane if you mean to go straight ahead. A right turn is not permitted on a red light. On designated bus lanes a sign at the beginning and end gives the time restrictions for use—usually during peak hours—if you are caught, you could be fined. The use of horns is prohibited between 11:30 PM and 7 AM. Seat belts are to be worn by law in the front and the back seats. Drunk-driving laws are strictly enforced and it is far safer to avoid alcohol altogether. The legal limit is 80 milligrams of alcohol, which roughly translated means two units of alcohol—two glasses of wine, one pint of beer, or one glass of whiskey.

Children under 12 must sit in the back seat of the car and be secured by a seatbelt. Children under 3 must be in the back seat, in a car seat.

THE CHANNEL TUNNEL

Short of flying, the Eurostar via the Chunnel is the fastest way to cross the English Channel—it's just 3 hours from London's Waterloo Station to Paris's Gare du Nord. You can take your car on the 35-minute journey through the Eurotunnel via Le Shuttle train, which operates between Folkestone, UK, and Calais, France. Reservations are not necessary. Once you've driven onto the shuttle you travel inside your car.

➤ CAR TRANSPORT: **Eurotunnel** (☎ 0870/535–3535 in the U.K., WEB ww2.eurotunnel.com).

➤ PASSENGER SERVICE: In the U.K.: **Eurostar** (☎ 0870/518–6186, WEB www.eurostar.co.uk). In the U.S.: **BritRail** (☎ 877/677–1066, WEB www.britrail.com). **Rail Europe** (☎ 877/456–7245; 800/361–7245 in Canada, WEB www.raileurope.com).

CHILDREN IN LONDON

There are lots of activities for children to enjoy in London, and museums and major attractions have made great strides in special interactive features and trails (particularly during summer and Christmas holidays). At many museums children now enjoy free admission, and between the great establishments there are masses of green spaces in the London parks. During the school holiday time, bookstores run story times; cinemas, concert halls, and theaters have plenty of programs to watch—and join in on. When packing, include things to keep children busy en route.

For information on events for kids in and around London, look out for *Kids Out!*, a monthly magazine available from newsagents and bookstores. The London Tourist Board's information line offers two options: What's on for Children and Places for Children to Go, both 60p per minute. The tourist board also publishes *Where to Take Children. Fodor's Around London with Kids* (available in bookstores everywhere) can help you plan your days together.

If you are renting a car, don't forget to **arrange for a car seat** (☞ Car Travel, Rules of the Road) when you reserve. For general advice about traveling with children, consult *Fodor's FYI: Travel with Your Baby* (available in bookstores everywhere).

➤ LOCAL INFORMATION: ***Kids Out!*** (☎ 020/7813–6018). **Visitorcall** ("What's on for Children," ☎ 09064/123404 or "Places for Children to Go," ☎ 09064/123424).

BABY-SITTING

Baby-sitting agencies offer the easiest way to find qualified baby-sitters. Most agencies use off-duty nurses, nannies, school teachers, or mothers who are usually over 19 years old. Baby-sitting costs about £5–£7 per hour.

➤ AGENCIES: **Childminders** (☎ 020/7935–2049 (daytime and Sundays); 020/7935–3000 (evenings), WEB www.babysitter.co.uk). **Nanny Connection** (✉ Collier House, 163–169 Brompton Rd., London SW3 1PY, ☎ 020/7591–4444, WEB www.londonnannycompany.co.uk). **The Nanny Service** (✉ 6 Nottingham St., London W1M 3RB, ☎ 020/7935–3515, WEB www.nannyservice.co.uk). **Universal Aunts** (✉ Box 304, London SW4 0NN, ☎ 020/7738–8937).

FLYING

When booking, **confirm carry-on allowances** if you're traveling with infants. In general, for babies charged 10% of the adult fare you are allowed one carry-on bag and a collapsible stroller; if the flight is full, the stroller may have to be checked or you may be limited to less.

Experts agree that it's a good idea to use safety seats aloft for children weighing less than 40 pounds. Airlines set their own policies: U.S. carriers usually require that the child be ticketed, even if he or she is young enough to ride free, since the seats must be strapped into regular seats. Do **check your airline's policy about using safety seats during takeoff and landing.** Safety seats are not allowed everywhere in the plane, so get your seat assignments as early as possible.

When reserving, **request children's meals or a freestanding bassinet** (not available at all airlines) if you need them. But note that bulkhead seats, where you must sit to use the bassinet, may lack an overhead bin or storage space on the floor.

FOOD

Chinatown is welcoming to children—as well as a colorful and interesting experience—and the many Italian restaurants and pasta and pizza places are practical. The key is to avoid the high-class establishments unless your children behave impeccably; you won't find a children's menu there, anyway. The Pizza Express chain is family-friendly. At Smollensky's Balloon and Sweeny Todd's, clowns and magicians provide entertainment on the weekends. Hard Rock Cafe and Capital Radio Café have lively, musical atmospheres. The Rainforest Café has waterfalls and thundering jungle fun. Babe Ruth is sporty with screens showing baseball coverage.

➤ BEST CHOICES: **Babe Ruth** (✉ O2 Centre, Finchley Rd., NW3, ☎ 020/7433–3388). **Capital Radio Café** (✉ Leicester Sq., WC2, ☎ 020/7484–8888). **Hard Rock Cafe** (✉ 150 Old Park La., W1, ☎ 020/7629–0382). **Rainforest Café** (✉ 20 Shaftesbury Ave., W1, ☎ 020/7434–3111). **Smollensky's Balloon** (✉ 1 Dover St., W1, ☎ 020/7491–1199). **Sweeny Todd's** (✉ 3–5 Tooley St., SE1, ☎ 020/7407–5267).

LODGING

Most hotels in London allow children under a certain age to stay in their parents' room at no extra charge, but others charge for them as extra adults; be sure to **find out the cutoff age for children's discounts.**

The following hotels offer family rooms and/or cots, baby-sitting service, and children's portions and high chairs in the restaurant.

➤ BEST CHOICES: **Basil Street Hotel** (✉ Basil St., Knightsbridge, SW3 1AH, ☎ 020/7581–3311). **Edward Lear** (✉ 30 Seymour St., Bayswater, W1H 5WD, ☎ 020/7402–5401). **Elizabeth Hotel** (✉ 37 Eccleston Sq., Victoria, SW1V 1PB, ☎ 020/7828–6814). **Forte Hotels** (☎ 0345/404040 central reservations). **Forte Posthouse Kensington** (✉ Wrights La., W8 5SP, ☎ 020/7937–8170).

PUBS

Most pubs tend to be child-friendly, but most have restricted hours for children. At some pubs, children between the ages of 14 and 17 can enter bar areas; children younger than 14 can only be admitted, with an adult, if the pub has a Children's Certificate. At others, anyone who is younger than 21 is not allowed in a bar after 6 PM. The Web site www.pubs.com is helpful for sorting out the various restrictions, and lists many pubs that are child-friendly.

SIGHTS & ATTRACTIONS

The Tower of London, Tower Bridge Experience, London Dungeon, Madame Tussaud's, the Natural History Museum, and Pollock's Toy Museum are just a handful of sights to excite children. Places that are especially appealing to children are indicated by a rubber-duckie icon (🐤) in the margin.

SUPPLIES & EQUIPMENT

Baby formula and disposable diapers (or nappies as they are called in Britain) are widely available at supermarkets and pharmacies. Both premixed and powder formulas are available. The most popular brands are Hipp and Sma, both of which cost about £9 for 900 grams. Pampers and Huggies nappies are available in all sizes and varieties. A pack of 94 diapers for a baby costs about £13 whereas a pack of 15 pull-ups cost £5.

TRANSPORTATION

On trains and buses, children pay half or reduced fares; children under five go for free. Car-rental companies may have child seats available. By law, where there are seat belts in front and back, children must use them, but it is the responsibility of the driver to ensure that they do. Children do not need a child seat if they are over age five and are 1.5 m in height, but they must wear an adult seat belt. Children must be three to sit in the front seat, and if under 1.5 m in height will need a child seat or adult strap, whichever is available.

COMPUTERS ON THE ROAD

If you're traveling with a laptop, carry a spare battery and adapter: new batteries and replacement adapters are expensive, although if you do need to replace them head to Tottenham Court Road (W1), which is lined with computer specialists. John Lewis department store and Selfridges, on Oxford Street (W1), also carry a limited range. Never plug your computer into any socket before asking about surge protection. Some hotels do not have built-in current stabilizers, and extreme electrical fluctuations and surges can short your adapter or even destroy your computer. IBM sells an invaluable pen-size modem tester that plugs into a telephone jack to check if the line is safe to use.

CONCIERGES

Concierges, found in many hotels, can help you with theater tickets and dinner reservations: a good one with connections may be able to get you seats for a hot show or prime-time dinner reservations at the restaurant of the moment. You can also turn to your hotel's concierge for help with travel arrangements, sightseeing plans, services ranging from aromatherapy to zipper repair, and emergencies. **Always tip** a concierge who has been of assistance (☞ Tipping).

CONSUMER PROTECTION

Whether you're shopping for gifts or purchasing travel services, **pay with a major credit card** whenever possible, so you can cancel payment or get reimbursed if there's a problem (and you can provide documentation). If you're doing business with a particular company for the first time, **contact your local Better Business Bureau and the attorney general's offices** in your state and (for U.S. businesses) the company's home state as well. Have any complaints been filed? Finally, if you're buying a package or tour, always **consider travel insurance** that includes default coverage (☞ Insurance).

➤ BBBs: **Council of Better Business Bureaus** (✉ 4200 Wilson Blvd., Suite 800, Arlington, VA 22203, ☎ 703/276–0100, FAX 703/525–8277, WEB www.bbb.org).

CUSTOMS & DUTIES

When shopping abroad, **keep receipts** for all purchases. Upon reentering the country, **be ready to show**

customs officials what you've bought. If you feel a duty is incorrect, appeal the assessment. If you object to the way your clearance was handled, note the inspector's badge number. In either case, first ask to see a supervisor. If the problem isn't resolved, write to the appropriate authorities, beginning with the port director at your point of entry.

IN AUSTRALIA

Australian residents who are 18 or older may bring home A$400 worth of souvenirs and gifts (including jewelry), 250 cigarettes or 250 grams of tobacco, and 1,125 ml of alcohol (including wine, beer, and spirits). Residents under 18 may bring back A$200 worth of goods. Prohibited items include meat products. Seeds, plants, and fruits need to be declared upon arrival.

➤ INFORMATION: **Australian Customs Service** (Regional Director, ✉ Box 8, Sydney, NSW 2001, ☎ 02/9213–2000, FAX 02/9213–4000, WEB www.customs.gov.au).

IN CANADA

Canadian residents who have been out of Canada for at least seven days may bring home C$750 worth of goods duty-free. If you've been away fewer than seven days but more than 48 hours, the duty-free allowance drops to C$200; if your trip lasts 24–48 hours, the allowance is C$50. You may not pool allowances with family members. Goods claimed under the C$750 exemption may follow you by mail; those claimed under the lesser exemptions must accompany you. Alcohol and tobacco products may be included in the seven-day and 48-hour exemptions but not in the 24-hour exemption. If you meet the age requirements of the province or territory through which you reenter Canada, you may bring in, duty-free, 1.5 liters of wine, or liquor *or* 24 12-ounce cans or bottles of beer or ale. If you are 19 or older you may bring in, partially duty-free, 200 cigarettes and 50 cigars. Check ahead of time with the Canada Customs Revenue Agency or the Department of Agriculture for policies regarding meat products, seeds, plants, and fruits.

You may send an unlimited number of gifts (only one gift per recipient, however) worth up to C$60 each duty-free to Canada. Label the package UNSOLICITED GIFT—VALUE UNDER $60. Alcohol and tobacco are excluded.

➤ INFORMATION: **Canada Customs and Revenue Agency** (✉ 2265 St. Laurent Blvd. S, Ottawa, Ontario K1G 4K3, ☎ 204/983–3500 or 506/636–5064; 800/461–9999 in Canada, WEB www.ccra-adrc.gc.ca).

IN NEW ZEALAND

All homeward-bound residents may bring back NZ$700 worth of souvenirs and gifts; passengers may not pool their allowances, and children can claim only the concession on goods intended for their own use. For those 17 or older, the duty-free allowance also includes 4.5 liters of wine or beer; one 1,125-ml bottle of spirits; and either 200 cigarettes, 250 grams of tobacco, 50 cigars, *or* a combination of the three up to 250 grams. Meat products, seeds, plants, and fruits must be declared upon arrival to the Agricultural Services Department.

➤ INFORMATION: **New Zealand Customs** (✉ Head Office, The Customhouse, 17-21 Whitmore St., Box 2218, Wellington, ☎ 09/359–6655, FAX 09/359–6735, WEB www.customs.govt.nz).

IN THE U.K.

There are two levels of duty-free allowance for entering Britain: one for goods bought outside the European Union (E.U.) and the other for goods bought within the E.U. (Austria, Belgium, Denmark, Finland, France, Germany, Greece, the Irish Republic, Italy, Luxembourg, the Netherlands, Portugal, Spain, and Sweden).

Of goods bought outside the E.U. you may import duty-free: 200 cigarettes or 100 cigarillos or 50 cigars or 250 grams of tobacco; 2 liters of table wine and, in addition, (a) 1 liter of alcohol over 22% by volume (most spirits), (b) 2 liters of alcohol under 22% by volume (fortified or sparkling wine or liqueurs), or (c) 2 more liters of table wine; 60 milliliters of perfume; ¼ liter (250 ml) of toilet water; and other goods up to a value of

£145, but not more than 50 liters of beer or 25 cigarette lighters.

Of goods bought within the E.U., you should not exceed (unless you can prove they are for personal use): 800 cigarettes, 400 cigarillos, 200 cigars, and 1 kilogram of tobacco, plus 10 liters of spirits, 20 liters of fortified wine, 90 liters of wine, and 110 liters of beer.

No animals or pets of any kind can be brought in without a lengthy quarantine. The penalties are severe and are strictly enforced. Similarly, fresh meats, plants and vegetables, controlled drugs, and firearms and ammunition may not be brought into the U.K.

➤ INFORMATION: **HM Customs and Excise** (Customer Helpline, ☎ 0845/010–9000).

IN THE U.S.

U.S. residents who have been out of the country for at least 48 hours (and who have not used the $400 allowance or any part of it in the past 30 days) may bring home $400 worth of foreign goods duty-free; the duty-free allowance drops to $200 for fewer than 48 hours.

U.S. residents 21 and older may bring back 1 liter of alcohol duty-free. In addition, regardless of your age, you are allowed 200 cigarettes and 100 non-Cuban cigars. Antiques, which the U.S. Customs Service defines as objects more than 100 years old, enter duty-free, as do original works of art done entirely by hand, including paintings, drawings, and sculptures. You may also send packages home duty-free, with a limit of one parcel per addressee per day (except alcohol or tobacco products or perfume worth more than $5). You can mail up to $200 worth of goods for personal use; label the package PERSONAL USE and attach a list of its contents and their retail value. If the package contains your used personal belongings, mark it PERSONAL GOODS RETURNED to avoid paying duties. You may send up to $100 worth of goods as a gift; mark the package UNSOLICITED GIFT. Mailed items do not affect your duty-free allowance on your return.

➤ INFORMATION: **U.S. Customs Service** (for inquiries, ✉ 1300 Pennsylvania Ave. NW, Washington, DC 20229, WEB www.customs.gov, ☎ 202/354–1000; for complaints, ✉ Customer Satisfaction Unit, 1300 Pennsylvania Ave. NW, Room 5.5A, Washington, DC 20229; for registration of equipment, ✉ Office of Passenger Programs, 1300 Pennsylvania Ave. NW, Room 5.4D, Washington, DC 20229, ☎ 202/927–0530).

DINING

The restaurants we list are the cream of the crop in each price category. Restaurants are indicated in the text by ✕.

CATEGORY	COST*
££££	over £22
£££	£16–£22
££	£9–£15
£	under £9

**per person for a main course at dinner, excluding drinks, service, and VAT*

MEALS & SPECIALTIES

In London, local could mean any global flavor, but for pure Britishness, roast beef probably tops the list. If you want the best-value traditional Sunday lunch, go to a pub. The traditional accompaniment of Yorkshire pudding is a savory batter baked in the oven until crisp, served with a rich dark gravy. More tummy liners include shepherd's pie, made with stewed minced lamb and a mashed potato topping, baked until lightly browned on top; and steak and kidney pie, chunks of beef and pigs' kidneys braised in a thick gravy and topped with a light puff-pastry crust. Sweet bread-and-butter pudding is served hot, the layers of bread and dried fruit baked in a creamy custard until lightly crisp. The fish in fish-and-chips is usually cod or haddock, served with thick chips. A ploughman's lunch in a pub is crusty bread, English cheese (strong flavored with bite—cheddar, blue Stilton, crumbly white Cheshire, smooth red Leicester), and pickles with a side salad garnish. English cream tea consists of scones served with jam and thick cream and sandwiches made with wafer-thin slices of cucumber—and of course plenty of tea.

Local cafés serving the traditional English breakfast of eggs, bacon, beans, half a grilled tomato, and strong tea are often the cheapest—and best—places for breakfast. For lighter morning fare (or for real brewed coffee), try the Continental-style sandwich bars offering croissants and other pastries.

At lunch, you can grab a sandwich between sights, pop into the local pub, or sit down in a proper restaurant. Dinner, too, has no set rules, but a three-course meal is standard in most mid-range or high-end restaurants. Pre- or post-theater menus, offering two or three courses for a set price, are usually a good value. Note that most pubs do not have any waitstaff and you are expected to go to the bar and order a beverage and your meal and inform them of your table number.

MEALTIMES

In London you could find breakfast all day, and perhaps all night, but it is generally served between 7:30 and 10. Workmen's cafés and sandwich bars for office workers are sometimes open from 7:30, smarter cafés from 9–10:30. Lunch is between noon and 2 and restaurant sittings will be booked within that time. Tea—often a meal in itself—is taken between 4 and 5:30, dinner or supper between 7:30 and 9:30, sometimes earlier. In London's theaterland, 6–6:30 is the time for pre-theater suppers, and 10 onwards for post-theater meals. Many ethnic restaurants, especially Indian, serve food until midnight. Sunday is proper lunch day, and some restaurants will open for lunch only. Unless otherwise noted, the restaurants listed in this guide are open daily for lunch and dinner, but some restaurants do not open on Sundays (or Mondays—a fish-and-chip shop worth its salt will not be open on Monday) at all.

PAYING

American Express, Diners Club, MasterCard, and Visa are accepted almost everywhere, but a pub, small café, or ethnic restaurant (such as Indian or Chinese) might not take credit cards.

RESERVATIONS & DRESS

Reservations are always a good idea; we mention them only when they're essential or not accepted. Book as far ahead as you can, and reconfirm as soon as you arrive. (Large parties should always call ahead to check the reservations policy.) We mention dress only when men are required to wear a jacket or a jacket and tie.

WINE, BEER, AND SPIRITS

The cheapest and best range of alcohol is in the supermarkets, but in the middle of town, go to an informative, friendly wine merchant, or off-license shop, such as Oddbin's, which sells wine from around the world, and beer, too. For beer, bitters, or ale, go to a pub. Though now licensed to stay open later, most pubs close at 11 PM or midnight.

The English aren't known for their wine-producing skills, but, you can get plenty of real ale and lager in London's bars and pubs. The beer-drinking scene here starts with a pint at the end of the work day, so if you want a taste of it, visit a pub then.

DISABILITIES & ACCESSIBILITY

Compared to New York City, London has a way to go in helping people with disabilities, but it is moving toward making the city more accessible. Many tourist attractions and hotels are updating facilities, although traveling around is a problem. Most Underground (subway) stations have vast escalators and steps; contact the London Transport information line for their booklet, "Access to the Underground," which gives facts about elevators and ramps at individual tube stations, and information about buses and Braille maps. The grand, regal London Black Cabs are perfectly accommodating in their spacious interiors for people in wheelchairs. More good news is that many London hotels have wheelchair ramps. The London Tourist Board (☞ Visitor Information) also produces an updated newsletter, *London for All,* available from Tourist Information Centres. Note that the British Tourist Authority and the London Tourist Board will provide lists of London hotels for people with disabilities; these hotels often post the sign H at their door to welcome such travelers.

Artsline provides information on the accessibility of arts venues (theaters and cinemas) and events. For holiday bookings and special deals on equipped hotel rooms, contact Holiday Care Service or Can Be Done travel agency. RADAR, or the Royal Association for Disability and Rehabilitation, is command central for travel information and advice on accommodations throughout the British Isles and Europe. DIAL or the Disablement Information and Advice Line offers information on local groups in the United Kingdom that can offer advice. Tripscope covers the ground on all transport questions. Wheelchair Travel & Access Mini Buses advise on where to find converted cars to rent, including chauffeured minibuses and cars with hand controls.

➤ LOCAL RESOURCES: **Artsline** (✉ 54 Chalton St., London, NW1, ☎ 020/7388–2227, WEB www.artsline.org.uk). **Can Be Done** (✉ 7-11 Kensington High St., London, W8 5NP, ☎ 020/8907–2400, WEB www.canbedone.co.uk). **DIAL,** ☎ 01302/310–123). **Holiday Care Service** (✉ Imperial Bldg., Victoria Rd., Horley, Surrey RH6 7PZ, ☎ 01293/774–535; minicom 01293/776–943). **London Transport's Unit for Disabled Passengers** (✉ 172 Buckingham Palace Rd., London SW1 9TN, ☎ 020/7918–3312, FAX 020/7918–3876, WEB www.londontransport.co.uk). **RADAR** (✉ 12 City Forum, 250 City Rd., London, EC1, ☎ 020/7250–3222, WEB www.radar.org.uk). **Tripscope** (✉ Alexandra House, Albany Rd., Brentford Middlesex, TW8, ☎ 0845/758–5641, WEB www.justmobility.co.uk/tripscope). **Wheelchair Travel & Access Mini Buses** (✉ 1 Johnston Green, Guildford Surrey, GU2 6XS, ☎ 01483/233–640, WEB www.wheelchair-travel.co.uk).

LODGING

If you book directly through Holiday Care (☞ *Disabilities & Accessibility*), rates at some hotels with special facilities can be discounted.

➤ BEST CHOICES: **Copthorne Tara Hotel** (✉ Scarsdale Pl., Kensington, W8, ☎ 020/7937–7211).**Thistle Marble Arch** (✉ Bryanston St., W1, ☎ 020/7629–8040).

RESERVATIONS

When discussing accessibility with an operator or reservations agent, **ask hard questions.** Are there any stairs, inside *or* out? Are there grab bars next to the toilet *and* in the shower/tub? How wide is the doorway to the room? To the bathroom? For the most extensive facilities meeting the latest legal specifications, **opt for newer accommodations.** If you reserve through a toll-free number, consider also calling the hotel's local number to confirm the information from the central reservations office. Get confirmation in writing when you can.

SIGHTS & ATTRACTIONS

Tour Guides Ltd. can tailor a tour for you. The London Tourist Board has details of more easily accessible attractions. Suggested sights might include: London Planetarium, London Transport Museum, London Zoo, National Portrait Gallery, and Natural History Museum.

➤ CONTACTS: **Tour Guides Ltd.** (☎ 020/7495–5504).

TRANSPORTATION

London cabs have spacious interiors for wheelchair users. For other information, *see* Local Resources. Some buses are equipped to hold wheelchairs, but help is not usually at hand to get on one. At train stations, moving about can prove difficult, so contact the station in advance or get there early. You have to ask to use the elevators, which aren't open to the general public, and you'll also need help getting on and off the trains. For Underground or bus problems, write to London Transport.

➤ COMPLAINTS: **London Transport** (✉ Windsor House, 42-50 Victoria St., London SW1H 0TL).

TRAVEL AGENCIES

In the United States, the Americans with Disabilities Act requires that travel firms serve the needs of all travelers. Some agencies specialize in working with people with disabilities.

➤ TRAVELERS WITH MOBILITY PROBLEMS: **CareVacations** (✉ No. 5, 5110–50 Ave., Leduc, Alberta T9E 6V4, Canada, ☎ 780/986–6404 or 877/478–7827, FAX 780/986–8332, WEB www.carevacations.com), for group tours and cruise vacations. **Flying Wheels Travel** (✉ 143 W. Bridge St., Box 382, Owatonna, MN 55060, ☎ 507/451–5005 or 800/535–6790, FAX 507/451–1685, WEB www.flyingwheelstravel.com).

➤ TRAVELERS WITH DEVELOPMENTAL DISABILITIES: **New Directions** (✉ 5276 Hollister Ave., Suite 207, Santa Barbara, CA 93111, ☎ 805/967–2841 or 888/967–2841, FAX 805/964–7344, WEB www.newdirectionstravel.com).

DISCOUNTS & DEALS

Be a smart shopper and **compare all your options** before making decisions. A plane ticket bought with a promotional coupon from travel clubs, coupon books, and direct-mail offers or on the Internet may not be cheaper than the least expensive fare from a discount ticket agency. And always keep in mind that what you get is just as important as what you save.

DISCOUNT RESERVATIONS

To save money, **look into discount reservations services** with Web sites and toll-free numbers, which use their buying power to get a better price on hotels, airline tickets, even car rentals. When booking a room, always **call the hotel's local toll-free number** (if one is available) rather than the central reservations number—you'll often get a better price. Always ask about special packages or corporate rates.

When shopping for the best deal on hotels and car rentals, **look for guaranteed exchange rates,** which protect you against a falling dollar. With your rate locked in, you won't pay more, even if the price goes up in the local currency.

➤ AIRLINE TICKETS: ☎ **800/FLY–ASAP.** ☎ **800/AIRFARE,** WEB www.1800airfare.com. **International Marketing & Travel Concepts** (☎ 404/240–0949, FAX 800/790–4682, WEB www.imtc-travel.com).

➤ HOTEL ROOMS: **Hotel Reservations Network** (☎ 800/715–7666, WEB www.hoteldiscount.com). **International Marketing & Travel Concepts** (☎ 404/240–0949, FAX 800/790–4682, WEB www.imtc-travel.com). **Steigenberger Reservation Service** (☎ 800/223–5652, WEB www.srs-worldhotels.com). **Travel Interlink** (☎ 800/888–5898, WEB www.travelinterlink.com). **Turbotrip.com** (☎ 800/473–7829, WEB www.turbotrip.com).

PACKAGE DEALS

Don't confuse packages and guided tours. When you buy a package, you travel on your own, just as though you had planned the trip yourself. Fly/drive packages, which combine airfare and car rental, are often a good deal. Discount passes, such as London Pass, are available from the Britain Visitor Centre and Tourist Information Centre branches; many offer local transportation, entrance to museums, movie theaters, and galleries, and tours at considerable savings.

If you **buy a rail/drive pass,** you may save on train tickets and car rentals. All Eurail- and Europass holders get a discount on Eurostar fares through the Channel Tunnel.

ELECTRICITY

To use electric-powered equipment purchased in the United States or Canada, **bring a converter and adapter.** The electrical current in London is 220/240 volts (coming into line with the rest of Europe at 230 volts), 50 cycles alternating current (AC); wall outlets take three-pin plugs, and shaver sockets take two round, oversize prongs.

If your appliances are dual-voltage, you'll need only an adapter. Don't use 110-volt outlets marked FOR SHAVERS ONLY for high-wattage appliances such as blow-dryers. Most laptops operate equally well on 110 and 220 volts and so require only an adapter. For converters, adapters, and advice, contact the British Airways Travel Shop.

➤ CONTACTS: **British Airways Travel Shop** (✉ 156 Regent St., W1, ☎ 020/7434–4725).

EMBASSIES

➤ AUSTRALIA: **Australia House** (✉ Strand, London WC2, ☎ 020/7379–4334, WEB www.australia.org.uk).

➤ CANADA: **MacDonald House** (✉ 38 Grosvenor St., London W1, ☎ 020/7258–6600, WEB www.canada.org.uk).

➤ NEW ZEALAND: **New Zealand House** (✉ 80 Haymarket, London SW1, ☎ 020/7930–8422, WEB www.newzealandhc.org.uk).

➤ UNITED STATES: **American Embassy** (✉ 24 Grosvenor Sq., London W1, ☎ 020/7499–9000, WEB www.usembassy.org.uk); for passports, go to the **U.S. Passport Unit** (✉ 55 Upper Brook St., London W1, ☎ 020/7499–9000).

EMERGENCIES

If you need to report a theft or an attack (London is a relatively safe city) go to the nearest police station (listed in the Yellow Pages or the local directory). For severe emergencies, dial 999 for police, fire, or ambulance (be prepared to give the telephone number you're calling from). National Health Service hospitals give free, 24-hour treatment in Accident and Emergency sections, where delays can be an hour or more. Prescriptions are valid only if made out by doctors registered in the United Kingdom.

➤ DOCTORS & DENTISTS: **Accident & Emergency Dental Repairs Service** (☎ 020/7834–2522). **Doctor's Call** (☎ 020/8900–1000). **Eastman Dental Hospital** (✉ 256 Gray's Inn Rd., WC1, ☎ 020/7915–1000). **Medical Express** (✉ 117A Harley St., W1, ☎ 020/7499–1991).

➤ HOSPITALS: **Charing Cross Hospital** (✉ Fulham Palace Rd., W6, ☎ 020/8846–1234). **Royal Free Hospital** (✉ Pond St., Hampstead NW3, ☎ 020/7794–0500). **St. Thomas' Hospital** (✉ Lambeth Palace Rd., SE1, ☎ 020/7928–9292). **University College Hospital** (✉ Grafton Way, WC1, ☎ 020/7387–9300).

➤ HOT LINES: **Samaritans** (☎ 020/7734–2800). **Victim Support** (☎ 020/7735–9166; 020/7582–5712 after office hours).

➤ LATE-NIGHT PHARMACIES: **Bliss the Chemist** (✉ 5 Marble Arch, W1, ☎ 020/7723–6116).

ETIQUETTE & BEHAVIOR

The British stiff upper lip is more relaxed, but on social occasions the rule is to observe and then go with the flow. If you're visiting a family home, a gift of flowers is welcome. If it's for a meal, then take a bottle of wine perhaps, and maybe some candy for the children—but not necessarily all three. Kissing on greeting is still too forward and Continental for most Brits. A warm handshake is just fine. For goodbyes, if the atmosphere warrants, a quick one-cheek kiss is appropriate. The British can never say please, thank you, or sorry too often; to thank your host, a phone call or thank-you card does nicely.

BUSINESS ETIQUETTE

In business, punctuality is of prime importance, so if you anticipate a late arrival, call ahead. On dinners, it is not assumed that spouses will attend unless prearranged, and if you proffered the invitation it is usually assumed that you will pick up the tab. If you are the visitor, however, it's good form for the host to do the taking. Alternatively, play it safe and offer to split the check.

GAY & LESBIAN TRAVEL

The main gay communities are in the center of London (Soho, Old Compton St., and west to Kensington and Earls Court). There is a thriving social scene of clubs and cafés, and the best notice board for gay life and services is Gay's the Word. There's a thriving social scene of clubs and cafés; for London event notices, contact Gay's the Word bookshop. The *Pink Paper,* available at libraries, large bookstores, and gay bars, and *Time Out* both have comprehensive London listings. The British Tourist Authority has a brochure and Web site for gay and lesbian travelers. The round-the-clock London Lesbian & Gay Switchboard is a font of information on London's gay scene. Hotel front desks should serve any couples with courtesy, but using the travel agents listed below should send you to the right direction.

➤ CONTACTS: **British Tourist Authority** (☎ 877/857–2464, WEB www.gaybritain.org). **Gay's the Word** (✉ 66 Marchmont St., WC1N 1AB, ☎ 020/7278–7654, WEB www.gaystheword.co.uk). **London's Lesbian & Gay Switchboard** (☎ 020/7837–7324).

➤ Gay- & Lesbian-Friendly Travel Agencies: **Kennedy Travel** (✉ 314 Jericho Turnpike, Floral Park, NY 11001, ☎ 516/352–4888 or 800/237–7433, FAX 516/354–8849, WEB www.kennedytravel.com). **Now Voyager** (✉ 4406 18th St., San Francisco, CA 94114, ☎ 415/626–1169 or 800/255–6951, FAX 415/626–8626, WEB www.nowvoyager.com). **Skylink Travel and Tour** (✉ 1006 Mendocino Ave., Santa Rosa, CA 95401–4330, ☎ 707/546–9888 or 800/225–5759, FAX 707/546–9891), serving lesbian travelers.

GUIDEBOOKS

Plan well and you won't be sorry. Guidebooks are excellent tools—and you can take them with you. You may want to check out color-photo-illustrated *Fodor's Exploring London,* thorough on culture and history, and pocket-size *Citypack London,* with a supersize city map. *Fodor's upCLOSE London* is loaded with budget options. All are available at on-line retailers and bookstores everywhere.

HEALTH

Great Britain enjoys high standards of health, from safe drinking water to pasteurized foods. That noted, to ensure a pleasant trip, all travelers should pack medicines to help cope with diet changes and consequent irregularity, although these are also readily available over the counter in British pharmacies. If you take prescription drugs, keep a supply in your carry-on luggage and make a list of all your prescriptions to keep on file at home while you are abroad. You will not be able to renew a U.S. prescription at a pharmacy in Britain. Prescriptions are accepted only if issued by a U.K.-registered physician.

In recent years, there has been concern in Great Britain (and, indeed, throughout Europe) about Bovine Spongiform Encephalopathy (BSE), commonly known as "Mad Cow Disease," a fatal disease believed to have spread to cattle through the use of feed enriched with body parts of sheep infected with a related disease. It is possible for humans to contract Creutzfeldt-Jakob Disease, an extremely rare, fatal, brain-wasting illness, by eating meat from infected cattle. Although the chance of catching the disease is extremely small, you may wish to avoid eating beef or choose beef or beef products, such as solid pieces of muscle meat (as opposed to burgers or sausages), that might have a reduced opportunity for contamination with tissues that might harbor the BSE agent. For more information, contact the Centers for Disease Control and Prevention.

➤ Contacts: **Centers for Disease Control and Prevention** (☎ 877/394–8747, WEB www.cdc.gov).

HOLIDAYS

Standard holidays include: New Year's Day, Good Friday, Easter Monday, May Day (first Monday in May), spring and summer bank holidays (last Monday in May and August, respectively), Christmas, and Boxing Day (day after Christmas). On Christmas Eve and New Year's Eve some shops, restaurants, and businesses close early. Some museums and tourist attractions are also closed then. If you want to book a hotel room during this period, make sure you do it well in advance, and check to see whether the hotel restaurant will be open.

INSURANCE

The most useful travel-insurance plan is a comprehensive policy that includes coverage for trip cancellation and interruption, default, trip delay, and medical expenses (with a waiver for preexisting conditions).

Without insurance you will lose all or most of your money if you cancel your trip, regardless of the reason. Default insurance covers you if your tour operator, airline, or cruise line goes out of business. Trip-delay covers expenses that arise because of bad weather or mechanical delays. Study the fine print when comparing policies.

If you're traveling internationally, a key component of travel insurance is coverage for medical bills incurred if you get sick on the road. Such expenses are not generally covered by Medicare or private policies. Australian citizens need extra medical coverage when traveling abroad.

Always **buy travel policies directly from the insurance company**; if you buy them from a cruise line, airline, or tour operator that goes out of business you probably will not be covered for the agency or operator's default, a major risk. Before making any purchase, **review your existing health and home-owner's policies** to find what they cover away from home.

➤ TRAVEL INSURERS: In the U.S.: **Access America** (✉ 6600 W. Broad St., Richmond, VA 23230–1702, ☎ 800/729–6021, FAX 804/673–1491, WEB www.etravelprotection.com). **Travel Guard International** (✉ 1145 Clark St., Stevens Point, WI 54481, ☎ 715/345–0505 or 800/826–4919, FAX 800/955–8785, WEB www.travelguard.com).

➤ INSURANCE INFORMATION: In the U.K.: **Association of British Insurers** (✉ 51–55 Gresham St., London EC2V 7HQ, U.K., ☎ 020/7600–3333, FAX 020/7696–8999, WEB www.abi.org.uk). In Canada: **RBC Travel Insurance** (✉ 6880 Financial Dr., Mississauga, Ontario L5N 7Y5, Canada, ☎ 905/791–8700, 800/668–4342 in Canada, FAX 905/816–2498, WEB www.royalbank.com). In Australia: **Insurance Council of Australia** (✉ Level 3, 56 Pitt St., Sydney NSW 2000, ☎ 03/9614–1077, FAX 03/9614–7924, WEB www.ica.com.au). In New Zealand: **Insurance Council of New Zealand** (✉ Box 474, Wellington, New Zealand, ☎ 04/472–5230, FAX 04/473–3011, WEB www.icnz.org.nz).

LODGING

London now ranks as one of the world's most expensive hotel capitals. Finding budget accommodations—especially during July and August—can be difficult; you should try to book well ahead if you are visiting during these months. Many London hotels offer special off-season (October–March) rates, however. The lodgings we list are the cream of the crop in each price category.

Properties are assigned price categories based on the range from their least-expensive standard double room at high season (excluding holidays) to the most expensive. We always list the facilities that are available—but we don't specify whether they cost extra: when pricing accommodations, always ask what's included and what costs extra. Hotels are indicated in the text by 🏨.

CATEGORY	COST*
££££	over £230
£££	£160–£230
££	£100–£160
£	under £100

**All prices are for a double room, VAT included.*

Assume that hotels operate on the **European Plan** (EP, with no meals) unless we specify that they use the **Continental Plan** (CP, with a Continental breakfast), or the **Breakfast Plan** (BP, with a full breakfast).

APARTMENT RENTALS

If you want a home base that's roomy enough for a family and comes with cooking facilities, **consider a furnished rental.** These can save you money, especially if you're traveling with a group. Home-exchange directories sometimes list rentals as well as exchanges. In Britain, apartments are called flats. If you want to deal directly with local agents in Britain, get a personal recommendation from someone who has used the company, as, unlike hotels, there is no accredited system for standards. The London Tourist Board also has accommodation lists.

➤ INTERNATIONAL AGENTS: **At Home Abroad** (✉ 405 E. 56th St., Suite 6H, New York, NY 10022–2466, ☎ 212/421–9165, FAX 212/752–1591, WEB www.athomeabroadinc.com). **Hideaways International** (✉ 767 Islington St., Portsmouth, NH 03801, ☎ 603/430–4433 or 800/843–4433, FAX 603/430–4444, WEB www.hideaways.com; membership $99). **Hometours International** (✉ Box 11503, Knoxville, TN 37939, ☎ 865/690–8484 or 800/367–4668, WEB http://thor.he.net/~hometour/). **Interhome** (✉ 1990 N.E. 163rd St., Suite 110, N. Miami Beach, FL 33162, ☎ 305/940–2299 or 800/882–6864, FAX 305/940–2911, WEB www.interhome.com). **Villanet** (✉ 1251 NW 116th St., Seattle, WA 98177, ☎ 206/417–3444 or 800/964–1891, FAX 206/417–1832, WEB www.rentavilla.com). **Villas and Apartments Abroad** (✉ 1270 Avenue of the Americas, 15th floor, New York, NY

10020–1700, ☎ 212/897–5045 or 800/433–3020, FAX 212/897–5039, WEB www.ideal-villas.com). **Villas International** (✉ 4340 Redwood Highway, Suite D309, San Rafael, CA 94903, ☎ 415/499–9490 or 800/221–2260, FAX 415/499–9491, WEB www.villasintl.com).

➤ LOCAL AGENTS: **The Apartment Service** (✉ 5 Francis Grove, Wimbledon, SW19 4DT, ☎ 020/8944–1444, FAX 020/8944–6744, WEB www.apartmentservice.com; American agent: **Keith Prowse & Co.,** ✉ 234 W. 44th St., Suite 1000, New York, NY 10036, ☎ 212/398–1430 or 800/669–8687, FAX 212/302–4251). **John D. Wood** offers short lets in Chelsea and area (2 Jubilee Pl., SW3 3TQ, ☎ 020/7352–3333), which can be viewed on the Web site WEB www.shortlet.co.uk. **The Landmark Trust** (☎ 01628/825–925, WEB www.landmarktrust.co.uk) for good-quality cottages in unusual and historic buildings. **The Short Let Company** (✉ 20 Montpelier St., SW7, ☎ 020/7589–2429, WEB www.shortletco.com).

➤ RENTAL LISTINGS: **Loot** (☎ 08700/434–343, WEB www.loot.com) is available at newsstands.

B&BS

B&Bs are often large, attractive family homes that are almost like small hotels. These aren't corporate facilities, so you should be prepared to accept some charming quirks. Choose carefully from accredited agencies, as some so-called B&Bs could be simply unfortunate hostels for refugees and homeless.

➤ RESERVATION SERVICES: **Bulldog Club** (✉ 14 Dewhurst Rd., Kensington W14 0ET, ☎ 020/7371–3202, FAX 020/7371–2015, WEB www.bulldogclub.com). **Uptown Reservations** (✉ 41 Paradise Walk, Chelsea SW3 4JL, ☎ 020/7351–3445, FAX 020/7351–9383, WEB www.uptownres.co.uk). **At Home in London** (✉ 70 Black Lion Ln., Hammersmith W6 9BE, ☎ 020/8748–1943, WEB www.athomeinlondon.co.uk). **Coach House London Vacation Rentals** (✉ 2 Tunley Rd., Balham SW17 7QJ, ☎ 020/8772–1939, WEB www.vacrent.cwc.net). **London B&B** (✉ 437 J St., Suite 210 San Diego, CA 92101, ☎ 800/872–2632, WEB www.londonbandb.com). **Host & Guest Service** (✉ 103 Dawes Rd., Chelsea SW6 7DU, ☎ 020/7385–9922, WEB www.host-guest.co.uk). **Primrose Hill B&B** (✉ 14 Edis St., Regent's Park NW1 8LG, ☎ 020/7722–6869).

HOME EXCHANGES

If you would like to exchange your home for someone else's, **join a home-exchange organization,** which will send you its updated listings of available exchanges for a year and will include your own listing in at least one of them. It's up to you to make specific arrangements.

➤ EXCHANGE CLUBS: **Green Theme International** (✉ 94 Fore St. Bodmin, Cornwall PL31 2HR, ☎ FAX 01208/873–123, WEB www.gti-home-exchange.com; $30–$78 per year and on-line access. **HomeLink International** (✉ Linfield House, Gorse Hill Rd., Virginia Water, Surrey GU25 4AS, ☎ 01344/842–642; U.S. representative: Vacation Exchange Club, Box 650, Key West, FL 33040, ☎ 305/294–1448 or 800/638–3841, WEB www.homelink.org; $98 per year). **Intervac U.S.** (✉ 30 Corte San Fernando, Tiburon, CA 94920, ☎ 415/435–7440 or 800/756–4663, FAX 415/386–6853, WEB www.intervacus.com; $93 yearly fee includes one catalogue and on-line access).

HOSTELS

No matter what your age, you can **save on lodging costs by staying at hostels.** In some 4,500 locations in more than 70 countries around the world, Hostelling International (HI), the umbrella group for a number of national youth-hostel associations, offers single-sex, dorm-style beds and, at many hostels, rooms for couples and family accommodations. Membership in any HI national hostel association, open to travelers of all ages, allows you to stay in HI-affiliated hostels at member rates; one-year membership is about $25 for adults (C$30 in Canada, £12.50 in the U.K., $52 in Australia, and $40 in New Zealand); hostels run about $10–$25 per night. Members have priority if the hostel is full; they're also eligible for discounts around the world, even on rail and bus travel in some countries.

Hostels in London are generally clean but noisy and full of student backpackers. Most have dorm rooms that sleep about a dozen people with a few double and triple rooms reserved for small groups.

➤ ORGANIZATIONS: **Hostelling International—American Youth Hostels** (✉ 733 15th St. NW, Suite 840, Washington, DC 20005, ☎ 202/783–6161, FAX 202/783–6171, WEB www.hiayh.org). **Hostelling International—Canada** (✉ 400–205 Catherine St., Ottawa, Ontario K2P 1C3, Canada, ☎ 613/237–7884, FAX 613/237–7868, WEB www.hostellingintl.ca). **Youth Hostel Association of England and Wales** (✉ Trevelyan House, 8 St. Stephen's Hill, St. Albans, Hertfordshire AL1 2DY, U.K., ☎ 0870/870–8808, FAX 01727/844–126, WEB www.yha.org.uk). **Australian Youth Hostel Association** (✉ 10 Mallett St., Camperdown, NSW 2050, Australia, ☎ 02/9565–1699, FAX 02/9565–1325, WEB www.yha.com.au). **Youth Hostels Association of New Zealand** (✉ Level 3, 193 Cashel St., Box 436, Christchurch, New Zealand, ☎ 03/379–9970, FAX 03/365–4476, WEB www.yha.org.nz).

HOTELS

Riding the crest of a media wave, Great Britain has become more popular than ever as a vacation destination, so be sure to **reserve hotel rooms months in advance.** In this edition, all hotels listed have private bath unless otherwise noted. Most hotels have rooms with "en suite" bathrooms—as private bathrooms are called in Great Britain—although some older ones may have only washbasins; in this case, showers and bathtubs (and toilets) are usually just down the hall. When you book a room in the mid-to-lower price categories, it's best to confirm your request for a room with en suite facilities. In London room rates generally do not include breakfast. Tourist Information Centres will reserve rooms for you, usually for a small fee. A great many hotels offer special weekend and off-season bargain packages. Travelers sensitive to noise should ask for rooms away from the street with double-glazed windows. There are several systems that grade hotels in Britain. The English Tourist Board (ETB) presently uses crowns, while the AA and RAC motoring organizations award stars. Some are awarded more for service than individual room facilities. For a good standard of comfort, look at three stars and above. Modern hotels usually have air-conditioning, and if you wish to have a double bed, you should specify.

➤ TOLL-FREE NUMBERS: **Best Western** (☎ 800/780–7234, WEB www.bestwestern.com). **Choice** (☎ 800/424-6423, WEB www.choicehotels.com). **Clarion** (☎ 800/252–7466, WEB www.choicehotels.com). **Comfort** (☎ 800/228–5150, WEB www.choicehotels.com). **Days Inn** (☎ 800/325–2525, WEB www.daysinn.com). **Heritage Hotels** (☎ 888/892–0038, WEB www.heritagehotels.co.uk). **Hilton** (☎ 800/445–8667, WEB www.hilton.com). **Holiday Inn** (☎ 800/465–4329, WEB www.sixcontinentshotels.com/holiday-inn). **Howard Johnson** (☎ 800/406–1411, WEB www.hojo.com). **Hyatt Hotels & Resorts** (☎ 800/233–1234, WEB www.hyatt.com). **Inter-Continental** (☎ 888/591–1234, WEB www.interconti.com). **Le Meridien** (☎ 800/543–4300, WEB www.lemeridien-hotels.com). **Nikko Hotels International** (☎ 800/645–5687, WEB www.nikkohotels.com). **Quality Inn** (☎ 800/228–5151, WEB www.choicehotels.com). **Radisson** (☎ 800/468–3571, WEB www.radisson.com). **Renaissance Hotels & Resorts** (☎ 888/236–2427, WEB www.renaissancehotels.com). **Sheraton** (☎ 888-625-5144, WEB www.starwood.com). **Sleep Inn** (☎ 800/753–3746, WEB www.choicehotels.com). **Travel Inn** (☎ 087/0238–3300 in the U.K., WEB www.travelinn.co.uk). **Westin Hotels & Resorts** (☎ 888-625-5144, WEB www.starwood.com).

MAIL & SHIPPING

Stamps may be bought from post offices (open weekdays 9–5:30, Saturday 9–noon), from stamp machines outside post offices, and from newsagents' stores and newsstands. Mailboxes are known as post or letter boxes and are painted bright red; large tubular ones are set on the edge of sidewalks, while smaller boxes are set into post-office walls.

Allow seven days for a letter to reach the United States and about ten days to two weeks to Australia or New Zealand by air mail. Surface mail service can take up to four or five weeks. Check the Yellow Pages for a complete list of branches.

➤ Post Offices: ✉ 17 Euston Rd., NW1. ✉ 125–131 Westminster Bridge Rd., SW1. ✉ 110 Victoria St., SW1. ✉ 15 Broadwick St., W1. ✉ 54 Great Portland St., W1. ✉ 43 Seymour St., Marble Arch, W1. ✉ The Science Museum, SW7. ✉ 24 William IV St., Trafalgar Sq., WC2.

OVERNIGHT SERVICES

➤ Major Services: **DHL** (✉ Unit 24 Mastmaker Court, Mastmaker Rd., London, E14 9UB, ☎ 0870/110–0300, WEB www.dhl.co.uk). **Federal Express** (✉ 27 Poland St., London, W1V 3DB, ☎ 0800/123800, WEB www.fedex.com). **Parcelforce** (☎ 0800/224466, WEB www.parcelforce.co.uk).

POSTAL RATES

Airmail letters up to 10 grams to North America cost 45p; postcards, 40p. The same rates apply to Australia and New Zealand. Letters within Britain are 27p for first-class, 19p for second-class. Always check rates before sending mail, as they are subject to change.

RECEIVING MAIL

If you're uncertain where you'll be staying, you can have mail sent to you at the London Main Post Office, c/o Poste Restante. The post office will hold international mail for one month. You can also collect letters at American Express.

➤ Contacts: **American Express** (✉ 6 Haymarket, SW1Y 4BS, ☎ 020/7930–4411). **London Main Post Office** (✉ 24–28 William IV St., WC2N 4DL).

SHIPPING PARCELS

Most department stores and retail outlets can ship your goods home. You should check your insurance for coverage of possible damage. If you want to ship goods yourself, use one of the overnight postal services, such as FedEx, DHL, or Parcelforce. Shipping to North America, New Zealand, or Australia can take anywhere from overnight to a month depending on how much you pay.

MEDIA

NEWSPAPERS & MAGAZINES

For the latest information about shops, restaurants, and art events, peruse Britain's glossy monthly magazines—*Tatler, Harpers & Queen, Vogue, Wallpaper, House & Garden, The Face,* and *Time Out*. The *London Times*, the *Evening Standard,* the *Independent,* and the *Guardian* have comprehensive Arts sections including reviews and advance news of future events. In addition, these newspapers have Web sites of their own, full of tips on what's hot and happening.

RADIO & TELEVISION

The main channels are BBC1 and BBC2 from the British Broadcasting Corporation. BBC2 is considered the more eclectic and artsy, with a higher proportion of alternative humor, drama, and documentaries. The independent channels are ITV (Independent Television), which is split into regional companies across the country: Carlton is the station for London and the southeast region. There are big-budget highbrow productions occasionally, but there are more mainstream soaps, both homegrown—*Brookside* and *Coronation Street* (which the Queen is rumored to watch)—and international (the Australian *Neighbors* and some U.S. daytime shows, such as *Oprah*). There are general-interest shows as well. Channel 4 is a mixture of mainstream and off-the-wall, while Channel 5 has a higher proportion of sports and films. Satellite and cable channels (many of which are beamed into hotel rooms) have increased the daily diet now available round the clock.

Radio has seen a similar explosion for every taste, from 24-hour classical music on Classic FM (100–102 MHz), and rock on Capital FM (95.8 MHz) and Branson's Virgin (105.8 MHz), or nostalgic on Heart (106.2 MHz), or talk-talk on Talk Radio (MW 1053 kHz)—and that is just a sample of the independents. The BBC's Radio 1 (FM98.8) is for the young and hip; 2 (FM89) for middle-of-the-roadsters;

3 (FM91.3) for classics, jazz, and arts; 4 (FM93.5) for news, current affairs, drama (such as The Archers radio soap), and documentary; 5 Live (MW693 kHz) for sports and news with phone-ins; and BBC World Service (MW648 kHz) for the best of the BBC.

MONEY MATTERS

A movie in the West End costs £6–£11 (at some cinemas less on Monday and at matinees); a theater seat, from £8.50 to about £35, more for hit shows; admission to a museum or gallery, around £5 (though some are free and others request a "voluntary contribution"); coffee, £1–£3; a pint of light (lager) beer in a pub, £2 and more; whiskey, gin, vodka, and so forth, by the glass in a pub, £2.50 and up (the measure is smaller than in the United States); house wine by the glass in a pub or wine bar, around £2, in a restaurant £3.50 or more; a Coke, around £1; a ham sandwich from a sandwich bar in the West End, £3; a 1-mi taxi ride, £4; an average Underground or bus ride, £1.60, a longer one £2.50. For standby theater tickets, many at half-price, go the tkts half-price ticket booth in Leicester Square for that day's shows; it is open Monday–Saturday, 10–7, Sun noon–3. There is a service charge of £2.50.

Prices throughout this guide are given for adults. Reduced fees—generally referred to as "concessions" throughout Great Britain—are usually available for children, students, and senior citizens. For information on taxes, *see* Taxes.

ATMS

A debit card, also known as a check card, deducts funds directly from your checking account and helps you stay within your budget. When you want to rent a car, though, you will need a credit card. Although you can usually *pay* for your car with a debit card, agencies will not allow you to *reserve* a car with a debit card.

Otherwise, the two types of plastic are virtually the same. Both will get you cash advances at ATMs worldwide if your card is properly programmed with your personal identification number (PIN). To increase your chances of happy encounters with cash machines in Great Britain, **make sure before leaving home that your card has been programmed for ATM use there**—ATMs in Great Britain accept PINs of four or fewer digits only; if your PIN is longer, ask about changing it. If you know your PIN as a word, learn the numerical equivalent, since most Great Britain keypads show numbers only, no letters. Most ATMs are on both the Cirrus and Plus networks. ATMs are available at most main-street banks, at most large supermarkets such as Sainsbury's and Tesco, some tube stops, most rail stations, and large shops like John Lewis or Virgin Megastore. Both credit and debit cards offer excellent, wholesale exchange rates. And both protect you against unauthorized use if the card is lost or stolen. Your liability is limited to $50, as long as you report the card missing.

CREDIT CARDS

Throughout this guide, the following abbreviations are used: **AE**, American Express; **DC**, Diners Club; **MC**, MasterCard; and **V**, Visa.

➤ REPORTING LOST CARDS: **American Express**(☎ 01273/696933). **Diners Club** (☎ 0800/460800). **MasterCard** (☎ 0800/964767). **Visa** (☎ 0800/895082).

CURRENCY

The unit of currency in Britain is the pound sterling (£), divided into 100 pence (p). The bills (called notes in Britain) are 50, 20, 10, and 5 pounds (Scotland and the Channel Islands have their own £1 bills). Coins are £2, £1, 50p, 20p, 10p, 5p, 2p, and 1p. At press time, the exchange rate was about Australian $2.82, Canadian $2.03, New Zealand $3.50, and U.S. $1.45 to the pound (also known as quid). Britain's entry into the European Union's currency—the euro—is still uncertain.

CURRENCY EXCHANGE

For the most favorable rates, **change money through banks.** The currency exchange at Marks & Spencer department stores is excellent as they usually have favorable rates and do not charge commission. Although ATM transaction fees may be higher abroad than at home, ATM rates are excellent because they are based on wholesale rates offered only by major banks. You won't do as well at exchange booths in airports or rail and bus stations, in hotels, in restaurants, or in stores. To avoid lines at airport exchange booths, **get a bit of local currency before you leave home.** The new-style U.S. bills are widely accepted.

➤ EXCHANGE SERVICES: **International Currency Express** (☎ 888/278–6628 for orders, WEB www.foreignmoney.com). **Thomas Cook Currency Services** (☎ 800/287–7362 for telephone orders and retail locations, WEB www.us.thomascook.com). Round-the-clock currency exchange: **Chequepoint** (548 Oxford St., ☎ 0207/723–1005; 2 Queensway, ☎ 0207/229–0093; 222 Earl's Court Rd., ☎ 0207/370–3238, WEB www.chequepoint.com/).

TRAVELER'S CHECKS

Do you need traveler's checks? It depends on where you're headed. If you're going to rural areas and small towns, go with cash; traveler's checks are best used in cities. Lost or stolen checks can usually be replaced within 24 hours. To ensure a speedy refund, buy your own traveler's checks—don't let someone else pay for them: irregularities like this can cause delays. The person who bought the checks should make the call to request a refund. Get checks in dollar denominations then exchange them into British pounds as you need cash.

PACKING

London can be cool, damp, and overcast, even in summer. You'll need a heavy coat for winter and a lightweight coat or warm jacket for summer. **Always bring an umbrella and, if possible, a raincoat.** Pack as you would for an American city: jackets and ties for expensive restaurants and nightspots, casual clothes elsewhere. Jeans are popular in London and are perfectly acceptable for sightseeing and informal dining. Blazers and sport jackets are popular here with men. For women, ordinary street dress is acceptable everywhere. If you plan to stay in budget hotels, take your own soap. Baggage carts are widely available at Heathrow and Gatwick, but in train stations, bus stations, and smaller airports you have to carry your own luggage.

In your carry-on luggage, **pack an extra pair of eyeglasses or contact lenses and enough of any medication** you take to last the entire trip. Prescriptions are valid only if made out by doctors registered in the United Kingdom. In luggage to be checked, **never pack prescription drugs or valuables.** And don't forget to carry with you the addresses of offices that handle refunds of lost traveler's checks. Check *Fodor's How to Pack* (available in bookstores everywhere) for more tips.

To avoid customs and security delays, carry medications in their original packaging; don't pack any sharp objects, including knives of any size or material, scissors, manicure tools, and corkscrews, or anything else that might arouse suspicion. If you need such objects on your trip, consider shipping them to your destination or buying them there.

CHECKING LUGGAGE

How many carry-on bags you can bring with you is up to the airline. Most allow two, but not always, so make sure that everything you carry aboard will fit under your seat or in the overhead bin. Get to the gate early, so you can board as soon as possible. Note that if you have a seat at the back of the plane, you'll probably board first, while the overhead bins are still empty.

If you are flying internationally, note that baggage allowances may be determined not by piece but by weight—generally 88 pounds (40 kilograms) in first class, 66 pounds (30 kilograms) in business class, and 44 pounds (20 kilograms) in economy.

Airline liability for baggage is limited to $2,500 per person on flights within the United States. On international flights it amounts to $9.07 per pound or $20 per kilogram for checked baggage (roughly $640 per 70-pound bag) and $400 per passenger for unchecked baggage. You can buy additional coverage at check-in for about $10 per $1,000 of coverage, but it excludes a rather extensive list of items, shown on your airline ticket.

Before departure, **itemize your bags' contents** and their worth, and label the bags with your name, address, and phone number. (If you use your home address, cover it so potential thieves can't see it readily.) Inside each bag, **pack a copy of your itinerary.** At check-in, **make sure that each bag is correctly tagged** with the destination airport's three-letter code. If your bags arrive damaged or fail to arrive at all, file a written report with the airline before leaving the airport.

PASSPORTS & VISAS

When traveling internationally, **carry your passport** even if you don't need one (it's always the best form of I.D.) and **make two photocopies of the data page** (one for someone at home and another for you, carried separately from your passport). If you lose your passport, promptly call the nearest embassy or consulate and the local police.

U.S. passport applications for children under age 14 require consent from both parents or legal guardians; both parents must appear together to sign the application. If only one parent appears, he or she must submit a written statement from the other parent authorizing passport issuance for the child. A parent with sole authority must present evidence of it when applying; acceptable documentation includes the child's certified birth certificate listing only the applying parent, a court order specifically permitting this parent's travel with the child, or a death certificate for the non-applying parent. Application forms and instructions are available on the Web site of the U.S. State Department's Bureau of Consular Affairs (www.travel.state.gov).

ENTERING GREAT BRITAIN

U.S. and Canadian citizens need only a valid passport to enter Great Britain for stays of up to six months. Australian citizens need a passport with at least six months' validity and can stay in Britain for up to six months without a visa when on vacation. New Zealand citizens need a valid passport and can stay up to six months on vacation. Every traveler should be prepared to show sufficient funds to support and accommodate themselves while in Britain and to show a return or onward ticket. Health certificates are not required.

PASSPORT OFFICES

The best time to apply for a passport or to renew is in fall and winter. Before any trip, check your passport's expiration date, and, if necessary, renew it as soon as possible.

➤ AUSTRALIAN CITIZENS: **Australian Passport Office** (☏ 02/131–232, WEB www.dfat.gov.au/passports).

➤ CANADIAN CITIZENS: **Passport Office** (☏ 800/567–6868 in Canada, WEB www.dfait-maeci.gc.ca/passport).

➤ NEW ZEALAND CITIZENS: **New Zealand Passport Office** (☏ 800/225–050, WEB www.passports.govt.nz).

➤ U.S. CITIZENS: **National Passport Information Center** (☏ 900/225–5674; 888/362–8668; calls are 35¢ per minute for automated service, $1.05 per minute for operator service; WEB www.travel.state.gov/passport services.html).

REST ROOMS

Public toilets are sparse in England. Most big cities do maintain public facilities that are clean and modern. If there is an attendant you are only expected to pay admission (usually 30p). Rail stations and department stores have public toilets, which occasionally charge a small fee. Most pubs, restaurants, and even fast-food chains reserve toilets for customer use only. Hotels and museums are usually a good place to find clean, free toilets. In London, in some upscale establishments, there are attendants who expect a small tip—about £1. On the road, gas station facilities are usually clean and welcoming.

SAFETY

Great Britain has a low incidence rate of violent crime. However, petty crime is on the rise and tourists are the target. **Don't wear a money belt or a fanny pack,** both of which peg you as a tourist. If you wear a backpack, don't store anything valuable in it. **Keep your wallet in your front pocket** where you can feel it and protect it. If you carry a purse, choose one with a zipper and a thick strap that you can drape across your body; adjust the length so that the purse sits in front of you at or above hip level. Store only enough money in the purse to cover casual spending. Distribute the rest of your cash and any valuables (including credit cards and your passport) between a deep front pocket, an inside jacket or vest pocket, and a hidden money pouch. Do not reach for the money pouch once in public. Keep bags away from the street where thieves on cycles could grab it. When paying at a shop or a restaurant **never put your wallet down or let your bag out of your hand.** When sitting on a chair in a public place, keep your purse on your lap. Never put your purse, bag, or coat under, beside, or on the back of your chair. Always **use the bag hooks in public toilet stalls** instead of putting your bag on the floor where it may snatched.

Don't wear expensive jewelry or watches as they are easily lifted. Keep all important documents (passport, credit cards, etc.) and money in separate places so that if you are robbed you don't lose everything. **Store your passport in the hotel safe** as you don't need to carry your passport as identification (you can use your driver's license). **Don't leave anything in your car**—take valuables with you and put everything else out of sight in your trunk. Even a coat on the back seat can be an invitation to a thief.

There have been terrorist incidents in England and Northern Ireland, and while U.S. citizens are not targeted, some have been injured. Since September 11th, bomb threats are taken even more seriously. Don't leave any bags unattended, as they may be viewed as a security risk and taken away by the authorities.

LOCAL SCAMS

Although scams do occur in Great Britain, they are not pervasive. **Pickpockets are the biggest problem for tourists.** They often work in pairs with one distracting you by asking for directions or the time, bumping into you, or pointing to a spill on your clothing while the other takes your valuables and wallet. Always take a licensed black taxi cab or a car service (sometimes called mini cabs) recommended by your hotel. Passengers have been robbed or overcharged by unlicensed drivers in fake cabs. Avoid using mini cab services offered by drivers on the street. In most cases, they will drive an indirect route and overcharge you. When withdrawing cash from an ATM, be sure to cover the number pad with one hand while inputting your PIN. Some thieves will learn your PIN, steal your card, and then withdraw money from your account. Always buy theater tickets from a reputable dealer. If you are driving in from a British port, beware of thieves posing as fake customs officials. They stop travelers after they have followed them away from the port. Then they flag them down and "confiscate illegal goods."

WOMEN IN LONDON

Women are not likely to be harassed. The usual precautions apply—be vigilant if walking alone at night and avoid dimly lit or deserted areas. In bars and nightclubs, women may be the target of "date rape" if their drinks are spiked with drugs. Women should keep an eye on their drinks at all times and not accept drinks from people that they don't know.

SENIOR-CITIZEN TRAVEL

To qualify for age-related discounts, **mention your senior-citizen status up front** when booking hotel reservations (not when checking out) and before you're seated in restaurants (not when paying the bill). Be sure to have identification on hand. When renting a car, ask about promotional car-rental discounts, which can be cheaper than senior-citizen rates.

➤ EDUCATIONAL PROGRAMS: **Elderhostel** (✉ 11 Ave. de Lafayette, Boston, MA 02111-1746, ☎ 877/426–8056, FAX 877/426–2166, WEB www.elderhostel.org). **Interhostel** (✉ 6 Garrison Ave., Durham, NH 03824, ☎ 603/862–2015 or 800/313–5327, FAX 603/862–1113, WEB www.learn.unh.edu).

SHOPPING

London is a global market: Europe's best labels and fashion boutiques can be found here, and several U.S. chain stores operate here as well. Department stores, including John Lewis, Selfridges, Debenhams, and Fenwicks, have a wide range of everyday items and goods that make great gifts for the folks back home. If you followed no other pursuit in London save shopping, you could really exercise your plastic—but the prices may well exhaust it. Yet in any shopping excursion, seek out original designs, ethnic finds (from the many craft markets and fairs), and history, which you'll find in abundance, since nearly every village has at least one antiques shop. Bargaining is generally nowhere to be found in London, even at the outdoor markets.

KEY DESTINATIONS

London is the center of the shopper's universe. Whatever department store, boutique, or specialty shop there is in the whole of the kingdom, you need look no further than London's Oxford and Regent Streets, Knightsbridge, and Kensington areas. Antiques hunters head for the capital's markets and auction rooms, particularly in the Portobello, Bermondsey, and Bond Street areas. For bespoke tailoring from top to toe, anything can be made to measure—at a price—on Savile Row and Jermyn Street. For fine china, department stores and specialty shops are fruitful hunting grounds. And for one-stop shopping for art, crafts, and beautiful clothes, head for Covent Garden.

But to seek out Britain's most famous products on their home turf, you must travel farther afield. If you're seeking true tartans, Shetland sweaters, shortbread, and whisky, Edinburgh should top your shopping itinerary. For Welsh wool rugs and woolen clothing, visit Cardiff and the Welsh folk museums. Torrington in Devon is the home of beautiful Dartington glass, and Caithness in Scotland and the Isle of Wight in the south also produce designs to rival the Venetians' Murano glass. Hay-on-Wye, on the Welsh border, is a bibliophiles' center; every other shop seems to be a book seller.

SMART SOUVENIRS

Shops in the museums, galleries, and stately homes in London and the rest of the country are good choices for interesting merchandise—museum-quality art replicas, stationary, and beautifully packaged food, such as jam, toffee, and tea. Bookshops and antiques stores offer a plethora of unique and interesting souvenirs. For British crafts and jewelry, the Victoria & Albert Museum shop is a smart choice, and for souvenirs with a historical bent, visit the British Museum shop. The London Transport Museum has a good selection of double-decker bus models and other transport memorabilia. Both Harrod's and the Fortnum & Mason food halls stock an interesting if expensive array of foodstuffs suitable for bringing home.

SIGHTSEEING TOURS

BUS TOURS

Guided sightseeing tours from the top of a double-decker bus, which are open-topped in summer, are a good introduction to the city, as they cover all the main central sights. There is a choice of companies, each providing daily tours departing (between 8:30 and 9 AM) from central points. You may board or alight at any of the numerous stops to view the sights, and reboard on the next bus. Tickets are bought from the driver and are good all day. Prices vary according to the type of tour—about £12–£15 for bus tours and £70 for a taxi tour.

➤ TOUR OPERATORS: **Big Bus Company** (☎ 0207/233–9533, WEB www.bigbus.co.uk). **Black Taxi Tour of London** (☎ 020/7289–4371, WEB www.londontours.uk.com). **Evan Evans** (☎ 020/7950–1777, WEB www.evanevans.co.uk). **London Bicycle Tour** (☎ 020/7928–6838, WEB www.londonbicycle.com). **London Pride** (☎ 020/7520–2050, WEB www.londonpride.co.uk). **Original London Sightseeing Tour** (☎ 020/8877–1722, WEB www.theoriginaltour.com).

BY CANAL

The tranquil side of London is to be found on narrow boats that cruise London's two canals, the Grand Union and Regent's Canal; most vessels operate on the latter, which runs between Little Venice in the west (nearest tube: Warwick Avenue on the Bakerloo Line) and Camden Lock (about 200 yards north of Camden Town tube station). Fares are about £5 for 1½-hour cruises.

➤ CRUISE OPERATORS: **Canal Cruises** (☎ 020/7485–4433). **Jason's Trip** (☎ 020/7286–3428). **London Waterbus Company** (☎ 020/7482–2550).

BY RIVER

All year round, but more frequently from April to October, boats cruise the Thames, offering a different view of the London skyline. Most leave from Westminster Pier, Charing Cross Pier, and Tower Pier. Downstream routes go to the Tower of London, Greenwich, and the Thames Barrier via Canary Wharf. Upstream destinations include Kew, Richmond, and Hampton Court (mainly in summer). Most of the launches seat between 100 and 250 passengers, have a public-address system, and provide a running commentary on passing points of interest. Depending upon the destination, river trips may last from one to four hours.

A Sail and Rail ticket combines the modern wonders of Canary Wharf by Docklands Light Railway with a trip on the river. Tickets are available year-round from Westminster Pier or DLR stations; ticket holders also get discounted tickets to the London Aquarium in Westminster and the National Maritime Museum in Greenwich.

Details on all river cruise operators are available from London River Services.

➤ RIVER CRUISE OPERATORS: **Catamaran Cruisers** (☎ 020/7925–2215). **London River Services** (☎ 020/7941–2400). **Sail and Rail** (☎ 020/7363–9700). **Thames Cruises** (☎ 020/7930–3373, WEB www.thamescruises.com). **Westminster Passenger Boat Services** (☎ 020/7930–4097).

WALKING TOURS

One of the best ways to get to know London is on foot, and there are many guided and themed walking tours from which to choose. If you wish to tailor your own tour, you might consider hiring a Blue Badge accredited guide. ZigZag tours offer Walkmans with a recorded tour that you can use to take your own guided walk.

➤ TOUR OPERATORS: **Architectural Dialogue** (☎ 0207/267–769). **Beatles Walks** (☎ 020/7624–3978, WEB www.walks.com). **Blue Badge** (☎ 020/7495–5504). **Citisights** (☎ 020/8806–4325). **Historical Walks** (☎ 020/8668–4019). **Jack the Ripper Mystery Walks** (☎ 020/8558–9446, WEB www.mysterywalks.co.uk). **Original London Walks** (☎ 020/7624–3978, WEB www.walks.com). **ZigZag Audio Tours** (☎ 020/7435–3736, WEB www.zigzagtours.com).

EXCURSIONS

London Regional Transport, Green Line, Evan Evans, and National Express all offer day excursions by bus to places within easy reach of London, such as Hampton Court, Oxford, Stratford, and Bath.

STUDENTS IN LONDON

Student discounts are available at all museums and some shops. Places that offer discounts will have a sign on the door stating so. Be sure to carry a student identification card as proof.

➤ I.D.S & SERVICES: **Council Travel** (CIEE; ✉ 633 Third Ave., New York, NY 10017, ☎ 888/268–6245, FAX 212/822–2649, WEB www.councilexchanges.org) for mail orders only, in the U.S. **Travel Cuts** (✉ 187 College St., Toronto, Ontario M5T 1P7, Canada, ☎ 866/246–9762, FAX 416/979–8167, WEB www.travelcuts.com).

TAXES

An airport departure tax of £20 (£10 for within U.K. and other EU countries) per person is payable and may be subject to more government tax increases, although it is included in the price of your ticket.

VALUE-ADDED TAX

The British sales tax (VAT, Value-Added Tax) is 17½%. The tax is almost always included in quoted prices in shops, hotels, and restaurants.

Most travelers can **get a VAT refund** by either the Retail Export or the more cumbersome Direct Export method. Many large stores provide these services, but only if you request them; they will handle the paperwork. For the Retail Export method, you must ask the store for Form VAT 407 (you must have identification—passports are best), to be given to customs at your last port of departure. (Lines at major airports can be long, so allow plenty of time.) The refund will be forwarded to you in about eight weeks, minus a small service charge, either in the form of a credit to your charge card or as a British check, which American banks usually charge you to convert. With the Direct Export method, the goods go directly to your home; you must have a Form VAT 407 certified by customs, police, or a notary public when you get home and then sent back to the store, which will refund your money. For inquiries, call the local Customs & Excise office listed in the London telephone directory.

When making a purchase, **ask for a VAT refund form** and find out whether the merchant gives refunds—not all stores do, nor are they required to. Have the form stamped like any customs form by customs officials when you leave the country or, if you're visiting several E.U. countries, when you leave the European Union. Be ready to show customs officials what you've bought (pack purchases together, in your carry-on luggage); budget extra time for this. After you're through passport control, take the form to a refund-service counter for an on-the-spot refund, or mail it back to the store or a refund service after you arrive home.

A refund service can save you some hassle, for a fee. Global Refund is a Europe-wide service with 130,000 affiliated stores and more than 700 refund counters—located at every major airport and border crossing. Its refund form is called a Shopping Cheque. The service issues refunds in the form of cash, check, or credit-card adjustment, minus a processing fee. If you don't have time to wait at the refund counter, you can mail in the form instead.

➤ VAT REFUNDS: **Global Refund** (✉ 99 Main St., Suite 307, Nyack, NY 10960, ☎ 800/566–9828, FAX 845/348–1549, WEB www.globalrefund.com).

TAXIS

Those big black taxicabs are as much a part of the London streetscape as the red double-decker buses, yet many have been replaced by the new boxy, sharp-edged model, and the beauty of others is marred by the advertising they carry on their sides. Hotels and main tourist areas have cab stands (just take the first in line), but you can also flag one down from the roadside. If the yellow FOR HIRE sign on the top is lit, the taxi is available. Cab drivers often cruise at night with their signs unlit so that they can choose their passengers and avoid those they think might cause trouble. If you see an unlit, passengerless cab, hail it: you might be lucky.

Fares start at £1.40 and increase by units of 20p per 281 yards or 55.5 seconds until the fare exceeds £8.60. After that, it's 20p for each 188 yards or 37 seconds. A 60p surcharge is added on weekday nights 8–midnight and until 8 PM on Saturday. Over Christmas and on New Year's Eve, it rises to £2—and there's 40p extra for each additional passenger. Tips are extra, usually 10%–15% per ride.

➤ TAXI COMPANIES: **Computer Cab** (☎ 020/7432–1432). **Dial-a-Cab** (☎ 020/7253–5000). **Radio Taxis** (☎ 020/7272–0272).

TELEPHONES

British Telecom runs the telephone service in Great Britain and is generally reliable.

AREA & COUNTRY CODES

The country code for Great Britain is 44. The former London area codes of 0171 and 0181 have been merged into one code—020—with the previous 7 or 8 denomination being added before the first digit of the old phone number, making an eight digit number. For example, 0171/222–3333 is now 020/7222–3333. The existing 0800 numbers have not changed; national information numbers of 0345 are now 0845. Details are on the Internet at www.numberchange.org. There is help available, within England, at 0800/

731–0202; from the United States, at 020/7634–8700.

When dialing Great Britain from abroad, drop the initial 0 from these local area codes. The country code is 1 for the United States and Canada, 61 for Australia, 64 for New Zealand, and 44 for the United Kingdom.

DIRECTORY & OPERATOR ASSISTANCE

For information anywhere in Britain, dial 192. For the operator, dial 100. For assistance with international calls, dial 155.

INTERNATIONAL CALLS

When calling from overseas to access a London telephone number, drop the 0 from the prefix and dial only 20 (or any other British area code) and then the eight-digit phone number. To give one example: Let's say you're calling Buckingham Palace—020/7839–1377—from the United States to inquire about tours and hours. First, dial 011 (the international access code), then 44 (Great Britain's country code), then 20 (London's center city code), then the remainder of the telephone number, 7839–1377.

LOCAL CALLS

You don't have to dial London's central area code (020) if you are calling inside London itself—just the new eight-digit telephone number.

LONG-DISTANCE CALLS

For long-distance calls within Britain, dial the area code (which begins with 01), followed by the number. The area-code prefix is only used when you are dialing from outside the city. In provincial areas, the dialing codes for nearby towns are often posted in the booth.

LONG-DISTANCE SERVICES

AT&T, MCI, and Sprint access codes make calling long distance relatively convenient, but you may find the local access number blocked in many hotel rooms. First ask the hotel operator to connect you. If the hotel operator balks, ask for an international operator, or dial the international operator yourself. One way to improve your odds of getting connected to your long-distance carrier is to travel with more than one company's calling card (a hotel may block Sprint, for example, but not MCI). If all else fails, call from a pay phone.

You can also pick up one of the many instant international phonecards from newsstands, which can be used from residential, hotel, and public pay phones. With these, you can call the United States for as little as 5p per minute.

➤ ACCESS CODES: **AT&T Direct** (In the United Kingdom, there are AT&T access numbers to dial the United States using three different phone types—Cable & Wireless: ☎ 0500/890011; British Telecom: ☎ 0800/890011; and AT&T: ☎ 0800/0130011; ☎ 800/435–0812 for other areas). **MCI WorldPhone** (in the U.K., dial ☎ 0800/890222 for the U.S. via MCI; 800/444–4141 for other areas). **Sprint International Access** (in the United Kingdom, there are Sprint access numbers to dial the United States using two different phone types—Cable & Wireless: ☎ 0500/890877; and British Telecom: ☎ 0800/890877; 800/877–4646 for other areas).

PHONE CARDS

Public card phones operate with British Telecom (BT) chip cards that you can buy from post offices or newsstands. They are ideal for longer calls; are composed of units of 20p; and come in values of £2, £5, £10, and £20. To use a card phone, lift the receiver, insert your card, and dial the number. An indicator panel shows the number of units used. At the end of your call, the card will be returned. Where credit cards are taken, slide the card through, as indicated. Beware of buying cards that are not inserted into the phone, but which require you to dial a free phone number. While some are legitimate, others are not. Be sure to get a BT card.

PUBLIC PHONES

There are three types of phones: those that accept (a) only coins, (b) only British Telecom (BT) phone cards, or (c) BT phone cards and credit cards.

The coin-operated phones are of the push-button variety; the workings of coin-operated telephones vary, but there are usually instructions on each unit. Most take 10p, 20p, 50p, and £1 coins. Insert the coins *before* dialing (minimum charge is 20p). If you hear a repeated single tone after dialing, the line is busy; a continual tone means the number is unobtainable (or that you have dialed the wrong—or no—prefix). The indicator panel shows you how much money is left; add more whenever you like. If there is no answer, replace the receiver and your money will be returned.

All calls are charged according to the time of day. Standard rate is weekdays 8 AM–6 PM; cheap rate is weekdays 6 PM–8 AM and all day on weekends, when it's even cheaper. A local call before 6 PM costs 15p for three minutes; this doubles to 30p for the same from a pay phone. A daytime call to the United States will cost 24p a minute on a regular phone (weekends are cheaper), 80p on a pay phone.

TIME

London is in Greenwich Mean Time so it is five hours ahead of New York City and six hours ahead of Chicago. For example, when it is 3 PM in New York, it is 8 PM in London. Sydney is 10 hours behind London time. Note that London and most European countries also move their clocks ahead for the one-hour differential when daylight saving time goes into effect (although they make the changeover several days after the United States).

TIPPING

Many restaurants and large hotels (particularly those belonging to chains) will automatically add a 10%–15% service charge to your bill, so **always check if tipping is necessary** before you hand out any extra money.

Do not tip movie or theater ushers, elevator operators, or bar staff in pubs—although you can always offer to buy them a drink. Washroom attendants may display a saucer, in which it's reasonable to leave 20p or so.

Here's a guide for other tipping situations. Restaurants: 10%–20% of the check for full meals if service is not already included (if paying by credit card, check that tip has not already been included before you fill in the total on your credit slip), a small token if you're just having coffee or tea. Taxis: 10%–15%, or perhaps a little more for a short ride. Porters: 50p–£1 per bag. Doormen: £1 for hailing taxis or for carrying bags to check-in desk. Bellhops: £1–£2 for carrying bags, £1–£2 for room service. Concierge: £1–2. Always pay the higher price for exceptional service or in a high-end hotel. Hairdressers: 10%–15% of the bill, plus £1–£2 for the hair-washer.

TOURS & PACKAGES

Because everything is prearranged on a prepackaged tour or independent vacation, you spend less time planning—and often get it all at a good price.

BOOKING WITH AN AGENT

Travel agents are excellent resources. But it's a good idea to collect brochures from several agencies as some agents' suggestions may be influenced by relationships with tour and package firms that reward them for volume sales. If you have a special interest, **find an agent with expertise in that area**; the American Society of Travel Agents (ASTA; ☞ Travel Agencies) has a database of specialists worldwide.

Make sure your travel agent knows the accommodations and other services of the place being recommended. Ask about the hotel's location, room size, beds, and whether it has a pool, room service, or programs for children, if you care about these. Has your agent been there in person or sent others whom you can contact?

Do some homework on your own, too: local tourism boards can provide information about lesser-known and small-niche operators, some of which may sell only direct.

BUYER BEWARE

Each year consumers are stranded or lose their money when tour operators—even large ones with excellent reputations—go out of business. So **check out the operator.** Ask several travel agents about its reputation, and try to **book with a company that has**

a consumer-protection program. (Look for information in the company's brochure.) In the United States, members of the National Tour Association and the United States Tour Operators Association are required to set aside funds to cover your payments and travel arrangements in the event that the company defaults. It's also a good idea to choose a company that participates in the American Society of Travel Agents' Tour Operator Program (TOP); ASTA will act as mediator in any disputes between you and your tour operator.

Remember that the more your package or tour includes the better you can predict the ultimate cost of your vacation. Make sure you know exactly what is covered, and **beware of hidden costs.** Are taxes, tips, and transfers included? Entertainment and excursions? These can add up.

➤ TOUR-OPERATOR RECOMMENDATIONS: **American Society of Travel Agents** (☞ Travel Agencies). **National Tour Association** (NTA; ✉ 546 E. Main St., Lexington, KY 40508, ☎ 859/226–4444 or 800/682–8886, WEB www.ntaonline.com). **United States Tour Operators Association** (USTOA; ✉ 275 Madison Ave., Suite 2014, New York, NY 10016, ☎ 212/599–6599 or 800/468–7862, FAX 212/599–6744, WEB www.ustoa.com).

TRAIN TRAVEL TO AND FROM LONDON

Privatization of rail service in Britain has produced some difficulties, with far more service delays and more accidents than in past years. Despite these concerns, the train system is extensive and helpful.

When traveling by train, **make a reservation whenever possible,** and specify if you require no-smoking or smoking; most trains have one or two carriages designated for smokers. On long-distance runs, some rail lines have buffet cars, whereas in others, you can purchase snacks from a mobile snack cart.

London has eight major train stations that serve as arteries to the rest of the country (and to Europe). All are served by the Underground. As a general rule of thumb, the stations' location in the city matches the part of the country they serve. Charing Cross serves southeast England, including Canterbury and Dover/Folkestone for Europe. Euston serves the Midlands, north Wales, northwest England, and western Scotland. King's Cross marks the end of the Great Northern Line, serving northeast England and Scotland. Liverpool Street serves East Anglia, including Cambridge and Norwich. Paddington mainly serves south Wales and the West Country, as well as Reading, Oxford, and Bristol. St. Pancras serves Leicester, Nottingham, and Sheffield in south Yorkshire. Victoria serves southern England, including Brighton, Dover/Folkestone, and the south coast. Waterloo serves southeastern destinations, including Portsmouth and Southampton. The Eurostar service to France and Belgium departs from Waterloo International, within Waterloo station.

Britain has some fabulously scenic rail routes, often on steam trains, which generally run from April to October. In Wales, the Vale of Rheidol Railway from Aberystwyth climbs up sheer rock faces to Devil's Bridge. In the north of England, the Settle-to-Carlisle Railway travels the Yorkshire Dales; in the west country, the West Somerset Railway's Dunster-to-Minehead route takes in glorious coastline; and in the east, the Romney Marsh-to-Dymchurch runs along the marshland, skirting the Kent coast.

CLASSES

Some trains have first-class and reserved seats (for which there is a small charge, depending on the rail company). Check with National Rail Enquiries for details.

CUTTING COSTS

To save money, **look into rail passes.** But be aware that if you don't plan to cover many miles you may come out ahead by buying individual tickets.

Apex tickets, bought seven days in advance, provide savings. Many discount passes are also available, such as the Young Person's Railcard (for which you must be under 26 and provide two passport-size photos) and the Family Travelcard, which can be bought from most mainline stations.

If you plan to travel by train in Great Britain, **consider purchasing a BritRail Pass,** which gives unlimited travel over the entire British rail network and will save you money. You must **buy your BritRail Pass before you leave home.** They are available from most travel agents or from BritRail or Rail Europe; check their Web sites for complete details (☞ Discount Passes). Note that EurailPasses are not honored in Britain and that the rates listed here are subject to change; year to year, slight increases are usually the order of the day.

BritRail passes come in two varieties. The Classic pass allows travel within consecutive days; the FlexiPass allows travel days within a set period of time. The cost of a BritRail Classic pass adult ticket for 8 days is $265 standard and $400 first-class; for 15 days, $400 standard and $600 first-class; for 22 days, $505 and $760; and for a month, $600 and $900. The cost of a BritRail FlexiPass adult ticket for four days travel in two months is $235 standard and $350 first-class; eight days travel in two months $340 standard and $510 first-class; and 15 days travel in two months $514 standard and $770 first-class. Prices drop by about 25% for off-peak travel passes between October and March. Students, seniors, and 16–25s passes are discounted. (These are U.S. dollar figures; Canadian prices will be a bit higher.)

If you want the flexibility of a car combined with the speed and comfort of the train, try BritRail/Drive (from $473 for one adult, with a $166 supplement for additional adults and $72.50 for children 5–15); this gives you a three-day BritRail FlexiPass and three vouchers valid for Hertz car rental from more than 100 locations throughout Great Britain. A six-day rail pass with seven days of car rental is also available (from $958 car and driver, with $241 adult supplement, $105 children, with a current "free child per adult" deal for children under 5 traveling gratis). Prices listed are for compact, automatic transmission cars, with first-class seats; other options—manual transmission, larger cars, etc.—are available at different prices. If you call your travel agency or Hertz's international desk (☞ Car Rental), the car of your choice will be waiting for you at the station as you alight from your train.

Many travelers assume that rail passes guarantee them seats on the trains they wish to ride. Not so. You need to **book seats ahead even if you are using a rail pass**; seat reservations are required on some European trains, particularly high-speed trains, and are a good idea on trains that may be crowded—particularly in summer on popular routes. You will also need a reservation if you purchase sleeping accommodations. Bassinets are not available for infants and children under five ride the rails for free.

➤ DISCOUNT PASSES: **BritRail** (☎ 877/677–1066, WEB www.britrail.net). **DER Travel Services** (✉ 9501 W. Devon Ave., Rosemont, IL 60018, ☎ 800/782–2424, FAX 800/282–7474 for information; 800/860–9944 for brochures, WEB www.der.com). **Rail Europe** (✉ 226 Westchester Ave., White Plains, NY 10604, ☎ 877/456–7245, WEB www.raileurope.com; ✉ 94 Cumberland St., Toronto, Ontario M5R 1A3, ☎ 416/482–1777 or 800/361–7245; ✉ 179 Piccadilly, London W1V 0BA, ☎ 0870/584–8848).

FARES & SCHEDULES

The monthly *OAG Rail Guide* (about £6.95 and available from WH Smith branches and most larger main line rail stations) covers all national rail services and Eurostar, including private, narrow-gauge, and steam lines, as well as special services, buses, ferries, and rail-based tourist facilities. You can find timetables of rail services in Britain and some ferry services in the *Thomas Cook European Timetable,* issued monthly and available at travel agents and some bookstores in the United States.

Delays have become a national joking matter, particularly since a renovation of rails and rolling stock. National Rail Enquiries provides an up-to-date state-of-the-railways schedule. Rail travel is expensive: for instance, a round-trip ticket to Bath from London can cost around £60 per person at peak times. The fee reduces to around £30 at other times, so it's best to travel before or after the frantic business commuter rush (before 4 PM and after 10 AM). Reserving your ticket in advance is always recommended. Even a reservation 24 hours in advance can provide a substantial discount. Look into cheap day returns if you are planning to travel a roundtrip in one day. Credit cards are accepted for train fares paid both in person and by phone.

➤ TRAIN INFORMATION: **BritRail Travel** (in the U.S., ☎ 800/677–8585). **Eurostar** (☎ 0990/186186). **National Rail Enquiries** (☎ 0845/748–4950; outside the United Kingdom ☎ 0161/236–3522).**Rail Europe** (☎ 0870/584–8848).

RESERVATIONS

Reservations should be made on all train trips longer than one hour. If they are short hop trains just outside of London, then in most cases the train company will not allow reserved seats. To reserve a seat call the National Rail Enquiries (☞ Fares & Schedules) to determine which train company covers your destination, and then call the train company to book a ticket. You can also book tickets at the station from which the train leaves. Call National Rail Enquiries to determine this.

TRANSPORTATION AROUND LONDON

By far the easiest and most practical way to get around is on the Underground or "tube." This subway system runs daily from early morning to night and provides a comprehensive service throughout the center with lines out to the suburbs. Tube fares can work out to be higher than bus fares, but if you are traveling a lot around town, then you should investigate buying a Travelcard pass, which gives you discounted flexible travel on the tube, plus bus and some overground rail travel (☞ Underground Tube Travel).

The overground rail system is a network that connects outlying districts and suburbs to the center. Prices are comparable to the Underground, and you can easily transfer between the Underground and other connecting rail lines at many tube stations. Some passes are good for both the Underground and the rail system, so check at the point of purchase.

If you want to see the city, buses crisscross all over town. Their routes are more complicated than the tube, but by reading the route posted on the main bus stop and watching the route on the front of the bus, you won't go far wrong. Bus travel prices are cheaper than the tube the farther you travel, but be prepared to get stuck in traffic, even though designated lanes for buses and taxis should speed up the journey. Services are frequent, but if you become frustrated and flag down a taxi, the fare can clock up to three times the price of a similar bus fare for the same distance. If you're traveling with several people, however, riding in a taxi is relatively inexpensive and is more comfortable and convenient.

TRAVEL AGENCIES

A good travel agent puts your needs first. Look for an agency that has been in business at least five years, emphasizes customer service, and has someone on staff who specializes in your destination. In addition, **make sure the agency belongs to a professional trade organization.** The American Society of Travel Agents (ASTA)—the largest and most influential in the field with more than 26,000 members in some 170 countries—maintains and enforces a strict code of ethics and will step in to help mediate any agent-client disputes involving ASTA members if necessary. ASTA (whose motto is "Without a travel agent, you're on your own") also maintains a Web site that includes a directory of agents. (If a travel agency is also acting as your tour operator, *see* Buyer Beware *in* Tours & Packages.)

➤ LOCAL AGENT REFERRALS: **American Society of Travel Agents** (ASTA; ☎ 800/965–2782 24-hr hot line, FAX 703/739–7642, WEB www.astanet.com). **Association of British Travel Agents** (✉ 68–71 Newman St., London W1T 3AH, U.K., ☎ 020/7637–2444, FAX 020/7637–0713,

WEB www.abtanet.com). **Association of Canadian Travel Agents** (✉ 130 Albert St., Suite 1705, Ottawa, Ontario K1P 5G4, Canada, ☎ 613/237–3657, FAX 613/237–7052, WEB www.acta.net). **Australian Federation of Travel Agents** (✉ Level 3, 309 Pitt St., Sydney NSW 2000, Australia, ☎ 02/9264–3299, FAX 02/9264–1085, WEB www.afta.com.au). **Travel Agents' Association of New Zealand** (✉ Level 5, Paxus House, 79 Boulcott St., Wellington 10033, New Zealand, ☎ 04/499–0104, FAX 04/499–0827, WEB www.taanz.org.nz).

UNDERGROUND TUBE TRAVEL

London's extensive Underground system has color-coded routes, clear signage, and extensive connections. Trains run out into the suburbs, and all stations are marked with the London Underground circular symbol. Trains are all one class; smoking is *not* allowed on board or in the stations.

Some lines have branches, so check which branch you need. Electronic platform signs tell you the final stop and route of the next train and how many minutes you'll have to wait for the train to arrive. Commute time is from about 8 AM–10 AM and 4:30 PM–6:30 PM on weekdays.

Starting in 2003, repairs on the Circle, District, Hammersmith, City, and Metropolitan lines could shut down service. Passengers will be moved onto buses.

FARES & SCHEDULES

London is divided into six concentric zones (ask at Underground ticket booths for a map and booklet, which give details of the ticket options), so make sure to buy a ticket for the correct zone or you may be liable for an on-the-spot fine (£10 at press time).

You can buy a single or return ticket, the equivalent of a one-way and a round-trip, for travel anytime on the day of issue. Singles vary in price from £1.60 to £3.60. If you are planning several trips in one day then consider a Travelcard, which is good for unrestricted travel on both tube and bus and some overground railways; these are valid weekdays after 9:30 AM, weekends, and on all public holidays, but cannot be used on airbuses or for certain special services. Other options are: One Day Travelcard (£4.10–£5); Weekend Travelcards, for the two days of the weekend and on any two consecutive days during public holidays (£6.10–£7.50); Family Travelcards, which are one-day tickets for one or two adults with one to four children (£2.70–£3.30 with one child, additional children cost 60p each); or the Carnet, a book of 10 single tickets valid for central Zone 1 (£10) to use anytime over a year. The Visitor's Travelcard may be bought in the United States and Canada for three, four, and seven days' travel; it is the same as the LT (London Transport) Card and has a booklet of discount vouchers to London attractions. In the United States, the Visitor's Travelcard costs $25, $32, and $49, respectively; in Canada, C$29, C$36, and C$55, respectively. Apply to travel agents or, in the United States, to BritRail Travel International.

Trains begin running just after 5 AM Monday–Saturday; the last services leave central London between midnight and 12:30 AM. On Sunday, trains start two hours later and finish about an hour earlier. Frequency of trains depends on the route and the time of day, but normally you should not have to wait more than 10 minutes in central areas.

There are LT Travel Information Centres at the following tube stations: Euston, Hammersmith, King's Cross, Liverpool Street, Oxford Circus, Piccadilly Circus, St. James's Park, and Victoria, open 7:15 AM–10 PM; and at Heathrow (in Terminals 1, 2 and 4), open 6 AM–3 PM. For travelers with disabilities, get the free leaflet, "Access to the Underground."

➤ UNDERGROUND INFORMATION: **"Access to the Underground"** (☎ 020/7918–3312). **BritRail Travel International** (✉ 1500 Broadway, New York, NY 10036, ☎ 212/382–3737, WEB www.britrail.com). **London Transport** (☎ 020/7222–1234, WEB www.londontransport.co.uk).

VISITOR INFORMATION

The main London Tourist Information Centre is at Victoria Station Forecourt, and also at Heathrow Airport (Terminals 1, 2, and 3).

Britain Visitor Centre, open weekdays 9–6:30, weekends 10–4, provides details about travel, accommodations, and entertainment for the whole of Britain, but you need to visit the center in person to get information. Londonline (accessible only in Britain) is the London Tourist Board's 24-hour phone service—it's a premium-rate (60p/minute at all times) recorded information line, with different numbers for theater, events, museums, sports, getting around, etc.

The London Tourist Board's Londonline phone guide to London gives information about events, theater, museums, transport, shopping, and restaurants. There is a separate phone number for regular updates on what's happening this week. There is also a faxback service, enabling you to have the major events calendar faxed to you. Just dial the number and press start/receive after the tone; after a short pause the pages will process through. Londonline charges start at 60p per minute at all times, plus any hotel/pay-phone surcharge. Note that this service is accessible only in the United Kingdom.

The official Web site of the British Tourist Authority is www.visitbritain.com.

➤ IN THE U.S.: **British Tourist Authority (BTA)** (✉ 551 5th Ave., 7th floor, New York, NY 10176, ☎ 212/986–2200 or 800/462–2748, WEB www.travelbritain.org; ✉ 625 N. Michigan Ave., Suite 1510, Chicago, IL 60611, ☎ 800/462–2748).

➤ U.S. GOVERNMENT ADVISORIES: **U.S. Department of State** (✉ Overseas Citizens Services Office, Room 4811 N.S., 2201 C St. NW, Washington, DC 20520, ☎ 202/647–5225 for interactive hot line, WEB http://travel.state.gov/travel/html); enclose a self-addressed business-size envelope.

➤ IN CANADA: **British Tourist Authority** (✉ 5915 Airport Rd., Suite 120, Mississauga, Ontario L4V 1T1, ☎ 905/405–1720 or 888/847–4885, WEB www.visitbritain.com/ca).

➤ IN LONDON: **Britain Visitor Centre** (✉ 1 Regent St., Piccadilly Circus, SW1Y 4NX, ☎ no phone, WEB www.visitbritain.com). **London Tourist Information Centre** (✉ Victoria Station Forecourt, ☎ no phone, WEB www.londontouristboard.com). **Londonline** ☎ 09068/663–344.

WEB SITES

Do check out the World Wide Web when planning your trip. You'll find everything from weather forecasts to virtual tours of famous cities. Be sure to **visit Fodors.com** (www.fodors.com), a complete travel-planning site. You can research prices and book plane tickets, hotel rooms, rental cars, vacation packages, and more. In addition, you can post your pressing questions in the Travel Talk section. Other planning tools include a currency converter and weather reports, and there are loads of links to travel resources.

For more information specifically on London, visit one of the following:

The official London Web site is www.londontouristboard.com, which has links to many helpful Web sites, including the BBC and London Transport. Also useful is the Evening Standard Online (www.thisislondon.com). For travel around the United Kingdom by bus, check out gobycoach.com.

For London events and news months in advance, visit the following culture and entertainment Web sites: www.timeout.com, www.officiallondontheatre.co.uk, and www.ukcalling.co.uk.royal-albert. For the hotel scene in London, visit www.demon.co.uk/hotel-uk. For the full array of walking tours offered by the excellent Original London Walks, try www.walks.com. For walks in and around the city, with maps to download, head to www.londonwalking.com.

WHEN TO GO

The heaviest tourist season in Britain runs mid-April–mid-October, with another peak around Christmas—though the tide never really ebbs. Spring is the time to see the countryside and the royal London parks and gardens at their freshest; early summer to catch the roses and full garden splendor; fall to enjoy near-ideal exploring conditions. The British take their vacations mainly in July and August, and the resorts are crowded. London in summer, however, though full of visitors, is also full of interesting things to see and do. But be warned: air-conditioning is rarely found in places other than department stores, modern restaurants, hotels, and cinemas in London, and in a hot summer you'll swelter. Winter can be rather dismal and is frequently wet and usually cold, but all the theaters, concerts, and exhibitions go full speed.

CLIMATE

London's weather has always been contrary, and in recent years it has proved red-hot and cool by turns. It is virtually impossible to forecast what the pattern might be, but you can be fairly certain that it will not be what you expect. The main feature of the British weather is that it is generally mild—with some savage exceptions, especially in summer. It is also fairly damp—though even that has been changing in recent years, with the odd bout of drought. The following list includes the average daily maximum and minimum temperatures for London.

➤ FORECASTS: **Weather Channel Connection** (☏ 900/932–8437, 95¢ per minute from a Touch-Tone phone).

LONDON

Jan.	43F	6C	May	62F	17C	Sept.	65F	19C
	36	2		47	8		52	11
Feb.	44F	7C	June	69F	20C	Oct.	58F	14C
	36	2		53	12		46	8
Mar.	50F	10C	July	71F	22C	Nov.	50F	10C
	38	3		56	14		42	5
Apr.	56F	13C	Aug.	71F	21C	Dec.	45F	7C
	42	6		56	13		38	4

FESTIVALS AND SEASONAL EVENTS

Top seasonal events in and around London include the Chelsea Flower Show in May, Derby Day at Epsom Racecourse, Wimbledon Lawn Tennis Championships and Henley Regatta in June, and the London Arts Season, which combines many events in theater, art, and music with good deals on hotels and meals out.

There is a complete list of ticket agencies in *Britain Events,* available in person only from the Britain Visitor Centre. When in London, check the weekly magazine *Time Out,* available at newsstands, for an ongoing calendar of special events. Or, for 60p per minute, call London Tourist Board's Visitorcall service, which offers the latest on events throughout the city.

➤ MID-DEC: The **Olympia International Show Jumping Championships** (☏ 020/7370–8209), an international equestrian competition, takes place in Olympia's Grand Hall.

➤ DEC. 31: **New Year's Eve at Trafalgar Square** is a huge, freezing, sometimes drunken slosh through the fountains to celebrate the new year. Unorganized by any official body, it is held in the ceremonial heart of London under an enormous Christmas tree, which is a gift from the people of Norway and set up from early December to early January. Unlike Americans, however, most Brits celebrate New Year's Eve at home.

➤ JAN. 1: The **London Parade** is a good ole U.S.-style extravaganza complete with cheerleaders, floats, and marching bands, led by the Lord Mayor of London. It starts on the south side of Westminster Bridge at 12:30, passing Parliament Square, Whitehall, Trafalgar Square, Lower Regent Street, Piccadilly, and finishing in Berkeley Square around 3 PM. No tickets are required.

➤ LAST SUNDAY IN JAN: **Charles I Commemoration** is held on the anniversary of the monarch's execution and brings out Londoners dressed in 17th-century garb for a march tracing his last walk from St. James's Palace to the Banqueting House in Whitehall.

➤ MAR. 17–28 AND SEPT. 15–24: The **Chelsea Antiques Fair** is a twice-yearly fair with wide range of pre-1830 pieces for sale. ✉ *Old Town Hall, King's Rd., Chelsea, SW3 4PW,* ☎ *01444/482–514.*

➤ END-MAR: **Head of the River Boat Race** offers the spectacle of 420 eight-man crews from Oxford and Cambridge universities dipping their 6,720 oars in the Thames as they race from Mortlake to Putney. The best view is from Surrey Bank above Chiswick Bridge (tube to Chiswick); check *Time Out* for the starting time, which depends on the tide. The **Oxford versus Cambridge University Boat Race** takes place often the week after, over the same 4½ mi course, carrying on a tradition going back to around 1829. In 1912 both boats sank spectacularly.

➤ EARLY APR: **Chaucer Festival** (☎ 01227/470379) allows Londoners to don medieval garb and parade from Southwark Cathedral to the Tower of London, where jugglers and strolling minstrels party the day away.

➤ MID-APR: **London Marathon** is a New York–style marathon through London's streets. Runners from 68 countries start in Greenwich and Blackheath at 9–9:30 AM, then run via Docklands and Canary Wharf, the Tower of London and Parliament Square to finish in the Mall.

➤ END-MAR: **British Antique Dealers' Association Fair,** the newest of the major fairs, is large and prestigious, with many affordable pieces. ✉ *Duke of York's Headquarters, King's Rd., Chelsea SW3,* ☎ *020/7589–6108.*

➤ APR. 21: **Queen's Birthday** earns a showy 41-gun salute at Hyde Park. In June (☞ Trooping the Colour), Elizabeth II's ceremonial b-day is celebrated by Trooping the Colour.

➤ MID-MAY: **Punch and Judy Festival** is held on the second Sunday in May and offers a May Fayre Procession in the morning, services at St. Paul's Church, then puppet shows until dusk. A lovely event for children of all ages. ✉ *Covent Garden Piazza, London, WC2,* ☎ *020/7375–0441.*

➤ MID-MAY: **Royal Windsor Horse Show** (☎ 01753/860–633) is a major show-jumping event attended by some members of the Royal Family.

➤ MAY 23–26: **Chelsea Flower Show,** Britain's most prestigious flower show, is always graced by the Royals and covers 22 acres. ✉ *Royal Hospital Rd., Chelsea, SW3,* ☎ *020/7630–7422.*

➤ LATE MAY–LATE AUG: **Glyndebourne Festival Opera** is a unique opportunity to see international stars in a bucolic setting. Tickets go fast and early booking starts on May 2nd. ✉ *Glyndebourne Festival Opera, Lewes, Sussex BN8 5UU,* ☎ *01273/815–000.*

➤ LATE MAY–LATE AUG: **Shakespeare Under the Stars** gives you the chance to see the Bard's plays performed at Regent's Park Open Air Theatre. Performances are usually Monday–Saturday at 8 PM, with matinees on Wednesday, Thursday, and Saturday. ✉ *Inner Circle, London, NW1,* ☎ *020/7486–2431.*

➤ EARLY JUNE: **Beating Retreat by the Guards Massed Bands** is when more than 500 musicians parade at Horse Guards, Whitehall. Tickets from Household Division Fund, ✉ *Horse Guards, London SW1A 2AX,* ☎ *020/7414–2271.*

➤ EARLY JUNE: **Derby Day** is the best-known event on the horse-racing calendar. Information from United Racecourses Ltd., ✉ *Epsom Downs Racecourse, Epsom, Surrey KT18 5LQ,* ☎ *013727/26311.*

➤ MID-JUNE: The **Grosvenor House Antiques Fair** is one of the most prestigious antiques fairs in Britain. ✉ *Grosvenor House Hotel, Park La., London W1A 3AA,* ☎ *020/7399–8100.*

➤ MID-JUNE: **Royal Meeting at Ascot** brings the horsey set and their enormous hats out in force during the third week in June (Tuesday–Friday; Thursday is the high-fashion Ladies Day). General admission is available but reserve months in advance; for tickets to the Royal Enclosure (you must be sponsored), write to: ✉ *Protocol Office, American Embassy, 24 Grosvenor Sq., London W1A*

1AE. General admission: ✉ *Ascot Racecourse, Ascot, Berkshire SL5 7JN*, ☏ *01344/876–876*.

➤ MID-JUNE: **Trooping the Colour,** Queen Elizabeth's colorful official birthday parade, is held at Horse Guards, Whitehall, usually on the second or third Saturday of June. Write for tickets *only* between January 1 and February 28, enclosing a self-addressed stamped envelope. ✉ *Ticket Office, Headquarters, Household Division, Horse Guards, London SW1A 2AX*, ☏ *020/7414–2479*.

➤ MID JUNE–EARLY SEPT: **Kenwood Lakeside Concerts** offers fireworks and classical concerts under the stars in the park of London's regal stately house. ✉ *Kenwood House, Hampstead La., London, NW3*, ☏ *020/7973–3427*.

➤ LATE JUNE–EARLY JULY: **Henley Royal Regatta** (☏ 01491/572153), an international rowing event and top social occasion, takes place at Henley-upon-Thames, Oxfordshire.

➤ LATE JUNE–EARLY JULY: **The Wimbledon Lawn Tennis Championships,** held at the All England Lawn Tennis and Croquet Club in Wimbledon. Write early to enter the lottery for tickets for Centre and Number One courts; tickets for outside courts are available daily at the gate. ✉ *Church Rd., Wimbledon, London SW19 5AE*, ☏ *020/8946–2244*.

➤ EARLY JULY: **Hampton Court Palace Flower Show** is a five-day event that nearly rivals the Chelsea Flower Show for glamour. ✉ *East Molesey*, ☏ *020/7834–4333; 0870/906–3791 ticket agency*.

➤ MID-JULY–MID-SEPT: **Henry Wood Promenade Concerts** is a marvelous series of concerts at the Royal Albert Hall. ✉ *Box Office, Royal Albert Hall, Kensington Gore, London, SW7 2AP*, ☏ *020/7589–8212*.

➤ LATE AUG: **Notting Hill Carnival** (☏ 020/8964–0544) is one of the liveliest street festivals in England. Caribbean foods, reggae music, and street parades are part of the swirling event, usually held on the last Sunday and Monday in August.

➤ SEPT: **Open House** (☏ 020/7267–7697) is a rare one-day chance to view historic London interiors of buildings usually closed to the public, organized by Architectural Dialogue.

➤ LATE SEPT: **The Great River Race** fills the Thames with more than 250 boats from Chinese dragonboats to Viking longboats. The boats race from Ham House in Richmond through the center of London to Greenwich pier.

➤ EARLY OCT: **Pearly Harvest Festival Service** draws a crowd of costermongers to the Church of St. Martin-in-the-Fields on the first Sunday in October. The Pearly Kings and Queens strut their famous costumes. ✉ *Trafalgar Square, London, WC2*, ☏ *020/7930–0089*.

➤ EARLY NOV: **London to Brighton Veteran Car Run** (☏ 01753/681736) is a run from Hyde Park in London to the seaside town of Brighton in East Sussex.

➤ EARLY NOV: **Lord Mayor's Procession and Show** (☏ 020/7332–1456) is a procession, for the lord mayor's inauguration, that takes place from the Guildhall in the City to the Royal Courts of Justice.

➤ NOV. 5: **Guy Fawkes Day** celebrates a foiled 1605 attempt to blow up Parliament. Fireworks are presented throughout London, but the place to be is the bonfire festivity on Primrose Hill near Camden Town.

1 DESTINATION: LONDON

From Cosmopolitan to Cockney: A City of Villages

What's Where

Pleasures and Pastimes

Fodor's Choice

Great Itineraries

FROM COSMOPOLITAN TO COCKNEY: A CITY OF VILLAGES

LONDON IS AN ENORMOUS CITY—600 square mi—on a tiny island, accommodating about 7 million inhabitants, one-eighth of the entire population of England, Scotland, and Wales, but to many travelers it never *really* feels big. It is fashioned on a different scale from other capital cities, as if, given the English penchant for modesty and understatement, it felt embarrassed by its size. Each of the 32 boroughs that compose the whole has its own character, lore, and rhythm. There is the heraldic splendor of Westminster, the chic of artistic Chelsea, the architectural elegance of Belgravia and Mayfair, the cosmopolitan charm of Soho, and the East End, home base of the Cockney—to name just a few. Stay here long enough and Professor Higgins' feat of deducing Eliza Dolittle's very street of birth from the shape of her vowels will seem like nothing special. It's a cliché, but London really is a city of villages.

London's contrasts can best be savored by strolling from one district to another. First pick a starting point such as Piccadilly Circus, face in the direction of the area of central London you want to explore, and start moving. To the north runs Regent Street, curving up one side of ritzy, mostly residential Mayfair. To the south is Lower Regent Street, leading toward Whitehall, the parks, and the palaces. To the east are Shaftesbury Avenue and Leicester Square, for theaters and Soho; to the west is Piccadilly itself, heading out to Hyde Park and Knightsbridge. This is also a great place to board a double-decker sightseeing bus—just remember to have some sort of protective wrap handy: atop these buses it's *always* windy.

That's one of the best things about the city: everything has been seen before, and history is forever poking its nose in. Whatever you're doing, you're doing it on top of a past layered like striated rock. You can see the cross sections clearly sometimes, as in the City, where lumps of Roman wall nest in the postmodern blocks of the street helpfully named London Wall. Walk toward the Thames to Cheapside, which you can tell was the medieval marketplace if you know the meaning of "ceap" ("to barter"), and there's the little Norman church of St. Mary-le-Bow, rebuilt by Wren and then again after the Blitz, but still ringing the Bow Bells. Then look to your right, and you'll be gobsmacked by the dome of St. Paul's. Of course, all you really wanted was to find a place for lunch—nearly impossible on a weekend in this office wasteland.

Instead of going weak-kneed at the sights, Londoners are apt to complain about such privations while pretending simultaneously that no other city in the United Kingdom exists. Edinburghers and Liverpudlians can complain till Big Ben tolls 13, but Londoners continue to pull rank with a complacency that will amuse and infuriate you in equal measure. London definitely *used* to be important. The vein of water running through its center has always linked the city with the sea, and it once gave British mariners a head start in the race to mine the world's riches and bring them home. The river proved convenient for building not only palaces (at Westminster, Whitehall, Hampton Court, Richmond, Greenwich) but an empire, too.

The empire dissolved, but the first Thames bridge is still there, in almost the same spot that the emperor Claudius picked in AD 43, and although the current drab concrete incarnation dates only from 1972, it's still called London Bridge. The Tudor one was much better—a row of decapitated heads were supposedly stuck on poles above the gatehouse.

The old London Bridge lasted 600 years. Lined with shops and houses, it presided over a string of fairs *on* the Thames, when winters were colder and the water froze thick. Nowadays London rarely sees a snowfall, though Londoners talk endlessly about its possibility. People here are genuinely obsessed by the weather because there's so much of it, though most of it is damp. Snow varies the scenery, stops any tube train with an overground route, makes kids of everyone with a makeshift toboggan and access to a park (99% of the population), and fosters a community spirit normally proscribed by the city's geography and its citizens' cool. Winters were colder as recently as the '60s, when waiting for the crust to thicken enough to skate on the Round Pond in Kensington Gardens—now good only for model-boat sailors and duck feeders—was only a matter of time.

The corollary to London's temperate winter, though, is a fresh confidence in summer sufficient to support herds of sidewalk tables. Holland Park Avenue no longer has the monopoly on a Parisian-style milieu. All over town, an epidemic of Continental-style café chains serving croissants and *salade frisée* has devoured the traditional tobacco-stained pubs serving warm bitter and bags of pork scratchings. Most of the remaining pubs have turned into faux-Edwardian parlors with coffee machines and etchings or, more recently, wood-floored bars serving flavored vodkas and Tuscan food. The change has been going on for about a decade, and it suits London, as does its momentous discovery that restaurants are allowed to serve good food in smart surroundings and not charge the earth.

London is increasingly a European city, as if England were no longer stranded alone in the sea. In fact, ever since airplanes superseded ships, this island race has been undergoing an identity crisis, which reached its apogee in the '70s when Prime Minister Edward Heath sailed the country irrevocably into the Common Market. Occasionally Britain still holds out against some European Community legislation or other, attempting to reassert differences that are following executions at the Tower and British Colonial supremacy into history. But however much the social climate changes, London is built on a firm foundation. Until the ravens desert the Tower of London—which is when, they say, the kingdom will fall—London has Westminster Abbey and St. Paul's and the Houses of Parliament, the Georgian squares and grand Victorian houses, the green miles of parks, the river, the museums and galleries and theaters, and 32 boroughs of villages to keep it going.

— Kate Sekules

WHAT'S WHERE

Westminster and Royal London

All things start at Westminster, where there is as much history in a few acres as there is in many complete cities. The ancient Westminster Abbey, crammed with memorials and monuments to the great, and the good, can blind you to the spectacular Gothic splendor surrounding you. Whitehall is both an avenue and the heartbeat of the British government; here is the prime minister's official residence, No. 10 Downing Street, and the Horse Guards, where two mounted sentries of the queen's guard provide a memorable image. Whitehall leads to Trafalgar Square and the incomparable National Gallery, with the National Portrait Gallery just beside. From the grand Admiralty Arch, the Mall leads straight to Buckingham Palace, as unprepossessing on the outside as it is sumptuous inside. The streets are wide and the vistas are long—the perfect backdrop for the pomp and pageantry of royal occasions. With beautifully kept St. James's Park at its center, the Westminster area exudes dignity and offers frequent glimpses of pinnacles and towers over treetops and, of course, the deep tones of Big Ben counting off the quarter hours.

Belgravia

Just a short carriage ride from Buckingham Palace is London's most splendidly aristocratic enclave: Belgravia, a grande-dame neighborhood of block after block of grand, porticoed mansions. Built in the mid-1800s, it is residential, untouched by neon, with an authentic vintage patina. Most of its streets are lined with terraced row houses, all painted Wedgwood-china white (to signify they remain the property of the Duke of Westminster). Pedigree-proud locations include Belgrave Square, Grosvenor Crescent, and Belgrave Place, but also check out the chic alleyways, called "mews." No other spot in London will make you feel so much like warbling "On the Street Where You Live," from *My Fair Lady.*

Bloomsbury

The literary set that made the name Bloomsbury world famous has left hardly a trace, but this remains the heart of learned London. The University of London is here; so are the Law Courts and the British Museum. With the British Library parked just north at St. Pancras, a greater number of books can probably be found in Bloomsbury than in all the rest of London. Virginia Woolf and T. S. Eliot would be pleased to note that some of London's most beautiful domestic architecture, elegant houses that would have been familiar to Dr. Johnson, still line the area's prim squares. At one, Charles Dickens worked on *Oliver Twist* at a tall upright clerk's desk.

Bloomsbury is really part of Holborn, the core of Legal London. The Inns of Court are the finest group of historic buildings in the city, in an almost unspoiled setting. In Holborn, you'll also find Sir John Soane's Museum, a mansion that whisks you back to the mid-1800s.

Chelsea

Chelsea has always beckoned to freethinkers and fashion-fringers—from Sir Thomas More to Isadora Duncan (she couldn't find a place to stay her first night, so she decamped to the graveyard at Chelsea Old Church, which natives *still* insist is a lovely place to stay). Major sights include Christopher Wren's magisterial Royal Hospital—the site of the Chelsea Flower Show—and Cheyne Walk, where Henry James and Dante Gabriel Rossetti once lived. An extremely expensive place to live, the area continues to draw an army of weekend trendaholics to King's Road, whose boutiques gave birth to the paisleyed '60s and the pink-headed-punk '70s.

The City

Known as "the Square Mile," the City is to London what Wall Street is to Manhattan. As the site of the Celtic settlement the Romans called Londinium, this is the oldest part of London. Unfortunately, thanks to blocks of high-rise apartments and steel skyscrapers, it looks like the newest part. Yet within and around the capital-C City are some of London's most memorable attractions—St. Paul's Cathedral and storybook Tower Bridge. Charles and Diana tied the knot at St. Paul's but they could have found other equally beautiful options here, including St. Bride's (its distinctive multitiered spire gave rise to today's wedding cakes), St. Giles Without Cripplegate, and St. Mary-le-Bow. At the east border of the City is the legendary Tower of London, England's most perfectly preserved medieval fortress, where Sir Thomas More, Anne Boleyn, and the young princes Edward V and his brother Richard, nephews of Richard III, met untimely ends.

Covent Garden

Just east of Soho, Covent Garden is one of the busiest, most raffishly enjoyable parts of the city. Continental-style open-air cafés create a very un-English environment. Warehouses, once cavernous and grim, now accommodate fashion boutiques and a huge variety of shops favored by the "trendoisie." A network of narrow streets, arcades, and pedestrian malls, the area is dominated by the Piazza—scene of a food market in the 1830s and a flower market in the 1870s. Today the indoor-outdoor complex overflows with clothing shops and crafts stalls, and the re-modernized Royal Opera House opens onto the Piazza.

Docklands

The epicenter of London's modern growth is the Isle of Dogs, once a neighborhood fit only for canines. Now you'll find the space-age architecture (Canary Wharf's no. 1 Canada Square being the most prominent, literally), waterways from the old docks, and the nifty overhead electric Docklands Light Railway linking buildings to wharves. The Museum in Docklands traces the history of this quarter. The Thames Barrier strides across the river, between the east end on the north bank and Greenwich on the south bank, and its Visitor Centre and pedestrian walkway presents an exciting panorama. Venture further downstream to Woolwich for the story of the nation's gunnery defenses, which are memorialized at the museum Firepower!—part of the ancient royal dockyard buildings.

The East End

The 19th-century slums—immortalized by Charles Dickens and the evocative etchings of Gustave Doré—are a relic of the past. Today the area possesses a haunting beauty and a warm spirit of humor and friendliness. Sundays you'll find 21st-century versions of the medieval fair: Spitalfields Market and Petticoat Lane. Other fascinating sights include the Geffrye Museum—an overlooked cluster of wonderful historic interiors—Hawksmoor's Christ Church, and the Blind Beggar, the Victorian den of iniquity where Salvation Army founder William Booth was moved to preach his first sermon. Off the main thoroughfare, tap into the true pulse of East End life by exploring the lanes and alleys that still make up one of the world's most fascinating melting pots. Down by the river, sprawling eastward from Tower Bridge, the old docks have been regenerated into a modern landscape of glittering office developments. Most notable is Canary Wharf with its towering One Canada Square, the tallest building in Britain. The bright quayside building blocks are regenerating the heart of modern Docklands, with an elevated electric railway as its artery. The Museum in Docklands traces the maritime past.

Greenwich

A quick 8-mi jaunt down the Thames will bring you past the National Maritime Museum and the *Cutty Sark* to Greenwich's Royal Observatory, where, if time stood still, all the world's timepieces would be off. When you tire of straddling the hemispheres at the Greenwich Meridian, take a stroll through the acres of parkland that cover the area or, on weekends, the crafts and antiques markets. Sir Christopher Wren's Royal Naval College and Inigo Jones's Queen House both scale architectural heights, while Richard Rogers's now-closed Millennium Dome encapsulates modern style, for better or worse. The pretty streets of Greenwich house numerous bookstores and antiques shops.

Hampstead

One of the great glories of England is the English village, and on the northern outskirts of London you'll find one of the most fetching: Hampstead. The classic Georgian houses, picturesque streets, cafés, and delis attract arts and media types, and the plain wealthy. An amble along Church Row—possibly the finest terrace of 18th-century houses in London—will prove the pulling power of the area. London's most beautiful painting by Vermeer is on view at Kenwood House (whose park hosts grand concerts and fireworks in the summer), and the latest Mod Brit artists are shown at the Saatchi Collection. Here, too, are the Freud Museum and the Keats House, where the poet penned his immortal "Ode to a Nightingale." You can go bird-watching in the 800-plus emerald acres of Hampstead Heath. In the nearby neighborhood of St. John's Wood you can visit Abbey Road to snap the famed crossing outside the studios where John, Paul, George, and Ringo made history.

Hyde Park, Kensington Gardens

Together with St. James's Park and Green Park, these beautiful, leafy breathing spaces run to almost 600 acres. The handsome trees and quiet walks will refresh you as thoroughly as, centuries ago, these grounds refreshed Henry VIII after a hard day's shenanigans. In the Regency era, splendid horseflesh and equipages were the grand attraction; today, the soapbox orators at Hyde Park Corner (most oratorical on Sunday mornings) remain grand entertainment. Sooner or later everyone heads to the Long Water in Kensington Gardens for one of London's most beloved sights: the Peter Pan statue. Then circumnavigate the Round Pond, or swim in the Serpentine, or try to catch a glimpse of the Household Cavalry on Rotten Row.

Knightsbridge and Kensington

Within the district's cavalcade of streets lined with decorous houses are small, sleepy squares; delightful pubs nestled away in back lanes; and antiques shops, their windows aglow with the luminous colors of oil paintings. Not surprisingly, the capital's snazziest department stores are also here, Harrods and Harvey Nichols. Head first for the area's main attraction, the great museum complex of South Kensington. Raphael and Constable canvases, Ossie Clark couture, and William Morris chairs beckon at the Victoria and Albert Museum, a showcase for the decorative arts. Next to the V&A come two museums devoted to science, including the Natural History Museum. Most delightful are two historic homes: Leighton House, Lord Leighton's stunning Persian extravaganza, and the Linley Sambourne House, whose elegant Edwardian interiors were featured in *A Room with a View.* Regroup at Kensington Palace—its state rooms and royal dress collection are open to view—then repair to its elegant Orangery for a pot of Earl Grey.

Notting Hill and Holland Park

These are two of London's most fashionable, coveted residential areas. Notting Hill, around Portobello Road, is a trendsetting square mile of multiethnicity, galleries, small and exciting shops, and see-and-be-seen-in restaurants. The style-watching media dubbed the natives—musicians, novelists, and fashion plates—"Notting Hillbillies." If Notting Hill is for the young, neighboring Holland Park is entirely the opposite—the area's leafy streets are full of expensive white-stucco Victorians and lead to bucolic Holland Park itself.

Regent's Park

Helping to frame the northern border of the city, Regent's Park is home to the much-loved zoo and Regent's Park Open-Air Theatre. A walk around the perimeter of the park is a must for devotees of classical architecture; the payoff is a view of John Nash's Terraces, a grandiose series of white-stucco terraced houses, built around 1810 for the "People of Quality" who demanded London homes as nearly as possible resembling their grand country estates. In summer, be sure to take in the rose-bedecked Queen Mary's Gardens. Next, head over to the open-air theater for, perhaps, a picture-perfect performance of *A Midsummer Night's Dream*. Between the walkers, joggers, and playing children, watch out for airborne objects—softballs, footballs, and cricket balls.

St. James's and Mayfair

St. James's and Mayfair form the core of the West End, the city's smartest and most desirable central area, where there is no shortage of history and gorgeous architecture, custom-built for ogling the lifestyles of London's rich and famous. Although many will say Mayfair is only a state of mind, the heart of Mayfair has shifted from the 19th-century's Park Lane to Carlos Place and Mount Street. Of course, the shops of New and Old Bond streets lure the wealthy, but the window-shopping is free. Mayfair is primarily residential, with two public grand houses to see: Apsley House, the Duke of Wellington's home, once known as No. 1, London, and, on elegant Manchester Square, the Wallace Collection, situated in a palatial town house filled with old master paintings and fine French furniture. The district of St. James's—named after the centuries-old palace that lies at its center—remains the ultimate enclave of the old-fashioned gentleman's London. Here you'll find Pall Mall, with its many noted clubs, including the Reform Club, and Jermyn Street, where you can shop like the Duke of Windsor.

Soho and Theatreland

Once known infamously as London's red-light district, Soho these days is more stylish than seedy—now it's populated with film and record bigwigs (Sir Paul McCartney's offices are here). The area is not especially rich architecturally, but it is nonetheless intriguing. The density of Continental residents around quaint Soho Square means some of London's best restaurants—whether pricey Italian, budget Chinese, or the latest opening—are in the vicinity. Shaftesbury Avenue cuts through the southern part of Soho; this is Theatreland, where you'll find almost 50 West End theaters. It's beloved of those who admire Shakespeare, Maggie Smith, and *Phantom*. To the south lie Leicester Square, London's answer to Times Square, and Charing Cross Road, the bibliophile's dream.

The South Bank

Totally rebuilt after the bombs of World War II flattened the remains of medieval Southwark (only a few stones of the Bishop of Winchester's Palace still stand), the South Bank has undergone a renaissance. If William Shakespeare returned today, however, he would be delighted to find a complete reconstruction of his Globe Theatre, not far from where the original closed in 1642. In fact, this side of the Thames (walk along the riverside embankment for great views of the city) has become a perch for diehard culture vultures: the Design Museum is here, as is the gigantic Tate Modern gallery, a new use for an old power station. From here, the Millennium Bridge offers a picturesque pedestrian walkway to St. Paul's Cathedral. Also here is the South Bank Arts Complex—with its Royal National Theatre, Royal Festival Hall, and culinary hot spot with a view, the OXO Tower Restaurant. And who can resist the London Dungeon—a waxwork extravaganza featuring blood 'n' guts—where "a perfectly horrible experience" is guaranteed. Towering over all is the British Airways London Eye, the tallest observation wheel in Europe.

The Thames Upstream

The most powerful palaces—Chiswick, Kew Palace and Gardens, Osterley Park, Richmond, and Putney—were linked closely to London by the river. A river cruise along Father Thames to some of these famous places, enveloped with serenity and rolling greenery, makes an idyllic retreat from the city on a sweltering summer day. Stroll around and just enjoy the rural air or find your way out of the famous maze at Hampton Court Palace, England's version of Versailles.

PLEASURES AND PASTIMES

Food, Glorious Food: The Delights of Dining

London ranks among the world's top dining scenes. A new generation of chefs has precipitated a fresh approach to food preparation, which you could call "London style," though most refer to it as "Modern British."

Today, almost everything on the culinary front has changed. The old standards have been given a nouvelle spin—although roast suckling pig topped with strawberry-papaya and served on a bed of chili noodles may not be everyone's cup of tea. The nouvelle push has taken the starch—literally—out of many of the city's menus, and this new energy is even finding a vogue for old standbys like angels-on-horseback (crisp bacon wrapped around oysters).

Savvy Londoners looking for a dinner bargain go for the nearest tandoori house—this Indian food goes beyond the cliché into national-dish territory. Londoners have now enlarged their purview to encompass most of the world; in the space of two weeks, diners can cover as much tongue-tingling ground as in a two-week package tour of exotic, far-flung places.

In fact, so many people are eating ethnic that the indigenous caff (the British diner)—which offers such grab-and-gulp goodies as fish-and-chips, chip butties (Wonder Bread with margarine and fries), or chips and ketchup—has become less ubiquitous in central London than good sandwich bars. Today, such native delicacies as the cockles, winkles, and smoked eels found in the cockney stalls of the East End appear as just one more exotic cuisine in the pantheon.

Cheers!: The Pub Experience

Londoners could no more live without their "local" than they could forgo dinner. The pub—or public house, to give it its full title—is ingrained in the British psyche as social center, bolt-hole, second home. Pub culture—revolving around pints, pool, darts, and sports—is still male dominated; however, as a result of the gentrification trend started in the late '80s by the major breweries (which own most pubs), transforming many ancient smoke- and spittle-stained dives into fantasy Edwardian drawing rooms, women have been entering their welcoming doors in increasing numbers. This decade, the trend has been toward the bar, superficially identified by its cocktail list, creative paintwork, bare floorboards, and chrome fittings. The social function is the same: these are English pubs, but not as Londoners formerly knew them.

When doing a London pub crawl, you must remember one thing: arcane licensing laws forbid the serving of alcohol after 11 PM (10:30 on Sunday; there are different rules for restaurants)—a circumstance you see in action at 10 minutes to 11, when the "last orders" bell signals a stampede to the bar. After many decades, however, some relaxation of these unpopular laws is in evidence with weekend "extensions" being granted, especially in Soho, plus a slew of clubs/bars/pubs that get around them by charging a moderate cover after 11 PM.

The Performing Arts: From the Boards to the Bard

There is a strength and fluidity about the performing arts in London that makes them very difficult to pin down. An actor playing Lear with the Royal Shakespeare Company one day could quite possibly appear in a television farce the next; an opera that has played to the small exclusive audience at Glyndebourne in the English countryside might reappear the next week at the Royal Albert Hall, delighting millions through radio. In music and drama, opera and ballet, there are endless ways for you to enjoy yourself to the hilt.

THEATER

Shakespeare, of course, supplies the backbone to the theatrical life of the city. There can hardly have been a day since the one on which the Bard breathed his last when one of his plays, in some shape or form, was not being performed. On the London stage, they have survived being turned into musicals (from Purcell to rock), they have made the reputations of generations of famous actors (and broken not a few), and they have seen women playing Hamlet and men playing Rosalind. If the Bard of Bards remains the headliner at Stratford-upon-Barbican, the London theater scene is amazingly varied. From a West End *Oliver!* revival to an East End feminist staging of *Ben-Hur,* London remains a theatergoer's town.

MUSIC

London has four world-class orchestras. The London Symphony Orchestra is in residence at the Barbican Centre, while the London Philharmonic lives at the Royal Festival Hall—one of the finest concert halls in Europe. Between the Barbican and South Bank, there are concert performances almost every night of the year. The Barbican also presents chamber music concerts in partnership with such celebrated orchestras as the City of London Sinfonia. The Royal Albert Hall during the Promenade Concert season (July–September) is a don't-miss pleasure. Also look for the lunchtime concerts held throughout the city in either smaller concert halls, arts-center foyers, or churches; they usually cost less than £5 or are free. St. John's, Smith Square, and St. Martin-in-the-Fields are the major venues for these, and they also present evening concerts.

BALLET AND OPERA

The two key players in London's opera scene are The Royal Opera House in Covent Garden and the more innovative English National Opera, which presents English-language productions at the London Coliseum. The Royal Opera House's current theater has undergone a monumental renovation, and the building has been very well received. The renowned Royal Ballet, which performs classical and contemporary repertoire, now has a permanent home in The Royal Opera House's spectacular state-of-the-art Victorian theater.

Best Foot Forward: Walking Through London

London is a great walking city because so many of its real treasures are untouted details: tiny alleyways barely visible on the map; garden squares; churchyards; shop windows; sudden vistas of skyline or park. However, it is big—very big. And often rather damp. With the obvious precautions of comfortable, weatherproof shoes and an umbrella, this activity might well become your favorite pastime.

FODOR'S CHOICE

With so many special places in London, Fodor's writers and editors have their favorites. Here are a few that stand out. For detailed information about each entry, refer to the appropriate chapter.

Quintessential London

Afternoon Performance at Shakespeare's Globe. London at its Wellsian time-machine best, this open-to-the-skies reconstruction of Shakespeare's beloved "Wooden O" transports you back to Elizabethan London.

Beatles' Magical Mystery Tour. This wonderful stroll down Memory Lane offered by Original London Walks includes the London Palladium, No. 3 Savile Row—the Fab Four's London headquarters—and Abbey Road.

Changing of the Guard. Adding a dash of red to the gloomiest of London days, the colorful regiments of guards march in front of Buckingham Palace as the band plays.

Houses of Parliament at Sunset. Cross the Thames to Jubilee Gardens to see this view of London at its storybook best.

Sunday Afternoon at Speakers' Corner, Hyde Park. A space especially reserved for anyone with anything to say that must be said publicly makes for great entertainment. Speakers seem to be most oratorical on Sunday afternoons.

Tower Bridge at Night. A dramatically floodlighted Tower Bridge confronts you as you come out of the Design Museum on a winter's night. Have your camera ready.

Magnificent Museums

Apsley House. Known as No. 1 London, this was the residence of the Duke of Wellington, fabled conqueror of Napoléon. The house's centerpiece, the Waterloo Gallery, is one of the grandest rooms in Europe.

British Museum. You could move into this grand pile and never tire of all that it has to offer, from the Rosetta Stone to the sublime Elgin Marbles from ancient Greece.

National Gallery. Da Vincis, Rubenses, and Rembrandts fill the rooms here—the richest trove of old master paintings in Britain.

Sir John Soane's Museum. Eccentric architect of the Bank of England, Sir John left his house to the nation on the condition that nothing be changed. The result is a Regency-era phantasmagoria of colors, unusual perspectives, and objets d'art.

Spencer House. The London house to end all London houses, this glamorous Palladian mansion was built by Princess Diana's ancestors and proves that even the 18th-century Spencers were no slouches in the flash department.

Tate Britain. Works by British artists from the 16th century to the present are on display here and at the Tate's offspring, Tate Modern.

Dining

Gordon Ramsay at Claridge's. Nobody does it better than this hot spot's eponymous French-inspired chef, so most book months in advance for his incomparable concoctions. Expect, for a democratically priced three-course meal (dinner starts at £38), wonders like goose liver, scallops, and sautéed cuttlefish. ££££

La Tante Claire. Pierre Koffmann may be London's best chef, and he is practicing his seemingly effortless art at the Berkeley Hotel. The service is impeccable and the French wine list impressive, but food is the point. ££££

Rules. Come, escape from the 21st century. London's delicious answer to Maxim's in Paris, Rules enjoys an incomparable 19th-century milieu, one that has welcomed everyone from Dickens to the Prince of Wales. £££

Le Caprice. This glamorous place has stood the test of time—the food is great, the surroundings even better. The other reason everyone comes here is that everyone else does, which leads to the best celeb-watching in town. ££–£££

The Eagle. This superior pub, with wooden floors, a few sofas, and art on the walls, serves amazingly good-value Portuguese/Spanish food. £–££

Quality Chop House. The food at this converted greasy spoon is a glorious parody of caff food (bangers and mash, egg and chips); the seats resemble Victorian pews. £–££

Lodging

Claridge's. The same fine qualities that attracted the king of Morocco, among many others, to this world-renowned Mayfair hotel are sure to make you feel right at home, too. ££££

The Connaught. Admirers of this exclusive, ambassadorial landmark simply refuse to stay elsewhere. No wonder: discretion and luxury prevail. There's a grand Edwardian lobby, packed with oil paintings and antiques, and a magnificent oak staircase. ££££

Covent Garden Hotel. Painted silks, ottomans, and off-duty celebrities. No wonder discerning travelers now call this the most stylish hotel in London. ££££

The Dorchester. Off-the-scale opulence *and* charm. When you're not strutting down the catwalk in the Promenade lounge you'll want to admire the 1,500 square yards of gold leaf and 1,100 square yards of marble. ££££

The Savoy. Elizabeth Taylor spent her honeymoon here, and Hemingway and Gershwin were fixtures at the bar. Take a river suite at this historic, late-Victorian hotel overlooking the Thames—you'll get one of the best stays and views in London. ££££

Dorset Square Hotel. Tim and Kit Kemp, hoteliers extraordinaire, decanted the English country look into a fine pair of Regency town houses and then turned up the volume in the first of their four London addresses. £££–££££

myhotel bloomsbury. List your preferences (music, film) and get exactly the room you expect, and a personal assistant to boot. This individualist-oriented town house–style hotel even comes with a spa (think honey and ginger body wrap). £££

GREAT ITINERARIES

London in 5 Days

In a city with as many richly stocked museums and matchless marvels as London, you risk seeing half of everything or all of nothing. So use the efficient itineraries below to keep you on track as you explore both the famous sights and those off the beaten path. Although you'll need those familiar red double-decker buses and the Underground to cover long distances, you'll soon discover how London rewards those who stroll its streets. So that you don't show up somewhere and find you've missed the boat, shuffle the itinerary segments with the closing hours, listed below, in mind.

Day One. Spend your first day in Royal London, which contains much that is historic and traditional in British life. Beat the crowds and get an early start at magnificent, medieval Westminster Abbey—if Prince Charles becomes king, this is where he will be crowned. After an hour exploring the abbey, make the 15-minute walk (or tube it from Westminster to St. James's Park) to catch the Changing of the Guard at 11:20, outside Buckingham Palace. Don't dawdle—optimally you need to get there by 10:45. In season an alternative option is to tour Buck House itself, as the British quippingly call it. Next stroll down the Mall, enjoying the very view the monarch sees when she rides in her gilded coach to open Parliament every year. Passing King George IV's glorious Carlton House Terrace, walk through the Admiralty Arch into Trafalgar Square, the very center of the city. Spend an hour or two in the National Gallery, the finest art museum in the land. If you're interested in history or you'll have time on another day for the National Gallery, go instead to nearby St. Martin's Place and the National Portrait Gallery, a visual who's who of England. From Trafalgar Square, head south to Whitehall, which is lined with grand government buildings, the Baroque-era Banqueting House, outside of which King Charles I was beheaded, and the Horse Guards Parade (Her Majesty's mounted guardsmen make a great photo-op). Head past 10 Downing Street—the Prime Minister's residence—to the Houses of Parliament. To see them, you have two options: either wait in line for the limited seats available in the Strangers Gallery of either house (use the St. Stephen's Entrance opposite the abbey), or prebook a tour, which shows off all the State Rooms. Eventually you'll hear Big Ben signaling the approaching dinner hour, just in time for your reservation at Rules, London's most beautiful restaurant, and a feast in the same salon where Lillie Langtry and the Prince of Wales once dined.

It's best to do this tour on Tuesday or Wednesday. But remember that from August through March, the Changing of the Guard (usually a daily event) occurs only every other day; check schedules before you plan. Buckingham Palace is open daily in season—from late August to early October. When the Houses of Parliament are open to visitors, the House of Lords is closed from Thursday to Sunday, the House of Commons from Friday to Sunday; optimal times are complex, so check the Houses of Parliament schedule in Chapter 2. On Sunday the Banqueting House is closed, and Westminster Abbey (except for the museum) is open only to those attending services.

Day Two. Think of this day as London 101—a tour of the city's postcard sights. Begin at the British Museum (where you'll find the Elgin Marbles, Rosetta Stone, and the Sutton Hoo Treasure) and explore the adjacent treasures of bookish Bloomsbury, including the Dickens House Museum and the British Library (on Euston Road, 10 blocks north), then perhaps track the spirit of Virginia Woolf on verdant Bedford, Russell, and Bloomsbury squares. Now head southeast toward the Thames to visit the Regency delight that is Sir John Soane's Museum at Lincoln's Inn. Continue south to Fleet Street, then east to 17th-century St. Paul's Cathedral, the city's presiding spirit. Wander south through the crooked streets of Blackfriars to Blackfriars Bridge and cross the Thames to Southwark; stop at the Tate Modern art gallery or take in a play at Shakespeare's Globe, the most famous theater in the world. At day's end, journey along old Father Thames east to Le Pont de la Tour or west to the OXO Tower to enjoy a riverside dinner with London spectacularly illuminated at your feet.

Don't plan on doing Day Two on Sunday, when both the Dickens House Museum and Sir John Soane's Museum are closed. Note that Shakespeare's Globe stages plays in the open-air theater only from May to September.

Day Three. Explore St. James's and Mayfair, the core of London's West End, the smartest and most atmospheric central area of the city. From Piccadilly Circus go west on Piccadilly to splurge on breakfast at the Queen's grocers, Fortnum & Mason. For a brush with royalty, maybe even with Wills and Harry, detour several blocks to Prince Charles's Tudor-era home, St. James's Palace near St. James's Square, then continue on to palatial Spencer House, which once housed the ancestors of the late Princess of Wales. From Piccadilly travel north for some ritzy window-shopping on Bond Street, in the 19th-century Burlington Arcade, and along Savile Row, continuing on through beautiful Mayfair via Mount Street, Carlos Place—tea at the Connaught Hotel, anyone?—and Grosvenor Square. From here take Duke Street north to view the Fragonards and Halses at the Wallace Collection on Manchester Square. Keep going south to Park Lane and just before Hyde Park Corner visit Apsley House, flanked by the Wellington Arch and a statue of Achilles pointing to the Duke's time-burnished mansion. To the southwest is the splendidly aristocratic enclave of Belgravia, London at its most Upstairs, Downstairs.

Apsley House is closed on Monday and Spencer House is open only on Sunday.

Day Four. London legends populate this itinerary. First take a break from the city and travel up to its most famous "village," Hampstead. After taking in the picturesque houses, chic cafés, and Church Row—London's most complete Georgian street—move on to (if you're a Beatlemaniac) Abbey Road, in nearby St. John's Wood. Then tube it down to Baker Street, visit the Sherlock Holmes Museum or Madame Tussaud's (a must for kids), then go north to Regent's Park and its swooningly elegant Cumberland Terrace and Chester Terrace (101 Dalmatians' Dearly family, the "pets" of Pongo and Perdita, lived here on the Outer Circle). In the afternoon take the tube to Tower Hill and the legendary Tower of London to see the Crown Jewels and the eight Tower Ravens. At dusk cross the street to the Tower Hill tube stop to pick up a spine-chilling Jack the Ripper Mystery Walk through the East End.

Note that the East End Jack the Ripper tours begin at 7 PM.

Day Five. This segment of your itinerary is all about shopping, history, and priceless art. Begin at the "museum mile" of South Kensington. See either the Victoria and Albert Museum, or, if you have children in tow, opt for the Natural History Museum or the Science Museum. Head up Brompton Road for lunch in Knightsbridge and shopping at Harrods or Harvey Nichols. Afterward you can go north or south. To the north, in Kensington Gardens, you can salute the Peter Pan statue, then visit historic Kensington Palace, childhood home of Queen Victoria and repository of the Royal Dress Collection. Continuing on Kensington High Street to Holland Park you will come to Leighton House, home of the noted 19th-century orientalist painter Lord Leighton. Have dinner in sassy and sophisticated Notting Hill. Alternatively from Knightsbridge you might head south to historic Chelsea to charming Cheyne Walk and the Tate Britain. If you go this route you can ensure a gala finale for your stay by booking tickets to a play or musical in the West End's Theatreland. But by now you will have learned that London is the most wonderful free show in the world.

Any day but Tuesday you can tour Leighton House.

If You Have More Time

Spectacular day trips lie upriver and down. Easily reachable by boat along the Thames to the east is Greenwich, with attractions such as the *Cutty Sark*, a 19th-century clipper, and the not-to-be-missed National Maritime Museum. Westward on the

Thames from London lie destinations that take you back, not forward, in time: Chiswick House, Kew Gardens, Syon House, and the 17th-century Hampton Court Palace, half rose-red Tudor brick, half serenely classical, still buried deep in parkland.

If You Have 3 Days

Touring the largest city in England in the space of three days sounds difficult, but it's long enough to give you a tempting taste of the city. Follow the itineraries for Days One and Two above, then begin your third day at the legend-haunted Tower of London. After a morning tour, take the tube or a taxi to Hyde Park Circle to see one of London's most spectacular town houses, Apsley House. You're in posh Mayfair now, so stroll to the Burlington Arcade and Bond Street for some world-class shopping, then head north to view the treasures at the Wallace Collection. From Marble Arch take the tube to Kensington High Street and Kensington Palace. After touring the historic palace, repair to its Orangery for tea and a well-deserved time-out. Try the best of contemporary British cuisine in nearby Notting Hill or book an evening in Theatreland.

A Kid's Day Out

Although children can't fly over the town as Peter Pan and Wendy did so thrillingly, this tour will show them a London packed with wonders. Get an early start with a tube ride to the Tower of London, where you can see the fabled Beefeater guards (plus its eight resident ravens; be sure to say hello to Thor, who talks). Across the street see the lively presentation about the Thames in the Tower Bridge. Cross to the south bank and hang a left toward Butler's Wharf for lunch. If you have teens, stop on Tooley Street at the goriest museum in town: the London Dungeon, a hoot of a horror waxworks show. Recross the river to catch a ferry at Tower Pier for a thrilling 15-minute cruise to Waterloo Pier (or, as far as Westminster Pier, from which you can walk across Westminster Bridge and then backtrack to Waterloo Pier; if it's raining, tube it from Tower Hill to Waterloo Station). On the way, watch a film at the BFI London IMAX Cinema; ride British Airways London Eye, the world's largest observation wheel; and tour the London Aquarium. At day's end take the tube back to Piccadilly and have tea at Fortnum & Mason.

2 EXPLORING LONDON

If London contained only its landmarks—Buckingham Palace, Big Ben, the Tower of London—it would still rank as one of the world's top destinations. But England's capital is much more. It's a bevy of British bobbies, an ocean of black umbrellas, and an unconquered continuance of more than 2,000 years of history. A city that loves to be explored, London beckons with great museums, royal pageantry, and quirky historical hideaways. Visit the Duke of Wellington's house or track Jack the Ripper's shadow in Whitechapel. East End, West End, you'll find London is a dickens of a place.

Updated by Jacqueline Brown and Catherine Belonogoff

LONDON IS AN ANCIENT CITY whose history greets you at every turn. To gain a sense of its continuity, stand on Waterloo Bridge at the hour of sunset. To the east, the great globe of St. Paul's Cathedral glows golden in the fading sunlight as it has since the 17th century, still majestic amid the towers of glass and steel that hem it in. To the west stand the mock-medieval ramparts of Westminster—here you'll find the "Mother of Parliaments," which has met here or hereabouts since the 1250s. Past them both snakes the swift, dark Thames, as it flowed past the first Roman settlement here nearly 2,000 years ago.

For much of its history, innumerable epigrams and observations have been coined about London by both her enthusiasts and detractors. The great 18th-century writer and wit Samuel Johnson said that a man who is tired of London is tired of life. Oliver Wendell Holmes said, "No person can be said to know London. The most that anyone can claim is that he knows something of it." Simply stated, London is one of the most interesting places on earth. There is no other place like it in its agglomeration of architectural sins and sudden intervention of almost rural sights, in its medley of styles, in its mixture of the green loveliness of parks and the modern gleam of neon. Thankfully, the old London of Queen Anne and Georgian architecture can still be discovered under the hasty routine of later additions.

Discovering it takes a bit of work, however. Modern-day London still largely reflects its medieval layout, a willfully difficult tangle of streets. Even Londoners, most of whom own a copy of the indispensable A–Z street finder (they come under different names), get lost in their own city. But London's bewildering street pattern will be a plus if you want to experience its indefinable historic environment. London is a walker's city and will repay every moment you spend exploring on foot. The undaunted visitor who wants to penetrate beyond the city's crust is well advised to not only visit St. Paul's Cathedral and the Tower but also to set aside some time for random wandering. Walk in the back streets and mews around Park Lane and Kensington. Pass up Buckingham Palace for Kew, the smallest royal palace, beautifully situated in the botanical gardens. Take in the National Gallery, but don't forget London's "time machine" museums, such as the 19th-century homes of Linley Sambourne and Sir John Soane. For out-and-out glamour, pay a call on the palatial Wallace Collection and Apsley House, the historic residence of the Duke of Wellington. Abandon the city's standard-issue chain stores to discover unique shopping emporiums, such as the gentlemen's outfitters of St. James's. Getting off the beaten track will help you visualize the shape, or rather the various shapes, of Old London, a curious city that engulfed its own past for the sake of modernity but still lives and breathes the air of history.

Today, that sense of modernity can be seen (witness the rash of spectacular architecture which has revitalized old landmarks) and sensed all around. It is still, as *Vanity Fair* magazine proclaimed, "the coolest, hottest city in the world." London is now more than ever the *only* place to be, as *Newsweek* declared. The city's art, style, fashion, and dining scenes continue to make headlines around the world. London's chefs have become superstars; its fashion designers have conquered Paris (John Galliano and Stella McCartney have made their mark at Dior and Chloë, and young dazzler Julien Macdonald is establishing himself after Alexander McQueen's run at Givenchy); avant-garde artists have made waves at the august Royal Academy of Arts; the city's raging after-hours scene is packed with music mavens ready to catch the next big thing; and the theater (including the National Theatre) continues its tradition of radical, shocking productions, which barely seem to turn most hairs. Even Shakespeare embraces cool: the Bard's own, reborn Globe—the fabled "wooden O"—is functioning brilliantly on the bank of the Thames just 200 yards from where it stood in the 16th century; when the troupe here presented *Two Gentlemen of Verona,* cast members were costumed in Ray-Ban sunglasses and sneakers. And following that, the theater continues to bring an incisive, witty new edge to the classic repertoire.

On the other hand, while the outward shapes may be altered and the inner spirit may be warmer now than in years past, the bedrock of London's character and tradition remains the same. The British bobby is alive and well. The tall, red, double-decker buses still lumber from stop to stop, though their aesthetic match at street level, the glossy red telephone booth, is slowly disappearing. And teatime is still a hallowed part of the day, with, if you search hard enough, toasted crumpets still laced with sweet butter. Then, of course, there is that greatest living link with the past—the Royal Family. Don't let the tag "typical tourist" stop you from enjoying the pageantry of the Windsors, one of the greatest free shows in the world. Line up for the Changing of the Guard and poke into the Royal Mews for a look at the Coronation Coach, resting after its outing for Queen Elizabeth II's Golden Jubilee in 2002. Pomp reaches its zenith in mid-June when the queen celebrates her official birthday with a parade called Trooping the Colour. Royalty-watching is by no means restricted to fascinated foreigners. You only have to open the national newspapers to read reports of the latest rumors. Then again, more and more people are feeling that what goes on inside Buckingham Palace is no one's affair but the queen's.

In the end, the London you'll discover will surely include some of our enthusiastic recommendations, but be prepared to be taken by surprise as well. The best that a great city has to offer often comes in unexpected ways. Armed with energy and curiosity, and the practical information and helpful hints in the following pages, you can be sure of one thing: to quote Dr. Johnson again, you'll be able to find "in London all that life can afford."

New & Noteworthy

The post millennium building frenzy continues as museums and galleries strive to become more technological and visitor-friendly. Most of the major national collections (the Natural History Museum, Science Museum, Victoria & Albert Museum) have extended opening hours on at least one night a week, and free admission. New museums offer greater insights into the lifeblood of old London. The Museum in Docklands (opened in May 2002), set in the space-age, renovated quaysides of the Thames, delves into the history of the ancient port of London. Also in the east of the city, set in the grand buildings of the former royal arsenal next to Henry VIII's regal dockyard, Firepower! The Museum of Artillery (which opened in May 2001) turns the spotlight on the guns and hardware from early to modern warfare. And for the more fragile of ears: the genteel sounds of Handel, along with exhibitions, can be enjoyed in the small Handel House Museum (opened in November 2001), where the composer created some of his most famous pieces. The imposing Wellington Arch, built to commemorate the Iron Duke's military prowess (the huge stone monument on the green bit which makes up the bustling roundabout of Hyde Park Corner), can now be enjoyed from the inside. At the top of three floors of exhibition space, you'll find a room with a brilliant view across the treetops of Hyde Park.

Central London

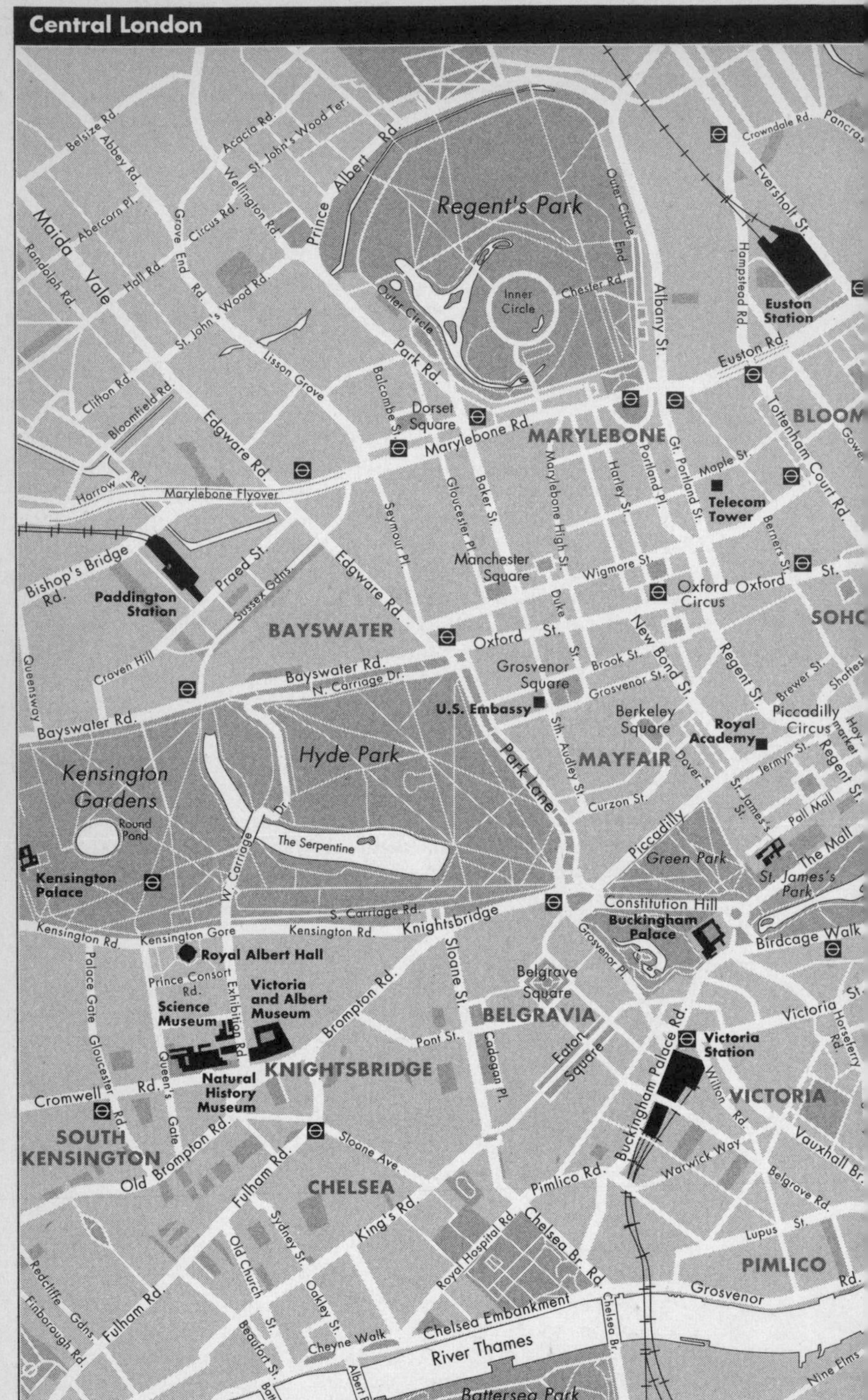

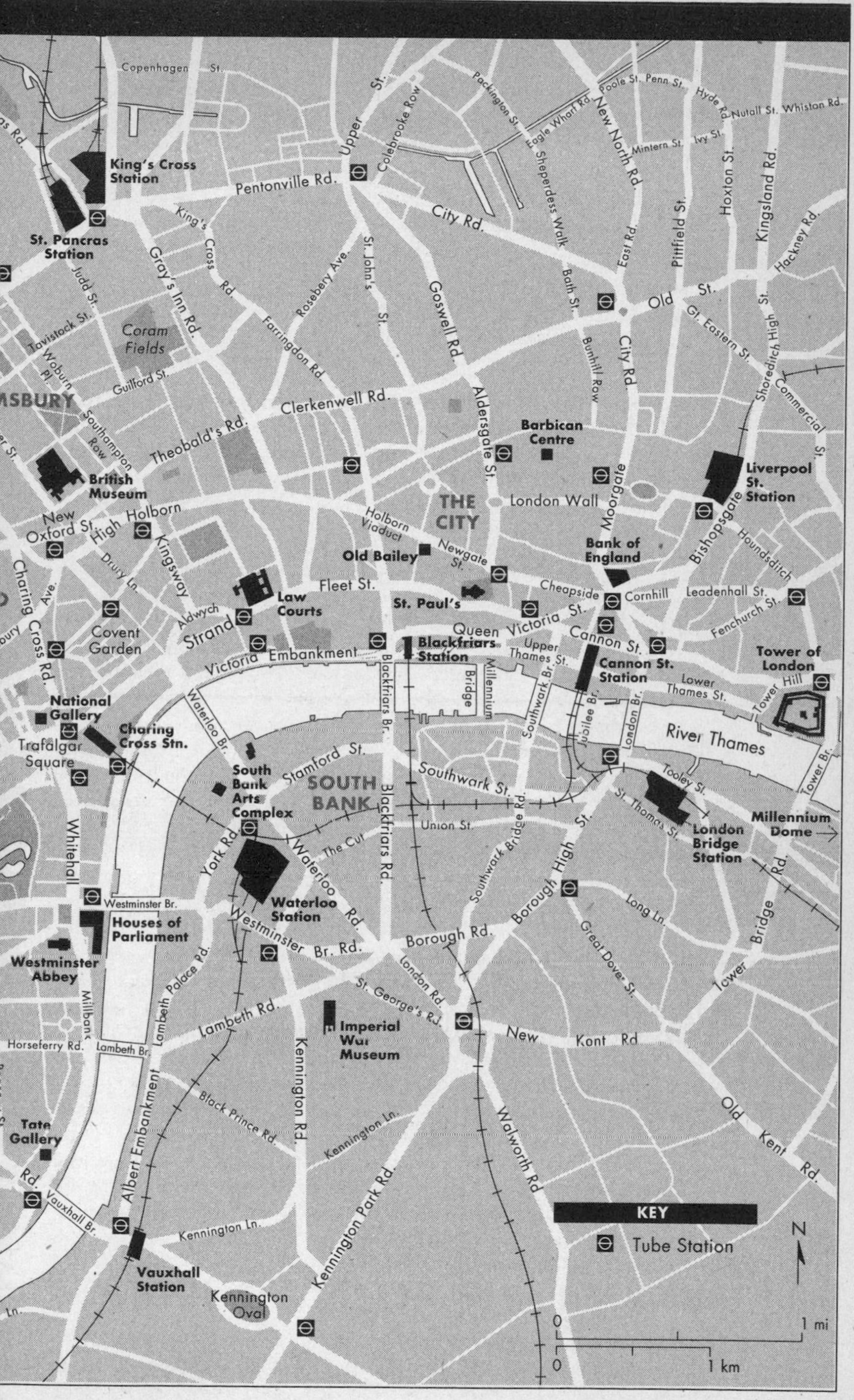
King's Cross Station
St. Pancras Station
Pentonville Rd.
City Rd.
Old St.
Goswell Rd.
Clerkenwell Rd.
Theobald's Rd.
Gray's Inn Rd.
Farringdon Rd.
Coram Fields
British Museum
New Oxford St.
High Holborn
Kingsway
Holborn Viaduct
Newgate St.
Old Bailey
Barbican Centre
London Wall
THE CITY
Moorgate
Liverpool St. Station
Bishopsgate
Bank of England
Fleet St.
St. Paul's
Cheapside
Cornhill
Leadenhall St.
Fenchurch St.
Law Courts
Aldwych
Strand
Covent Garden
Queen Victoria St.
Cannon St.
Blackfriars Station
Cannon St. Station
Tower of London
Tower Hill
Lower Thames St.
Victoria Embankment
National Gallery
Charing Cross Stn.
Trafalgar Square
Charing Cross Rd.
River Thames
Blackfriars Br.
Millennium Bridge
Southwark Br.
London Br.
Jubilee Br.
Tower Br.
Waterloo Br.
South Bank Arts Complex
SOUTH BANK
Stamford St.
Southwark St.
Union St.
Tooley St.
London Bridge Station
Millennium Dome
Whitehall
York Rd.
The Cut
Waterloo Rd.
Waterloo Station
Westminster Br.
Houses of Parliament
Westminster Abbey
Westminster Br. Rd.
Borough Rd.
Borough High St.
Blackfriars Rd.
Southwark Bridge Rd.
Long Ln.
Great Dover St.
Tower Bridge Rd.
Lambeth Palace Rd.
Lambeth Rd.
St. George's Rd.
London Rd.
Imperial War Museum
New Kent Rd.
Old Kent Rd.
Kennington Rd.
Black Prince Rd.
Kennington Ln.
Kennington Park Rd.
Walworth Rd.
Horseferry Rd.
Lambeth Br.
Albert Embankment
Tate Gallery
Vauxhall Br.
Vauxhall Station
Kennington Oval
KEY
Tube Station
N
0
1 mi
0
1 km

The opening of the surrealist museum Dalí Universe and the BFI London IMAX Cinema, not to mention Tate Modern, have made the South Bank a hot spot. In addition, the British Airways London Eye continues to offer unrivaled views of London and beyond from its see-through, podlike capsules.

At the Victoria & Albert Museum, a modernizing programme is under way, beginning with the updated British Galleries, which reopened in November 2001. This tour de force presents the story of art and design in Britain from Henry VIII to Queen Victoria, made more enlightening with period room settings and interactive-ware.

The Queen's outstanding collection of paintings, drawings, and sculpture—the Royal Collection—has twice as much exhibition space with the opening of a new extension in spring 2002. Even the unhung pieces can be viewed on screen in a state-of-the-art micro gallery.

Tate Britain has also completed bright new space, including an entrance that leads to the new Linbury Galleries on the lower floors, which will display changing exhibitions. There are new upper floors too, bringing some of the fabulous works by British artists (such as Turner and Gainsborough, and the more recent Bacon and Moore) to permanent view—many of them used to be consigned to storage.

To get you to the above-mentioned must-sees in Docklands is the ultra-modern Jubilee Underground line, with its futuristic-style stations. Architect Norman Foster's design at Canary Wharf is one of the award-winning examples. Many of the city's latest landmarks can be enjoyed along the scenic river route starting from one of the most recent piers, the Waterloo Pier, beside the London Eye. Bridge building also continues apace. One of the least attractive footbridges, the Hungerford, has been the site of a river crossing for people and horses to a marketplace since Brunel's suspension bridge was built in 1846. This was later dismantled due to lack of tolls (payment for crossing), and parts were used for Brunel's more famous suspension bridge, the Clifton, at Bristol. It wasn't until the 1950s that a walkway returned, parallel to the Charing Cross railway, but it was anything but pleasant. This has been remedied in the remodeled Hungerford Bridge, scheduled to open late summer 2002. If you're wondering about the significance behind the name, it's from a grand 17th-century marketplace built in the gardens of Edward Hungerford's old mansion, long before Charing Cross station. Also in celebration of the queen's Golden Jubilee in 2002 (and planned to be opened before the end of that year), the Jubilee Bridge is the first covered pedestrian bridge since the original London Bridge in medieval times. It has been built on previous Victorian foundations adjacent to Cannon Street rail lines over the river, and although the recycling principle seems less revolutionary than the dazzling, modern Millennium Bridge, at least it experienced less problems with stability. The latter's suspension structure caused much swaying and its almost immediate closure—but it reopened, with new shock absorbers, in early 2002.

WESTMINSTER AND ROYAL LONDON

This tour might be called "London for Beginners." If you went no farther than these few acres, you would see many of the most famous sights, from the Houses of Parliament, Big Ben, Westminster Abbey, and Buckingham Palace to two of the world's greatest art collections, housed in the National and Tate Britain galleries. You can truly call this area Royal London, as it is neatly bounded by the triangle of streets that make up the route that the queen usually takes when journeying from Buckingham Palace to the Abbey or to the Houses of Parliament on state occasions. The three points on this royal triangle are Trafalgar Square, Westminster, and Buckingham Palace. If you have time to visit only one part of London, undoubtedly this should be it. There is as much history in these few acres as in many entire cities, as the statues of kings, queens, soldiers, and statesmen that stand guard at every corner attest—this is concentrated sightseeing, so pace yourself. The main drawback to sightseeing here is that half the world is doing it at the same time. So, even if you're tired after a long day on your feet, try to come back in the evening, after the crowds have dispersed, to drink in the serenity and grandeur at your leisure. Not only does it make for a calmer experience, you'll also enjoy the floodlight beauty of many of these places by night.

Westminster is by far the younger of the capital's two centers, postdating the City by some 1,000 years. Edward the Confessor put it on the map when he packed up his court from its cramped City quarters and moved it west a couple of miles, founding the abbey church of Westminster—the minster west of the City—in 1050. Subsequent kings continued to hold court here until Henry VIII decamped to Whitehall Palace in 1512, leaving Westminster to the politicians. And here they are still, not in the palace, which burned almost to the ground in 1834, but in the Victorian mock-Gothic Houses of Parliament, whose 320-ft-high Clock Tower (Big Ben) is as much a symbol of London as the Eiffel Tower is of Paris.

Numbers in the text correspond to numbers in the margin and on the Westminster and Royal London map.

A Good Walk

Trafalgar Square ① is the obvious place to start for several reasons. It is the geographical core of London and a gathering point for many political demonstrations, a raucous New Year's Eve party, and the highest concentration of bus stops and pigeons in the capital. After taking in the instantly identifiable **Nelson's Column** ② in the center (read about the area on a plaque marking its 150th anniversary), head for the **National Gallery** ③, on the north side—this is Britain's greatest trove of masterpieces. Detour around the corner to see the **National Portrait Gallery** ④, a parade of the famous that can be very rewarding to anyone interested in what makes the British tick. East of the National Gallery, still on Trafalgar Square, see the much-loved church **St. Martin-in-the-Fields** ⑤; then, stepping through grand **Admiralty Arch** ⑥ down on the southwest corner, enter the royal pink road, the **Mall,** with St. James's Park on your left. On your right is the **Institute of Contemporary Arts** ⑦, known as the ICA and housed in the great Regency architect John Nash's **Carlton House Terrace** ⑧. At the foot of the Mall is one of London's most famous sights, **Buckingham Palace** ⑨, home, of course, to the monarch of the land and punctuated by the ornate, white-marble **Queen Victoria Memorial** ⑩. Turning left and left again, almost doubling back, follow the southern perimeter of St. James's Park around Birdcage Walk (the **Queen's Gallery** ⑪, with masterpieces from Her Majesty's vast art collection, is a few steps to the right at the side of the palace), passing **Wellington Barracks** ⑫, headquarters of the queen's guards, and, in turn, the hulking Home Office and **Queen Anne's Gate** ⑬. Cross Horse Guards Road at the eastern edge of the park and walk down Great George Street, with **St. Margaret's Church** ⑭ on your right. Continue across Parliament Square to come to another of the great sights of London, the **Houses of Parliament** ⑮, with Big Ben. A clockwise turn around the square brings you to yet another major landmark, breathtaking **Westminster Abbey** ⑯. Complete the circuit and head north up Whitehall, passing the **Cabinet War Rooms** ⑰, where you'll see a simple monolith in the middle of the street—the Cenotaph designed by Edwin Lutyens in 1920 in commemoration of the 1918 armistice. The gated alley on your left is **Downing Street** ⑱, where England's modest "White House" stands at No. 10. Soon after that, you pass **Horse Guards Parade** ⑲, the place where the queen's birthday is celebrated, in a festival called Trooping the Colour, with the classical Inigo Jones **Banqueting House** ⑳, scene of Charles I's execution, opposite. It's well worth it to backtrack a little ways down Whitehall and Abingdon Street, to Millbank and **Tate Britain** ㉑, the collection of British art.

TIMING

You could achieve this walk of roughly 3 mi in just over an hour, but you could just as easily spend a week's vacation on this route alone. Allow as much time as you can for the two great museums—the National Gallery requires at *least* two hours; the National Portrait Gallery can be whizzed round in less than one. Westminster Abbey can take half a day—especially in summer, when lines are long—both to get into and to get around in. In summer, you can get inside Buckingham Palace, too, a half-day's operation increased to a whole day if you see the Royal Mews and the Queen's Gallery or the Guards Museum. If the Changing of the Guard is a priority, make sure you time this walk correctly.

HOW TO GET THERE

This is an easy neighborhood to access, especially if you start at Trafalgar Square, where many buses stop. The central neighborhood tube stop, Charing Cross (on the Jubilee, Northern, and Bakerloo lines), exits at the beginning of Northumberland Avenue, on the southeast corner. Practically all buses stop around here, including Buses 3, 9, 11, 12, 16, 24, 29, 53, 88, 139, and 159. Just to the north of Trafalgar Square on Charing Cross Road is the Leicester Square tube stop (on the Northern and Piccadilly lines), which is just behind the galleries. Alternative tube stations on the south side are St. James's Park (on the District and Circle lines), which is the best for Buckingham Palace, or the next stop, Westminster, which deposits you right by the bridge, in the shadow of Big Ben.

Sights to See

❻ **Admiralty Arch.** Gateway to the Mall—no, not an indoor shopping center but one of the very grand avenues of London—this is one of London's stateliest urban set pieces. Situated on the southwest corner of Trafalgar Square, the arch, which was named after the adjacent Royal Navy headquarters, was designed in 1910 by Sir Aston Webb as part of a ceremonial route to Buckingham Palace. As you pass under the enormous triple archway—though not through the central arch, opened only for state occasions—the environment changes along with the color of the road, for you are exiting frenetic Trafalgar Square and entering the Mall (rhymes with shall)—the elegant avenue that leads directly to the palace. ✉ *The Mall, Cockspur St., Trafalgar Sq., Westminster SW1. Tube: Charing Cross.*

⓴ **Banqueting House.** This is all that remains today of the Tudor Palace of Whitehall, which was (according to one foreign visitor) "ill-built, and nothing but a heap of houses." James I commissioned Inigo Jones (1573–1652), one of England's great architects, to do a grand remodeling. Influenced during a sojourn in Tuscany by Andrea Palladio's work, Jones brought Palladian sophistication and purity back to London with him. The resulting graceful and disciplined classical style of

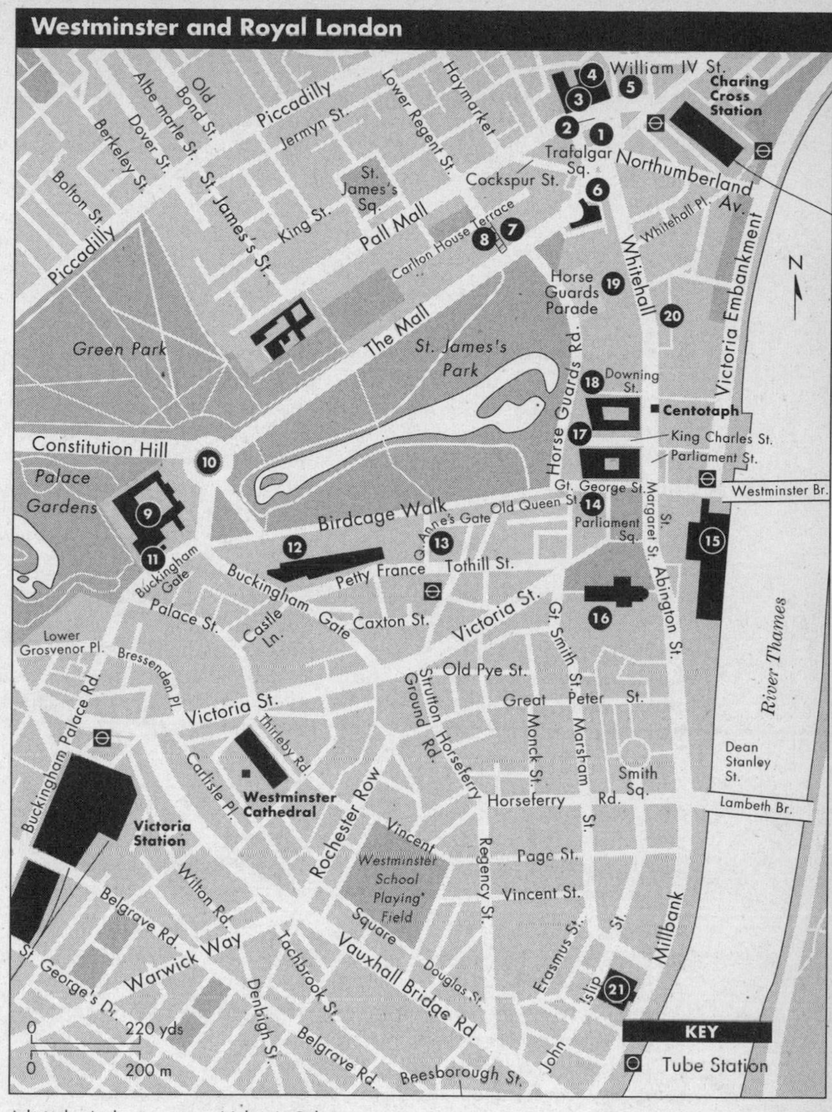

Admiralty Arch **6**

Banqueting House **20**

Buckingham Palace **9**

Cabinet War Rooms **17**

Carlton House Terrace **8**

Downing Street **18**

Horse Guards Parade **19**

Houses of Parliament **15**

Institute of Contemporary Arts (ICA) **7**

National Gallery . . . **3**

National Portrait Gallery **4**

Nelson's Column . . . **2**

Queen Anne's Gate **13**

Queen Victoria Memorial **10**

Queen's Gallery . . . **11**

St. Margaret's Church **14**

St. Martin-in-the-Fields **5**

Tate Britain **21**

Trafalgar Square . . . **1**

Wellington Barracks **12**

Westminster Abbey **16**

Banqueting House must have stunned its early occupants. In the quiet vaults beneath, James would escape the stresses of being a sovereign with a glass or two. His son, Charles I, enhanced the interior by employing the Flemish painter Peter Paul Rubens to glorify his father all over the ceiling. As it turned out, these allegorical paintings, depicting a wise monarch being received into heaven, were the last thing Charles saw before he was beheaded by Cromwell's Parliamentarians in 1649. But his son, Charles II, was able to celebrate the restoration of the monarchy in this same place 20 years later. ✉ *Whitehall, Westminster SW1,* ☎ *020/7930–4179,* WEB *www.hrp.org.uk.* 🎫 *£3.90, includes free audio guide.* ⏲ *Mon.–Sat. 10–5; closed on short notice for banquets, so call first. Tube: Charing Cross, Embankment, or Westminster.*

★ ❾ **Buckingham Palace.** Supreme among the symbols of London, indeed of Britain generally and of the Royal Family, Buckingham Palace tops many must-see lists—although the building itself is no masterpiece and has housed the monarch only since Victoria (1819–1901) moved here from Kensington Palace on her accession in 1837. Its great gray bulk sums up the imperious splendor of so much of the city: stately, magnificent, and ponderous. When Victoria moved in, the place was a mess. George IV, on his accession in 1820, had fancied the idea of moving to Buckingham House, his parents' former home, and had employed John Nash, as usual, to remodel it. The government authorized only "repair and improvement"; Nash, that tireless spendthrift, overspent his budget by about half a million pounds. George died, Nash was dismissed, and Edward Blore finished the building, adding the now familiar east front (facing the Mall). Victoria arrived to faulty drains and sticky doors and windows, but they did not mar her affection for the place, nor that of her son, Edward VII. The Portland stone facade dates only from 1913 (the same stone used for the Victoria Memorial outside the Palace and Admiralty Arch at the foot of the Mall), and the interior was renovated and redecorated only after it sustained World War II bomb damage. Indeed, compared to other great London residences, this is very much a Johnny-come-lately affair.

The palace contains 19 state rooms, 52 royal and guest bedrooms, 188 staff bedrooms, 92 offices, and 78 bathrooms—a prerequisite for the 450 people who work there, and the mere 50,000 who are entertained during the year. The state rooms are where much of the business of royalty is played out—investitures, state banquets, and receptions for the great and good. The royal apartments are in the north wing; when the queen is in residence, the royal standard is raised. The state rooms are on show from August to early October, a period when the Royal Family is away. A visit to the palace's west wing is a fascinating glimpse into another world: the fabulously gilt interiors are not merely museum pieces but pomp and pageantry at work. A tour starts from the Ambassadors' Court entrance, through to the **Entrée,** where portraits of past kings look down. The classical tone is set with Ionic columns in honeyed Bath stone, marble pillars in cool Carrara white, fine French and English furniture, and Chinese vases. Once through the **Grand Hall,** the **Grand Staircase,** and **Guard Room** (too small for the royal bodyguards—Yeoman of the Guard and Gentlemen-at-Arms in their traditional red and gold uniforms), the superlatives for the richness and elegance before your eyes could begin to wane. Prepare to be completely and utterly gilded out as Nash's ornate designs unfold through the numerous drawing rooms—each more jaw-dropping and neck-craning than the last—decorated with awesome ceilings and chandeliers, and magnificent objects brought from the Prince Regent's original palatial home, Carlton House. (Some of the most precious Sèvres porcelain in the world found its way here after the French Revolution.) The **Throne**

Room is opulent with gilt Baroque decor and the original 1953 coronation throne chairs. Queen Victoria used to hold balls here, but today it is the backdrop for royal wedding photographs and presentations. By now, when eyes are becoming glazed, the **Picture Gallery** is a restful feast of renowned art. The collection was begun by Charles I, and the works are periodically rearranged. Highlights among the many masterpieces are works by Rubens, Vermeer, Van Dyck, Cuyp, and Canaletto. The state rooms are graced with some of Her Majesty's most famous old master paintings, but other artwork is on view in the **Queen's Gallery** (which has been renovated extensively), near the south side of the palace. The palace tour continues through more galleries and drawing rooms filled with exquisite paintings and tapestries, culminating with the **State Dining Room** and its overly elaborate Blore ceiling. The table is sadly not set for a banquet with its usual crystal, gold, and silverware, but a solitary pair of ewers stands at attention.

From the State Dining Room there are views across the sweeping gardens, and unless you have an invitation to one of the queen's summer garden parties, the most you'll see of the magnificent 45-acre grounds is a walk along the south side of the palace garden. This addition to the tour gives views of the Garden (west) front of the palace and the 19th-century lake. The walled oasis has plenty of wildlife—it contains more than 350 types of wildflowers. Behind the front palace gates, the **Changing of the Guard,** with all the ceremony monarchists and children adore, remains one of London's best free shows and culminates in front of the palace. Marching to live music, the guards proceed up the Mall from St. James's Palace to Buckingham Palace. Shortly afterward, the replacement guard approaches from Wellington Barracks via Birdcage Walk. Then within the forecourt, the old guard symbolically hands over the keys to the palace to the replacement guard. The ceremony usually takes place on schedule, but the guards sometimes cancel owing to bad weather; check the signs in the forecourt or phone. Get there by 10:30 AM to grab a spot in the best viewing section at the gate facing the palace, since most of the hoopla takes place behind the railings in the forecourt. Be sure to prebook tour reservations of the palace with a credit card by phone. ✉ *Buckingham Palace Rd., St. James's SW1,* ☎ *020/7839–1377; 020/7799–2331 24-hr information; 020/7321–2233 credit-card reservations (subject to 50p booking charge),* WEB *www.royal.gov.uk.* 🎫 *£11.50 (prices change annually).* ⏲ *Early Aug.–early Oct., daily 9:30–4:15 (confirm dates, which are subject to queen's mandate). Changing of the Guard Apr.–July, daily 11:30 AM; Aug.–Mar., alternating days only 11:30 AM. AE, MC, V. Tube: Victoria or St. James's Park.*

🖐 ⓱ **Cabinet War Rooms.** It was from this small maze of 17 bomb-proof underground rooms—in back of the hulking Foreign Office—that Britain's World War II fortunes were directed. During air raids, the Cabinet met here—the Cabinet Room is still arranged as if a meeting were about to convene; in the Map Room, the Allied campaign is charted; the Prime Minister's Room holds the desk from which Winston Churchill (1874–1965) made his morale-boosting broadcasts; and the Telephone Room has his hot line to FDR. The great man only slept here on a number of occasions; he preferred the comfort of Downing Street, even at the height of the German blitz. ✉ *Clive Steps, King Charles St., Westminster SW1,* ☎ *020/7930–6961,* WEB *www.iwm.org.uk.* 🎫 *£5.* ⏲ *Apr.–Sept., daily 9:30–5:15; Oct.–Mar., daily 10–5:15. Tube: Westminster.*

❽ **Carlton House Terrace.** This is a glorious example of Regency architect John Nash's genius. Between 1812 and 1830, under the patron-

Close-Up

ROYAL ATTRACTIONS: WAITING FOR THE QUEEN

THE QUEEN AND THE ROYAL FAMILY attend approximately 400 functions a year, and if you want to know what she and the rest of the Royal Family are doing on any given date, turn to the *Court Circular,* printed in the major London dailies. But most want to see the royals in all their dazzling pomp and circumstance. For this, the best bet is the second Saturday in June, when the Trooping the Colour is usually held to celebrate the queen's official birthday. This spectacular parade begins when she leaves Buckingham Palace in her carriage and rides down the Mall to arrive at Horse Guards Parade at 11 exactly. If you wish to obtain one of the 7,000 seats to watch the Trooping the Colour rehearsal or the spectacle itself (no more than two seats per request, distributed by ballot), enclose a letter and stamped, self-addressed envelope or International Reply Coupon—from January to February 28 only—to **Ticket Office** (✉ Headquarters Household Division, Horse Guards, Westminster, London SW1A 2AX, ☎ 020/7414–2479). Of course, you can also just line up along the Mall with your binoculars!

Another time you can catch the queen in all her regalia is when she and the Duke of Edinburgh ride in state to Westminster to open the Houses of Parliament. The famous gilded coach that became such an icon of fairy-tale glamour at Elizabeth II's coronation parades from Buckingham Palace to Parliament, escorted by the brilliantly uniformed and superbly mounted Household Cavalry—on a clear day, it is to be hoped, for this ceremony takes place in late October or early November, depending on the exigencies of Parliament. But perhaps the nicest time to see the queen is during Royal Ascot, held at the racetrack near Windsor Castle—just a short train ride out of London—usually during the third week of June (Tuesday–Friday). After several races, the queen invariably walks down to the paddock on a special path, greeting race-goers as she proceeds. Americans wishing to reserve a seat in the Royal Enclosure should apply to the **American Embassy** (✉ 24 Grosvenor Square, Mayfair London W1) before the end of March. But remember: you must be sponsored by two guests who have attended Ascot at least seven times before!

age of George IV (Prince Regent until George III's death in 1820), Nash was the architect for the grand scheme of Regent Street and the sweep of neoclassical houses encircling Regent's Park. The Prince Regent, who lived at Carlton House, had plans to build a country villa at Primrose Hill (to the north of the park), connected by a grand road—hence Regent Street. Even though it was considered a most extravagant building for its time, Carlton House was demolished after the prince's accession to the throne. Nash's Carlton House Terrace, no less imposing, with white-stucco facades and massive Corinthian columns, was built in its place. It was a smart address, needless to say, and one that Prime Ministers Gladstone (1856) and Palmerston (1857–75) enjoyed. Today Carlton House Terrace building houses the Royal College of Pathologists (No. 2), the Royal Society (No. 6, whose members included Isaac Newton and Charles Darwin), the Turf Club (No. 5), and, at No. 12, the **Institute of Contemporary Arts,** better known as the ICA. ✉ *The Mall, St James's W1. Tube: Charing Cross.*

⓲ **Downing Street.** Looking like an unassuming alley but barred by iron gates at both its Whitehall and Horse Guards Road approaches, this is the location of the famous **No. 10,** London's modest version of the White House. Only three houses remain of the terrace built circa 1680 by Sir George Downing, who spent enough of his youth in America to graduate from Harvard—the second man ever to do so. **No. 11** is traditionally the residence of the chancellor of the exchequer (secretary of the treasury), and **No. 12** is the party whips' office. No. 10 has officially housed the prime minister since 1732. (The gates were former prime minister Margaret Thatcher's brainstorm.) Just south of Downing Street, in the middle of Whitehall, you'll see the **Cenotaph,** a stark white monolith designed in 1920 by Edward Lutyens to commemorate the 1918 armistice. On Remembrance Day (the Sunday nearest November 11) it is strewn with red poppies to honor the dead of both world wars and all British soldiers killed in action since, with the first wreath laid by the queen. ✉ *Whitehall, Westminster SW1. Tube: Westminster.*

⓳ **Horse Guards Parade.** Once the tiltyard of Whitehall Palace, where jousting tournaments were held, the Horse Guards Parade is now notable mainly for the annual Trooping the Colour ceremony, in which the queen takes the Royal Salute, her official birthday gift, on the second Saturday in June. (Like Paddington Bear, the queen has two birthdays; her real one is on April 21.) There is pageantry galore, with marching bands—the occasional guardsman fainting clean away from the heat building up under his weighty busby—and throngs of onlookers. Covering the vast expanse of the square that faces Horse Guards Road, opposite St. James's Park at one end and Whitehall at the other, the ceremony is televised. At the Whitehall facade of Horse Guards, the changing of two mounted sentries known as the **mounted guard** provides what may be London's most frequently exercised photo opportunity. ✉ *Whitehall, Westminster SW1.* ⏲ *Queen's mounted guard ceremony Mon.–Sat. 11 AM, Sun. 10 AM. Tube: Westminster.*

★ ⓯ **Houses of Parliament.** Overlooking the Thames, the Houses of Parliament are, arguably, the city's most famous and photogenic sight, with the Clock Tower—which everyone calls Big Ben—keeping watch on the corner and Westminster Abbey ahead of you across Parliament Square. The most romantic view of the complex is from the opposite (south) side of the river, a vista especially dramatic at night when the storybook spires, pinnacles, and towers of the great building are floodlighted green and gold—a fairy-tale vision only missing the presence of Peter Pan and Wendy on their way to Never-Never Land.

The Palace of Westminster, as the complex is still properly called, was established by Edward the Confessor in the 11th century, when he moved his court here from the City. It has served as the seat of English administrative power, on and off, ever since. In 1512, Henry VIII (1491–1547) abandoned it for Whitehall, and it ceased to be an official royal residence after 1547. At the Reformation, the Royal Chapel was secularized and became the first meeting place of the Commons. The Lords settled in the White Chamber. These, along with everything but the **Jewel Tower** and **Westminster Hall,** were destroyed in 1834 when "the sticks"—the arcane elmwood "tally" sticks notched for loans paid out and paid back, beneath the Lords' Chamber, on which the court had kept its accounts until 1826—were incinerated, and the fire got out of hand. Westminster Hall, with its remarkable hammer-beam roof, was the work of William the Conqueror's son, William Rufus. It is one of the largest remaining Norman halls in Europe, and its dramatic interior was the scene of the trial of Charles I.

After the 1834 fire, architects were invited to submit plans for new Houses of Parliament in the grandiose "Gothic or Elizabethan style." Charles Barry's were selected from among 97 entries, partly because Barry had invited the architect and designer Augustus Pugin to add the requisite neo-Gothic curlicues to his own Renaissance-influenced style. As you can see, it was a happy collaboration, with Barry's classical proportions offset by Pugin's ornamental flourishes—although the latter were toned down by Gilbert Scott when he rebuilt the bomb-damaged House of Commons after World War II. The two towers were Pugin's work. The **Clock Tower,** now virtually the symbol of London, was completed in 1858 after long delays due to bickering over the clock's design. (Barry designed the faces himself in the end.) It contains the 13-ton bell known as Big Ben, which chimes the hour (and the quarters). Some say Ben was "Big Ben" Caunt, heavyweight champ; others, Sir Benjamin Hall, the far-from-slim Westminster building works commissioner. At the southwest end of the main Parliament building is the 336-ft-high **Victoria Tower,** agleam from its restoration and cleaning. The rest of the complex was scrubbed down some years ago; the revelation of the honey stone under the dowdy, smog-blackened facades, which seemed almost symbolic at the time, cheered London up no end.

The building itself, which covers 8 acres, is a series of chambers, lobbies, and offices joined by more than 2 mi of passages. There are two Houses, Lords and Commons. The former has been downsized and reformed by Mr. Blair's Labour party. More than 100 hereditary peers (earls, lords, viscounts, and other aristocrats) failed to win the right to continue to be elected to their seats in the House of Lords. The House of Commons is made up of 659 elected Members of Parliament (MPs). The party with the most MPs forms the government, its leader becoming prime minister; other parties form the Opposition. Since 1642, when Charles I tried to have five MPs arrested, no monarch has been allowed into the House of Commons. The state opening of Parliament in November consequently takes place in the House of Lords. Visitors aren't allowed many places in the Houses of Parliament, though the Visitors' Galleries of the House of Commons do afford a view of the best free show in London, staged in the world's most renowned ego chamber. The opposing banks of green leather benches seat only 437 MPs—not that this is much of a problem, since absentees far outnumber the diligent. When MPs vote, they exit by the "Aye" or the "No" corridor, thus being counted by the party whips. When they speak, it is not directly to each other but through the Speaker, who also decides who will get the floor each day. Elaborate procedures notwithstanding, debate is often drowned out by amazingly raucous and immature jeers and insults.

Other public areas of the 1,100-room labyrinth are rather magnificently got up in high neo-Gothic style and punctuated with stirring frescoes commissioned by Prince Albert. You pass these en route to the Visitors' Galleries—if, that is, you are patient enough to wait in line for hours (the Lords line is shorter) or have applied in advance for the special "line of route" tour (open only to overseas visitors) by writing to the **Parliamentary Education Unit** (✉ House of Commons Information Office, House of Commons, Westminster, London SW1A 2TT) at least a month in advance of your visit. The tour takes you through the Queen's Robing Room, Royal Gallery, House of Lords, Central Hall (where MPs meet their constituents—the lucky ones get to accompany their MP to a prestigious tea on the terrace), House of Commons, and out into the spectacular Westminster Hall. Watch for the "VR" (Victoria Regina) monograms in the carpets and carving belying the "medieval" detailing as 19th-century work. Permits for tours of up to 16 people are available Friday afternoon between 3:30 and 5:30 while the House is sitting. The time to catch the action is Question Time—when the prime minister defends himself against the attacks of his "right honorable friends" on Wednesday between 3 and 3:30 PM (it's also live on BBC2). Foreigners are required to secure tickets from their respective embassies. The next best time to visit is either chamber's regular Question Time, held Monday–Thursday 2:30–3:30. The easiest time to get into the Commons is during an evening session—Parliament is still sitting if the top of the Clock Tower is illuminated.

For a special exhibition devoted to the "History of Parliament: Past and Present," head to the **Jewel Tower,** across the street from Victoria Tower, on Abingdon Street (also called Old Palace Yard), just south of Parliament Square. Not to be confused with the other famed jewel tower at the Tower of London, this was the stronghold for Edward III's treasure in 1366. It's also one of the original parts of the old Palace of Westminster and still retains some original beams; part of the moat and medieval quay still remain. (The tower is run by English Heritage, with a small charge for entry.) Be sure to have your name placed in advance on the waiting list for the twice-weekly tours of the **Lord Chancellor's Residence,** a popular attraction since its spectacular renovation. ✉ *St. Stephen's Entrance, St. Margaret St., Westminster SW1,* ☎ *020/7219–4272 Commons information; 020/7219–3107 Lords information; 020/7222–2219 Jewel Tower; 020/7219–2184 Lord Chancellor's Residence,* WEB *www.parliament.uk.* 🎫 *Free.* ⏲ *Commons Mon.–Thurs. 2:30–10, Fri. 9:30–3 (although not every Fri.); Lords Mon.–Thurs. 2:30–10; Lord Chancellor's Residence Tues. and Thurs. 10:30–12:30. Closed Easter wk, July–Oct., and 3 wks at Christmas. Tube: Westminster.*

7 **Institute of Contemporary Arts (ICA).** Behind its incongruous white-stucco facade, at No. 12 Carlton House Terrace, the ICA has provided a stage for the avant-garde in performance, theater, dance, visual art, and music since it was established in 1947. There are two cinemas, an underused library of video artists' works, a bookshop, a café and a bar, and a team of adventurous curators. ✉ *The Mall, St. James's W1,* ☎ *020/7930–3647,* WEB *www.ica.org.uk.* 🎫 *1-day, weekday membership £1.50; weekend, £2.50; additional charge for cinema screenings.* ⏲ *Daily noon–7:30, later for some events. Tube: Charing Cross or Piccadilly Circus.*

NEED A BREAK?

The **ICAfé** is windowless but brightly lighted, with a self-service counter offering good hot dishes, salads, quiches, and desserts. The bar upstairs, which serves baguette sandwiches, has a picture window overlooking the Mall. Both are packed before popular performances and are subject to the £1.50 one-day membership fee.

The Mall. This street was laid out around 1660 for the game of *pell mell* (a type of croquet crossed with golf), which also gave Pall Mall its name, and it quickly became the place to be seen. Samuel Pepys, Jonathan Swift, and Alexander Pope all wrote about it, and it continued as the beau monde's social playground into the early 19th century, long after the game it was built for had gone out of vogue. Something of the former style survives on those summer days when the queen is throwing a Buckingham Palace garden party: hundreds of her subjects throng the Mall, from the grand and titled to the humble and hardworking, all of whom have donned hat and frock to take afternoon tea with the monarch—or somewhere near her—on the lawns of Buck House. The old Mall still runs alongside the graceful, pink, 115-ft-wide avenue that replaced it in 1904 for just such occasions. ✉ *The Mall, St. James's SW1. Tube: Charing Cross, Green Park.*

★ ❸ **National Gallery.** Jan Van Eyck's *Arnolfini Portrait,* Leonardo da Vinci's *Madonna of the Rocks,* Velázquez's *Rokeby Venus,* Constable's *Hay Wain* . . . you get the picture. There are about 2,200 other paintings in this museum—many of them instantly recognizable and among the most treasured works of art anywhere. The museum's low, gray, colonnaded neoclassic facade fills the north side of Trafalgar Square. The institution was founded in 1824, when George IV and a connoisseur named Sir George Beaumont persuaded a reluctant government to spend £57,000 to acquire part of the philanthropist John Julius Angerstein's collection. These 38 paintings, including works by Raphael, Rembrandt, Titian, and Rubens, were augmented by 16 of Sir George's own and exhibited in Angerstein's Pall Mall residence until 1838, when William Wilkins's building was completed. By the end of the century, enthusiastic directors and generous patrons had turned the National Gallery into one of the world's foremost collections, with works from painters of the Italian Renaissance and earlier, from the Flemish and Dutch masters, the Spanish school, and of course the English tradition, including Hogarth, Gainsborough, Stubbs, and Constable.

The modern extension of the gallery, the Sainsbury Wing, designed by American architect Robert Venturi, houses the early Renaissance collection. (It was the only plan that appeased Prince Charles's traditionalist views, and at the time he described it as "A monstrous carbuncle on the face of a much-loved friend.") Occasionally, this wing hosts noted temporary exhibitions.

The gallery is really too overwhelming to absorb in a single viewing. It is wise to acquaint yourself with the layout—easy to negotiate compared with that of other European galleries—and plot a route in advance. The **Micro Gallery,** a computer information center in the Sainsbury Wing, might be the place to start. You can access in-depth information on any work here, choose your favorites, and print out a free personal tour map that marks the paintings you most want to see. Careful, though—you could spend hours in here scrolling through this colorful if pixelized history of art.

The following is a list of 10 of the most familiar works, to jog your memory, whet your appetite, and offer a starting point for your own exploration. The first five are in the Sainsbury Wing. In chronological order: (1) **Van Eyck** (circa 1395–1441), *The Arnolfini Portrait.* A solemn couple holds hands, the fish-eye mirror behind them mysteriously illuminating what can't be seen from the front view. (2) **Uccello** (1397–1475), *The Battle of San Romano.* In a work commissioned by the Medici family, the Florentine commander on a rearing white warhorse leads armored knights into battle against the Sienese. (3) **Bellini** (circa 1430–1516), *The Doge Leonardo Loredan.* The artist captured the Venetian doge's beatific expression (and snail-shell "buttons") at the beginning of his 20 years in office. (4) **Botticelli** (1445–1510), *Venus and Mars.* Mars sleeps, exhausted by the love goddess, oblivious to the lance wielded by mischievous putti and the buzzing of wasps. (5) **Leonardo da Vinci** (1452–1519), *The Virgin and Child.* This haunting black chalk cartoon is partly famous for having been attacked at gunpoint, and it now gets extra protection behind glass and screens. (6) **Caravaggio** (1573–1610), *The Supper at Emmaus.* A cinematically lighted, freshly resurrected Christ blesses bread in an astonishingly domestic vision from the master of chiaroscuro. (7) **Velázquez** (1599–1660), *The Toilet of Venus.* "The Rokeby Venus," named for its previous home in Yorkshire, has the most famously beautiful back in any gallery. She's the only surviving female nude by Velázquez. (8) **Constable** (1776–1837), *The Hay Wain.* Rendered overfamiliar by too many greeting cards, this is the definitive image of golden-age rural England. (9) **Turner** (1775–1851), *The Fighting Téméraire.* Most of the collection's other Turners were moved to the Tate Britain; the final voyage of the great French battleship into a livid, hazy sunset stayed here. (10) **Seurat** (1859–91), *Bathers at Asnières.* This static summer day's idyll is one of the pointillist extraordinaire's best-known works.

Glaring omissions from the above include some of the most popular pictures in the gallery, by Piero della Francesca, Titian, Holbein, Bosch, Brueghel, Rembrandt, Vermeer, Canaletto, Claude, Tiepolo, Gainsborough, Ingres, Monet, Renoir, and van Gogh. You can't miss the two most spectacular works on view—due to their mammoth size—Sebastiano del Piombo's *Sermon on the Mount* and Stubbs's stunning *Whistlejacket.* These great paintings aren't the only thing glowing in the rooms of the National Gallery—thanks to government patronage and lottery monies, salons here now gleam with stunning brocades and opulent silks. Rubens's *Samson and Delilah* has never looked better.

The collection of Dutch 17th-century paintings is one of the greatest in the world, and pieces by Hals, Hooch, Ruisdel, Hobbema, and Cuyp are shown in renewed natural light and gracious surroundings. There is also a program of temporary themed exhibitions where key works are loaned from other galleries of world renown. If you visit during the school vacations, there are special programs and trails for children that are not to be missed. Neither are the Ten Minute Talks, which illuminate the story behind a key work of art. Check the information desk, or Web site, for details. ✉ *Trafalgar Sq., Covent Garden WC2,* ☎ *020/7747–2885,* WEB *www.nationalgallery.org.uk.* 🎫 *Free; charge for special exhibitions.* ⏲ *Daily 10–6, Wed. until 9 (special exhibition in Sainsbury Wing, Wed. until 10); 1-hr free guided tour starts at Sainsbury Wing daily at 11:30 and 2:30 (and additionally 6:30 Wed.). Tube: Charing Cross or Leicester Sq.*

NEED A BREAK?

The **Brasserie** in the Sainsbury Wing of the National Gallery offers a fashionable lunch—mussels, gravlax, charcuterie, salads, a hot special—plus baguette sandwiches, pastries, tea, coffee, and wine, in a sophisticated, spacious room on the second floor.

★ ❹ **National Portrait Gallery.** An idiosyncratic collection that presents a potted history of Britain through its people, past and present, this museum is an essential visit for all history and literature buffs. The previously dark, dingy stairways and rooms have been remade into spacious light, bright galleries which are accessible via a state-of-the-art escalator, where you can view the paintings as you ascend to a skylit gallery displaying the oldest works in the Tudor Gallery. At the summit, a restaurant with classy British cuisine, open beyond gallery hours, will satiate skyline droolers. Here you'll see one of the best landscapes for real: a panoramic view of Nelson's Column and the backdrop along the Mall to the Houses of Parliament. Back in the basement are a lecture theater, computer gallery, bookshop, and café. The National Portrait Gallery has the largest cache of portraits in the world and, with the architectural face-lift, has doubled its exhibition space.

Throughout the gallery, the subject, not the artist, is the point; and there are numerous notable works. In the Tudor Gallery—a modern update on a Tudor long hall—is a Holbein cartoon of Henry VIII; Stubbs's self-portrait hangs in the refurbished 17th-century rooms; and Hockney's appears in the modern Balcony Gallery, mixed up with photographs, busts, caricatures, and amateur paintings. (The miniature of Jane Austen by her sister Cassandra, for instance, is the only likeness that exists of the great novelist.) Many of the faces are obscure and will be just as unknown to you if you're English, because the portraits outlasted their sitters' fame—not so surprising when the portraitists are such greats as Reynolds, Gainsborough, Lawrence, and Romney. But the annotation is comprehensive, the layout is easy to negotiate—chronological, with the oldest at the top—and there is a separate research center for those who get hooked on particular personages. Don't miss the Victorian and early 20th-century portrait galleries or the photography gallery. ✉ *St. Martin's Pl., Covent Garden WC2,* ☎ *020/7312–2463 recorded information,* WEB *www.npg.org.uk.* 💷 *Free.* ⏲ *Mon.–Wed., weekends 10–6; Thurs.–Fri. 10–9. Tube: Charing Cross or Leicester Sq.*

2 **Nelson's Column.** Trafalgar Square takes its name from the Battle of Trafalgar, Admiral Lord Horatio Nelson's great naval victory over the French, in 1805. Appropriately, the dominant landmark here is this famous column, a 145-ft-high granite perch from which E. H. Baily's 1843 statue of Nelson (1758–1805), one of England's favorite heroes, keeps watch; three bas-reliefs depicting his victories at Cape St. Vincent, the Battle of the Nile, and Copenhagen (and a fourth, his death at Trafalgar itself in 1805) sit around the base. All four bas-reliefs were cast from cannons he captured. The four majestic lions, designed by the Victorian painter Sir Edwin Landseer, were added in 1867. ✉ *Trafalgar Sq., Covent Garden WC2. Tube: Charing Cross or Leicester Sq.*

13 **Queen Anne's Gate.** Standing south of Birdcage Walk, by St. James's Park, are these two pretty 18th-century closes, once separate but now linked by a statue of the last Stuart monarch. (Another statue of Anne, beside St. Paul's, inspired the doggerel "Brandy Nan, Brandy Nan, you're left in the lurch, your face to the gin shop, your back to the church"—proving that her attempts to disguise her habitual tipple in a teapot fooled nobody.) ✉ *Queen Anne's Gate, Westminster SW1. Tube: St James's Park.*

10 **Queen Victoria Memorial.** You can't overlook this monument if you're near Buckingham Palace, which it faces from the traffic island at the west end of the Mall. The monument was conceived by Sir Aston Webb as the nucleus of his ceremonial route down the Mall to the Palace, and it was executed by the sculptor Thomas Brock, who was knighted on the spot when the memorial was revealed to the world in 1911. Many wonder why he was given that honor, since the thing is Victoriana incarnate: the frumpy queen glares down the Mall, with golden-winged Victory overhead and her siblings Truth, Justice, and Charity, plus Manufacture, Progress-and-Peace, War-and-Shipbuilding, and so on—in Osbert Sitwell's words, "tons of allegorical females . . . with whole litters of their cretinous children"—surrounding her. ✉ *The Mall and Spur Rd., St. James's. Tube: Victoria or St. James's Park.*

11 **Queen's Gallery.** This is the former chapel at the south side of Buckingham Palace, which has been open since 1962 for special, temporary exhibitions (focusing on small parts of the collection, such as Her Majesty's Michelangelo drawings). After a modernization program, the gallery reopened in June 2002, giving greater space and computer access to pictures both on show and in storage. The Standing Gallery will display a selection of paintings and the Graphic Art Gallery will exhibit drawings and watercolors, while the original main gallery will shows changing exhibitions including fine furniture, porcelain, and decorative arts. As only a part of the collection is hung at any one time, in the micro gallery you will be able to view other works in her

majesty's vast art collection on screen. The addition of a splendid Nash-style entrance, in tune with the grandeur of the collection, replaces the previous nondescript side door. Call for admission fee details. ✉ *Buckingham Palace Rd., St. James's SW1,* ☎ *020/7799–2331,* WEB *www.royal.gov.uk.* 🎟 *£6.50.* ⏲ *Daily. 10–5:30. Tube: Victoria or St. James's Park.*

Royal Mews. Unmissable children's entertainment, this museum is the home of Her Majesty's Coronation Coach. Standing nearly next door to the Queen's Gallery, the Royal Mews were designed by famed Regency-era architect John Nash. Mews were originally falcons' quarters (the name comes from their "mewing," or feather shedding), but horses gradually eclipsed birds of prey. Now some of the magnificent royal beasts live here alongside the fabulous bejeweled glass and golden coaches they draw on state occasions. ✉ *Buckingham Palace Rd., St. James's SW1,* ☎ *020/7839–1377,* WEB *www.royal.gov.uk.* 🎟 *£4.60.* ⏲ *Mon.–Thurs. noon–4, until 4:30 in summer (call for months), last admission 30 mins before closing. Closed royal and state occasions; call ahead. Tube: Victoria or St. James's Park.*

St. James's Park. With three palaces at its borders (the ancient Palace of Westminster, now the Houses of Parliament; the Tudor **St. James's Palace**; and Buckingham Palace), St James's Park is acclaimed as the most royal of the royal parks. It is also London's smallest, most ornamental park, as well as the oldest; it was acquired by Henry VIII in 1532 for a deer park. The land was marshy and took its name from the lepers' hospital dedicated to St. James. Henry VIII built the palace next to the park, which was used for hunting only—duelling and sword fights were forbidden. James I improved the land and installed an aviary and zoo (complete with crocodiles). Charles II (after his exile in France and because of his admiration for Louis XIV's formal Versailles Palace landscapes) had formal gardens laid out, with avenues, fruit orchards, and a canal. Lawns were grazed by goats, sheep, and deer. The Mall, alongside, also became used for the French croquet-type game of *paille-maille,* or pell mell. Its present shape more or less reflects what John Nash designed under George IV, turning the canal into a graceful lake (which was cemented in at a depth of 4 ft in 1855, so don't even think of swimming) and generally naturalizing the gardens. St. James's Park makes a spectacular frame for the towers of Westminster and Victoria—especially at night, when the illuminated fountains play and the skyline beyond the trees looks like a floating fairyland.

About 17 species of birds—including pelicans, geese, ducks, and swans (which belong to the queen)—now breed on and around Duck Island at the east end of the lake, attracting ornithologists at dawn. Later on summer days the deck chairs (which you must pay to use) are crammed with office workers lunching while being serenaded by music from the bandstands. But the best time to stroll the leafy walkways is after dark, with Westminster Abbey and the Houses of Parliament rising above the floodlighted lake. ✉ *The Mall or Horse Guards approach, or Birdcage Walk, St. James's SW1. Tube: St. James's Park or Westminster.*

St. John's in Smith Square. Completed around 1720, St. John's charmingly dominates Smith Square, an elegant enclave of perfectly preserved early 18th-century town houses that still looks like the London of Dr. Johnson. The Smith Square address is much sought after by MPs, especially of the Tory persuasion; No. 32 is the Conservative Party Headquarters. The Baroque church is well known to Londoners as a chamber-music venue; its popular lunchtime concerts are often broadcast on the radio. ✉ *North of Horseferry St., end of John Islip St., Westminster SW1,* ☎ *020/7222–1061.* WEB *www.sjss.org.uk.* ⏲ *Weekdays*

10–5 (may be closed during concert rehearsals), Sat. for concerts only. Tube: Westminster.

NEED A BREAK? In the Crypt of St. John's, Smith Square, is the **Footstool**—about the only place to find refreshments around here. It has varied, simply prepared snacks and meals through lunchtime, with a slightly more innovative touch in the evening for pre- and post-concert suppers. Open weekdays 11:30 AM–2:45 PM and 5:30 PM–10 PM. On Saturday, times for pre-concert meals and snacks vary according to the concert program.

14 **St. Margaret's Church.** Dwarfed by its northern neighbor, Westminster Abbey, this church was founded in the 12th century and rebuilt between 1486 and 1523. St. Margaret's is the parish church of the Houses of Parliament and much sought after for weddings: Samuel Pepys married here in 1655, Winston Churchill in 1908. The east Crucifixion window celebrates another union, the marriage of Prince Arthur and Catherine of Aragon. Unfortunately, it arrived so late that Arthur was dead and Catherine had married his brother, Henry VIII. Sir Walter Raleigh is among the notables buried here, only without his head, which had been removed at Old Palace Yard, Westminster, and kept by his wife, who was said to be fond of asking visitors, "Have you met Sir Walter?" as she produced it from a velvet bag. ✉ *Parliament Sq., Westminster SW1. Tube: Westminster.*

5 **St. Martin-in-the-Fields.** The small medieval chapel that once stood here, probably used by the monks of Westminster Abbey, was indeed surrounded by fields. These gave way to a grand rebuilding, completed in 1726, and St. Martin's grew to become one of Britain's best-loved churches. James Gibbs's classical temple-with-spire design became a familiar pattern for churches in early Colonial America. Though it seems dwarfed by the surrounding structures of Trafalgar Square, the spire is actually slightly taller than Nelson's Column, which it overlooks. It is a welcome sight for the homeless, who have sought soup and shelter here since 1914. The church is also a haven for music lovers; the internationally known Academy of St. Martin-in-the-Fields was founded here, and a popular program of lunchtime (free) and evening concerts continues today (tickets are available from the box office in the crypt). The church's musty interior is a wonderful place for music making—but the wooden benches can make it hard to give your undivided attention to the music. St. Martin's is often called the royal parish church, partly because Charles II was christened here. The crypt is a hive of lively activity, with a café, bookshop, plus the **London Brass-Rubbing Centre,** where you can make your own souvenir knight, lady, or monarch from replica tomb brasses, with metallic waxes, paper, and instructions provided for about £5; and the **St. Martin's Gallery,** showing contemporary work. There is also a crafts market in the courtyard behind the church. ✉ *Trafalgar Sq., Covent Garden WC2,* ☎ *020/7930–0089 or 020/7839–8362;* ☎ *020/7930–0089 or 020/7839–8362 for evening-concert credit-card bookings;* WEB *www.stmartin-in-the-fields.org.* ⏲ *Church daily 8–8; crypt Mon.–Sat. 10–8, Sun. noon–6; box office Mon.–Sat. 10–5. Tube: Charing Cross or Leicester Sq.*

NEED A BREAK? St. Martin's **Café-in-the-Crypt** serves full meals, sandwiches, snacks, and even wine by the glass, Monday–Saturday 10–8 and Sunday noon–8.

★ 21 **Tate Britain.** The gallery, which first opened in 1897, funded by the sugar magnate Sir Henry Tate, became Tate Britain with the opening of its younger sister gallery, Tate Modern, on the south bank of the Thames. As the name proclaims, great British artists from the 16th century to the present day are the focus. The building has been cleaned up, spruced up, and livened up, beginning with a modern approach at the reconstructed west entrance. This leads to the light, bright Linbury Galleries on the lower floors, which stage changing exhibitions. Additional upper floors, reached by a wide, sweeping staircase, bring many works to permanent view—many of which had been consigned to storage. The different rooms cover a massive range, some 500 years of art from the Tudor age to the up-to-the-minute Turner prize offerings. Each room has a theme and includes key works by major British artists: Van Dyck, Hogarth, and Reynolds rub shoulders with Rossetti, Sickert, Hockney, and Bacon, for example. Not to be missed is the improved, more generous selection of Constable landscapes, which compete with the famous Turners.

The Turner Bequest consists of J. M. W. Turner's personal collection; he left it to the nation on condition that the works be displayed together. The James Stirling–designed Clore Gallery (to the right of the main gallery) has fulfilled his wish since 1987, and it should not be missed. The annual Turner Prize gets artists and non-artists into a frenzy about what art has come to—or where it's going.

You can rent a "Tateinform," a hand-held audio guide, with commentaries by curators, experts, and some of the artists themselves. About a 20-minute walk south of the Houses of Parliament, the Tate is also accessible if you tube it to the Pimlico stop, then take a five-minute, signposted walk. A shuttle bus and boat service link Tate Britain with Tate Modern at Bankside across the river. ✉ *Millbank, Westminster SW1,* ☎ *020/7887–8000; 020/7887–8008 recorded information,* WEB *www.tate.org.uk.* 💴 *Free; special exhibitions £3–£7.* ⏲ *Daily 10–5:50. Tube: Pimlico.*

❶ **Trafalgar Square.** This is the center of London, by dint of a plaque on the corner of the Strand and Charing Cross Road from which distances on U.K. signposts are measured. It is the home of the **National Gallery** and of one of London's most distinctive landmarks, **Nelson's Column.** Permanently thronged with people—Londoners and tourists alike—and roaring traffic, it remains London's "living room." Great events, such as New Year's Eve, royal weddings, elections, and sporting triumphs will always see the crowds gathering in the city's most famous square.

The square is a commanding open space, built on the grand scale demanded by its central position in the capital of an empire that once reached to the farthest corners of the globe. Long ago, however, the site housed the Royal Mews, where Edward I (1239–1307) kept his royal hawks and lodged his falconers (not the numberless Edward the Confessor of Westminster Abbey fame, who died in 1066; this one, known as "Longshanks," died of dysentery in 1307). Later, all the kings' horses were stabled here, in increasingly smart quarters, until 1830, when John Nash had the buildings torn down as part of his Charing Cross Improvement Scheme. Nash exploited the square's natural incline—it slopes down from north to south—making it a succession of high points from which to look down the imposing carriageways that run dramatically away from it toward the Thames, the Houses of Parliament, and Buckingham Palace. Upon Nash's death, the design baton was passed to Sir Charles Barry and then to Sir Edwin Lutyens.

There's a pathetic history attached to the **equestrian statue of Charles I,** which stands near Whitehall on the southern slope of the square (on a pedestal *possibly* designed by Sir Christopher Wren and *possibly* carved by Grinling Gibbons). After Charles's High Treasurer ordered it (from Hubert le Sueur), the Puritan Oliver Cromwell tumbled Charles from the throne and commissioned a scrap dealer with the appropriate name of Rivett to melt the king down. Rivett apparently buried the statue in his garden and made a fortune peddling knickknacks wrought, he claimed, from its metal, only to produce the statue miraculously unscathed after the restoration of the monarchy—and to make more cash reselling it to the authorities. In 1767 Charles II had it placed where it stands today, near the spot where his father was executed in 1649. Each year, on January 30, the day of the king's death, the Royal Stuart Society lays a wreath at the foot of the statue.

Today, street performers enhance the square's intermittent feeling of celebration, which is strongest in December, first when the lights on the gigantic Christmas tree (an annual gift from Norway to thank the British for harboring its Royal Family during World War II) are turned on, and then, less festively, when thousands see in the New Year. ✉ *Trafalgar Sq., Covent Garden SW1. Tube: Charing Cross.*

⓬ **Wellington Barracks.** These are the headquarters of the Guards Division, the queen's five regiments of elite foot guards (Grenadier, Coldstream, Scots, Irish, and Welsh) who protect the sovereign and patrol her palace dressed in tunics of gold-purled scarlet and tall fur "busby" helmets of Canadian brown bearskin. If you want to learn more about the guards, visit the **Guards Museum**; the entrance is next to the Guards Chapel. ✉ *Wellington Barracks, Birdcage Walk, Westminster SW1,* ☎ *020/7414–3271.* 🎫 *£2.* ⏲ *Daily 10–4. Tube: St. James's Park.*

★ ⓰ **Westminster Abbey.** Marked by the teeming human contents of tour buses, off the south side of Parliament Square, this is where nearly all of England's monarchs have been crowned amid great heraldic splendor; most are buried here, too. The main nave, often crowded, is packed with memories, as it has witnessed many splendid royal ceremonies. As the most ancient of London's great churches, the place is crammed with spectacular medieval architecture. Other than the mysterious gloom of the vast interior, the first thing to strike most people is the fantastic proliferation of statues, tombs, and commemorative tablets: in parts, the building seems more like a stonemason's yard than a place of worship. But it is in its latter capacity that this landmark truly comes into its own. Although attending a service is not something to undertake purely for sightseeing reasons, it provides a glimpse of the abbey in its full majesty, accompanied by music from the Westminster choristers and the organ that Henry Purcell once played. During a service, you won't be bothered by the frequent and jarring loudspeaker announcements made during peak hours, requesting "a minute of silence" from the noisy masses.

The origins of Westminster Abbey are uncertain. The first church on the site may have been built as early as the 7th century by the Saxon king Sebert (who may be buried here, alongside his queen and sister); a Benedictine abbey was established in the 10th century. There were certainly preexisting foundations when Edward the Confessor was crowned in 1040, moved his palace to Westminster, and began building a church. Only traces have been found of that incarnation, which was consecrated eight days before Edward's death in 1066. (It appears in the Bayeaux Tapestry.) Edward's canonization in 1139 gave a succession of kings added incentive to shower the abbey with attention and improvements. Henry III, full of ideas from his travels in France, pulled it down and started again with Amiens and Rheims in mind. In fact, it was the master mason Henry de Reyns ("of Rheims") who, between 1245 and 1254, put up the transepts, north front, and rose windows, as well as part of the cloisters and chapter house; and it was his master plan that, funded by Richard II, was resumed 100 years later.

Belfry Tower 17
Chapel of St. Edward the Confessor; Henry V's Chantry 3
Chapter House 12
Coronation Chair. 2
Henry VII Chapel 7
High Altar . . . 5
Norman Undercroft and Museum. . . . 15
North Entrance 1
Organ Loft . . 10
Poet's Corner. 11
Pyx Chamber . . . 14
Royal Airforce Chapel 5
St. George Chapel 19
Sanctuary . . . 9
Sir Winston Churchill Memorial . . . 18
Stairs to Library. 13
Tomb of Elizabeth I . . . 4
Tomb of Henry II 6
Tomb of Mary, Queen of Scots 8
Tomb of the Unknown Warrior 16
West Entrance and Bookshop. . . 20

Westminster Abbey

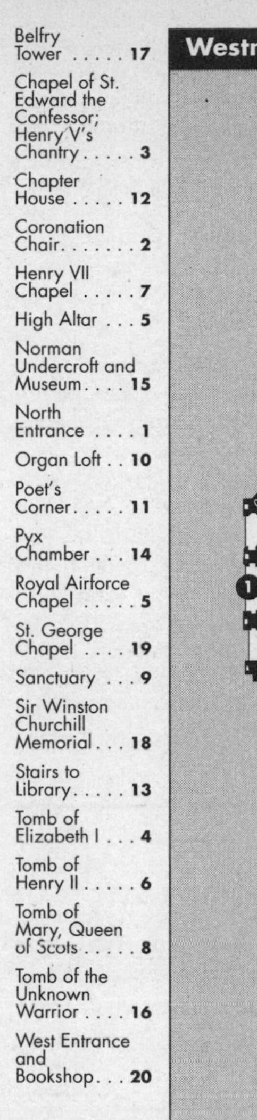

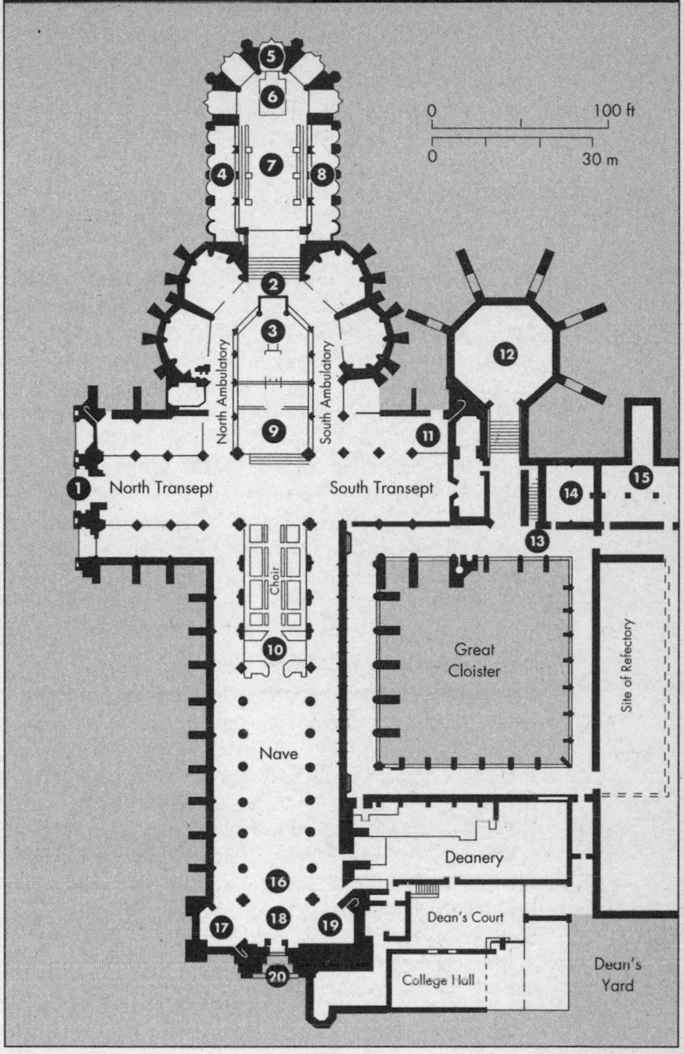

Henry V (reigned 1413–22) and Henry VII (1485–1509) were the chief succeeding benefactors. The abbey was eventually completed in 1532. After that, Sir Christopher Wren had a hand in shaping the place; his west towers were completed in 1745, 22 years after his death, by Nicholas Hawksmoor. The most riotous elements of the interior were, similarly, much later affairs.

There is only one way around the abbey, and as there will almost certainly be a long stream of shuffling tourists at your heels, you'll need to be alert to catch the highlights. Entering by the north door, the first thing you see on your left are the overbearing and extravagant 18th-century monuments of statesmen in the north transept and north-transept chapels. Look up to your right to see the painted-glass rose window, the largest of its kind. At many points the view of the abbey is crowded by the many statues and screens; to your right is the 19th- (and part 13th-) century choir screen, while to the left is the sacrarium, containing the medieval kings' tombs which screen the **Chapel of**

St. Edward the Confessor. Due to its incredibly ancient fragility, the shrine to the pre-Norman king known as Edward the Confessor is closed off (unless via a tour with the verger; details are available at the admission desk and there is a small extra charge), but continuing to the foot of the Henry VII Chapel steps you can still see the hot seat of power, the **Coronation Chair,** which has been briefly graced by nearly every regal posterior. Edward I ordered it around 1300; it used to shelter the Stone of Scone (pronounced "Skoon"), upon which Scottish kings had been crowned since time began, but this precious relic was returned to Scotland's Edinburgh Castle. The stone is to be returned to England, however, for the duration of future coronations.

Proceed up the steps into one of the architectural glories of Britain, the **Henry VII Chapel,** passing the huge white marble tomb of Elizabeth I, buried with her half sister, "Bloody" Mary I; then the tomb of Henry VII with his queen, Elizabeth of York, by the Renaissance master Torrigiano (otherwise known for having been banished from Florence after breaking Michelangelo's nose). Close by are monuments to the young daughters of James I; Sophia, who only lived for three days, is remembered by a single alabaster candle. An urn holds the purported remains of the so-called Princes in the Tower—Edward V and Richard. All around are magnificent sculptures of saints, philosophers, and kings, with wild mermaids and monsters carved on the choir-stall misericords (undersides) and with exquisite fan vaulting above—one of the miracles of Western architecture. (Keep an eye open for St. Wilgefort, who was so concerned to protect her chastity that she prayed to God for help and woke up one morning with a full growth of beard.)

The tombs and monuments with which Westminster Abbey is packed (some would say stuffed) began to appear at an accelerated rate starting in the 18th century (newest additions are ten 20th-century figures, including Martin Luther King, over the west door of the nave). One earlier occupant, though, was Geoffrey Chaucer, who in 1400 became the first poet to be buried in **Poets' Corner.** Most of the other honored writers have only their memorials here, not their bones: William Shakespeare and William Blake (who both had a long wait before the dean deemed them holy enough to be here at all), John Milton, Jane Austen, Samuel Taylor Coleridge, and William Wordsworth. Charles Dickens is both celebrated and buried in this crowded corner.

After the elbow battle you are guaranteed in Poets' Corner, you exit the main body of the abbey by a door from the south transept and south choir aisle to the comparative calm of the **cloisters,** where monks once strolled in contemplation and you may do the same. Go nearly all the way round and an archway leads to the quiet green **Dean's Yard,** where you can catch a fine view of the massive flying buttresses above. Also here is the entrance to Westminster School, formerly a monastic college, now one of Britain's finest public (which means the exact opposite to Americans) schools; Christopher Wren and Ben Jonson number among the old boys. Return to the cloisters and the abbey rooms used by monarchs of the Middle Ages (there's a separate small fee). The **Chapter House,** a stunning octagonal room supported by a central column and adorned with 14th-century frescoes, is where the King's Council and, after that, an early version of the Commons, met between 1257 and 1547. Underfoot is one of the finest surviving tiled floors in the country. The **Abbey Museum** is in the undercroft, which survives from Edward the Confessor's original church, and includes a collection of deliciously macabre effigies made from the death masks and actual clothing of Charles II and Admiral Lord Nelson (complete with eye patch) and the battle kit of shield, saddle, and helmet of Henry V at Agincourt, among other fascinating relics. The **Pyx Chamber,** or Chapel of the Pyx, next door, contains the abbey's treasure, just as it did when it was the royal strong room during the 13th century. In fact, the columns date back to the 11th century; the pyx was the name for the monks' box of gold and silver.

Returning to the abbey and the nave, look to the foot of the wall in the north aisle opposite the organ loft. All of Ben Jonson is buried here—upright in accord with his modest demand for a two-by-two-ft grave site (only his memorial is in Poets' Corner). ("O rare Ben Jonson," reads his epitaph, in a modest pun on the Latin *orare,* "to pray for.") James Watt and Michael Faraday are among the scientists with memorials; Sir Isaac Newton has both grave and memorial. There is only one painter: Godfrey Kneller, whose dying words were "By God, I will not be buried in Westminster."

The poignant **Tomb of the Unknown Warrior,** an anonymous World War I martyr, lies buried near the exit in memory of the soldiers fallen in both world wars. Nearby is one of the very few tributes to a foreigner, a plaque to Franklin D. Roosevelt. Note that photography is not permitted anywhere in the abbey. ✉ *Broad Sanctuary, Westminster SW1,* ☎ *020/7222–5152,* WEB *www.westminster-abbey.org.* 🎫 *Abbey £6; museum, Pyx Chamber, and Chapter House £2.50, £1 if you have bought a ticket to the abbey.* ⏲ *weekdays 9–4:45, Sat. 9–2:45 (last admission 1 hr before closing). Museum, Pyx Chamber daily 10:30–4. Chapter House 1 Apr.–31 Oct. 10–5:30, 1 Nov.–31 Mar. 10–4:30. Abbey closed weekdays and Sun to visitors during services. Tube: Westminster.*

Westminster Cathedral. This massive cathedral is hard to miss—once you are almost upon it, that is. It's in a 21-year-old paved square that has fallen on hard times. The cathedral is the seat of the Cardinal of Westminster, head of the Roman Catholic Church in Britain; consequently it is London's principal Roman Catholic church. The asymmetrical redbrick Byzantine hulk, dating only from 1903, is banded with stripes of Portland stone and abutted by a 273-ft-high campanile at the northwest corner, which you can scale by elevator. Faced with the daunting proximity of the heavenly Westminster Abbey, the architect, John Francis Bentley, flew in the face of fashion by rejecting neo-Gothic in favor of the Byzantine idiom, which still provides maximum contrast today—not only with the great church but with just about all of London. The interior is partly unfinished but worth seeing for its brooding mystery, its mosaics, and its noted Eric Gill reliefs depicting the stations of the cross. Just inside the main entrance is the tomb of Cardinal Basil Hume, who held the seat for more than 25 years. ✉ *Ashley Pl., Westminster,* ☎ *020/7798–9055.* 🎫 *Tower £2.* ⏲ *Cathedral daily 7–7. Tower Apr.–Sept., daily 9:30–5; Oct.–Mar., Thurs.–Sun. 9:30–5. Tube: Victoria.*

ST. JAMES'S AND MAYFAIR

St. James's and Mayfair form the very core of London's West End, the city's smartest central area. No textbook sights here; rather, these neighborhoods epitomize much of the flavor that is peculiarly London's—the sense of being in a great, rich, (once) powerful city is almost palpable as you wander along its posh and polished streets. Here is the highest concentration of grand hotels, department stores, exclusive shops, glamorous restaurants, commercial art galleries, auction houses, swanky offices—all accoutrements that give this area an unmistakable air of wealth and leisure, even on busy days.

A late-17th-century ghost in the streets of contemporary St. James's would not need to bother walking through walls because practically none have moved since he knew them. Its boundaries, clockwise from the north, are Piccadilly, Haymarket, the Mall, and Green Park: a neat rectangle, with a protruding spur satisfyingly located at Cockspur Street. The rectangle used to describe "gentlemen's London," where Sir was outfitted head and foot (but not in between, since the tailors were, and still are, north of Piccadilly in Savile Row) before repairing to his club. This has been a fashionable part of town from the first, largely by dint of the eponymous palace, St. James's, which was a royal residence—if not *the* palace—from the time of Henry VIII until the Victorian era, and this is the home of Prince Charles.

Mayfair, like St. James's, is precisely delineated—a trapezoid contained by, respectively, Oxford Street and Piccadilly on the north and south, Regent Street and Park Lane on the east and west. Within its boundaries are streets both broad and narrow, but mostly unusually straight and gridlike for London, making it fairly easy to negotiate.

Numbers in the text correspond to numbers in the margin and on the St. James's and Mayfair map.

A Good Walk

Starting in Trafalgar Square, you'll find Cockspur Street off the southwest corner; follow it to the foot of **Haymarket.** On your right is London's oldest shopping arcade, the splendid Regency Royal Opera Arcade, which John Nash finished in 1818. Now you come to **Pall Mall** ①, a showcase of 18th- and 19th-century patrician architecture; it also houses such famous gentlemen's retreats as the Reform Club, halfway along on the right (from which Phileas Fogg set out to go around the world). At the end of Pall Mall, you collide with the small, Tudor brick **St. James's Palace** ②. Continue along Cleveland Row by the side of the palace to spy on York House, home of the Duke and Duchess of Kent; then turn left into Stable Yard Road to Lancaster House, built for the Duke of York in the 1820s but more notable as the venue for the 1978 conference that led to the end of white rule in Rhodesia (now Zimbabwe); and Clarence House, designed by John Nash and built in 1825 for the Duke of Clarence (who became William IV) and, until her death in March 2002 home to the Queen Mother. Now, head north up along St. James's Street to St. James's Place, where, if you turn left, you can spot, at No. 27, one of London's most spectacular 18th-century mansions, **Spencer House** ③, home of Diana's ancestors; the interior can be viewed on tours given on Sunday only throughout the year (except August and January).

Cross back over St. James's Street to King Street—No. 8 is Christie's, the fine art auctioneers; Duke Street on the left harbors further exclusive little art salons—but straight ahead is **St. James's Square** ④, one of London's oldest squares and home of the London Library. Leave the square by Duke of York Street to the north, and turn left on **Jermyn Street** ⑤, the world center of gentlemen's paraphernalia shops. Set back from the street is the lovely **St. James's Church** ⑥. A right on Duke Street brings you to Piccadilly. Turn right again, and you'll pass the exclusive department store that supplies the queen's groceries, Fortnum & Mason, on the right, and the **Royal Academy of Arts** ⑦, opposite, with famous **Piccadilly Circus** ⑧ ahead. Turn around—Wellington Arch and **Apsley House (Wellington Museum)** ⑨, the gloriously opulent mansion the Duke of Wellington once called home, are ahead in the distance. Cross the street and head north up the shopping hub **Bond Street** ⑩, with **Burlington Arcade** ⑪ to the right. You could detour by turning right before you reach Oxford Street into Brook Street (the composer Handel lived at No. 25, the **Handel House Museum** ⑫), which leads to Hanover Square. Turning right down St. George Street brings you to the porticoes of St. George's Church, where Percy Bysshe Shelley and George Eliot, among others, had their weddings. A right turn after the church down Mill Street brings you into Savile Row, the fashionable center for custom-made suits and coats since the mid-19th century. No. 3 is a draw for Beatlemaniacs: the former headquarters of Apple Records and the site of John, Paul, George, and Ringo's legendary rooftop concert (the building now houses a financial institution and is not open to the public). Continuing from Savile Row to behind the Royal Academy is Albany Street, one of the smartest addresses since the turn of the 19th century. You can peer through the railings at the posh Henry Holland apartments built for fashionable bachelors, which included Byron, Prime Ministers Gladstone and Heath, Graham Greene, and latterly actor Terence Stamp. From Savile Row, head west on Grosvenor Street to Duke Street: slightly to the south you'll find a couple of Mayfair's beauty spots—Carlos Place (site of the Connaught) and neighboring Mount Row, both adorned with some veddy, veddy elegant residences. Here, too, is Mount Street, a pedigree-proud shopping avenue; take South Audley Street one block south to discover St. George's Gardens, a fine place for a picnic. Head over to Hyde Park to take in **Speakers' Corner** ⑬ and **Marble Arch** ⑭. Shop-till-you-droppers can then explore Oxford Street (**Selfridges** ⑮ and **Marks & Spencer** are here), while art lovers will want to continue north to Manchester Square for the magnificent **Wallace Collection** ⑯.

TIMING

Although this walk doesn't cover an enormous distance, you'll probably do a lot of doubling back and detouring down beckoning alleys—and into interesting shops. If you want to do more than window-shop, do a weekday jaunt, starting in the morning, so you get time for visits to the Royal Academy and the Wallace Collection or perhaps some of the commercial art galleries in and around Cork Street. The walk alone should take less than two hours. Add at least an hour for Apsley House, and another two for the Wallace Collection. Any of those could easily consume an afternoon, if you have one to spare. Shopping could take all week.

HOW TO GET THERE

You could start walking around this area from Trafalgar Square, or get the Piccadilly or Bakerloo Line to the Piccadilly Circus tube stop, the Piccadilly to the Hyde Park Corner stop, or the Central Line to any of the stops along Oxford Street—Marble Arch, Bond Street (also Jubilee Line), Oxford Circus (also Victoria and Bakerloo lines), or Tottenham Court Road (also Northern Line). The Green Park stop on the Piccadilly, Victoria, or Jubilee Line is also central to many of this neighborhood's sights. The best buses are 8, 9, 14, 19, 22, and 38 along Piccadilly, especially the 8, which loops around via New Bond Street to Oxford Street and skims the eastern border of Green Park down Grosvenor Place.

Sights to See

★ ❾ **Apsley House (Wellington Museum).** For Hyde Park Corner read "heroes corner"; even in the subway, beneath the turmoil of traffic, the Duke of Wellington's heroic exploits are retold in murals. The years of war against the French, and the subsequent final defeat of Napoléon at the Battle of Waterloo in 1815 made Wellington—Arthur Wellesley—the greatest soldier and statesman in the land. The house is flanked by imposing statues: opposite is the 1828 Decimus Burton **Wellington Arch** with the four-horse chariot of peace as its pinnacle (cleaned and renovated by English Heritage, and now open to the public as an exhibition area and viewing platform). Cast from captured French guns, the legendary **Achilles** statue points the way with thrusting shield to the ducal mansion from the tip of Hyde Park. Once known, quite simply, as No. 1, London, this was long celebrated as the best address in town. Built by Robert Adam and later refaced and extended, this housed the Duke of Wellington from 1817 until his death in 1852. As the Wellington Museum, it has been kept as the "Iron Duke" liked it—even the railings outside are painted pale green as the duke once had them—his uniforms and weapons, his porcelain and plate, and his extensive art collection are displayed heroically. Unmissable, in every sense (and considered rather too athletic for the time), is the gigantic Canova statue of a nude (but fig-leafed) Napoléon Bonaparte, Wellington's archenemy, which presides over the grand staircase that leads to the many elegant reception rooms. The most stunning is the Waterloo Gallery, where the annual banquet for officers who fought beside Wellington was held. With its heavily sculpted and gilded ceiling, its feast of old master paintings on red damask walls, and commanding gray candelabra, it is a veritable orgy of opulence. Apsley House installed iron shutters in 1830 after rioters, protesting the duke's opposition (he was briefly prime minister) to the Reform Bill, broke the windows. Yes, the British loved him for defeating Napoléon, but mocked him with the name Iron Duke—referring not only to his military prowess but to his indomitable will. ✉ *Wellington Arch, Hyde Park Corner,* ☎ *020/7499–5676,* WEB *www.apsleyhouse.org.uk.* ⏲ *Tue.–Sun. 11–5.* 🎟 *£4.50. Tube: Hyde Park Corner.*

Berkeley Square. As anyone who's heard the old song knows, the name rhymes with "starkly." Not many of its original mid-18th-century houses are left, but look at Nos. 42–46 (especially No. 44, which the architectural historian Sir Nikolaus Pevsner thought London's finest terraced house) and Nos. 49–52 to get some idea of why it was once London's top address—not that it's in the least humble now. Snob nightclub Annabels is one current resident. ✉ *Berkeley Sq., Mayfair W1. Tube: Green Park.*

10 **Bond Street.** This world-class shopping haunt is divided into northern "New" (1710) and southern "Old" (1690) halves. On New Bond Street you'll find **Sotheby's,** the world-famous auction house, at No. 35. But there are other ways to flirt with financial ruin on Old Bond Street: the mirror-lined Chanel store, the vainglorious marble acres of Gianni Versace, and the boutique of the more sophisticated Gucci, plus Tiffany's British outpost and art dealers Colnaghi, Léger, Thos. Agnew, and Marlborough Fine Arts. **Cork Street,** which parallels the top half of Old Bond Street, is where London's top dealers in contemporary art have their galleries—where you're welcome to browse. ✉ *Tube: Bond Street or Green Park.*

11 **Burlington Arcade.** Perhaps the finest of Mayfair's enchanting covered shopping alleys is the second oldest in London, built in 1819 for Lord Cavendish, to stop the hoi polloi from throwing rubbish into his garden at Burlington House, which is behind the arcade. It's still patrolled by top-hatted beadles, who preserve decorum by preventing you from singing, running, or carrying open umbrellas. ✉ *Piccadilly, Mayfair W1. Tube: Green Park or Piccadilly Circus.*

Faraday Museum, Royal Institution. Although there is no plaque outside indicating that the museum is situated here, the front reception desk will point you toward the basement, where you'll find a reconstruction of the laboratory where the physicist Michael Faraday discovered electromagnetic induction in 1831—with echoes of Frankenstein.

St. James's and Mayfair

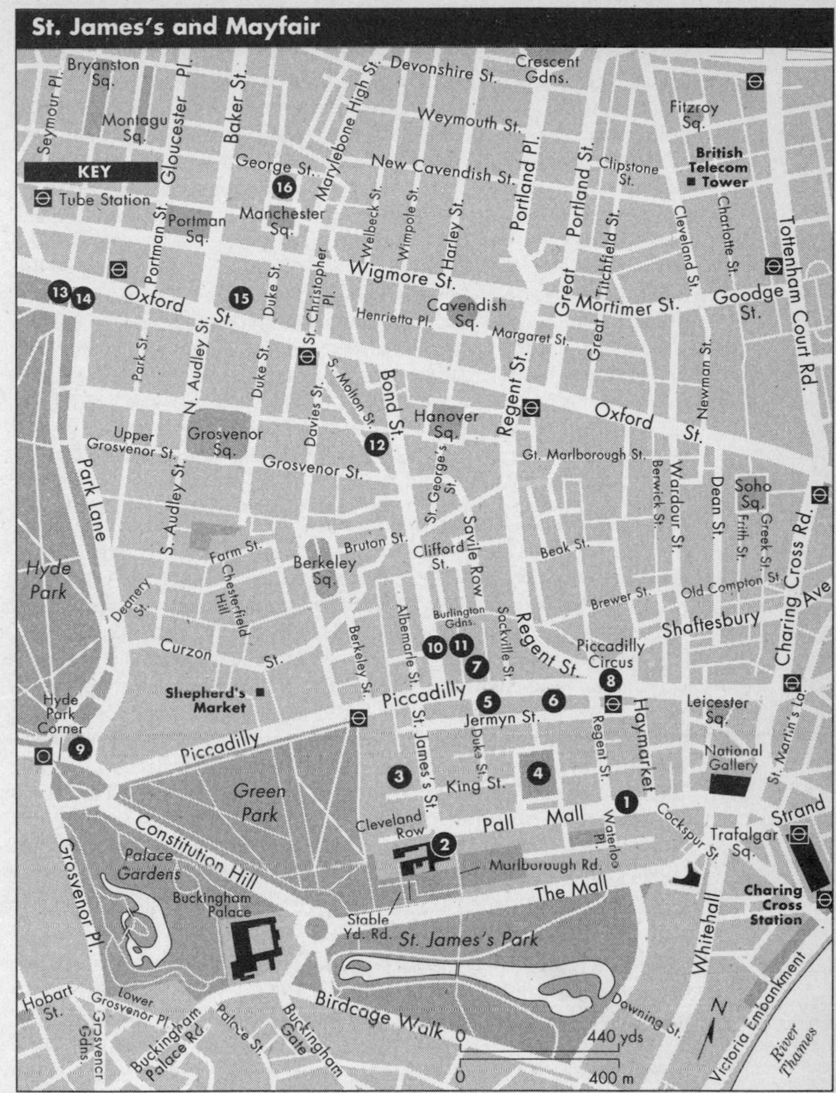

✉ *21 Albermarle St., Mayfair W1,* ☎ *020/7409–2992,* WEB *www.ri.ac.uk.* *£1.* ⏲ *Weekdays 10–5. Tube: Green Park.*

12 **Handel House Museum.** The former home of the composer, where he lived for over 30 years until his death in 1759, is a celebration of his genius. It's the first museum in London solely dedicated to one composer, and that is made much of with room settings in the contemporary fine Georgian style. You can linger over original manuscripts (there are more to be seen in the British Library) and gaze at portraits, accompanied by live music—if the adjoining music rooms are being used by musicians in rehearsal. Some of the composer's most famous pieces were created here, including *Messiah* and *Music for the Royal Fireworks.* The museum occupies both no. 25 and the adjoining house, where life in Georgian London is displayed in exhibit space (another musical star, Jimi Hendrix, lived here for a brief time in the sixties, although all that remains of his presence is a blue plaque outside the house). ✉ *25 Brook St., Mayfair W1,* ☎ *020/7495–1685,* WEB *www.handelhouse.org.* *£4.50.* ⏲ *Tues.–Sat. 10–6, Thurs. 10–8, Sun. (and Bank Holiday Mons.) 12–6. Tube: Bond St.*

Grosvenor Square. This square (pronounced "*Grove*-na") was laid out in 1725–31 and is as desirable an address today as it was then. Americans certainly thought so—from John Adams, the second president, who as ambassador lived at No. 38, to Dwight D. Eisenhower, whose wartime headquarters was at No. 20. Now the ugly '50s block of the U.S. Embassy occupies the entire west side, and a British memorial to Franklin D. Roosevelt stands in the center. The little brick chapel used by Eisenhower's men during World War II, the 1730 Grosvenor Chapel, stands a couple of blocks south of the square on South Audley Street, with the entrance to pretty **St. George's Gardens** to its left. Across the gardens is the headquarters of the English Jesuits as well as the society-wedding favorite, the mid-19th-century Church of the Immaculate Conception, known as Farm Street because that is the name of the street on which it stands. ✉ *Mayfair W1. Tube: Bond St.*

5 **Jermyn Street.** This is where the gentleman purchases his traditional fashion accessories. He buys his shaving sundries and hip flask from Geo. F. Trumper; briar pipe from Astley's; scent from Floris (for women, too—both the Prince of Wales and his mother are Floris customers), whose interiors are exceedingly historic and beautiful, or Czech & Speake; shirts from Turnbull & Asser; and deerstalkers and panamas from Bates the Hatter. Don't forget the regal cheeses from Paxton & Whitfield (founded in 1740 and a legend among dairies). Shop your way east along Jermyn Street, and you're practically in Piccadilly Circus. ✉ *St. James's SW1. Tube: Piccadilly Circus.*

14 **Marble Arch.** The name denotes both the traffic whirlpool where Bayswater Road segues into Oxford Street and John Nash's 1827 arch, which moved here from Buckingham Palace in 1851. Search the sidewalk on the traffic island opposite the cinema to find the stone plaque that marks (roughly) the place where the Tyburn Tree stood for four centuries, until 1783. This was London's central gallows, a huge wooden structure with hanging accommodations for 21. Hanging days were holidays, the spectacle supposedly functioning as a crime deterrent. Oranges, gingerbread, and gin were sold, alongside "personal favors," to vast, rowdy crowds, and the condemned, dressed in finery for his special moment, was treated more as hero than as villain. Cross over (or under—there are signs to help in the labyrinth) to the northeastern corner of Hyde Park to Speakers' Corner. ✉ *Park La., Mayfair W1. Tube: Marble Arch.*

NEED A BREAK? Smarter than the usual street café, **Sotheby's Café** (✉ 34–35 New Bond St., Mayfair W1) is a cut above, as you would expect of this classy auction house in the chic shopping quarter of Bond Street. Lunches, such as the lobster club sandwich, aren't terribly cheap, but service is included in the tab.

7 **Pall Mall.** Like its near-namesake, *the* Mall, Pall Mall rhymes with "shall" and derives its name from the cross between croquet and golf that the Italians, who invented it, called *pallo a maglio* and the French, who made it chic, called *palle-maille.* In England it was taken up with enthusiasm by James I, who called it "pell mell" and passed it down the royal line, until Charles II turned the dusty alley into a proper road so the ball could be seen clearly. Needless to say, Catherine Street, as Pall Mall was officially named (after Charles's queen, Catherine of Braganza), was *very* fashionable. No. 79 must have been one of its livelier addresses, since Charles's gregarious mistress, Nell Gwynne, lived there. The king gave her the house when she complained about being a mere leaseholder, protesting that she had "always conveyed free under the Crown" (as it were); it remains, to this day, the only privately owned bit of Pall Mall's south side. Stroll slowly, the better to appreciate the creamy facades and perfect proportions along this showcase of 18th- and 19th-century British architecture.

Notable examples are two James Barry–designed buildings, the **Travellers' Club** and the **Reform Club,** both representatives of the upper-class gentleman's retreat that made St. James's the club land of London. The Reform is the most famous club of all, thanks partly to Jules Verne's Phileas Fogg, who accepted the around-the-world-in-80-days bet in its smoking room and was thus soon qualified to join the Travellers'. And—hallelujah—women can join the Reform. The RAC Club (for Royal Automobile Club, but it's never known as that), with its marble swimming pool, and the Oxford and Cambridge Club complete the Pall Mall quota; there are other, even older establishments—Brooks's, the Carlton, Boodles, and White's (founded in 1736, the oldest of all)—in St. James's Street around the corner, alongside *the* gentleman's bespoke (custom) shoemaker, Lobb's, and, at No. 6, *the* hatter, James Lock, which has one of the most historic store facades in the city—you half expect Lord Byron or Anthony Trollope to walk out the door. Waterloo Place, around the corner, is a continuation of this gentleman's quarter. ✉ *St. James's SW1. Tube: Piccadilly Circus.*

8 **Piccadilly Circus.** New York has its Times Square, in Venice it's Piazza San Marco, and London has Piccadilly Circus. As natives say, if you stand here long enough, you will meet everyone you know. The name came into use during the early 17th century, when a humble tailor on the Strand named Robert Baker sold an awful lot of picadils—a collar ruff all the rage in courtly circles—and built a house with the proceeds. Snobs dubbed his new-money mansion Piccadilly Hall, and the name stuck. As for "Circus," that refers not to the menagerie of backpackers and camera-clickers clustered around the steps of **Eros** but to the circular junction of five major roads.

Eros, London's favorite statue and symbol of the *Evening Standard* newspaper, is not in fact the Greek god of erotic love at all, but the angel of Christian charity, commissioned in 1893 from the young sculptor Alfred Gilbert as a memorial to the philanthropic Earl of Shaftesbury (the angel's bow and arrow are a sweet allusion to the earl's name). It cost Gilbert £7,000 to cast the statue he called his "missile of kindness" in the novel medium of aluminum, and because he was paid only £3,000, he promptly went bankrupt and fled the country. (Not to worry—he was knighted in the end.) Around Eros, London roars on—this hub includes a very large branch of Tower Records, the tawdry Trocadero Centre (video arcades, food courts, chain stores), and a perpetual traffic jam. Beneath the blight, however, is beauty: just behind the modern bank of neon advertisements are some of the most elegant Edwardian-era buildings in town. ✉ *Mayfair W1. Tube: Piccadilly Circus.*

Portland Place. The elegant throughway to Regent's Park was London's widest street in the 1780s, when brothers Robert and James Adam designed it. The first sight to greet you here, drawing the eye around the awkward corner, is the curvaceous portico and pointy Gothic spire of **All Souls Church,** one part of Nash's Regent Street plan that remains. It is now the venue for innumerable concerts and Anglican services broadcast to the nation by the British Broadcasting Corporation. The 1931 block of Broadcasting House next door is where you'll find the BBC's five radio stations. It curves, too, if less beautifully; you'll see an Eric Gill sculpture of Shakespeare's Ariél (aerial—get it?) over the entrance, from which the playful sculptor was obliged to excise a portion of phallus lest it offend public decency—which the modified model did in any case. At No. 66, opposite the Chinese Embassy, the Royal Institute of British Architects has a small exhibitions gallery devoted to shows from its esteemed members. Here, too, if you need a break, is a tasteful branch of a Patisserie Valerie café. ✉ *Marylebone W1. Tube: Oxford Circus or Great Portland St.*

Regent Street. This curvaceous thoroughfare was conceived by John Nash and his patron, the Prince Regent—the future George IV—as a kind of ultra-catwalk from the Prince's palace, Carlton House, to Regent's Park (then called Marylebone Park). The section between Piccadilly and Oxford Street was to be called the Quadrant and lined with colonnaded shops purveying "articles of fashion and taste," in a big PR exercise to improve London's image as the provincial cousin of smarter European capitals. The scheme was never fully implemented, and what there was fell into such disrepair that, early this century, Aston Webb (of the Mall route) collaborated on the redesign you see today. It is still a major shopping street. Hamleys, the gigantic toy emporium, is fun; and since 1875 there has been Liberty, which originally imported silks from the East then diversified to other Asian goods, and is now best known for its "Liberty print" cottons, its jewelry department, and—still—its high-class Asian imports. The mock-Tudor interior, with stained glass and beams taken from battleships, is worth a look. ✉ *Mayfair W1. Tube: Piccadilly Circus or Oxford Circus.*

7 **Royal Academy of Arts.** Burlington House was built in the Palladian style for the Earl of Burlington around 1720, and it is one of the few surviving mansions from that period. The chief occupant today is the Royal Academy of Arts (RA), and one of its famed members, Sir Joshua Reynolds, is shown in statue complete with artist's palette in hand, in the academy courtyard. The academy owns a major collection of works by Academicians past and present as well as its most prized piece, the *Taddeo Tondo* (a sculpted disk) by Michelangelo of the Madonna and Child, on display in the Sackler Wing. The RA mounts a continuous program of internationally renowned loan exhibitions such as, in recent years, Sensation (1997), Monet in the 20th Century (1999), Van Dyck (1999), and the Genius of Rome (2001). Every June, the RA puts on the **Summer Exhibition,** a huge and always surprising collection of sculpture and painting by the young (and older) artists of today, with about 1,000 things crammed into every cranny. Craving art now? Try the shop; it's one of the best museum stores in town. ✉ *Burlington House, Piccadilly, Mayfair W1,* ☎ *020/7300–8000;*

020/7300–5760 recorded information, WEB *www.royalacademy.org.uk.* 🎫 *Admission varies according to exhibition.* ⏲ *Sat.–Thurs. 10–6, Fri. 10–10. Tube: Piccadilly Circus or Green Park.*

NEED A BREAK?

The **Royal Academy Restaurant** has hot dishes at lunchtime, very good vegetarian options, and an extensive salad selection that is inexpensive for such a swish location. Desserts and cakes are masterpieces. It's a popular place to meet for a bite throughout the day, as you can eat here without paying admission but still drink in the artistic atmosphere. It's open weekdays 10–5:30, with a dinner menu on Friday from 6:15–10:30.

❻ **St. James's Church.** Recessed from the street behind a courtyard, the church is filled most days with an antiques and crafts market. Completed in 1684, this was the last of Sir Christopher Wren's London churches and his own favorite. It contains one of Grinling Gibbons's finest works, an ornate limewood reredos (the screen behind the altar). The organ is a survivor of Whitehall Palace and was brought here in 1691. A 1940 bomb scored a direct hit here, but the church has been completely restored, albeit with a fiberglass spire. It's a lively place, offering all manner of lectures and concerts. The courtyard hosts different markets: Tues. antiques and small collectibles; Wed.–Sat. arts and crafts. ✉ *Piccadilly, St. James's W1,* ☎ *020/7381–0441 for concert program and tickets. Tube: Piccadilly Circus or Green Park.*

❷ **St. James's Palace.** With its solitary sentry posted at the gate, this surprisingly small palace of Tudor brick was once a home for many British sovereigns, including the first Elizabeth and Charles I, who spent his last night here before his execution. Today it is the residence of another Charles—the future King Charles III (that is, if the current Prince of Wales makes it to Westminster Abbey). His front door actually debouches right onto the street, but he always uses a back entrance. Matters to ponder as you look (you can't go in): the palace was named after a hospital for women lepers, which stood here during the 11th century; Henry VIII had it built; foreign ambassadors to Britain are still accredited to the Court of St. James's even though it has rarely been a primary royal residence; and the present queen made her first speech here. Friary Court out front is a splendid setting for Trooping the Colour, part of the Changing of the Guard ceremony. Everyone loves to take a snap of the scarlet-coated guardsman standing sentinel outside the imposing Tudor gateway. ✉ *Friary Court, St. James's SW1. Tube: Green Park.*

❹ **St. James's Square.** One of London's oldest and leafiest squares was also the most snobbish address of all when it was laid out around 1670, with 14 resident dukes and earls installed by 1720. Since 1841, No. 14—one of the several 18th-century residences spared by World War II bombs—has housed the **London Library,** founded by Thomas Carlyle, and which, with its million or so volumes, is considered the best private humanities library in the land. You can go in and read the famous authors' complaints in the comments book—but not the famous authors' books, unless you join, at £100 a year. ✉ *St. James's SW1. Tube: Piccadilly Circus.*

⓯ **Selfridges.** With its row of massive Ionic columns, this huge store was opened three years after Harry Gordon Selfridge came to London from Chicago in 1906. Now British-run, Selfridges rivals Harrods in size and stock, and it is finally rivaling its glamour, too, since investing in major face-lift operations. ✉ *400 Oxford St., Mayfair W1,* ☎ *020/7629–1234,* WEB *www.selfridges.co.uk.* ⏲ *Mon.–Fri. 10–8, Sat. 9:30–8, Sun. 11:30–6. Tube: Marble Arch or Bond St.*

Shepherd Market. Though it looks like a quaint and villagelike tangle of streetlets, this was anything *but* quaint when Edward Shepherd laid it out in 1735 on the site of the orgiastic, two-week-long May Fair (which gave the whole district its name). Now there are sandwich bars, pubs and restaurants, boutiques and nightclubs, and a (fading) red-light reputation in the narrow lanes. ✉ *Curzon and Shepherd Sts., Mayfair W1. Tube: Green Park.*

★ 13 **Speakers' Corner.** This corner harbors one of London's most public spectacles. Here, on Sunday afternoons, anyone is welcome to mount a soapbox and declaim upon any topic. It's an irresistible showcase of eccentricity, one such being the (deceased) "Protein Man," who, wearing his publicity board, proclaimed the eating of meat, cheese, and peanuts led to uncontrollable acts of passion that would destroy Western civilization. The pamphlets he sold for four decades the length and breadth of Oxford Street are now collector's items. ✉ *Cumberland Gate, Park La., Mayfair W1. Tube: Marble Arch.*

★ 3 **Spencer House.** Ancestral abode of the Spencers—Diana, Princess of Wales's family—this great mansion is perhaps the finest example of 18th-century elegance, on a domestic scale, extant in London. Superlatively restored by Lord Rothschild, the house was built in 1766 for the first Earl Spencer, heir to the first Duchess of Marlborough. A gorgeous Doric facade, complete with a pediment adorned with classical statues, announces at once Earl Spencer's passion for the Grand Tour and the classical antiquities of the past. Inside, James "Athenian" Stuart decorated the gilded State Rooms, including the Painted Room, the first completely Neoclassic room in Europe. The most ostentatious part of the house (and the Spencers did not shrink from ostentation—witness the £40,000 diamond shoe buckles the first countess proudly wore) is the florid bow window of the Palm Room: covered with stucco palm trees, it conjures up both ancient Palmyra and modern Miami Beach. ✉ *27 St. James's Pl., St. James's SW1,* ☎ *020/7499–8620,* WEB *www.spencerhouse.co.uk.* 🎫 *£6.* ⏲ *Sept.–Dec. and Feb.–July, Sun. 10:45–4:45 (guided tour leaves approx. every 25 mins; tickets on sale Sun. at 10:30). Tube: Green Park.*

★ 16 **Wallace Collection.** Assembled by four generations of Marquesses of Hertford and given to the nation by the widow of Sir Richard Wallace, bastard son of the fourth, this collection of art and artifacts is important, exciting, undervisited—and free. As at the Frick Collection in New York, Hertford House itself is part of the show: the fine late-18th-century mansion, built for the Duke of Manchester, contains a basement floor with educational activities, several galleries, and a courtyard, covered by a glass roof, with exhibit space and an upscale restaurant.

The first marquess was a patron of Sir Joshua Reynolds, the second bought Hertford House, the third—a flamboyant socialite—favored Sèvres porcelain and 17th-century Dutch painting; but it was the eccentric fourth marquess who, from his self-imposed exile in Paris, really built the collection, snapping up Bouchers, Fragonards, Watteaus, and Lancrets for a song (the French Revolution having rendered them dangerously unfashionable), augmenting these with furniture and sculpture and sending his son Richard out to do the deals. With 30 years of practice behind him, Richard Wallace continued acquiring treasures after his father's death, scouring Italy for majolica and Renaissance gold, then moving most of it to London. Look for Rembrandt's portrait of his son, the Rubens landscape, Gainsborough and Romney portraits, the Van Dycks and Canalettos, the French rooms, and of course the porcelain. The highlight is Fragonard's *The Swing,* which conjures up the 18th-century's let-them-eat-cake frivolity better than any other painting around. Don't forget to smile back at Frans Hals's *Laughing Cavalier* in the Big Gallery or pay your respects to Thomas Sully's enchanting *Queen Victoria,* which resides in a rouge-pink salon (just to the right of the main entrance). There is a fine collection of armor and weaponry in the basement as a break from all the upstairs gentility. ✉ *Hertford House, Manchester Sq., Mayfair W1,* ☎ *020/7935–0687,* WEB *www.the-wallace-collection.org.uk.* *Free.* ⏲ *Mon.–Sat. 10–5, Sun. noon–5. Tube: Bond St.*

Waterloo Place. This is a long rectangle off Pall Mall, punctuated by the Duke of York Memorial Column atop the Duke of York Steps and littered with statues, among them Florence Nightingale, the "Lady with the Lamp" nurse-heroine of the Crimean War; Captain R. F. Scott, who led a disastrous Antarctic expedition in 1911–12 and is here frozen in a bronze by his wife; Edward VII, mounted; George VI; and, as usual, Victoria, here in terra-cotta. Flanking Waterloo Place and looking onto Pall Mall are two of the gentlemen's clubs for which St. James's came to be known as Clubland: the **Athenaeum** and the former United Service Club, a favorite haunt of the Duke of Wellington, now the **Institute of Directors.** The latter was built by John Nash in 1827–28 but was given a face-lift by Decimus Burton 30 years later to match it up with the Athenaeum across the way, which he had designed. It's fitting that you gaze on the Athenaeum first, since it was—and is—the most elite of all the societies. (It called itself "the Society" until 1830 just to rub it in.) Most prime ministers and cabinet ministers, archbishops, and bishops have belonged; the founder, John Wilson Croker (the first to call the British right-wingers "Conservatives"), decreed it the club for artists and writers, and so literary types (Sir Arthur Conan Doyle, Rudyard Kipling, J. M. Barrie—the posh ones) have graced its lists, too. Women are barred. Most clubs will tolerate female guests these days, but few admit women members, and anyway it's almost impossible to become a member unless you have the connections—which, of course, is the whole point. ✉ *Regent St., Pall Mall, St. James's SW1. Tube: Piccadilly Circus.*

SOHO AND COVENT GARDEN

An area delineated by Regent Street, Coventry and Cranbourn streets, Charing Cross Road, and the eastern half of Oxford Street encloses Soho, the most fun part of the West End. This appellation, unlike the New York neighborhood's similar one, is not an elision of anything but a blast from the past—derived (supposedly) from the shouts of "So ho!" that royal huntsmen in Whitehall Palace's parklands were once heard to cry. One of Charles II's illegitimate sons, the Duke of Monmouth, was an early resident, his dubious pedigree setting the tone for the future: for many years, Soho was London's center of strip shows, peep shows, clip joints, sex shops, and brothels. The mid-'80s brought legislation that granted expensive licenses to a few such establishments and closed down the rest; most prostitution had already been ousted by the 1959 Street Offences Act. Only a cosmetic smear of red-light activity remains now, plus one or two purveyors of fetish wear for trendy club-goers.

These clubs, which cluster around the Soho grid, are the diametric opposite of the St. James's gentlemen's museums—they cater to youth, and post tyrannical fashion police at the door. Another breed of Soho club is the strictly members-only media haunts (the Groucho, the Soho House, Fred's, Brown's, Black's), salons for carefully segregated strata of high-income hipsters. The same crowd populates the astonishing selection of restaurants, but then so do the rest of London and all its visitors.

It was after the First World War, when London households relinquished their resident cooks en masse, that Soho's gastronomic reputation was established. It had been a cosmopolitan area since the first immigrant wave of French Huguenots arrived in the 1680s. More French came fleeing the revolution during the late 18th century, then the Paris Commune of 1870, followed by Germans, Russians, Poles, Greeks, and (especially) Italians, and, much later, Chinese. Pedestrianized Gerrard Street, south of Shaftesbury Avenue, is the hub of London's compact Chinatown, with restaurants, dim sum houses, Chinese supermarkets, and Chinese New Year's celebrations, plus a brace of scarlet pagoda-style archways and a pair of phone booths with pictogram dialing instructions.

The former Covent Garden Market became the Covent Garden Piazza, with the Central Market in the middle, in 1980, and it still functions as the center of a neighborhood—one that has always been alluded to as "colorful." It was originally the "convent garden" belonging to the Abbey of St. Peter at Westminster (later Westminster Abbey). The land was given to the first Earl of Bedford by the Crown after the Dissolution of the Monasteries in 1536. The earls—later promoted to dukes—of Bedford held on to the place right up until 1918, when the 11th duke managed to off-load what had by then become a liability. In between, the area enclosed by Long Acre, St. Martin's Lane, Drury Lane, and assorted streets north of the Strand had gone from the height of fashion (until the snobs moved west to brand-new St. James's) to a period of arty-literary bohemia during the 18th century, followed by an era of vice and mayhem, once more to become vegetable provisioner to London when the market building went up in the 1830s, followed by the Flower Market in 1870 (Eliza Dolittle's haunt in Shaw's *Pygmalion* and Lerner and Loewe's musical version, *My Fair Lady*).

Still, it was no Mayfair, what with 1,000-odd market porters spending their 40 shillings a week in the alehouses, brothels, and gambling dens that had never quite disappeared. By the time the Covent Garden Estate Company took over the running of the market from the 11th duke, it seemed as if seediness had set in for good, and when the fruit-and-veg trade moved out to the bigger, better Nine Elms Market in Vauxhall in 1974, it left behind a decrepit wasteland. But this is one of London's success stories: the Greater London Council (now defunct) stepped in with a dream of a rehabilitation plan—not unlike the one that was tried, though less successfully, in the Parisian equivalent, Les Halles. By 1980 the transformation was complete.

Numbers in the text below correspond to numbers in the margin and on the Soho and Covent Garden map.

A Good Walk

Soho, being small, is easy to explore, though it's also easy to mistake one narrow, crowded street for another, and even Londoners go astray here. Enter from the northwest corner, Oxford Circus, and head south for about 200 yards down Regent Street, turn left onto Great Marlborough Street, and head to the top of **Carnaby Street** ①. Turn right off Broadwick Street into Berwick (pronounced "Berrick") Street, famed as central London's best fruit-and-vegetable market. Then step through tiny Walker's Court (a hookers' haunt); cross Brewer Street, named for two extinct 18th-century breweries; and you'll have arrived at Soho's hip (and very gay) hangout, Old Compton Street. From here, Wardour, Dean, Frith, and Greek streets lead north, all of them bursting with restaurants and clubs. Either of the last two leads north to **Soho Square** ②, but head one block south instead, to Shaftesbury Avenue, heart of theaterland, across which you'll find Chinatown's main

HOW TO USE THIS GUIDE

Great trips begin with great planning, and this guide makes planning easy. It's packed with everything you need—insider advice on hotels and restaurants, cool tools, practical tips, essential maps, and much more.

COOL TOOLS

Fodor's Choice Top picks are marked throughout with a star.

Great Itineraries These tours, planned by Fodor's experts, give you the skinny on what you can see and do in the time you have.

Smart Travel Tips A to Z This special section is packed with important contacts and advice on everything from how to get around to what to pack.

Good Walks You won't miss a thing if you follow the numbered bullets on our maps.

Need a Break? Looking for a quick bite to eat or a spot to rest? These sure bets are along the way.

Off the Beaten Path Some lesser-known sights are worth a detour. We've marked those you should make time for.

POST-IT® FLAGS

Dog-ear no more!

ICONS AND SYMBOLS

Watch for these symbols throughout:

★	Our special recommendations
✕	Restaurant
🏨	Lodging establishment
✕🏨	Lodging establishment whose restaurant warrants a special trip
🐥	Good for kids
☞	Sends you to another section of the guide for more information
✉	Address
☎	Telephone number
FAX	Fax number
WEB	Web site
🎟	Admission price
⏲	Opening hours
$-$$$$	Lodging and dining price categories, keyed to strategically sited price charts. Check the index for locations.
①❶	Numbers in white and black circles on the maps, in the margins, and within tours correspond to one another.

ON THE WEB

Continue your planning with these useful tools found at **www.fodors.com**, the Web's best source for travel information.

"Rich with resources." —*New York Times*

"Navigation is a cinch." —*Forbes* "Best of the Web" list

"Put together by people bursting with know-how."
—*Sunday Times* (London)

Create a Miniguide Pinpoint hotels, restaurants, and attractions that have what you want at the price you want to pay.

Rants and Raves Find out what readers say about Fodor's picks—or write your own reviews of hotels and restaurants you've just visited.

Travel Talk Post your questions and get answers from fellow travelers, or share your own experiences.

On-Line Booking Find the best prices on airline tickets, rental cars, cruises, or vacations, and book them on the spot.

About our Books Learn about other Fodor's guides to your destination and many others.

Expert Advice and Trip Ideas From what to tip to how to take great photos, from the national parks to Nepal, Fodors.com has suggestions that'll make your trip a breeze. Log on and get informed and inspired.

Smart Resources Check the weather in your destination or convert your currency. Learn the local language or link to the latest event listings. Or consult hundreds of detailed maps—all in one place.

drag, Gerrard Street. Below Gerrard Street is **Leicester Square** ③, and running along its west side is Charing Cross Road, the bibliophile's dream. You'll find some of the best of the specialist bookshops in little Cecil Court, running east just before Trafalgar Square.

The easiest way to find the **Covent Garden Piazza** ④ and market building is to walk down Cranbourn Street, next to the Leicester Square tube, then down Long Acre, and turn right at James Street. Around here are **St. Paul's Church** ⑤—the actors' church—the **London's Transport Museum** ⑥, and the **Theatre Museum** ⑦, as well as plenty of shops and cafés. (If your aim is to shop, Neal Street, Floral Street, the streets around Seven Dials, and the Thomas Neal's mall all reward exploration.) From Seven Dials, veer 45 degrees south onto Mercer Street, turning right on Long Acre, then left onto Garrick Street, past the **Garrick Club** ⑧, left onto Rose Street, and right onto Floral Street. At the other end you'll emerge onto Bow Street, right next to the **Royal Opera House** ⑨ and the **Bow Street Magistrates' Court** ⑩. Continuing on and turning left onto Russell Street, you reach Drury Lane and the **Theatre Royal, Drury Lane** ⑪.

At the end of Drury Lane is the Aldwych, a great big croissant of a potential traffic accident, with a central island on which stand three hulking monoliths: India House, Melbourne House, and the handsome 1935 Neoclassic Bush House, headquarters of the BBC World Service. Stranded on traffic islands to the west are the 1717 St. Mary-le-Strand; James Gibbs's (of St. Martin-in-the-Fields fame) first public building, inspired by the Baroque churches of Rome; and Wren's St. Clement Danes (with a tower appended by Gibbs), whose 10 bells peal the tune of the nursery rhyme "Oranges and lemons, Say the bells of St. Clements . . ." even though the bells in the rhyme belong to the St. Clements in Eastcheap. Inside is a book listing 1,900 American airmen who were killed during World War II. Heading west, perhaps stopping at **Somerset House** ⑫ and the **Courtauld Institute Gallery** within, walk the ¾-mi traffic-clogged Strand to the southern end, where you take Villiers Street down to the Thames. See the historic York Watergate, once the gateway leading from the Duke of Buckingham's garden to the river steps, and **Cleopatra's Needle** ⑬ by Victoria Embankment Gardens; cross the gardens northwest to the **Adelphi** ⑭, circumnavigating the Strand by sticking to the embankment walk; and you'll soon reach Waterloo Bridge, where (weather permitting) you can catch some of London's most glamorous views, toward both the City and Westminster around the Thames bend.

TIMING

The distance covered here is around 5 mi if you include the lengthy walk down the Strand and riverside stroll back. Skip that and it's barely a couple of miles, but you will almost certainly get lost, because the streets in both Covent Garden and Soho are winding, chaotic, and not logically disposed. Although getting lost is half the fun, it does make it hard to predict how long this walk will take. You can whiz round both neighborhoods in an hour, but if the area appeals at all, you'll want all day—for shopping, lunch, the Theatre and Transport museums, and the Courtauld Galleries. One way to do it is to start at Leicester Square at 2 PM, when the Half Price Theatre Booth opens; pick up tickets for later; and then walk, shop, and eat in between.

HOW TO GET THERE

A popular way to get to Soho is to hop on the Northern Line to Tottenham Court Road and walk south down Charing Cross Road, then west along Old Compton Street into the district proper, or eastward, by turning left at Shaftesbury Avenue, over to the Covent Garden area.

The Covent Garden tube stop is on the Piccadilly Line; Leicester Square—the nearest tube to Soho—is on the Northern and Piccadilly lines. The best Soho buses are Buses 3, 8, 10, 12, 13, 15, 23, 38, 73, 139, 159, and 176 to Charing Cross Road and Shaftesbury Avenue; for Covent Garden, get those listed above or the ones that stop along the Strand: Buses 9, 11, 13, 15, and 23.

Sights to See

14 **Adelphi.** This regal riverfront row of houses was the work of London's Scottish architects—all four of them. John, Robert, James, and William Adam, being brothers, gave rise to the name, from the Greek *adelphoi,* meaning brothers. All the late-18th-century design stars were roped in to beautify the interiors, but the grandeur gradually eroded, and today very few of the 24 houses remain; Nos. 1–4 Robert Street, and No. 7 Adam Street are the best. ✉ *The Strand, Covent Garden WC2. Tube: Charing Cross or Temple.*

10 **Bow Street Magistrates' Court.** This was where the prototype of the modern police force first operated. Known as the Bow Street Runners (because they chased thieves on foot), they were the brainchild of the second Bow Street magistrate—none other than Henry Fielding, the author of *Tom Jones* and *Joseph Andrews*. The late-19th-century edifice on the site went up during one of the market improvement drives. It now houses three courts, including that of the Metropolitan Chief Magistrate, who hears all extradition applications. ✉ *Bow St., Covent Garden WC2. Tube: Covent Garden.*

1 **Carnaby Street.** The '60s synonym for swinging London fell into a post-party depression, reemerging sometime during the 1980s as the main drag of a public-relations invention called West Soho. Blank stares would greet anyone asking directions to such a place, but it is geographically logical, and the tangle of streets—Foubert's Place, Broadwick Street, Marshall Street—do cohere, at least in type of merchandise (youth accessories, mostly, with a smattering of up-and-coming, happening designer boutiques and fashionable restaurants). Broadwick Street is also notable as the birthplace, at No. 74, in 1758, of the great visionary poet and painter William Blake. At age 26 he relocated back to this house for a year to sell prints next door, at No. 72 (now an ugly tower block), and then remained a Soho resident on Poland Street. ✉ *Soho W1. Tube: Oxford Circus.*

13 **Cleopatra's Needle.** Off the triangular-handkerchief Victoria Embankment Gardens, where office sandwich-eaters and people who call it home coexist, is London's *very oldest thing,* predating its arbitrary namesake, and London itself, by centuries. The 60-ft pink granite obelisk was erected at Heliopolis, in lower Egypt, in about 1475 BC, then moved to Alexandria, where in 1819 Mohammed Ali, the Turkish viceroy of Egypt, rescued it from its fallen state and presented it to the British. The British, though grateful, had not the faintest idea how to get the 186-ton gift home, so they left it there for years until an expatriate English engineer contrived an iron pontoon to float it to London via Spain. The sphinxes are a later, British addition. Future archaeologists will find an 1878 time capsule underneath, containing the morning papers, several Bibles, a railway timetable, some pins, a razor, and a dozen photos of Victorian pinup girls. ✉ *Embankment, Covent Garden WC2. Tube: Charing Cross or Embankment.*

Courtauld Institute Gallery. One of London's most beloved art collections, the Courtauld is set in the grounds of the renovated, grand 18th-century classical **Somerset House.** Founded in 1931 by the textile magnate Samuel Courtauld, this is London's finest Impressionist and

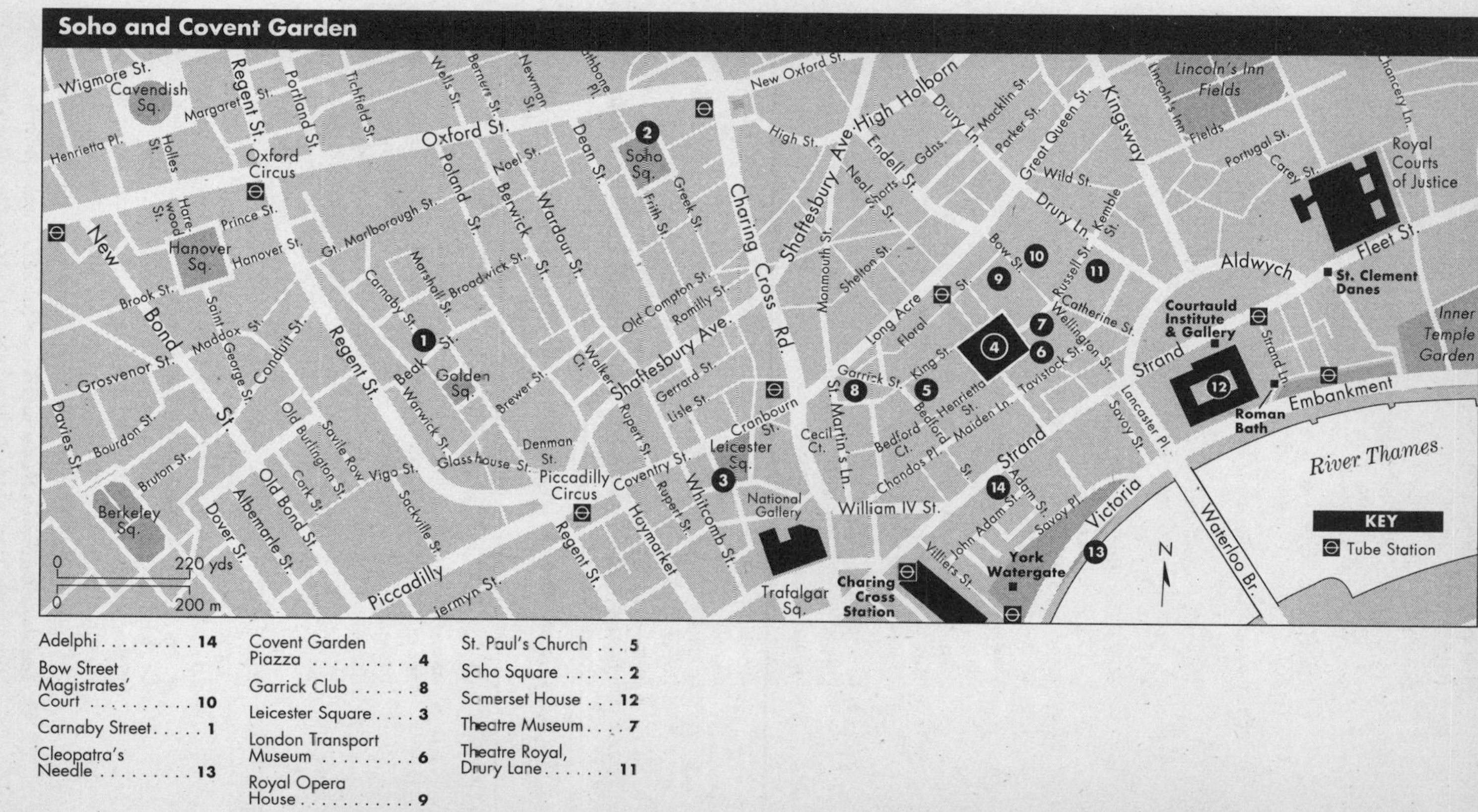

Adelphi 14
Bow Street Magistrates' Court 10
Carnaby Street 1
Cleopatra's Needle 13
Covent Garden Piazza 4
Garrick Club 8
Leicester Square 3
London Transport Museum 6
Royal Opera House 9
St. Paul's Church . . . 5
Scho Square 2
Scmerset House . . . 12
Theatre Museum 7
Theatre Royal, Drury Lane 11

Post-Impressionist collection, ranging from Bonnard to Van Gogh (Manet's *Bar at the Folies-Bergère* is the star), with bonus post-Renaissance works thrown in. Botticelli, Brueghel, Tiepolo, and Rubens are also represented, thanks to the exquisite bequest of Count Antoine Seilern's Princes Gate collection. ✉ *The Strand, Covent Garden WC2,* ☎ *020/7848–2526,* WEB *www.courtauld.ac.uk.* 🎟 *£4; free Mon. 10–2.* ⏲ *Daily 10–6 (last admission 5:15), Fri. 10–9 late July–early Sept. Tube: Covent Garden, Holborn, or Temple.*

4 **Covent Garden Piazza.** The restored 1840 market building around which Covent Garden pivots is known as the Piazza. Inside, the shops are mostly higher-class clothing chains, plus a couple of cafés and some knickknack stores that are good for gifts. There's a superior crafts market on most days, too. If you turn right, you'll reach the indoor **Jubilee Market,** with stalls selling clothing, army surplus gear, more crafts, and more knickknacks. At yet another market off to the left (on the way back to the tube), the leather goods, antiques, and secondhand clothing stalls are a little more exciting. In summer it may seem that everyone you see around the Piazza (and the crowds are legion) is a fellow tourist, but there is still plenty of office life in the area, and Londoners continue to flock here. By the church in the square, street performers—from global musicians to jugglers and mime artists—play to the crowds. ✉ *Covent Garden WC2. Tube: Covent Garden.*

8 **Garrick Club.** Named for the 18th-century actor and theater manager David Garrick, this club is, because of its literary-theatrical bent, more louche than its St. James's brothers, and famous actors, from Sir Laurence Olivier down, have always been proud to join—along with Dickens, Thackeray, and Trollope, in their time. Find the **Lamb & Flag** down teeny Rose Street to the left. Dickens drank in this pub, better known in its 17th-century youth as the Bucket of Blood, owing to the bare-knuckle boxing matches held upstairs. (You'll find that many London pubs claim Dickens as an habitué, and it's unclear whether they exaggerate or the author was the city's premier sot.) ✉ *15 Garrick St., Covent Garden WC2. Tube: Leicester Sq. or Covent Garden.*

3 **Leicester Square.** This square (pronounced "Lester") is showing no sign of its great age. Looking at the neon of the major movie houses, the fast-food outlets (plus a useful Häagen-Dazs café), and the disco entrances, you'd never guess it was laid out around 1630. By the 19th century it was already bustling and disreputable, and now it's usually one of the only places crowded after midnight—with suburban teenagers, backpackers, and London's swelling ranks of the homeless. That said, it is not a threatening place, and the liveliness can be quite cheering. In the middle is a statue of a sulking Shakespeare, clearly wishing he were somewhere else and perhaps remembering the days when the cinemas were live theaters—burlesque houses, but live all the same. Here, too, are figures of Hogarth, Reynolds, and Charlie Chaplin, and underneath, but not visible, is a £22 million electrical substation. One landmark certainly worth visiting is the **Society of London Theatre ticket kiosk,** on the southwest corner, which sells half-price tickets for many of that evening's performances. On the northeast corner, in Leicester Place, stands the church of **Notre Dame de France,** with a wonderful mural by Jean Cocteau in one of its side chapels. ✉ *Covent Garden WC2. Tube: Covent Garden.*

6 **London's Transport Museum.** Housed in the old Flower Market at the southeast corner of the Covent Garden Piazza, this museum tells the story of mass transportation in the capital, and it is much better than it sounds. It is particularly child-friendly, with lots of touch-screen interactive material; live actors in costume (including a Victorian horse-

dung collector, though you should go early to see them); old rolling stock; period smells and sounds; and, best of all, a tube-driving simulator. There's also a café and a shop selling the wonderful old London Transport posters, plus mugs, socks, bow ties, and so on, printed with that elegant London tube map, designed by Harry Beck in 1933 and still in use today. ⊠ *Piazza, Covent Garden WC2,* ☎ *020/7379–6344,* WEB *www.ltmuseum.co.uk.* 🎟 *£5.95.* ⏲ *Sat.–Thurs. 10–6, Fri. 11–6 (last admission 5:15). Tube: Covent Garden.*

Neal Street. One of Covent Garden's most intriguing shopping streets begins north of Long Acre, catercorner to the tube station, and is closed to traffic halfway down. Here you can buy everything you never knew you needed—apricot tea, sitars, vintage aviators' jackets, silk kimonos, Alvar Aalto vases, halogen desk lamps, shoes with heel lower than toe, collapsible top hats, and so on. To the left off Neal Street, on Earlham Street, is Thomas Neal's—a new, upmarket, designerish clothing and housewares mall named after the founder (in 1693) of the star-shape cobbled junction of tiny streets just past there, called Seven Dials—a surprisingly residential enclave, with lots going on behind the tenement-style warehouse facades. The small and intimate **Donmar Warehouse Theatre** is part of the complex; it presents a radical range of theater—such as Nicole Kidman in *The Blue Room.* Turning left onto the next street off Neal Street, Shorts Gardens, you come to Neal's Yard (note the comical, water-operated wooden clock), originally just a whole-foods wholesaler and now an entire holistic village, with therapy rooms, an organic bakery and dairy, a great vegetarian café, and a medical herbalist's shop reminiscent of a medieval apothecary. ⊠ *Covent Garden WC2. Tube: Covent Garden.*

9 **Royal Opera House.** Here, in days of yore, Joan Sutherland brought down the house as Lucia di Lammermoor, and Rudolf Nureyev and Margot Fonteyn became the greatest ballet duo of all time. For such delights, seats were top dollar—nearly £100—or just one-twentieth of that lordly amount. Whatever the price, it was worth it if you loved the red-and-gold Victorian surroundings, which always managed to give a very special feel to the hush that precedes the start of a performance. London's premier opera venue was designed in 1858 by E. M. Barry, son of Sir Charles, the House of Commons architect. This is actually the third theater on the site. The first opened in 1732 and burned down in 1808; the second opened a year later under the aegis of one John Anderson, only to succumb to fire in 1856 (Anderson, who had lost two theaters already, had an appalling record when it came to keeping the limelights apart from the curtains).

The entire building was overhauled spectacularly as a modern, practical, technologically streamlined opera house in 2000, while keeping the magic of the grand Victorian theater. Without doubt, the glass and steel Floral Hall (so badly damaged by fire in the 1950s it was used only for storing scenery) is the most wonderful feature; you can wander around and drink in (literally, in the foyer café) the interior during the day. The same is true of the Amphitheatre Bar and Piazza concourse, which give a splendid panorama across the city. There are free lunchtime chamber concerts and lectures as part of the policy to dispel the elitist tag the House is claimed to hold. Behind the scenes, the Royal Ballet can finally enjoy a much updated and more spacious home. ⊠ *Bow St., Covent Garden,* ☎ *020/7240–1200 or 020/7304–4000,* WEB *www.royaloperahouse.org. Tube: Covent Garden.*

5 **St. Paul's Church.** If you want to commune with the spirits of Vivien Leigh, Noël Coward, Edith Evans, and Charlie Chaplin, this might be the place. Memorials to them and many other theater greats are

found in this 1633 work of the renowned Inigo Jones, which has always been known as "the actors' church" thanks to the neighboring theater district and St. Paul's prominent parishioners (well-known actors often read the lessons at services). Fittingly, its portico was where the opening scene for *Pygmalion* was staged. St. Paul's Church (Wren's mammoth St. Paul's cathedral is eastward in the City) is across the Covent Garden Piazza, often picturesquely punctuated with street entertainers—those who have passed auditions for this most coveted of London's street venues. ✉ *Bedford St., Covent Garden WC2. Tube: Covent Garden.*

❷ **Soho Square.** Laid out about 1680, this square was fashionable during the 18th century. Only two of the original houses still stand, plus the 19th-century central garden. It's now a place of peace and offices (among them Paul McCartney's music publishers and Bloomsbury Publishing). That isn't a Tudor landmark in the center but a Tudor-style thatch-and-daub Victorian gardener's hut—an almost fairy-tale sight to enjoy during a take-out lunch in the park. ✉ *Soho W1. Tube: Tottenham Court Rd.*

NEED A BREAK?

Take any excuse you can think of to visit either of these food landmarks. They're both cafés, but there the similarity ends. **Maison Bertaux** (✉ 28 Greek St., Soho) has been dispensing savory and sweet delights since the end of the 19th century, in surroundings reminiscent of a faded French *salon de thé* on two floors. **Pâtisserie Valerie** (✉ 44 Old Compton St., Soho) serves divine gâteaux, milles-feuilles, croissants, éclairs, and more. Valerie majors on chocolate laden cakes (the window display alone is a cake-lovers orgy). Enjoy this, along with Italian coffee, in a cramped, lively ground-floor room.

⓬ **Somerset House.** An old royal palace once stood on the site, but the 18th-century building that finally replaced it was the work of Sir William Chambers (1726–96) during the reign of George III. It was built to house government offices, principally those of the Navy; for the first time in over one hundred years, these gracious rooms are on view for free, including the Seamen's Waiting Hall and the Nelson Stair. In addition, the Navy Commissioners' Barge has returned to dry dock at the Water Gate. The rooms are on the south side of the building, by the river, while the **Courtauld Institute Gallery** occupies most of the north building, facing the busy Strand. Between is the cobbled Italianate courtyard, where Admiral Nelson used to walk, which is the scene of concerts and other cultural events. Cafés and a restored river terrace adjoin the property, and a stone-and-glass footbridge leads up to Waterloo Bridge, which crosses the river.

In the vaults of the house is **The Gilbert Collection,** a museum of intricate works of silver, gold snuff boxes, and Italian mosaics. The micromosaics on tables, portrait miniatures, and jewelry are made in such fine detail that you might think they're painted, so be glad if you're offered a magnifying glass—it's the best way to fully appreciate the fine detail. The **Hermitage Rooms** contain permanent exhibition space for some of the treasures from the State Hermitage Museum in Russia. The opening show consisted of a selection of jewels, antiquities, portraits, and miniatures amassed by Catherine the Great, one of the greatest collectors of all time. ✉ *The Strand, Covent Garden WC2,* ☎ *020/7845–4600 information line,* WEB *www.somerset-house.org.uk.* 🎟 *Somerset House free; Gilbert Collection £5, Courtauld Institute Gallery £4, Hermitage Rooms £6. Visit two collections, save £1; visit all three, save £2.* ⏲ *Daily 10–6 (last admission 5:15). Tube: Charing Cross.*

Strand. Remember Judy Garland doing Burlington Bertie in Chaplin drag, walking down the Strand with gloves in hand, in *A Star Is Born?* William Hargreaves's song was a popular number in the Strand music halls that put the street on the map afresh in the early 1900s. Now its presence on maps is about all that the characterless Strand has to recommend it. ✉ *Covent Garden WC2. Tube: Charing Cross.*

7 **Theatre Museum.** This mostly below-ground museum aims to re-create the excitement of theater itself. There are usually programs in progress allowing children to get in a mess with makeup or have a giant dressing-up session. Permanent exhibits paint a history of the English stage from the 16th century to Mick Jagger's jumpsuit, with tens of thousands of theater playbills and sections on such topics as Hamlet through the ages and pantomime—the peculiar British theatrical tradition whereby men dress as ugly women (as distinct from RuPaul) and girls wear tights and play princes. There's a little theater in the bowels of the museum and a ticket desk for "real" theaters around town, plus an archive holding video recordings and audiotapes of significant British theatrical productions. ✉ *7 Russell St., Covent Garden WC2,* ☎ *020/7943–4700,* WEB *www.theatremuseum.org.* *Free.* *Tues.–Sun. 10–6 (last admission 5:30). Tube: Covent Garden.*

11 **Theatre Royal, Drury Lane.** This is London's best-known auditorium and almost its largest. Since World War II, its forte has been musicals (past ones have included *The King and I, My Fair Lady, South Pacific, Hello, Dolly!,* and *A Chorus Line*)—though David Garrick, who managed it from 1747 to 1776, made its name by reviving the works of the by-then-obscure William Shakespeare. It enjoys all the romantic accessories of a London theater—a history of fires (it burned down three times, once in a Wren-built incarnation), riots (in 1737, when a posse of footmen demanded free admission), attempted regicides (George II in 1716 and his grandson George III in 1800), and even sightings of the most famous phantom of theaterland, the Man in Grey (in the Circle, matinees). The entrance is on Catherine Street. ✉ *Catherine St., Covent Garden WC2. Tube: Covent Garden.*

BLOOMSBURY AND LEGAL LONDON

The character of an area of London can change visibly from one street to the next. Nowhere is this so clear as in the contrast between fun-loving Soho and intellectual Bloomsbury, a mere 100 yards to the northeast, or between arty, trendy Covent Garden and—on the other side of Kingsway—sober Holborn. Both Bloomsbury and Holborn are almost purely residential and should be seen by day. The first district is best known for its famous flowering of literary-arty bohemia, personified by the clique known as the Bloomsbury Group during this century's first three decades, and for the British Museum and the University of London, which dominate it now. The second sounds as exciting as, say, a center for accountants or dentists, but don't be put off—filled with magnificently ancient buildings, it's more interesting and beautiful than you might suppose.

Let's get the Bloomsbury Group out of the way since you can't visit them and nothing exists to mark its territory beyond a sprinkling of blue plaques. (These government-sponsored tablets commemorate persons who enhanced "human welfare or happiness" and have been dead for at least 20 years.) There's also a plaque in Bloomsbury Square saying nothing about this elite core of writers and artists except that they lived around here. The chief Bloomsburies were Virginia Woolf, E. M. Forster, Vanessa and Clive Bell, Duncan Grant, Dora Carrington, Roger Fry, John Maynard Keynes, and Lytton Strachey, with satellites including Rupert Brooke and Christopher Isherwood. They agreed with G. E. Moore's philosophical notion that "the pleasures of human intercourse and the enjoyment of beautiful objects . . . form the rational ultimate end of social progress." True to their beliefs, when they weren't producing beautiful objects, the friends enjoyed much human intercourse, as has been exhaustively documented, not least in Virginia Woolf's own diaries. All you need do to find out more about them is to read the "Review" supplements of the Sunday broadsheets, which are forever running Bloomsbury exposés as if they were fresh gossip.

More clearly visible than those literary salons is the time-warp territory of interlocking alleys, gardens and cobbled courts, and town houses and halls where London's legal profession grew up. The Great Fire of 1666 razed most of the city but spared the buildings of legal London, and the whole neighborhood oozes history. What is best about the area is that it lacks the commercial veneer of other historic sites, mostly because it still is very much the center of London's legal profession. Barristers, berobed and bewigged, may add an anachronistic frisson to your sightseeing, but they're only on their way to work.

They are headed for one of the four Inns of Court: Gray's Inn, Lincoln's Inn, Middle Temple, and Inner Temple. Those arcane names are simply explained. The inns were just that: lodging houses for the lawyers who, back in the 14th century, clustered together here so everyone knew where to find them and ultimately took over the running of the inns themselves. The temples were built on land owned by the Knights Templar, a chivalric order founded during the First Crusade in the 11th century; their 12th-century Temple Church still stands here. Few barristers (British for trial lawyers) still live in the inns, but nearly all keep chambers (British for barristers' offices) here, and all are still obliged to eat a requisite number of meals in the hall of "their" inn during training—no dinner, no career. They take exams, too.

Numbers in the text correspond to numbers in the margin and on the Bloomsbury and Legal London map.

A Good Walk

From Russell Square tube stop, walk south down Southampton Row and west on Great Russell Street, passing **Bloomsbury Square** on the left, en route to London's biggest and most important collection of antiquities, the **British Museum** ①. Leaving this via the back exit leads you to Montague Place, which you should cross to Malet Street, straight ahead, to reach the **University of London** ②. On the left after you pass the university buildings is the back of the Royal Academy of Dramatic Art, or RADA (its entrance is on Gower Street), where at least half of the most stellar British thespians got their training, with **University College** ③ following at the top of Malet Place. For a delightful detour, head west over to Scala Street (just one block west from the Goodge Street tube stop, then one block north on Charlotte Street) to find the delightful Victorian-era wonders of **Pollock's Toy Museum** ④. The streets around here and Fitzroy Square, built by the Adam brothers, are known as Fitzrovia, so named by literary soaks who drank at the Fitzroy Tavern on Charlotte Street. Back around the university, head over to Gordon Street to reach Gordon Square. For the prettiest little street with picturesque 19th-century shop fronts, divert to Woburn Walk (Irish poet Yeats lived at No. 5). If you're interested in Asian art, stop in at the **Percival David Foundation of Chinese Art** ⑤; if you want to check out the spectacular **British Library** ⑥, head north up to Euston Road. Otherwise, continue south down busy Woburn Place, veering left down Guilford Street to reach Coram's Fields, home of the **Thomas**

Coram Foundation; then turn left south of there on Guilford Place, then right to Doughty Street and the **Dickens House Museum** ⑦. Two streets west, parallel to Doughty Street, is Lamb's Conduit Street (whose pretty pub, the Lamb, Dickens inevitably frequented).

At the bottom of Lamb's Conduit Street you reach Theobalds Road, where you enter the first of the Inns of Court, **Gray's Inn** ⑧. From here, emerge onto High Holborn (pronounced "Hoe-bun"); heavy with traffic, it is the main route from the City to the West End and Westminster and still the center of London's diamond and jewelry trade. Pass another ghost of former trading, **Staple Inn** ⑨, and turn left down tiny Great Turnstile Row to reach **Lincoln's Inn** ⑩, where you pass the Hall and continue around the west side of New Square to Carey Street, which leads you round into Portugal Street. Here you'll find the Old Curiosity Shop, probably one of the rare places in London Dickens did *not* frequent. Recross to the north side of Lincoln's Inn Fields to **Sir John Soane's Museum** ⑪ or walk the other way on Carey Street to reach the **Royal Courts of Justice** ⑫, which run through to the Strand. Off to the left is Fleet Street and the 1610 **Prince Henry's Room** ⑬. Cross the Strand to **Temple** ⑭, and pass through the elaborate stone arch to Middle Temple Lane, which you follow past **Temple Church** ⑮ to the Thames.

TIMING

This is a substantial walk of 3 to 4 mi, and it has two distinct halves. The first half, around Bloomsbury, is not so interesting on the surface, but it includes a major highlight of London, the British Museum, where you could easily add 1 mi to your total and certainly at least two hours. The Dickens House is also worth a stop. The second half, legal London, is a real walker's walk, with most of the highlights in the building architecture and surroundings. The exception is Sir John Soane's Museum, which will absorb an extra hour. The walk alone can be done comfortably in two hours and is best on a sunny day.

HOW TO GET THERE

The best tube stops for the Inns of Court are Holborn on the Central and Piccadilly lines (surface and walk east up High Holborn, then south), or Chancery Lane on the Central Line. For the British Museum, Tottenham Court Road (Northern and Central lines) and Russell Square (Piccadilly Line) are equidistant. Bus 7 is the best bus for the BM; for the Inns of Court, get Bus 8, 17, 25, 45, 46, or 243 to High Holborn or Bus 17, 19, 38, 45, 46, 55, or 243 to Theobalds Road.

Sights to See

Bloomsbury Square. This was laid out in 1660, making it the earliest of the Bloomsbury squares, although none of the original houses remain; what is most remarkable about it now is that you can always find a parking spot in the huge underground garage. You'll find it by exiting the tube at Tottenham Court Road—a straight, very ugly street where London buys its electrical appliances, hi-fi equipment, and computer accessories—and taking Great Russell Street east. Bloomsbury is dotted with squares—Gordon, Tavistock, Bedford, and Brunswick are some of the more picturesque ones. ✉ *Bloomsbury WC1. Tube: Tottenham Court Rd.*

❻ **British Library.** Since 1759, the British Library had always been housed in the British Museum on Gordon Square. But space ran out long ago. The collection of around 18 million volumes now has a home in state-of-the-art surroundings, and if you are a researcher, it's a wonderful place to work (special passes are required). The library's treasures are on view to the general public: Magna Carta, a Gutenberg Bible, Jane Austen's writings, Shakespeare's First Folio, and musical manuscripts

British Library 6
British Museum 1
Dickens House Museum 7
Gray's Inn 8
Lincoln's Inn 10
Percival David Foundation of Chinese Art 5
Pollock's Toy Museum 4
Prince Henry's Room 13
Royal Courts of Justice 12
Sir John Soane's Museum 11
Staple Inn 9
Temple 14
Temple Church 15
University College 3
University of London 2

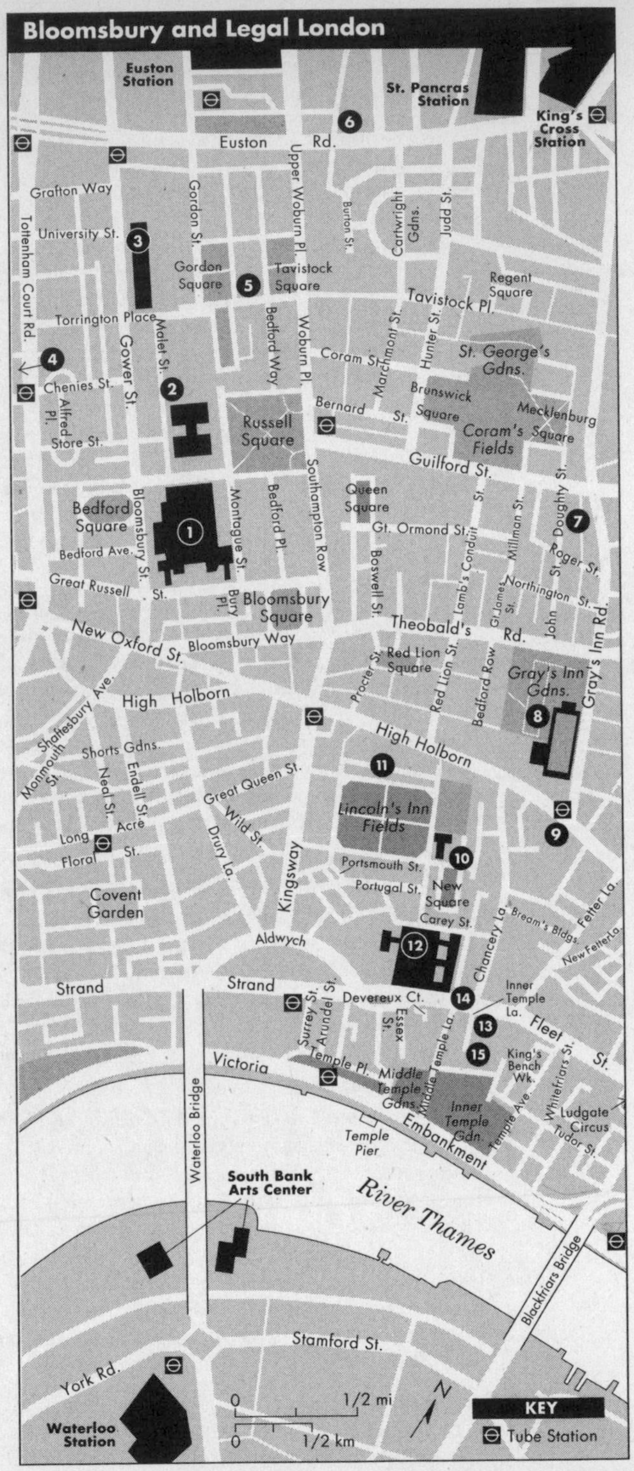

by Handel and Sir Paul McCartney are on show in the John Ritblat Gallery. Also in the gallery are headphones—you can listen to some of the most interesting snippets in a small showcase of the **National Sound Archive** stored here (it's the world's the largest collection, but is not on view), such as the voice of Florence Nightingale, and an extract from the Beatles' last tour interview. The Workshop of Words, Sound & Images explores the vitality of the living word, and on weekends and during school vacations there are hands-on demonstrations of how a book comes together. Feast your eyes also on the six-story glass tower that holds the 65,000-volume collection of George III, plus a permanent exhibition of rare stamps. And if all that wordiness is just too much, you can relax in the library's piazza or restaurant and take in one of the occasional free concerts in the amphitheater. ✉ *96 Euston Rd., Bloomsbury NW1,* ☎ *020/7412–7332,* WEB *www.bl.uk.* 💳 *Free.* ⏲ *Mon. and Wed.–Fri. 9:30–6, Tues. 9:30–8, Sat. 9:30–5; Sun. 11–5. Tube: Euston or King's Cross.*

★ ❶ **British Museum.** With a facade like a great temple, this celebrated treasure house—filled with plunder of incalculable value and beauty from around the globe—is housed in a ponderously dignified Greco-Victorian building that makes for a suitably grand impression. Inside you'll find some of the greatest relics of humankind: the Elgin Marbles, the Rosetta Stone, the Sutton Hoo Treasure—everything, it seems, but the Ark of the Covenant. Now 250 years old, the museum has undergone great changes to modernize and update many of the galleries. The focal point is the unmissable Great Court, a brilliant techno-classical design with a vast glass roof, which highlights and reveals the museum's best-kept secret—an inner courtyard, which, for more than 150 years had been used for storage. The revered Reading Room, after many years of closure, is a wonderful sight with its restored blue and gold dome, and ancient tomes lining the walls, contrasted with banks of computer screens. The museum space is vast, split into nearly 100 galleries—if you want to orienteer comprehensively, buy a Visit Guide for £2.50, directly as you go in, or keep asking one of the museum staff if you want to avoid having a search party sent out to rescue you.

The collection began in 1753, when Sir Hans Sloane, physician to Queen Anne and George II, bequeathed his personal collection of curiosities and antiquities to the nation. It then quickly grew, thanks to enthusiastic kleptomaniacs after the Napoleonic Wars—most notoriously the seventh Earl of Elgin, who acquired the marbles from the Parthenon and Erechtheum during his term as British Ambassador in Constantinople in the days when Greece was part of the Turkish Empire.

The enormous building, with its classical Greek-style facade featuring figures representing the Progress of Civilization, was finished in 1847, the work of Sir Robert Smirke. Wherever you go, there are marvels, but certain objects and collections are more important, rarer, older, or downright unique, and because you may wish to include these in your wanderings, here follows a highly edited overview (in order of encounter) of the BM's greatest hits:

Close to the entrance, in Room 4, is the **Rosetta Stone,** found in 1799 and carved in 196 BC with a decree of Ptolemy V in Egyptian hieroglyphics, demotic, and Greek. It was this multilingual inscription that provided the French Egyptologist Jean-François Champollion with the key to deciphering hieroglyphics.

Perhaps the **Elgin Marbles** ought not to be here, but since they are you can find them in Room 18 in the Parthenon Galleries. Carved around 440 BC, these beautiful, graceful decorations are displayed along with an in-depth, high-tech exhibit of the Acropolis, and bring to the fore the rumbling debate on whether the Greeks should reclaim their spectacular sculptural heritage (the handless, footless Dionysus who used to recline along its east pediment is especially well known). While you're in the west wing, you can see one of the Seven Wonders of the Ancient World—in fragment form, unfortunately—in Room 21: the **Mausoleum of Halikarnassos.** This 4th-century tomb of Mausolus, King of Caria, was the original "mausoleum."

Upstairs are some of the most popular galleries, especially beloved by children: Rooms 62–63, where the **Egyptian mummies** live. The Roxie Walker Galleries have a fascinating collection of relics from the Egyptian realm of the dead—in addition to real corpses, wrapped mummies, and mummy cases, there is a menagerie of animal companions and curious items which were buried alongside them.

Proceeding clockwise, you'll come to Room 49, where the **Mildenhall Treasure** glitters in the refurbished Weston Gallery of Roman Britain. This haul of 4th-century Roman silver tableware was found beneath the sod of a Suffolk field in 1942. Next door, in Room 41, is the equally splendid **Sutton Hoo Treasure,** including swords and helmets, bowls and buckles, all encrusted with jewels—which was buried at sea with (they think) Redwald, King of the Angles, in the 7th century and excavated from a Suffolk field in 1938–39.

In Room 50 lies Pete Marsh, so named by the archaeologists who unearthed the **Lindow Man** from a Cheshire peat marsh. He was ritually slain, probably as a human sacrifice, in the 1st century and lay perfectly pickled in his bog until 1984. In the upper level of the museum is the Money Gallery, which holds ancient coins and medals. Back on the ground floor, in Room 26, the **Chase Manhattan Gallery of North America** has one of the largest collections of native culture outside the North American continent, going back to the earliest hunters 10,000 years ago. Other recent, notable additions to the museum are: the Korea Foundation Gallery (Room 67), which delves into the art and archaeology of the country, including precious porcelain (much admired by today's artist potters), and colorful, intricately worked screens; and the Sainsbury African Galleries, which present a staggering 200,000 objects, including intricate pieces of old ivory, gold, and wooden masks and carvings—highlighting such ancient kingdoms as the Benin and Asante. Make sure to join at least one of the free "Eyeopener" 50-minute tours by museum guides (details at the information desk)—they do just what they say. ✉ *Great Russell St., Bloomsbury WC1,* ☎ *020/7636–1555,* WEB *www.thebritishmuseum.ac.uk.* 🎫 *Free (suggested donation of £2).* ⏲ *Museum Sat.–Wed. 10–5:30, Thurs.–Fri. 10–8:30. Great Court Mon. 9–6, Tues.–Wed 9–9, Thurs.–Sat. 9–11, Sun. 9–9. Tube: Tottenham Court Rd., Holborn, or Russell Sq.*

NEED A BREAK?

The British Museum's self-service **restaurant and café** get very crowded, but serve a reasonably tasty menu beneath a plaster cast of a part of the Parthenon frieze that Lord Elgin didn't remove. The restaurant is open Monday–Saturday noon–4:30, Sunday noon–5:30; the café, Monday–Saturday 10–3. There is also a café in the concourse of the Great Court, which keeps the museum's extended opening hours.

7 **Dickens House Museum.** This is the only one of the many London houses Charles Dickens (1812–70) inhabited that's still standing, and it would have had a real claim to his fame in any case because he wrote *Oliver Twist* and *Nicholas Nickleby* and finished *Pickwick Papers* here between 1837 and 1839. The house looks exactly as it would have in

Dickens's day, complete with first editions, letters, and a tall clerk's desk (where the master wrote standing up, often while chatting with visiting friends and relatives). There's a treat for Lionel Bart fans—his score of *Oliver!* Down in the basement is a replica of the Dingley Dell kitchen from *Pickwick Papers.* ✉ *48 Doughty St., Bloomsbury WC1,* ☎ *020/7405–2127,* WEB *www.dickensmuseum.com.* 🎟 *£4.* ⏲ *Mon.–Sat. 10–5. Tube: Chancery La. or Russell Sq.*

8 **Gray's Inn.** Although the least architecturally interesting of the four Inns of Court and the one most damaged by German bombs in the 1940s, this still has its romantic associations. In 1594, Shakespeare's *Comedy of Errors* was performed for the first time in its hall—which was lovingly restored after World War II and has a fine Elizabethan screen of carved oak. You must make advance arrangements to view the Tudor-style Gray's Inn's Hall (apply in writing, in advance, to the administrator, the Under Treasurer), but you can stroll around the secluded and spacious gardens, first planted by Francis Bacon in 1606. ✉ *Gray's Inn Rd., Holborn, Bloomsbury,* ☎ *020/7458–7800.* ⏲ *Weekdays 10–4. Tube: Holborn or Temple.*

★ 10 **Lincoln's Inn.** There's plenty to see at one of the oldest, best-preserved, and most comely of the Inns of Court—from the Chancery Lane Tudor brick gatehouse to the wide-open, tree-lined, atmospheric Lincoln's Inn Fields and the 15th-century chapel remodeled by Inigo Jones in 1620. The wisteria-clad New Square, London's only complete 17th-century square, is not the newest part of the complex; in fact, the oldest-looking buildings are the 1845 Hall and Library, which you must obtain the porter's permission to enter. ✉ *Chancery La., Bloomsbury WC2,* ☎ *020/7405–1393.* ⏲ *Gardens weekdays 7–7, chapel weekdays noon–2:30; public may also attend Sun. service in chapel at 11:30 during legal terms. Tube: Chancery La.*

5 **Percival David Foundation of Chinese Art.** This collection, belonging to the University of London, is dominated by ceramics from the Sung to Qing dynasties—from the 10th to the 19th century, in other words. It's on **Gordon Square,** which Virginia Woolf, the Bells, John Maynard Keynes (all at No. 46), and Lytton Strachey (at No. 51) called home for a while. ✉ *53 Gordon Sq., Bloomsbury WC1,* ☎ *020/7387–3909.* 🎟 *Free.* ⏲ *Weekdays 10:30–5. Tube: Russell Sq.*

4 **Pollock's Toy Museum.** For some, this will merit a visit whether they have children or not. A charmingly small museum in a warren of rooms in an 18th-century town house, Pollock's is crammed with antique dolls, dollhouses, and teddy bears. Best of all are the fabulous little toy theaters that Pollock made famous during the Victorian era—more than a few of England's most famous actors grew up playing with these cardboard delights. Even better: you can still buy reproductions of these cut-and-paste theater kits in the toy store on the premises. (Bring lots of money if you want to purchase some of the antique kits still for sale.) ✉ *1 Scala St., Bloomsbury W1,* ☎ *020/7636–3452.* WEB *www.pollocksweb.co.uk.* 🎟 *£3.* ⏲ *Mon.–Sat. 10–5. Tube: Goodge St.*

13 **Prince Henry's Room.** This is the Jacobean half-timber house built in 1610 to celebrate the investiture of Henry, James I's eldest son, as Prince of Wales; it's marked with his coat of arms and a PH on the ceiling. It's an entrance to the lawyers' sanctum, Temple, where the Strand becomes Fleet Street, and you can go in to visit the small Samuel Pepys exhibition. ✉ *17 Fleet St., Bloomsbury EC4,* ☎ *020/7936–2710.* 🎟 *Free.* ⏲ *Mon.–Sat. 11–2. Tube: Temple.*

12 **Royal Courts of Justice.** Here is the vast Victorian Gothic pile containing the nation's principal law courts, with 1,000-odd rooms running

off 3½ mi of corridor. And here are heard the most important civil law cases—that's everything from divorce to fraud, with libel in between—and you can sit in the viewing gallery to watch any trial you like, for a live version of *Court TV.* The more dramatic criminal cases are heard at the Old Bailey. Other sights are the 238-ft-long main hall and the compact exhibition of judges' robes. Check out the gift shop also, where useful items (such as umbrellas) are emblazoned with the royal courts' crest. ✉ *The Strand, Bloomsbury WC2,* ☎ *020/7947–6000,* WEB *www.open.gov.uk.* 🎫 *Free.* ⏲ *Weekdays 9:30–4:30 (during Aug. there are no sittings and public areas close at 2:30). Tube: Temple.*

★ ⓫ **Sir John Soane's Museum.** Guaranteed to raise a smile from the most blasé and footsore tourist, this museum hardly deserves the burden of its dry name. Sir John (1753–1837), architect of the Bank of England, bequeathed his house to the nation on condition that nothing be changed. He obviously had enormous fun with his home, having had the means to finance great experiments in perspective and scale and to fill the space with some wonderful pieces. There are also different exhibitions on subjects as broad and as varied as Sir John's interests: from early architecture to more modern art. In the Picture Room, for instance, two of Hogarth's *Rake's Progress* series are among the paintings on panels that swing away to reveal secret gallery pockets with more paintings. Everywhere mirrors and colors play tricks with light and space, and split-level floors worthy of a fairground fun house disorient you. In a basement chamber sits the vast 1300 BC sarcophagus of Seti I, lighted by a domed skylight two stories above. When Sir John acquired this priceless object for £2,000, he celebrated with a three-day party. ✉ *13 Lincoln's Inn Fields, Bloomsbury WC2,* ☎ *020/7405–2107,* WEB *www.soane.org.* 🎫 *Free.* ⏲ *Tues.–Sat. 10–5; also 6–9 on the first Tues. of every month. Tube: Holborn.*

❾ **Staple Inn.** Despite its name, this is not an inn of court but the former wool staple, where wool was weighed and traded and its merchants were lodged. It is central London's oldest surviving Elizabethan half-timber building and, thanks to extensive restoration, with its overhanging upper stories, oriel windows, and black gables striping the white walls, looks the same as it must have in 1586 when it was brand new. ✉ *Holborn, Bloomsbury WC1.* ⏲ *Courtyard weekdays 9–5. Tube: Chancery La.*

⓮ **Temple.** The entrance to Temple—the collective name for **Inner Temple** and **Middle Temple,** and the exact point of entry into the City—is marked by a young bronze griffin, the **Temple Bar Memorial** (1880). He is the symbol of the City, having replaced (sadly) a Wren gateway (though you can't deny he makes a splendidly heraldic snapshot). In the buildings opposite is an elaborate stone arch through which you pass into Middle Temple Lane, past a row of 17th-century timber-frame houses, and on into Fountain Court. This lane runs all the way to the Thames, more or less separating the two Temples, past the sloping lawns of Middle Temple Gardens, on the east border of which is the Elizabethan **Middle Temple Hall.** If it's open, don't miss that hammerbeam roof, among the finest in the land. ✉ *Middle Temple La., Bloomsbury,* ☎ *020/7427–4800.* ⏲ *Weekdays 10–11:30 and (when not in use) 3–4. Tube: Temple.*

⓯ **Temple Church.** Featuring "the Round"—a rare circular nave—this church was built by the Knights Templar in the 12th century. The Red Knights (so called after the red crosses they wore—you can see them in effigy around the nave) held their secret initiation rites in the crypt here. Having started poor, holy, and dedicated to the protection of pilgrims, they grew rich from showers of royal gifts, until in the 14th century they were charged with heresy, blasphemy, and sodomy, thrown into the Tower,

Close-Up

BLUE PLAQUE ATTACK!

AS YOU WANDER AROUND LONDON, you'll see lots of small, blue, oval-shape plaques on the sides and facades of buildings, describing which famous, semifamous, or obscure but brilliant person once lived there. The first was placed outside Lord Byron's birthplace (now no more) by the Royal Society of Arts. There are around 700 blue plaques, erected by different bodies—you may even find some green ones which originated from Westminster City Council—but English Heritage now maintains the responsibility. Below are some of the highlights:

James Barrie (100 Bayswater Rd., Hyde Park, W2); Hector Berlioz (58 Queen Anne St., Marylebone, W1); Elizabeth Barrett Browning (50 Wimpole St., Marylebone, W1); Robert Browning (17 Warwick Crescent, Hyde Park, W2); Frederic Chopin (4 St. James's Place, St. James's, W1); Captain James Cook (88 Mile End Rd., Mile End, E1); Sir Winston Churchill (28 Hyde Park Gate, Kensington, SW7); T. S. Eliot (3 Kensington Court Gardens, Kensington); Mahatma Gandhi (20 Baron's Court Rd., West Kensington, W14); George Frederic Handel (25 Brook St., Mayfair, W1); Karl Marx (28 Dean St., Soho, W1); Wolfgang Amadeus Mozart (180 Ebury St., Belgravia, SW1); Sir Isaac Newton (87 Jermyn St., St. James's, SW1); Florence Nightingale (10 South St., Mayfair, W1); George Bernard Shaw (29 Fitzroy Sq., Bloomsbury, W1); Percy Bysshe Shelley (15 Poland St., Soho, W1); Mark Twain (23 Tedworth Sq., Chelsea, SW3); Oscar Wilde (34 Tite St., Chelsea, SW3); William Butler Yeats (23 Fitzroy Rd., Camden, NW1).

and stripped of their wealth. You might suppose the church to be thickly atmospheric, but Victorian and postwar restorers have tamed its air of antique mystery. Still, it's a very fine Gothic-Romanesque church, whose 1240 chancel ("the Oblong") has been accused of perfection. ✉ *The Temple, Bloomsbury EC4,* ☎ *020/7353–1736.* ⏲ *Wed.–Sat. 11–4, Sun. 1–4, and closures for special services. Tube: Temple.*

Thomas Coram Foundation. Capt. Thomas Coram devoted half his life to setting up a sanctuary and hospital, which he called the Foundling Hospital, for London's street orphans. He was a remarkable man, a master mariner and shipbuilder who, having played a major role in the colonization of Massachusetts, returned to London in 1732 to encounter sights he could not endure—babies and children "left to die on dung hills." Petitioning the lunching ladies of his day and their lords, he raised the necessary funds to set up what became the most celebrated good cause around, thanks partly to the sparkling benefactors he attracted. Currently this site is closed; the Foundling Museum is refurbishing the rooms and collection, which should reopen for tours in April 2004. ✉ *40 Brunswick Sq., Bloomsbury WC2,* ☎ *020/7841–3600. Currently closed to visitors; call to determine if museum has reopened. Tube: Russell Sq.*

3 **University College.** Set in a satisfyingly classical edifice designed by the architect of the National Gallery, William Wilkins, the college has within its portals the **Slade School of Fine Art,** which did for many of Britain's artists what the nearby Royal Academy of Dramatic Art (on Gower Street)

did for its actors. On view inside is a fine collection of sculpture by an alumnus, John Flaxman. You can also see more Egyptian artifacts, if you didn't get enough at the neighboring British Museum, in the **Petrie Museum** (☎ 020/7679–2884), accessed from Malet Place, on the first floor of the DMS Watson building. It houses an outstanding, huge collection of fascinating objects of Egyptian archaeology—jewelry, toys, papyri, and some of the world's oldest garments. It has proved so popular with schoolchildren that it is now open Saturday 10–1 in addition to Tuesday–Friday 1–5. The South Cloisters contain one of London's weirder treasures: the clothed skeleton of one of the university's founders, Jeremy Bentham, who bequeathed himself to the college. ✉ *Bloomsbury WC1. Tube: Euston Sq. or Goodge St.*

❷ **University of London.** This relatively youthful institution grew out of the need for a nondenominational center for higher education (Oxford and Cambridge both demanded religious conformity to the Church of England). It was founded by Dissenters in 1826, with its first examinations held 12 years later. Jews and Roman Catholics were not the only people admitted for the first time to an English university—women were, too, though they had to wait 50 years (until 1878) to sit for a degree. ✉ *Russell Sq., Bloomsbury WC1. Tube: Russell Sq.*

Wig and Pen Club. The club—another of those St. James's–style affairs, this time for "men of justice, journalists, and businessmen of the City" (plus former U.S. presidents Nixon and Reagan)—has its home in the only Strand building to have survived the Great Fire of 1666. ✉ *229–230 The Strand, Bloomsbury WC2. Tube: Aldwych or Temple.*

THE CITY

You may have assumed you had entered the City of London when your plane touched down at Heathrow, but note that capital letter: the City of London is not the same as the city of London. The "capital-C" City is an autonomous district, separately governed since William the Conqueror's time, and despite its compact size (it's known as the Square Mile), it remains the financial engine of Britain and one of the world's leading centers of trade. The City, however, is more than just London's Wall Street: it is also the neighborhood where you'll find two of London's most notable sights, the Tower of London and St. Paul's, one of the world's greatest cathedrals—truly a case of the money changers' encompassing the temple! Temple Bar marks the western edge of the district, which does cover 677 acres, though not in a remotely straight-sided fashion. The curvy shape described by its boundaries—Smithfield in the north, Aldgate and Tower Hill in the east, and the Thames in the south—resembles nothing so much as an armadillo, with Temple Bar at snout level.

The City is London's most ancient part, although there is little remaining to remind you of that beyond a scattering of Roman stones. It was Aulus Plautius, Roman ruler of Britain under Claudius, who established the Romans' first stronghold on the Thames halfway through the 1st century AD. The name "Londinium," though, probably derives from the Celtic *Lyn-dun,* meaning "fortified town on the lake," which suggests far earlier settlement. It was really only after Edward the Confessor moved his court to Westminster in 1060 that the City gathered momentum. As Westminster took over the administrative role, the City was free to develop the commercial heart that still beats strong.

The Romans had already found Londinium's position handy for trade—the river being navigable yet far enough inland to allow for its defense—but it was the establishment of crafts guilds in the Middle Ages, followed in Tudor and Stuart times by the proliferation of great trading companies (the Honourable East India Company, founded in 1600, was the star), that really started the cash flowing.

Three times the City has faced devastation—and that's not counting "Black Monday," when the pound sterling crashed. The Great Fire of 1666 spared practically none of the labyrinthine medieval streets—a blessing in disguise, actually, because the Great Plague of the year before had wiped (or driven) out most of the population and left a terrible mess in the cramped, downright sordid houses. With the wind in the west, they said, you could smell London from Tilbury. The fire necessitated a total reconstruction, in which Sir Christopher Wren had a big hand, contributing not only his masterpiece, St. Paul's Cathedral, but 49 parish churches as well.

A third wave of destruction, after the plague and the fire, was dealt by German bombers during the Second World War. In 57 nights devoted to the City, they wrought as much havoc as the Great Fire had managed. The ruins were rebuilt, but slowly and with no overall plan, creating an awkward patchwork of old and new, interesting and flagrantly awful. The City's colorful past can be hard to visualize in the midst of today's gray reality, but there are clues. Wander through its maze of streets and you will come across ancient coats of arms and street names redolent of life in the Middle Ages: Ropemaker Street, Pudding Lane, Jewry Street, and Fish Street. During the week, the place is overrun with people—but since a mere 8,000 or so people call it home today, the City is deserted on weekends, with most restaurants shuttered and streets forlorn and windswept. It's this swing from hectic activity to near total silence that accounts for much of the City's unique sensibility. Where else does the Lord Mayor, clad in ceremonial robes and chain of office, ride in an 18th-century coach—on the Lord Mayor's Show day in celebration of the annually elected office—past buildings in which satellite communications have long since become routine?

Numbers in the text correspond to numbers in the margin and on the City map.

A Good Walk

Begin (literally) at the gateway to the City. Until the 18th century there were eight such gates, of which only one survives; the others exist in name only (Cripplegate, Ludgate, Bishopsgate, Moorgate, and so on). The surviving one is Temple Bar, a bronze griffin on the Strand opposite the Royal Courts of Justice, at which the sovereign has to ask permission to enter the City from the Lord Mayor. Walk east to **Fleet Street** and turn left on Bolt Court to Gough Square and **Dr. Johnson's House** ①, passing **Ye Olde Cheshire Cheese** ② on Wine Office Court en route back to Fleet Street and the journalists' church, **St. Bride's** ③. The end of Fleet Street is marked by the messy traffic intersection called Ludgate Circus, which you should cross to Ludgate Hill to reach **Old Bailey** ④ and the Central Criminal Courts.

Continuing along Ludgate Hill, you come to **St. Paul's Cathedral** ⑤, Wren's masterpiece. A unique, pedestrian-only bridge by Norman Foster, the **Millennium Bridge** ⑥, is in clear view from St. Paul's Churchyard. Then retrace your steps to Newgate Street, to the road called Little Britain, where you'll see the archway to **St. Bartholomew the Great Church** ⑦ on the left and come to London's meat market, Smithfield, at the end. Cross Aldersgate Street and take the right fork to London Wall, named for the Roman rampart that stood along it. It's a dismal street, now dominated by postmodern architect Terry Farrell's late-'80s follies, but about halfway along you can see a section of 2nd- to 4th-century wall at St. Alphege Garden. There's another bit in an appropriate spot back at the start of London Wall, outside the **Museum of London** ⑧; and behind that are the **Barbican Centre** ⑨, an important arts center of gray concrete, and **St. Giles Without Cripplegate** ⑩. You can walk all around here without touching the ground (well, ground level).

Back on London Wall, turn south into Coleman Street, then right onto Masons Avenue to reach Basinghall Street and the **Guildhall** ⑪; then follow Milk Street south to Cheapside ("cheap" derives from the Old English via Middle English *chep*, for trade); it was on this street that the bakers of Bread Street, the cobblers of Cordwainer Street, the goldsmiths of Goldsmiths Row, and all their brothers gathered to sell their wares. Here is another symbolic center of London, the church of **St. Mary-le-Bow** ⑫. Walk to the east end of Cheapside, where seven roads meet, and you will be facing the **Bank of England** ⑬. Turn your back on the bank, and there's the Lord Mayor's Palladian-style residence, Mansion House. Wren's **St. Stephen Walbrook Church** ⑭ rises behind it and the **Royal Exchange** ⑮ stands between Threadneedle Street and Cornhill. Farther down Cornhill to Lime Street is **Lloyd's of London** ⑯.

Now head down Queen Victoria Street, where you'll pass the remains of the Roman **Temple of Mithras** ⑰; then, after a sharp left turn onto Cannon Street, you'll come upon the **Monument** ⑱, Wren's memorial to the Great Fire of London. Just south of there is **London Bridge** ⑲. Turn left onto Lower Thames Street, for just under a mile's walk—passing Billingsgate, London's principal fish market for 900 years (until 1982), and the Custom House, built early in the last century—to the **Tower of London** ⑳, which may be the single most unmissable of London's sights. **Tower Bridge** ㉑, just outside it, isn't bad either.

TIMING

This is a marathon. Unless you want to be walking all day without a chance to do justice to London's most famous sights, the Tower of London and St. Paul's Cathedral—not to mention the Museum of London, Tower Bridge, and the Barbican Centre—you should consider splitting the walk into segments. Conversely, if you're not planning to go inside, this walk makes for a great day out, with lots of surprising vistas, river views, and history. The City is a wasteland on weekends and after dark, so choose your time. There's a certain romantic charm to the streets when they're deserted, but it's hard to find lunch.

HOW TO GET THERE

This is a big and confusing area, with, however, several tube stops that will deposit you within walking distance of most sights. They are the following: on the Central Line, the Bank and St. Paul's stops; on the District and Circle lines, the Monument, Cannon Street, and Mansion House stops (plus Blackfriars, which is a little off-center). The Moorgate and Barbican stops (Circle, Metropolitan, Hammersmith, and City lines) are the nearest to the theaters of the Barbican Centre, while the next stop west, Farringdon, is best for exploring Clerkenwell. Finally, the only sensible way to get to the Tower of London is via the District and Circle lines to the Tower Hill stop. As for buses, Nos. 4, 11, 15, 17, 23, 26, 76, and 172 deposit you centrally, by St. Paul's. For the Barbican Centre, Buses 4, 56, 172, 141, 172, and 271 to Moorgate are best.

Sights to See

⓭ **Bank of England.** Known familiarly for the past couple of centuries as "the Old Lady of Threadneedle Street," after someone's parliamentary quip, the bank, which has been central to the British economy since 1694, manages the national debt and the foreign exchange reserves, issues banknotes, sets interest rates, looks after England's gold, and

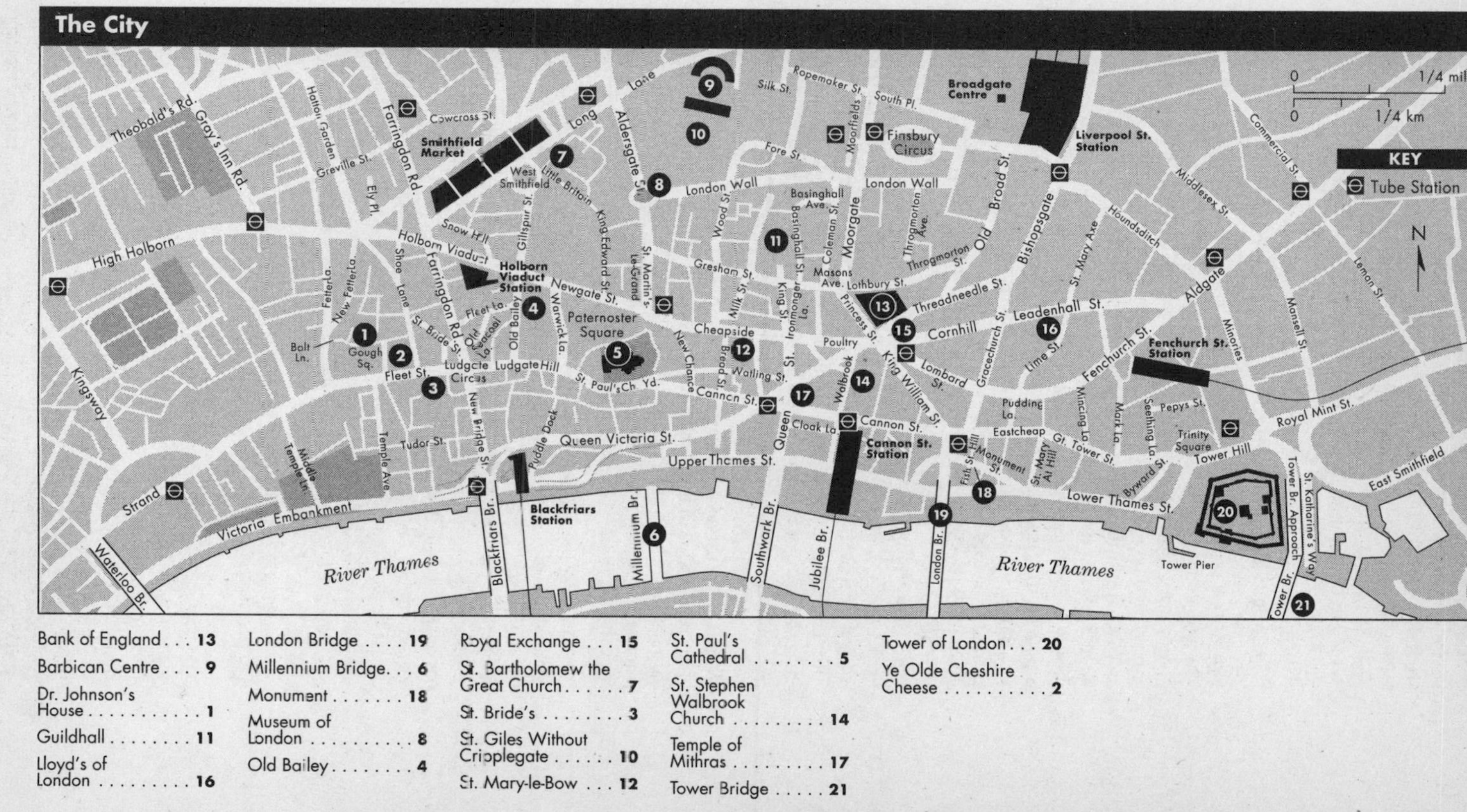
The City
0 1/4 mile
0 1/4 km
KEY
Tube Station
N
Theobald's Rd.
Gray's Inn Rd.
High Holborn
Kingsway
Strand
Waterloo Br.
Victoria Embankment
River Thames
Hatton Garden
Greville St.
Ely Pl.
Farringdon Rd.
Cowcross St.
Smithfield Market
West Smithfield
Long Lane
Little Britain
Aldersgate St.
Snow Hill
Holborn Viaduct
Holborn Viaduct Station
Giltspur St.
King Edward St.
St. Martin's-le-Grand
Fetter La.
New Fetter La.
Shoe Lane
St. Bride St.
Fleet La.
Old Seacoal La.
Old Bailey
Warwick La.
Newgate St.
Paternoster Square
Bolt Ln.
Gough Sq.
Fleet St.
Ludgate Circus
Ludgate Hill
St. Paul's Ch. Yd.
New Bridge St.
Tudor St.
Temple Ave.
Middle Temple Ln.
Puddle Dock
Queen Victoria St.
Blackfriars Br.
Blackfriars Station
Millennium Br.
Upper Thames St.
New Change
Cheapside
Bread St.
Watling St.
Cannon St.
Gresham St.
Milk St.
Wood St.
London Wall
Silk St.
Ropemaker St.
South Pl.
Moorfields
Finsbury Circus
Fore St.
Basinghall Ave.
Basinghall St.
Coleman St.
Moorgate
King St.
Ironmonger La.
Queen St.
Masons Ave.
Lothbury St.
Princess St.
Poultry
Walbrook
Cloak La.
Cannon St. Station
Southwark Br.
Jubilee Br.
Throgmorton Ave.
Throgmorton St.
Old Broad St.
Broadgate Centre
Liverpool St. Station
Bishopsgate
Threadneedle St.
Cornhill
Lombard St.
King William St.
Gracechurch St.
Leadenhall St.
St. Mary Axe
Lime St.
Fenchurch St.
Pudding La.
Eastcheap
Fish St. Hill
Monument St.
St. Mary At Hill
Gt. Tower St.
London Br.
Lower Thames St.
Mincing La.
Mark La.
Seething La.
Pepys St.
Byward St.
Trinity Square
Tower Hill
Tower Pier
Fenchurch St. Station
Houndsditch
Middlesex St.
Commercial St.
Aldgate
Minories
Mansell St.
Leman St.
Royal Mint St.
East Smithfield
Tower Br. Approach
St. Katharine's Way
Tower Br.
Bank of England . . . 13
Barbican Centre 9
Dr. Johnson's House 1
Guildhall 11
Lloyd's of London 16
London Bridge 19
Millennium Bridge. . . 6
Monument 18
Museum of London 8
Old Bailey 4
Royal Exchange . . . 15
St. Bartholomew the Great Church 7
St. Bride's 3
St. Giles Without Cripplegate 10
St. Mary-le-Bow . . . 12
St. Paul's Cathedral 5
St. Stephen Walbrook Church 14
Temple of Mithras 17
Tower Bridge 21
Tower of London . . . 20
Ye Olde Cheshire Cheese 2

regulates the country's banking system. Sir John Soane designed the Neoclassic hulk in 1788, wrapping it in windowless walls, which are all that survives of his building. It is ironic that an executive of so sober an institution should have been Kenneth Grahame, author of *The Wind in the Willows*. This and other facets of the bank's history are traced in the Bank of England Museum. ✉ *Bartholomew La., The City EC4,* ☎ *020/7601–5545,* WEB *www.bankofengland.co.uk.* 🎫 *Free.* ⏲ *Weekdays and Lord Mayor's Show day (second Sat. in Nov.) 10–5. Tube: Bank or Monument.*

9 **Barbican Centre.** With two theaters; the London Symphony Orchestra and its auditorium; the Guildhall School of Music and Drama; a major art gallery for touring and its own special exhibitions; two cinemas; a convention center; an upscale restaurant, cafés, and literary bookshops; and apartments for a hapless two-thirds of the City's residents (most part-time), the Barbican is an enormous concrete maze Londoners love to hate. In 2001 the Royal Shakespeare Company announced that it would stage plays in the West End rather than only in the Barbican. The name comes from a defensive fortification of the City, and defensive is what Barbican apologists (including architects Chamberlain, Powell, and Bon) became when the complex was finally revealed in 1982. There ensued an epidemic of jokes about getting lost forever in the Barbican bowels and even though you can follow yellow lines, Oz-like, on the floors, it is still difficult to navigate. Londoners accept the place, because of its imaginative contents. Actors rate the theater acoustics especially high, and the steep rake of the seating makes for a good stage view. The dance and music programs are adventurous without straying too far from core favorites. Try to sample some of the Barbican's annual dance, drama, and music fest between May and October, which attracts top-billing international performers. The exhibitions in the **Barbican Art Gallery** are extremely popular and often showcase modern, populist topics ranging from the Shaker movement to *Star Wars* the movie. Also worth a look are the free displays in the Concourse Gallery.

Negotiating the winding walkways of the residential section, spotting stray sculptures and water gardens, then descending to the lower depths of the Centre (where you find the studio auditorium, aptly named the Pit), all has its charm. Secreted on an upper floor is an enormous, lush conservatory in a towering glass palace, spacious enough for full-grown trees to flourish. Although not often open to the public, you may be able to get into a tour. These are conducted for a minimum of 10 people and must be booked in advance. ✉ *Silk St., The City EC2,* ☎ *020/7638–8891; 020/7628–3351 RSC backstage tour,* WEB *www.barbican.org.uk.* 🎫 *Barbican Centre free; art gallery £3–£5.* ⏲ *Barbican Centre Mon.–Sat. 9 AM–11 PM, Sun. noon–11 PM; gallery Mon.–Sat. 10–7:30, Sun. noon–7:30; conservatory weekends noon–5:30 when not in use for private function (call first). Tube: Moorgate or Barbican.*

NEED A BREAK? The Barbican Centre's **Waterside Café** has salads, sandwiches, and pastries; they're unremarkable but are served in a tranquil, enclosed concrete (naturally) waterside terrace. Sometimes customers are serenaded by practice sessions of the Guildhall School of Music and Drama's orchestra next door.

1 **Dr. Johnson's House.** This is where Samuel Johnson lived between 1746 and 1759, while in the worst of health, compiling his famous dictionary in the attic. Like Dickens, he lived all over town, and as Dickens House is the only one of his houses still extant, this is the only one of Johnson's residences remaining today. It is an appropriately 17th-

century house, exactly the kind of place you would expect the Great Bear, as Johnson was nicknamed, to live. It is a shrine to the man possibly more attached to London than anyone else ever, and it includes a first edition of his dictionary among the Johnson and Boswell mementos. When you're done, repair around the corner in Wine Office Court to the famed Ye Olde Cheshire Cheese pub, once Johnson and Boswell's favorite watering hole. ✉ *17 Gough Sq., The City EC4,* ☎ *020/7353–3745.* WEB *www.drjh.dircon.co.uk.* 🎫 *£4.* ⏲ *May–Sept., Mon.–Sat. 11–5:30; Oct.–Apr., Mon.–Sat. 11–5. Tube: Blackfriars or Chancery La.*

Fleet Street. This famous street follows the course of, and is named after, one of London's ghost rivers. The Fleet, so called by the Anglo-Saxons, spent most of its centuries above ground as an open sewer, offending local nostrils until banished below in 1766. It still flows underfoot, now a sanctioned section of London's sewer system. The street's sometime nickname, "Street of Shame," has nothing to do with the stench. It refers to the trade that made it famous: the press. Since the end of the 15th century, when Wynkyn de Worde set up England's first printing press here, and especially after 1702, when the first newspaper, the *Daily Courant,* moved in, followed by (literally) all the rest, "Fleet Street" has been synonymous with newspaper journalism. The papers themselves all moved out during the 1980s, but the British press is still collectively known as "Fleet Street." To find a relic from the old days, check out the black-glass-and-chrome Art Deco *Daily Mirror* building. ✉ *The City EC4. Tube: Blackfriars or St. Paul's.*

11 **Guildhall.** In the symbolic nerve center of the City, the Corporation of London ceremonially elects and installs its Lord Mayor as it has for 800 years. The Guildhall was built in 1411, and though it failed to avoid either the 1666 or 1940 flames, its core survived. Since then, the exterior has had embellishments added during the '70s. The fabulous hall is a psychedelic patchwork of coats of arms and banners of the City Livery Companies, which inherited the mantle of the medieval trade guilds, to which history owes the invention of the City in the first place. Actually, this honor belongs to two giants, Gog and Magog, the pair of mythical beings who founded ancient Albion and the city of New Troy, upon which London was said to be built, and who glower upon the incoming lord mayor's inaugural November banquet from their west-gallery grandstand in 9-ft-high painted lime-wood form.

To the right of Guildhall Yard is the **Guildhall Art Gallery,** the corporation's collection. It includes portraits from the 16th century (royals and statesmen) and the present, and a fair sprinkling of weighty battlescapes from the 18th century for good measure. London landscapes give a picture of the old City in days gone by, and there are a couple of surprises in the form of pre-Raphaelite beauties. The 1970s west wing houses the **Guildhall Library**; it has mainly City-related books and documents, plus a collection belonging to one of the Livery Companies, the Worshipful Company of Clockmakers, with more than 600 timepieces on show, including a skull-faced watch that belonged to Mary, Queen of Scots. It's one of the most important horological collections in the country. ✉ *Gresham St., The City EC2,* ☎ *020/7606–3030; 020/7332–1632 gallery; 020/7332–3700 recorded information,* WEB *www.cityoflondon.gov.uk.* 🎫 *Free; gallery £2.50.* ⏲ *Mon.–Sat. 9:30–5; Clockmakers Collection weekdays 9:30–4:45; gallery Mon.–Sat. 10–5, Sun. noon–4. Print room and bookshop closed Sat. Tube: St. Paul's, Moorgate, Bank, or Mansion House.*

16 **Lloyd's of London.** Richard Rogers's (of Paris Pompidou Centre fame) fantastical steel-and-glass medium-rise of six towers around a vast atrium,

with his trademark inside-out ventilation shafts, stairwells, and gantries, may be the most exciting modern structure erected in London. The building is best seen at night, when cobalt and lime spotlights make it leap out of the deeply boring gray skyline as though it were Carmen Miranda at a wake. The institution that commissioned this fabulous £163 million fun house has been trading in insurance for two centuries and is famous the world over for several reasons: (1) having started in a coffeehouse; (2) insuring Betty Grable's legs; (3) accepting no corporate responsibility for losses, which are carried by its investors; (4) having its "Names"—the rich people who underwrite Lloyd's losses; (5) seeming unassailable for a very long time . . . ; (6) losing £2.9 billion in 1990; (7) causing, with its losses, the financial ruination, and worse, of many Names. ✉ *1 Lime St., The City EC3. Tube: Bank, Monument, Liverpool St., or Aldgate.*

19 **London Bridge.** Dating from only 1972, this bridge replaced the 1831 Sir John Rennie number that now graces Lake Havasu City, Arizona, the impulse purchase of someone at the McCulloch Oil Corporation, who (rumor has it) was under the impression that he'd bought the far more picturesque Tower Bridge. The version before that one, the first in stone and the most renowned of all, stood for 600 years after it was built in 1176, the focus of many a gathering thanks to the shops and houses crammed along its length, not to mention the boiled and tar-dipped heads of traitors that decorated its gatehouse after being removed in the Tower of London. Before *that* the Saxons had put up a wooden bridge; it collapsed in 1014, which was probably the origin of the refrain "London Bridge is falling down." Nobody is sure of the exact location of the very earliest London Bridge—the Roman version around whose focus London grew—but it was certainly very close to the 100-ft-wide, three-span, prestressed concrete cantilever one that you see today. ✉ *The City EC3, SE1. Tube: London Bridge or Monument.*

6 **Millennium Bridge.** This is not just another bridge, but the first pedestrian-only bridge to open in central London in more than century, the last being Tower Bridge in 1894. Designed by Norman Foster and sculptor Anthony Caro, thousands lined up to enjoy the so-called "blaze of light" built of aluminum and steel on its opening day. This unique bridge has only one moving part—it pivots upward when it opens for ships passing below. A stabilization problem led to the closing of the bridge, but reparation work opened the bridge in time for the queen's Golden Jubilee celebrations. The bridge connects the old City—St. Paul's Cathedral area—with the Tate Modern art gallery. On the south bank side, the bridge marks the middle of the Millennium Mile, a newly devised walkway taking in a clutch of popular sights. The views are breathtaking: from the bridge, you can look downriver to the Tower of London, Tower Bridge, and beyond, and up to Somerset House, with the London Eye and Big Ben rising above the river's bend. You'll also have perhaps the best-ever view of St. Paul's Cathedral. ✉ *Peters Hill, The City EC4, SE1. Tube: Mansion House, Blackfriars, or Southwark.*

18 **Monument.** Commemorating the "dreadful visitation" of the Great Fire of 1666, this is the world's tallest isolated stone column. It is the work of Wren, who was asked to erect it "On or as neere unto the place where the said Fire soe unhappily began as conveniently may be." And so here it is—at 202 ft, exactly as tall as the distance it stands from Farriner's baking house in Pudding Lane, where the fire started. Above the viewing gallery (311 steps up—a better workout than any StairMaster) is a flaming bronze urn with a cage around it to prevent suicidal jumps, which were a trend for a while in the 19th century. ✉ *Monument St.,*

The City EC3, ☎ *020/7626–2717.* 🎫 *£1.50; combination ticket gives £1 discount off entry to Tower Bridge.* ⏲ *Daily 10–5:40 (hrs subject to change; phone before visiting). Tube: Monument.*

8 **Museum of London.** If there's one place to get the history of London sorted out, it's here—although there's a great deal to sort out: Oliver Cromwell's death mask, Queen Victoria's crinolined gowns, Selfridges's Art Deco elevators, and the Lord Mayor's coach are just some of the goodies here. Various fascinating exhibitions—from London Bodies (magnetically gruesome) to early Briton king Alfred the Great and the life and times of the Rothschilds—regularly entice more crowds. The museum appropriately shelters a section of the 2nd- to 4th-century London wall, which you can view from a window inside, near the Roman monumental arch the museum's archaeologists reconstructed a mere two decades ago. Anyone with the least interest in how this city evolved will adore this museum, especially said reconstructions and the dioramas—like one of the Great Fire (flickering flames! sound effects!), a 1940s air-raid shelter, a Georgian prison cell, a Roman living room, and a Victorian street complete with fully stocked shops—as well as the Catwalk, which guides you interactively through the ages. There are special Sunday and holiday sessions that allow children to handle and discover many objects not on view. The museum is also updating its exhibition space, where World City takes the major spotlight. Celebrating the dynamic spirit that characterized life in Victorian London, the gallery charts changes from the French Revolution to the First World War, including the formation of the police, the underground railway, and, the first (very authoritarian) proper schools. Another addition is the Medieval Gallery—a time journey to an age when London depended on the Thames. Illustrated by many important, recent finds, such as boat structures, fragments of clothes and shoes, and skeletal remains from the Black Death, it gives a new perspective on these early times in the thriving capital. ✉ *London Wall, The City EC2,* ☎ *020/7600–0807,* WEB *www.museumoflondon.org.uk.* 🎫 *Free.* ⏲ *Mon.–Sat. 10–5:50, Sun. noon–5:50. Tube: Barbican.*

4 **Old Bailey.** This, the present-day **Central Criminal Court,** is where Newgate Prison stood from the 12th century right until the beginning of the 20th century. Few survived for long in the version pulled down in 1770. Those who didn't starve were hanged, or pressed to death in the Press Yard, or they succumbed to the virulent gaol (the archaic British spelling of "jail") fever—any of which must have been preferable to a life in the stinking, subterranean, lightless Stone Hold or to the robberies, beatings, and general victimization endemic in what the novelist Henry Fielding called the "prototype of hell." The next model lasted only a couple of years before being torn down by raving mobs during the anti-Catholic Gordon Riots of 1780, to be replaced by the Newgate that Dickens visited several times (obviously between pubs) and described in several novels. In fact, Fagin ended up in the Condemned Hold here in *Oliver Twist,* from which he would have been taken to the public scaffold that replaced the Tyburn Tree and stood outside the prison until 1868. The Central Criminal Court replaced Newgate in 1907. The most famous and most interesting feature of the solid Edwardian building is the gilded statue of blind Justice perched on top, scales in her left hand, sword in her right. Ask the doorman which current trial is likely to prove juicy, if you're that kind of ghoul—you may catch the conviction of the next Crippen or Christie (England's most notorious wife-murderers, both tried here). Cameras are not allowed in the court. Check the day's hearings on the sign outside. There are some restrictions on entry (children under 14 are not allowed); call the information line first. ✉ *New-*

gate St., The City EC4, ☎ *020/7248–3277 information.* ⏲ *Public Gallery weekdays 10–1 and 2–4:30 (line forms at Newgate St. entrance). Tube: Blackfriars.*

15 **Royal Exchange.** Inhabiting the isosceles triangle between Threadneedle Street and Cornhill, this is the third version to have stood here but the first to have been blessed by Queen Victoria—at its 1844 opening. Sir William Tite designed the massive templelike building—its pediment featuring 17 limestone figures (Commerce, plus merchants) supported by eight sizable Corinthian columns—to house the then-thriving futures market. The market has now moved on, leaving the Royal Exchange, which you may no longer enter, as a monument to money. ⊠ *Cornhill and Threadneedle St., The City EC3. Tube: Bank.*

7 **St. Bartholomew the Great Church.** Reached via a perfect half-timber gatehouse atop a 13th-century stone archway, this is one of London's oldest churches. Along with its namesake on the other side of the road, St. Bartholomew's Hospital, the Norman church was founded by Rahere, Henry I's court jester. At the Dissolution of the Monasteries, Henry VIII had most of it torn down; the Romanesque choir loft is all that survives from the 12th century. ⊠ *West Smithfield, The City EC1,* ☎ *020/7606–5171.* ⏲ *Weekdays 8:30–5, Sat. 10:30–1:30, Sun. 2–6. Tube: Barbican.*

3 **St. Bride's.** From afar, study the extraordinary steeple of this church—its uniquely tiered shape gave rise, legend has it, to the traditional wedding cake. This, the first of Wren's city churches, did not escape wartime bomb damage and was reconsecrated only in 1960 after a 17-year-long restoration. As St. Paul's (in Covent Garden) is the actors' church, so St. Bride's belongs to journalists, many of whom have been buried or memorialized here, as reading the wall plaques will tell you. Even before the press moved in, it was a popular place to take the final rest. By 1664 the crypts were so crowded that diarist Samuel Pepys had to bribe the grave digger to "justle together" some bodies to make room for his deceased brother. Now the crypts house a museum of the church's rich history, and a bit of Roman sidewalk. ⊠ *Fleet St., The City EC4,* ☎ *020/7353–1301.* 🎫 *Free.* ⏲ *Weekdays 8–5, Sat. 9–5, Sun. between services at 11 and 6:30. Tube: Chancery La.*

10 **St. Giles Without Cripplegate.** Standing south of the Barbican complex, this is one of the only City churches to have withstood the Great Fire, only to succumb to the Blitz bombs three centuries later. The tower and a few walls survived; the rest was rebuilt to the 16th-century plan during the 1950s, and now the little church struggles hopelessly for attention among the Barbican towers, whose parishioners it tends. Past parishioners include Oliver Cromwell, married here in 1620, and John Milton, buried here in 1674. St. Giles was the patron saint for cripples, hence Cripplegate. ⊠ *Fore St., The City EC2.* ⏲ *Weekdays 9:30–5:30, Sun. 8–5:30. Tube: Barbican or Moorgate.*

12 **St. Mary-le-Bow.** Wren's 1673 church has one of the most famous sets of bells around—a Londoner must be born within the sound of Bow Bells to be a true cockney. The origin of that idea was probably the curfew rung on the Bow Bells during the 14th century, even though "cockney" only came to mean Londoner three centuries later, and then it was an insult. The Bow takes its name from the bow-shape arches in the Norman crypt. ⊠ *Cheapside, The City EC2.* ⏲ *Mon.–Thurs. 6:30–5:45, Fri. 6:30–4, weekends special services only. Tube: Mansion House.*

Adm. Collingwood. **21**
Adm. Howe . **20**
All Soul's Chapel **1**
The American Chapel. **13**
Bishop's Throne **18**
Chapel of Modern Martyrs **11**
Chapel of St. Michael and St. George . . **27**
Crypt Entrance. . . . **19**
Dean's Vestry **16**
The Donne Effigy. **15**
Dr. Johnson . . **8**
Duke of Wellington . . . **5**
General Gordon Monument . . . **4**
Geometric Staircase . . . **28**
High Altar . . **12**
J.M.W. Turner **22**
The Lady Chapel. **14**
Lord of Leighton Monument . . . **3**
Lord Mayor's Stall. **17**
Lord Mayor's Vestry **6**
Minor Canons' Vestry **9**
Nelson. **23**
St. Dunstan's Chapel **2**
St. Paul's Watch Memorial Stone. **26**
Sanctuary Screens **10**
Sir John Moore **24**
Sir Joshua Reynolds **7**
Staircase to Whispering Gallery, Dome and Golden Gallery **25**

St. Paul's Cathedral

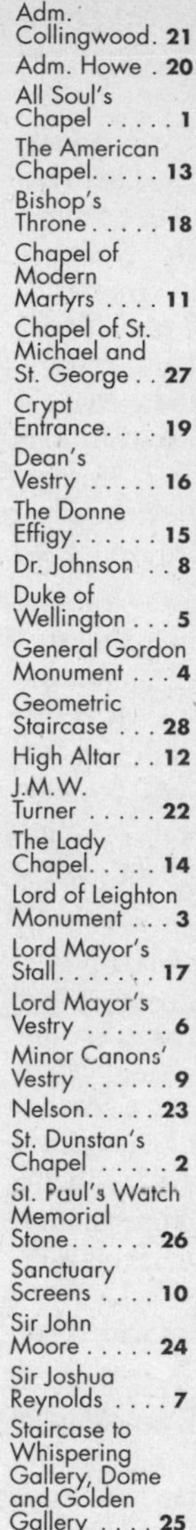

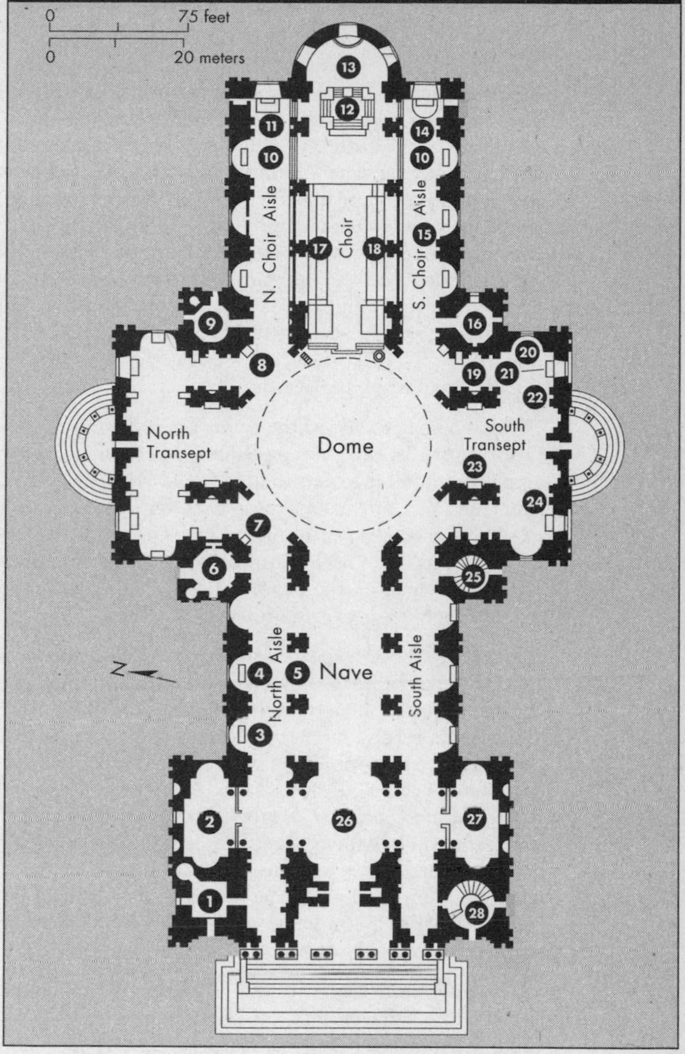

NEED A BREAK? The **Place Below** is below the church, in St. Mary-le-Bow's crypt, and gets packed with City workers weekdays at lunchtime—the self-service soup and quiche are particularly good. Lunches are served from 10:30 until 2:30, weekdays only. It's also open for breakfast (from 7:30) and morning coffee.

★ ❺ **St. Paul's Cathedral.** The symbolic heart of London, St. Paul's will take your breath away. In fact, its dome—the world's third largest—will already be familiar, since you see it peeping through on the skyline from many an angle, riding high (although now nudged by skyscrapers) over the rooftops of the City, just as it does in Canaletto's 18th-century views of the Thames. The cathedral is, of course, the masterpiece of Sir Christopher Wren (1632–1723), completed in 1710 after 35 years of building and much argument with the Royal Commission, then, much later, miraculously (mostly) spared by the World War II bombs. Wren had originally been commissioned to restore Old St. Paul's, the Norman cathedral that had replaced, in its turn, three earlier versions, but the Great Fire left so little of it standing that a new cathedral was deemed necessary.

Wren's first plan, known as the "New Model," did not make it past the drawing board, while the second, known as the "Great Model," got as far as the 20-ft oak rendering you can see here today before it, too, was rejected, whereupon Wren is said to have burst into tears. The third, however, known as the Warrant Design (because it received the royal warrant), was accepted, with the fortunate coda that the architect be allowed to make changes as he saw fit. Without that, there would be no dome, because the approved design had featured a steeple. Parliament felt that building was proceeding too slowly (in fact, 35 years is lightning speed, as cathedrals go) and withheld half of Wren's pay for the last 13 years of work. He was pushing 80 when Queen Anne finally coughed up the arrears.

When you enter and see the dome from the inside, you may find that it seems smaller than you expected. You aren't imagining things—it *is* smaller, and 60 ft lower, than the lead-covered outer dome. Between the inner and outer domes is a brick cone, which supports the familiar 850-ton lantern, surmounted by its golden ball and cross. Nobody can resist making a beeline for the dome, so we'll start beneath it, standing dead center, on the beautiful sunburst floor, Wren's focal mirror of the magnificent design above.

Now climb the 259 spiral steps to the **Whispering Gallery.** This is the part of the cathedral with which you bribe children, who are fascinated by the acoustic phenomenon: whisper something to the wall on one side, and a second later it transmits clearly to the other side, 107 ft away. The only problem is identifying "your" whisper from the cacophony of everyone else's. Look down onto the nave from here, and up to the frescoes of St. Paul by Sir James Thornhill (who nearly fell off while painting them), before ascending farther to the Stone Gallery, which encircles the outside of the dome and affords a spectacular panorama of London. Up again (careful—you will have tackled 627 steps altogether), and you reach the Golden Gallery, from which you can view the lantern through a circular opening called the oculus.

Back downstairs there are the inevitable monuments and memorials to see, though fewer than one might expect because Wren didn't want his masterpiece cluttered up. The poet John Donne, who had been Dean of St. Paul's for his final 10 years (he died in 1631), lies in the south choir aisle; his is the only monument remaining from Old St. Paul's. There is Wren's own memorial, with an epitaph by his son (who also worked on the building) that reads succinctly: LECTOR, SI MONUMENTUM REQUIRIS, CIRCUMSPICE (READER, IF YOU SEEK HIS MONUMENT, LOOK AROUND YOU). The vivacious choir-stall carvings nearby are the work of Grinling Gibbons, as is the organ, which Wren designed and Handel played. The painters Sir Joshua Reynolds and J. M. W. Turner are commemorated, as is George Washington. The American connection continues behind the high altar in the **American Memorial Chapel,** dedicated in 1958 to the 28,000 GIs stationed here who lost their lives in World War II.

A visit to the **crypt** brings you to Wren's tomb (also with his son's epitaph), the black marble sarcophagus containing Admiral Nelson (who was pickled in alcohol for his final voyage here from Trafalgar), and an equestrian statue of the Duke of Wellington on top of his grandiose tomb. A café and gift shop are also in the crypt. Finally, to catch

Wren's facade and dome at its most splendid, remember to make a return trip to see St. Paul's at night. ✉ *St. Paul's Churchyard, Ludgate Hill, The City EC4,* ☎ *020/7236–4128,* WEB *www.stpauls.co.uk.* 🎫 *Cathedral, crypt, ambulatory, and gallery £6.* ⏲ *Cathedral Mon.–Sat. 8:30–4 (closed occasionally for special services); ambulatory, crypt, and gallery Mon.–Sat. 9–5:15. Shop and Crypt Café also Sun. 10:30–5. Tube: St. Paul's.*

14 **St. Stephen Walbrook Church.** This is the parish church many think is Wren's best, by virtue of its practice dome, which predates the big one at St. Paul's by some 30 years. Two inside sights warrant investigation: Henry Moore's 1987 central stone altar, which sits beneath the dome ("like a lump of Camembert," say critics), and, well, a telephone—an eloquent tribute to that genuine savior of souls, Rector Chad Varah, who founded the Samaritans, givers of phone aid to the suicidal, here in 1953. ✉ *Walbrook St., The City EC4.* ⏲ *Mon.–Thurs. 10–4, Fri. 10–3. Tube: Bank or Cannon St.*

17 **Temple of Mithras.** This minor place of pilgrimage in the Roman City was unearthed on a building site in 1954 and was taken, at first, for an early Christian church. In fact, worshipers here favored Christ's chief rival during the 3rd and 4th centuries: Mithras, the Persian god of light. Mithraists aimed for all the big virtues but still were not appreciated by early Christians, from whom their sculptures and treasures had to be concealed. These devotional objects are now on display back at the Museum of London, while here, on Queen Victoria Street, not far from the Bank of England, you can see the foundations of the temple itself. ✉ *Temple Court, Queen Victoria St., The City EC4. Tube: Bank.*

★ 21 **Tower Bridge.** Despite its venerable, nay, medieval, appearance, this is a Victorian youngster. Constructed of steel, then clothed in Portland stone, it was deliberately styled in the Gothic persuasion to complement the Tower next door, and it is famous for its enormous bascules—the "arms," which open to allow large ships through. Nowadays this rarely happens, but when river traffic was dense, the bascules were raised about five times a day.

The exhibition, **Tower Bridge Experience,** is a fun tour back in time in the company of "Harry Stoner," an animatronic bridge construction worker worthy of Disneyland, to witness the birth of the Thames's last downstream bridge. History and engineering lessons are painlessly absorbed as you meet the ghost of the bridge's architect, Sir Horace Jones; see the bascules work; and wander the walkways with their grand upstream–downstream views annotated by interactive video displays. Be sure to hang on to your ticket and follow the signs to the Engine Rooms for part two; here the original steam-driven hydraulic engines gleam, and a cute rococo theater is the setting for an Edwardian-style music-hall production of the bridge's story. One of the natural highlights is the glorious view from up high on the covered walkway between the turrets, watching the world go by on the river. ☎ *020/7403–3761,* WEB *www.towerbridge.org.uk.* 🎫 *£6.25; combination ticket with Monument, £6.75.* ⏲ *Apr.–Oct., daily 10–6:30 (last entry at 5:15); Nov.–Mar., daily 9:30–5:15 (last entry at 4). Tube: Tower Hill.*

★ 20 **Tower of London.** This has top billing on many tourist itineraries for good reason. Nowhere else does London's history come to life so vividly as in this minicity of melodramatic towers stuffed to bursting with heraldry and treasure, the intimate details of lords and dukes and princes and sovereigns etched in the walls (literally in some places, as you'll see), and quite a few pints of royal blood spilled on the stones. New systems ensure that lines are minimal, so you'll be able to put in

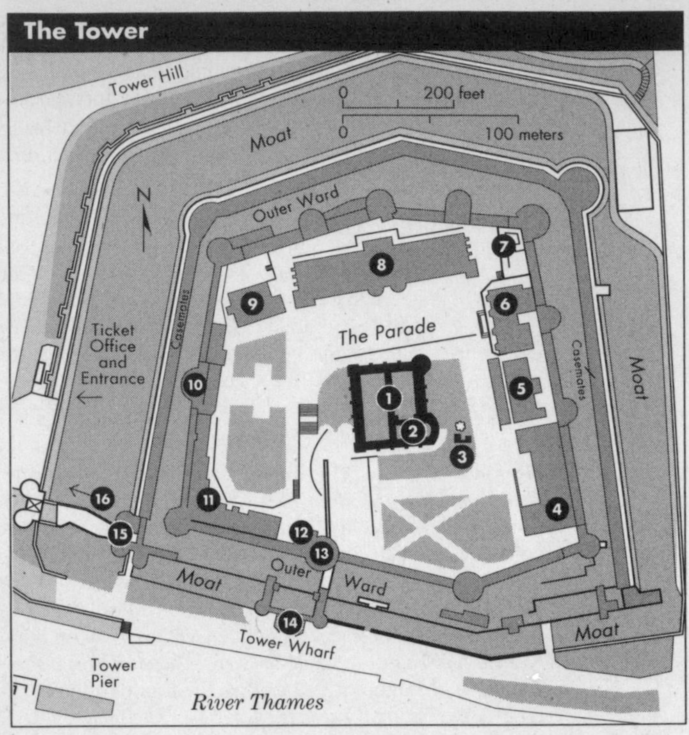

place all those grisly torture scenes you saw in the film *Elizabeth*. And thankfully, you need no longer spend all day in line for the prize exhibit, the Crown Jewels, since they can be seen in glass cabinets on both sides, where moving walkways hasten progress at the busiest times.

The reason the Tower holds the royal gems is that it is still one of the royal palaces, although no monarch since Henry VII has called it home. It has also housed the Royal Mint, the Public Records, the Royal Menagerie (which formed the basis of London Zoo), and the Royal Observatory, although its most renowned and titillating function has been, of course, as a jail and place of torture and execution.

A person was mighty privileged to be beheaded in the peace and seclusion of **Tower Green** instead of before the mob at Tower Hill. In fact, only seven people were ever important enough—among them Anne Boleyn and Catherine Howard, wives two and five, respectively, of Henry VIII's six; Elizabeth I's friend Robert Devereux, the Earl of Essex; and the nine-day queen, Lady Jane Grey, aged 17. Tower Green's other function was as a corpse dumping ground when the chapel just got too full. The executioner's block—with its bathetic forehead-size dent—and his axe, along with the equally famous rack and the more obscure "scavenger's daughter" (which pressed a body nearly to death), plus assorted thumbscrews, "iron maidens," and so forth, have moved to the Royal Armouries in Leeds, Yorkshire. (Fans of this horrifying niche of heavy metal might also want to pay a call on the London Dungeon attraction, just across the Thames).

You should know about the excellent free and fact-packed tours that depart every half hour or so from the Middle Tower. They are conducted by the 39 Yeoman Warders, better known as Beefeaters—ex-servicemen dressed in resplendent navy-and-red (scarlet-and-gold on special occasions) Tudor outfits. Beefeaters have been guarding the tower since Henry VII appointed them in 1485. One of them, the Yeoman Ravenmaster, is responsible for making life comfortable for Hardey, George, Hugine, Mumin, Cedric, Odin, Thor (who talks), and Gwylem—the Tower Ravens. This used to be a delicate duty, because if they were to desert the tower (goes the legend), the kingdom would fall. Today, the tower takes no chances: the ravens' wings are clipped.

In prime position stands the oldest part of the tower and the most conspicuous of its buildings, the **White Tower.** This central keep was begun in 1078 by William the Conqueror; by the time it was completed, in 1097, it was the tallest building in London, underlining the might of those victorious Normans. Henry III (1207–72) had it whitewashed, which is where the name comes from, then used it as a barracks and as housing for his menagerie, including the first elephant ever seen in the land.

The spiral staircase—winding clockwise to help the right-handed swordsman defend it—is the only way up, and here you'll find the **Royal Armouries,** Britain's national museum of arms and armor, with about 40,000 pieces on display. One of the tower's original functions was as an arsenal, supplying armor and weapons to the kings and their armies. Henry VIII started the collection in earnest, founding a workshop at Greenwich as a kind of bespoke tailor of armor to the gentry, but the public didn't get to see it until the second half of the 17th century, during Charles II's reign—which makes the Tower Armouries Britain's oldest public museum.

Here you can see weapons and armor from Britain and the Continent, dating from Saxon and Viking times right up to our own. Among the highlights are four suits of armor Henry VIII commissioned to fit his ever-increasing bulk, plus one for his horse. The medieval warhorse was nothing without his *shaffron,* or head protector, and here you'll find a 500-year-old example, one of the oldest pieces of horse armor in the world. Don't miss the tiny armors on the third floor—one belonging to Henry's son (who survived in it to become Edward VI) and another just a bit more than 3 ft tall. The impressive, carved Line of Kings is not to be missed. The **New Armouries** have been renovated into a restaurant.

Most of the interior of the White Tower has been much altered over the centuries, but the **Chapel of St. John the Evangelist,** downstairs from the armories, is a pure example of 11th-century Norman—very rare, very simple, and very beautiful. The other fortifications and buildings surrounding the White Tower date from the 11th to 19th centuries. Starting from the main entrance, you can't miss the **moat.** Until the Duke of Wellington had it drained in 1843, this was a stinking, stagnant mush, obstinately resisting all attempts to flush it with water from the Thames. Now there's a little raven graveyard in the grassed-over channel, with touching memorials to some of the old birds (who are not known for their kind natures, by the way, and you risk a savage pecking if you try to befriend them).

Across the moat, the **Middle Tower** and the **Byward Tower** form the principal landward entrance, with **Traitors' Gate** a little farther on to the right. This is the London equivalent of Venice's Bridge of Sighs, which led to the cells in the Doge's Palace. Unlike the Venetian monument, Traitors' Gate is not architecturally beautiful but was the last walkway of daylight before condemned prisoners were doomed to darkness and death in the dungeons. During the period when the Thames was London's chief thoroughfare, this was the main entrance to the Tower.

Immediately opposite Traitors' Gate is the former Garden Tower, better known since about 1570 as the **Bloody Tower.** Its name comes from one of the most famous unsolved murders in history, the saga of the "little princes in the Tower." In 1483 the uncrowned boy king Edward V and his brother Richard were left here by their uncle, Richard of Gloucester, after the death of their father, Edward IV. They were never seen again, Gloucester was crowned Richard III, and in 1674 two little skeletons were found under the stairs to the White Tower. The obvious conclusions have always been drawn—and were, in fact, even before the skeletons were discovered.

Another famous inmate was Sir Walter Raleigh, who was kept here from 1603 to 1616. It wasn't such an ordeal, as you'll see when you visit his spacious rooms, where he kept two servants, had his wife and two sons live with him (the younger boy was christened in the Tower chapel), and amused himself by writing his *History of the World*. Unfortunately, he was less lucky on his second visit in 1618, which terminated in his execution at Whitehall.

Next to the Bloody Tower is the circular **Wakefield Tower,** which dates from the 13th century and once contained the king's private apartments. It was the scene of another royal murder in 1471, when Henry VI was killed in mid-prayer. Henry founded Eton College and King's College, Cambridge, and they haven't forgotten: every May 21, envoys from both institutions mark the anniversary of his murder by laying white lilies on the site.

The most dazzling and most famous exhibits in the Tower are, of course, the **Crown Jewels,** now housed in the **Jewel House, Waterloo Block.** Here you get so close to the fabled gems you feel you could polish them (if it weren't for the wafers of bulletproof glass), and they are enhanced by laser lighting, which nearly hurts the eyes with sparkle. Before you meet them in person, you are given a high-definition-film preview, which features scenes from Elizabeth's 1953 coronation.

It's commonplace to call these baubles priceless, but it's impossible not to drop your jaw at the notion of their worth. They were, in fact, stolen once—by Col. Thomas Blood, in 1671—though taken only as far as a nearby wharf. The colonel was given a royal pension instead of a beating, fueling speculation that Charles II, short of ready cash as usual, had had his hand in the escapade somewhere. These days security is as fiendish as you'd expect, behind secure double doors of incredible thickness, since the jewels—even though they would be impossible for thieves to sell—are *so* priceless.

A brief résumé of the top jewels: finest of all is the **Royal Sceptre,** containing the earth's largest cut diamond, the 530-carat Star of Africa. This is also known as Cullinan I, having been cut from the South African Cullinan, which weighed 20 ounces when dug up from a De Beers mine at the beginning of the century. Another chip off the block, Cullinan II, lives on the **Imperial State Crown** that Prince Charles is due to wear at his coronation—the same one that Elizabeth II wore in her coronation procession; it was made for Victoria's coronation in 1838. Aside from its 2,800 diamonds, you'll find the Black Prince's ruby, which Henry V was supposed to have worn at Agincourt and which is actually an imposter—it's no ruby but, rather, a semiprecious spinel. The other most famous gem is the Koh-i-noor, or "Mountain of Light," which adorns the late **Queen Mother's crown.** When Victoria was presented with this gift horse in 1850, she looked it in the mouth, found it lacking in glitter, and had it chopped down to almost half its weight.

An addendum to the major jewels in the Martin Tower is accurately called "Crowns and Diamonds." See naked crown frames—the coronation crown of George IV, George I's Imperial State Crown, Victoria's State Crown—surrounded by 12,500 loose diamonds on permanent loan from De Beers. It's a graphic illustration of how the Royals once had to rent the stones that would adorn their headpiece on the big day.

The little chapel of **St. Peter ad Vincula** is the second church on the site, and conceals the remains of some 2,000 people executed at the Tower, Anne Boleyn and Catherine Howard among them. Being traitors, they were not so much buried as dumped under the flagstones, but the genteel Victorians had the courtesy to rebury their bones during renovations.

One of the more evocative towers is **Beauchamp Tower,** built west of Tower Green by Edward I (1272–1307). It was soon designated as a jail for the higher class of miscreant, including Lady Jane Grey, who is thought to have added her Latin graffiti to the many inscriptions here.

Just south of the Beauchamp Tower is an L-shape row of half-timber Tudor houses, with the **Queen's House** at the center. Built for the governor of the Tower in 1530, this place saw the interrogation or incarceration of several celebrated prisoners, including Anne Boleyn and the Gunpowder Plot conspirators. The Queen's House also played host to the Tower's last-ever prisoner, Rudolph Hess, the Nazi who parachuted over Scotland on a spy mission and was taken prisoner here.

Allow at least three hours to explore, and arrive early in summer to beat the huge crowds. You can buy your ticket at any tube stop to save time, too. Don't forget to stroll along the battlements before you leave; from them, you get a wonderful overview of the whole Tower of London. For tickets to Ceremony of the Keys (locking of main gates, nightly at 10), write well in advance to the Resident Governor and Keeper of the Jewel House (at the Queen's House, address below). Give your name, the dates you wish to attend (including alternate dates), and number of people (up to seven) in your party, and enclose a self-addressed, stamped envelope. Yeoman Warder guides leave daily from Middle Tower, subject to weather and availability, at no charge, about every 30 minutes until 3:30 in summer, 2:30 in winter. ✉ *H. M. Tower of London, Tower Hill, The City, EC3,* ☎ *020/7709–0765 or 020/7680–9004 (recorded information),* WEB *www.hrp.org.uk.* 🎟 *£11.30.* ⏲ *Mar.–Oct., Mon.–Sat. 9–5, Sun. 10–5; Nov.–Feb., Tues.–Sat. 9–4, Sun.–Mon. 10–4 (the Tower closes 1 hr after last admission time and all internal buildings close 30 mins after last admission). Tube: Tower Hill.*

❷ **Ye Olde Cheshire Cheese.** This is one of the many places in which that acerbic compiler of the first dictionary, Dr. Johnson, drank (like Dickens, he is claimed by many a pub). This was, in fact, his "local," around the corner from his house. It retains a venerable open-fires-in-tiny-rooms charm when not too packed with tourists. Among 19th-century writers who followed Johnson's footsteps to the bar here were Mark Twain and, yes, Charles Dickens. ✉ *145 Fleet St., The City EC4,* ☎ *020/7373–6170.* ⏲ *Mon.–Sat. 11–11, Sun. noon–3 and 6–10. Tube: Blackfriars.*

THE EAST END

Made famous by Dickens and infamous by Jack the Ripper, the East End remains one of London's most hauntingly evocative neighborhoods. There is a good argument for considering it the real London, since East Enders are born "within the sound of Bow Bells" and are therefore

Close-Up

DOCKLANDS: THE RENAISSANCE BY THE RIVER

BUT FOR THE RIVER, ROMAN LONDINIUM, with its sea link to the rest of the world, would not have grown into a world power. Trade and people came and went on the water from the port, or Pool of London (some of the early American settlers to Virginia set sail from Blackwall, one of the numerous wharves and quaysides along the river). Life was played out by the riverside; palaces—such as Lambeth, Greenwich, Somerset House, Westminster, and Whitehall—redolent of Venice, were built. Henry VIII built dockyards at Woolwich and Deptford to relieve congestion at Billingsgate (fish market). Dock warehouses sprang up during the 18th century from the trade with the Indies for tea and coffee, spices, and silks (some now converted into museums and malls, such as Hay's and Butler's wharves). Along with others, West India and East India Docks were built in the 19th century, extending London's port some miles east, to Millwall and the Isle of Dogs. Trade took a gradual downturn, leading to the docks' degeneration, after World War II, when larger vessels pushed trade further downriver to Tilbury. It took a driverless railway and Britain's tallest building to start a renaissance.

Once a desolate and dirty quarter of the east end (which could be why it's called the Isle of Dogs, as only a dog might live there) is a modern piece of real estate, a peninsula of waterways with cutting-edge architecture, offices, water-based leisure and cultural activities, restaurants, and bars.

The best way to explore is on the Docklands Light Railway, whose elevated track appears to skim over the water past the swanky glassy buildings where the railway is reflected in the windows. By foot, the Thames Path has helpful plaques along the way, with nuggets of historical information. Canary Wharf, 1 Canada Square (not open to the public), embodies the bold architecture of the Docklands, but a visit to one of the original dockside warehouses at West India Quay, to the Museum in Docklands (020/7001–9800), tells the story of days when boats and sailors, rather than blue-chip outfits, were all around here. Everything you could want to know about this fascinating place can be discovered in a series of displays and interactive zones: the water zone, dockwork, building, and early years. Some exhibits are scary—one, for example, reveals the grisly tortures meted out to pirates.

Farther along the river, approached from the south side, and also covering the life cycle of the river in a hands-on exhibition, is the Thames Barrier Visitor Centre (020/8305–4188, Charlton station). The views of the monster steel flood-restraining shells stretching across the river, with the Millennium Dome in the background, are quite surreal.

If you have time to travel farther downstream to the old Royal Dockyard at Woolwich, you'll find, adjacent to it, a brilliant exhibition of the Royal Artillery, *Firepower!* (020/8855–7755, Woolwich Arsenal station). Complete with smoke and sound effects, it explores the role of the gunner in film, from the discovery of gunpowder to the Gulf War. Also on show are tanks and guns—some complete with battle scars, and most with individual investigative touch-screen storyboards. Housed in the old regal buildings of the Royal Arsenal leading down to the river shore, there's a powerful sense of the Thames and its lingering effect on the capital's history.

cockneys through and through (not to mention models for the characters of England's favorite soap opera, *EastEnders*). The district began as separate villages—Whitechapel and Spitalfields, Shoreditch, Mile End, and Bethnal Green—melding together during the population boom of the 19th century, a boom that was shaped by French Huguenot and Jewish refugees, by poverty, and, in the past several decades, by a growing Bengali community. Whitechapel is where the Salvation Army was founded and the original Liberty Bell was forged, but, of course, what everyone remembers about it is that its Victorian slum streets were stalked by the most infamous serial killer of all, Jack the Ripper. Many outfitters offer walking tours of "Jack's London." Two centuries earlier, neighboring Spitalfields provided sanctuary for the French Huguenots. They had fled here after the Edict of Nantes (which had allowed them religious freedom in Catholic France) was revoked in 1685, and had found work in the nascent silk industry, many of them becoming prosperous master weavers. Today, as it turns out, Spitalfields is one of London's most cutting-edge neighborhoods, with stylish boutiques and artists setting up shop. All in all, prosperous is not really the word for the East End of today, but what the area lacks in traditional tourist attractions it makes up for in history and urban romance of a sublime sort.

Numbers in the text correspond to numbers in the margin and on the East End map.

A Good Walk

The easiest way to reach Whitechapel High Street is via the District Line to Aldgate East tube stop. Turn left out of the station. Behind No. 90 Whitechapel High Street once stood George Yard Buildings, where Jack the Ripper's first victim, Martha Turner, was discovered in August 1888. Nowadays you'll come across the **Whitechapel Art Gallery** ① instead. Continue east until you reach Fieldgate Street on the right, where you'll find the **Whitechapel Bell Foundry** ②; then, retracing your steps, turn right onto Osborn Street, which soon becomes **Brick Lane**③.

Brick Lane itself and the narrow streets running off it offer a paradigm of the East End's development. Its population has always been in flux, with some moving in to find refuge here as others were escaping its poverty. Just before the start of Brick Lane you can take a short detour (turn left, then right) to see the birthplace of one who did just that. Flower and Dean streets, past the ugly 1970s housing project on Thrawl Street and once the most disreputable street in London, was where Abe Sapperstein, founder of the Harlem Globetrotters, was born in 1908. On the west end of **Fournier Street** ④, see Nicholas Hawksmoor's masterpiece, **Christ Church, Spitalfields** ⑤, and some fine early Georgian houses; then follow Wilkes Street north of the church, where you'll find more 1720s Huguenot houses, and turn right onto Princelet Street, once important to the Jewish settlers. Where No. 6 stands now, the first of several thriving Yiddish theaters opened in 1886, playing to packed houses until the following year, when a false fire alarm, rung during a January performance, ended with 17 people being crushed to death and so demoralized the theater's actor-founder, Jacob Adler, that he moved his troupe to New York. Adler played a major role in founding that city's great Yiddish theater tradition—which, in turn, had a significant effect on Hollywood. The Spitalfields Centre occupies and is raising funds to restore and open to the public the house at No. 19 Princelet Street, which harbored French Huguenots (the upper windows are wider than usual so the Huguenot silk weavers had light to work) and, later, Polish Jews (behind its elegant Georgian door, Jacob

Davidson, a shoe warehouseman, formed the Loyal United Friendly Society and a tiny synagogue). Spitalfields' grand Georgian houses were crammed with lodgings and workshops for the poor and persecuted. As you walk these quiet streets now, where many of the doors and window shutters have fresh, gleaming paint, there is an air of intellectual restoration and respect for heritage. It's an enclave of mysterious beauty.

Now you reach Brick Lane again and the **Black Eagle Brewery** ⑥. Turn left at Hanbury Street, where, in 1888, behind a seedy lodging house at No. 29, Jack the Ripper left his third mutilated victim, "Dark" Annie Chapman. A double murder followed, and then, after a month's lull, came the death on this street of Marie Kelly, the Ripper's last victim and his most revolting murder of all. He had been able to work indoors this time, and Kelly, a young widow, was found strewn all over the room, charred remains of her clothing in the fire grate. (Of course, Jack the Ripper's identity never has been discovered, although to this day theories are still bandied about—the latest one taken up by historians fingers Francis Twomblety, an American quack doctor.)

Now turn onto Lamb Street and the two northern entrances to **Spitalfields Market** ⑦ or turn left on Commercial Street to Folgate Street and **Dennis Severs's House** ⑧. Elder Street, just off Folgate, is another gem of original 18th-century houses. On the south and east side of Spitalfields Market are yet more time-warp streets that are worth a wander, such as Gun Street, where artist Mark Gertler (1891–1939) lived at No. 32. (If you have kids, they might have fun—and learn something, too—going to **Spitalfields City Farm** ⑨ a few blocks away.) Go back west through Folgate Street to reach Shoreditch High Street, where you can catch Bus 22A, 22B, or 149 north to Kingsland Road, or get there across Bethnal Green Road, left, then right onto Club Row, to **Arnold Circus** ⑩ and then two streets north, to **Columbia Road** ⑪. Cross Hackney Road and slip up Waterson Street—that's about a ½-mi walk. On Kingsland Road, you'll come to the row of early 18th-century almshouses that are the **Geffrye Museum** ⑫. Head east about 500 yards on Hackney Road (Cremer Street, south of the museum, gets you there), to reach **Hackney City Farm** ⑬. Going south down Warner Place (across Hackney Road opposite the farm entrance), you come to Old Bethnal Green Road, at the end of which a right turn brings you to the **Bethnal Green Museum of Childhood** ⑭.

Now you can catch either Bus 106 or 253 or walk south about ½ mi down Cambridge Heath Road as far as the Mile End Road. Turning left, you'll pass several historical landmarks that provide more food for thought than thrills for the senses. On the north side of the street are the former **Trinity Almshouses** ⑮, with the statue of William Booth on the very spot where the first Salvation Army meetings were held. Behind you, on the northwest corner of Cambridge Heath Road is the **Blind Beggar** ⑯ pub, with the **Royal London Hospital** ⑰ a few yards to the left and its Archives behind. The **Ragged School Museum** ⑱ is off our map, but easily walked from Mile End tube stop via Stepney Green and Ben Jonson Road, or from the Trinity Almshouses.

TIMING

This is a long walk, and not for everyone. The East End isn't picturesque, and the sights are anything but world famous. However, those who get pleasure from discovery and an adventurous route will enjoy these hidden corners. If you visit on a Sunday morning, the East End has a festive air: about half the neighborhood sprouts hundreds of market stalls (especially in and around Middlesex Street, Brick Lane, and Columbia Road). After shopping, you could go on to take brunch among cows and sheep on a farm, then play at being Georgians in a restored, candlelit 18th-century town house. You would miss out on a few weekday-only sights, but—as a Victorian peep-show barker might say—yer pays yer money and yer takes yer choice. A weekday focus for your jaunt might well be the excellent Whitechapel Gallery, the Geffrye Museum, or the Bethnal Green Museum of Childhood, any of which will take an hour or two. Aside from visits, the walk alone is a three-hour marathon, done at a brisk pace. The suggested bus links might be appealing, since the in-between parts aren't going to win tourism awards.

HOW TO GET THERE

The best tube stop to start from is Whitechapel or Aldgate East on the District/Hammersmith and City lines or Aldgate on the Metropolitan and Circle lines. Buses 8, 25, 26, 35, 47, 48, and 78 are useful. To continue up into the northern part of the area, around Shoreditch and Spitalfields, including the Geffrye Museum (get the 22A or B or the 67 for that), get Buses 8, 22A, 22B, 26, 35, 47, 48, 55, 67, 78, and 242 to the junction of Shoreditch High Street and Bishopsgate.

Sights to See

10 **Arnold Circus.** A perfect circle of Arts and Crafts–style houses around a central raised bandstand, this is the core of the Boundary Estate—"model" housing built by Victorian philanthropists and do-gooders for the slum-dwelling locals and completed as the 20th century began. It's of special interest to architecture buffs. ✉ *East End E2. Tube: Liverpool St. or Old St.*

14 **Bethnal Green Museum of Childhood.** This is the East End outpost of the Victoria & Albert Museum—in fact, this entire iron, glass, and brown-brick building was transported here from South Kensington in 1875. Since then, believe it or not, its contents have grown into the biggest toy collection in the world. The central hall is a bit like the Geffrye Museum zapped into miniature: here are dollhouses (some royal) of every period. Each genre of plaything has its own enclosure, so if teddy bears are your weakness, you need waste no time with the train sets. The museum's title is justified upstairs, in the fascinating—and possibly unique—galleries on the social history of childhood from baby dolls to Beanie Babies. Free art "carts" of goodies are available Saturdays and Sundays for children over the age of 3 with a ticket from the admission desk. There's also a soft-play area for little kids so the "big" ones can gaze longer at the museum's collection, a daily dressing-up area with old-fashioned clothes, and floor-size board games such as Snakes and Ladders—guaranteed to send parents into a world of nostalgia, and children to a tranquil land before techno took its hold. ✉ *Cambridge Heath Rd., East End E2,* ☎ *020/8983–5200; 020/8980–2415 recorded information.* WEB *www.museumofchildhood.org.uk.* *Free.* *Sat.–Thurs. 10–5:50; art workshop Sat. and Sun. 11, noon, 2, 3. Tube: Bethnal Green.*

6 **Black Eagle Brewery.** This is the only one of the former East End breweries still standing. It is a very handsome example of Georgian and 19th-century industrial architecture, too, along with its mirrored 1977 extension. It belonged to Truman, Hanbury, Buxton & Co., which in 1873 was the largest brewery in the world (the English always did like their bitters). The building now houses the East End Tourism Trust offices and the present Truman brewery's administration. You can't go in except to look at the old stables and vat house on the east side. The old brewery canteen used to be the **Brick Lane Music Hall** (✉ 134–146 Curtain Rd., East End, ☎ 020/7739–9996), but this has now moved to larger premises a couple of roads away; there, you'll find East End

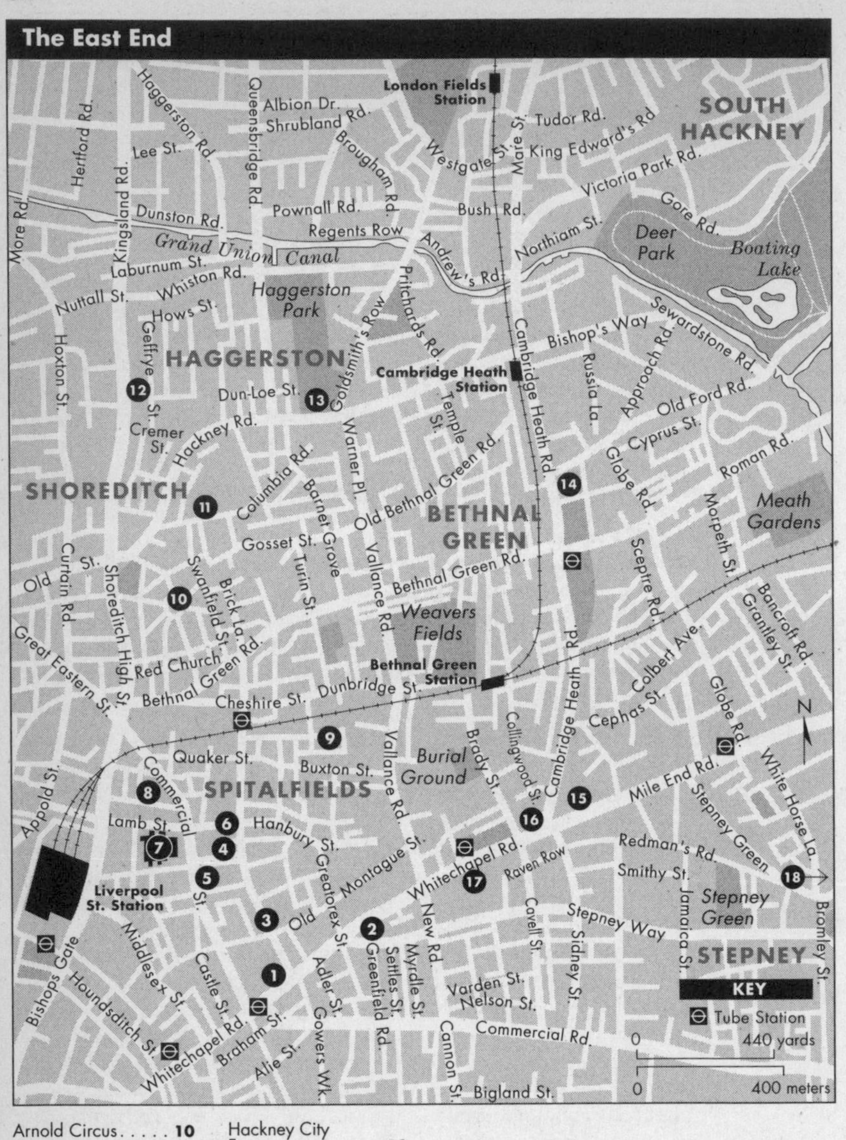

Arnold Circus 10
Bethnal Green Museum of Childhood 14
Black Eagle Brewery 6
The Blind Beggar 16
Brick Lane 3
Christ Church, Spitalfields. 5
Columbia Road . . . 11
Dennis Severs's House 8
Fournier Street 4
Geffrye Museum. . . 12
Hackney City Farm. 13
Ragged School Museum 18
Royal London Hospital. 17
Spitalfields City Farm. 9
Spitalfields Market 7
Trinity Almshouses. 15
Whitechapel Art Gallery 1
Whitechapel Bell Foundry. 2

Jewish fare (such as latkes, or potato pancakes) and an old-fashioned laugh-a-minute cabaret show on tap. ✉ *91 Brick La., East End E1. Tube: Aldgate East or Shoreditch.*

16 **The Blind Beggar.** This is the Victorian den of iniquity where Salvation Army founder William Booth preached his first sermon. Also, on the south side of the street stands a stone inscribed, HERE WILLIAM BOOTH COMMENCED THE WORK OF THE SALVATION ARMY, JULY 1865, marking the position of the first Sally Army platform, while back by the pub, a statue of William Booth stands where the first meetings were held. Booth didn't supply the pub's main claim to fame, though. The Blind Beggar's real notoriety dates only from March 1966, when Ronnie Kray—one of the Kray twins, the former gangster kings of London's East End underworld—shot dead rival "godfather" George Cornell in the saloon bar. The original Albion Brewery was next door, celebrated home to the first bottled brown ale. ✉ *337 Whitechapel Rd., East End E1. Tube: Whitechapel.*

3 **Brick Lane.** This street has, in its time, seen the manufacture of bricks (during the 16th century, when it was named), beer, and bagels, but nowadays it is the center of the East End's Bengali community. (You can still get the bagels, though, at No. 159, the 24-hour **Beigel Bake.**) All along here you'll see shops selling psychedelic saris and stacks of sticky Indian sweets, video stores renting Indian movies, and Bengali, Bangladeshi, and Pakistani restaurants, popular among Londoners for the most authentic and least expensive curries in town. On Sunday morning the entire street is packed with stalls in a companion market to the nearby Petticoat Lane. ✉ *Brick La., East End E1. Tube: Aldgate East or Shoreditch.*

5 **Christ Church, Spitalfields.** This is the 1729 masterpiece of Wren's associate, Nicholas Hawksmoor. Hawksmoor built only six London churches; this one was commissioned as part of Parliament's 1711 "Fifty New Churches Act." The idea was to score points for the Church of England against such nonconformists as the Protestant Huguenots. (It must have worked; in the churchyard, you can still see some of their gravestones, with epitaphs in French.) The Spitalfields district once flourished thanks to the silk-weaving trade of its émigré population, but as the silk industry declined (19th-century machinery had made hand weaving obsolete), the church fell into disrepair and its gardens even acquired a reputation as a tramps' ground (and the sobriquet "Itchy Park"). By 1958 the structure was crumbling to bits and had to be closed. It was saved from demolition—but only just—and reopened in 1987. Restoration work on the exterior is now complete, although the interior work continues. Opening hours are restricted to those listed below, although you can also admire the interior during the Spitalfields Festival in June and December, when there are lunchtime and evening concerts; call ☎ 020/7377–0287 for details. There is always a fine view of the colonnaded portico and tall spire from Brushfield Street to the west. ✉ *Commercial St., East End E1,* ☎ *020/7247–7202, 020/7373–1362 ticket line for concerts.* 🎟 *Free; charge for concerts.* ⏲ *Weekdays noon–2, Sun. services. Tube: Aldgate East.*

11 **Columbia Road.** On Sundays, this narrow street gets buried under forests of potted palms, azaleas, ivy, ficus, freesia, tiger lilies, carnations, roses, and hosts of daffodils in London's main plant and flower market. Prices are ultralow, and lots of the Victorian shop windows around the stalls are filled with horticultural wares—terra-cotta pots, vases, gardening tools, hats, and antiques. ⏲ *Sun. 7–2. Tube: Old St., then Bus 55.*

★ 8 **Dennis Severs's House.** Ever want to feel what Ebenezer Scrooge felt when the three ghosts visited him? Enter this extraordinary time machine of a house—a Georgian terrace belonging to the eponymous performer-designer-scholar from Escondido, California, who dedicated his life not only to restoring his house but also to raising the ghosts of a fictitious Jervis family that might have inhabited it over the course of two centuries. Severs, who died a few years ago, lived a replica of Georgian life, without electricity but with a butler in full 18th-century livery to light the candles and lay the fires—for the Jervises. His assistant still carries on the tradition. The rooms are shadowy set pieces of rose-laden Victorian wallpapers, Jacobean paneling, Georgian wing chairs, Baroque carved ornaments, "Protestant" colors (upstairs), and "Catholic" shades (downstairs). Once a month there is an open house on Sunday and next day, Monday; but for the following Mondays of the month, reservations are essential, when the house is viewed by candlelight. Private visits by special arrangement are possible. ✉ *18 Folgate St., East End E1,* ☎ *020/7247–4013.* WEB *www.dennisservershouse.co.uk.* 💵 *£7 for Sun. open house, £5 for Mon. open house; £10 for candlelit Mon. evenings.* ⏲ *1st Sun. of month 2–5, 1st Mon. noon–2. Call for hrs for other Mons. (reservations required). Tube: Liverpool St.*

4 **Fournier Street.** This contains fine examples of the neighborhood's characteristic Georgian terraced houses, many of them built by the richest of the early 18th-century Huguenot silk weavers (see the enlarged windows on the upper floors). Most of those along the north side of Fournier Street have now been restored by conservationists; others still contain textile sweatshops—only now the workers are Bengali. On the Brick Lane corner is the **Jamme Masjid,** where local Muslims worship. UMBRA SUMMUS (WE ARE SHADOWS) announces the inscription above the entrance, an apt epitaph for the successive communities that have had temporary claim on the building. Built in 1742 as a Huguenot chapel, it converted to Methodism in 1809, only to become the Spitalfields Great Synagogue when the Orthodox Machzikei Hadath sect bought it in 1897. ✉ *East End E1. Tube: Liverpool St.*

★ 12 **Geffrye Museum.** This is a small and perfectly formed museum that re-creates domestic English interiors of every period from Elizabethan through postwar '50s utility, up to the more familiar 20th century, all in sequence, so that you walk through time. The best thing about the Geffrye (named after the 17th-century Lord Mayor of London whose land this was) is that its rooms are not the grand parlors of the gentry one normally sees in historic houses but copies of real family homes, as if talented movie-set designers had been let loose instead of academic museum curators. There's also a walled, scented herb garden and a full program of accessible lectures, including regular "bring a room to life" talks. ✉ *Kingsland Rd., East End E2,* ☎ *020/7739–9893,* WEB *www.geffrye-museum.org.uk.* 💵 *Free.* ⏲ *Tues.–Sat. 10–5, Sun. noon–5. Tube: Old St., then Bus 243; Liverpool St., then Bus 149, 242, or 243A.*

13 **Hackney City Farm.** This one is smaller than the city farm at Spitalfields, and so are its animals. Bees and butterflies are the stars here, along with the kinds of wildflowers they like, as well as an ecologically sound pond. If you're walking this route, drop in and buy a pot of London honey. ✉ *1A Goldsmiths Row, East End E2,* ☎ *020/7729–6381.* 💵 *Free.* ⏲ *Tues.–Sun. 10–4:30. Tube: Bethnal Green.*

18 **Ragged School Museum.** In its time, this was the largest school in London and a place where impoverished children could escape their deprived homes to get free education and a good meal. The museum re-creates the children's experiences with a time-capsule classroom, dating from

the 1880s. Even after their short school career, the students were helped to find their first jobs, and hopefully a way out of their poverty trap. At home, they were probably living in one room with the rest of their usually large family, eking out a sad life with little future prospect of improvement. The school was their passport to a better life.

It's an eye-opener for adults, and a fun time-travel experience for kids who get the chance to work with such materials as scratchy slates and chalks—just like Victorian kids did more than 100 years ago, in one of the many organized workshops. There are guided tours, an exhibit on the history of the area, a bookshop, and a café overlooking the canal, where you can take stock of the facilities young students have at their disposal today. ✉ *46–50 Copperfield Rd., East End EC3,* ☎ *020/8980–6405,* WEB *www.raggedschoolmuseum.org.uk.* 🎟 *Free.* ⏲ *Wed.–Thurs. 10–5, first Sun. of month 2–5.*

17 **Royal London Hospital.** Founded in 1740, the Royal London was once as nasty as its then-neighborhood near the Tower of London. Waste was carried out in buckets and dumped in the street; bedbugs and alcoholic nurses were problems; but according to hospital records patients didn't die—they were "relieved." Anyone who lived but refused to give thanks to both the hospital committee and God went on a blacklist, to be banned from further treatment. In 1757, the hospital moved to its present site, the building of which is the core of the one you see today. By then it had become one of the best hospitals in London, and it was enhanced further by the addition of a small medical school in 1785, and again, 70 years later, an entire state-of-the-art medical college. Thomas John Barnado, who went on to found the famous Dr. Barnado's Homes for Orphans, came to train here in 1866. Ten years later, the hospital grew to become the largest in the United Kingdom, and now, though mostly rebuilt since World War II, it remains one of London's most capacious. To get an idea of the huge medical leaps forward, walk through the main entrance and garden to the crypt of St. Augustine with St. Philip's Church (alternatively, go direct two blocks south to the entrance on Newark Street), to the **Royal London Hospital Archives** (⏲ weekdays 10–4:30), whose displays of medical paraphernalia, objects, and documentation illustrate the 250-year history of this East London institution. ✉ *Whitechapel Rd., East End E1,* ☎ *020/7377–7608.* WEB *www.rlhleagueofnurses.org.uk, www.bartsandthelondon.org.uk.* 🎟 *Free.* ⏲ *Hospital and garden daily 9–6. Tube: Whitechapel.*

9 **Spitalfields City Farm.** This is just what it sounds like—a sliver of rural England squashed between housing projects. It's one of about a dozen such places in London, which exist to educate city kids in country matters. A tiny farm shop sells freshly laid eggs and farm recipes. ✉ *Weaver St., off Pedley St., East End E1,* ☎ *020/7247–8762.* 🎟 *Free.* ⏲ *Tues.–Sun. 10:30–5. Tube: Shoreditch or Liverpool St.*

7 **Spitalfields Market.** There's been a market here since the mid-17th century, but the current version is overflowing with crafts and design shops and stalls, a sports hall, restaurants and bars (with a pan-world palette, from Spanish tapas to Thai), and different-purpose markets every day of the week. The nearer the weekend, the busier it all gets, culminating in the Sunday arts-and-crafts and green market—the best day to go. There's also a burgeoning events program with arts and concerts. ✉ *65 Brushfield St., East End E1,* ☎ *020/7377–1496.* 🎟 *Free.* ⏲ *Daily 10–7; market stalls weekdays 10–3, Sun. 9:30–5. Tube: Liverpool St.*

OFF THE BEATEN PATH

SUTTON HOUSE – Homerton (part of Hackney, east of London) hasn't much to recommend it, but Sutton House has survived the inroads of modern block estates. When it was built in 1535, it was surrounded by fields and a country village. Now run by the National Trust, the mansion was first owned by Ralph Sadleir, an important courtier to Henry VIII. The Tudor linen-fold paneling in the parlor is some of the finest in London and can only be seen elsewhere in Hampton Court; the carved stone fireplaces are also original. The painted stairwell with its wall friezes has been carefully preserved. The kitchen, which has fascinating cooking implements of the time, leads onto a cobbled Italianate courtyard—you could be a thousand miles from deepest Hackney. There's a café, a gift shop, and exhibitions—including a computer on which you can read a copy of a local Victorian child's diary. It's a special place that transports you light-years away from the thronging traffic and ugly apartment blocks just outside. ✉ *2 Homerton High St., East End E9,* ☎ *020/8986–2264,* 💷 *£2.10.* ⏲ *Wed., Sun, Bank Hol. Mon. 11:30–5:30.* WEB *www.nationaltrust.org.uk. Tube: Highbury and Islington, then Bus 377 or 30; Whitechapel, then Bus 106 or 253.*

15 **Trinity Almshouses.** This square row of cottages, with a chapel, around a grass lawn called Trinity Green, was built (possibly with Wren's help) in 1695 for "28 decayed Masters and Commanders of Ships or ye widows of such," bombed during World War II, and restored by the London County Council. Between the almshouses and the Stepney Green tube station is the well-concealed, oldest Jewish cemetery in Britain (known as the Velho, which means old) founded by the Sephardic community in 1657 after Cromwell allowed Jews to resettle in the country. (If you would like to view the cemetery, call the **Bevis Marks Spanish and Portuguese Synagogue,** ☎ 020/7289–2573, for an appointment.) ✉ *Mile End Rd., East End E1. Tube: Whitechapel or Stepney Green.*

1 **Whitechapel Art Gallery.** Housed in a spacious 1901 Art Nouveau building, this has an international reputation for its shows, which are often on the cutting edge of contemporary art. The American painter Jackson Pollock exhibited here in the 1950s, as did pop artist Robert Rauschenberg in the '60s, and David Hockney had his first solo show here in the '70s. Other exhibitions highlight the local community and culture, and there are programs of lectures, too. The Whitechapel Café serves remarkably inexpensive, home-cooked, whole-food hot meals, soups, and cakes. ✉ *Whitechapel High St., East End E1,* ☎ *020/7522–7888.* WEB *www.whitechapel.org.* 💷 *Free (fee for some exhibitions).* ⏲ *Tues. –Fri. 11–5 (Wed. 11–8), Sat.–Sun. 11–6. Tube: Aldgate East.*

2 **Whitechapel Bell Foundry.** It may be off the beaten track, but this working foundry was responsible for some of the world's better-known chimes. Before moving to this site in 1738, the foundry cast Westminster Abbey's bells (in the 1580s), but its biggest work, in every sense, was the 13-ton Big Ben, cast in 1858 by George Mears and requiring 16 horses to transport it from here to Westminster. The foundry's other important work was casting the original Liberty Bell (now in Philadelphia) in 1752, and both it and Big Ben can be seen in pictures, along with exhibits about bell making, in a little museum in the shop. Note: the actual foundry is off-limits, for health and safety reasons, but in the small front shop you can buy bell paraphernalia and browse through the historic photos. There are guided tours of the foundry on Saturday morning only, but bookings are usually made months in advance (call for information and fees). ✉ *34 Whitechapel Rd., East End E1,* ☎ *020/7247–2599.* ⏲ *Weekdays 8:30–5:30. Tube: Aldgate East.*

OFF THE BEATEN PATH

WILLIAM MORRIS GALLERY – An 18th-century house in northeast London where the artistic polymath William Morris (1834–96)—craftsman, painter, and writer—lived for eight years, this gallery contains many examples of his work and that of his fellow artisans in the Arts and Crafts movement. The shop sells Morris prints on stationery and other artsy gifts. ✉ *Water House, Lloyd Park, Forest Rd., East End,* ☎ *020/8527-3782,* WEB *www.lbwf.gov.uk/wmg.* ⏲ *Tues.–Sat. 10–1 and 2–5, 1st Sun. of month 10–1 and 2–5. Tube: Walthamstow Central, then 15-min walk down Hoe St., turn left at Forest Rd.*

THE SOUTH BANK

That old, snide North London quip about needing a passport to cross the Thames is no longer heard. For decades, natives never ventured beyond the watery curtain that divides the city in half; tourists, too, rarely troubled with the area unless they were departing from Waterloo Station. But lately, a host of attractions is drawing even the most ardent northerners across the great divide. The adjunct branch of the Tate Gallery, Tate Modern, is the star; a grim exterior—a functional 1930s power station—within which is a place for inspiration and creativity. At the South Bank Centre, the world's largest observation wheel, officially called the British Airways London Eye, gives you a 25-minute flight over the city. Even looked at from a great height, the South Bank—which occupies the riverside stretch between Waterloo Bridge and Hungerford Bridge—still isn't beautiful, but if it's culture you're hunting for, this complex of theaters and museums is fantastic. Today, developers and local authorities have expanded the South Bank's potential farther east with an explosion of attractions that are turning this once-neglected district into one of London's most happening neighborhoods. The 1980s brought renovations and innovations such as Gabriel's Wharf, London Bridge City, Hay's Galleria, and Butler's Wharf; the '90s arrived, and so did such headline-making sights as the spectacular reconstruction of Shakespeare's Globe—the most famous theater in the world—the OXO Tower, and the London Aquarium. The South Bank has since become a dazzling perch for culture vultures.

Actually, it is fitting that so much of London's artistic life should once again be centered here on the South Bank—back in the days of Ye Olde London Towne, **Southwark** was the city's oldest "suburb": though just across London Bridge, it was conveniently outside the City walls and laws and therefore the ideal location for the theaters, taverns, and cockfighting arenas that served as after-hours entertainment in the Middle Ages. The Globe Theatre, in which Shakespeare acted and held shares, was one of several established here after theaters were banished from the City in 1574 for encouraging truancy in young apprentices and for being generally rowdy. In truth, the Globe was as likely to stage a few bouts of bearbaiting as the latest interpretations of Shakespeare. Today, at the reconstructed "Wooden O," of course, you can just see the latter.

Numbers in the text correspond to numbers in the margin and on the South Bank map.

A Good Walk

Start scenically at the south end of Tower Bridge, finding the steps on the east (left) side, which descend to the start of a pedestrians-only street, Shad Thames. Now turn your back on the bridge and follow this quaint path between cliffs of the good-as-new warehouses, which are now **Butler's Wharf** ① but were once the seedy, dingy, dangerous shadow lands where Dickens killed off Bill Sikes in *Oliver Twist.* See the foodies' center, the Gastrodrome, and the **Design Museum** ②; then, just before you get back to Tower Bridge, turn away from the river (along Horsleydown Lane), follow Tooley Street, and take either the right turn at Morgan Lane to **HMS *Belfast*** ③ or continue to **Hay's Galleria** ④, with London Bridge and the **London Dungeon** ⑤ beyond. Next, turn left onto Joiner Street underneath the arches of London's first (1836) railway, then right onto St. Thomas Street, where you'll find the **Old Operating Theatre Museum** ⑥. **Southwark Cathedral** ⑦ is just across Borough High Street, past the organic Saturday Borough Market and past another of the South Bank's office developments, St. Mary Overy's Dock, down Cathedral Street. See the west wall, with a rose-window outline of Winchester House, the palace of the Bishops of Winchester until 1626, built into it, and take a tour of the little ***Golden Hinde*** ⑧ and the **Clink** ⑨ next door. Continue to the end of Clink Street onto Bankside, where Jubilee Bridge, built to celebrate the queen's 50 years of reign, offers the latest pedestrian access linking north and south banks of the river. Detouring left up Rose Alley, where in 1989 the remains of the famous Jacobean **Rose Theatre** were unearthed, you can view a compact exhibition which charts the latest finds in this continuing excavation. Just before you reach the place to imbibe culture, you come to **Vinopolis** ⑩, the world's first leisure complex celebrating wine. Then head to the next little alley, New Globe Walk, where there is much to see: the reconstruction of that most famous of Jacobean theaters, **Shakespeare's Globe Theatre** ⑪. Next along Bankside is the 17th-century Cardinal's Wharf, where, as a plaque explains, Wren lived while St. Paul's Cathedral was being built; then Bankside Power Station, now the **Tate Modern** ⑫ at Bankside and **Bankside Gallery** ⑬. Stretching from the Tate back across the river to the St. Paul's Cathedral steps in the City is the Millennium Bridge, a pedestrian bridge across the Thames.

Now you reach your sixth bridge on this walk, Blackfriars Bridge, which you pass beneath to join the street called Upper Ground, spending some time in the Coin Street Community Builders' fast-emerging neighborhood, where you'll find the **OXO Tower** ⑭ and Gabriel's Wharf, a marketplace of shops and cafés. Farther along Upper Ground, you reach the South Bank Centre, with the **Royal National Theatre** ⑮ first, followed by the National Film Theatre, the **Royal Festival Hall** ⑯, and the **Hayward Gallery** ⑰. The **BFI London IMAX Cinema** ⑱ sits just down Waterloo road behind the building complex. Carry on round the curve of the river, passing another restored footbridge, this time the Hungerford running parallel to the Charing Cross rail line, and you come to the magnificent **British Airways London Eye** ⑲. You'll find distractions all over this section of the walk, especially in summer—secondhand-book stalls, entertainers, and a series of plaques annotating the buildings opposite. When you've passed the South Bank Centre, look across the river for the quintessential postcard vista of the Houses of Parliament, which continues past Westminster Bridge to St. Thomas's Hospital. Next, you reach the former County Hall, which now houses the **London Aquarium** ⑳ and the surrealist museum **Dalí Universe** ㉑. Farther along the river, beyond the **Florence Nightingale Museum** ㉒, **Lambeth Palace** ㉓ stands by Lambeth Bridge, with the **Museum of Garden History** ㉔ in St. Mary's next door. If you take a detour to the right off Lambeth Road, you could be "doing the Lambeth Walk" down the street of the same name. A cockney tradition ever since the 17th century, when there was a spa here, the Sunday stroll was immortalized in a song from the 1937 musical *Me and My Girl*. A little farther east along Lambeth Road you reach the **Imperial War Museum** ㉕.

TIMING

On a fine day, this 2- to 3-mi walk makes a very scenic wander, since you're following the south bank of the great Thames nearly all the way. Fabulous views across to the north bank take you past St. Paul's and the Houses of Parliament, and you pass—under, over, or around—no fewer than 10 bridges, from the Tower to Lambeth. It's bound to take far longer than a couple of hours because there is so much to see. The BFI London IMAX Cinema, Tate Modern, the Imperial War Museum, Shakespeare's Globe, the Hayward Gallery, the Design Museum, and the London Aquarium could each take a good deal more than an hour (depending on your interests), while the London Dungeon doesn't take long, unless you have kids in tow—which is why you'd go in at all. The other museums on this route—the Clink, Rose Theatre, Dalí Universe, Garden History, Old Operating Theatre, Florence Nightingale, the South Bank Centre foyers, and the Bankside Gallery—are compact enough to squeeze together. You can finish this walk with a flourish by going to one of three theatres—the Lytleton, the Cottesloe, or the Olivier—at the National Theatre complex, to the National Film Theatre, or to Shakespeare's Globe, but remember that the theaters stay dark on Sundays. Dinner or a riverside drink at the OXO Tower Brasserie, the Gastrodrome restaurants, or the People's Palace is another idea for a big finish.

HOW TO GET THERE

The tube stop to use is London Bridge on the Jubilee or Northern line, though you could also start at Monument on the District and Circle lines and walk across London Bridge to the beginning of the walk. At the end of the walk you'll end up at Waterloo on the Northern and Bakerloo lines. You could also leave on the Embankment stop (same lines, plus District and Circle) or Charing Cross (the Jubilee and Northern lines) by walking across the Charing Cross pedestrian bridge. Buses that take you into the rather confusing territory behind the South Bank Centre include Buses 1, 68, 76, 168, 171, 176, 178, and 188. For farther downstream, near Shakespeare's Globe, get the 21, 35, 40, 47, or 133 to Tooley Street, or get the tube to Blackfriars and walk across that bridge (offering a particularly scenic walk) to the latest addition to the Jubilee Line, Southwark station, or to Mansion House and walk across Southwark Bridge. The latter is the best way to the OXO Tower.

Sights to See

13 **Bankside Gallery.** Two artistic societies—the Royal Society of Painter-Printmakers-Etchers and the Royal Watercolour Society—have their headquarters here. Together they mount exhibitions of current members' work, usually for sale, alongside artists' materials and books. ⊠ *48 Hopton St., The South Bank SE1,* ☎ *020/7928–7521.* 🎟 *£3.50.* ⏲ *Tues.–Fri. 10–5, Sat. –Sun. 11–5. Tube: Blackfriars or Southwark.*

18 **BFI London IMAX Cinema.** With the largest screen in London—the height of five doubledecker buses and a width that completely fills your eye—the IMAX Cinema guarantees an eyeful of technological and celluloid innovation. Choose from 2D or 3D films. Soon to be encompassed within the complex here (projected 2005): the re-invented Museum of the Moving Image, and the National Film Theatre. ⊠ *Waterloo Bridge at Stamford St., The South Bank SE1,* ☎ *020/7902–1234,* WEB *www.bfi.org.uk.* 🎟 *£6.40.* ⏲ *Sun.–Thurs. noon–8:45, Fri.–Sat. noon–10. Tube: Waterloo, Exit 5.*

19 **British Airways London Eye.** If you long to see London from a different perspective, this giant ride, the fourth highest structure in London, will give you the chance.. At 500 ft, the highest observation wheel in the world towers over the South Bank from the Jubilee Gardens next to County Hall. The fainthearted may want to pass up the 25-minute slow-motion hover over the city, although you'd hardly know you were moving at all. On a clear day you can take in a range of up to 25 mi, including some of the most famous sites—aerial views of

The South Bank

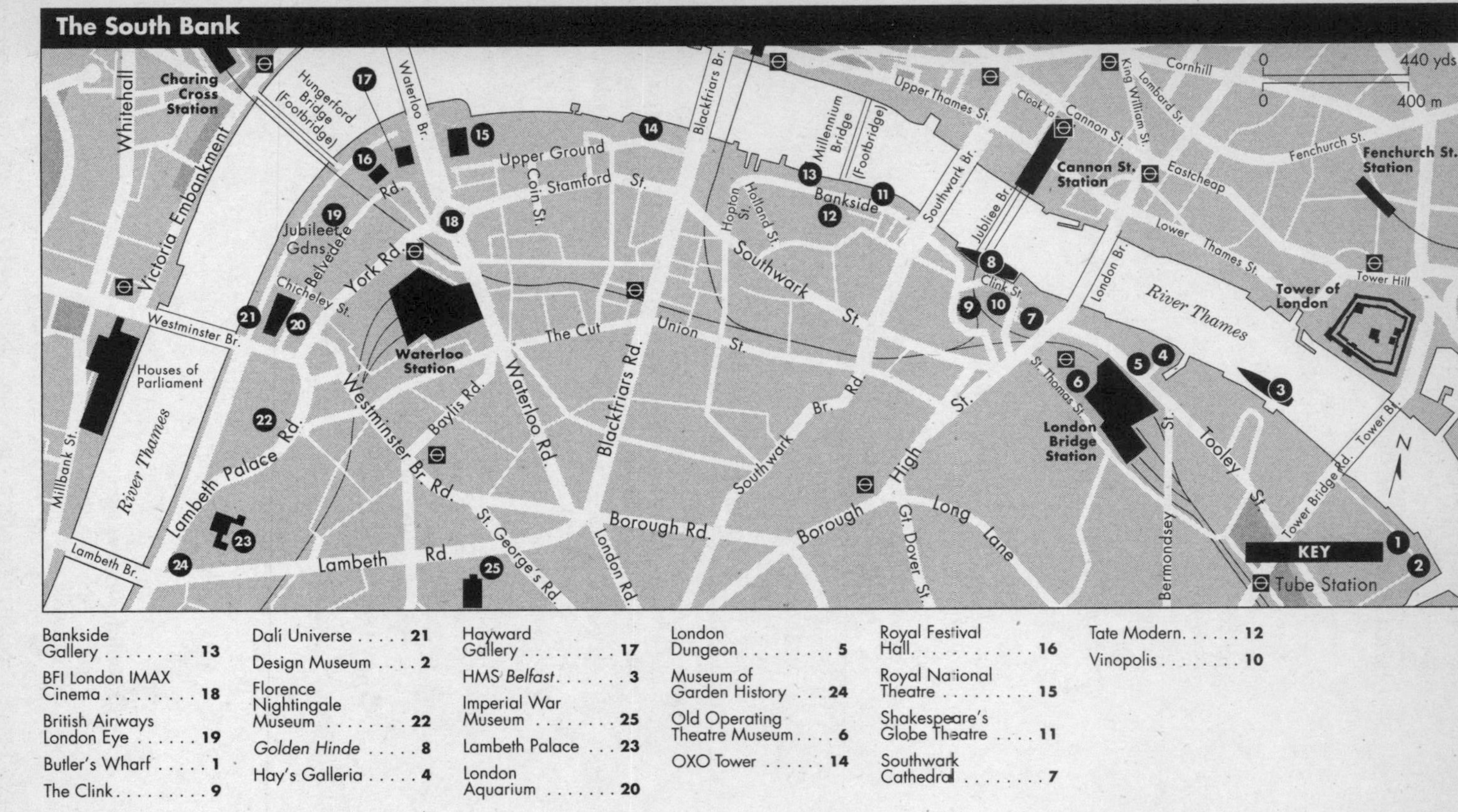

Bankside Gallery 13
BFI London IMAX Cinema 18
British Airways London Eye 19
Butler's Wharf 1
The Clink. 9
Dalí Universe 21
Design Museum 2
Florence Nightingale Museum 22
Golden Hinde 8
Hay's Galleria 4
Hayward Gallery 17
HMS *Belfast*. 3
Imperial War Museum 25
Lambeth Palace . . . 23
London Aquarium 20
London Dungeon 5
Museum of Garden History . . . 24
Old Operating Theatre Museum 6
OXO Tower 14
Royal Festival Hall. 16
Royal National Theatre 15
Shakespeare's Globe Theatre 11
Southwark Cathedral 7
Tate Modern. 12
Vinopolis 10

St. Paul's and Big Ben give London landmarks a fascinating new angle. ✉ *Jubilee Gardens, The South Bank SE1,* ☎ *0870/500–0600,* WEB *www.ba-londoneye.com.* 🎟 *£8.50.* ⏲ *Apr.–Oct., daily 9–sunset; Nov.–Mar., daily 10–6. Tube: Waterloo.*

1 **Butler's Wharf.** An '80s development that is maturing gracefully, this wharf is full of deluxe loft-style warehouse conversions and swanky buildings housing restaurants and galleries. People flock here thanks partly to London's saint of the stomach, Sir Terence Conran (also responsible for high-profile central London restaurants Bibendum, Mezzo, and Quaglino's). He has given it his "Gastrodrome" of four restaurants (including the fabulous Pont de la Tour), a vintner's, a deli, and a bakery. ✉ *The South Bank SE1. Tube: London Bridge or Tower Hill, then walk across river.*

9 **The Clink.** Giving rise to the term "clink," which still means jail, this institution was originally the prison attached to Winchester House, palace of the Bishops of Winchester until 1626. One of five Southwark prisons, it was the first to detain women, most of whom were called "Winchester geese"—another euphemism meaning prostitutes. The world's oldest profession was endemic in Southwark, especially around the bishops' area of jurisdiction, which was known as "the Liberty of the Clink." Their graces' sensible solution was to license prostitution rather than ban it, but a Winchester goose who flouted the rules ended up in the Clink. Now there is a museum tracing the history of prostitution in "the Liberty" and showing what the Clink was like during its 16th-century prime. ✉ *1 Clink St., The South Bank SE1,* ☎ *020/7403–6515,* WEB *www.clink.co.uk.* 🎟 *£4.* ⏲ *Daily 10–6 (last admission 5:30). Tube: London Bridge.*

21 **Dalí Universe.** This truly surrealist museum has the largest collection of Salvador Dalí's sculpture and a great many of his drawings, paintings, and lithographs. Dalí-inspired furniture is even on display. Neatly arranged into three areas, Sensuality and Femininity, Religion and Mythology, and Dreams and Fantasy, the museum reflects Dalí's eclectic work. Hitchcock fans will be mesmerized by the *Spellbound* painting made especially for the eponymous 1945 movie. ✉ *County Hall, Riverside Building, Westminster Bridge Rd., The South Bank SE1,* ☎ *020/7620–2720,* WEB *www.daliuniverse.com.* 🎟 *£8.50.* ⏲ *Daily 10–5:30. Tube: Waterloo or Westminster.*

2 **Design Museum.** This was the first museum in the world (it opened in 1989) to elevate everyday design and design classics to the status of art by placing them in their social and cultural context. On the top floor, the Collection traces the evolution of mass-produced goods, with display cases full of telephones and washing machines, plates and hi-fi equipment, computers and Coke bottles, and plenty of backup material, from ads to films. Alongside the Collection, the regularly revamped Review looks deeply into a particular aspect of the consumer durable. Special exhibitions are held downstairs on the first floor, and there's also a program of lectures and events, as well as the very good Blueprint Café, a funky restaurant with its own river terrace and superb views of London. ✉ *28 Shad Thames, The South Bank SE1,* ☎ *020/7403–6933, 020/7940–8790 recorded information,* WEB *www.designmuseum.org.* 🎟 *£5.50.* ⏲ *Daily 10–5:45 (last admission 5:15). Tube: London Bridge or Bermondsey.*

OFF THE BEATEN PATH

DULWICH PICTURE GALLERY – A highly distinguished small gallery, the Dulwich has impressive works by Rembrandt, Van Dyck, Rubens, Poussin, and Gainsborough, among others, with three critically acclaimed international loan exhibitions each year. Anyone who fell in love with Sir John Soane's house may wish to make the short overground train journey (12 minutes from London Bridge or Victoria) here, since this gallery was also designed by the visionary architect—it is also in sparkling form after a major face-lift. You'll also enjoy wandering around Dulwich Village, with its handsome 18th-century houses strung out along its main street. Most of the land around here belongs to the famous local school, the Dulwich College Estate, founded in the early 17th century by the actor Edward Alleyn, and this keeps strict control of modern development. Opposite the gallery, Dulwich Park is a well-kept municipal park with a particularly fine display of rhododendrons in late May. ✉ *College Rd., The South Bank,* ☎ *020/8693–5254.* WEB *www.dulwichpicturegallery.org.uk.* 🎫 *£4; free on Fri.* ⏲ *Tues.–Fri. 10–5, weekends 11–5. British Rail: West Dulwich (from Victoria) or North Dulwich (from London Bridge).*

---

22 **Florence Nightingale Museum.** Here you can learn all about the founder of the first school of nursing, that most famous of health-care reformers, "the Lady with the Lamp." See the reconstruction of the barracks ward at Scutari, Turkey, where she tended soldiers during the Crimean War (1854–56) and earned her nickname. Here you also find a Victorian East End slum cottage showing what she did to improve living conditions among the poor—and the famous lamp. The museum is in **St. Thomas's Hospital,** which was built in 1868 to the specifications of Florence Nightingale. Most of it was bombed to bits in the Blitz, then rebuilt to become one of London's teaching hospitals. ✉ *2 Lambeth Palace Rd., The South Bank SE1,* ☎ *020/7620–0374,* WEB *www.florence-nightingale.co.uk.* 🎫 *£4.80.* ⏲ *Mon.–Fri. 10–5 (last admission 4), Sat.–Sun. 11:30–4:30 (last admission 3:30). Tube: Waterloo or Westminster, then walk over bridge.*

8 ***Golden Hinde.*** Sir Francis Drake circumnavigated the globe in this little galleon, or one just like it. This exact replica made a 23-year round-the-world voyage—much of it spent along U.S. coasts, both Pacific and Atlantic—and has settled here to continue its educational purpose. If you want information along with your visit, book a tour in advance. ✉ *St. Mary Overie Dock, Cathedral St., The South Bank SE1,* ☎ *020/7403–0123,* WEB *www.goldenhinde.co.uk.* 🎫 *£2.50.* ⏲ *Daily 9:30–5:30. Tube: London Bridge or Mansion House.*

4 **Hay's Galleria.** Hay's Wharf was built by Thomas Cubitt in 1857 on the spot where the port of London's oldest wharf had stood since 1651. It was once known as "London's larder" on account of the quantity of edibles that landed here. It then wound down gradually and closed in 1970. In 1987 it was reborn as this Covent Garden–like parade of bars and restaurants, offices, shops and craft stalls, all weatherproofed by an arched glass atrium roof supported by tall iron columns. The centerpiece is a fanciful kinetic sculpture by David Kemp, *The Navigators,* which looks like the skeleton of a pirate schooner crossed with a dragon and spouts water from various orifices. Needless to say, jugglers, string quartets, and crafts stalls abound. This courtyard hub of the developing London Bridge City needed all the help it could get in its early days, but it has settled in nicely now with its captive crowd of office workers from the adjacent developments. ✉ *2 Battle Bridge La., The South Bank SE1,* ☎ *020/7940–7770,* WEB *www.haysgalleria.co.uk. Tube: London Bridge.*

17 **Hayward Gallery.** This is one of the city's major art-exhibition spaces, its bias fixed firmly in the 20th century. The stained and windowless bunker tucked behind the South Bank Centre concert halls has been the brunt of most of the criticism of Thames-side buildings, enduring con-

stant threats to flatten it and start again. But it's still here, topped by its multicolor neon tube sculpture, the most familiar landmark on the South Bank skyline. ✉ *South Bank Complex, The South Bank SE1,* ☎ *020/7928–3144,* WEB *www.hayward-gallery.co.uk.* 🎟 *Admission varies according to exhibition.* ⏲ *Thurs.–Mon. 10–6, Tues.–Wed. 10–8. Tube: Waterloo.*

3 **HMS *Belfast*.** At 656 ft, this is one of the largest and most powerful cruisers the Royal Navy has ever had. It played an important role in the D-Day landings off Normandy, left for the Far East after the war, and has been becalmed here since 1971. On board there's an outpost of the **Imperial War Museum,** which tells the Royal Navy's story from 1914 to the present and shows you what life on a World War II battleship was like, from mess decks and bakery to punishment cells and from operations room to engine room and armaments. ✉ *Morgan's La., Tooley St., The South Bank SE1,* ☎ *020/7940–6300,* WEB *www.hmsbelfast.org.uk.* 🎟 *£5.40.* ⏲ *Mid-Mar.–Oct., daily 10–6; Nov.–mid-Mar., daily 10–5 (last admission 45 mins before closing). Tube: London Bridge.*

OFF THE BEATEN PATH

HORNIMAN MUSEUM – This educational museum of anthropology, which also manages to be fun, is set in 16 acres of gardens in South London with well-displayed ethnographic and natural history collections. Recent additions include an aquarium stocked with endangered species and the African Worlds section. Extended gallery space has been built to include galleries for world cultures and temporary exhibitions; the Centre for Understanding, with hands-on displays for younger visitors; and a café and shop. ✉ *100 London Rd., Forest Hill,* ☎ *020/8699–1872,* WEB *www.horniman.ac.uk.* 🎟 *Free.* ⏲ *Mon.–Sat. 10:30–5:30, Sun. 2–5:30. British Rail: Forest Hill (from London Bridge or Victoria).*

25 **Imperial War Museum.** Despite its title, this museum of 20th-century warfare does not glorify bloodshed but attempts to evoke what it was like to live through the two world wars. Of course, there is hardware and interactive material for martial-minded children—a Battle of Britain Spitfire, a German V2 rocket, tanks, guns, submarines—but there is an equal amount of war art (David Bomberg, Henry Moore, John Singer Sargent, Graham Sutherland, to name a few), poetry, photography, and documentary film footage. One very affecting exhibit is *The Blitz Experience,* which is just what it sounds like—a 10-minute taste of an air raid in a street of acrid smoke with sirens blaring and searchlights glaring. There is also a permanent Holocaust exhibition, funded from a generous lottery grant. More recent wars attended by British forces are thoughtfully commemorated, too, right up to the Gulf War.

The museum is housed in an elegant domed and colonnaded building, erected in the early 19th century to house the Bethlehem Hospital for the Insane, better known as the infamous Bedlam. By 1816, when the patients were moved here, they were no longer kept in cages to be taunted by tourists (see the final scene of Hogarth's *Rake's Progress* at Sir John Soane's Museum for some sense of how horrific it was), since reformers—and George III's madness—had effected more humane standards of confinement. Bedlam moved to Surrey in 1930. ✉ *Lambeth Rd., The South Bank SE1,* ☎ *020/7416–5320,* WEB *www.iwm.org.uk.* 🎟 *Free.* ⏲ *Daily 10–6. Tube: Lambeth North.*

23 **Lambeth Palace.** For 800 years, this has been the London base of the Archbishop of Canterbury, head of the Church of England. Much of the palace is hidden behind great walls, and even the Tudor gatehouse, visible from the street, is closed to the public, but you can stand here

and absorb the historical vibrations echoing from momentous events. These include the 1381 storming of the palace during the Peasants' Revolt against the poll tax and the 1534 clash of wills when Thomas More refused to sign the Oath of Supremacy claiming Henry VIII (and not the pope) as leader of the English Church, for which he was sent to the Tower and executed for treason the following year. Adjacent to this house is the Museum of Garden History. ✉ *Lambeth Palace Rd., The South Bank SE1,* WEB *www.archbishopofcanterbury.org. Tube: Waterloo.*

20 **London Aquarium.** County Hall was the original name of this curved, colonnaded Neoclassic hulk, which, with the interference of two world wars, took 46 years (1912–58) to build. It once housed London's local government, the Greater London Council (GLC), which mutated out of the London County Council in 1965 and disbanded in 1986. After a £25 million injection, a three-level aquarium (full of sharks and stingrays) was installed. There are also educational exhibits and piscine sights previously unseen on these shores. It is not the biggest aquarium you've ever seen—especially if you've been to SeaWorld—but the exhibit is well arranged on several subterranean levels, with areas for different oceans, water environments, and climate zones, including a stunning coral reef, and the highlight: the rain forest, which is almost like the real thing. ✉ *County Hall, Riverside Building, Westminster Bridge Rd., The South Bank SE1,* ☎ *020/7967–8000,* WEB *www.londonaquarium.co.uk.* *£8.75.* *Daily 10–6 (last admission 5). Tube: Westminster or Waterloo.*

5 **London Dungeon.** Here's the goriest, grisliest, gruesomest museum in town, where realistic waxwork people are subjected in graphic detail to all the historical horrors the Tower of London merely tells you about. Tableaux depict famous bloody moments—like Anne Boleyn's decapitation or the martyrdom of St. George—alongside the torture, murder, and ritual slaughter of lesser-known victims, all to a soundtrack of screaming, wailing, and agonized moaning. London's times of deepest terror—the Great Fire and the Great Plague—are brought to life, too, and so are its public hangings. And did you ever wonder what a disembowelment actually looks like? See it here. Naturally, children absolutely adore this place, but be warned—nervous kiddies may find it too truly frightening. Expect long lines. ✉ *28–34 Tooley St., The South Bank SE1,* ☎ *020/7403–7221.* WEB *www.thedungeons.com.* *£10.95.* *1 Apr.–14 Jul., daily 10–5:30; 15 Jul.–3 Sept. 10–8; 4 Sept.–Mar., daily 10–5. Tube: London Bridge.*

24 **Museum of Garden History.** Housed in St. Mary's Church, next to Lambeth Palace, this museum was founded in 1977 (when the church was deconsecrated) by the Tradescant Trust. The trust is named after John Tradescant (circa 1575–1638), botanist extraordinaire, who brought to these shores the lilac, larch, and jasmine, and a spiderwort named *Tradescantia* in his honor. In the nave are changing horticultural exhibitions, supplemented by a reconstructed—or regrown—17th-century knot garden. Tradescant's tomb in the graveyard is carved with scenes from his worldwide plant-discovery tours and surrounded with the plants he discovered. William Bligh, captain of the *Bounty,* is buried nearby—appropriately enough, as the *Bounty* was on a breadfruit-gathering mission when the crew mutinied in 1787. ✉ *Lambeth Palace Rd., The South Bank SE1,* ☎ *020/7401–8865,* WEB *www.museumgardenhistory.org.* *Suggested donation £2.50.* *Feb.–mid Dec. Daily 10:30–5. Tube: Waterloo.*

National Film Theatre (NFT). The National Film Theatre is in the process of renovation, although programs will continue throughout the work. The NFT has easily the best repertory programming in London, favoring obscure, foreign, silent, forgotten, classic, noir, and short films over blockbusters. For details on **British Film Institute** activities, you can phone the events line at ☏ 087/0240–4050. ✉ *South Bank Centre, The South Bank SE1,* ☏ *020/7401–2636,* WEB *www.bfi.org.uk. Tube: Waterloo.*

NEED A BREAK?

There are many options along the South Bank for a quick bite or a fancy meal. **OXO Tower Brasserie** (✉ OXO Tower Wharf, Bargehouse St., The South Bank SE1, ☏ 020/7803–3888) is the more low-key and slightly cheaper half of the famous OXO Tower restaurant. Besides a menu of tasty Asian-inspired morsels, it offers floor-to-ceiling windows with an unbeatable vista of the Thames and its north bank dotted with famous sites like Big Ben, St. Paul's Cathedral, and Westminster Abbey. If OXO Tower is too crowded or too expensive, try the street-level and far more proletariat **People's Palace** (✉ Royal Festival Hall, South Bank Centre, The South Bank SE1, ☏ 020/7928–9999).

6 **Old Operating Theatre Museum.** All that remains of one of England's oldest hospitals, which stood here from the 12th century until the railway forced it to move in 1862, is the room where women went under the knife. The theater was bricked up and forgotten for a century but has now been restored into an exhibition of early 19th-century medical practices: the operating table onto which the gagged and blindfolded patients were roped; the box of sawdust underneath for catching their blood; the knives, pliers, and handsaws the surgeons wielded; and—this was a theater in the round—the spectators' seats. Next door is a sweeter show: the **Herb Garret,** with displays of medicinal herbs used during the same period. ✉ *9A St. Thomas St., The South Bank SE1,* ☏ *020/7955–4791,* WEB *www.thegarret.org.uk.* 🎫 *£3.75.* ⏲ *Daily 10:30–5:30. Tube: London Bridge.*

14 **OXO Tower.** This might very well turn out to be the 21st-century version of Big Ben—a wonderfully renovated Art Deco–era tower, filled with designers' workshops overlooking the Thames. Long a London landmark to the cognoscenti, the OXO has graduated from its former incarnations as a power-generating station and warehouse into a vibrant community of artists' and designers' workshops, a pair of restaurants and cafés, as well as five floors of the best low-income housing in the city, via a £20 million plan by Coin Street Community Builders. There's a rooftop viewing gallery (a balcony for observation) for a super river vista (St. Paul's to the east, and Somerset House to the west), and a performance area on the first floor, which comes alive all summer long—as does the entire surrounding neighborhood. All the designers and artisans have been selected by totally nondemocratic methods, meaning the work is of incredibly high standard. They all rely on you to disturb them whenever they're open. Don't be shy—they really mean it; you will be most welcome, whether buying, commissioning, or just browsing. The biggest draw remains the OXO Tower Restaurant extravaganza for a meal or a martini. ✉ *Bargehouse St., The South Bank SE1,* ☏ *020/7401–3610.* 🎫 *Free.* ⏲ *Studios and shops Tues.–Sun. 11–6. Tube: Blackfriars or Waterloo.*

Rose Theatre. If you are thrilled by the reconstruction of Shakespeare's Globe, then you'll be fascinated by an even earlier model of which much of the original is still in existence. Built in 1587, this theater preceded its near neighbor, the Globe, which opened in 1599. It did not have as illustrious a history as the Globe, and was soon closed in 1606. The ancient diaries of celebrated Elizabethan actor Edward Alleyn (who went on to establish Dulwich College) explain much of how the theater looked, the costumes, and the plays performed at the Rose, and as a result more is known about this small theater than about the Globe. The original foundations were uncovered in 1989 but put back under wraps until just recently. As the exhibition, which opened 10 years later, shows, there is much more to be found to this fascinating little theater. English Heritage has added its weight to a big dig adjacent to the exhibition site, which has revealed the theater's Tudor timbers; further archaeological treasures could soon be on show—watch this space. ✉ *56 Park St., The South Bank SE1,* ☎ *020/7593–0026,* WEB *www.rosetheatre.org.uk.* *£4; joint ticket available with entrance to Shakespeare's Globe Theatre museum.* *Apr.–Sept. daily 11–5. Tube: Southwark; or Blackfriars, then walk across Blackfriars Bridge.*

16 **Royal Festival Hall.** This is the largest auditorium of the South Bank Centre, with superb acoustics and a 3,000-plus capacity. It is the oldest of the riverside blocks, raised as the centerpiece of the 1951 Festival of Britain, a postwar morale-boosting exercise. The London Philharmonic resides here; symphony orchestras from the world over like to visit; and choral works, ballet, serious jazz and pop, and even films with live accompaniment are staged. Also featured are a multiplicity of foyers with free rotating exhibitions; a good, independently run restaurant, the People's Palace; free jazz in the main foyer on Sunday, and a very fine bookstore. The next building you come to also contains concert halls, one medium and one small, the **Queen Elizabeth Hall** and the **Purcell Room,** respectively. Both offer predominantly classical recitals of international caliber, with due respect paid to 20th-century composers and the more established jazz and vocal artists. ✉ *South Bank Centre, The South Bank SE1,* ☎ *020/7960–4242,* WEB *www.rfh.org.uk. Tube: Waterloo.*

15 **Royal National Theatre.** When it opened in 1976, Londoners generally felt the same way about this low-slung, multilayered block the color of heavy storm clouds and designed by Sir Denys Lasdun that they would feel a decade later about the far nastier Barbican Centre. But whatever its merits or demerits as a landscape feature (and architects have subsequently given it an overall thumbs-up, rejecting the derogatory-sounding term "brutalist"), the Royal National Theatre—still abbreviated colloquially to the pre–royal warrant "NT"—has wonderful insides.

Three auditoriums occupy the complex. The biggest one, the **Olivier,** is named after Sir Laurence, chairman of the first building commission and first artistic director of the National Theatre Company, formed in 1962. (In between the first proposal of a national theater for Britain and the 1949 formation of that building commission, an entire century had passed.) The **Lyttelton** theater has a traditional proscenium arch, while the little **Cottesloe** mounts studio productions and new work in the round. Interspersed with the theaters is a multilayered foyer with exhibitions, bars, and restaurants, and free entertainment. The whole place is lively six days a week. The Royal National Theatre Company does not rest on its laurels: it attracts many of the nation's top actors (Anthony Hopkins, for one, does time here) in addition to launching future stars. Because it is a repertory company, you'll have several plays from which to choose even if your London sojourn is short, but, tickets or not, wander around and catch the buzz. ✉ *South Bank, The South Bank SE1,* ☎ *020/7452–3000 box office,* WEB *www.nt-online.org.* *Tour £3.50.* *1-hr tour of theater backstage Mon.–Sat. at 10:15, 12:30, and 5:30; foyer Mon.–Sat. 10 AM–11 PM. Tube: Waterloo.*

★ 11 **Shakespeare's Globe Theatre.** Three decades ago, Sam Wanamaker—then an aspiring actor—pulled up in Southwark in a cab and was amazed to find that the fabled Shakespeare's Globe Playhouse didn't actually exist. Worse, a tiny plaque was the only sign on the former site of the world's most legendary theater. So appalled was he that London lacked a center for the study and worship of the Bard of Bards, Wanamaker worked ceaselessly, until his death, to raise funds for his dream—a full-scale reconstruction of the theater. The dream was realized when an exact replica of Shakespeare's open-roof Globe Playhouse (built in 1599; incinerated in 1613) was created, using authentic Elizabethan materials and craft techniques—green oak timbers joined only with wooden pegs and mortise and tenon joints; plaster made of lime, sand, and goat's hair; and the first thatched roof in London since the Great Fire. In addition, a second, indoor theater has been added, built to a design of the 17th-century architect Inigo Jones. The whole complex stands 200 yards from the original Globe on the appropriate site of the 17th-century Davies Amphitheatre, admittedly more a bull-baiting, prizefighting sort of venue than a temple to the legitimate stage, but at least Samuel Pepys immortalized it in his diaries.

The Globe is a celebration of the great Bard's life (1564–1616) and work, an actual rebirth of his "wooden O" (see *Henry V*), where his plays are presented in natural light (and sometimes rain) to 1,000 people on wooden benches in the "bays," plus 500 "groundlings," who stand on a carpet of filbert shells and clinker, just as they did nearly four centuries ago. For any theater buff, this stunning project is unmissable. Although the open-air Globe Theatre offers performances only during the summer season (generally mid-May to mid-September), it can be viewed year-round if you take the helpful tour offered by the **Shakespeare's Globe Exhibition Centre,** an adjacent museum that provides fascinating background material on both the Elizabethan theater and the actual construction of the modern-day Globe. The **New Shakespeare's Globe Exhibition** is touted as the largest ever to focus on Shakespeare, his work, and his contemporaries; this "all-singing, all-dancing" exhibition is housed in the Underglobe, beneath the Globe site. ✉ *New Globe Walk, Bankside, The South Bank SE1,* ☎ *020/7902–1500; 020/7401–9919 box office; 020/7902–1500 New Shakespeare's Globe Exhibition,* FAX *020/7401–8261,* WEB *www.shakespeares-globe.org.* 🎫 *£7; joint ticket available to Rose Theatre exhibition (see above).* ⏲ *Museum daily 9–4, plays May–Sept. (call for performance schedule). Tube: Southwark, then walk to Blackfriars bridge and descend the steps; Mansion House, then walk across Southwark Bridge; or Blackfriars, then walk across Blackfriars Bridge.*

7 **Southwark Cathedral.** Pronounced "Suth-uck," this is the second-oldest Gothic church in London, after Westminster Abbey, with parts dating back to the 12th century. Although it houses some remarkable memorials, not to mention a program of lunchtime concerts, it is seldom visited. It was promoted to cathedral status only in 1905; before that it was the priory church of St. Mary Overy (as in "over the water"—on the South Bank). Look for the gaudily renovated 1408 tomb of the poet John Gower, friend of Chaucer, and for the Harvard Chapel. Another notable buried here is Edmund Shakespeare, brother of William. ✉ *Montague Close, The South Bank SE1,* ☎ *020/7367–6700,* WEB *www.dswark.org.* 🎫 *Free.* ⏲ *Daily 8–6. Tube: London Bridge.*

12 **Tate Modern.** This much-anticipated offspring of the Tate Gallery opened in May 2000 resides in the Bankside Power Station. Shuttered for decades, the station has glowered magnificently on its Thames-side site ever since it was built in the 1930s. Now it has been renovated by Swiss architects Herzog & de Meuron to make a dazzling venue for some of the Tate's overflowing treasures. For decades, the old Millbank Gallery of the Tate Britain had been so overstuffed the curators had to resort to a revolving menu of paintings and sculpture. The power station (designed by the same man who created the famous red tele-

phone box) and its 8½-acre site now house the surplus, running from classic works by Matisse, Picasso, Dalí, Moore, Bacon, and Warhol to the most-talked-about British artists of today. ✉ *25 Summer St., The South Bank SE1,* ☎ *020/7887–8000,* WEB *www.tate.org.uk.* 💰 *Free.* ⏲ *Sun.–Thurs. 10–6, Fri.–Sat 10–10. Tube: Blackfriars or Southwark.*

10 **Vinopolis.** The Brits are perhaps not the first nation you would expect to erect a monument to wine, but here it is—Vinopolis, City of Wine. Spread over 2 acres between the Globe Theatre and London Bridge, its arched vaults promise multimedia tours of the world's wine cultures, tastings, retail shops, an art gallery, restaurants, and a wine school. You can learn about wine production and history, and then have a chance to put your newfound knowledge to the test in the Tasting Halls. The four restaurants claim to offer more wines by the glass than anywhere else in the city, and you can, of course, buy from an enormous selection of world vintages, many of them available for delivery. Keep in mind that the last entry is two hours before the scheduled closing time. ✉ *1 Bank End St., The South Bank,* ☎ *087/0444–4777,* WEB *www.vinopolis.co.uk.* 💰 *£11.50 (£10.50 when booked in advance).* ⏲ *Mon. 11–9, Tues.–Fri. 11–6, Sat. 11–8, Sun. 11–6. Tube: London Bridge.*

CHELSEA AND BELGRAVIA

Chelsea is where J. M. W. Turner painted his sunsets and John Singer Sargent his society portraits, where Oscar Wilde wrote *The Importance of Being Earnest,* and where Mary Quant cut her first miniskirt. Today, Chelsea is a neighborhood as handsome as its real estate is costly. Strolling its streets, you will often notice gigantic windows adorning otherwise ordinary houses. They are remnants of Chelsea's 19th-century bohemian days, when they served to bring light into artists' studios; now they are mostly used to hike property values a few notches higher. This is the place—the King's Road in particular—that gave birth to Swinging '60s London, then to '70s punk youth culture. The millennial version of this colorful thoroughfare is not really the center of anything, but it's hard not to like wandering down it.

Chelsea's next-door neighborhood is aristocratic Belgravia, with the King's Road and Knightsbridge as its respective southern and northern borders, Sloane Street and Grosvenor Place its western and eastern ones, and vast Belgrave Square—where many embassies are located—in the middle. Diagonally across the square, Belgrave Place will lead past grand mansions (all painted Wedgwood-white to denote that they, like every other house in this district, are the property of England's richest landowners, the Dukes of Westminster) through to Eaton Square, the aptly chosen locale for the TV series *Upstairs, Downstairs.* It is no accident that this whole neighborhood of wealth and splendor is grouped around the back of Buckingham Palace—many titled peers wished to live adjacent to the Court. Belgravia is relatively young: it was built between the 1820s and the 1850s by the builder-developer-entrepreneur Thomas Cubitt (who had as great an influence on the look of London in his day as Wren and Nash had in theirs), under the patronage of Lord Grosvenor, and was intended to rival Mayfair for spectacular snob value and expense. Today it still does.

Numbers in the text correspond to numbers in the margin and on the Chelsea and Belgravia map.

A Good Walk

Start at **Cheyne Walk** ①, stretching in both directions from Albert Bridge, going all the way west to see the statue of Thomas More, then doubling back for a left turn into Cheyne Row to reach **Carlyle's**

House ②. Where the east end of Cheyne Walk runs into Royal Hospital Road, you'll find the **Chelsea Physic Garden** ③, while a right after the garden on Royal Hospital Road brings you to the **National Army Museum** ④. Royal Hospital Road takes its name from the institution next door to the museum, the magnificent **Royal Hospital** ⑤. A left turn from here up Franklin's Row and Cheltenham Terrace brings you to famous **King's Road** ⑥, which you could follow east until you reach the beginning of Belgravia: Sloane Square, named after Sir Hans Sloane, whose collection founded the British Museum and who bought the manor of Chelsea in 1712. Cross the square more or less in a straight line, and follow Cliveden Place for a taste of Belgravia. The grand, white-stucco houses have changed not at all since the mid-19th century, and Eaton Square, which you'll soon come upon, remains such a desirable address that the rare event of one of its houses' coming on the market makes all the property pages. Its most famous residents were fictional, of course, as the enduringly popular period soap *Upstairs, Downstairs* was set here. A left turn on **Belgrave Place** ⑦ brings you to Belgrave Square, dense with embassies, but the best thing to do around here is follow your nose. Other than Palladian-perfect mansions, chic alleys, and magnificent Georgian squares—in addition to Belgrave and Eaton, the smaller Lowndes, Cadogan, Trevor, Brompton, and Montpelier—there are no particular Belgravia sights. After taking in Belgrave Place and the picturesque mews next to Eaton Place, however, you might continue eastward on Belgrave Place, walk south several blocks on Eaton Place, and head for the lovely warren of streets and alleys around Chester Row and Minerva Mews.

TIMING

This may read like a short hop, but the walk above covers a good 2 to 3 mi. If you explore side streets, you could double the figure—and exploring these streets is the best aspect of these neighborhoods, which are primarily residential and expensive. The houses along the way will detain you, and the shops will for longer; even though King's Road isn't what it used to be, it's still fruitful. In summer you'll want to spend time in the Physic Garden or around the Royal Hospital, so make sure you're heading out on one of the opening days. If you're dead set on the Physic Garden, that means Wednesday or Sunday afternoon from April to October.

HOW TO GET THERE

Chelsea is notoriously ill-served by tube stops. To start the walk at Cheyne Walk, take the tube to Earl's Court on the District Line then take Bus 328 on Earl's Court Road to its terminus at World's End on King's Road. From there walk away from the bus on King's Road and take a right on Glebe Place to reach Cheyne Row and Carlyle's House. Alternatively, if you're more interested in shopping than sightseeing you can take the District and Circle lines to Sloane Square, then strike out by foot along King's Road. Or catch a bus (11, 19, 22, 137, or 211). Farther down toward the river, around World's End and Fulham, the 19, 49, 319, and 345 are the buses to look for. The edge of Belgravia farthest from Chelsea is accessible from Hyde Park Corner on the Piccadilly Line. Buses 2, 8, 9, 10, 14, 16, 19, 22, 36, 38, 52, 73, 74, 82, and 137 also stop there. Choose a bus that appears on both lists for travel between the two neighborhoods.

Sights to See

❼ **Belgrave Place.** One of the main arteries of Belgravia—London's swankiest neighborhood—Belgrave Place is lined with grand, imposing Regency-era mansions (now mostly embassies). Walk down this street toward Eaton Place to pass two of Belgravia's most beautiful mews—

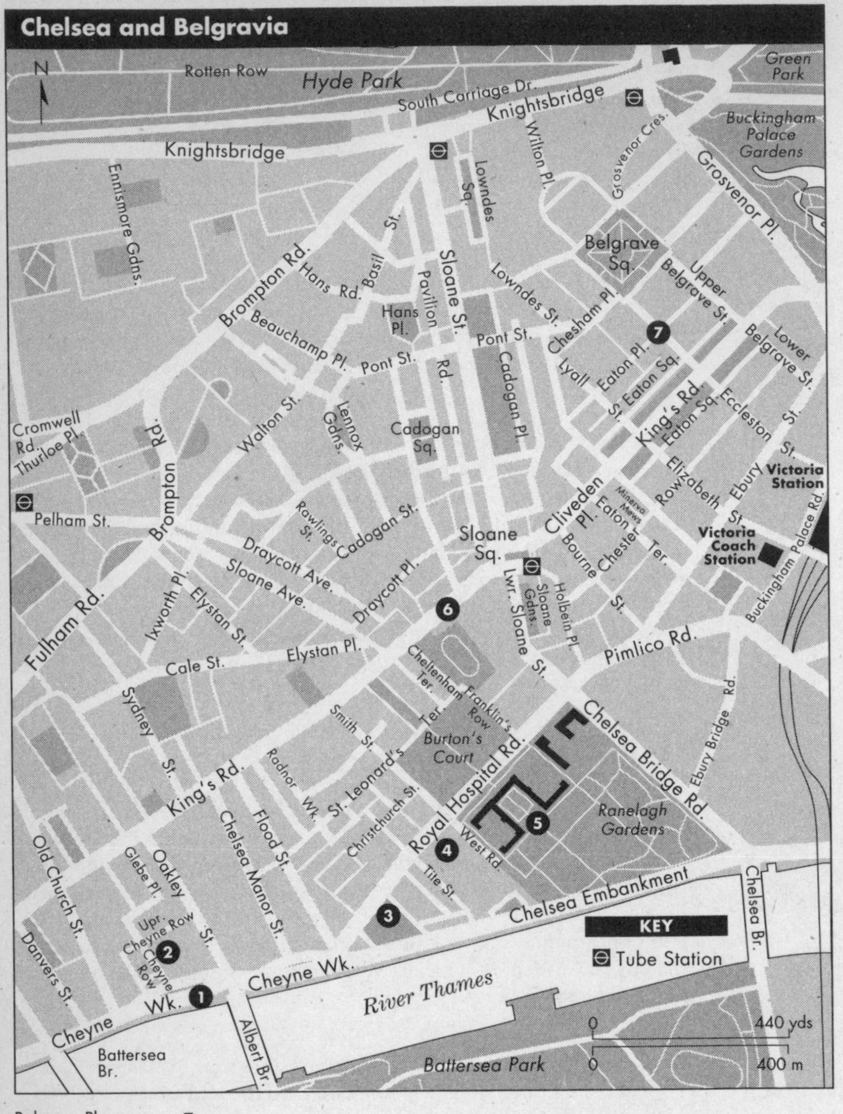

- Belgrave Place **7**
- Carlyle's House **2**
- Chelsea Physic Garden **3**
- Cheyne Walk. **1**
- King's Road **6**
- National Army Museum **4**
- Royal Hospital **5**

Eaton Mews North and Eccleston Mews, both fronted by grand Westminster-white rusticated entrances right out of a 19th-century engraving: there are few other places where London is both so picturesque and elegant.

❷ **Carlyle's House.** This house hosted a thriving salon of 19th-century authors, attracted by the fame of Thomas Carlyle (1795–1881)—author of a blockbuster history of the French Revolution that is now almost forgotten and the amusing *Sartor Resartus* and by the wit of his wife, the poet Jane Carlyle. Dickens, Thackeray, Tennyson, and Browning were regular visitors, and you can see the second-floor drawing room where they met just as they saw it, complete with leather armchair, decoupage screen, fireplace, and oil lamps, all in ruddy Victorian hues. ✉ *24 Cheyne Row, Chelsea SW3,* ☎ *020/7352–7087 or 014/9475–5559.* 🎫 *£3.30.* ⏲ *Apr.–Oct., Wed.–Sun. 11–4:30. Tube: Sloane Sq., then walk down King's Rd. or take Bus 11, 19, 22, 49, 219, or 249.*

❸ **Chelsea Physic Garden.** First planted by the Society of Apothecaries in 1673 for the study of medicinal plants, these gardens are still in use for the same purpose today. The herbs and shrubs and flowers, planted to a strict plan but tumbling over the paths nevertheless, are interspersed with woodland areas, England's first rock garden, and ancient trees, some of which were tragically uprooted in a 1987 storm. In the middle stands a statue of Sir Hans Sloane, physician to Queen Anne and George II, whose collection formed the basis of the British Museum and who saved the garden from closing in 1722, making sure nobody would ever be allowed to build over it. ✉ *Swan Walk, 66 Royal Hospital Rd., Chelsea SW3,* ☎ *020/7352–5646,* WEB *www.cpgarden.demon.co.uk.* 🎫 *£4.* ⏲ *Apr.–Oct., Wed. noon–5 and Sun. 2–6; daily noon–5 during Chelsea Flower Show (3rd wk of May). Tube: Sloane Sq., then walk down King's Rd., or take Bus 11, 19, 22, 319, 211 or 239 (get off at Chelsea Old Town Hall).*

★ ❶ **Cheyne Walk.** Its name rhymes with "rainy." Expect to find some beautiful Queen Anne houses (particularly Norman Shaw's ornamental 1876 Cheyne House, to the right off Albert Bridge) and a storm of blue plaques marking famous ex-residents' homes. George Eliot died at No. 4 in 1880; Dante Gabriel Rossetti annoyed the neighbors of No. 16 with his peacock collection (there's still a clause in the lease banning the birds); Henry James died at Carlyle Mansions (after the King's Head and Eight Bells pub), and later residents were T. S. Eliot and Ian Fleming. The western reaches were painters' territory, most notably of James McNeill Whistler, who lived at No. 96 and then No. 101, and J. M. W. Turner, who used No. 119 as a retreat, shielding his identity behind the name Adm. "Puggy" Booth. Also toward the western end, outside the Church of All Saints, is a golden-faced statue of **Thomas More** (who wouldn't sign the Oath of Supremacy at Lambeth Palace in 1534 and was executed as a traitor), looking pensive and beatific on a throne facing the river, a 1969 addition to the Walk.

❻ **King's Road.** This was where the miniskirt first strutted its stuff in the '60s and where Vivienne Westwood and Malcolm McLaren clothed the Sex Pistols in bondage trousers from their shop, "Sex," in 1975, thus spawning punk rock. Westwood, one of Britain's most innovative fashion stars, still runs her shop at No. 430, where the road, fittingly, kinks. Both boutique and neighborhood are called **World's End,** possibly because Chelsea-ites believe that's what happens here. The Fulham district begins around this stretch, full of yuppie singles and places to shop. The other end of King's Road, leading into Sloane Square, has various fashion stores (no longer style-setters, on the whole) and some rather good antiques shops and markets along the way. The

Pheasantry, at No. 152, is recognizable by some over-the-top Grecian statuary in a fancy portico. Named in its mid-19th-century pheasant-breeding days, it had a phase from 1916 to 1934 as a ballet school where Margot Fonteyn and Alicia Markova learned first position. Now it's a branch of the ubiquitous Pizza Express. The Peter Jones department store marks the exit from the north of Chelsea and the beginning of Belgravia: Sloane Square. Conran's trendy restaurant **Bluebird,** at No. 352, is a great place to stop for lunch.

4 **National Army Museum.** This museum covers the history of British land forces from the Yeoman of the Guard (the first professional army, founded in 1485 and ancestors of the Tower's Beefeaters) to the present. It is best explained in its current exhibit, titled "The Rise of the Redcoat," which takes you from Henry V (1413–22) all the way to George III (1760–1820). A great deal of effort is made to convey the experience of those who lived through the wars, with the use of videos, interactives, wonderful model armies, and scenic effects, and a visit will enhance anyone's grasp of London's history and its personages. There is also a busy program, throughout the year, of special events, using actors in period dress and real-life soldiers from the modern army. ✉ *Royal Hospital Rd., Chelsea SW3,* ☎ *020/7730–0717, 020/7730–0717 for special events,* WEB *www.national-army-museum.ac.uk.* 🎟 *Free.* ⏲ *Daily 10–5:30. Tube: Sloane Sq.*

5 **Royal Hospital.** The hospice for elderly and infirm soldiers was founded by Charles II in 1682—some say after a badgering from his soft-hearted, high-profile mistress, Nell Gwynne, but more probably as an act of expedience. His troops had hitherto enjoyed not so much as a meager pension and were growing restive after the civil wars of 1642–46 and 1648. Charles wisely appointed the great architect of burned-out City churches, Sir Christopher Wren, to design this small village of brick and Portland stone set in manicured gardens (which you can visit) surrounding the Figure Court—named after the 1692 bronze figure of Charles II dressed up as a Roman soldier—and the Great Hall (dining room) and chapel. The latter is enhanced by the choir stalls of Grinling Gibbons (who did the bronze of Charles, too), the former by a vast oil of Charles on horseback by Antonio Verrio, and both are open to inspection.

No doubt you will run into some of the 400-odd residents. Despite their advancing years, these "Chelsea Pensioners" are no shrinking violets. In summer and for special occasions they sport dandy scarlet frock coats with gold buttons, medals, and natty tricorne hats, and since they are of proven good character (a condition of entry, along with old age and loyal service), they might offer to show you around—in which case you may wish to supplement their daily beer and tobacco allowance with a tip.

May is the important month at the Royal Hospital. The 29th is Oak Apple Day, when the pensioners celebrate Charles II's birthday by draping oak leaves on his statue and parading around it in memory of a hollow oak tree that expedited the king's miraculous escape from the 1651 Battle of Worcester. In the same month, and usually the third week in May, the Chelsea Flower Show, the year's highlight for thousands of garden-obsessed Brits, is also held here. Run by the Royal Horticultural Society, the mammoth event takes up a vast acreage here, and the surrounding streets throng with visitors. ✉ *Royal Hospital Rd., Chelsea SW3,* ☎ *020/7730–0161,* WEB *www.chelseapensioners.org.uk.* 🎟 *Free.* ⏲ *Weekdays 10–noon and 2–4, weekends 10–noon. Closed Dec. 24–26, Good Friday, May Day. Tube: Sloane Sq.*

KNIGHTSBRIDGE, KENSINGTON, AND HOLLAND PARK

Even in these supposedly democratic days, you still sometimes hear people say that the *only* place to live in London is in the grand residential area of the Royal Borough of Kensington. True, the district is an endless cavalcade of streets lined with splendid houses with pillared porches, but there are other fetching attractions here as well—some of the most fascinating museums in London, stylish squares, elegant antiques shops, and Kensington Palace (formerly the home of Diana, Princess of Wales, and of Queen Victoria when she was a girl)—which helped to put the district on the map. South and west of this historic edifice, you'll find the stamping grounds of the Sloane Rangers—a quintessentially London type of gilded youth whose upper-class accents make English sound like a foreign language. They tend to haunt salubrious Knightsbridge, east of Belgravia and north of Chelsea, offering as it does about equal doses of elite residential streets and ultra-shopping venues. To its east is one of the highest concentrations of important artifacts anywhere, the Museum Mile of South Kensington, with the rest of Kensington offering peaceful strolls and a noisy main street. The Holland Park neighborhood is worth visiting for its big, fancy, tree-shaded houses and its exquisite and unexpected park.

Kensington first became the Royal Borough of Kensington (and Chelsea) by virtue of a king's asthma. William III, who suffered terribly from the Thames mists over Whitehall, decided in 1689 to buy Nottingham House in the rural village of Kensington so that he could breathe more easily; and besides, his wife and co-monarch, Mary II, felt confined by water and wall at Whitehall. Courtiers and functionaries and society folk soon followed where the crowns led, and by the time Queen Anne was on the throne (1702–14), Kensington was overflowing. In a way, it still is, because most of its grand houses, and the Victorian ones of Holland Park, have been divided into apartments or else are serving as foreign embassies.

Numbers in the text correspond to numbers in the margin and on the Knightsbridge, Kensington, and Holland Park map.

A Good Walk

This is an all-weather walk—museums and shops for rainy days, grass and strolls for sunshine. When you surface from the Knightsbridge tube station—one of London's deepest—you are immediately engulfed by the manic drivers, professional shoppers, and ladies-who-lunch who make up the local population. If you're in a shopping mood, start with Harvey Nichols—right at the tube—and its six floors of total fashion. Sloane Street, leading south, is strung with the boutiques of big-name European designers, while **Harrods** ① is found to the west down Brompton Road; continue west down this road, pausing at Beauchamp (pronounced "Bee-chum") Place and Walton Street if shopping is your intention. Presently, at the junction of Brompton and Cromwell roads, you'll come to the pale, Italianate **Brompton Oratory** ②, which marks the beginning of museum territory, with the vast **Victoria & Albert Museum** ③, the **Natural History Museum** ④, and the child-friendly **Science Museum** ⑤ behind it. (The neighborhood's three large museums, incidentally, can also be reached via a long underground passage from the South Kensington tube station.) Turn left to continue north up Exhibition Road, a kind of unfinished cultural main drag that was Prince Albert's conception, toward the road after which British moviemakers named their fake blood, Kensington

Gore, to reach the giant, round Wedgwood china–box of the **Royal Albert Hall** ⑥, the glittering **Albert Memorial** ⑦ opposite, and the **Royal College of Art** ⑧ next door.

Now follow **Kensington Gardens** (which is what this western neighbor of Hyde Park is called) west to its end, and a little farther, perhaps detouring into the park to see **Kensington Palace** ⑨ and, behind it, one of London's rare, private "Millionaires' Row" sanctuaries, **Kensington Palace Gardens** ⑩. Turn off Kensington High Street down little Derry Street, with the offices of London's local paper, the *Evening Standard,* on the left and what was once Derry and Tom's department store—it closed down in the '70s—on the right. (The best part of the store was its magical roof garden, complete with palm trees, ponds, and flamingos; it's still there, now part of a nightclub owned by Richard Branson, the high-profile London figure also responsible for the Virgin Megastores, Virgin Atlantic Airways, etc.). Take a turn around peaceful **Kensington Square** ⑪; then, returning to High Street, either follow Kensington Church Street up to Notting Hill Gate—with the little 1870 St. Mary Abbots Church on its southwest corner and a cornucopia of expensive antiques in its shops all along the way—or take the longer, scenic route.

To do this, turn left off Kensington Church Street onto Holland Street, admiring the sweet 18th-century houses (Nos. 10, 12–13, and 18–26 remain). As you cross Hornton Street you'll see to your left an orange-brick 1970s building, the Kensington Civic Centre (donor of parking permits, home of the local council); Holland Street becomes the leafy Duchess of Bedford's Walk, with Queen Elizabeth College, part of London University, on the right. Turn left before Holland Park into Phillimore Gardens (perhaps detouring east into Phillimore Place to see No. 44, where Kenneth Grahame, author of *The Wind in the Willows,* lived from 1901 to 1908), then left again into Stafford Terrace to reach **Linley Sambourne House.** Step back to High Street and turn right. For a tranquil time-out, head past the gates into **Holland Park** ⑫. Exit the park at the gate by the tennis courts (near the Orangery) onto Ilchester Place, follow Melbury Road a few yards, and turn right onto Holland Park Road to reach **Leighton House** ⑬. Late in the 19th century, Melbury Road was a veritable colony of artists, though the Victorian muse they followed failed to appeal to later sensibilities, and they're now an obscure bunch—except for Dickens's illustrator, Marcus Stone, who had No. 8 built in 1876. From here you could turn right onto Addison Road to see the Technicolor tiles rioting over Sir Ernest Debenham's Peacock House at No. 8 (he founded the eponymous Oxford Street department store). If you continue north, you reach plane tree–lined Holland Park Avenue, main thoroughfare of an expensive residential neighborhood that provides more pleasant strolling territory, if you feel you haven't walked enough.

TIMING

This walk is at least 4 mi long and is almost impossible to achieve without venturing inside somewhere. The best way to approach these neighborhoods is to treat Knightsbridge shopping and the South Kensington museums at one go. The rest of the tour works as a scenic walk on a fine day, because places to see—such as Leighton House and Kensington Palace—are less time-consuming than the V&A and the Natural History, and Science museums. During "term time," these are populated by more or less orderly school parties during the week, while weekends and school vacations see them fill up with more random arrangements of children. The parks are best in the growing seasons—early spring for crocuses and daffodils and summer for roses—and in the fall, when the foliage show easily rivals New England's. Kensington Gardens closes its gates at sundown, though you can get into Holland Park later in summer, thanks to the restaurant and the Open Air Theatre.

HOW TO GET THERE

There are many tubes here, but which you choose will depend on which part you want. Knightsbridge on the Piccadilly Line, Kensington High Street on the District and Circle, and Holland Park on the Central Line are the best ones. The best buses between Kensington High Street and Knightsbridge are Buses 9, 10, and 52. From Kensington to Holland Park, get the 9, 27, 28, or 31.

Sights to See

7 **Albert Memorial.** The Victorian era is epitomized in this neo-Gothic shrine to Prince Albert. The 14-ft bronze statue looks as if it were created yesterday, thanks to a brilliant restoration by English Heritage. During the war, the statue was deliberately blackened to avoid attracting Zeppelins to Kensington Palace, then the natural elements caused much damage. It took 1,000 20-page books of gold leaf to bring it to its present glory. Albert's grieving widow, Queen Victoria, had this elaborate confection erected on the spot where his Great Exhibition had stood a mere decade before his early death from typhoid fever in 1861. ✉ *Kensington Gore, opposite Royal Albert Hall, Hyde Park, Kensington. Tube: Knightsbridge.*

2 **Brompton Oratory.** This is a late product of the mid-19th-century English Roman Catholic revival led by John Henry Cardinal Newman (1801–90), who established the oratory in 1884 and whose statue you see outside. Architect Herbert Gribble, a previously unknown 29-year-old, won the competition to design the place, an honor that you may conclude went to his head when you see the vast, incredibly ornate interior. It is punctuated by treasures far older than the church itself, like the giant *Twelve Apostles* in the nave, carved from Carrara marble by Giuseppe Mazzuoli in the 1680s and brought here from Siena's cathedral. ✉ *Brompton Rd., Kensington,* ☎ *020/7808–0900.* *Free.* ⏲ *6:30 AM–8 PM. Services Mon.–Fri. 7, 8, 10, 12:30, and 6; Sat. 7, 8, 10, and 6; Sun. 7, 8:30, 11, 12:30, 4:30, and 7. Tube: South Kensington.*

1 **Harrods.** Just in case you don't notice it, this well-known shopping destination frames its domed terra-cotta Edwardian outline in thousands of white lights each night. The 15-acre Egyptian-owned store's sales weeks are world class, and inside it's as frenetic as that of a stock market floor. Its motto, *Omnia, omnibus, ubique* (Everything, for everyone, everywhere) is not too far from the truth. Visit the pet department, a highlight for children, and don't miss the extravagant Food Hall, with its stunning Art Nouveau tiling in the neighborhood of meat and poultry and continuing on in the fishmongers' territory, where its glory is rivaled by displays of the sea produce itself. This is the place to acquire your green-and-gold souvenir Harrods bag, as food prices are surprisingly competitive. ✉ *87–135 Brompton Rd., Knightsbridge SW1,* ☎ *020/7730–1234,* WEB *www.harrods.com.* ⏲ *Mon.–Sat. 10–7, Sun. noon–6. Tube: Knightsbridge.*

NEED A BREAK? **Pâtisserie Valerie** (✉ 215 Brompton Rd., Knightsbridge SW3, ☎ 020/7832–9971), just down the road from Harrods, keeps in tune with your posh day out offering light café meals and splendid pastries and coffee.

12 **Holland Park.** The former grounds of the Jacobean Holland House opened to the public only in 1952. Since then, many treats have been laid on within its 60 acres. Holland House itself was nearly flattened

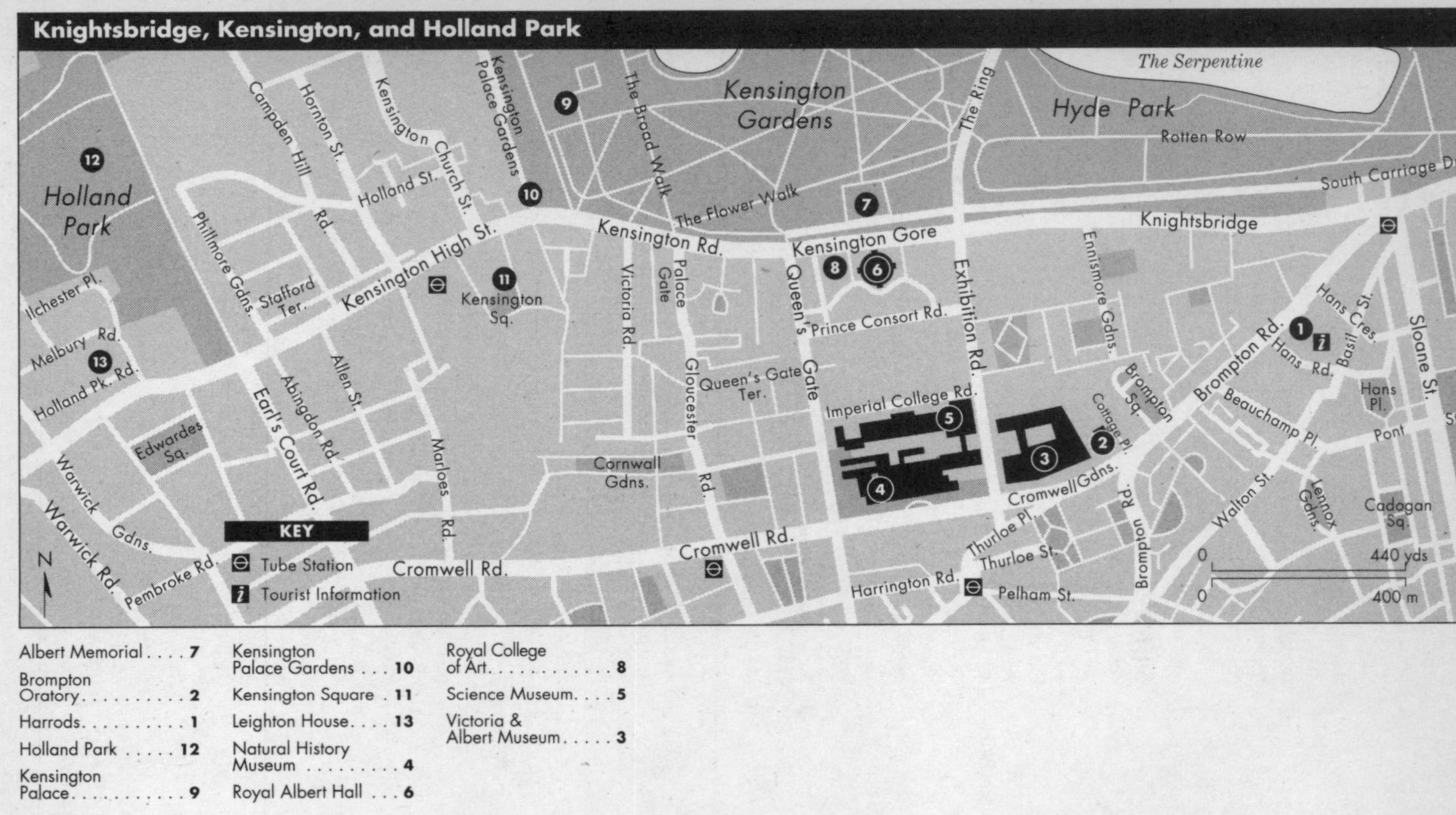

Albert Memorial 7
Brompton Oratory 2
Harrods. 1
Holland Park 12
Kensington Palace. 9
Kensington Palace Gardens . . . 10
Kensington Square . 11
Leighton House. . . . 13
Natural History Museum 4
Royal Albert Hall . . . 6
Royal College of Art. 8
Science Museum. . . . 5
Victoria & Albert Museum 3

by World War II bombs, but the east wing remains, now incorporated into a youth hostel and providing a fantastical stage for the April–September **Open Air Theatre** (☏ 020/7602–7856 box office). The glass-walled Orangery also survived to host art exhibitions and wedding receptions, while next door, the former Garden Ballroom has become the upmarket Belvedere restaurant; nearby is a lovely café. From the Belvedere's terrace you see the formal Dutch Garden, planted by Lady Holland in the 1790s with the first English dahlias. North of that are woodland walks; lawns populated by peacocks, guinea fowl, and the odd, awkward emu; a fragrant rose garden; great banks of rhododendrons and azaleas, which bloom profusely in May; a well-supervised children's Adventure Playground; and even a Japanese water garden, legacy of the London Festival of Japan. If that's not enough, you can watch cricket on the Cricket Lawn on the south side or tennis on the several courts. ⏲ *Daily dawn–dusk. Tube: Holland Park or High St. Kensington.*

OFF THE BEATEN PATH

KENSAL GREEN CEMETERY – Heralding itself as "London's first necropolis," this West London cemetery was established in 1832 and beats the more famous Highgate for atmosphere, if only because it is less populated by the living. Within its 77 acres are more freestanding mausoleums than in any other cemetery in Britain, some of them almost the size of small churches and most of them constructed while their future occupants were still alive. Those who balked at burial but couldn't afford a mausoleum of their own could opt for a spot in the catacombs, and these, with their stacks of moldering caskets, are a definite highlight for seekers of the macabre, though they can only be seen as part of a tour. In the cemetery you'll find the final resting places of the novelists Trollope, Thackeray, and Wilkie Collins; of the great 19th-century engineer Isambard Kingdom Brunel; and of Decimus Burton, Victorian architect of the Athenaeum Club, the Wellington Arch, and the Kew Gardens greenhouses. ✉ *Harrow Rd., Kensal Green W10,* ☏ *020/8969–0152; 020/7402–2749 tours.* ⏲ *Mon.–Sat. 9–4:30, Sun. 10–5; tours Sun. 2 PM (including the catacombs on the 1st and 3rd Sun. of the month).* 🎫 *£5. Tube: Kensal Green.*

★ 9 **Kensington Palace.** The long history of this palace has been eclipsed in the last few years by—some might say its most famous inhabitant—the late Princess Diana. She resided here, so this was where the crowds flocked with millions of flower tributes when the tragic news of her death was heard. To date, no lasting memorial has been erected in her name, although a wonderful children's playground with an innovative Peter Pan, Neverland theme, has proved extremely popular. The playground can be found close to the Peter Pan statue in Kensington Gardens. Socially speaking, Kensington was put on the map when King William III, "much incommoded by the Smoak of the Coal Fires of London," decided in the 17th century to vacate Whitehall and relocate to a new palace outside the center city in the "village" of Kensington. Twelve years of renovation were needed before William and Mary could move in, and it continued to undergo all manner of refurbishment during the succeeding three reigns. By coincidence, these monarchs happened to suffer rather ignominious deaths. William III fell off his horse when it stumbled on a molehill, and succumbed to pleurisy in 1702. Then, in 1714, Queen Anne (who, you may recall, was fond of brandy) suffered an apoplectic fit thought to have been brought on by overeating. Next, George I, the first of the Hanoverian Georges, had a stroke said to have been caused by "a surfeit of melons"—admittedly not at Kensington, but in a coach carrying him to Hanover in 1727. Worst of all, in 1760, poor George II burst a blood vessel while on the toilet.

But the royal curtain here always rang up on a remarkable changing cast of characters, no more so than when the 18-year-old Princess Victoria of Kent was called from her bed in June 1837 by the Archbishop of Canterbury and the Lord Chamberlain. She was told that her uncle, William IV, was dead, and she was to be queen. The state rooms where Victoria had her ultrastrict upbringing have been renovated, although, for the decor-factor, the King's Apartments are the best part of the (compulsory) guided tour. Look out for Tintorettos and Van Dycks among the canvases; see the Mortlake tapestries commissioned by Charles I; and look at the ceiling in the Cupola Room: it appears to be domed but is actually as flat as a pancake. This palace is an essential stop for royalty vultures because it's the only one where you may actually catch a glimpse of the real thing. The Duke and Duchess of Gloucester and Prince and Princess Michael of Kent all have apartments here, as did Princess Margaret and, of course, Diana. In the palace's ultra-civilized Orangery you can buy an expensive cup of tea and enjoy the festive hall where many Windsor birthday parties and weddings were held.

Extending back centuries, the **Royal Ceremonial Dress Collection** showcases state and occasional dresses, hats, and shoes worn by Britain's Royal Family. Diana-watchers will note the difference between the regal if dowdy garments of Her Majesty the Queen compared to the glittering, contemporary fashions of her daughter-in-law. Other dazzlers of note are the coronation robes of Queen Mary and George V and a regal mantua—a 6-ft-wide court dress. ✉ *The Broad Walk, Kensington Gardens, Kensington W8,* ☎ *020/7937–9561,* WEB *www.hrp.org.uk.* 🎫 *£8.80, including admission to the Dress Collection.* ⏲ *Mar.–Oct., daily 10–6; Nov.–Feb., daily 10–5 (last admission 1 hr before closure). Tube: High St. Kensington.*

10 **Kensington Palace Gardens.** Starting behind Kensington Palace, this is one of London's rare private roads, guarded and gated both here and at the Notting Hill Gate end. If you walk it, you will see why it earned the nickname "Millionaires' Row"—it is lined with palatial white-stucco houses designed by a selection of the best architects of the mid-19th century. The novelist William Makepeace Thackeray, author of *Vanity Fair,* died in 1863 at No. 2—which now houses the Israeli embassy.

11 **Kensington Square.** Laid out around the time William moved to Kensington Palace up the road, this is one of London's most venerable squares. A few early 18th-century houses remain, with Nos. 11 and 12 the oldest.

NEED A BREAK? Revel in the regal surroundings while sipping a cup of tea and daintily nibbling tasty treats at the **Orangery** (✉ Kensington Palace, Kensington W8, ☎ 020/7376–0239).

13 **Leighton House.** This was the home of Frederic Leighton (1830–96)—painter, sculptor, and president of the Royal Academy. The prize room here is the incredible Arab Hall. George Aitchison designed this Moorish fantasy in 1879 to show off Leighton's valuable 13th- to 17th-century Islamic tile collection, and, adorned with marble columns, dome, and fountain, it is exotic beyond belief. The rest of the rooms are more conventionally, stuffily Victorian, but they do contain many paintings by Leighton, plus those of Edward Burne-Jones, John Millais, and other leading Pre-Raphaelites. ✉ *12 Holland Park Rd., Kensington W14,* ☎ *020/7602–3316.* 🎫 *Free.* ⏲ *Wed.–Mon. 11–5:30. Tube: High St. Kensington.*

Linley Sambourne House. Stuffed with delightful Victorian and Edwardian antiques, fabrics, and paintings, this is one of the most charming 19th-century London houses extant—small wonder that it was used in Merchant and Ivory's *A Room with a View.* In the 1870s it was the home of the political cartoonist Edward Linley Sambourne. ✉ *18 Stafford Terr., Kensington W8,* ☏ *020/7602–3316.* 🎫 *Free.*

4 **Natural History Museum.** Architect Alfred Waterhouse had relief panels scattered across the outrageously ornate French Romanesque–style terra-cotta facade of this museum, depicting extant creatures to the left of the entrance, extinct ones to the right. Inside, that categorization is sort of continued in reverse, with dinosaurs on the left and the Ecology Gallery on the right. Both of these renovated exhibits (the former with life-size moving dinosaurs, the latter complete with "moonlit rain forest") make essential viewing in a museum that, realizing it was becoming crusty, has invested millions in a superb modernization program, featuring more of the wow-power and interactives necessary to secure interest from younger visitors; and it succeeds.

You'll find, in the Creepy Crawlies Gallery, a super-enlarged scorpion so nightmarish that it makes tarantulas seem cute (8 out of 10 animal species, one learns here, are arthropods). Other wonderful bits include the Human Biology Hall, which you arrive at through a birth-simulation chamber; the full-size blue whale; and the moving dinosaur diorama. The Earth Galleries are also unmissable, with ambitious exhibits about the structure of the planet: The Power Within with an earthquake simulation, Restless Surface, and Visions of the Earth. Understandably, this place usually resembles a grade-school recess. In the basement, quieter, more absorbing hands-on activities are on offer in the Investigate section, which allows you to do just that with actual objects, from old bones to bugs. ✉ *Cromwell Rd., Kensington SW7,* ☏ *020/7942–5000,* WEB *www.nhm.ac.uk.* 🎫 *Free.* ⏲ *Mon.–Sat. 10–5:50, Sun. 11–5:50. Tube: South Kensington.*

6 **Royal Albert Hall.** This domed, circular 8,000-seat auditorium (as well as the Albert Memorial, opposite) was made possible by the Victorian public, who donated funds for it. More money was raised, however, by selling 1,300 future seats at £100 apiece—not for the first night but for every night for 999 years. (Some descendants of purchasers still use the seats.) The Albert Hall is best known for its annual July–September Henry Wood Promenade Concerts (the "Proms"), with bargain-price standing (or promenading, or sitting-on-the-floor) tickets sold on the night of concert. ✉ *Kensington Gore, Kensington SW7,* ☏ *020/7589–8212,* WEB *www.alberthall.co.uk.* 🎫 *Prices vary with event. Tube: South Kensington.*

8 **Royal College of Art.** Housed in a glass-dominated building designed by Sir Hugh Casson in 1973, the RCA provides great contrast with the Victoriana surrounding it, including the Albert Hall next door. Famous in the 1950s and '60s for processing David Hockney, Peter Blake, and Eduardo Paolozzi, the college is still one of the country's foremost art and design schools, and there's usually an exhibition, lecture, or event going on here that's open to the public. ✉ *Kensington Gore, Kensington SW7,* ☏ *020/7590–4125,* WEB *www.rca.ac.uk.* 🎫 *Free.* ⏲ *Weekdays 10–6 (call to check times). Tube: South Kensington.*

5 **Science Museum.** This, the third of the great South Kensington museums, stands behind the Natural History Museum in a far plainer building. It has loads of hands-on exhibits, with entire schools of children apparently decanted inside to interact with them; but it is, after all,

painlessly educational. Highlights include the Launch Pad gallery, which demonstrates basic scientific principles (try the plasma ball, where your hands attract "lightning"—if you can get them on it); *Puffing Billy,* the oldest steam locomotive in the world; and the actual *Apollo 10* capsule. The newest attraction is the Wellcome Wing, a £45 million addition devoted to contemporary science, medicine, and technology, which also includes a 450-seat IMAX cinema. ✉ *Exhibition Rd., Kensington SW7,* ☎ *020/7942–4000,* WEB *www.sciencemuseum.org.uk.* 🎫 *Free.* ⏲ *Daily 10–6. Tube: South Kensington.*

★ ❸ **Victoria & Albert Museum.** Recognizable by the copy of Victoria's imperial crown on the lantern above the central cupola, this institution is always referred to as the V&A. It is a huge museum, showcasing the applied arts of all disciplines, all periods, all nationalities, and all tastes, and it is a wonderful, generous place to get lost in, full of innovation and completely devoid of pretension. The collections are *so* catholic that confusion is a hazard—one minute you're gazing on the Jacobean oak four-poster Great Bed of Ware (one of the V&A's most prized possessions, given that Shakespeare immortalized it in *Twelfth Night*) and the next you're in the 20th-century end of the equally celebrated Dress Collection, coveting a Jean Muir frock you could actually buy at nearby Harrods. The £31 million British Galleries are the latest addition to the museum. The galleries showcase 400 years of British art and design from 1500 to 1900. Displays include George Gilbert Scott's model of the Albert Memorial and the first-ever English fork made in 1632. Information about how a 16th-century bed was made and how women got into carriages with hoop skirts is also provided.

Prince Albert, Victoria's adored consort, was responsible for the genesis of this permanent version of the 1851 Great Exhibition, and his queen laid its foundation stone in her final public London appearance, in 1899. From the start, the V&A had an important role as a research institution, and that role continues today, with many resources available to scholars, designers, artists, and conservators. Two such resources are the Textiles and Dress 20th Century Reference Centre, with ingenious space-saving storage systems for thousands of bolts of cloth, and the Textile Study Galleries, which perform the same function for 2,000 years' worth of the past.

Follow your own whims around the enormous gallery space, but try to reach the spectacular Glass Gallery, where a collection spanning four millennia is reflected between room-size mirrors under young designer Danny Lane's breathtaking glass balustrade. Recent additions include the Raphael Galleries, housing seven massive cartoons the painter completed in 1516 for his Sistine Chapel tapestries, and the Silver Galleries, displaying six centuries of English silver. The museum stays open late on Wednesdays and the last Friday of every month for Late View—a kind of museum salon, with lectures (for a fee) and a wine bar. ✉ *Cromwell Rd., Kensington SW7,* ☎ *020/7942–2000,* WEB *www.vam.ac.uk.* 🎫 *Free.* ⏲ *Daily 10–5:45; Late View Wed. 6:30–9:30, last Fri. of the month 6–10. Tube: South Kensington.*

NEED A BREAK? Indulge in a true national tradition—the English breakfast—at the **New Restaurant at the V&A** (✉ Cromwell Rd., Kensington SW7, ☎ 020/7581–2159), served here daily from 11 until 1. There's also a Sunday Roast, from 1 until 2:45, complete with occasional live musicians, from jazz to harp.

HYDE PARK, KENSINGTON GARDENS, AND NOTTING HILL

The royal parks of Hyde Park and Kensington Gardens are among London's unique features: great swaths of green in the middle of the city, where it really is possible to escape from London's fast pace. Although some of this territory was covered in the Knightsbridge, Kensington, and Holland Park tour, this is another option for visiting the royal parks (without the museums) that also takes in Portobello Road and Notting Hill. The description "royal" is somewhat paradoxical, for today these are the most democratic of places, where Londoners from all walks of life come to relax (and let off steam as soapbox orators). Although it's probably been centuries since any major royal had a casual stroll here, these parks remain the property of the Crown, and it was the Crown that saved them from being devoured by the city's late-18th-century growth spurt. North of the pair of parks—which are separate entities, although the boundary is virtually invisible—lies Bayswater. Farther northwest lies Notting Hill, a trendsetting square mile of multiethnicity, music, and markets, with lots of restaurants to see and be seen in and younger, more egalitarian, and more adventurous versions of Cork Street's commercial modern-art galleries. The style-watching media has dubbed the local residents Notting Hillbillies. The whole area has mushroomed around one of the world's great antiques markets, Portobello Road.

A Good Walk

Where else would you enter Hyde Park but at **Hyde Park Corner**? The most impressive of the many entrances is the Hyde Park Screen by Apsley House, usually called **Decimus Burton's Gateway** because it was he who designed this triple-arched monument in 1828. The next gate along to the north, a gaudy unicorns-and-lions-rampant number, was a 90th-birthday gift to Elizabeth the Queen Mother and is therefore the **Queen Mother's Gate.** Follow the southern perimeter along the sand track called **Rotten Row,** now used by the Household Cavalry, which lives at the **Knightsbridge Barracks** to the left.

Follow Rotten Row west to the **Serpentine.** When you pass its **Bridge** you leave Hyde Park and enter **Kensington Gardens** and its **Serpentine Gallery.** En route to the formal garden at the end of the Long Water, the **Fountains,** you pass statues of **Peter Pan** and the horse and rider called **Physical Energy.** Continuing westward, you reach **Round Pond** and Kensington Palace. Follow the Broad Walk north past the playground on the left and leave the park by Black Lion Gate; you are almost opposite Queensway, a rather peculiar, cosmopolitan street of ethnic confusion, late-night cafés and restaurants, a skating rink, and the Whiteleys shopping-and-movie mall. Turn left at the end into Westbourne Grove, however, and you've entered Notting Hill; you'll reach the famous **Portobello Road** after a few blocks. Turn left for the Saturday antiques market and shops, right to reach the Westway and the flea market. For Notting Hill's grandest houses, stroll over to Lansdowne Road, Lansdowne Crescent, and Lansdowne Square—two blocks west of Kensington Park Row.

TIMING

This is a route that changes vastly on weekends. Saturday is Portobello Road's most fun day, so you may prefer to start at the end and work backward, using the parks for relaxation after your shopping exertions. Do the same on Friday if you're a flea-market fan. Sunday, the Hyde Park and Kensington Gardens railings all along Bayswater Road are hung with very bad art, which may slow your progress; this is also prime

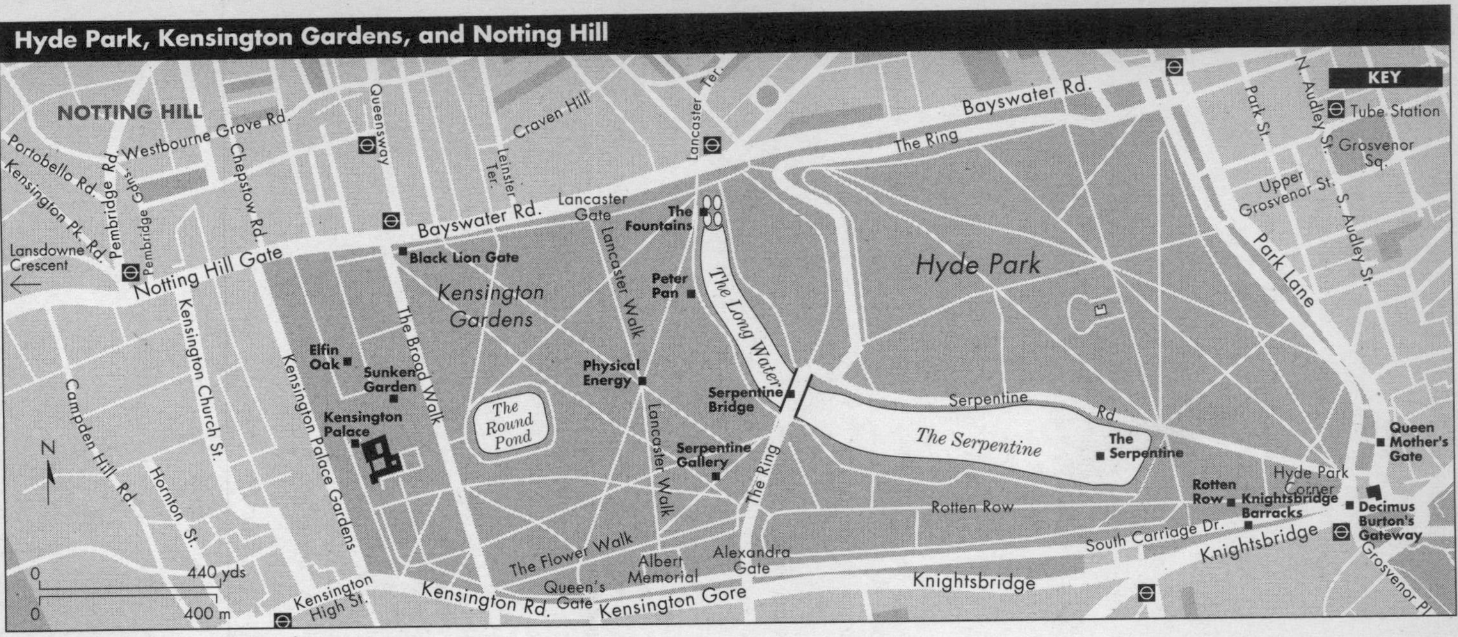
Hyde Park, Kensington Gardens, and Notting Hill
KEY
Tube Station
NOTTING HILL
Portobello Rd.
Kensington Pk. Rd.
Pembridge Rd.
Pembridge Gdns.
Westbourne Grove Rd.
Chepstow Rd.
Queensway
Leinster Ter.
Craven Hill
Lancaster Ter.
Bayswater Rd.
The Ring
Park St.
N. Audley St.
Grosvenor Sq.
Upper Grosvenor St.
S. Audley St.
Park Lane
Lansdowne Crescent
Notting Hill Gate
Lancaster Gate
The Fountains
Black Lion Gate
Kensington Gardens
Lancaster Walk
Peter Pan
The Long Water
Hyde Park
Kensington Church St.
Kensington Palace Gardens
The Broad Walk
Elfin Oak
Sunken Garden
Kensington Palace
The Round Pond
Physical Energy
Serpentine Bridge
Serpentine Rd.
The Serpentine
Queen Mother's Gate
Hyde Park Corner
Serpentine Gallery
The Ring
Rotten Row
Knightsbridge Barracks
Decimus Burton's Gateway
Campden Hill Rd.
Hornton St.
South Carriage Dr.
Knightsbridge
Grosvenor Pl.
The Flower Walk
Albert Memorial
Alexandra Gate
Queen's Gate
Kensington Rd.
Kensington Gore
Kensington High St.
N
0
440 yds
0
400 m

perambulation day for locals. Whatever your priorities, this is a long walk if you explore every corner, with the perimeter of the two parks alone covering a good 4 mi and about half as far again around the remainder of the route. You could cut out a lot of park without missing out on essential sights and walk the whole thing in a brisk three hours.

HOW TO GET THERE

For Hyde Park and Kensington Gardens, get off the Central Line at Queensway or Lancaster Gate, or enter the park from Hyde Park Corner on the Piccadilly Line. If you want Portobello Market and environs, the best tube stop is Ladbroke Grove or Westbourne Park (Hammersmith and City lines), and then ask directions; the Notting Hill stop on the District, Circle, and Central lines is also an option. Buses for the area include Buses 12, 70, and 94 for seeing anything off Bayswater Road or Buses 27, 28, 31, and 52 for penetrating the depths of Notting Hill.

Sights to See

Hyde Park. Along with the smaller St. James's and Green parks to the east, Hyde Park started as Henry VIII's hunting grounds. He more or less stole the land for his own personal pleasure from the monks at Westminster in the 1536 Dissolution of the Monasteries. James I was more generous and allowed the public in at the beginning of the 17th century, as long as they were "respectably dressed." Nowadays, as you can see if you're here in the summer, you may wear whatever you like—a bathing suit will do. Along its south side runs **Rotten Row.** It was Henry VIII's royal path to the hunt—hence the name, a corruption of *route du roi.* It's still used by the Household Cavalry, who live at the **Knightsbridge Barracks**—a high-rise and a long, low, ugly red block—to the left. This is the brigade that mounts the guard at Buckingham Palace, and you can see them leave to perform this duty in full regalia, plumed helmet and all, at around 10:30, or await the return of the exhausted ex-guard about noon. Sunday's **Speaker's Corner** in the park near Marble Arch is an unmissable spectacle of vehement, sometimes comical, and always entertaining orators. From June to August, Hyde Park is the venue for the Royal Parks Summer Festival with live jazz evenings, opera, and plays all over the park. ☎ *020/7298–2100,* WEB *www.royalparks.co.uk.* ⊙ *Daily 5 AM–midnight. Tube: Hyde Park Corner, Lancaster Gate, Marble Arch, or Knightsbridge.*

Kensington Gardens. More formal than neighboring Hyde Park, Kensington Gardens was first laid out as palace grounds. The paved Italian garden at the top of the Long Water, the **Fountains,** is a reminder of this, though of course **Kensington Palace** itself is the main clue to the gardens' royal status, with its early 19th-century Sunken Garden north of the palace complex, complete with a living tunnel of lime trees (i.e., linden trees) and golden laburnum. Several statues are worth looking out for: George Frampton's 1912 ***Peter Pan*** is a bronze of the boy who lived on an island in the Serpentine and never grew up and whose creator, J. M. Barrie, lived at 100 Bayswater Road, not 500 yards from here. Southwest of Peter at the intersection of several paths is George Frederick Watts's 1904 bronze of a muscle-bound horse and rider, entitled ***Physical Energy.*** By the Princess Diana Memorial Playground, close to the Round Pond, is the remains of a tree carved with scores of tiny woodland creatures, Ivor Innes's ***Elfin Oak.*** The **Round Pond** acts as a magnet for model-boat enthusiasts and duck feeders. WEB *www.royalparks.co.uk.* ⊙ *Daily dawn–dusk. Tube: Lancaster Gate or Queensway.*

Notting Hill. Currently the best place to wear sunglasses, smoke Gauloises, and contemplate the latest issue of *Wallpaper,* "the Hill" now ranks as London's coolest neighborhood (for this week, at least). Centered on the Portobello Road antiques market, this district is bordered to the west by Lansdowne Crescent—lined by the Hill's poshest 19th-century terraced row houses—and to the east by Chepstow Road, with Notting Hill Gate and Westbourne Grove Road marking south and north boundaries. In between, Rastafarians rub elbows with wealthy young Brits (a.k.a. "Trustafarians"), and residents like fashion designer Rifat Ozbek, CNN's Christiane Amanpour, and historian Lady Antonia Fraser can be spotted at the chic shops on Westbourne Grove and in the lively café on Kensington Park Road. There are no historic sites here, so explore just to savor the flavor. *Tube: Notting Hill Gate or Ladbroke Grove.*

Portobello Road. Tempted by tassels, looking for a 19th-century snuff spoon, an ancient print of North Africa, or a dashingly Deco frock (just don't believe the dealer when he says the Vionnet label just fell off), or hunting for a gracefully Georgian silhouette of the Earl of Chesterfield? Head to Portobello Road, world famous for its Saturday antiques market (arrive at about 9 AM to find the real treasures-in-the-trash; after 10, the crowds pack in wall to wall). Actually, the Portobello Market is three markets: antiques, "fruit and veg," and a flea market. The street begins at Notting Hill Gate, though the antiques stalls start a couple of blocks north, around Chepstow Villas. Lining the sloping street are also dozens of antiques shops and indoor markets, open most days—in fact, serious collectors will want to do Portobello on a weekday, when they can explore the 90-some antiques and art stores in relative peace. Where the road levels off, around Elgin Crescent, youth culture and a vibrant neighborhood life kick in, with all manner of interesting small stores and restaurants interspersed with the fruit and vegetable market. This continues to the Westway overpass ("flyover" in British), where London's best flea market (high-class, vintage, antique, and secondhand clothing; jewelry; and junk) happens Fridays and Saturdays, then on up to Golborne Road. There's a strong West Indian flavor to Notting Hill, with a Trinidad-style Carnival centered along Portobello Road on the August bank-holiday weekend. *Tube: Notting Hill Gate or Ladbroke Grove.*

Serpentine Gallery. Influential on the trendy art circuit, this gallery hangs several exhibitions of modern work a year, often very avant-garde, indeed, and always worth a look. It overlooks the west bank of the **Serpentine,** a beloved lake, much frequented in summer, when the south-shore Lido resembles a beach and the water is dotted with hired rowboats. Walk the bank, and you will soon reach the picturesque, stone **Serpentine Bridge,** built in 1826 by George Rennie, which marks the boundary between Hyde Park and Kensington Gardens. ✉ *Kensington Gardens, Kensington W2,* ☎ *020/7402–6075,* WEB *www.serpentinegallery.org.* *Free.* ⏲ *Daily 10–6; call to check if open. Tube: Lancaster Gate.*

REGENT'S PARK AND HAMPSTEAD

Regent's Park and Hampstead in North London contain some of the prettiest and most rural parts of the city, as well as some of the most aristocratic architecture in the world (thanks to the terraces and town houses of John Nash, 19th-century design whiz) and some important historical sights. For the sheer pleasure of idle exploring, these city districts are hard to beat. All told, this section covers a large area. It starts from the Georgian houses superimposed on medieval Maryburne; continues around John Nash's Regency facades and his park; stretches on into North London's canal-side youth center; climbs up the hill to the city's chicest, most expensive "village"; and finishes, fittingly, at its most famous cemetery.

Marylebone Road (pronounced "Marra-le-bun" after Queen Mary *le bon*) these days is remarkable mostly for its permanent traffic jam, some of it heading to Madame Tussaud's. At the east end is the first part of John Nash's impressive Regent's Park scheme, the elegantly curvaceous Park Crescent (1812–18), which Nash planned as a full circus at the northern end of his ceremonial route from St. James's. Like most of the other Nash houses around the park, it was wrecked during World War II, reconstructed, and rebuilt behind the repaired facade in the 1960s. Northeast of the park, Camden Town is the neighborhood that houses London's highest concentration of single people in their twenties.

The cliché about Hampstead is that it is just like a pretty little village—albeit one with designer shops, expensive French delicatessens, restaurants, cafés, cinemas, and so on. In fact, like so many other London neighborhoods, Hampstead did start as a separate village, when plague-bedeviled medieval Londoners fled the city to this clean hilltop 4 mi away. By the 18th century, its reputation for cleanliness had spread so far that its water was being bottled and sold to the hoi polloi down the hill as the Perrier of its day. That was the beginning of Hampstead's heyday as an artistic and literary retreat attracting many famous writers, painters, and musicians to its leafy lanes—as it still does. Just strolling around here is rewarding: not only are the streets incredibly picturesque, they also offer some of London's best Georgian buildings.

Numbers in the text correspond to numbers in the margin and on the Regent's Park and Hampstead map.

A Good Walk

Begin at the tube station whose name will thrill the Sherlock Holmes fan: Baker Street—the **Sherlock Holmes Museum** ① is at No. 221B, of course. Turn left and follow the line of tour buses past **Madame Tussaud's** ② and the **London Planetarium**; then go to the end of Harley Street—an English synonym for private (as opposed to state-funded) medicine because it is lined with the consulting rooms of the country's top specialist doctors—to Park Crescent and, across the street, **Regent's Park** ③. Enter along the Outer Circle and turn left on Chester Road. Straight ahead are Queen Mary's Gardens, the lake, and the **Regent's Park Open-Air Theatre** ④.

If you want to take a look at the most elegant street in London, head straight ahead up Chester Road to **Cumberland Terrace** (1827), the porticoed white-stucco structure that overlooks the eastern edge of the park like a Grecian temple. This is one of architect Joseph Nash's most famous Regency-era creations. His most elegant urban stage set, however, is reached by continuing two blocks south, where **Chester Place** (1825) debouches into a cream-colored, magnificent triumphal arch, with its name emblazoned across the top of the arch. Nash aficionados will want to continue eight blocks to the north to see Park Village East and West, two streets that are lined with enchanting "villas" in the 19th-century mode.

If you haven't made this architectural detour outside the park to see Nash's buildings, continue within the park from Regent's Park Open-Air Theatre along Chester Road until the Broad Walk, and then make a left. Look west past the mock-Tudor prefab tearoom for one of London's rare, uninterrupted open vistas toward the London Central Mosque; and then continue on to the **London Zoo** ⑤. From here, you can take a round-trip detour on the water bus and spy on the back gardens along the **Grand Union Canal** (which everyone calls the Regent's Canal) to Little Venice. This canal is flanked with enormous white wedding-cake houses, separated from the banks with willow trees and long gardens, making it a beautiful strolling location. Alternatively you can walk along the whole canal, past the animals in the zoo down to Camden Lock, one of Britain's largest markets.

North of the zoo, cross Prince Albert Road to the man-made Primrose Hill, a high point (literally, at 206 ft) and the best place to be on the night of November 5, when London's biggest bonfire burns a Guy Fawkes effigy and the council puts on a spectacular fireworks display. Heading east from here (the easiest route is Regent's Park Road, then left down Parkway, past the **Jewish Museum** ⑥), brings you to the center of Camden Town. Turn left at the foot of Parkway, and battle your way north along Camden High Street (actually, the crowds are unbearably dense only on the weekend) to **Camden Lock** ⑦. From here you can keep going east, although it's less scenic, to King's Cross, site of one of London's main train stations, the British Library building, the city's highest concentration of streetwalkers, and the **London Canal Museum** ⑧.

Back at the Lock, you could walk up Haverstock Hill or travel three stops on the Northern Line from Camden Town tube station (make sure you take the Edgware branch) to Hampstead. Cross High Street to Heath Street and turn right to Church Row, said to be London's most complete Georgian street. At the west end is the 1745 "village" church of St. John's, where the painter John Constable is buried. Just south of the tube station, Flask Walk is another beautiful street, narrow and shop-lined at the High Street end, then widening after you pass the Flask—the pub it is named for. This place has a pretty courtyard and was described by Samuel Richardson in his 18th-century novel *Clarissa* as "a place where second-rate persons are to be found, often in a swinish condition." Nearby Well Walk was where a spring surfaced, its place now marked by a dried-up fountain. John Constable lived here, as well as John Keats (in, of course, **Keats House** ⑨) and, later, D. H. Lawrence. Head some blocks north to regal **Fenton House,** a National Trust property with some lovely gardens; then amble around the corner and alongside Fenton House to reach Admiral's Walk, where you may gaze at the house with a roof that echoes the quarterdeck of a ship immortalized in *Mary Poppins*. About 15-minutes' walk farther along East Heath Road you'll find the Gothic manse that inspired Hell Hall in *One Hundred and One Dalmatians*. You now have two choices: if you've had enough fresh air, walk all the way down Fitzjohn's Avenue and visit the **Freud Museum** ⑩, where Sigmund Freud lived and worked, and then continue down Finchley Road to the impressive **Saatchi Collection** ⑪, a huge, cavernous gallery space; Beatles aficionados will head posthaste, instead, to the fabled **Abbey Road Studios** ⑫. If you've been blessed with a clear London day, take advantage and follow the long walk northeast up Spaniards Road, traversing **Hampstead Heath** to Hampstead Lane, to the bucolic oasis of **Kenwood House** ⑬, well worth a visit for its setting alone. To the east of Hampstead, and also topping a hill, is the former village of Highgate, which has some fine houses, especially along its Georgian High Street, and retains its peaceful period surroundings. But it is most famous for **Highgate Cemetery** ⑭.

TIMING

You may well want to divide this tour into segments, using the (notoriously inefficient) Northern Line of the tube to jump between the Regent's Park and Hampstead neighborhoods. It will take you at least three or even four hours to cover the full length of this walk on foot.

There are several approaches. In summer, with children, you might consider a North London jaunt in Regent's Park, the zoo, Camden Lock, and a canal trip, a day's worth of sightseeing. If you wanted to add Madame Tussaud's and the planetarium, you'd have a frenetic day, especially in summer, because you might be in line for over an hour. You could start a summer's day without children at the other end, with Hampstead Heath, Kenwood House, a stroll around Hampstead, and a pub or two on the agenda. Teenagers and youth might want to spend all day shopping in Camden Town. Both Camden and Hampstead are usually fairly busy during the week as well, for in addition to being shopping havens they are residential neighborhoods. Bear in mind that much of this itinerary may be washed out by rain.

HOW TO GET THERE

For Regent's Park, go to Regent's Park tube station (on the Bakerloo Line), though Camden Town on the Northern Line, with a walk up Parkway, is almost as close. Hampstead is best accessed from the Hampstead tube stop. Make sure you get on the right branch of the Northern Line—you want the Edgware branch. Buses for Regent's Park include Buses 18, 27, and 30 along the Marylebone Road or Buses 13, 82, 113, 139, and 274 to Lord's Cricket Ground. Take the 274 for the zoo. For Hampstead, catch the 268.

Sights to See

★ ⓬ **Abbey Road Studios.** The most famous Beatles site in London, this is the fabled studio where the Fab Four recorded their entire output. The studios themselves are closed to the public, but many travelers journey here to see the famous traffic crossing used by the group on the cover of their *Abbey Road* album. ✉ *3 Abbey Rd., Hampstead NW8,* WEB *www.abbeyroad.co.uk. Tube: St. John's Wood.*

❼ **Camden Lock.** What was once just a pair of locks on the Grand Union Canal has now developed into London's third-most-visited tourist attraction. It's a vast honeycomb of markets that sell just about everything, but mostly crafts, clothing (vintage, ethnic, and young designer), and antiques. Here, especially on a weekend, the crowds are dense, young, and relentless. You may tire of the identical T-shirts, pants, boots, vintage wear, and cheap leather on their backs and in the shops. Camden does have its charms, though. Gentrification has layered over a once overwhelmingly Irish neighborhood, vestiges of which coexist with the youth culture. Charm is evident in sections of the market itself as well as in other markets, including the bustling fruit-and-vegetable market on Inverness Street. Along the canal are some stylish examples of Nicholas Grimshaw architecture (architect of Waterloo Station), as well as the MTV offices with their designer graffiti. ✉ *Camden Lock, Camden High St., Camden Town NW1,* WEB *www.camdenlock.net.* ⏲ *Weekends. Tube: Camden Town or Chalk Farm.*

NEED A BREAK?

You will not go hungry in Camden Town. Among the countless cafés, bars, pubs, and restaurants, the following stand out for good value and good food: **Marine Ices** (✉ 8 Haverstock Hill, Camden Town NW3, ☎ 020/7482–9003) has a window dispensing ice cream to strollers, and pasta, pizza, and sundaes inside. **Bar Gansa** (✉ 2 Inverness St., Camden Town NW1, ☎ 020/7267–8909) offers Spanish tapas—small dishes for sharing. **Cottons Rhum Shop, Bar and Restaurant** (✉ 55 Chalk Farm Rd., Camden Town NW1, ☎ 020/7482–1096) is a Caribbean island in miniature, with great rum cocktails and jerk chicken.

Fenton House. This is Hampstead's oldest surviving house. Now a National Trust property, it has an interesting collection of antiques and period interiors, along with some 17th century–style gardens. Baroque enthusiasts can join a tour of the large collection of keyboard instru-

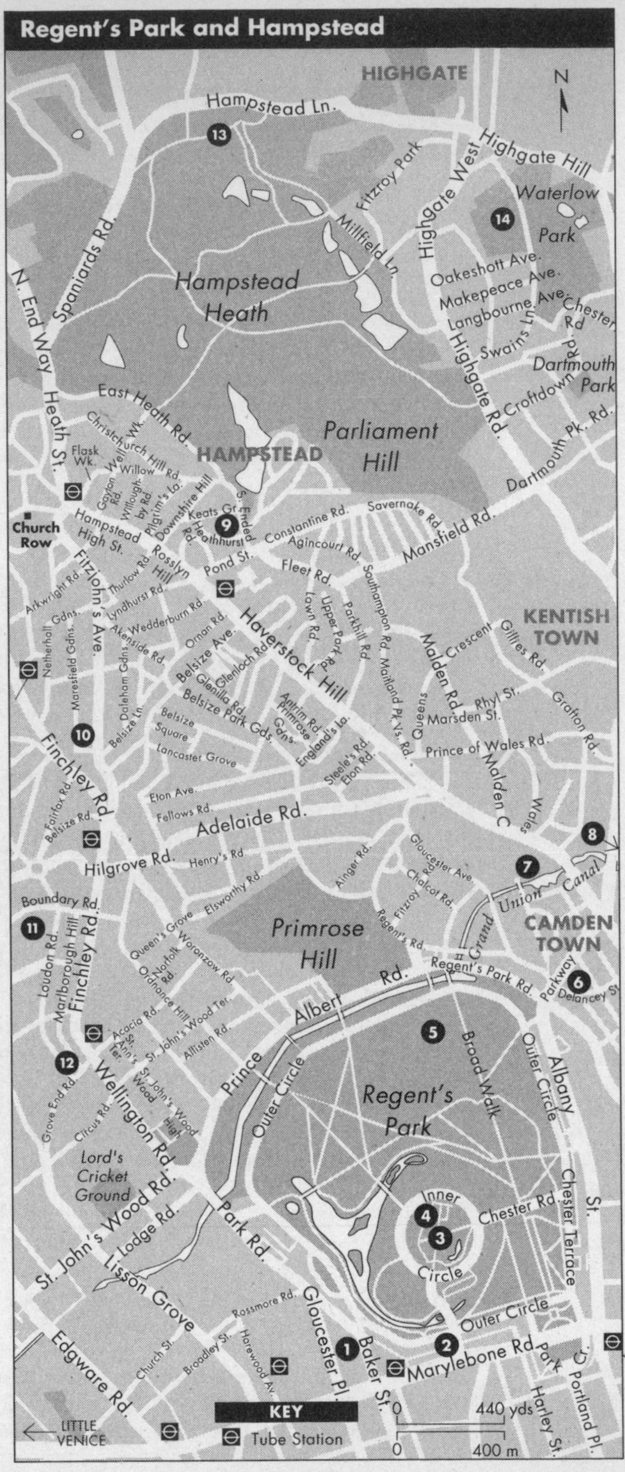

Regent's Park and Hampstead
HIGHGATE
N
Hampstead Ln.
Highgate Hill
Highgate West
Fitzroy Park
Waterlow Park
Millfield Ln.
Spaniards Rd.
N. End Way
Hampstead Heath
Oakeshott Ave.
Makepeace Ave.
Langbourne Ave.
Chester Rd.
Swains Ln.
Dartmouth Park
Croftdown Rd.
Highgate Rd.
Dartmouth Pk. Rd.
East Heath Rd.
Parliament Hill
HAMPSTEAD
Heath St.
Christchurch Hill Rd.
Well Wk.
Flask Wk.
Willow Rd.
Gayton Rd.
Willoughby Rd.
Pilgrim's La.
Downshire Hill
Keats Gr.
S. End Rd.
Heathhurst Rd.
Church Row
Hampstead High St.
Rosslyn Hill
Constantine Rd.
Savernake Rd.
Mansfield Rd.
Agincourt Rd.
Pond St.
Fleet Rd.
Southampton Rd.
Maitland Pk. Vs. Rd.
Fitzjohn's Ave.
Arkwright Rd.
Thurlow Rd.
Lyndhurst Rd.
Wedderburn Rd.
Akenside Rd.
Lawn Rd.
Upper Park Rd.
Parkhill Rd.
Haverstock Hill
Ornan Rd.
Belsize Ave.
Glenloch Rd.
Glenilla Rd.
Belsize Park Gds.
Antrim Rd.
Primrose Gdns.
England's La.
Netherhall Gdns.
Maresfield Gdns.
Daleham Gdns.
Belsize Ln.
Belsize Square
Lancaster Grove
KENTISH TOWN
Malden Rd.
Crescent
Gillies Rd.
Queens
Rhyl St.
Marsden St.
Grafton Rd.
Prince of Wales Rd.
Malden C.
Wales
Steele's Rd.
Eton Rd.
Finchley Rd.
Fairfax Rd.
Belsize Rd.
Eton Ave.
Fellows Rd.
Adelaide Rd.
Hilgrove Rd.
Henry's Rd.
Elsworthy Rd.
Ainger Rd.
Gloucester Ave.
Chalcot Rd.
Fitzroy Rd.
Regent's Rd.
Grand Union Canal
CAMDEN TOWN
Boundary Rd.
Loudon Rd.
Marlborough Hill
Queen's Grove
Norfolk Rd.
Woronzow Rd.
Ordnance Hill
Primrose Hill
Albert Rd.
Regent's Park Rd.
Parkway
Delancey St.
Acacia Rd.
St. Ann's Ter.
St. John's Wood Ter.
Allitsen Rd.
Prince
Outer Circle
Broad Walk
Albany St.
Grove End Rd.
Wellington Rd.
Circus Rd.
St. John's Wood High St.
Regent's Park
Lord's Cricket Ground
St. John's Wood Rd.
Lodge Rd.
Park Rd.
Inner Circle
Chester Rd.
Chester Terrace
Lisson Grove
Rossmore Rd.
Gloucester Pl.
Baker St.
Marylebone Rd.
Park Cr.
Portland Pl.
Harley St.
Edgware Rd.
Church St.
Broadley St.
Harewood Av.
LITTLE VENICE
KEY
Tube Station
0 440 yds
0 400 m

Close-Up

STRAWBERRY BEATLES FOREVER: A TRIP TO ABBEY ROAD

FOR COUNTLESS BEATLEMANIACS and baby boomers, No. 3 Abbey Road is one of the most beloved spots in London. Here, outside the legendary Abbey Road Studios, is the most famous zebra crossing in the world. Immortalized on the Beatles' 1969 *Abbey Road* album, this footpath became a mod monument when, on August 8 of that year, John, Paul, George, and Ringo posed—walking symbolically *away* from the recording facility—for photographer Iain Macmillan for the famous album shot.

Today, many fans venture to Abbey Road to leave their signatures on the white-stucco fence that fronts the studio facility. "God Is a Beatle!," "Why don't you do it in the road?," and "Strawberry Beatles Forever" are a few of the flourishes left.

The recording facility's Studio 2 is where the Beatles recorded their entire output, from "Love Me Do" onward, including, most momentously, *Sgt. Pepper's Lonely Hearts Club Band* (early 1967). Since this was the Beatles' professional home for much of their career, many of their most famous photos were taken here.

Today, tourists like to Beatle-ize themselves by taking the same sort of photo, but be careful: rushing cars make Abbey Road a dangerous intersection. Currently, there are few places in London that commemorate the Fab Four, so the best way Beatle-lovers can enjoy the history of the group is to take one of the smashing walking tours offered by the **Original London Walks** (☏ 020/7624–3978), including "The Beatles In-My-Life Walk" (11:20 AM at the Baker Street underground on Saturday and Tuesday) and "The Beatles Magical Mystery Tour" (10:55 AM at Dominion Theater underground Exit, Tottenham Court Road, on Sunday and Thursday).

Abbey Road is in the elegant neighborhood of St. John's Wood, just a 10 minute ride on the tube from central London. Take the Jubilee subway line to the St. John's Wood tube stop, head southwest three blocks down Grove End Road, and—especially if you were one of the 63 million people who tuned in to the *Ed Sullivan Show* on February 8, 1964, and grew up with the Beatles—be prepared for a heart-stopping vista right out of Memory Lane.

ments, given by the curator. Call ahead for details. ✉ *Hampstead Grove, Hampstead NW3,* ☏ *020/7435–3471,* WEB *www.nationaltrust.org.uk.* 🎫 *£4.40.* ⏲ *Mar., weekends 2–5; Apr.–Oct., Wed.–Fri. 2–5, weekends 11–5. Tube: Hampstead.*

10 **Freud Museum.** The father of psychoanalysis lived here for only a few months, between his escape from Nazi persecution in his native Vienna in 1938 and his death in 1939. Many of his possessions emigrated with him and were set up by his daughter, Anna (herself a pioneer of child psychoanalysis), as a shrine to her father's life and work. Four years after Anna's death in 1982 the house was opened as a museum. It replicates Freud's famous consulting rooms, particularly through the presence of *the couch*. You'll find Freud-related books, lectures, and study

groups here, too. ✉ *20 Maresfield Gardens, Hampstead NW3,* ☎ *020/7435–2002,* WEB *www.freud.org.uk.* 🎫 *£4.* ⏲ *Wed.–Sun. noon–5. Tube: Swiss Cottage or Finchley Rd.*

Hampstead Heath. For an escape from the ordered prettiness of Hampstead, head to the heath—a wild park, which spreads for miles to the north. From here you'll get stunning views of London. On the southwest corner stands the rebuilt version of a famous inn, once Dickens's favorite haunt, **Jack Straw's Castle** (✉ North End Way, Hampstead NW3, ☎ 020/7435–8885). It is named after the Peasants' Revolt leader who hid out and was captured here in 1381 after destroying Sir Robert Hales's residence and priory, the Priory of St. John. Hales was hated for enforcing the poll tax, which led to the uprising—and which, when reintroduced by Margaret Thatcher, proved equally unpopular the second time around. Another historic pub stands off the northwest edge, on Hampstead Lane. The **Spaniards Inn** (✉ Spaniards Rd., Hampstead NW3, ☎ 020/8731–6571) is little changed since the early 18th century, when (they say) the notorious highwayman Dick Turpin hung out here. Keats also drank here, as did Shelley and Byron.

14 **Highgate Cemetery.** The older west side of this sprawling early Victorian graveyard, featuring many an overwrought stone memorial, can be visited only by a tour given by the Friends of Highgate Cemetery—a group of volunteers who virtually saved the place from ruin. The shady streets of the dead, Egyptian Avenue and the Circle of Lebanon, are particularly Poe-like, but the famous graves are mostly on the newer, less atmospheric east side. This side can be wandered freely. Karl Marx's enormous black bust is probably the most-visited site, but George Eliot is also buried here. This is not London's oldest cemetery—that distinction belongs to Kensal Green, with its spine-chilling catacombs and Gothic mausoleums. ✉ *Swains La., Highgate, Highgate N6,* ☎ *020/8340–1834,* WEB *www.highgate-cemetery.org.* 🎫 *Prices on request.* ⏲ *Call for opening times and visitor information; hrs vary according to whether a funeral service is scheduled. Tube: Archway.*

6 **Jewish Museum.** This museum tells a potted history of the Jews in London from Norman times, though the bulk of the exhibits date from the end of the 17th century (when Cromwell repealed the laws against Jewish settlement) and later. The museum holds a world-renowned collection of ceremonial art. The museum's branch in Finchley covers social history, with changing exhibitions, and permanent exhibits and tape archives on the Holocaust, in the words of survivors. ✉ *Raymond Burton House, 129 Albert St., Camden Town NW1,* ☎ *020/7284–1997,* WEB *www.jewmusm.ort.org.* 🎫 *£3.50.* ⏲ *Sun. 10–5, Mon.–Thurs. 10–4. Tube: Camden Town.*

9 **Keats House.** Here you can see the plum tree under which the young Romantic poet composed "Ode to a Nightingale," many of his original manuscripts, his library, and other possessions he managed to acquire in his short life. It was in February 1820 that Keats coughed blood up into his handkerchief and exclaimed, "I know the color of that blood; it is arterial blood. I cannot be deceived in that color. That drop of blood is my death warrant. I must die." He left this house in September, moved to Rome, and died of consumption there, in early 1821, at age 25. ✉ *Keats House, Wentworth Pl., Keats Grove, Hampstead NW3,* ☎ *020/7435–2062.* 🎫 *£3 (valid for one year).* ⏲ *Apr.–Oct., Tues.–Sun. noon–5; Nov.–Mar., Tues.–Sun. noon–4. Tube: Hampstead.*

NEED A BREAK?

Hampstead is full of restaurants, including a few that have been here forever. Try the **Coffee Cup** (✉ 74 Hampstead High St., Hampstead NW3, ☎ 020/435–7565), which has been serving English breakfasts all day to a hip crowd of locals since the 1950s, from 8 till late (and you can get steak sandwiches and pasta, too). The **Hampstead Tea Rooms** (✉ 9 South End Rd., Hampstead NW3, ☎ 020/7435–9563) has been run by the same owners for over 30 years, selling sandwiches, pies, pastries and cream cakes, on drool view in the window. For a more substantial but still speedy meal on the hoof, stop at the **Hampstead Creperie** (✉ 77 Hampstead High St., Hampstead NW3, ☎ 020/7372–0081), which serves authentic sweet and savory French crepes from a little cart on the street. The quaintest pub in Hampstead, complete with fireplace and timber frame, is the **Hollybush** (✉ 22 Holly Mount, Hampstead NW3, ☎ 020/7435–2892), which dates back to 1807. Tucked away on a side street, it is open until 11 each night and serves traditional English lunches and dinners, often to the accompaniment of live Irish music.

13 **Kenwood House.** Perfectly and properly Palladian, this mansion was first built in 1616 and remodeled by Robert Adam in 1764. Adam refaced most of the exterior and added the gaudy library, which, with its curved painted ceiling, rather garish coloring, and gilded detailing, is the sole highlight of the house for decor buffs. What is unmissable here is the **Iveagh Bequest,** a collection of paintings that the Earl of Iveagh gave the nation in 1927, starring a wonderful Rembrandt self-portrait and works by Reynolds, Van Dyck, Hals, Gainsborough, and Turner. Top billing goes to Vermeer's *Guitar Player,* one of the most beautiful paintings in the world. In front of the house, a graceful lawn slopes down to a little lake crossed by a trompe-l'oeil bridge—all in perfect 18th-century upper-class taste. The rest of the grounds are skirted by Hampstead Heath. Nowadays the lake is dominated by its concert bowl, which stages a summer series of orchestral concerts, including an annual performance of Handel's *Music for the Royal Fireworks,* complete with fireworks. ✉ *Hampstead La., Hampstead NW3,* ☎ *020/8348–1286.* WEB *www.english-heritage.org.uk.* 🎫 *Free.* ⏲ *Easter–Aug., Sat.–Tues. and Thurs. 10–6, Wed. and Fri. 10:30–6; Dec.–Easter, Sat.–Tues. and Thurs. 10–4, Wed. and Fri. 10:30–5; Sept.–Nov. Sat.–Tues. and Thurs. 10–4, Wed. and Fri. 10:30–4. Tube: Golder's Green, then Bus 210.*

8 **London Canal Museum.** Here, in a former ice storage house, you can learn about the rise and fall of London's once extensive canal network. Outside, on the Battlebridge Basin, float the gaily painted narrow boats of modern canal dwellers—a few steps and a world away from King's Cross, which remains one of London's least salubrious neighborhoods. The quirky little museum is accessible from Camden Lock if you take the towpath. ✉ *12–13 New Wharf Rd., Camden Town N1,* ☎ *020/7713–0836,* WEB *www.canalmuseum.org.uk.* 🎫 *£2.50.* ⏲ *Tues.–Sun. 10–3:45. Tube: King's Cross.*

London Planetarium. This domed building stands right next to Madame Tussaud's, but it could hardly provide greater contrast with the waxworks (though you can save a bit of cash by combining them in a single visit). Inside the dome, exact simulations of the night sky are projected by the Digistar Mark 2 and accompanied by gosh-wow-fancy-that narration. The shows, which change daily, are good enough to addict children to astronomy. There are also regular laser shows and rock music extravaganzas. Beat the crowds by calling in advance for timed entry tickets to both Madame Tussaud's and the Planetarium. ✉ *Marylebone Rd., Regent's Park NW1,* ☎ *087/0400–3000 for timed entry tickets,* WEB *www.london-planetarium.com.* 🎫 *£6.75, combined ticket with Madame Tussaud's £16.45.* ⏲ *Weekdays 10–5:30, weekends 9:30–5:30; show every 30 mins; last show 5. Tube: Baker Street.*

5 **London Zoo.** The zoo opened in 1828 and peaked in popularity during the 1950s, when more than 3 million people passed through its turnstiles every year. A modernization program to attract a wider range of visitors progresses gradually. Many traditional cages remain, but for instance, in order that they can live in more natural space, the elephants have been moved to the "safari" branch of the zoo in the countryside, Whipsnade. One of the more modern highlights is the Web of Life—a conservation and education center set in a glass pavilion. And to ensure that the celebration of life does not go unheralded, the zoo has taken on a poet-in-residence, the young but highly acclaimed Tobias Hill. If you get the chance, catch one of his readings or popular children's workshops at the zoo.

Zoo highlights (unchanged over the years) include the Rhino Pavilion (which closely resembles the South Bank Arts Complex); the graceful Snowdon Aviary, spacious enough to allow its tenants free flight; and the 1936 Penguin Pool, where feeding time sends small children into raptures. The reptile house is a special draw for Harry Potter fans—it's where Harry discovers he can talk to snakes, and that he can make magic happen. New thrills include a desert swarming with locusts; a rain forest alive with butterflies, bats, and hummingbirds; and a cave lighted by fireflies. This is the headquarters of the Zoological Society of London, and much work is done here in wildlife conservation, education, and the breeding of endangered species. The emphasis has been shifted onto this aspect of the exhibits. The first step along this road was the Children's Zoo, which shows how people and animals live together; it has domestic animals from around the world. For animal encounter sessions with keepers, and feeding times, check the information board at admission. ✉ *Regent's Park NW1,* ☎ *020/7722–3333,* WEB *www.londonzoo.co.uk.* *£8:50.* *Mar.–Oct., daily 10–5:30; Nov.–Feb., daily 10–4. Tube: Camden Town, then Bus 74.*

2 **Madame Tussaud's.** This—one of London's busiest sights—is nothing more and nothing less than the world's premier exhibition of lifelike waxwork models of celebrities. Madame T. learned her craft while making death masks of French Revolution victims, and in 1835 set up her first show of the famous ones near this spot. Nowadays, Super Stars of entertainment, in their own hall of the same name, outrank any aristo in popularity, along with the newest segment, The Spirit of London, and a Time Taxi Ride that visits every notable Londoner from Shakespeare to Benny Hill. But top billing still goes to the murderers in the Chamber of Horrors, who stare glassy-eyed at visitors—one from an electric chair, one sitting next to the tin bath where he dissolved several wives in quicklime. What, aside from ghoulish prurience, makes people stand in line to invest in London's most expensive museum ticket? It is the thrill of rubbing shoulders with Shakespeare, Martin Luther King Jr., the queen, and the Beatles—most of them dressed in their very own outfits—in a single day. Beat the crowds by calling in advance for timed entry tickets. ✉ *Marylebone Rd., Regent's Park NW1,* ☎ *087/0400–3000 for timed entry tickets,* WEB *www.madame-tussauds.com.* *£14, combined ticket with planetarium £16.45.* *Sept.–June, weekdays 10–5:30, weekends 9:30–5:30; July–Aug., daily 9:30–5:30. Tube: Baker St.*

★ 3 **Regent's Park.** The youngest of London's great parks, Regent's Park was laid out in 1812 by John Nash, who worked for his patron, the Prince Regent (hence the name), who was crowned George IV in 1820. The idea was to re-create the feel of a grand country residence close to the center of town, with all those magnificent white-stucco terraces facing in on the park. As you walk the Outer Circle, you'll see how successfully

Nash's plans were carried out, although the focus of it all—a palace for the prince—was never actually built (George was too busy fiddling with the one he already had, Buckingham Palace). The most famous and impressive of Nash's terraces would have been in the prince's line of vision from the planned palace. **Cumberland Terrace** has a central block of Ionic columns surmounted by a triangular Wedgwood-blue pediment that is like a giant cameo. Snow-white statuary personifying Britannia and her empire (the work of the on-site architect, James Thomson) single it out from the pack. The noted architectural historian Sir John Summerson described it thus: "the backcloth as it were to Act III, and easily the most breathtaking architectural panorama in London."

As in all London parks, planting here is planned with the aim of having something in bloom in all seasons, but if you hit the park in May, June, or July, head first to the Inner Circle. Your nostrils should lead you to **Queen Mary's Gardens,** a fragrant 17-acre circle that riots with roses in summer and heather, azaleas, and evergreens in other seasons. The **Broad Walk** is a good vantage point from which to glimpse the minaret and golden dome of the **London Central Mosque** on the far west side of the park. If it's a summer evening or a Sunday afternoon, witness a remarkable phenomenon. Wherever you look, the sport being enthusiastically played is not cricket but softball, now Britain's fastest-growing participant sport (bring your mitt). You're likely to see cricket, too, plus a lot of dog walkers—not for nothing did Dodie Smith set her novel *A Hundred and One Dalmatians* in an Outer Circle house. ☎ *020/7486–7905,* WEB *www.royalparks.co.uk.*

❹ **Regent's Park Open-Air Theatre.** They have mounted Shakespeare productions here every summer since 1932; everyone from Vivien Leigh to Jeremy Irons has performed here. *A Midsummer Night's Dream* is the one to catch—never is that enchanted Greek wood more lifelike than it is here, augmented by genuine bird squawks and a rising moon. The park can get chilly, so bring a blanket; rain stops the play only when heavy. ✉ *Open-Air Theatre, Regent's Park NW1,* ☎ *020/7486–2431.* ⏲ *June–Aug., evening performances 7:30, matinees 2:30. Tube: Baker St. or Regent's Park.*

⓫ **Saatchi Collection.** This blinding white space is all crisp angles and quietness, the better to contemplate the front lines of contemporary painting, installations, and sculpture—by the likes of Lucian Freud, Paula Rego, Damien Hirst, Rachel Whiteread, Janine Antoni—collected by the advertising mogul. ✉ *98A Boundary Rd., St. John's Wood NW8,* ☎ *020/7624–8299.* 🎫 *£5.* ⏲ *Thurs.–Sun. noon–6. Tube: Swiss Cottage or St. John's Wood.*

❶ **Sherlock Holmes Museum.** You know you've reached this museum when you see the actor dressed as a Victorian policeman outside and the sign that claims this as 221B Baker Street, the address of Arthur Conan Doyle's fictional detective. Inside, "Holmes's housekeeper" conducts you into a series of Victorian rooms full of Sherlock-abilia. It's all so realistic, you may actually begin to believe in Holmes's existence. ✉ *221B Baker St., Regent's Park NW1,* ☎ *020/7935–8866,* WEB *www.sherlock-homes.co.uk.* 🎫 *£6.* ⏲ *Daily 9:30–6. Tube: Baker St.*

2 Willow Road. Modern movement master Ernö Goldfinger put this house up in the 1930s, and the National Trust has now kindly restored it and filled it with important (and currently very trendy) modernist furniture and art. Note that there are limited visitor hours with timed tickets because the house is small. ✉ *2 Willow Rd., Hampstead NW1,* ☎ *020/7435–6166,* WEB *www.nationaltrust.org.uk.* 🎫 *£4.* ⏲ *Mar.–Oct., Thurs.–Sat. noon–5; Nov.–Dec., Sat. noon–5. Tube: Hampstead.*

GREENWICH

About 8 mi downstream from central London—which means seaward, to the east—lies a neighborhood that has recently had front-page fame thrust upon it. Once a sleepy, charming self-contained village with elegant, perfectly proportioned buildings and tall ships anchored at the river bank, Greenwich became the site of the Millennium Dome and, consequently, synonymous with the millennium. The Dome—either a spectacular monument to mankind or, according to some British critics, a dazzling waste of £758 million of public money—is now closed to the public and has been on offer to several companies; its future remained unclear at press time. Greenwich really scored on transportation when it became the center of the millennium universe. Now there are more roads leading to it than to Rome—but don't try driving there, as all new routes are strictly public transportation. Take the Jubilee Line extensions, and if you're an architecture buff, get out at every stop—each one was designed by a different cutting-edge architect.

Greenwich has many attractions. Spreading both grandly and elegantly beside the river are the colonnades and pediments of Sir Christopher Wren's Royal Naval College and Inigo Jones's Queen's House, both of which seem to be part of a complex of Grecian temples transported to the Thames. Here, too, is the Old Royal Observatory, which measures time for the entire planet, and the Greenwich Meridian, which divides the world in two—you can stand astride it with one foot in either hemisphere. This is also where the millennium officially started (when this clock said so). The National Maritime Museum and the proud clipper ship *Cutty Sark* thrill seafaring types, and landlubbers can stroll the green acres of parkland that surround the buildings, the quaint 19th-century houses, and the weekend crafts and antiques markets.

Numbers in the text correspond to numbers in the margin and on the Greenwich map.

A Good Walk

To start your walk, take the Docklands Light Railway (DLR) or a ferry to Cutty Sark station and begin your tour with the **Cutty Sark** ①. Follow King William Walk and then take a right on College Approach toward Wren's majestic **Royal Naval College** ②. The **Queen's House** ③, followed by the **National Maritime Museum** ④ sit just down King William Walk on Romney Road. Now head up the hill in Greenwich Park, overlooking the Naval College and Maritime Museum, to the **Old Royal Observatory** ⑤ and the **Ranger's House** ⑥. Walking back through the park toward the river, you'll enter the pretty streets of Greenwich Village to the west. There are plenty of bookstores and antiques shops for browsing and, at the foot of Crooms Hill, the modern Greenwich Theatre—a West End theater, despite its location, that mounts well-regarded, often star-spangled productions—and the **Fan Museum** ⑦ opposite. Finish up at the excellent **Village Market** ⑧ and the Victorian **Greenwich Market** ⑨ by the *Cutty Sark,* on College Approach. If you've still energy and time, a visit to the Thames Barrier Visitors' Centre is a fun way to explore the banks of the Thames.

TIMING

The boat trip takes about an hour from Westminster Pier (next to Big Ben), or 25 minutes from the Tower of London, so figure in enough time for the round-trip. There are such riches here, especially if the maritime theme is your thing, that whatever time you allow will seem halved. If the weather's good, you'll be tempted to stroll aimlessly around the quaint village streets, too, and maybe take a turn in the park. If you want to take in the markets, you'll need to come on a weekend.

HOW TO GET THERE

Once, Greenwich was thought of as remote by Londoners, with only the river as a direct route. Now, with extended transport links in the form of the Docklands Light Railway and the tube's Jubilee Line, getting here is both easy and inexpensive. The quickest route to Greenwich is the tube to Canary Wharf and the Docklands Light Rail (or DLR, the driverless elevated train with good views of the Docklands) to the *Cutty Sark*. You can also exit the DLR at Island Gardens and walk under the Thames to Greenwich for a thrill.

The river connections to Greenwich mean that the journey to Greenwich is fun in itself, for you will then get the best possible vista of the Royal Naval College, with the Queen's House behind. On the way, the boat glides past famous sights on the London skyline (there's a guaranteed spine chill on passing the Tower) and the ever-changing docklands, and there's always a cockney navigator enhancing the views with wise-guy commentary. **Ferries** from central London to Greenwich take 30–55 minutes and leave from various piers: from Charing Cross and Tower piers (☎ 020/7987–1185), from Westminster Pier (☎ 020/7930–4097), and from the Thames Barrier Pier (☎ 020/8305–0300).

Sights to See

1 ***Cutty Sark.*** This romantic clipper was built in 1869, one of fleets and fleets of similar wooden tall-masted clippers that plied the seven seas in the 19th century, trading in exotic commodities—tea, in this case. The *Cutty Sark*, the last to survive, was also the fastest, sailing the China–London route in 1871 in only 107 days. Now the photogenic vessel lies in dry dock, a museum of one kind of seafaring life—and not a comfortable kind for the 28-strong crew, as you'll see. The collection of figureheads is amusing, too. ⊠ *King William Walk, Greenwich SE10,* ☎ *020/8858–3445,* WEB *www.cuttysark.org.uk.* *£3.50.* *Daily 10–5 (last admission 4:30). DLR: Cutty Sark.*

7 **Fan Museum.** In two newly restored houses dating from the 1820s, opposite the Greenwich Theatre, is this highly unusual museum. The 2,000 fans here, which date from the 17th century onward, compose the world's only such collection, and the history and purpose of these often exquisitely crafted objects are satisfyingly explained. It was the personal vision—and fan collection—of Helene Alexander that brought it into being, and the workshop and conservation and study center that she has also set up ensure that this anachronistic art has a future. ⊠ *12 Croom's Hill, Greenwich SE10,* ☎ *020/8858–7879,* WEB *www.fan-museum.org.* *£3.50.* *Tues.–Sat. 11–5, Sun. noon–5. DLR: Greenwich.*

9 **Greenwich Market.** You'll find this Victorian covered crafts market by the *Cutty Sark*, on College Approach. Established as a fruit and vegetable market in 1700, and granted a royal charter in 1849, the glass-roofed market now offers arts and crafts everyday except Thursday, when it becomes one of London's premier antiques and collectibles markets. Shopping for crafts is a pleasure, as in most cases you're buying directly from the artist. ⊠ *College Approach, Greenwich SE10,* ☎ *020/7515–7153.* *Wed.–Sun. 9:30–5:30, Thurs. 9–5. DLR: Cutty Sark.*

4 **National Maritime Museum.** One of Greenwich's star attractions contains everything to do with the British at sea, in the form of paintings, models, maps, globes, sextants, uniforms (including the one Nelson died in at Trafalgar, complete with bloodstained bullet hole), and—best of all—actual boats, including a collection of ornate, gilded royal barges. There is an immense glazed roof, creating an indoor courtyard. ⊠ *Romney Rd., Greenwich SE10,* ☎ *020/8858–4422,* WEB *www.nmm.ac.uk.* *Free.* *Mon.–Sun. 10–5. DLR: Greenwich.*

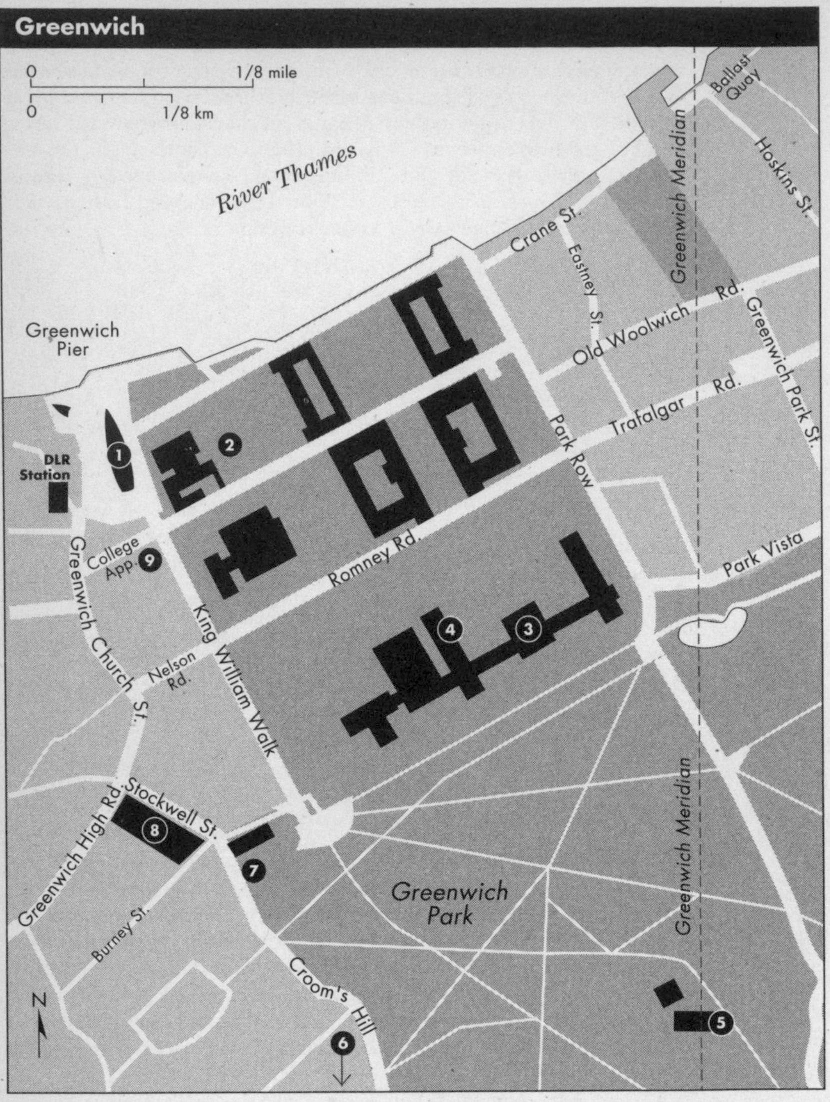

Cutty Sark **1**
Fan Museum **7**
Greenwich Market **9**
National Maritime Museum **4**
Old Royal Observatory **5**
Queen's House **3**
Ranger's House **6**
Royal Naval College **2**
Village Market **8**

5 **Old Royal Observatory.** Founded in 1675 by Charles II, this imposing institution was designed the same year by Christopher Wren for John Flamsteed, the first Astronomer Royal. The red ball you see on its roof has been there only since 1833. It drops every day at 1 PM, and you can set your watch by it, as the sailors on the Thames always have. This Greenwich Timeball, along with the Gate Clock inside the observatory, is the most visible manifestation of Greenwich Mean Time—since 1884, the ultimate standard for time around the world. Greenwich is on the **prime meridian** at 0° longitude. A brass line laid among the cobblestones here marks the meridian, one side being the eastern, one the western hemisphere. In 1948 the Old Royal Observatory lost its official status: London's glow had grown too intense, and the astronomers moved to Sussex, while the Astronomer Royal decamped to Cambridge. They left various telescopes, chronometers, and clocks for you to view in their absence. An excellent exhibition on the solution to the problem of measuring longitude includes John Harrison's famous clocks, H1–H4, now in working order. ✉ *Greenwich Park, Greenwich SE10,* ☎ *020/8858–4422,* WEB *www.rog.nmm.ac.uk.* 🎫 *Free.* ⏲ *Daily 10–5. DLR: Greenwich.*

★ 3 **Queen's House.** The queen for whom Inigo Jones began designing the house in 1616 was James I's Anne of Denmark, but she died three years later, and it was Charles I's French wife, Henrietta Maria, who inherited the building when it was completed in 1635. It is no less than Britain's first classical building—the first, that is, to use the lessons of Italian Renaissance architecture—and is therefore of enormous importance in the history of English architecture. Inside, the Tulip Stair, named for the fleur de lys–style pattern on the balustrade, is especially fine, spiraling up, without a central support, to the Great Hall. The Great Hall itself is a perfect cube, exactly 40 ft in all three directions, decorated with paintings of the Muses, the Virtues, and the Liberal Arts. ✉ *Romney Rd., Greenwich SE10,* ☎ *020/8293–9618.* WEB *www.nmm.ac.uk.* 🎫 *Free.* ⏲ *Daily 10–5. DLR: Cutty Sark.*

NEED A BREAK? After a long walk, the historic **Trafalgar Tavern** (✉ Park Row, Greenwich SE10, ☎ 020/8858–2437), with excellent views of the Thames, is a grand place to have a pint and some upmarket pub grub. In warm weather, the riverside terrace offers outdoor seating overlooking the Millennium Dome. At **Goddard's Ye Olde Pie House** (✉ 45 Greenwich Church St., Greenwich SE10), pie and mash are the only things on the menu.

6 **Ranger's House.** This handsome, early 18th-century mansion, which was the Greenwich Park Ranger's official residence during the 19th century, now houses collections of Jacobean portraits. The Wernher Collection, a magnificent and internationally important collection of European art which includes fine old master pieces and Renaissance jewelry, is also on permanent display. Concerts are regularly given here, too. It stands just outside the park boundaries, on the southwest side of **Greenwich Park,** one of London's oldest royal parks. It had been in existence for more than 200 years before Charles II commissioned the French landscape artist Le Nôtre (who was responsible for Versailles and for St. James's Park) to redesign it in what was, in the 1660s, the latest French fashion. Look also for Queen Elizabeth's Oak on the east side, around which Henry VIII and his second queen, Anne Boleyn, Elizabeth I's mother, are said to have danced. ✉ *Chesterfield Walk, Blackheath, Greenwich SE10,* ☎ *020/8853–0035,* WEB *www.english-heritage.org.uk.* 🎫 *Free.* ⏲ *Apr.–Sept., daily 10–1 and 2–6; Oct.–Mar., Wed.–Sun. 10–1 and 2–4. DLR: Cutty Sark.*

★ 7 **Royal Naval College.** Begun by Christopher Wren in 1694 as a home, or hospital (as in the Chelsea Royal Hospital, not Charing Cross Hospital), for ancient mariners, it became instead a school for young ones in 1873. Today the University of Greenwich has classes here. You'll notice how the structures part to reveal the Queen's House across the central lawns. Wren, with the help of his assistant, Nicholas Hawksmoor, was at pains to preserve the river vista from the house, and there are few more majestic views in London than the awe-inspiring symmetry he achieved. Behind the college are two buildings you can visit. The **Painted Hall,** the college's dining hall, derives its name from the Baroque murals of William and Mary (reigned 1689–95; William alone 1695–1702) and assorted allegorical figures, the whole supported by trompe-l'oeil pillars that Sir James Thornhill (who decorated the inside of St. Paul's dome, too) painted between 1707 and 1717. In the opposite building stands the **College Chapel,** which was rebuilt after a fire in 1779 and is altogether lighter, in a more restrained, neo-Grecian style. At Christmas 1805, Admiral Nelson's body was brought from the Battle of Trafalgar to lie in state here. ✉ *Royal Naval College, King William Walk, Greenwich SE10,* ☎ *0800/389–3341 recorded information; 020/8269–4747,* WEB *www.greenwichfoundation.org.uk.* 🎫 *£3; free after 3:30 Mon.–Sat. and all day Sun..* ⏲ *Mon.–Sat. 10–5, Sun. 12:30–5 (last admission 4:15). DLR: Cutty Sark.*

8 **The Village Market.** If you're visiting on the weekend, this market on Stockwell Street near the Fan Museum and Greenwich Theatre is open for business. It has a lot of bric-a-brac and books, too, and it's well known among the cognoscenti as a good source for vintage clothing. **Antiques Market.** Just on the opposite block to the Village Market, more vintage shopping can be found in the weekend Antiques Market, on Greenwich High Road, where you can browse among the "small collectibles." It's a weekenders' market haven, where you can find some original and inspired gifts. To make sure you don't miss a bargaining opportunity, get a visitors' map from the Tourist Information Centre by the *Cutty Sark* to orient your way around the profusion of markets. ✉ *Stockwell St., Greenwich SE10,* ☎ *020/8858–0808.* ⏲ *Weekends 9–5. DLR: Cutty Sark.*

OFF THE BEATEN PATH

THAMES BARRIER VISITORS' CENTRE – Learn what comes between London and its famous river—a futuristic-looking metal barrier that has been described as the eighth wonder of the world. Multimedia presentations, a film on the Thames' history, working models, and views of the barrier itself put the importance of the relationship between London and its river in perspective. ✉ *Unity Way, Eastmoor St., Woolwich SE18,* ☎ *020/8305–4188.* WEB *www.environment-agency.gov.uk.* 🎫 *£1.* ⏲ *Daily 10:30–4:30. British Rail: Charlton (from London Bridge).*

UPSTREAM FROM LONDON

The Thames is Britain's longest river. It winds its way through the Cotswolds, beyond Oxford and past majestic Windsor Castle—here far more the lazy, leafy country river than the dark-gray urban waterway you see in London. Once you leave the city center, going west, or upstream, you reach a series of former villages—Chiswick, Kew, Richmond, Putney—that, apart from the roar of aircraft coming in to land at Heathrow a few miles farther west, are still peaceful, almost rural, especially in places where parkland rolls down to the riverbank. In fact, it was really only at the beginning of the 20th century that London proper expanded to encompass these villages. The royal palaces and grand houses that dot the area were built as country residences with easy access to London by river.

TIMING

Each of the places listed here could easily absorb a whole day of your time, and Hampton Court is especially huge.

HOW TO GET THERE

Access is fairly easy: the District Line of the underground runs out to Kew and Richmond, as does Network SouthEast from Waterloo, which also serves Twickenham and Hampton Court. For Chiswick House or Hogarth's House, take British Rail to Chiswick station or take the District Line to Turnham Green. Both options require walking to reach the destination, but Chiswick station is a bit closer to the houses. British Rail also runs trains to Kew Bridge, which is convenient to Strand-on-the-Green. For Kew Gardens, take the District Line heading toward Richmond and get off at Kew Gardens. British Rail also stops nearby; from the station it's a pleasant walk down a tree-lined residential avenue to the gardens.

A pleasant if slow way to go is by river. Boats depart from **Westminster Pier,** just by Big Ben (☎ 020/7930–4097) for Kew (1½ hours), Richmond (2–3 hours), and Hampton Court (4 hours) several times a day in summer, less frequently from October through March. As you can tell from those sailing times, the boat trip is worth taking only if you make it an integral part of your day out, and even then, be aware that it can get very breezy on the water and that the scenery going upstream is by no means constantly fascinating.

Chiswick and Kew

Chiswick is the nearest Thames-side destination to London, with Kew just a mile or so beyond it. Much of Chiswick, developed at the beginning of the 20th century, is today a nondescript suburb. Incongruously stranded among the terraced houses, however, a number of fine 18th-century houses and a charming little village survive. The village atmosphere of Kew is still distinct, making this one of the most desirable areas of outer London. What makes Kew famous, though, are the Royal Botanic Gardens.

A Good Walk

Start your walk at the Italianate **Chiswick House** on Burlington Lane. Then follow Burlington Lane and take a left onto Hogarth Lane, which is anything but a lane, to reach **Hogarth's House.** Chiswick's Church Street (reached by an underpass from Hogarth's House) is the nearest thing to a sleepy country village street in all of London, despite its proximity to the Great West Road. Follow it down to the Thames and turn left at its foot to reach the sturdy 18th-century riverfront houses of Chiswick Mall. The ½-mi walk along here takes you far away from mainstream London and into a world of elegance and calm. You will pass several riverside pubs as you head along this stretch of the Thames toward Hammersmith Bridge. The Dove is the prettiest, if the most crowded, with its terrace hanging over the water. The food is better at the Blue Anchor, which you'll reach first.

There's a similarly peaceful walk to be had about 1 mi to the west along the 18th-century river frontage of Strand-on-the-Green, whose houses look over the narrow towpath to the river, their tidy brick facades covered with wisteria and roses in summer. Right before you reach Kew Bridge, you may be ready for a break at the Bell & Crown, where crowds congregate on summer days to watch the Thames roll by. Strand-on-the-Green ends at Kew Bridge, opposite which is Kew Green, where local teams play cricket on summer Sundays. All around it are fine 18th-century houses, and, in the center, a church in which the painters Thomas Gainsborough and John Zoffany (1733–1810) are buried. **Kew Gardens** and **Kew Palace** are just a short walk away over the Kew Bridge.

Sights to See

★ **Chiswick House.** Built circa 1725 by the Earl of Burlington (the Lord Burlington of Burlington House, Piccadilly, home of the Royal Academy, and, of course, the Burlington Arcade) as a country residence in which to entertain friends, and as a kind of temple to the arts, this is the very model of a Palladian villa, inspired by the Villa Capra near Vicenza in northeastern Italy. The house fans out from a central octagonal room in perfect symmetry, guarded by statues of Burlington's heroes, Palladio himself and his disciple Inigo Jones. Burlington's friends—Pope, Swift, Gay, and Handel among them—were well qualified to adorn a temple to the arts. Burlington was a great connoisseur and an important patron of the arts, but he was also an accomplished architect in his own right, fascinated by—obsessed with, even—the architecture and art of the Italian Renaissance and ancient Rome, with which he'd fallen in love during his Italian grand tour. Along with William Kent (1685–1748), who designed the interiors and the rambling gardens here, Burlington did a great deal toward the dissemination of Palladian ideals around Britain: Chiswick House sparked enormous interest, and you'll see these forms reflected in hundreds of later English stately homes both small and large. ✉ *Burlington La., Chiswick W4,* ☎ *020/8995–0508,* WEB *www.english-heritage.org.uk.* 🎫 *£3.50.* ⏲ *Apr.–Sept., daily 10–6; Oct.–Mar., Wed.–Sun. 10–4. Closed first two weeks in Jan. Tube: Turnham Green.*

Hogarth's House. This is where the painter lived from 1749 until his death in 1764. Unprotected from the six-lane Great West Road, which remains a main route to the West Country, the poor house is besieged by the surrounding traffic, but it's worth visiting for its little museum consisting mostly of the amusingly moralistic engravings for which Hogarth is best known, including the most famous of all, the *Rake's Progress* series of 1735. ✉ *Hogarth La., Chiswick W4,* ☎ *020/8994–6757.* 🎫 *Free.* ⏲ *Apr.–Sept., Tues.–Fri. 1–5, weekends 1–6; Oct.–Mar., Tues.–Fri. 1–4, weekends 1–5. Tube: Turnham Green.*

NEED A BREAK?

Pubs are the name of the game here at Chiswick's portion of the Thames. Many pubs sit on the bank of the river, offering watery vistas to accompany stout pints of brew. The **Bell & Crown** (✉ 72 Strand-on-the-Green, Chiswick W4, ☎ 020/8994–4164) is the first pub on the riverside path from Kew Bridge, with a riverside conservatory to check those breezes. The **Blue Anchor** (✉ 13 Lower Mall, Hammersmith W6, ☎ 020/8748–2639) is a cozy 18th-century watering hole, with rowing memorabilia lining the walls. The **Dove** (✉ 19 Upper Mall, Hammersmith W6, ☎ 020/8748–5405) retains the charm of its 300-year plus heritage. If you can find a place on the tiny terrace it's a tranquil place to watch the energetic oarsmen.

★ **Kew Gardens.** The Royal Botanic Gardens at Kew are a spectacular 300 acres of public gardens, containing more than 60,000 species of plants. In addition, this is the country's leading botanical institute, with strong royal associations. Until 1840, when Kew Gardens was handed over to the nation, it had been the grounds of two royal residences: the White House (formerly Kew House) and Richmond Lodge, or the Dutch House. George II and Queen Caroline lived at Richmond Lodge in the 1720s, while their eldest son, Frederick, Prince of Wales, and his wife, Princess Augusta, came to the White

House during the 1730s. The royal wives were keen gardeners. Queen Caroline got to work on her grounds, while next door Frederick's pleasure garden was developed as a botanical garden by his widow after his death. She introduced all kinds of "exotics," foreign plants brought back to England by botanists. Caroline was aided by a skilled head gardener and by the architect Sir William Chambers, who built a series of temples and follies, of which the crazy 10-story **Pagoda** (1762), visible for miles around, is the star turn. The celebrated botanist Sir Joseph Banks (1743–1820) then took charge of Kew, which developed rapidly in both its roles—as a landscaped garden and as a center of study and research.

The highlights of a visit to Kew are the two great 19th-century greenhouses filled with tropical plants, many of which have been there as long as their housing. Both the **Palm House** and the **Temperate House** were designed by Sir Decimus Burton, the first opening in 1848, the second in 1899; the latter was the biggest greenhouse in the world, and today contains the largest greenhouse plant in the world, a Chilean wine palm rooted in 1846. You can climb the spiral staircase almost to the roof and look down on this and the dense tropical profusion from the walkway. The **Princess of Wales Conservatory,** the latest and the largest plant house at Kew, was opened in 1987 by Princess Diana. Under its bold glass roofs, designed to maximize energy conservation, there are no fewer than 10 climatic zones.

The **Centre for Economic Botany** is housed in the Joseph Banks Building, the majority of which is devoted to Kew's research collection on economic botany and to its library. But the public can enjoy exhibitions here on the theme of plants in everyday life. (There is no admission charge, and the center is open Monday–Saturday 9:10–4:30 and Sunday 9:30–5:30.) The plant houses make Kew worth visiting even in the depths of winter, but in spring and summer the gardens come into their own. In late spring the woodland nature reserve of Queen Charlotte's Cottage Gardens is carpeted in bluebells; a little later, the Rhododendron Dell and the Azalea Garden become swathed in brilliant color. High summer brings glorious displays of roses and water lilies, while fall is the time to see the heather garden, near the pagoda. Whatever time of year you visit, something is in bloom, and your journey is never wasted. The main entrance is between Richmond Circus and the traffic circle at Mortlake Road. ✉ *Kew Rd., Kew,* ☎ *020/ 8940–1171,* WEB *www.kew.org.* 💳 *£5.* ⏲ *Gardens Apr.–Oct., weekdays 10–6, weekends, 9:30–7:30; greenhouse Apr.–Oct., daily 9:30–5:30; Nov.–Mar., daily 10–4. Tube: Kew Gardens.*

Kew Palace. To this day quietly domestic, Kew Palace remains the smallest royal palace in the land. The palace house and gardens offer a glimpse into the 17th century. ✉ *Kew Gardens, Kew.*

NEED A BREAK?

Maids of Honour (✉ 288 Kew Rd., Kew), the most traditional of Old English tearooms, is named for the famous tarts invented here and still baked by hand on the premises. Tea is served in the afternoon, Tuesday–Saturday 2:45–5:30.

Richmond

Named after the palace Henry VII built here in 1500, Richmond is still a welcoming and extremely pretty riverside "village," with many handsome (and expensive) houses, antiques shops, a Victorian theater, London's grandest stately home, and, best of all, the largest of London's royal parks.

Sights to See

★ **Ham House.** Ham House stands to the west of Richmond Park, overlooking the Thames and nearly opposite the oddly named Eel Pie Island. The house was built in 1610 by Sir Thomas Vavasour, knight marshal to James I, then refurbished later the same century by the Duke and Duchess of Lauderdale, who, although not particularly nice (a contemporary called the duchess "the coldest friend and the most violent enemy that ever was known"), managed to produce one of the finest houses in Britain at the time. Now that £2 million has been sunk into restoring Ham House—a project overseen by the National Trust—its splendor can be appreciated afresh. The formerly empty library has been filled with 17th- and 18th-century volumes; the original decorations in the Great Hall, Round Gallery, and Great Staircase have been replicated; and all the furniture and fittings, on permanent loan from the V&A, have been cleaned and restored. The 17th-century gardens merit a visit in their own right. You can reach Ham from Richmond on Bus 65 or 371, or by one of Greater London's most pleasant rural walks, lasting half an hour or so, along the eastern riverbank south from Richmond Bridge. ✉ *Ham St., Richmond,* ☎ *020/8940–1950,* WEB *www.guidetorichmond.co.uk.* 🎫 *House £5, gardens free.* ⏲ *House Mar.–Oct., Sat.–Wed. 1–5; gardens daily 10:30–dusk. Tube: Richmond.*

Marble Hill House. On the northern bank of the Thames, almost opposite Ham House, stands another mansion, this one a near-perfect example of a Palladian villa. Marble Hill House was built in the 1720s by George II for his mistress, the "exceedingly respectable and respected" Henrietta Howard. Later the house was occupied by Mrs. Fitzherbert, who was secretly married to the Prince Regent (later George IV) in 1785. Marble Hill House was restored in 1901 and opened to the public two years later, looking very much like it did in Georgian times. A ferry service operates during the summer from Ham House across the river; access by foot is a half-hour walk south along the west bank from Richmond Bridge. ✉ *Richmond Rd., Twickenham, Richmond,* ☎ *020/8892–5115,* WEB *www.english-heritage.org.uk.* 🎫 *£3.30.* ⏲ *Apr.–Sept., daily 10–6; Oct.–Mar., Wed.–Sun. 10–4 (subject to change; call before visiting). Tube: Richmond.*

Richmond Park. Charles I enclosed this one in 1637 for hunting purposes, as with practically all the other parks. Unlike the others, however, Richmond Park still has wild red and fallow deer roaming its 2,470 acres of grassland and heath and the oldest oaks you're likely to see—vestiges of the forests that encroached on London from all sides in medieval times. White Lodge, inside the park, was built for George II in 1729. Edward VIII was born here; now it houses the Royal Ballet School. You can walk from the park past the fine 18th-century houses in and around Richmond Hill to the river, admiring first the view from the top. At the Thames, you may notice Quinlan Terry's Richmond Riverside development, which met with the approval of England's architectural adviser, Prince Charles, for its classical facades and was vilified by many others for playing it safe. *Tube: Richmond.*

NEED A BREAK? The **Cricketers** (✉ Maids of Honour Row, Richmond Green, Richmond, ☎ 020/8940–4372) serves a good pub lunch. The modern, partially glass-roofed **Caffé Mamma** (✉ 24 Hill St., Richmond, ☎ 020/8940–1625) is a good spot for inexpensive Italian food.

★ **Syon House.** Home to Their Graces the Duke and Duchess of Northumberland, this is one of England's most sumptuous stately houses, and it is certainly the only one that's reachable by the London Underground. Several tube stops away from the center city on the District

Line, the house is set in a 55-acre park landscaped by Capability Brown. The core of the house is Tudor—two of Henry VIII's queens, Catherine Howard and Lady Jane Grey, made pit stops here before they were sent to the Tower—but the house was redone in the Georgian style in 1761 by famed decorator Robert Adam. He had just returned from studying the sites of classical antiquity in Italy and created two rooms here worthy of any Caesar: the entryway is an amazing study in black and white, pairing neoclassic marbles with antique bronzes, while the Ante-Room contains 12 enormous verdantique columns surmounted by statues of gold—this, no less, was meant to be a waiting room for the duke's servants and retainers. The Red Drawing Room is covered with crimson Spitalfields silk, while the Long Gallery is one of Adam's noblest creations (it was used by Cary Grant and Robert Mitchum for a duel in the 1958 film *The Grass Is Greener*). Elsewhere on the grounds are a nature center, a butterfly house, and a Victorian glass conservatory that is famous among connoisseurs for its Victorian charm. ✉ *Syon Park, Brentford, Brentford,* ☎ *020/8560–0881,* WEB *www.guidetorichmond.co.uk.* 🎫 *£6.25.* ⏲ *House early Apr.–late Oct., Wed.–Thurs. and Sun. 11–5; gardens daily 10–dusk. Tube: Gunnersbury, then take Bus 237 or 267 to Brentlea stop.*

Hampton Court Palace

★ Some 20 mi from central London, on a loop of the Thames upstream from Richmond, stands one of London's oldest royal palaces, more like a small town in size and requiring a day of your time to do it justice. Follow at least one of the themed routes on their map. The magnificent Tudor brick house was begun in 1514 by Cardinal Wolsey, the ambitious and worldly lord chancellor (roughly, prime minister) of England and archbishop of York. He wanted it to be the absolute best palace in the land, and in this he succeeded so effectively that Henry VIII grew deeply envious, whereupon Wolsey felt obliged to give Hampton Court to the king. Henry moved in in 1525, adding a great hall and chapel, and proceeded to live much of his rambunctious life here. James I made further improvements at the beginning of the 17th century, but by the end of the century the palace was getting rather run-down. Plans were drawn up by the joint monarchs William III and Mary II to demolish the building and replace it with a still larger and more splendid structure, in conscious emulation of the great palace of Versailles outside Paris. However, the royal purse wouldn't stretch quite that far. It was decided to keep the original buildings but add a complex adjoining them at the rear, for which Wren was commissioned, and his graceful south wing is one of the highlights of the whole palace. (A serious fire badly damaged some of Wren's chambers in 1986, but they were restored, with some of the Tudor features he had covered up uncovered again.) William and, especially, Mary loved Hampton Court and left their mark on the place—see their fine collections of Delftware and other porcelain.

The site beside the slow-moving Thames is perfect. The palace itself—steeped in history, hung with priceless paintings, full of echoing, cobbled courtyards and cavernous Tudor kitchens (complete with deer pies and cooking pots), not to mention the ghost of Catherine Howard screaming her innocence of adultery to an unheeding Henry VIII—is set in a fantastic arrangement of ornamental gardens, lakes, and ponds. Among the horticultural highlights are an Elizabethan knot garden, Henry VIII's Pond Garden, the enormous conical yews around the Fountain Garden, and the Great Vine near the Banqueting House, planted in 1768 and still producing black Hamburg grapes, which you can buy in season. Best of all is the celebrated maze, which you enter to the north of the palace. It was planted in 1714 and is truly fiendish.

Royalty ceased living here with George III; poor George preferred the seclusion of Kew, where he was finally confined in his madness. The private apartments that range down one side of the palace are now occupied by pensioners of the Crown. Known as "grace and favor" apartments, they are among the most coveted homes in the country, with a surfeit of peace and history on their doorsteps. ✉ *East Molesey,* ☎ *020/8977–8441,* WEB *www.hrp.org.uk.* *Apartments and maze £10.50, maze alone £2.30, grounds free.* ⏲ *State apartments Apr.–Oct., Tues.–Sun. 9:30–6, Mon. 10:15–6; Nov.–Mar., daily 9:30–4:30; grounds daily 7–dusk. British Rail: Hampton Court Station from Waterloo. Tube: Richmond, then bus R68.*

3 DINING

No longer would Somerset Maugham be justified in warning, "If you want to eat well in England, have breakfast three times a day." England is one of the hottest places around for restaurants of every cultural flavor, with London at its epicenter. Nearly everyone in town is passionate about food and will love to tell you where they've eaten recently—even Lord Lloyd Webber, composer of *Cats* and *Phantom of the Opera,* has added restaurant critic to his expanding repertoire of roles. After feasting on modern British cuisine, visit one (or two or three) of London's fabulous pubs for a nightcap. Hit the right one on the right night and watch that legendary British reserve melt away.

Updated by
Alex Wijeratna

AS ANYONE WHO READS the Sunday papers knows, London has had a restaurant boom or, rather, a restaurant revolution. Londoners wonder: how far can it go? How many new, talked-out gastrodomes can the *caput mundi* support? Nothing seems to slow the onslaught. More than ever, London loves its restaurants—all 6,700 of them—from its be-here, right now eateries to its tiny neighborhood joints, from pubs where young foodniks find their feet to swank trendsetters where celebrity chefs launch their ego flights. You, too, will be smitten, since you will be spending, on average, 25% of your travel budget on eating out.

To appreciate London's culinary rise, it helps to recall that at one time it was understood that the British ate to live while the French lived to eat. Change was slow in coming after the Second World War, when steamed puddings and boiled sprouts were still consumed on a daily basis by tweed-and-flannel-wrapped Brits. When people thought of British cuisine, fish-and-chips came to mind. The latter was a dish that tasted best wrapped in newspaper (a spoilsport bureaucracy decreed that this wasn't sanitary, so the days of peeping at the latest murder news through a film of oil came to an end). Then there was always shepherd's pie, ubiquitously available in pubs—though not made, according to the song from *Sweeney Todd,* "with real shepherd in it." Visitors used to arrive in London and joke that the reason Britain conquered half the world was that its residents probably wanted some decent food. Didn't Britain invade India for a good curry?

Today, culinary London has been transformed. New menus seem to evolve every 10 minutes as chefs outdo each other creating hot spots that are all about the buzz of "being there." Sir Terence Conran began it all with Quaglino's, the first of the megarestaurants. His 480-seat Mezzo was the biggest restaurant in Europe, though he topped that with Bluebird, complete with grocery store, fishmonger, florist, and food market.

The greatest ambition, though, belongs to Marco Pierre White; unfortunately for genius hunters, he's hung up his apron for good, although his 11-restaurant empire is everywhere: the Criterion, Mirabelle, and Quo Vadis, are all his creations.

Happily, the vogue has turned against mega-eateries—intimacy is all. Take super-chef Jean-Christophe Novelli. He downsized—he pulled back from running three big joints to concentrate on just one, Maison Novelli, in Clerkenwell.

The haute cuisine scene is thriving. La Tante Claire is happy at the Berkeley Hotel in Knightsbridge, Michel Bourdin excels at the Connaught Hotel, and Gordon Ramsay powers away at Claridges. There are, of course, many more stars of the celebrity category (gobby Jamie Oliver—"The Naked Chef"—is everywhere); you can read about all of them when you get here by picking up any newspaper. To keep up with the changes, each has reviewers aplenty. Read up on the best places in *Time Out* or the food supplements in the newspapers, especially the Saturday and Sunday editions.

London also does a good job of catering to people interested more in satisfying their appetites without breaking the bank than in following the latest food trends. We've struck a balance in our listings between these extremes, and have included hip and happening places, neighborhood spots, ethnic alternatives, and old favorites. There are about 80 cuisines on offer in London, and ethnic restaurants have always been a good bet here, especially the thousands of Indian restaurants, since Londoners see a good curry as their birthright. Londoners are busy broadening their range to encompass Malaysian, Spanish, and Turkish places, a drove of Thai and Vietnamese restaurants, a North African pack, and a wave of Japanese places. With all this going on, traditional British food, when you track it down, appears as one more exotic cuisine in the pantheon.

As for cost, the democratization of restaurants does not necessarily mean smaller checks, and London is not an inexpensive city. A modest meal for two can cost £70 (about $100). Damage-control strategies include making lunch your main meal—the top places have bargain lunch menus, halving the price of evening à la carte—and ordering a second appetizer instead of an entrée, to which few places object. (Note that an appetizer, usually known as a "starter" or "first course," is sometimes called an "entrée," as it is in France, and an entrée in England is dubbed the "main course" or simply "mains.") Seek out fixed-price menus, and watch for hidden extras on the check: cover, bread, or vegetables charged separately, and service. Many restaurants exclude service charges from the menu (which the law obliges them to display outside), then add 10%–15% to the check, or else stamp SERVICE NOT INCLUDED along the bottom, in which case you should add the 10%–15% yourself. Don't pay twice for service—unscrupulous restaurateurs may add service, then leave the total on the credit-card slip blank, hoping for more.

Two caveats: first, although the chance of contracting so-called Mad Cow Disease is small, you may wish to avoid eating beef or to select beef with a reduced risk of contamination. Second, beware of Sundays. Many restaurants are closed, especially in the evening; likewise public holidays. Over the Christmas period, London virtually shuts down—only hotels will be prepared to feed you. When in doubt, call ahead. It's a good idea to book a table at all times, but you'll have gotten the idea by now.

CATEGORY	COST*
££££	over £22
£££	£16–£22
££	£9–£15
£	under £9

**per person for a main course at dinner, excluding drinks, service, and VAT*

Bloomsbury

ECLECTIC

££ ✕ **Providores.** Kiwi Peter Gordon, who made Pacific Rim fusion cuisine famous at the Sugar Club, is back with Providores. Here you'll have a charming meal upstairs from the trendy ground-floor Tapa Rooms—get the sweet potato and miso, the cassava fritters, and the roast *chioca* (a tuber similar to Jerusalem artichokes). ✉ *109 Marylebone High St., Bloomsbury W1,* ☎ *020/7935–6175. AE, MC, V. Tube: Baker St.*

FRENCH

£££–££££ ✕ **John Burton-Race.** Consider this restaurant a gourmand's playground—if you want to blow out on top-line ingredients, it's hard to find a better place to eat. JB-R came down from Berkshire to crack London when he opened this restaurant in the Landmark hotel. Go à la carte or splash out on the six-course menu gourmand (£220 for two, with wine); the coquilles Saint Jacques (scallops with oysters and caviar) and lobster with creamy leek sauce stand out amongst the

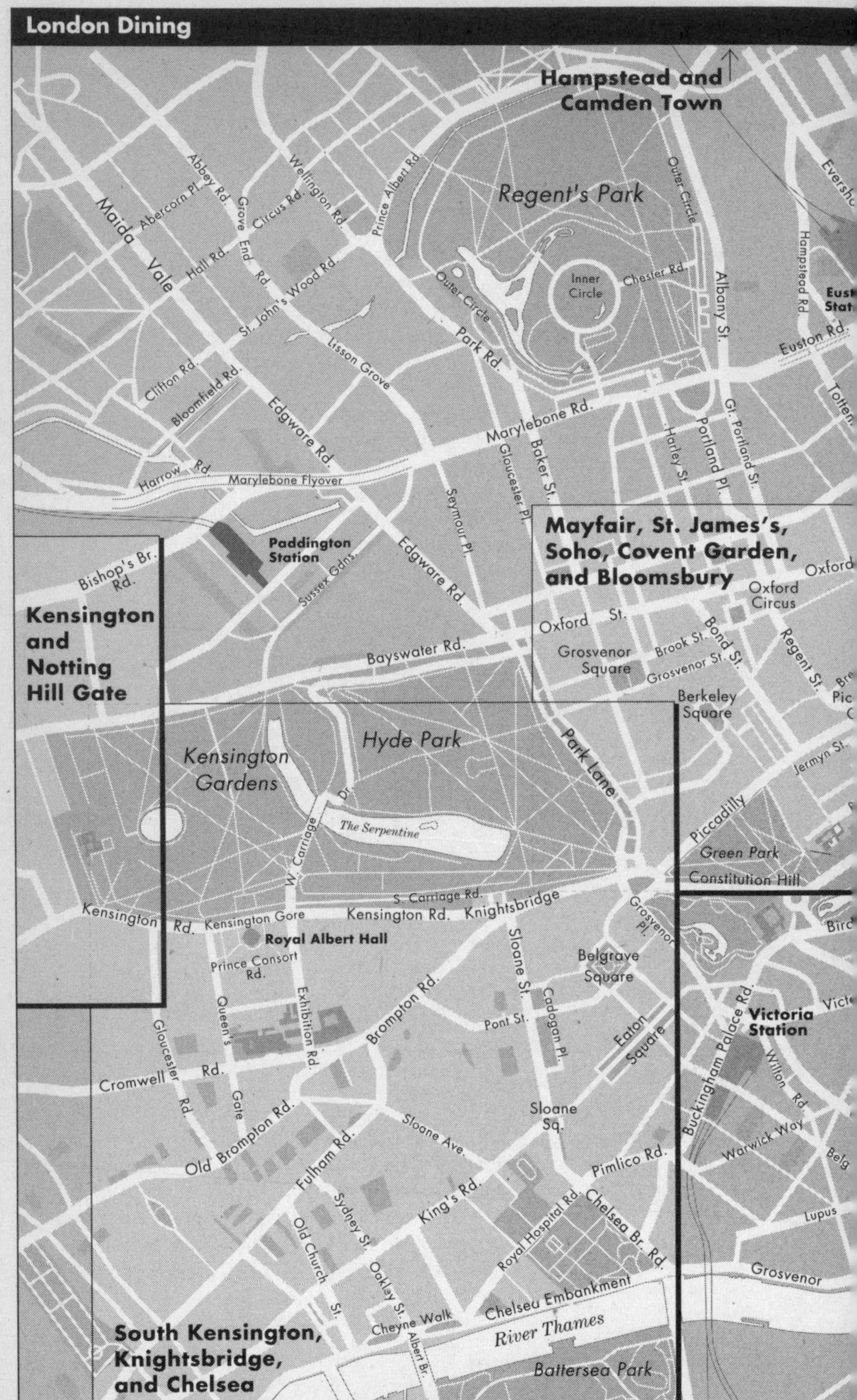
London Dining
Hampstead and Camden Town
Regent's Park
Mayfair, St. James's, Soho, Covent Garden, and Bloomsbury
Kensington and Notting Hill Gate
Paddington Station
Hyde Park
Kensington Gardens
The Serpentine
Royal Albert Hall
Green Park
Victoria Station
South Kensington, Knightsbridge, and Chelsea
River Thames
Battersea Park
Maida Vale
Abbey Rd.
Abercorn Pl.
Grove End Rd.
Circus Rd.
Wellington Rd.
Prince Albert Rd.
Outer Circle
Inner Circle
Chester Rd.
Albany St.
Hampstead Rd.
Euston Rd.
Hall Rd.
St. John's Wood Rd.
Lisson Grove
Park Rd.
Clifton Rd.
Bloomfield Rd.
Edgware Rd.
Marylebone Rd.
Baker St.
Gloucester Pl.
Harley St.
Portland Pl.
Gt. Portland St.
Harrow Rd.
Marylebone Flyover
Seymour Pl.
Bishop's Br. Rd.
Sussex Gdns.
Oxford St.
Oxford Circus
Grosvenor Square
Brook St.
Bond St.
Grosvenor St.
Regent St.
Bayswater Rd.
Berkeley Square
Park Lane
Jermyn St.
Piccadilly
Constitution Hill
W. Carriage Dr.
S. Carriage Rd.
Kensington Rd.
Kensington Gore
Knightsbridge
Grosvenor Pl.
Sloane St.
Belgrave Square
Prince Consort Rd.
Exhibition Rd.
Brompton Rd.
Pont St.
Cadogan Pl.
Eaton Square
Buckingham Palace Rd.
Wilton Rd.
Queen's Gate
Gloucester Rd.
Cromwell Rd.
Old Brompton Rd.
Sloane Sq.
Sloane Ave.
Warwick Way
Fulham Rd.
King's Rd.
Pimlico Rd.
Sydney St.
Royal Hospital Rd.
Chelsea Br. Rd.
Old Church St.
Oakley St.
Grosvenor
Chelsea Embankment
Cheyne Walk
Albert Br.

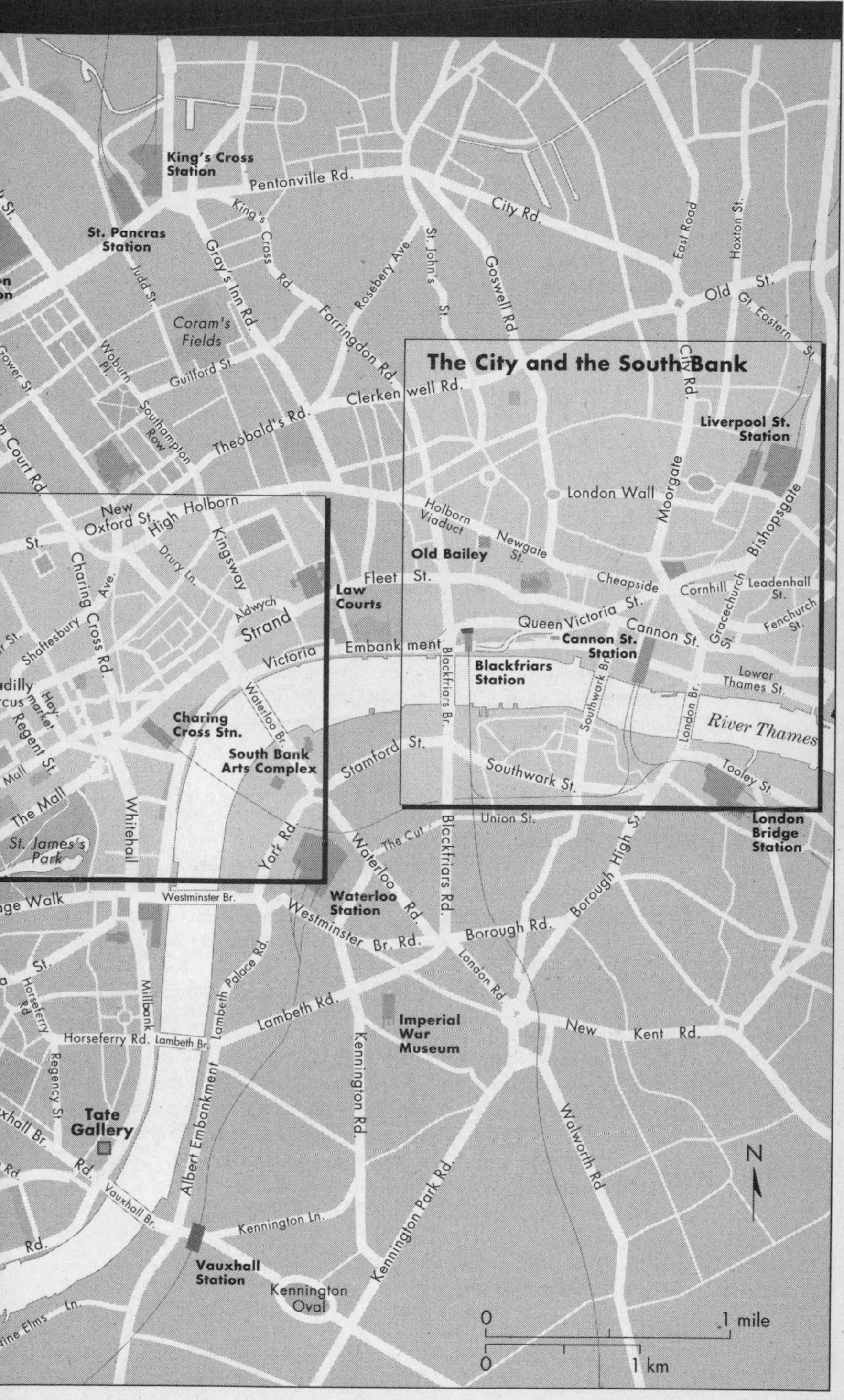

The City and the South Bank
King's Cross Station
St. Pancras Station
Pentonville Rd.
City Rd.
King's Cross Rd.
Gray's Inn Rd.
Judd St.
Coram's Fields
Woburn Pl.
Guilford St.
Southampton Row
Gower St.
Theobald's Rd.
Clerkenwell Rd.
Farringdon Rd.
Rosebery Ave.
St. John's St.
Goswell Rd.
East Road
Hoxton St.
Old St.
Gt. Eastern St.
City Rd.
Liverpool St. Station
London Wall
Moorgate
Bishopsgate
Holborn Viaduct
Newgate St.
Old Bailey
New Oxford St.
High Holborn
Kingsway
Drury Ln.
Charing Cross Rd.
Shaftesbury Ave.
Fleet St.
Law Courts
Aldwych
Strand
Cheapside
Cornhill
Leadenhall St.
Gracechurch St.
Fenchurch St.
Queen Victoria St.
Cannon St.
Cannon St. Station
Victoria Embankment
Blackfriars Br.
Blackfriars Station
Lower Thames St.
Southwark Br.
London Br.
River Thames
Haymarket
Regent St.
Waterloo Br.
Charing Cross Stn.
South Bank Arts Complex
Stamford St.
Southwark St.
Tooley St.
London Bridge Station
The Mall
St. James's Park
Whitehall
York Rd.
Union St.
The Cut
Blackfriars Rd.
Borough High St.
Waterloo Rd.
Waterloo Station
Westminster Br.
Westminster Br. Rd.
Borough Rd.
London Rd.
Lambeth Palace Rd.
Millbank
Horseferry Rd.
Lambeth Br.
Lambeth Rd.
Imperial War Museum
Kennington Rd.
New Kent Rd.
Regency St.
Tate Gallery
Albert Embankment
Walworth Rd
Vauxhall Br.
Kennington Ln.
Kennington Park Rd.
Vauxhall Station
Kennington Oval
N
0
1 mile
0
1 km

overall excellence. The sommelier knows the way through the huge wine list (heavy on France) and the service is expert and attentive. ✉ *222 Marylebone Rd., Bloomsbury NW1,* ☎ *020/7723–7800. AE, DC, MC, V. Closed Sun. Tube: Marylebone.*

££–£££ ✕ **Chez Gérard.** One of an excellent chain of steak-frites restaurants (there are 10 across London), this one has widened the choice on the Gallic menu to include more for non–red meat eaters: smoked salmon and cream-cheese roulade and poached eggs, for instance. Steak, served with shoestring fries and béarnaise sauce, remains the reason to visit, though. ✉ *8 Charlotte St., Bloomsbury W1,* ☎ *020/7636–4975. AE, DC, MC, V. Tube: Goodge St.*

££–£££ ★ ✕ **Elena's L'Etoile.** Elena Salvoni presided for years over L'Escargot in Soho, where she made so many friends she opened her own restaurant. This understated century-old place is one of London's few remaining unreconstructed French-bistro restaurants. The traditional dishes of duck braised with cabbage, salmon fish cakes, *coqueletrôti* (roast chicken), crème brûlée, and apple tart are joined by newer treats, and most diners are guaranteed a warm smile from Elena, even if you're not one of the politician-journalist-actor regulars. ✉ *30 Charlotte St., Bloomsbury W1,* ☎ *020/7636–7189. AE, DC, MC, V. Closed Sun., no lunch Sat. Tube: Goodge St.*

££–£££ ✕ **Villandry.** Heaven for food lovers, Villandry is an exclusive food hall—with a renowned dining room out the back. This tempting cave of wonders heaves with fancy French pâtés, Continental cheeses, fruit tarts, biscuits, organic vegetables, and breads galore. There's a tearoom café, a bar, and a fashionable dining room in which to enjoy the exquisite offerings; breakfast, lunch, and dinner are served daily. ✉ *170 Great Portland St., Bloomsbury W1,* ☎ *020/7631–3131. AE, DC, MC, V. Tube: Great Portland St.*

JAPANESE

£ ★ ✕ **Wagamama.** London adores the Japanese noodles in this big basement. It's high-tech, high volume, and high turnover, with a fast-moving line at the door. You can choose ramen in or out of soup (topped with sliced meats) or "raw energy" dishes and juices. This formula has proved so successful that they now sport clothing, so grateful diners can *wear* Wagamama. Other branches are at 10A Lexington Street (☎ 020/7292–0990), near Piccadilly Circus, and 101A Wigmore Street (☎ 020/7409–0111). ✉ *4A Streatham St., Bloomsbury WC1,* ☎ *020/7323–9223. Reservations not accepted. AE, DC, MC, V. Tube: Tottenham Court Rd.*

SEAFOOD

£–££ ★ ✕ **North Sea Fish Restaurant.** Come here and nowhere else for the British national dish of fish-and-chips—battered and deep-fried whitefish with thick fries shaken with salt and vinegar. It's tricky to find—three blocks south of St. Pancras station, down Judd Street. They only serve freshly caught fish, which you can order grilled—though that would defeat the purpose. You can take out or eat in. ✉ *7–8 Leigh St., Bloomsbury WC1,* ☎ *020/7387–5892. AE, DC, MC, V. Closed Sun. Tube: Russell Sq.*

Camden Town and Hampstead

CAFÉS

£ ✕ **Coffee Cup.** A Hampstead landmark for about as long as anyone can remember, this smoky, dingy, uncomfortable café is lovable and cheap, and therefore always packed. You can get anything (beans, eggs, kippers, mushrooms) on toast, grills, sandwiches, cakes, fry-ups, etc.—nothing healthy or fashionable whatsoever. There are tables outside in summer. This place has no liquor license. ✉ *74 Hampstead High St.,*

Hampstead NW3, ☎ 020/7435–7565. Reservations not accepted. No credit cards. Tube: Hampstead.

GREEK

£–££ ★ ✕ **Lemonia.** It shines as a superior version of London Greek—large and light, friendly, and packed every evening. Besides the usual *mezedes* (appetizers), *souvlaki* (kebabs), *stifado* (beef stewed in wine), and so on, there are interesting specials: quail, perhaps, or *gemista* (stuffed vegetables). Lemonia is on a pleasant street near Regent's Park. ✉ *89 Regent's Park Rd., Euston NW1, ☎ 020/7586–7454. Reservations essential. MC, V. No lunch Sat., no dinner Sun. Tube: Chalk Farm.*

TURKISH

£ ✕ **Gallipoli II.** The restaurant's charms are well known to locals—it's a noisy, packed, darkly lit, and altogether fun neighborhood restaurant with bags of style. Things are squished and crammed, and the rule is very much "room for one more." The *meze* (a spread of small dishes) is the best first act: it's bursting with flavor, and color (the *kisir,* crushed wheat with walnut and onion, and falafel are particularly good). Keep the hot breads from the oven coming and you won't need much more. The bone-of-lamb *incik* (boiled with red, green, and white peppers) is tender and the baklava is worth the indulgence. ✉ *120 Upper St., Islington N1, ☎ 020/7359–1578. Reservations essential. MC, V.*

Chelsea

AMERICAN/CASUAL

££ ✕ **Cactus Blue.** Go for dinner or go for a weekend brunch, but go—American southwestern food is happening in London these days, and this Tex-Mex place has attitude. You can find the buzz on split levels bathed in ochre hues, with a gamut of cacti on the stairs. On offer are tequilas, beers, and Baja wines, which help slide down yummy crab cakes and quesadillas. ✉ *86 Fulham Rd., Chelsea SW3, ☎ 020/7823–7858. AE, DC, MC, V. Tube: South Kensington.*

££ ✕ **PJ's Grill.** When you enter you'll feel like you've adopted the Polo Joe lifestyle—wooden floors and stained glass, a slowly revolving propeller from a 1911 Vickers Vimy flying boat, and polo memorabilia. But the place is relaxed, friendly, and efficient. The menu, which includes all-American staples (crab cakes, steaks, smoked ribs), salads, pecan pie, and brownies, will please all but vegetarians. PJ's stays open late, and the bartenders can mix anything. Brunch is popular. ✉ *52 Fulham Rd., Chelsea SW3, ☎ 020/7581–0025. AE, DC, MC, V. Tube: South Kensington.*

£ ✕ **Chelsea Bun Diner.** Get fed heaps of food for very little money at this hybrid of an American diner and an English greasy spoon. Expect a huge menu with huge portions—burgers, salads, potato skins, many breakfasts (New York, San Francisco, Lumberjack, All-Day English Full), pastas, and pies. ✉ *9A Limerston St., Chelsea SW10, ☎ 020/7352–3635. Reservations not accepted. V. Tube: Sloane Sq., then Bus 11, 19, 22, or 31.*

CONTEMPORARY

££–£££ ✕ **Bluebird.** From Sir Terence Conran comes a gastrodome—foodmarket, florist, fruit stand, butchers, kitchen shop, and café-restaurant. The place is blue and white, light, and not in the least cozy, and the food is slightly formulaic: mussels, coriander, lime leaf; or partridge and Savoy cabbage; then chocolate cake and espresso ice cream. Go for the synergy and visual excitement—Conran's chefs tend to promise more than they deliver. ✉ *350 King's Rd., Chelsea SW3, ☎ 020/7559–1000. Reservations essential. AE, DC, MC, V. Tube: Sloane Sq.*

FRENCH

££££ ✕ **Aubergine.** William Drabble is building his reputation here, and his ★ signature dishes are accomplished and often gamey—boudin of wood pigeon with foie gras, turnip, and jus truffle; Mansergh lamb with onions, garlic, and rosemary. The restaurant looks simply alluring—it's bathed in the hues of impressionist Provence. For a thrifty option, come for lunch. ✉ *11 Park Walk, Chelsea SW10,* ☎ *020/7352–3449. Reservations essential. AE, DC, MC, V. Closed Sun., no lunch Sat. Tube: South Kensington.*

££££ ✕ **Gordon Ramsay.** Ramsay whips up a storm with white beans, ★ girolles, foie gras, scallops, and truffles. He's Britain's current number one, and it hasn't gone unnoticed: tables here are booked months in advance. For £80, blow out on the seven-course option, for £65 wallow in three dinner courses, or plump for lunch (£35 for three courses) for a gentler check. ✉ *68–69 Royal Hospital Rd., Chelsea SW3,* ☎ *020/7352–4441. Reservations essential. AE, DC, MC, V. Closed weekends. Tube: Sloane Sq.*

££–£££ ✕ **La Poule au Pot.** One of London's most romantic restaurants, La ★ Poule au Pot is superb for proposals or romantic evenings. The "Chelsea Set"—and Americans—love this candlelit corner of France in Belgravia. The country cooking is fairly good, not spectacular. The *poule au pot* (stewed chicken) and *lapin à la moutarde* (rabbit with mustard) are strong and hearty, and there are fine classics, such as beef bourguignonne and French onion soup. The service comes with bonhomie. ✉ *231 Ebury St., Knightsbridge SW1,* ☎ *020/7730–7763. Reservations essential. AE, DC, MC, V. Tube: Sloane Sq.*

££ ✕ **La Brasserie.** This is a convenient choice if you're on South Kensington museum visits. Opening hours are long. You can get everything from fish soup to tarte tatin here. There's a good buzz here on Sunday mornings, when the entire well-heeled neighborhood sits around reading the papers and sipping cappuccino. You can't hang out at peak dining hours, however. The food's reliable, if a little overpriced. ✉ 272 *Brompton Rd., South Kensington SW3,* ☎ *020/7584–1668. AE, DC, MC, V. Tube: South Kensington.*

INDIAN

££–£££ ✕ **Chutney Mary.** London's stalwart Indian restaurant provides a fantasy version of the British Raj, all giant wicker armchairs and palms. Dishes like masala lamb and Goan chicken curry (with mint and coriander) intermingle with the more familiar North Indian dishes—*kosha mangsho* (slow-cooked Bengali lamb with red chilies and cinnamon) and *dum ka murgh* (a classic chicken curry from Hyderabad). Servers are deferential, and desserts are usually worth leaving room for. The three-course Sunday brunch is a good value at £15. ✉ *535 King's Rd., Chelsea SW10,* ☎ *020/7351–3113. Reservations essential. AE, DC, MC, V. Tube: Fulham Broadway.*

The City and the South Bank

AMERICAN/CASUAL

£ ✕ **Fatboy's Diner.** One for the kids, this is a 1941 chrome trailer transplanted from the banks of the Susquehanna in Pennsylvania and now secreted, unexpectedly, in a back street, complete with an Astroturf "garden." A '50s jukebox accompanies the dogs, burgers, and fries. ✉ *23 Horner Sq., Spitalfields Market, The City E1,* ☎ *020/7375–2763. Reservations not accepted. No credit cards. Tube: Liverpool St.*

CONTEMPORARY

££–£££ ✕ **Maison Novelli.** Jean-Christophe Novelli is a hero of the Modern ★ Brit movement, and has drawn foodies from the day his restaurant

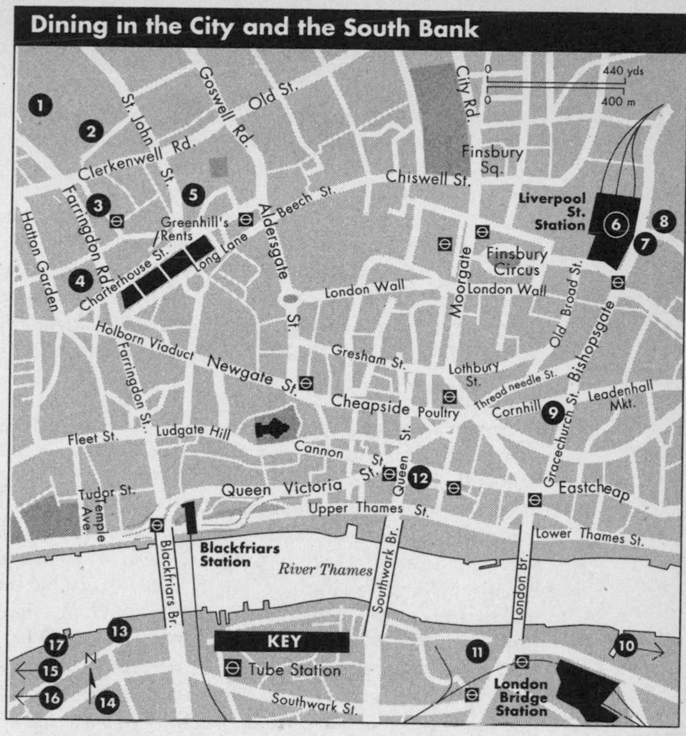

opened in buzzing Clerkenwell. These days, gladly, Novelli has downsized and is back running the kitchen after almost burning out, expanding his empire across London. Favorites include glazed goat cheese, celeriac, and mozzarella terrine; roast filet of beef; Beaufort cheese, garlic, and tomatoes; and the famed pig's trotter stuffed "following the mood of the day." You can also come by an elegant sea bass with chorizo or truffle oil, or pan-fried halibut with mussel sauce. ✉ *29–31 Clerkenwell Green, The City EC1,* ☎ *020/7251–6606. Reservations essential. AE, DC, MC, V. Tube: Farringdon.*

££–£££ ✕ **OXO Tower Brasserie and Restaurant.** London has a room with a view—and *such* a view. On the eighth floor of the OXO Tower near the South Bank is this elegant space, run by the folks who put the Fifth Floor at Harvey Nichols on the map and featuring Euro-Asia food with the latest trendy ingredients (acorn-fed black-pig charcuterie with tomato and pear chutney; Dover sole with sea urchin butter). The ceiling slats turn from white to blue, but who notices, with the London Eye wheel and St. Paul's dazzling you across the water? The Brasserie is slightly less expensive than the restaurant, but both have great river views. The terrace tables in summertime are probably the best panoramic places in London. ✉ *Barge House St., The South Bank SE1,* ☎ *020/7803–3888. AE, DC, MC, V. Tube: Waterloo.*

££–£££ ★ ✕ **St. John.** This former smokehouse, converted by owner-chef Fergus Henderson, has soaring white walls, schoolroom lamps, stone floors, iron railings, and plain wooden chairs. Some find Henderson's chutzpah scary: one appetizer is sliced pig spleen, although the imaginativeness of others—bone marrow and parsley salad; smoked eel, beetroot, and horseradish—excuses this austerity. Entrées (lamb and parsnip; haddock and fennel; deviled crab) appear nude on the plate, but always have style. Expect an all-French wine list with plenty of affordable bottles, plus lots of Malmseys and ports. The pastry chef's chocolate slice belongs in the brownie hall of fame. ✉ *26 St. John St., The City EC1,*

☎ *020/7251–0848. Reservations essential. AE, DC, MC, V. Closed Sun and Sat dinner. Tube: Farringdon.*

EASTERN EUROPEAN

££ ✕ **Baltic.** To eat well in Southwark while you're on safari to the Tate Modern, come to Baltic, opposite the great modern Southwark tube station. Here you'll find a bustling vodka-party playground—a good spot for a drink at the bar or a decent east European meal in a sexy venue. Owned by the man behind Wodka in Kensington, Baltic serves fine blinis—with herring, smoked salmon, or caviar—and great *leniwe* (potato dumplings) and gravlax. The vodkas, not surprisingly, are strong, fruity, wild, and wicked: rose petal, rowan berry, Siberian, peppercorn, Bison grass, rye, honey. ✉ *74 Blackfriars Rd., The South Bank SE1,* ☎ *020/7928–1111. AE, MC, V Tube: Southwark.*

ENGLISH

££–£££ ✕ **People's Palace.** Thank goodness for this place—now you can have a civilized meal during your South Bank arts encounter. Run independently from the Royal Festival Hall et al., it has remarkably low prices considering it commands the greatest river view in town (apart from OXO). There are occasional mistakes here, but the more British the dish, the more reliable it proves to be: veal, skate wings, pecan and banana pudding—all these are fine. Service is flaky, but the soaring space makes up for everything. ✉ *Royal Festival Hall, Level 3, The South Bank SE1,* ☎ *020/7928–9999. AE, DC, MC, V. Tube: Waterloo.*

£–££ ★ ✕ **Quality Chop House.** Converted from one of the most gorgeous "greasy spoon" caffs in town, this place retains the Victorian fittings (including pewlike seats, which you have to share). It is not luxurious, but the grub is glorious cafeteria food—bangers and mash turns out to be homemade Toulouse sausage with veal gravy and fluffy potatoes; egg and chips are not even remotely greasy. You'll also find posh dishes: salmon cakes and rump steak. There's plenty of fish on the menu—scallops, oysters, clams, and jellied eels. ✉ *94 Farringdon Rd., The City EC1,* ☎ *020/7837–5093. Reservations essential. MC, V. No lunch Sat. Tube: Farringdon.*

£ ✕ **Konditor & Cook.** Very useful for theatrical forays over the river, this cafeteria in the Young Vic theater serves full meals a cut above the tired quiche you might expect. Black ravioli stuffed with crab as well as potato cakes and smoked salmon and Toulouse sausages with mash are the kind of dishes to expect, but the pies and cakes—from the bakery around the corner, which supplies half of London—are the standouts. ✉ *Young Vic Theatre, 66 The Cut, The South Bank SE1,* ☎ *020/7620–2700. MC, V. Closed Sun. Tube: Waterloo or Southwark.*

£ ✕ **Simpson's Tavern.** A bastion of English tradition, this back-alley chophouse was founded in 1759 and only admitted women after 1916. It's popular with traders and stockbrokers who come for traditional fare: steak and kidney pie, liver and bacon, chops from the grill, Simpson's salmon cakes, or the house specialty—"Stewed Cheese"—of melted Cheddar cheese with bechamel and Worcestershire sauce sauce spread on toast. It's always full at lunch, so come early. ✉ *38½ Cornhill, at Ball Ct., The City EC3,* ☎ *020/7626–9985. Reservations not accepted. AE, DC, MC, V. No dinner. Closed Sat.–Sun.*

FRENCH

£££–££££ ★ ✕ **Le Pont de la Tour.** Le Pont de la Tour comes into its own in summer, when sitting at the outside tables feels heavenly. Inside you'll find a wine merchant, bakery and deli; a seafood bar; a brasserie; and this diner-style restaurant, smart as the captain's table. Fish and seafood (lobster salad, halibut and hollandaise) and meat and game (Denham-estate venison and Gressingham duck) feature heavily. Prune-and-

Armagnac tart could finish a glamorous—and expensive—meal. ✉ *36D Shad Thames, Butler's Wharf, The South Bank SE1,* ☏ *020/7403–8403. Reservations essential. AE, DC, MC, V. Tube: Tower Hill.*

JAPANESE

£ ✕ **Moshi Moshi Sushi.** London digs sushi like New Yorkers did a decade back, and this joint above Platform One in Liverpool Street station set the fish train chugging. The shtick here is that you pick *tekka* or *kappa maki* (tuna or seaweed rolls) or *maguro* (tuna), *sake* (salmon), *saba* (mackerel), etc.—off a conveyor belt that snakes around the counter. At the end, you count up your plates to pay. The sushi's okay, but this is not really the place for a sophisticated evening. ✉ *Unit 24 Liverpool St. Station, The City EC2,* ☏ *020/7247–3227. Reservations not accepted. DC, MC, V. Closed weekends. Tube: Liverpool St.*

MEDITERRANEAN

££–£££ ★ ✕ **Moro.** Up the road from the City, at the cusp of Clerkenwell and Sadler's Wells, is Exmouth Market—a cluster of shops, an Italian church, and more and more good places like Moro. The menu includes a mélange of Spanish and North African flavors. Spiced meats, cured Serrano hams, salt cod, and other delicacies seasoned with herbs are the secret to Moro's success. The only downside is the persistent noise. But then again, that's part of the buzz. ✉ *34–36 Exmouth Market, The City EC1,* ☏ *020/7833–8336. Reservations essential. AE, DC, MC, V. No dinner Sun. Tube: Farringdon.*

£–££ ★ ✕ **The Eagle.** It's the gastro-pub of gastro-pubs, and it belongs in the "Restaurants" section by virtue of the amazingly good-value Portuguese-Spanish food. There are about nine dishes—a pasta, two vegetarian, and/or risotto always among them. Quite a few places in London charge three times the price for similar food; there's a welcome trend toward pubs serving good meals—one that the Eagle all but started. ✉ *159 Farringdon Rd., The City EC1,* ☏ *020/7837–1353. Reservations not accepted. AE, DC, MC, V. Tube: Farringdon.*

SEAFOOD

££–£££ ✕ **Bill Bentley's.** You can see from the bare walls and the arched ceiling that this once housed a wine merchant's vaults. There are another four City-based branches in London, all equally old-fashioned in feel and all serving classic boarding school–like fish dishes and seafood platters. ✉ *Swedeland Ct., 202 Bishopsgate, The City EC2,* ☏ *020/7283–1763. Reservations essential. AE, DC, MC, V. Closed weekends. Tube: Liverpool St.*

££ ★ ✕ **fish!** A sensation on the London scene and a remarkable diner—sleek and modern—it sits in the shadow of Southwark Cathedral, across the road from Borough Market (where lots of the British gangster flick *Lock, Stock and Two Smoking Barrels* was filmed). The fish at fish! is excellent, and politically correct. The langoustine are creel-caught, the salmon organic, and scallops landed by divers. There are eight types on the menu, including swordfish, brill, skate, and turbot. The splish-splosh formula has struck a chord; six new fish! have come on-stream. Call for locations. ✉ *Cathedral St., The South Bank SE1,* ☏ *020/7234–3333. AE, DC, MC, V. Tube: London Bridge.*

££ ✕ **Livebait.** Although no longer as fantastic as when it was independently run, this fish restaurant still packs them in, serving English seafood with British ales by the pint (cockles and mussels alive-alive-o!), home-baked breads (beetroot, garlic, or turmeric), and all sorts of fish: broiled, baked, stewed, and generally combined in clever ways. There are branches in Covent Garden, Wandsworth, the City, Fulham, and Notting Hill. ✉ *41–43 The Cut, The South Bank SE1,* ☏ *020/7928–7211. Reservations essential. AE, DC, MC, V. Closed Sun. Tube: Southwark.*

££ ✕ **Sweetings.** Uniquely English, Sweetings is a time warp from the old City of London (established 1886). There are things Sweetings doesn't do: dinner, reservations, weekends, coffee. It does, however, do seafood. It's not far from St. Paul's, and City gents come for "luncheon." They like tankards of "Black Velvet" (Guinness and champagne) and are reassured by potted shrimps, whitebait, haddock and poached eggs, Welsh rarebit, and roe on toast. The West Mersey oysters are good, and the puddings old school favorites—spotted dick and steamed syrup pudding. ✉ *39 Queen Victoria St., The City EC4,* ☎ *020/7248–3062. Reservations not accepted. AE, MC, V. Closed weekends, no dinner. Tube: Mansion House.*

Covent Garden

AMERICAN

£–££ ★ ✕ **Joe Allen.** Long hours (thespians flock here after the curtains fall in theaterland) and a welcoming interior mean New York Joe's London branch still swings after more than two decades. The fun menu helps: roasted poblano chillies and black bean soup are typical starters; entrées include barbecue ribs and London's only available corn muffins, or monkfish with sun-dried-tomato salsa. There are Yankee desserts, too—such as grilled banana bread with ice cream and hot caramel sauce. ✉ *13 Exeter St., Covent Garden WC2,* ☎ *020/7836–0651. Reservations essential. AE, MC, V. Tube: Covent Garden.*

£–££ ✕ **Maxwell's.** London's first-ever burger joint, now more than a quarter-century old, cloned itself and then grew up. Here's the result, a happy place under the Royal Opera House serving the kind of food you're homesick for: quesadillas and nachos, Buffalo chicken wings, barbecued ribs, chef's salad, and a burger to die for. ✉ *8–9 James St., Covent Garden WC2,* ☎ *020/7836–0303. AE, DC, MC, V. Tube: Covent Garden.*

BELGIAN

££–£££ ✕ **Belgo Centraal.** Have mussels and *frites* (fries) in vast quantities, served with your choice of 101 Belgian beers (Trappist-brewed, white, or light) by people dressed as monks in a hall like a refectory in a monastery. Also eat *stoemp* (mashed potatoes and cabbage) with steak; Chimay-beer sausages; lobster; or roast chicken. The luxury index is low, but your check probably will be, too. ✉ *50 Earlham St., Covent Garden WC2,* ☎ *020/7813–2233. AE, DC, MC, V. Tube: Covent Garden.*

CAFÉS

£ ✕ **Pret a Manger.** You'll fall over this sandwich chain's cafés wherever you go, and you'll be grateful because the freshness of the chicken breast and avocado on granary bread, the Peking duck wrap, lemon cake, banana bread, almond croissant, and so on, are tops. There's even sushi. ✉ *78 St. Martin's La., Covent Garden WC2,* ☎ *020/7379–5335. No credit cards. Tube: Covent Garden.*

CONTEMPORARY

£££ ★ ✕ **The Ivy.** It's many Londoners' favorite restaurant. In a deco room with blinding-white tablecloths, and Hodgkins on the walls, the celebrated and the wannabes eat Caesar salad, roast grouse, Thai baked sea bass, and rice pudding with Armagnac prunes or sticky toffee pudding. For star-trekking ("Don't look now, dear, but there's Ralph Fiennes") this is the primo spot in London. The weekend three-course lunch is a snip at £17.50. ✉ *1 West St., Covent Garden WC2,* ☎ *020/7836–4751. Reservations essential. AE, DC, MC, V. Tube: Covent Garden.*

££–£££ ★ ✕ **Bank.** City and fashionable folk flock to this vast eatery with its spectacular chandelier and equally dazzling menu. Seared fish and confit of duck; French beans and Parmesan cheese; mousses, brûlées, and nursery puddings—these are just a few examples of its fast-changing world palette, which has a definitive mod-Brit touch. It's not a steal price-wise, but dishes never fail to please. ✉ *1 Kingsway, Covent Garden WC2,* ☎ *020/7379–9797. Reservations essential. AE, DC, MC, V. Tube: Holborn.*

CONTINENTAL

£££–££££ ✕ **Savoy Grill.** The grill continues in the first rank of power-dining locations. Politicians, newspaper barons, and tycoons like the comforting food and impeccably discreet, attentive service in the low-key, rather dull, yew-paneled salon. On the menu, an omelet Arnold Bennett (with cheese and smoked haddock) is perennial, and such standards as beef Wellington and saddle of lamb are joined by risotto. Diners can give their dancing shoes a workout at the weekly "Stompin' at the Savoy." ✉ *Strand, Covent Garden WC2,* ☎ *020/7836–4343. Reservations essential. Jacket and tie. AE, DC, MC, V. Closed Sun., no lunch Sat. Tube: Covent Garden.*

ENGLISH

£££ ★ ✕ **Rules.** Come, escape from the 21st century. This is probably the single most beautiful dining salon in London. More than 200 years old (it opened in 1798), this gorgeous institution has welcomed everyone from Dickens to Lillie Langtry and the Prince of Wales. The menu includes fine historical dishes—try the steak and kidney pudding for a taste of the 18th century. Happily, the decoration is delicious: plush red banquettes and lacquered Regency yellow walls crammed with oil paintings and engravings. For a main dish, try something from the list of daily specials, which will, in season, include game from Rules' Teesdale estate. ✉ *35 Maiden La., Covent Garden WC2,* ☎ *020/7836–5314. AE, DC, MC, V. Tube: Covent Garden.*

FRENCH

£££–££££ ✕ **Admiralty.** It is a restaurant worthy of exhibition halls and the grand courtyard setting of Somerset House, just off the Strand. London is turning away from anything-goes fusion food and is now interested in purer cuisines. Admiralty does fantastic French cuisine—very simply. The snail ravioli in Chablis, with artichokes and roasted garlic, is a classic French starter, and the monkfish and asparagus dish tastes as fine as it looks on the plate. Political heavyweights flock here for the serious, splendid cooking, and their hard hearts melt when they glimpse the steaming hot chocolate *moelleux* (pudding). ✉ *Somerset House, Strand Covent Garden, WC2,* ☎ *020/7845–4646. AE, DC, MC, V. Closed Sun. Tube: Charing Cross.*

£–££ ✕ **Café Flo.** Expect unpretentious baguette sandwiches, steak frites, or *poisson-frites* (fish and fries), tarts, espresso, fresh orange juice, simple set-price weekend menus—everything for the Francophile on a budget. There are branches of this brasserie in Hampstead, Islington, Ludgate Hill, St. Paul's, Fulham, Richmond, and Kensington. ✉ *50–51 St. Martin's La., Covent Garden WC2,* ☎ *020/7836–8289. AE, MC, V. Tube: Covent Garden.*

INDIAN

£ ✕ **India Club.** Defying all convention, this Indian canteen is going strong after 50 years. It has been described as "strange to the point of weird," but idiosyncratic is more generous. You'll find it in the Strand Continental Hotel. It's not pretty—Formica, linoleum, faded photos—but it's a favorite of University of London students, BBC World Service workers, and bods from the Indian High Commission. You have to be a member of the hotel drinking club (£1) to get a beer from the bar (down two flights), so stick with the lassies and the *masala dosai* (pancakes stuffed with onion and potato). ✉ *143 The Strand, Covent Garden WC2,* ☎ *020/7836–0650. Reservations not accepted. No credit cards. Tube: Charing Cross.*

ITALIAN

££ ✕ **Orso.** It shares, with its Italian sister, Joe Allen, the same snappy staff and glitzy clientele of showbiz types and hacks. The Tuscan menu changes daily, but it always includes excellent pizza and pasta dishes—plus entrées based, perhaps, on grilled rabbit or roast sea bass and first courses of deep-fried zucchini flowers stuffed with ricotta. Food here is never boring, much like the place itself. Orsino, at 119 Portland Road, W11, is a stylish offshoot, serving much the same food. ✉ *27 Wellington St., Covent Garden WC2,* ☎ *020/7240–5269. Reservations essential. AE, MC, V. Tube: Covent Garden.*

£–££ ✕ **Bertorelli's.** Across from the stage door of the Royal Opera House, Bertorelli's is quietly chic; the food is tempting; and the menu is just innovative enough: sea bass with walnut pesto and monkfish ragout with fennel, wonder beans, Swiss chard, and lime butter are two typical dishes. There is a café-bar downstairs and a restaurant upstairs. Even more decorous and delicious is the branch at 19–23 Charlotte Street (and do check out its amazing marble-clad restrooms). ✉ *44A Floral St., Covent Garden WC2,* ☎ *020/7836–3969. AE, DC, MC, V. Closed Sun. Tube: Covent Garden.*

PAN-ASIAN

£££–££££ ✕ **Asia de Cuba.** It's a trendy restaurant, in a trendy hotel, in the trendiest city in the world. Asia de Cuba is the lead restaurant at Ian Schrager's St. Martins Lane Hotel. The Philippe Starck–designed restaurant is sexy and loud—check the dangly light bulbs, the Latino music, stacks of library books, portable TVs, and satin-clad pillars. The food is Pan-Asian fusion and you're encouraged to share (like the Brits do with curry). The Thai beef salad with Asian greens and coconut is delicious, as is the lobster with rum and red curry. Schrager is right: hotels (and their restaurants) are the new disco. ✉ *St. Martins Lane Hotel, 45 St. Martin's La., Covent Garden WC2,* ☎ *020/7300–5588. AE, DC, MC, V. Tube: Leicester Sq.*

SEAFOOD

££–££££ ✕ **J Sheekey.** This is where the stars go (you know, Cate Blanchett, Johnny Depp) when rubbernecking at the Ivy (along with Le Caprice, run by the owners of J Sheekey) becomes tedious. Sleek, discreet, and clublike, and in the heart of theaterland, the popularity of this seafood haven is evidenced by the photos on the walls—Peter O'Toole, Chaplin, Coward, Sellers. And J Sheekey charms: cracked tiles, lava-rock bar tops, American oak paneling. Sample the wonderful jellied eels, pickled herrings, Dover sole, and fish pie. To save money, try the weekend set lunch for £13.50. ✉ *28–32 St. Martin's Ct., Covent Garden WC2,* ☎ *020/7240–2565. AE, DC, MC, V. Tube: Leicester Sq.*

£–££ ✕ **Rock & Sole Plaice.** The appalling pun announces central London's only fish-and-chips joint, complete with inside seating. In addition to salmon, sole, and plaice, there's the usual cod and haddock, battered, deep-fried, and served with fries, ready for the salt and vinegar shakers. ✉ *47 Endell St., Covent Garden WC2,* ☎ *020/7836–3785. AE, DC, MC, V. Tube: Covent Garden.*

VEGETARIAN

£ ✕ **Food for Thought.** Despite being a simple basement restaurant with no liquor license that seats 50, Food for Thought is extremely popular. You'll almost always find a line of people down the stairs. The menu—stir-fries, casseroles, salads, and desserts—changes daily, and each dish is freshly made. ✉ *31 Neal St., Covent Garden WC2,* ☎ *020/7836–0239. Reservations not accepted. No credit cards. Closed Christmas week. Tube: Covent Garden.*

Hammersmith

ITALIAN

££–££££ ★ ✕ **River Café.** Touted as having the best Italian food in Europe outside Italy, this superstar restaurant started a trend with its single-estate olive oils and simple roasts and pastas. Chefs Rose Gray and Ruth Rogers believe in snappingly fresh ingredients, so you get salmon with Sicilian lemons, Tuscan bread soup with *cavolo nero* (black leaf cabbage) and Swiss chard, and one of London's highest checks. But remember, if you snag a reservation: this is in distant Hammersmith, and you can be stranded if you haven't booked a taxi. Note: last food orders are at 9:30 PM. ✉ *Thames Wharf Studios, Rainville Rd., Hammersmith W6,* ☏ *020/7381–8824. Reservations essential. AE, DC, MC, V. Tube: Hammersmith.*

Kensington and Notting Hill Gate

AMERICAN/CASUAL

£–££ ✕ **Tootsies.** A superior burger place, Tootsies is dark but cheerful. Rock music plays in the background, usually accompanied by a neighborhood buzz. Alternatives to the burgers, which come with great fries, are big salads, steaks, BLTs, and chicken divertissements. The usual ice creams and pies will do for dessert. There are branches in Fulham, Chiswick, Wimbledon, Kew Barnes, Hampstead, and Richmond. ✉ *120 Holland Park Ave., Holland Park W11,* ☏ *020/7229–8567. Reservations not accepted. AE, MC, V. Tube: Holland Park.*

CONTEMPORARY

££££ ✕ **Clarke's.** There's no choice on the evening menu at Sally Clarke's restaurant; her four-course dinners contain ultrafresh ingredients, plainly but perfectly cooked, accompanied by home-baked breads. The flower-and-art-speckled room is similarly home-style, if home is one of the big white stucco-fronted Kensington houses you see around here. ✉ *124 Kensington Church St., Notting Hill W8,* ☏ *020/7221–9225. Reservations essential. AE, DC, MC, V. Closed Sun. and 2 wks in Aug., no lunch Sat. Tube: Notting Hill Gate.*

££–£££ ✕ **Pharmacy.** Yes, it's one of those trendy places where the bar is larger than the restaurant. In this case, the bar seats 140 and is shaped like a gigantic aspirin. Yes, this spot looks like its namesake, and even the menu looks fab—but then, Damien Hirst, Brit artist extraordinaire, was involved in setting up the place. The menu highlights "comfort food" and ranges from carpaccio of whitefish with ginger and sesame to roast Dorset lamb with puy lentils and baked quince with suckling pig. If you can't snag a table, just have fun at the bar and order the drink called "Blood Transfusion." ✉ *150 Notting Hill Gate, Notting Hill W11,* ☏ *020/7221–2442. AE, DC, MC, V. Tube: Notting Hill Gate.*

CONTINENTAL

££ ✕ **The Belvedere.** There can be no finer setting for a summer supper or a sunny Sunday brunch than a window table—or a balcony one if you luck out—at this stunning restaurant in the middle of Holland Park. The menu has good Aberdeen Angus beef with snails and pommes frites, and although things are a little pricey, you won't fail to enjoy the conservatory-like room. ✉ *Holland Park off Abbotsbury Rd., Holland Park W8,* ☏ *020/7602–1238. Reservations essential. AE, DC, MC, V. No dinner Sun. Tube: Holland Park.*

ENGLISH

££–£££ ✕ **Julie's.** This sweet 1960s throwback (with a pop-star past) has two parts: a wine bar and a basement restaurant, both decorated with Victorian ecclesiastical furniture. Jean Shrimpton, Terence Stamp, Bryan Ferry, Jerry Hall, and even Sean Connery and Michael Caine used to come in the old days (now it's their children who turn up). The cooking is old-fashioned English (pheasant-and-hare terrine, sea bass and parsnips). The Sunday lunches are popular, and in summer there's a garden room for al fresco eating. ⊠ *137 Portland Rd., Holland Park W11,* ☏ *020/7727–7985. AE, MC, V. No lunch Sat. Tube: Holland Park.*

FRENCH

££–£££ ✕ **Chez Moi.** Sophisticated French food is served in a dark red and black dining room that demands romantic behavior. There are "traditional" dishes that Chez Moi's fans have depended on for a quarter-century—like rack of lamb with Dijon mustard and bread crumbs, and filet mignon with port sauce—as well as more novel dishes, such as Thai chicken and seared seafood, which take their cue from Asia. The desserts are hit-or-miss, but ample chocolates are brought with the coffee. ⊠ *1 Addison Ave., Holland Park W11,* ☏ *020/7603–8267. Reservations essential. AE, DC, MC, V. Closed Sun., no lunch Sat. and Mon. Tube: Holland Park.*

GREEK

£ ✕ **Costa's Fish Restaurant.** Come for good value and down-to-earth Greek food: grilled fish and *kleftiko* (roast lamb on the bone). The place is homey and happy, and there's a tiny garden open in summer. ⊠ *18 Hillgate St., Notting Hill W8,* ☏ *020/7727–4310. No credit cards. Closed Sun. and 3 wks in summer. Tube: Notting Hill Gate.*

MIDDLE EASTERN

£–££ ✕ **Alounak.** Alounak has a raffish air, but its Iranian food is tried and tested. Middle Eastern locals come here for the superior hot bread and kebabs that emerge from the clay oven by the door. Try the *joojeh* kebab or the *zereshk polo* (chicken with rice and Iranian forest berries). Take the Iranian black tea and the Persian sweets, but don't bother with the sour yogurty drinks—they're not to everyone's liking. ✉ *44 Westbourne Grove, Bayswater W2,* ☎ *020/7229–0416. MC, V. Tube: Queensway.*

£–££ ★ ✕ **Yas.** This friendly Persian restaurant has an oven by the door, from which lavish bread is brought steaming to your table. Eat this with *panir o sabzi* (white cheese with herbs), hummus, *borani-e esfenaj* (yogurt and spinach), or any of the dips and salads; then have a grilled chicken or lamb dish or the daily special—like Sunday's *baghali polow* (lamb shank, broad beans, dill, and rice). Yas, which is opposite Olympia Exhibition Centre, is open until 5 AM every day. ✉ *7 Hammersmith Rd., Notting Hill W14,* ☎ *020/7603–9148. AE, DC, MC, V. Tube: Olympia.*

CONTEMPORARY

££–£££ ✕ **The Cow.** Not *another* Conran. The Cow belongs to Tom, son of Sir Terence, although it's a million miles from Quag's and Mezzo. A chic gastro-pub, it comprises a faux-Dublin back-room bar that serves oysters, salmon cakes, and baked brill. Upstairs the chef whips up Anglo-French specialties—cod and mash is one temptation. Notting Hillbillies love the house special—a half-dozen Irish rock oysters with a pint of Guinness. ✉ *89 Westbourne Park Rd., Notting Hill W2,* ☎ *020/7221–5400. Reservations essential. AE, MC, V. Tube: Westbourne Park.*

££–£££ ✕ **First Floor.** Popular for its inventive food and its unusual style—it looks like a bombed church inhabited by distressed nobility—First Floor serves a great brunch on weekends. Otherwise go for seared tuna and asparagus or chicken and butternut salad. ✉ *186 Portobello Rd., Notting Hill W11,* ☎ *020/7243–0072. Reservations essential. AE, DC, MC, V. Tube: Notting Hill Gate.*

££–£££ ★ ✕ **Kensington Place.** Being a favorite among the local glitterati keeps KP packed and noisy. A huge plate-glass window and mural are backdrops to fashionable food—grilled foie gras with sweet-corn pancake and baked tamarillo with vanilla ice cream are perennials—but it's the buzz that draws the crowds. ✉ *201 Kensington Church St., Notting Hill W8,* ☎ *020/7727–3184. AE, DC, MC, V. Tube: Notting Hill Gate.*

£–££ ✕ **Prince Bonaparte.** Forget bangers and mash. At this foodie pub that draws in the crowds, you'll get salmon with beans, a yummy toffee pudding, and lots of interesting beers. Singles take over during the week; young families move in on the weekends. As the night wears on, the place—with large windows, church pews, and farmhouse tables—becomes a lively preclub stop (complete with thumping music on weekends). ✉ *80 Chepstow Rd., Notting Hill W2,* ☎ *020/7313–9491. AE, MC, V. Tube: Notting Hill Gate, Westbourne Park.*

POLISH

££ ★ ✕ **Wódka.** This smart restaurant serves modern Polish food. It's popular with elegant locals and celebs, and often seems like it's hosting one big dinner party. Alongside the salmon, herring, caviar, and eggplant blinis you might find venison sausages or roast duck. Order a carafe of the purest vodka in London; it's encased in ice and is flavored (with bison grass, cherries, and rowanberries) by the owner, who, being a Polish prince, is not unreasonably qualified to do this. ✉ *12 St. Alban's Grove, Kensington W8,* ☎ *020/7937–6513. Reservations essential. AE, DC, MC, V. No lunch weekends. Tube: High Street Kensington.*

Knightsbridge

CONTEMPORARY

£–££ ✕ **The Enterprise.** A hot spot for hooray Henrys and brash bucks—near Harrods and Brompton Cross, the Enterprise is filled with decorative types who complement the striped wallpaper, Edwardian side tables covered with baskets and farmhouse fruit, vintage books piled up in the windows, white linen and fresh flowers on the tables. The menu is fairly subtle—seared butterfish, quail and grapes, and baby artichokes—and the heartiness of the room contributes to a fun experience. ✉ *35 Walton St., South Kensington SW3,* ☎ *020/7584–3148. AE, MC, V. Tube: Kensington.*

FRENCH

££££ ✕ **The Capital.** The clublike dining room sports a grown-up atmosphere. Service is formal. Chef Eric Chavot carries out classy French cooking, and most of his dishes never fail to astonish. These include a saddle of rabbit a la Provencal and sea bass and basil minestrone. Desserts follow the same exciting route. Set-price menus at lunch (£26.50) make it somewhat more affordable. ✉ *22–24 Basil St., Knightsbridge SW3,* ☎ *020/7589–5171. Reservations essential. AE, DC, MC, V. Tube: Knightsbridge.*

££££ ★ ✕ **La Tante Claire.** Pierre Koffmann still reigns over La Tante Claire, so expect brilliant standards of haute cuisine. From the *carte,* you might choose langostine tails, grilled scallops, or Koffmann's signature dish of pigs' feet with sweetbreads and wild mushrooms. As every expense-accounter knows, the set lunch (£29) is a genuine bargain. Lunch reservations must be made three to four days in advance; dinner reservations three to four weeks. ✉ *Berkeley Hotel, Wilton Pl., Knightsbridge SW1,* ☎ *020/7823–2003. Reservations essential. Jacket and tie. AE, DC, MC, V. Closed Sun., no lunch Sat. Tube: Knightsbridge.*

££–£££ ✕ **Brasserie St. Quentin.** French expatriates and locals alike frequent this popular slice of Paris. Every inch of the Gallic menu is explored—queen scallops, escargots, fillet of beef brioche, tart Tatin—in the bourgeois provincial comfort so many London chains (the Dômes, the Cafés Rouges) try for but fail to achieve. ✉ *243 Brompton Rd., Knightsbridge SW3,* ☎ *020/7589–8005. AE, DC, MC, V. Tube: Knightsbridge.*

ITALIAN

££££ ✕ **Zafferano.** Princess Margaret, Joan Collins, and any number of Cartier brooch–wearing Belgravians flock to this place, London's best exponent of *cucina nuova.* The fireworks are in the kitchen, and *what* fireworks: pheasant with rosemary and black truffle, venison with mushrooms, and cod with lentils and parsley sauce. The desserts are *delizioso,* especially the Sardinian pecorino pastries served with ice cream and the panettone pudding. ✉ *15 Lowndes St., Knightsbridge SW1,* ☎ *020/7235–5800. Reservations essential. AE, DC, MC, V. Tube: Knightsbridge.*

£££ ✕ **Isola.** An island of glam in Knightsbridge, Isola guns to be the coolest restaurant in London—so don't be surprised to see Joseph Fiennes in a corner. Upstairs you'll find Iso-bar—a banquette-and-booth wine bar; downstairs is larky fine dining—you sit at leather "compromise sofas" amid the sparkle of chrome and mirrors. Try the rack of lamb and potato gratin or the carpaccio of Scottish beef. ✉ *145 Knightsbridge, Knightsbridge SW1,* ☎ *020/7838–1044. Reservations essential. AE, DC, MC, V. Tube: Knightsbridge.*

££–£££ ✕ **San Lorenzo.** This well-heeled trattoria is nothing special food-wise, but it may be the ticket if you're keen to spot the occasional celebrity or to gaze into the world of ladies who lunch. The usual Italian dishes are here, but they often make a nod to fashion—try any of the veal dishes. ✉ *22 Beauchamp Pl., Knightsbridge SW3,* ☎ *020/7584–1074. No credit cards. Closed Sun. Tube: South Kensington.*

PORTUGUESE

£–££ ✕ **Caravela.** Lower-ground-floor Caravela is one of London's few Portuguese restaurants. You can get *caldo verde* (cabbage soup), *bacalhau* (salt-cured cod), and other typical dishes while listening (Wednesday through Saturday) to the national music, fado—desperately sad songs belted out at thrash-metal volume. ✉ *39 Beauchamp Pl., Knightsbridge SW3,* ☎ *020/7581–2366. AE, DC, MC, V. Tube: South Kensington.*

THAI

££££ ✕ **Nahm.** London at last has a wonderful, world-class Thai restaurant—manned by Australian chef David Thompson. The cuisine's the thing at Nahm. All sorts of ingredients make it into Thompson's dishes: betel leaves, galangal, samphire, Chinese chives, and black sticky rice. Don't leave without trying the yam makreva salad (grilled green eggplant with eggs and dried prawns); oysters with chilies, shredded ginger, lime, and sorrel; or jungle curry with monkfish, coriander, and deep-fried shallots. ✉ *Halkin Hotel, Halkin St., Knightsbridge SW1,* ☎ *020/7333–1234. AE, DC, MC, V Tube: Hyde Park Corner.*

Mayfair

AMERICAN/CASUAL

££ ✕ **Smollensky's on the Strand.** This American-style bar-restaurant is useful for those with children in tow, especially at lunch on weekends, when the young are fed burgers and "Kids' Koktails" and are taken off your hands by sundry clowns and magicians. The grown-ups' menu favors red meat, with several cuts of steak, all served with fries and a choice of sauces. There are potato skins, salads, sandwiches—from New England to New Mexico—and a couple of vegetarian choices. ✉ *105 The Strand, Mayfair W1,* ☎ *020/7497–2101. AE, DC, MC, V. Tube: Charing Cross.*

£ ✕ **Condotti.** In a neighborhood not known for its casual dining options, this elegant pizzeria is a breath of fresh air. Anyone familiar with Pizza Express will know the menu already—because this also belongs to the founder of that chain. The Veneziana (with onions, pine nuts, sultanas, and capers) is everyone's favorite, and a donation goes to the Venice in Peril Fund when you order it. Or try the King Edward, with a potato base instead of bread, and check out the Paolozzis on the walls. ✉ *4 Mill St., Mayfair W1,* ☎ *020/7499–1308. AE, DC, MC, V. Tube: Oxford Circus.*

CONTEMPORARY

£££–££££ ✕ **Greenhouse.** Tucked away behind the Mayfair mansions in a cobbled mews is where you'll find this elegant salon for people who like their food big and strong. You sit among extravagant greenery and men in lilac and black—with chauffeurs to match—to partake of modern European cooking: duck livers with snail and red onion jelly, sea bass sag aloo, onion bhargee, and coconut risotto. The chocolate fondant with peanut butter ice cream is a treat. ✉ *27A Hay's Mews, Mayfair W1,* ☎ *020/7499–3331. Reservations essential. AE, DC, MC, V. No lunch Sat. Tube: Green Park.*

ENGLISH

£–££ ✕ **Browns.** Unpretentious, crowd-pleasing, child-friendly English feeding gets done at the former establishment of the bespoke tailors Messrs. Cooling and Wells, now converted to Edwardian style by the group

Dining in Mayfair, St. James's, Soho, Covent Garden, and Bloomsbury

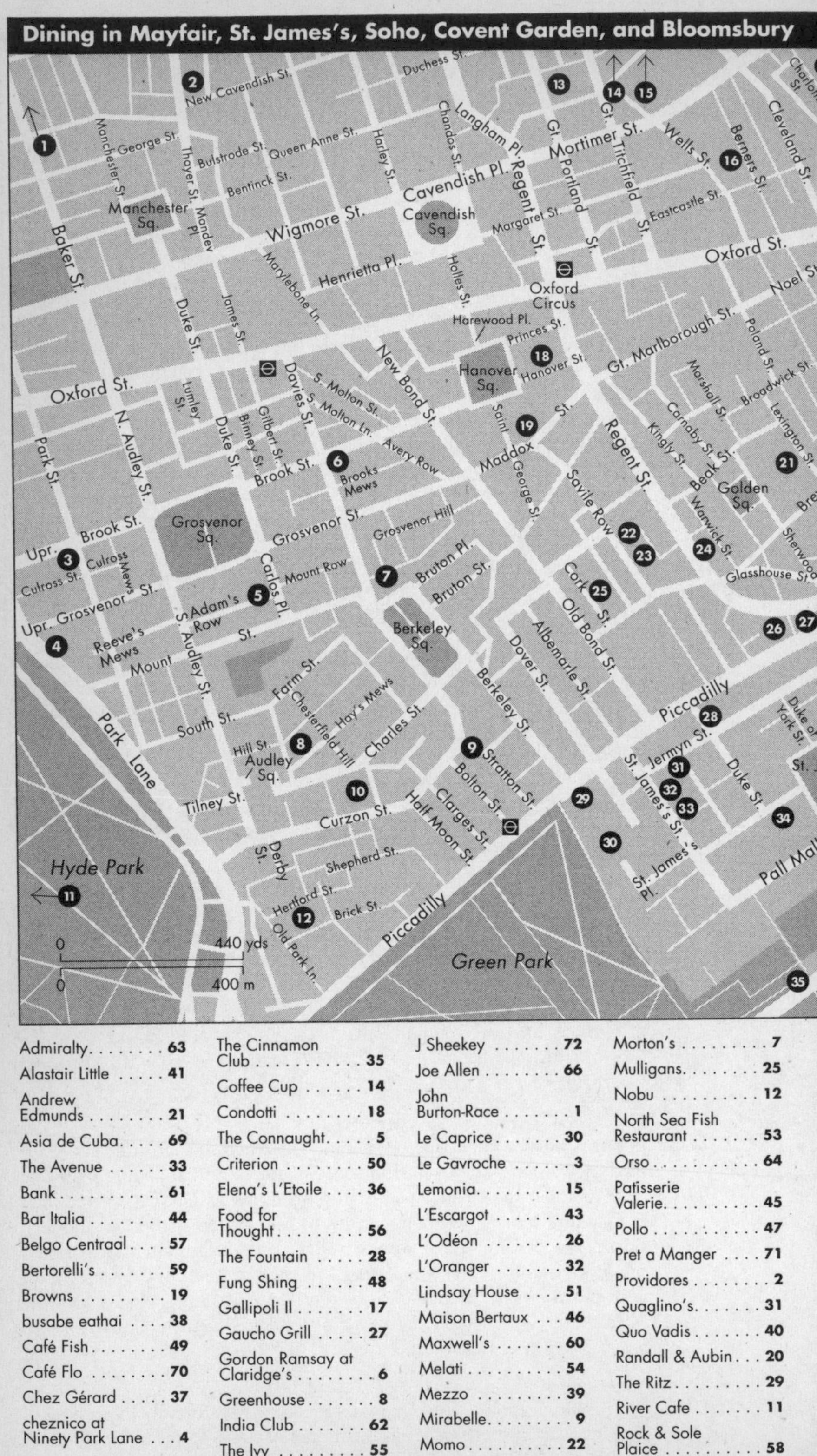

Admiralty 63
Alastair Little 41
Andrew Edmunds 21
Asia de Cuba. 69
The Avenue 33
Bank 61
Bar Italia 44
Belgo Centraal 57
Bertorelli's 59
Browns 19
busabe eathai 38
Café Fish 49
Café Flo 70
Chez Gérard 37
cheznico at Ninety Park Lane . . . 4
The Cinnamon Club 35
Coffee Cup 14
Condotti 18
The Connaught. 5
Criterion 50
Elena's L'Etoile 36
Food for Thought 56
The Fountain 28
Fung Shing 48
Gallipoli II 17
Gaucho Grill 27
Gordon Ramsay at Claridge's 6
Greenhouse 8
India Club 62
The Ivy 55
J Sheekey 72
Joe Allen 66
John Burton-Race 1
Le Caprice 30
Le Gavroche 3
Lemonia. 15
L'Escargot 43
L'Odéon 26
L'Oranger 32
Lindsay House 51
Maison Bertaux . . . 46
Maxwell's 60
Melati 54
Mezzo 39
Mirabelle. 9
Momo 22
Morton's 7
Mulligans. 25
Nobu 12
North Sea Fish Restaurant 53
Orso 64
Patisserie Valerie. 45
Pollo 47
Pret a Manger 71
Providores 2
Quaglino's. 31
Quo Vadis 40
Randall & Aubin . . . 20
The Ritz 29
River Cafe 11
Rock & Sole Plaice 58

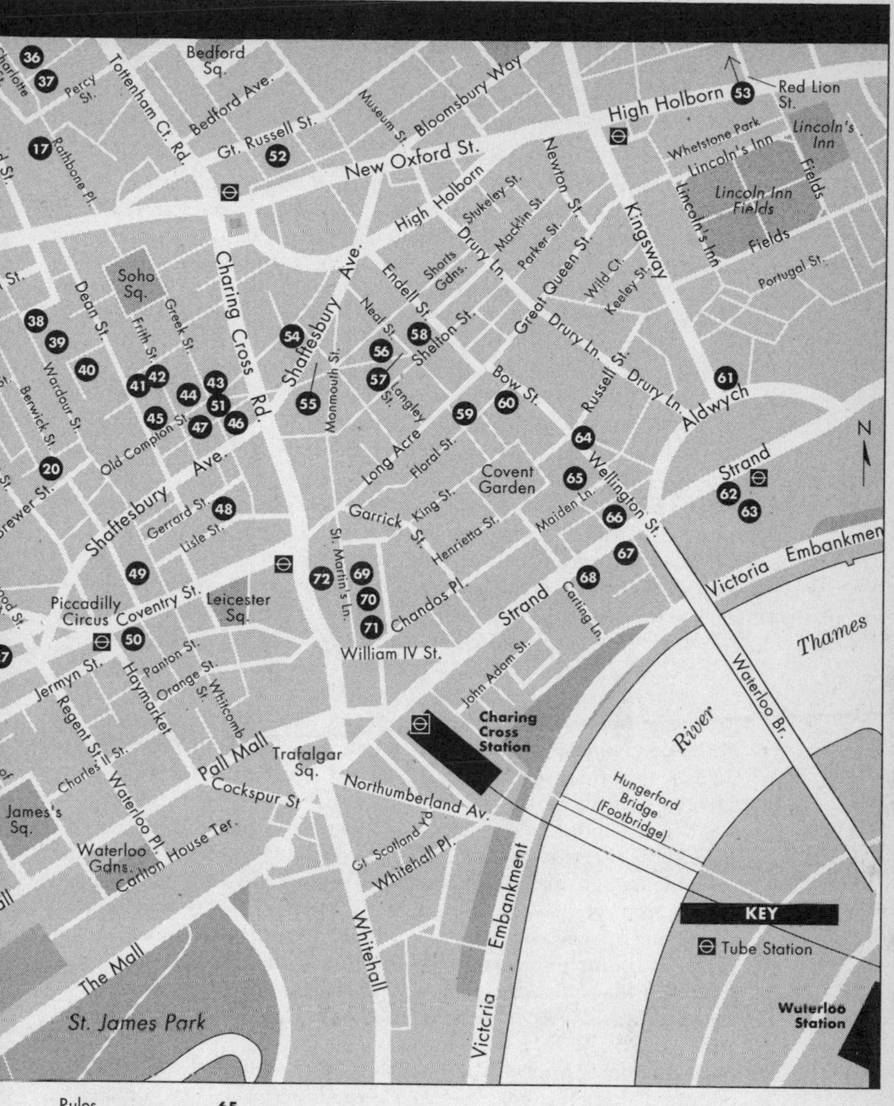

Rules **65**

Savoy Grill **68**

Smollensky's on the Strand **67**

Spoon **16**

The Square **34**

Sugar Club **24**

Tamarind **10**

Villandry **13**

Wagamama. **52**

Wok Wok **42**

Zinc Bar & Grill . . . **23**

behind the successful regional Browns eateries (the Oxford and Cambridge ones are student standbys). The classic Browns steak and Guinness pie is still on the menu, but king prawns, lamb shanks, roasted peppers, salads, and pastas predominate. ✉ *47 Maddox St., Mayfair W1,* ☎ *020/7491–4565. AE, DC, MC, V. Tube: Oxford Circus.*

FRENCH

££££ ✕ **cheznico at Ninety Park Lane.** Those with refined palates and deep pockets should not miss Nico Ladenis's exquisite cuisine, served in a suitably hushed, plush Louis XV dining room next to the Grosvenor House Hotel. Autodidact Nico is one of the world's great chefs, and he's famous for knowing it. The stately food has heavenly light touches—try tortellini with langoustines and lobster sauce. There's no salt on the tables—ask for some at your peril. It's all more affordable in daylight, when you can choose from set lunch menus (£35 for two courses). Otherwise expect to pay £62 or £72 for a 4- or 10-course dinner, respectively. ✉ *90 Park La., Mayfair W1,* ☎ *020/7409–1290. Reservations essential. Jacket and tie required. AE, DC, MC, V. Closed Sun., no lunch Sat. Tube: Marble Arch.*

££££ ★ ✕ **The Connaught.** The mahogany-paneled Connaught remains London's most-respected traditional dining room, with French chef Michel Bourdin still in charge more than 25 years. There's nothing wild here, only the mushrooms and fabulous game—venison, guinea fowl, pigeon—presented with traditional trimmings. "Luncheon dishes" from the trolley follow a pattern according to day-of-the-week (if it's Wednesday, it must be beef). The Connaught is by no means a fashionable place, but it's never out of fashion. ✉ *Carlos Pl., Mayfair W1,* ☎ *020/7499–7070. Reservations essential. Jacket and tie. AE, DC, MC, V. Tube: Green Park.*

££££ ✕ **Gordon Ramsay at Claridge's.** London's finest chef Gordon Ramsay is so precise that he's installed CCTV monitors in the kitchen at Claridge's to keep tabs on the diners out the front. Sit at the chef's table—a 6–8–seat booth in the kitchen—and watch the heat and the drama. They do breakfasts, stunning three-course lunches for £21, and impeccable set dinners for £38 and £48. Try the eight-hour roast shoulder of lamb or braised halibut. Book months in advance, as the restaurant has become popular with the fickle-fashion dining scene. Arrive early for dinner and grab a drink at the art deco bar—the coolest cocktail lounge in London. ✉ *Claridge's Hotel, Brook St., Mayfair W1,* ☎ *020/7499–0099. Reservations essential. Jacket required. AE, DC, MC, V. Tube: Bond St.*

££££ ★ ✕ **Le Gavroche.** Michel Roux has the family cooking gene—he runs one of London's finest restaurants. He's a master of classical cooking—formal, flowery, decorated. The set lunch is relatively affordable at £40 (for canapés, three courses, plus mineral water, a half a bottle of wine, coffee, and petits fours). In fact, it's the only way to eat here if you don't have an expense account—which most patrons do. Book at least one week in advance. ✉ *43 Upper Brook St., Mayfair W1,* ☎ *020/7408–0881. Reservations essential. AE, DC, MC, V. Closed Sun., no lunch Sat., closed 10 days at Christmas. Tube: Marble Arch.*

£££–££££ ★ ✕ **The Square.** Philip Howard's sophisticated set menus, in the modern French haute tradition, include such dishes as foie gras with caramelized endive and muscat grapes or crab lasagne with shellfish and basil, followed perhaps by a saddle of lamb with shallot puree, or a steamed turbot with champagne sauce. All dishes are arranged carefully and symmetrically. The clientele is heavy on business types who appreciate impeccable service, complete with a friendly (and necessary—the wine list has the heft of a novel) sommelier. ✉ *6–10 Bruton St., Mayfair W1,* ☎ *020/7495–7100. Reservations essential. AE, DC, MC, V. No lunch weekends. Tube: Green Park.*

££–£££ ✕ **L'Odéon.** It's an odd contribution to London's mania for giant restaurants: a former airline office, with long, low dimensions peculiarly reminiscent of an aircraft. Food is elevated French bistro–style with the usual modish Italian additions—grilled fish and meats, wild mushrooms on brioche toast—and is far more affordable in set-menu form, available for lunch and before 7 PM. Take a table by the huge arched windows if you want to people-watch. ✉ *65 Regent St., Mayfair W1,* ☎ *020/7287–1400. AE, DC, MC, V. Tube: Piccadilly Circus.*

££–£££ ★ ✕ **Mirabelle.** Marco Pierre White does what he does best at Mirabelle—taking over an old establishment, licking it into shape, and turning its fortunes around. The environment is lavish, while the food is an excellent interpretation of French with a hint of Italian. Expect lots of exceptional seafood (lemon sole with tartare sauce and creamed potatoes), and some remarkably good meat creations (steak with snails stands out). The fondant chocolate dessert is a gutsy knockout, as is the pineapple tart with fromage blanc and ice cream. ✉ *56 Curzon St., Mayfair W1,* ☎ *020/7499–4636. Reservations essential. AE, DC, MC, V. Tube: Green Park.*

£–££ ✕ **Criterion.** You'll love the glamour of this spectacular, neo-Byzantine mirrored marble hall, which first opened in 1874. It's heavy on the awe factor, with dishes to match, and Marco Pierre White's team scores highly. Some of his well-known dishes appear on a menu whose divisions include one headed "Farinaceous Dishes"—where you'll find his ballotine of salmon with herbs and *fromage blanc,* for instance. The soaring golden ceiling, oil paintings, and attentive Gallic service adds up to a first-rate night out. ✉ *Piccadilly Circus, St. James's W1,* ☎ *020/7930–0488. AE, DC, MC, V. Tube: Piccadilly Circus.*

INDIAN

££££ ✕ **Tamarind.** Some say Tamarind serves the best curry in London; expect to see lots of posh Indians here. The Mayfair basement is a sumptuous place, with golden arches, framed textiles, gilded staircases, and copper plates. It's expensive, but dishes like *machchi ka sula* (salmon and monkfish) and *dal bukhari* (creamy black lentils) are presented with precision. Try the puddings—they're sweet and good. ✉ *20 Queen St., Mayfair W1,* ☎ *020/7629–3561. AE, DC, MC, V. Tube: Green Park.*

IRISH

££–£££ ✕ **Mulligans.** Mulligans is straight out of Dublin, down to the draught Guinness. Downstairs, in the upscale restaurant, order traditional dishes such as roasted partridge and chestnuts or Irish stew with homey accompaniments like "champ and colcannon" (buttery mashed potatoes with cabbage), then a big rice pudding brûlée with whiskey-soused prunes and Irish coffee cheesecake. ✉ *13–14 Cork St., Mayfair W1,* ☎ *020/7409–1370. AE, DC, MC, V. Closed weekends. Tube: Green Park.*

JAPANESE

££££ ✕ **Nobu.** Bulging with stars, Nobu is London's sexiest destination restaurant, where Boris Becker famously had sex with a waitress in a broom cupboard ("It was just poom-pah-boom!" he said.) Nobu Matsuhisa wows with new-style sashimi with a Peruvian touch—they sell 300 lbs of Alaskan black cod every day. Nobu is in the Metropolitan, a hip hotel, with staff, attitude, clientele, and prices to match. Ubon, a sister restaurant (backwards for "Nobu") operates in Canary Wharf. ✉ *Metropolitan Hotel, 19 Old Park La., Mayfair W1,* ☎ *020/7447–4747. Reservations essential. AE, DC, MC, V. No lunch weekends. Tube: Hyde Park.*

St. James's

CONTEMPORARY

£££ ✕ **Quaglino's.** "Quags" is *the* out-of-towners' post-theater or celebration destination. To the cognoscenti it's *history,* but it never fails to impress first-timers. The gigantic restaurant has a glamorous staircase, "Crustacea Altar," and large bar, and hosts live jazz. The food is pan-European with Asian trimmings—crab with mirin and soy; tuna with black bean and lime. Desserts are somewhere between the Paris bistro and the English nursery (Pavlova and berries and sticky toffee pudding), and wine from the Old World (France, Italy) and the New (Australia, the United States). ✉ *16 Bury St., St. James's SW1,* ☎ *020/7930–6767. Reservations essential. AE, DC, MC, V. Tube: Green Park.*

££–£££ ✕ **The Avenue.** The large and swanky Avenue was London's first restaurant to be owned by committee. Unlike the horse designed by committee (a camel), it has worked out well, emulating New York singles-heavy, dining-as-theater glamour. The food is pretty good—generic Euro-Brit with the usual rash of Mediterranean-vegetarian starters and sides. Set menus are competitively priced, but the content doesn't always deliver. ✉ *7–9 St. James's St., St. James's SW1,* ☎ *020/7321–2111. AE, DC, MC, V. Tube: Green Park.*

££–£££ ★ ✕ **Le Caprice.** Secreted behind the Ritz, Le Caprice commands the deepest loyalty of any restaurant in London because it gets everything right: the glossy Eva Jiricna interior; the perfect service; the menu, halfway between Euro-peasant and fashion plate. This food—crispy duck and watercress salad; San Daniele ham and figs—has no business being so good. Frequented by Clive James, Joan Collins, David Bowie, and Helena Bonham Carter, Le Caprice has the best people-watching in town (apart from at its sister restaurant, the Ivy). ✉ *Arlington House, Arlington St., St. James's SW1,* ☎ *020/7629–2239. Reservations essential. AE, DC, MC, V. Tube: Green Park.*

CONTINENTAL

££££ ✕ **The Ritz.** This palace of marble, gilt, and trompe l'oeil would moisten Marie Antoinette's eye; add the view over Green Park and the Ritz's sunken garden, and it seems beside the point to eat. But the cuisine stands up to the visual onslaught, with super-rich morsels—foie gras, lobster, truffles, caviar, all served with a flourish. Englishness is wrested from Louis XVI by a daily roast "from the trolley." A three-course lunch at £35 and a four-course dinner at £51 make the check more bearable than the £59 you'll pay for the Friday and Saturday dinner-dance (a dying tradition). ✉ *150 Piccadilly, St. James's W1,* ☎ *020/7493–8181. Reservations essential. Jacket and tie. AE, DC, MC, V. Tube: Green Park.*

ENGLISH

£–£££ ★ ✕ **The Fountain.** At the back of Fortnum & Mason is the old-fashioned Fountain, as frumpy and popular as a boarding-school matron, serving delicious light meals and ice-cream sodas. During the day, go for the Welsh rarebit or Fortnum's steak-and-ale pie; in the evening, a no-frills steak is a typical option. It's just the place for afternoon tea and ice-cream sundaes after the Royal Academy or Bond Street shopping, and for pretheater meals. ✉ *181 Piccadilly, St. James's W1,* ☎ *020/7734–8040. AE, DC, MC, V. Closed Sun. Tube: Green Park.*

FRENCH

£££–££££ ★ ✕ **L'Oranger.** The food here reaches gobsmacking perfection: ravioli of mushroom and asparagus; hake with clam sauce; fig tartlette with pear and cinnamon ice cream. The conservatory is highly romantic, plus there's a little courtyard where the last duel in London was fought. The all-French waiters are courteous and not snobby. ✉ *5 St. James's*

St., St. James's SW1, ☏ *020/7839–3774. Reservations essential. AE, DC, MC, V. Closed Sun., no lunch Sat. Tube: Green Park.*

£££–£££ ✕ **Morton's.** Try Morton's if you're near Berkeley Square and fancy an elegant meal. The dining room is one of the nicest in London, and the cooking is worthy of the setting. It's not cheap, mind you, not for a starter of foie gras with grapes, walnuts, and dandelion; an entrée of risotto of wild mushrooms; or the tournedos Rossini (excellent though it may be). Downstairs you'll find a raucous members-only bar. Watch out for the foxy Mayfair ladies, the roué business brokers, and cufflinked boozers. ✉ *28 Berkeley Sq., Mayfair W1,* ☏ *020/7493–7171. Reservations essential. AE, DC, MC, V. Tube: Green Park.*

INDIAN

££ ✕ **The Cinnamon Club.** MPs, politicos, and spin doctors flock here for the posh Indian nosh in the converted Old Westminster Library—hence the wooden floors, high ceilings, double doors, and book-lined galleries. It's only a block away from Westminster Abbey and the House of Commons. The food is tasty and elaborate (loin of rabbit with cottage cheese and dried fruit or Goan spiced duck with curry-leaf flavored semolina)—but generally the calmer, less complex the dish, the better. Get the lamb tikka. ✉ *Old Westminster Library, Great Smith St., St. James's SW1,* ☏ *020/7222–2555. MC, V. St. James's Park.*

LATIN

££ ✕ **Gaucho Grill.** They say Gaucho Grill serves the best steaks in London, but that's probably overstating it. Nevertheless, this chain of Argentinian chophouses (the other locations are Canary Wharf, Hampstead, Chancery Lane, and the City) are reasonably priced and unreconstructed in their reverence for meat. The steaks are flown vacuum packed from Buenos Aires, and are cut to order. There is not much for vegetarians, but it's great for a beef fix. ✉ *19 Swallow St., St. James's W1,* ☏ *020/7734–4040. AE, DC, MC, V. Tube: Piccadilly Circus.*

NORTH AFRICAN

££–£££ ✕ **Momo.** It's a hot ticket—if you can book a table, go. Algerian-born Mourad Mazouz—Momo to friends—stormed beau London with his casbah-like North African restaurant, set in a cul-de-sac behind Regent Street. The seats are low and placed close together, and there's a resident DJ, and often live North African music. Downstairs is the members-only Kemia Bar, and next door is Mô—a Moroccan tearoom, open to all. The menu, based on pastilla, tagine, and couscous, doesn't match the excitement of the scene; but the lamb merguez is a winner. The restaurant CD, *Arabesque Zoudge,* is now on sale. ✉ *23–25 Heddon St., St James's W1,* ☏ *020/7434–4040. Reservations essential. AE, DC, MC, V. Tube: Piccadilly Circus.*

SEAFOOD

£–££ ★ ✕ **Zinc Bar & Grill.** The open zinc bar at this fun and underrated brasserie-rotisserie off Regent Street heaves with music and PR girls. Try a dozen rock oysters, crab or lobster, or calves' liver with bacon and gravy. Or sip a "Pink Zinc"—champagne and raspberry liqueur. There are good pretheater and prix-fixe deals. ✉ *21 Heddon St., St. James's W1,* ☏ *020/7255–8899. AE, DC, MC, V. Tube: Piccadilly Circus.*

Soho

CAFÉS

£ ✕ **Maison Bertaux.** On two floors in central Soho, this French patisserie is not in the least dainty, but it is the kind of place to refuel after a shopping trek, with a savory pastry at lunchtime, a Danish mid-morning, or even an early supper (it closes at 8 PM). The ancient rivalry with Valerie, around the corner, continues. ✉ *28 Greek St., Soho W1,* ☎ *020/7437–6007. No credit cards. Tube: Leicester Sq.*

£ ✕ **Patisserie Valerie.** Beloved of film-biz people, students, shoppers, and just about everyone, this dimly lit pastry shop and café is cherished because nothing has changed in years. The cakes are wondrous creations: dark *foret noir* (black forest gateaux with Morello cherries), cortinas (creamy sponge cakes with rum and white chocolate), or classic almond croissants (£1.30). Drool at the window, it's a chocoholic's Shangri-la. Valerie has also taken over the historic eatery, the Sagne, at 105 Marylebone High Street—the interior there has retained a French-*sud* time warp. ✉ *44 Old Compton St., Soho W1,* ☎ *020/7437–3466. AE, DC, MC, V. Tube: Leicester Sq.*

CHINESE

££–£££ ★ ✕ **Fung Shing.** This cool-green restaurant is a hefty cut above the Lisle–Wardour Street crowd of Chinese restaurants in terms of both service and food. The better Chinatown food choices are supplemented by some even more exciting dishes: especially fine is the crispy baby squid with Chinese sausage, and the salt-baked chicken, served on or off the bone with a bowl of intense broth, is essential. Reserve a table in the back room conservatory. ✉ *15 Lisle St., Soho WC2,* ☎ *020/7437–1539. AE, DC, MC, V. Tube: Leicester Sq.*

CONTEMPORARY

££££ ✕ **Alastair Little.** Little, one of London's most original chefs, draws inspiration from practically everywhere (Thailand, Japan, Scandinavia, France, and North Africa, but chiefly Italy), and nearly always brings it off brilliantly. His restaurant is soft-lit and minimalist (modern prints and tables close together), and the menu changes twice daily (for lunch and dinner). You can expect a simple starter of nettle soup and decent fish (like smoked eel, pancetta, horseradish and potato cakes), but beyond that it's hard to predict. Look for Little's cheaper restaurant—with the same name—next to the Ladbroke Grove Tube stop. ✉ *49 Frith St., Soho W1,* ☎ *020/7734–5183. AE, DC, MC, V. Closed Sun., no lunch Sat. Tube: Leicester Sq.*

££–£££ ✕ **Quo Vadis.** Andy Warhols adorn the former house of Karl Marx at Quo Vadis in central Soho. Downstairs, in the restaurant, the Modern European food is seriously impressive; highlights include baked cod with fennel and courgette fritters, and the roasted lobster with garlic bulbs, champagne jelly, and passion fruit. Artistry does not come cheap, but there are affordable fixed-price lunches for £14.50–£17.50. ✉ *26–29 Dean St., Soho W1,* ☎ *020/7439–4809. Reservations essential. AE, DC, MC, V. Tube: Leicester Sq., Tottenham Court Rd.*

££–£££ ✕ **Sugar Club.** David Selex's global, eclectic menu is picking up well from Peter Gordon, who made his name here and introduced Londoners to Australasian fusion cooking. Among the exotic dishes you'll find are buffalo *bocconcini* (mozzarella balls) and tamarillo, or lamb shanks with parsnip puree and *grimolata* (parsley, garlic, and lemon zest). The black sea bream sashimi with sesame and ginger is a hit with the restaurant's fans. It's one of those places so loved by the chatterati that you have to reserve way ahead—two weeks is recommended. ✉ *21 Warwick St., Soho W1,* ☎ *020/7437–7776. Reservations essential. AE, DC, MC, V. Tube: Oxford Circus, Piccadilly Circus.*

CONTINENTAL

££–£££ ✕ **L'Escargot.** This ever-popular media haunt serves Anglo-French food in a ground-floor brasserie and a more formal upstairs restaurant. Reasonably priced wine from a comprehensive list is sure to go well with partridge and cepes, or simple poached or grilled fish. L'Escargot is relaxed and reliable. ✉ *48 Greek St., Soho W1,* ☎ *020/7437–2679. AE, DC, MC, V. Closed Sun. Tube: Leicester Sq.*

ECLECTIC

££–£££ ✕ **Andrew Edmunds.** Good food at realistic prices defines this perpetually jammed, softly lit restaurant—though you'll wish it were larger and the seats more forgiving. Tucked away behind Oxford and Carnaby streets, it's a favorite with the film and media lunch crowd, who like the daily-changing set menu. Starters and main courses range from a taste of Ireland through the Mediterranean to the Middle East. ✉ *46 Lexington St., Soho W1,* ☎ *020/7437–5708. AE, MC, V. Tube: Oxford Circus, Piccadilly Circus.*

££–£££ ✕ **Mezzo.** Sir Terence Conran's 480-seater rolls on, much maligned and beloved by turns. The young office and evening crowds still like to hang out here (live jazz plays every night). The contemporary food includes confit duck leg with brown lentils and Madiera sauce, monkfish saltimbocca, and orange and lemon tart. The upstairs bar area includes a Southeast Asian restaurant—called Mezzonine—where wasabi-seared tuna and bean sprouts and salmon and chili can be taken more informally. ✉ *100 Wardour St., Soho W1,* ☎ *020/7314–4000. AE, DC, MC, V. Tube: Leicester Sq.*

FRENCH

£££–££££ ✕ **Spoon.** A disco vibe permeates London's grooviest destination, in the Sanderson Hotel. Designed by Philippe Starck, the great Alain Ducasse's first London foray has become the place to be seen. Diners pick 'n' mix ingredients; ask for help, or go for the chef-decides "Sexy Spoon" option (£95 each, with wine). The soups are sublime—shellfish, or potato and truffle—and the meats tender and juicy. The 80-ft Long Bar is the place for checking out the talent. ✉ *Sanderson Hotel, 50 Berners St., Covent Garden W1,* ☎ *020/7300–1444. Reservations essential. AE, DC, MC, V. Tube: Oxford Circus.*

IRISH

£££ ✕ **Lindsay House.** You'll love Lindsay House—some of the most elegant and idiosyncratic dining in London. Great Irishman Richard Corrigan has brought his bluff country charm to the heart of Soho and set up a Georgian town house of immense quirkiness and personality. Prime Minister Tony Blair and other Cabinet ministers are said to know its charms. You might have an amusette of celeriac soup or a pre-dessert of Amaretto-soaked figs. Waiters glide through the warren of rooms of the paneled, rickety house. Corrigan enjoys using hearty flavors—he likes to wrap rabbit and black pudding in Bayonne ham, he excels with Irish beef with mash and snail butter, and his white asparagus and langoustine dish can't be bettered. The petit fours with coffee will send you home happy. ✉ *21 Romilly St., Soho W1,* ☎ *020/7439–0450. AE, DC, MC, V. Closed Sun. Tube: Leicester Sq.*

ITALIAN

£ ✕ **Bar Italia.** A well-established Frith Street caffeine and stand-up snack stop is an oasis for photographers and admen, Soho-ites, theatergoers, and clubbers—both early birds and late-nighters. Expect chocolate cake, strong cappuccino, and espresso. The walls are full of Italian hardmen, singers, and old-school sporting heroes. It's the number-one place to watch Italy play in the football World Cup. ✉ *22 Frith St., Soho W1,* ☎ *020/7437–4520. AE, DC, MC, V. Tube: Leicester Sq.*

£ ✕ **Pollo.** A boisterous Italian café that's been around forever, and through which all Londoners pass during their student and/or clubbing days, Pollo is good for a quick feed with a bottle of house plonk pretheater or for an afternoon spaghetti carbonara. Beware of the evening crowds, though—it's no fun unless you're 18 and in art school.

✉ *20 Old Compton St., Soho W1,* ☎ *020/7734–5917. No credit cards. Tube: Leicester Sq.*

MALAYSIAN

£ ✕ **Melati.** What amounts to a Malaysian café with wooden tables and, usually, lines at the door, is a useful place when you don't want to spend too much but are looking for a taste thrill. Whole stuffed squid and a tofu omelet, stir-fried vegetables, and the inevitable *nasi goreng* (spicy fried rice with tiny shrimp, onions, and garlic) are among the standout dishes. ✉ *21 Great Windmill St., Soho W1,* ☎ *020/7437–2745. AE, MC, V. Tube: Leicester Sq.*

PAN-ASIAN

£ ✕ **Wok Wok.** Decorated in bright, primary colors, with friendly service and a menu of fresh soups, noodles, stir-fries, and rice dishes from all over Asia (Thailand, Vietnam, Malaysia, China, Japan, and Indonesia), this central branch of a small chain will continue to thrive, especially given the reasonable cost. ✉ *10 Frith St., W1,* ☎ *020/7437–7080. AE, DC, MC, V. Tube: Leicester Sq.*

SEAFOOD

££–£££ ✕ **Café Fish.** This cheerful, bustling restaurant has an encyclopedic selection of fish—marlin, bream, salmon, and monkfish—arranged on the menu according to cooking method (char-grilled, steamed). The Mediterranean and Asian accents usually delight. Try the bar and canteen on the ground floor for a cornucopia of shellfish; in the upstairs restaurant you can linger longer over the likes of cod and shrimp. This spot is great for pretheater. ✉ *36–40 Rupert St., Soho W1,* ☎ *020/7287–8989. AE, DC, MC, V. Tube: Piccadilly Circus.*

££–£££ ★ ✕ **Randall & Aubin.** Consultant chef Ed Baines shreds the rest—he has become London's coolest TV chef. The ex-Armani model's converted French butcher's shop (with white tiles, meat hooks, and marble table tops) runs one of London's buzziest champagne-oyster bars—bang in the bosom of Soho's sexland. Go for the Loch Fyne oysters or half a lobster with chips. Peak time, it can take 10 minutes at the bar waiting for a seat. Watch out Thursday to Saturday for the transvestite cabaret. ✉ *16 Brewer St., Soho W1,* ☎ *020/7287–4447. Reservations not accepted. AE, DC, MC, V. Tube: Piccadilly Circus.*

THAI

£ ✕ **busabe eathai.** One of the best cheap spots in Soho, this superior Thai canteen is outfitted with rattans, benches, hardwood tables, low lights, and paper lampshades. It's no less seductive for its communal tables. The menu includes noodles, curries, stir-fries, rice, and sides. Try chicken with butternut squash, green curry chicken, or seafood vermicelli (prawns, squid, scallops). The mantra here is *gan gin gan yuu,* which means "as you eat, so you are." There's no smoking. ✉ *106–110 Wardour St., Soho W1,* ☎ *020/7255–8686. Reservations not accepted. AE, MC, V. Tube: Leicester Sq.*

South Kensington

CONTEMPORARY

££–££££ ★ ✕ **Bibendum.** This converted Michelin showroom, adorned with art deco prints and brilliant stained glass, remains one of London's dining showplaces. Chef Matthew Harris cooks with Euro-Brit flair. Try herring with horseradish, any of the risottos, steak au poivre, or sea bass and salsa verde. Here, too, are brains and tripe as they ought to be cooked. The £28.50 set-price menu at lunchtime is money well spent. ✉ *Michelin House, 81 Fulham Rd., South Kensington SW3,* ☎ *020/*

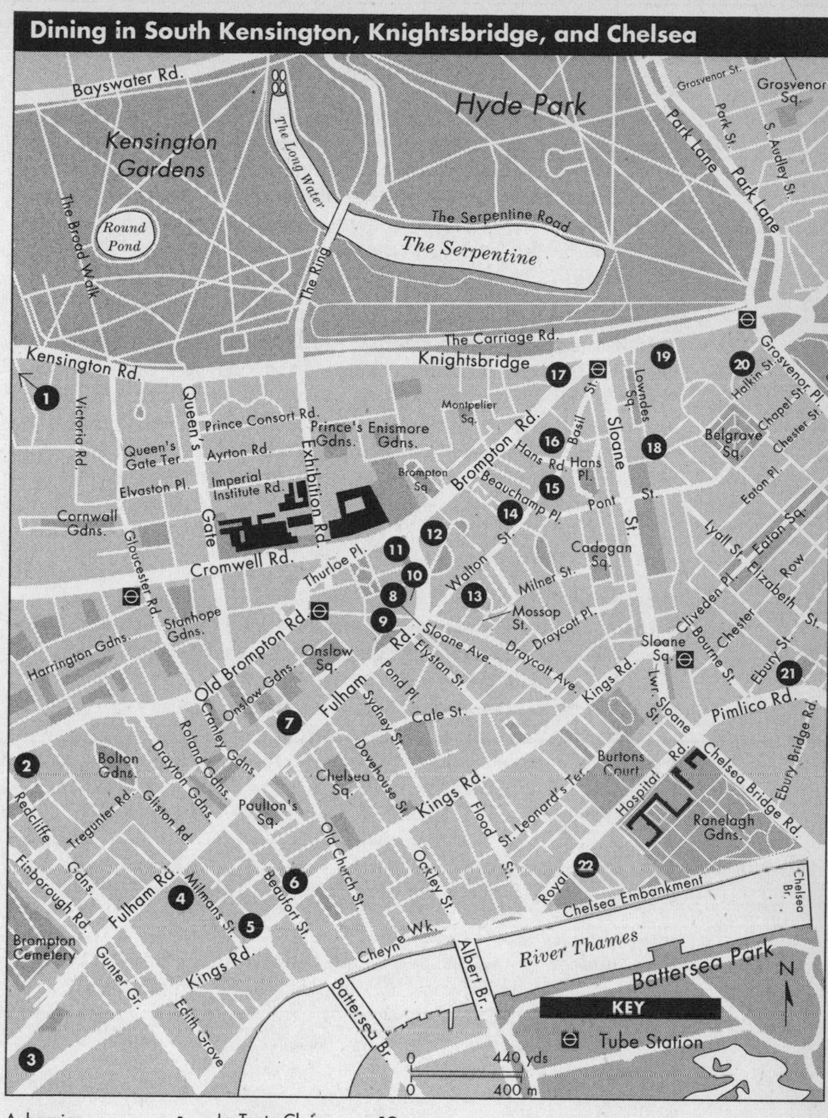

Aubergine 4
Bibendum 8
Bluebird 6
Brasserie St. Quentin 12
Cactus Blue 7
The Capital 16
Caravela 14
Chelsea Bun Diner. 5
Chutney Mary 3
The Collection 11
The Enterprise 13
Gordon Ramsay . . . 22
Isola 17
La Brasserie 10
La Poule au Pot. . . . 21
La Tante Claîre 19
Lou Pescadou 2
Nahm 20
PJ's 9
San Lorenzo. 15
Zafferano 18
Zaika 1

7581–5817. Reservations essential. AE, DC, MC, V. Tube: South Kensington.

FRENCH

££ ★ ✕ **Lou Pescadou.** Imagine a little slice of the South of France, in sea-theme surroundings and with an emphatically French staff. Fish predominates here, and the menu changes often—don't miss the *soupe de poisson* (fish soup) with croutons and *rouille* (rose-color, garlicky mayonnaise) if it's featured. The French-dominated wine list can be pricey. ✉ *241 Old Brompton Rd., South Kensington SW5,* ☎ *020/7370–1057. Reservations essential. AE, DC, MC, V. Tube: Earl's Court.*

INDIAN

££ ✕ **Zaika.** At one of London's finest Indian restaurants, Vineet Bhatia pushes the boundaries of Indian cuisine by mixing old flavors with modern needs. The restaurant is dark, refined, and subtle. You can't top the starter of *dhungar machli tikka* (tandoor-smoked salmon with mustard and dill), nor can you better the scallops in coconut milk, with masala mashed potato. Sign off with chocolate samosas ("chocomosas") and Indian ice cream. ✉ *1 Kensington High Street, South Kensington W8,* ☎ *020/7351–7823. Reservations essential. AE, MC, V. Tube: High Street Kensington.*

MEDITERRANEAN

££ ✕ **The Collection.** Enter this former Katharine Hamnett shop through the spotlighted tunnel over the glass drawbridge, and you'll find yourself engulfed by a fashionable crowd. The huge warehouse setting, adorned with industrial wood beams and steel cables, a vast bar, and a suspended gallery, makes a great theater for people-watching. Well-dressed wannabes peck at Mediterranean food seasoned with Japanese and Thai accents. ✉ *264 Brompton Rd., South Kensington SW3,* ☎ *020/7225–1212. AE, DC, MC, V. Tube: South Kensington.*

Brunch and Afternoon Tea

Supposedly, brunch is catching on among Londoners, while the afternoon ritual, often mistakenly referred to as "high tea," is dying out. Tea—the drink—however, is so ingrained in the national character that tea—the meal—will always have a place in the capital, if only as an occasional celebration, a children's treat, or something you do when your American friends are in town. Reserve for all these, unless otherwise noted.

Brunch

Butlers Wharf Chop House. What you'll get here, at £15.95 for three courses, is brunch that's as British as brunch ever gets, with lobster mayonnaise, Stilton and celery soup, and a fabulous Thames-side setting. ✉ *36E Shad Thames, The South Bank SE1,* ☎ *020/7403–3403. AE, DC, MC, V.* ⏲ *Brunch served Sat. and Sun. noon–4. Tube: Tower Hill.*

Christopher's. Imagine you're in Manhattan at this superior Covent Garden purveyor of American food—it serves everything from pancakes, steak, eggs, and fries to salmon cakes and Caesar salad. ✉ *18 Wellington St., Covent Garden WC2,* ☎ *020/7240–4222. AE, DC, MC, V.* ⏲ *Brunch served Sat. and Sun. 11:30–4:30. Tube: Covent Garden.*

★ **Joe Allen.** A hangout famous among theater people, Joe Allen is a place to refuge from the lovely British weather and down some Bloody Marys. Supplement that with a grilled chicken sandwich or a salad of spicy sausage, shrimp, and new potatoes. ✉ *13 Exeter St., Covent Garden WC2,* ☎ *020/7836–0651. Reservations essential. AE, MC, V.* ⏲ *Brunch served Sat. and Sun. 11:30–4. Tube: Covent Garden.*

Veeraswamy. It's been here for years, but the Chutney Mary group from Chelsea has taken it over and given it a makeover. The result is great, and what better way to try the delights here than the Sunday brunch menu (£15 for three courses). You'll be so taken with the aromatic fish and chicken dishes and mod-Euro/trad-Indian desserts, you'll be coming back for dinner. ✉ *Victory House, 101 Regent St., St. James's W1,* ☎ *020/7734–1401. AE, DC, MC, V.* ⏲ *Brunch served Sun. 12:30–3. Tube: Regent Street.*

Afternoon Tea

Note that Claridge's and the Savoy require jacket and tie.

Brown's Hotel. Brown's does rest on its laurels somewhat, with a packaged aura and nobody around but fellow tourists who believe this to be the most famous. Still, everyone swears by the divine armchairs here. For £23 you get sandwiches, a scone with cream and jam, tart, fruitcake, and shortbread. Champagne tea is £33. ✉ *33 Albermarle St., Mayfair W1,* ☎ *020/7518–4108. AE, DC, MC, V.* ⏲ *Tea served daily 2–6. Tube: Green Park.*

Claridge's. This is the real McCoy, with liveried footmen proffering sandwiches, scones, and superior pâtisseries (£19 or £22) in the palatial yet genteel Foyer, to the sound of the resident "Hungarian orchestra" (actually a string quartet). ✉ *Brook St., Mayfair W1,* ☎ *020/7629–8860. AE, DC, MC, V.* ⏲ *Tea served daily 3–5:30. Tube: Bond Street.*

Fortnum & Mason. Upstairs at the Queen's grocers, three set teas are ceremoniously offered: standard afternoon tea (sandwiches, scone, cakes, £17.50), old-fashioned high tea (the traditional nursery meal, adding something more robust and savory, £19.50), and champagne tea (£23). ✉ *St. James's Restaurant, 4th floor, 181 Piccadilly, St. James's W1,* ☎ *020/7734–8040. AE, DC, MC, V.* ⏲ *Tea served Mon.–Sat. 3–5:45. Tube: Green Park.*

Harrods. For sweet-toothed people, the Georgian Restaurant Room at this ridiculously well-known department store has a high tea that will give you a sugar rush for a week. ✉ *Brompton Rd., Knightsbridge SW3,* ☎ *020/7730–1234. AE, DC, MC, V.* ⏲ *Tea served Mon.–Sat. 3:45–5:30. Tube: Knightsbridge.*

The Orangery at Kensington Palace. This Georgian, gorgeous, sunlight-flooded (assuming the sun is out), yes, orangery is the perfect place for a light lunch or for tea. You can get homemade soups and quiche, cakes, shortbread, pastries, and pots of Earl Grey. Go when it's balmy, or you'll freeze. ✉ *Kensington Gardens, Holland Park W8,* ☎ *020/7376–0239. AE, MC, V. Closes at 5, Oct.–Easter; at 6, Easter–Sept. Tube: High Street Kensington or Queensway.*

The Ritz. The Ritz's huge, stagey, and sometimes cold and overly formal Palm Court offers tiered cake stands, silver pots, a harpist, and Louis XVI chaises, plus a great deal of rococo gilt and glitz, all for £27. Reserve at least four weeks ahead, more for weekends. ✉ *150 Piccadilly, St. James's W1,* ☎ *020/7493–8181. AE, DC, MC, V.* ⏲ *Tea served daily 1:30–5:30. Tube: Green Park.*

The Savoy. The glamorous Thames-side hotel does one of the most pleasant teas (£23 or £29); its triple-tiered cake stands are packed with goodies and its tailcoated waiters are wonderfully polite. ✉ *The Strand, Covent Garden WC2,* ☎ *020/7836–4343. AE, DC, MC, V.* ⏲ *Tea served daily 3–5:30. Tube: Charing Cross.*

Pubs

Even today, when television keeps so many people glued to their hearth and home, the pub, or public house, or "local" is still a vital part of British life. It also should be a part of the tourist experience, as there are few better places to meet the natives in their local habitat. There are hundreds of pubs in London, but the best—ever fewer of which still have original Victorian etched glass, Edwardian panels, and Art Nouveau carvings—are listed below.

Gastro-pub fever is still sweeping London. At many places, char-grills are installed in the kitchen out back, while up front the faded wallpapers are replaced by abstract paintings and food mavens galore. Some of the following also serve nouveau pub grub, but whether you have Moroccan chicken or the ploughman's special, you'll want to order a pint. What Americans call beer Brits call lager. However, the main Brit pub drink is "bitter"—usually warm. Today, there is a movement to bring back the traditionally prepared ale that is much less gassy. There's also plenty of other potations—stouts like Guinness and Murphy's are thick, pitch-black brews you'll either love or hate; ciders, made from apples, are an alcoholic drink in Britain (Bulmer's and Strongbow are the names to remember); shandies are a mix of lager and lemonade sodas; while black and tans are a blend of lager and stout named for the distinctive uniforms worn by early 20th-century British troops. Discuss your choices of drink with the barman, turn to your neighbor, raise the glass, and utter that most pleasant of toasts, "Cheers."

Arcane licensing laws forbid the serving of alcohol after 11 PM (10:30 on Sunday; different rules for restaurants) and have created, some argue, a nation of alcoholics, driven to down more pints than is decent in a limited time—a circumstance you see in action at 10 minutes to 11, when the "last orders" bell signals a stampede to the bar. That noted, "lock-ins" are an old tradition—pubs that lock the front door after hours and ask remaining customers to leave by the side door—that bobbies tend to overlook. The list below offers a few pubs selected for central location, historical interest, a pleasant garden, music, or good food, but you might just as happily adopt your own temporary local.

The Albert. Positively heaving with pubishness, the Albert must have been designed to be *the* complete and authentic London pub, with its burnished wood, walls adorned with Victorian prints about the evils of drinking, and a "division bell" (which calls back members of Parliament in time for a vote). The food in the restaurant upstairs is so good reservations are usually required. ✉ *52 Victoria St., St. James's SW1,* ☎ *020/7222–5577. Tube: St. James's Park.*

Black Friar. A step from Blackfriars tube stop, this spectacular pub has an Arts and Crafts interior that is entertainingly, satirically ecclesiastical, with inlaid mother-of-pearl, wood carvings, stained glass, and marble pillars all over the place. In spite of the finely lettered temperance tracts on view just below the reliefs of monks, fairies, and friars, there are, needless to say, a nice group of beers on tap from independent brewers. ✉ *174 Queen Victoria St., The City EC4,* ☎ *020/7236–5474. Tube: Blackfriars.*

Crown and Goose. This is an art-bedecked Camden Town local, where armchairs augment the tables and coffee and herb tea the beers, and good food (steak in baguettes, smoked chicken salad, baked and stuffed mushrooms) is served to the crowds. ✉ *100 Arlington Rd., Camden Town NW1,* ☎ *020/7485–8008. Tube: Camden Town.*

Dove Inn. Read the list of famous ex-regulars, from Charles II and Nell Gwynn to Ernest Hemingway as you wait for a beer at this very popular, very comely 16th-century riverside pub by Hammersmith Bridge. If it's too full, stroll upstream to the Old Ship or the Blue Anchor. ✉ *19 Upper Mall, Hammersmith W6,* ☎ *020/8748–5405. Tube: Hammersmith.*

French House. In the pub where the French Resistance convened during World War II, Soho hipsters and eccentrics rub shoulders now—more than shoulders, actually, because this tiny, tricolor-waving, photograph-lined pub is always filled to bursting with theater luvvies and literary bods. ✉ *49 Dean St., Soho W1,* ☎ *020/7437–2799. Tube: Piccadilly Circus.*

George Inn. The inn sits in a courtyard where Shakespeare's plays were once staged. The present building dates from the late 17th century and is central London's last remaining galleried inn. Dickens was a regular—the inn is featured in *Little Dorrit*. Entertainments include Shakespeare performances, medieval jousts, and morris dancing. ✉ *77 Borough High St., The South Bank SE1,* ☎ *020/7407–2056. Tube: London Bridge.*

Island Queen. Gigantic caricature pirates leer down at you from the ceiling in this sociable Islington pub, which offers home-cooked food, a busy pool table, and a fab jukebox. The playwright Joe Orton frequented the place; he lived—and died, murdered by his lover—next door. ✉ *87 Noel Rd., Islington N1,* ☎ *020/7704–7631. Tube: Angel.*

Jack Straw's Castle. Straw was a leader of the Peasants Revolt of 1381, and he was hanged nearby. In Tudor times this was a favorite hangout for highwaymen, but by the 19th century it had become picturesque and respectable; artists painted charming views from it, and Dickens (inevitably) stayed here. Sadly, it was blitzed during World War II, but was rebuilt in 1963. Come to admire the views over Hampstead Heath and drink in the large courtyard. ✉ *North End Way, Hampstead NW3,* ☎ *020/7435–8885. Tube: Hampstead.*

The Lamb. Another of Dickens's locals is now a picturesque place for a pint in summer, when you can drink on the patio. ✉ *94 Lamb's Conduit St., The City WC1,* ☎ *020/7405–0713. Tube: Farringdon.*

Lamb & Flag. This 17th-century pub was once known as "The Bucket of Blood" because the upstairs room was used as a ring for bare-knuckle boxing. Now it's a trendy, friendly, and bloodless pub, serving food (lunchtime only) and real ale. It's on the edge of Covent Garden, off Garrick Street. ✉ *33 Rose St., Covent Garden WC2,* ☎ *020/7497–9504. Tube: Covent Garden.*

Mayflower. An atmospheric 17th-century riverside inn, with exposed beams and a terrace, this is practically the very place from which the Pilgrims set sail for Plymouth Rock. The inn is licensed to sell American postage stamps. ✉ *117 Rotherhithe St., The South Bank SE16,* ☎ *020/7237–4088. Tube: Rotherhithe.*

Museum Tavern. Across the street from the British Museum, this gloriously Victorian pub makes an ideal resting place after the rigors of the culture trail. With lots of fancy glass—etched mirrors and stained-glass panels—gilded pillars, and carvings, the heavily restored hostelry once helped Karl Marx to unwind after a hard day in the Library. He could have spent his *Kapital* on any one of six beers available on tap. ✉ *49 Great Russell St., Bloomsbury WC1,* ☎ *020/7242–8987. Tube: Tottenham Court Rd.*

Princess Louise. This fine, popular pub has an over-the-top Victorian interior—glazed terra-cotta, stained and frosted glass, and a glorious painted ceiling. It's not all show, either; the food is a cut above normal pub grub, and there's a good selection of real ales. ✉ *208 High Holborn, Holborn WC1,* ☎ *020/7405–8816. Tube: Holborn.*

Prospect of Whitby. Named after a ship, this is London's oldest riverside pub, dating from 1520. Once upon a time it was called "The Devil's Tavern" because of the low-life criminals—thieves and smugglers—who congregated here. It's ornamented with pewter ware and nautical objects. ✉ *57 Wapping Wall, The City E1,* ☎ *020/7481–1095. Tube: Wapping.*

St. James Tavern. This pretty pub is steps from Piccadilly Circus and five major West End theaters; another plus is that it stays open until 1 AM Tuesday through Saturday. The interior has lovely hand-painted Doulton tiles depicting Shakespearean scenes. The kitchen prides itself on its fish-and-chips. ✉ *45 Great Windmill St., Soho W1,* ☎ *020/7437–5009. Tube: Piccadilly Circus.*

Sherlock Holmes. This pub used to be known as "The Northumberland Arms," and Arthur Conan Doyle popped in regularly for a pint. It figures in *The Hound of the Baskervilles,* and you can see the hound's head and plaster casts of its huge paws among other Holmes memorabilia in the bar. ✉ *10 Northumberland St., Euston WC2,* ☎ *020/7930–2644. Tube: Charing Cross.*

Spaniards Inn. Another historic, oak-beamed pub on Hampstead Heath? Yes, but this one has a gorgeous rose garden, scene of the tea party in Dickens's *Pickwick Papers.* Dick Turpin, the highwayman, frequented the inn; you can see his pistols on display. Shelley, Keats, and Byron hung out here, as did Dickens. It's extremely popular, especially on Sundays, when Londoners take to the heath in search of fresh air. ✉ *Spaniards Rd., Hampstead NW3,* ☎ *020/8731–6571. Tube: Hampstead.*

Star Tavern. In the heart of elegant Belgravia, this pub has a postcard-perfect Georgian-era facade. The inside is charming, too; Victorian furnishings and two roaring fireplaces make this a popular spot. ✉ *6 Belgrave Mews West, Belgravia SW1,* ☎ *020/7235–3019. Tube: Victoria.*

Windsor Castle. Rest here if you're on a Kensington jaunt, and save your appetite for the food, especially on Sunday, when they do a traditional roast. On other days expect oysters, salads, fish cakes, and steak sandwiches. In winter a fire blazes; in summer, an exquisite patio garden awaits. ✉ *114 Campden Hill Rd., Notting Hill W8,* ☎ *020/7727–8491. Tube: Notting Hill Gate Park.*

Ye Bunch of Grapes. This traditional (smoky, noisy, and anti-chic) pub has been popular since Victoria was on the throne. It's in the heart of Shepherd Market, the village-within-Mayfair, and is still home-away-from-home for a full deck of London characters. ✉ *16 Shepherd Market, Mayfair W1,* ☎ *020/7499–1563. Tube: Green Park.*

Ye Olde Cheshire Cheese. Yes, it is a tourist trap, but it's also the most historic of all London pubs (it dates from 1667) and it deserves a visit for its sawdust-covered floors, low wood-beam ceilings, and the 14th-century crypt of Whitefriars' monastery under the cellar bar. But if you want to see the set of 17th-century pornographic tiles that once adorned upstairs, you must get special permission from the brewery to see them at the British Museum. This was the most regular of Dr. Johnson's and Dickens's *many* locals. ✉ *145 Fleet St., The City EC4,* ☎ *020/7353–6170. Tube: Chancery Lane.*

4 LODGING

Queen Elizabeth hasn't invited you this time? No matter. Staying at one of London's grande-dame hotels is the next best thing to being a guest at the palace—some say even better. Resplendent furnishings, armies of pampering staff—the Windsors should have it so good. Even the more affordable hotels convey an inimitable British style: tea makers and pastel wallpaper, Victorian-style parlors and country-house antiques.

Updated by Catherine Belonogoff

STANDING IN THE PARLORLIKE lobby—burnished oak paneling, time-stained antiques, chintz-softened sofas, the distant tinkle of teacups in the air—a century seems to slip away. The concierge whispers that Queen Victoria used to visit—she, too, probably got willingly lost in the corridors and crannies. In the grand salon sit ancient Chippendale desks that once bore the concentrated energy of the empire's Kiplings and Hardys. Set near a crackling fire, a roomy leather Chesterfield beckons you to approach its quilted field. Yes, Olde London Towne fantasies may be fading fast in the light of Blair's Britain, but when it comes time to rest your head, the old-fashioned continues to entice. Who wouldn't want to lounge in a brocade armchair while a frock-coated retainer serves cream tea? Or enjoy coffee, toast, and croissants in a handmade bed in your powder-blue and white Syrie Maugham–esque boudoir as the Thames flows lazily past your French windows? Choose one of London's heritage-rich hotels—Brown's and Claridge's supply perfect parlors; the Savoy has that river view—and these fantasies can, and always will, be fulfilled.

Still, faster times are bringing more changes to the London hotel scene than there have been in years. Hotels are springing up in places not previously considered "touristy," meaning your stay need not be confined to the bustle and noise of the West End or the exclusive nabes (so exclusive you will find few Brits native to these areas) of Kensington or Knightsbridge. And the variety is not limited to location. Immaculately designed, entirely contemporary hotels now are challenging luxurious, old, chintzy favorites while nationwide budget chains take on the B&B scene, offering clean and functional accommodations at friendly prices. Chain hotels with cookie-cutter furnishings, and all modern conveniences, have moved to the center of town, attracted by Chunnel travelers and other inter-Europe wayfarers. So you no longer need to blow your entire budget on your bed.

Still, if you want to do just that, London is the place. Prices can soar into the empyrean here, but many of the best hotels are worth it. Take the Connaught, a landmark whose regulars wouldn't *dream* of staying anywhere else. Its Edwardian lobby, created in 1897, is unadulterated by things modern; grand and faded, it's filled with oil paintings and antiques. In contrast to this dowager-aunt type are hotels such as the Pelham and Covent Garden—most of them renovated town houses, aglitter with sensationally atmospheric Regency-style interiors and richly appointed with stunning furnishings. Designed to be the very epitome of English country-housedom, these newer boutique hotels appeal to clientele bent on revisiting the landed gentry culture. Waving the banner SMALL IS BEAUTIFUL, they have stolen a march on the genteel sleeping beauties—the Claridges, the Savoys, and the Dorchesters—who have launched a broad counterattack. The Sultan of Brunei sank tens of millions into refurbishing the Dorchester; a Hunt heiress sponsored a complete makeover of the Lanesborough; and the Connaught, Savoy, and Claridge's have each been renovated to the tune of a mint. Paying top dollar, of course, does not always mean you'll get stately grandeur—several places have moved away from Regency flounces and Laura Ashley–isms into neo-Bauhaus minimalism. The Halkin was the first frill-free grand hotel; now add the ultra-fashionable Metropolitan, the understated Hempel, and the grand Great Eastern near groovy Spitalfields market and the gray expanse of the City. At the other end of the scale, things can be almost as trendy. In design-crazy London, even hostels have become stylish—just look at the Generator.

Where you stay can affect your experience significantly. For instance, the West End is equivalent to downtown, but it covers a lot of ground. There's a great deal of difference between, say, posh Park Lane and bustling, touristy Leicester Square, yet both are in the West End. Hotels in Mayfair and St. James's are central and yet distant in both mileage and sensibility from funky, youthful neighborhoods like Notting Hill and Camden Town and from major tourist sights like the Tower of London, St. Paul's Cathedral, and the Kensington museums. On the edges of the West End, Soho and Covent Garden are crammed with eateries and entertainment options.

South Kensington, Kensington, Chelsea, and Knightsbridge are all patrician and peaceful, which will give you a more homey feeling than anything in the West End, while Belgravia is superelegant, geographically and atmospherically about halfway between the extremes. From Bloomsbury it's a short stroll to the shops and restaurants of Covent Garden, to Theatreland, and to the British Museum. From here, it's a short bus ride to Camden and Regent's Park, too, and Hampstead and Islington are close enough to explore easily. Bayswater is a particularly affordable haven. It's barely considered a real neighborhood by Londoners, but everything is accessible from there. Notting Hill and Holland Park are worth considering as bases if you want something more down-home plus the antiques of Portobello Road.

The general custom these days in all but the bottom end of the scale is for rates to be quoted for the room alone (which, unless otherwise noted, is with bath); breakfast, whether Continental or "full English," usually comes at extra cost. We've noted at the end of each review if breakfast is included in the rate (CP for Continental breakfast daily and BP for full breakfast daily). Note: while some establishments may offer a hearty breakfast, others may offer little more than coffee and rolls; check ahead about what's offered if breakfast is important to you. VAT and service charges are usually included. All hotels listed here are graded according to their weekday, high-season rates. Remember there may be significant discounts at the weekend and off-season. Like those in most other European countries, British hotels are obliged by law to display a tariff at the reception desk. Study it carefully if you have not booked ahead. And make sure to make reservations well in advance.

CATEGORY	COST*
££££	over £230
£££	£160–£230
££	£100–£160
£	under £100

**All prices are for a double room, VAT included.*

Bayswater and Notting Hill Gate

££££ ★ **The Halcyon.** Discretion, decadent furnishings, and disco divas make this expensive, enormous, wedding-cake Edwardian building a desperately desirable place to stay while in London. The Blue Room has moons and stars, the Egyptian Suite is canopied like a bedouin tent, one room has heraldic motifs, and the Halcyon Suite has its own conservatory. All rooms are very large, with the high ceilings and big windows typical of the grand houses here—a 10-min tube ride from the West End and steps from London's most exquisite park. The French restaurant, Aix, is very well regarded, as is the Oasis bar. ✉ *81 Holland Park W11 3RZ,* ☎ *020/7727–7288,* FAX *020/7229–8516,* WEB *www.halcyon-hotel.co.uk. 42 rooms. Restaurant, room service, minibars, in-room safe, cable TV with movies, in-room VCRs, Internet, parking (fee), meeting room, bar. AE, DC, MC, V. Tube: Holland Park.*

London Lodging *(Boxes Refer to Detail Maps)*

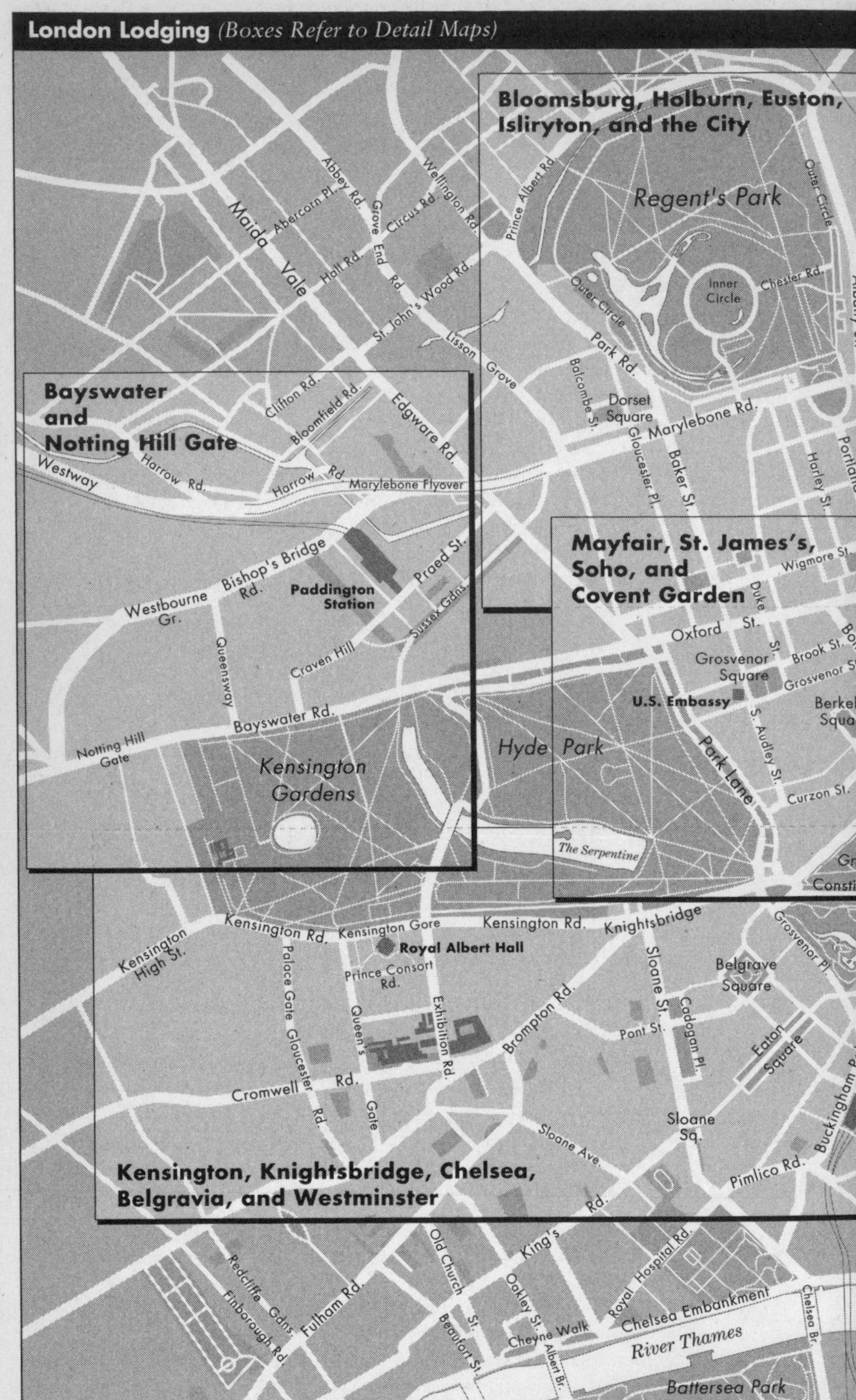

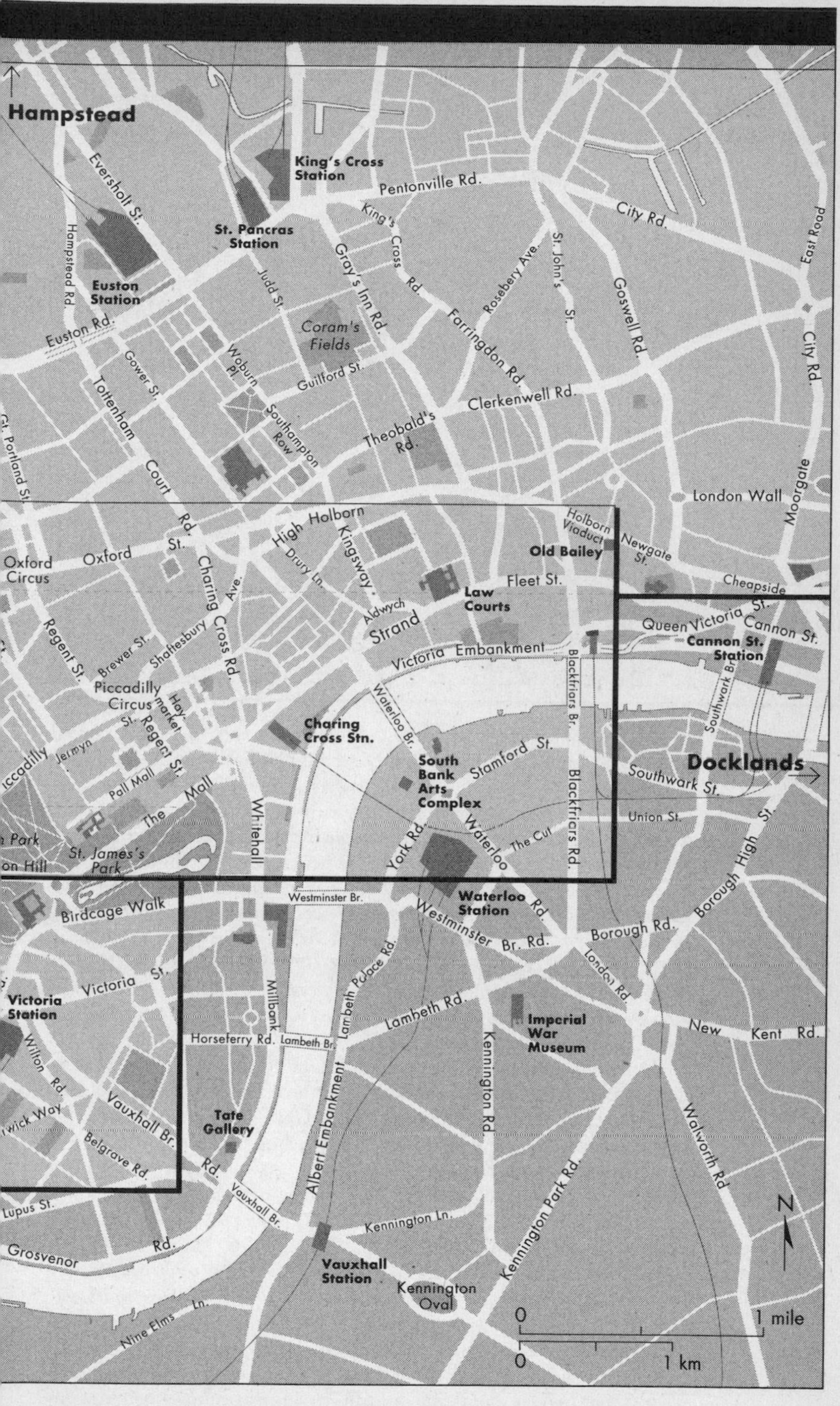
Hampstead
King's Cross Station
St. Pancras Station
Euston Station
Eversholt St.
Hampstead Rd.
Euston Rd.
Pentonville Rd.
City Rd.
East Road
King's Cross Rd.
Gray's Inn Rd.
Judd St.
Rosebery Ave.
St. John's St.
Goswell Rd.
Farringdon Rd.
Coram's Fields
Guilford St.
Woburn Pl.
Gower St.
Tottenham Court Rd.
Southampton Row
Theobald's Rd.
Clerkenwell Rd.
City Rd.
Gt. Portland St.
London Wall
Moorgate
High Holborn
Holborn Viaduct
Newgate St.
Old Bailey
Oxford Circus
Oxford St.
Charing Cross Rd.
Drury Ln.
Kingsway
Fleet St.
Cheapside
Law Courts
Aldwych
Strand
Queen Victoria St.
Cannon St.
Cannon St. Station
Regent St.
Brewer St.
Shaftesbury Ave.
Victoria Embankment
Blackfriars Br.
Piccadilly Circus
Haymarket
Regent St.
Waterloo Br.
Charing Cross Stn.
Southwark Br.
Docklands
Piccadilly
Jermyn St.
Pall Mall
South Bank Arts Complex
Stamford St.
Southwark St.
The Mall
Blackfriars Rd.
Union St.
St. James's Park
Green Park
Constitution Hill
Whitehall
York Rd.
Waterloo Rd.
The Cut
Borough High St.
Birdcage Walk
Westminster Br.
Waterloo Station
Westminster Br. Rd.
Borough Rd.
Victoria St.
London Rd.
Victoria Station
Millbank
Lambeth Palace Rd.
Lambeth Rd.
Imperial War Museum
Horseferry Rd.
Lambeth Br.
New Kent Rd.
Kennington Rd.
Wilton Rd.
Vauxhall Br. Rd.
Warwick Way
Belgrave Rd.
Tate Gallery
Albert Embankment
Walworth Rd.
Kennington Park Rd.
Lupus St.
Vauxhall Br.
Kennington Ln.
N
Grosvenor Rd.
Vauxhall Station
Kennington Oval
Nine Elms Ln.
0
1 mile
0
1 km

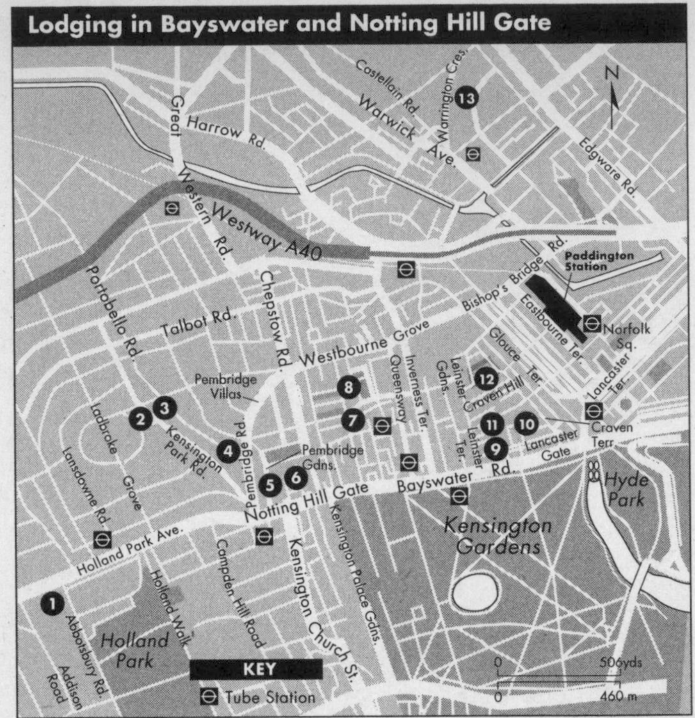

£££ 🏨 **The Hempel.** This is a prime contender for the "most glamorous hostelry in London" prize. Anouska Hempel did the lush and lavish Blakes, then did a 180-degree turn into these stunning, crisp, clean, white-on-white-on-white spaces—and no kidding about spaces. There's nothing jarring or extraneous, and no visible means of support beneath the furniture. Naturally, the Hempel appeals greatly to showbizzy style hounds. Elton John (remember when he went Zen and sold all his gew-gaws?) was one of the first party-throwers in the restaurant here. But beware: the minimalist sensibility is not for everyone. ✉ *31–35 Craven Hill Gardens, Bayswater W2 3EA,* ☎ *020/7298–9000,* FAX *020/7472–4666,* WEB *www.the-hempel.co.uk. 43 rooms. Restaurant, bar, room service, in-room safes, cable TV with movies, in-room VCRs, parking (fee). AE, DC, MC, V. Tube: Lancaster Gate.*

£££–££££ 🏨 **Westbourne Hotel.** This trendy Notting Hill hotel bills itself as an "urban inn." The Georgian building and the friendly staff ensure a level of coziness, while British artwork (such as Gavin Turk and Dan Macmillan) showcased in the bedrooms lends the hotel an urban touch. The walled patio garden creates a Zen retreat space and the unobtrusive dark wood, clean lines, and gray-and-white base color scheme keeps the feeling modern. Each room has a DVD player. ✉ *165 Westbourne Grove, Notting Hill W11 2RS,* ☎ *020/7243–6008,* FAX *020/7229–7201.* WEB *www.zoohotels.com. 20 rooms. Bar, room service, cable TV, in-room data ports, Internet, business services, no-smoking rooms. AE, MC, V. CP. Tube: Notting Hill Gate.*

£££ 🏨 **Pembridge Court.** In a colonnaded white-stucco Victorian row house, this sweet, cozy hotel has scatter cushions and books, quirky Victoriana, two resident cats, and framed fans from the neighboring Portobello Market. Bedrooms have a great deal of swagged floral drapery, but are sumptuous nonetheless. ✉ *34 Pembridge Gardens, Notting Hill W2 4DX,* ☎ *020/7229–9977,* FAX *020/7727–4982; 800/709–9882 in U.S.,* WEB *www.pemct.co.uk. 20 rooms. Restaurant, bar,* *room service, cable TV, no-smoking rooms, parking (fee). AE, DC, MC, V. BP. Tube: Notting Hill Gate.*

£££ **The Portobello.** This small, eccentric place has long been a favorite of high-style mavens in the music and design worlds, and a tinge of the groovy early '70s still adheres to the corners. The two adjoining Victorian houses back onto a beautiful large garden shared with the neighbors. The Cabin Rooms are minute. Many bigger rooms have Victorian claw-foot bathtubs, though the famous round-bed suite has the pièce de résistance of the bath world—an Edwardian "bathing machine," all knobs and shiny brass pipes. ✉ *22 Stanley Gardens, Notting Hill W11 2NG,* ☎ *020/7727–2777,* FAX *020/7792–9641,* WEB *www.portobello-hotel.co.uk. 24 rooms. Restaurant, bar, room service, minibars, cable TV, in-room VCRs, business services, Internet. AE, DC, MC, V. CP. Closed 10 days at Christmas. Tube: Notting Hill Gate.*

££–£££ **Abbey Court.** A very elegant little hotel in a gracious white Victorian mansion, in a quiet street off Notting Hill Gate, Abbey Court is deep in the era of Victoria—deep-red wallpapers, Murano glass, gilt-framed mirrors, framed prints, mahogany, and plenty of antiques. The sitting room and the pretty conservatory are lovely places to relax. Bathrooms look the part but are entirely modern: gray Italian marble, with brass fittings and whirlpool baths. There's 24-hour room service. ✉ *20 Pembridge Gardens, Notting Hill W2 4DU,* ☎ *020/7221–7518,* FAX *020/7792–0858,* WEB *www.abbeycourthotel.co.uk. 22 rooms. Room service, no air-conditioning, fans, in-room data ports, cable TV, no-smoking rooms. AE, DC, MC, V. CP. Tube: Notting Hill Gate.*

££–£££ **Colonnade.** You'll find this lovely town house in quiet, residential Little Venice, near a canal filled with colorful narrowboats. If you're looking for a quiet abode, this is it. From the Freud suite (Sigmund visited in 1938) to the rooms with four poster beds or balconies, you'll find rich brocades, velvets, and antiques. It's a former home, so each room is different; some are split-level. A bathrobe and slippers, a bowl of apples, a CD player, and a trouser press add a touch of luxury. ✉ *2 Warrington Crescent, Bayswater W9 1ER,* ☎ *020/7286–1052,* FAX *020/7286–1057,* WEB *www.etontownhouse.com. 43 rooms. Room service, minibars, in-room safe, in-room data ports, cable TV, business services, parking (fee). AE, DC, MC, V. BP. Tube: Warwick Avenue.*

££ **The Commodore.** This peaceful boutique hotel made up of three converted Victorians is close to the Columbia but deeper in the big leafy square known as Lancaster Gate. It's a find of a very different stripe, as you'll notice on entering the cozy, carpeted lounge. There are 16 new Executive rooms; the rest are Victorian and contemporary. Try to get one of the amazing Deluxe rooms—as superior to the regular ones as Harrods is to Kmart, but priced the same. Three of these are split-level, all large, all different, all with something special—like a walk-in closet with its own stained-glass window. One (No. 11) is a duplex, entered through a secret mirrored door off a lemon-yellow hallway with palms and Greek statuary. Ask about special offers on weekends. ✉ *50 Lancaster Gate, Bayswater W2 3NA,* ☎ *020/7402–5291,* FAX *020/7262–1088,* WEB *www.commodore-hotel.com. 83 rooms. Restaurant, bar, some in-room data ports, some in-room safes, minibars, cable TV, gym, business services. AE, MC, V. CP. Tube: Lancaster Gate.*

££ **Mornington Lancaster.** Swedes run this Best Western hotel, and their Scandinavian aesthetic shows. Rooms are clean cut, with simple, modern furnishings and tea/coffeemakers. Plaid fabric lends an English touch. Hyde Park is within walking distance. ✉ *12 Lancaster Gate, Bayswater W2 3LG,* ☎ *020/7262–7361,* FAX *020/7706–1028,* WEB *www.mornington.com. 66 rooms. Bar, in-room data ports, cable TV* *with movies, meeting room, no-smoking rooms. AE, DC, MC, V. BP. Tube: Lancaster Gate.*

£–££ **Vancouver Studios.** This little hotel is run like an apartment building—rooms are actually studios with kitchenettes, and the front door has a security entry system. Each studio has daily maid service as well as room service. ✉ *30 Prince's Sq., Bayswater W2 4NJ,* ☎ *020/7243–1270,* FAX *020/7221–8678,* WEB *www.vienna-group.co.uk. 45 rooms. Room service, kitchenettes, in-room data ports, laundry service, business services. AE, DC, MC, V. CP. Tube: Bayswater or Queensway*

£ **The Columbia.** The public rooms in these five adjoining Victorians are as big as museum halls. The clean, high-ceiling bedrooms, some of which are very large (three to four beds) and have park views and balconies, offer TVs, hair dryers, tea/coffeemakers, direct-dial phones, and safes. The design tends to teak veneer, khaki-beige-brown color schemes, and avocado bathroom suites, but who expects Regency Revival at these prices? It's popular with tour groups. ✉ *95–99 Lancaster Gate, Bayswater W2 3NS,* ☎ *020/7402–0021,* FAX *020/7706–4691,* WEB *www.columbiahotel.co.uk. 103 rooms. Restaurant, bar, no air-conditioning, meeting room. AE, MC, V. BP. Tube: Lancaster Gate.*

£ **Garden Court Hotel.** Built in 1870, the hotel consists of two 19th-century town houses in a quiet Victorian garden square. It's run by a very hospitable owner. Each of the comfortable rooms has a character of its own, complete with some original Victorian fittings. Rooms with toilet and shower cost £30 more. The paved garden is relaxing in good weather and the owners are eager to please. ✉ *30–31 Kensington Gardens Sq., Bayswater W2 4BG,* ☎ *020/7229–2553,* FAX *020/7727–2749,* WEB *www.gardencourthotel.co.uk. 32 rooms, some without bath. No air-conditioning, fans, cable TV. MC, V. BP. Tube: Bayswater or Queensway.*

£ **The Gate.** It's absolutely teeny—just a house at the very top of Portobello Road, off Notting Hill Gate. The plain bedrooms have refrigerators, TVs, direct-dial phones, and tea/coffee facilities, plus bath (unless you opt for a smaller, £10-cheaper, shower-only room), and Continental breakfast brought directly to your room. ✉ *6 Portobello Rd., Notting Hill W11 3DG,* ☎ *020/7221–0707,* FAX *020/7221–9128,* WEB *www.gatehotel.com. 6 rooms, some with shower. No air-conditioning, fans. MC, V. CP. Tube: Notting Hill Gate.*

Bloomsbury, Holborn, Euston, and the City

££££ **Great Eastern.** Another style coup for designer and gourmand Sir Terence Conran, the Great Eastern Hotel is a sturdy pillar of the modern establishment. There are four restaurants—offering sushi, fish, brasserie, and haute cuisine—two bars, a gym, private dining and function rooms, a florist, and a Ren bath products shop. Some of the rooms look out over Liverpool Street and Bishopsgate. Others look inward to the stained-glass dome of the Aurora restaurant or the Gallery. All rooms have a CD player; you can request a VCR or DVD player. ✉ *Liverpool St. at Bishopsgate, The City E2M 7QN,* ☎ *020/7618–5010,* FAX *020/7618–5011,* WEB *www.great-eastern-hotel.co.uk. 246 rooms, 21 suites. 4 restaurants, 2 bars, 12 dining rooms, some in-room fax, some in-room VCRs, in-room data ports, in-room safe, cable TV, gym, spa, cinema, business services, no-smoking rooms. AE, DC, MC, V. Tube: Liverpool St.*

££££ **Renaissance Chancery Court.** This landmark building, built by the Pearl Assurance Co. in 1914, has been transformed into a beautiful hotel. What were once offices are now spacious bedrooms kitted out with all the latest gadgets. The former banking halls now house a modern restaurant and a clubby bar. The use of marble is extensive from the floors in public spaces to the massive staircase (there are elevators,

Lodging in Bloomsbury, Holburn, Euston, Islington, and the City

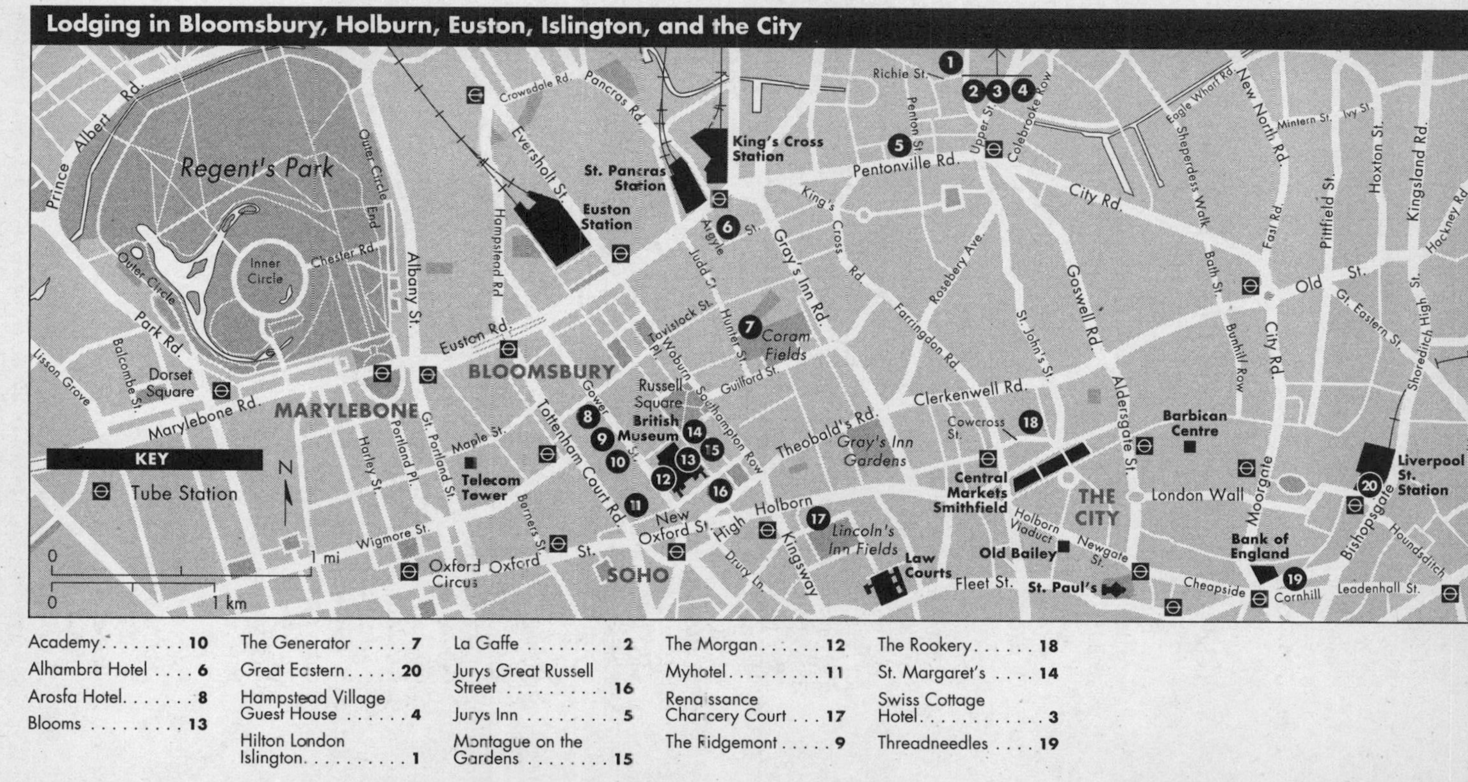

Academy 10	The Generator 7	La Gaffe 2	The Morgan 12	The Rookery 18
Alhambra Hotel 6	Great Eastern 20	Jurys Great Russell Street 16	Myhotel 11	St. Margaret's 14
Arosfa Hotel. 8	Hampstead Village Guest House 4	Jurys Inn 5	Renaissance Chancery Court . . . 17	Swiss Cottage Hotel 3
Blooms 13	Hilton London Islington 1	Montague on the Gardens 15	The Ridgemont 9	Threadneedles 19

too) to the bathrooms. So striking is the architecture that the building has been featured in the film *Howard's End* and many BBC productions. ✉ *252 High Holborn, Holborn WC1V 7EN,* ☎ *020/7829–9888,* FAX *0207/829–9889. 356 rooms, 14 suites. Restaurant, room service, in-room data ports, in-room safes, minibars, cable TV with video games, spa, bar, laundry service, concierge, business services, meeting rooms. AE, MC, V. Tube: Holborn.*

££££ **The Rookery.** Set in the City district, the 18th-century Rookery is just a step away from the Jerusalem Tavern, from which it is said the Knights of St. John left to fight the Crusades. From the magnificent Rook's Nest, the hotel's duplex suite, you can relax in a claw-foot bath set in the corner of the bedroom or have a magnificent view of the City's ancient buildings. Each beautiful, bijoux-sized double room has an antique carved wooden headboard and period furnishings, including exquisite salvaged wooden pieces. The conservatory, with its small patio garden, is an especially nice place to unwind with a beverage from the honor bar. ✉ *Peter's La. at Cowcross St., The City EC1M 6DS,* ☎ *020/7336–0931,* FAX *020/7336–0932.* WEB *www.rookeryhotel.com. 33 rooms. Bar, room service, minibar, cable TV, in-room VCRs and movies, business services, meeting rooms. AE, MC, V. Tube: Farringdon.*

££££ **Threadneedles.** Owned by the same people as the Academy in Bloomsbury and the Colonnade in Bayswater, Threadneedles is the first boutique hotel in the City. The building, affectionately called the "Old Lady of Threadneedle Street," is a former bank and the hotel has kept the banking hall and has reused the mahogany panels from the original interior in its "heritage wing." If you have business in the City, Threadneedles can't be beat for luxury. ✉ *5 Threadneedle, The City EC2R 8BD,* ☎ *0207/432–8451,* WEB *www.etontownhouse.com. 70 rooms. Restaurant, bar, exercise equipment, meeting rooms. AE, DC, MC, V. BP. Tube: Bank.*

£££–££££ **Montague on the Gardens.** Converted from a row of 1830s Georgian town houses, the Montague keeps the antique look alive with its period furnishings and collection of objets d'art. Standard double rooms are small, but there are plenty of cozy public areas in which to unwind. The bar hosts jazz evenings and the sitting room is filled with comfy, flowery furniture. The best views are from the small terrace and conservatories where you can look out on a stretch of lawn running an entire city block. What the hotel lacks in space, it makes up for with its charming floral and fabric decorating scheme. ✉ *15 Montague St., Bloomsbury WC1B 5BJ,* ☎ *020/7637–1001,* FAX *020/7637–2516,* WEB *www.redcarnationhotels.com. 93 rooms, 11 suites. Restaurant, bar, room service, in-room data ports, minibars, cable TV, exercise equipment, sauna, bar, concierge. AE, DC, MC, V. Tube: Russell Sq.*

£££ **Academy.** These three joined-up Georgian houses, boasting a little patio garden and a fashion-conscious mirrored and wood-floor basement restaurant, Alchemy, supply the most sophisticated and hotel-like facilities in the Gower Street "hotel row." The comfortable bedrooms have a TV, direct-dial phones, and tea/coffeemakers. Like most of the hotels in this section, the Academy neighbors the British Museum and University of London, a perk that appeals to culture vultures on a budget and affluent students. ✉ *21 Gower St., Bloomsbury WC1E 6HG,* ☎ *020/7631–4115,* FAX *020/7636–3442,* WEB *www.etontownhouse.com. 48 rooms. Restaurant, bar, room service, minibars, no-smoking rooms. AE, DC, MC, V. BP. Tube: Goodge St.*

£££ **Blooms.** This white Georgian town house hotel is a home away from home. Rooms in the back of the hotel look out onto a leafy green garden, and some have a four poster bed. The Theatre Royal and Lords room work off drama and cricket themes, and the rest of the rooms, though small, offer reasonable accommodation in a great location next to the British Museum. ✉ *7 Montague St., Bloomsbury WC1B 5BP,*

☎ *020/7323–1717,* FAX *020/7636–6498,* WEB *www.bloomshotel.com. 27 rooms. Restaurant, bar, room service. AE, DC, MC, V. BP. Tube: Goodge St.*

£££ **Jurys Great Russell Street.** Originally designed by architect Sir Edwin Lutyens for the Young Women's Christian Association in the early 1930s, today this neo-Georgian building stands proudly restored as an upscale hotel. Throughout the reception area and lounge, much of the original design, including reproduction furniture, has been retained. Deep burgundy and light tan beautifully complement the dark wood features throughout the hotel. Rooms are fairly spacious and have a classy 1930s look to them, though they have all of the perks of the 21st century. ✉ *16-22 Great Russell St., Bloomsbury WC1B 3NN,* ☎ *020/7347–1000,* FAX *020/7347–1001,* WEB *www.jurysdoyle.com. 170 rooms, 6 suites. Restaurant, in-room data ports, minibars, cable TV, bar, room service. AE, DC, MC, V. Tube: Tottenham Court Rd.*

£££ ★ **myhotel bloomsbury.** Before you arrive, you'll be asked to fill out a preferences sheet so that your room is just as you like it. If anything should go wrong, no need to call the front desk, just contact your personal assistant for help. Rooms are minimalist with wooden floors and simple color schemes. Superior doubles, which go up to ££££, are bigger and have a separate sitting room. For the most space, book one of the two penthouse apartments in "myspace" on the top floor. From the "jinja" spa to the library stocked with CDs, books, and free beverages, myhotel's new approach succeeds brilliantly. ✉ *11–13 Bayley St., Bedford Sq., Bloomsbury WC1 B3HD,* ☎ *020/7667–6000,* FAX *020/7667–6001,* WEB *www.myhotels.co.uk. 76 rooms. Restaurant, room service, cable TV with movies, exercise equipment, spa, library, business services, no-smoking floors. AE, DC, MC, V. Tube: Tottenham Court Rd.*

£ **Alhambra Hotel.** One of the best bargains in Bloomsbury, this family-run hotel has singles as low as £32 and doubles as low as £45. Rooms tend to be small and look stylistically dated, but are clean and a good value. Some rooms have a shower; some have a shower and toilet. The hotel is spread across several properties on the street, some of which are newer than others. ✉ *17–19 Argyle St., Bloomsbury WC1H 8EJ,* ☎ *020/7837–9575,* FAX *020/7916–2476,* WEB *www.alhambrahotel.com. 52 rooms. AE, DC, MC, V. BP. Tube: King's Cross.*

£ **Arosfa Hotel.** The friendly owners, Mr. and Mrs. Dorta, mark this B&B directly opposite Waterstone's bookstore apart from the Gower Street hotel pack—that, and the fact that this was once the home of Pre-Raphaelite painter Sir John Everett Millais. Rooms are simple and spotless, and are equipped with TVs and sinks, but not necessarily with their own showers. Those at the back are far quieter, though newly installed double glazing somewhat tames the Gower Street din. ✉ *83 Gower St., Bloomsbury WC1E 6HJ,* ☎ *020/7636–2115,* FAX *020/7636–2115. 16 rooms, 2 with shower. No phones, no air-conditioning, no smoking. MC, V. BP. Tube: Goodge St.*

£ **The Generator.** Easily the grooviest youth hostel in town, this former police barracks has a friendly, funky, and international vibe. Talking Heads, the Internet café, provides handy maps and leaflets, plus a chance to get on-line. The Generator Bar has cheap drinks and a rowdy, young clientele, and the Fuel Stop cafeteria provides inexpensive meals. Rooms—designed on a prison-cell theme complete with bunk beds and dim views—are simple but clean. There are singles, twins, and dormitory rooms. This is an excellent choice for the youthful and adventurous traveler. ✉ *MacNaghten House, Compton Pl. off Tavistock Pl., Bloomsbury WC1H 9SD,* ☎ *020/7388–7666,* FAX *020/7388–7644,* WEB *www.the-generator.co.uk. 217 rooms without bath. Restaurant, bar, Internet, no-smoking rooms. MC, V. BP. Tube: Russell Sq.*

£ ★ **The Morgan.** This is a Georgian row-house hotel, family run with charm and panache. Rooms are small and functionally furnished, yet friendly and cheerful overall, with phones and TVs. The five newish apartments are particularly pleasing: three times the size of normal rooms (and an extra £15 per night), complete with kitchens and private phone lines. The tiny, paneled breakfast room is straight out of an 18th-century doll's house. The back rooms overlook the British Museum. ✉ *24 Bloomsbury St., Bloomsbury WC1B 3QJ,* ☎ *020/7636–3735,* FAX *020/7636–3045. 15 rooms with shower, 5 apartments. MC, V. BP. Tube: Tottenham Court Rd. or Russell Sq.*

£ **The Ridgemount.** The kindly British owners, Mr. and Mrs. Rees, make you feel at home. Rooms tend to have a 1970s style, but offer a cheap sleep in a reasonable neighborhood. The public areas, especially the family-style breakfast room, are cluttered Victorian-style parlors. Some rooms overlook a leafy garden and 14 have an en-suite bathroom for about £15 extra per night. ✉ *65 Gower St., Bloomsbury WC1E 6HJ,* ☎ *020/7636–1141,* FAX *0207/636–2558,* WEB *www.ridgemounthotel.co.uk. No phones, no-smoking rooms. 33 rooms, 14 with bath. MC, V. BP. Tube: Goodge St.*

£ **St. Margaret's.** A popular hotel near the British Museum, St. Margaret's offers well-lit rooms with high ceilings, telephones, and TVs in a Georgian-era building. The friendly Italian family that runs the hotel is sure to welcome you by name if you stay long enough. Know that prices are higher for one-night stays. Back rooms have garden views. ✉ *26 Bedford Pl., Bloomsbury WC1B 5JL,* ☎ *020/7636–4277,* FAX *020/7323–3066. 64 rooms, 12 with bath. No air-conditioning, no-smoking rooms. MC, V. BP. Tube: Russell Sq.*

Hampstead and Islington

£££ **Hilton London Islington.** This purpose-built hotel next door to the Islington Business Design Centre has a modern lobby, complete with restaurant and free newspapers, which perfectly complements the media-filled and trendy borough of Islington. The hotel has standard, good-sized rooms with climate control, satellite TV, and trouser presses, plus, in many of them, panoramic skyline views. The in-house gym and spa are an added bonus for weary travelers. ✉ *53 Upper St., Islington N1 OUY,* ☎ *020/7354–7700,* FAX *020/7354–7711,* WEB *www.hilton.com. 178 rooms, 6 suites. Restaurant, bar, gym, spa, meeting room. BP. AE, DC, MC, V. Tube: Angel.*

££ **Swiss Cottage Hotel.** It's a little out of the way on a peaceful street behind the Swiss Cottage tube stop, but this charming hotel will suit those who like to stay in a residential district, save a little on the check, and still have their home comforts. The lounge and reception area are stuffed with antiques and reproductions, and are smilingly staffed. In summer, French windows open from the bar and the breakfast room. Bedrooms are in Victorian style, most are good-sized, and all come with full English breakfast. ✉ *4 Adamson Rd., Swiss Cottage, Euston NW3 3HP,* ☎ *020/7722–2281,* FAX *020/7483–4588,* WEB *www.swisscottagehotel.co.uk. 54 rooms. Bar, room service, cable TV, business services, meeting room, no-smoking rooms. AE, DC, MC, V. BP. Tube: Swiss Cottage.*

£–££ **La Gaffe.** A short walk up one of Hampstead's magnificent hills, La Gaffe is run by Italian Bernardo Stella, who has been welcoming people back to these early 18th-century shepherds' cottages for more than 20 years—and his restaurant has been going for nearly 40. Make no mistake, rooms are tiny, with showers only, but the popular wine bar and restaurant, which (naturally) serve Italian food, are yours to enjoy. Between the two wings of the hotel is a raised patio for summer. ✉ *107–111 Heath St., Hampstead NW3 6SS,* ☎ *020/7435–*

8965, FAX 020/7794–7592, WEB www.lagaffe.co.uk. 18 rooms with shower. Restaurant, bar, café, no air-conditioning, fans. AE, MC, V. CP. Tube: Hampstead.

£ **Hampstead Village Guesthouse.** This eccentric Victorian guesthouse offers distinctive and comfortable rooms cluttered with antiques and curiosities. The Blue Room has its own free-standing tub, and the Yellow Room has a roof terrace and a canopy bed. You are encouraged to relax in the garden or play with the resident dog, Marley. Families will appreciate the separate garden studio, which houses up to five people and has its own kitchenette. Book ahead for this hot property. Breakfast costs £7 extra. ✉ *2 Kemplay Rd., Hampstead NW3 1SY,* ☎ *020/7435–8679, FAX 020/7794–0254, WEB www.hampsteadguesthouse.com. 8 rooms. No air-conditioning, parking (fee), no smoking. No credit cards. Tube: Hampstead.*

£ **Jurys Inn.** Just a 10-minute walk to King's Cross and St. Pancras stations, this nondescript, purpose-built hotel provides low-priced accommodations in a trendy neighborhood. Upper Street and its quiet cafés, lively bars, and international restaurants are close by. The rooms are standard but very spacious, and accommodate up to three adults or a family of four. ✉ *60 Pentonville Rd., Islington N1 9LA,* ☎ *020/7282–5500, FAX 020/7282–5511, WEB www.jurysdoyle.com. 229 rooms. Restaurant, bar, cable TV. AE, DC, MC, V. Tube: Angel or King's Cross.*

Kensington

££££ ★ **Blakes.** Blakes is another world. Designed by owner Anouska Hempel, each room is a fantasy packed with precious Biedermeier, Murano glass, and modern pieces collected from all over the world. Cinematic mood lighting, featuring recessed halogen spots, compounds the impression that you, too, are a movie star living in a big-budget biopic. The foyer sets the tone with its piles of cushions, Phileas Fogg valises and trunks, black walls, rattan, and bamboo. ✉ *33 Roland Gardens, South Kensington SW7 3PF,* ☎ *020/7370–6701, FAX 020/7373–0442, WEB www.smallchichotels.com. 52 rooms. Restaurant, room service, in-room safe, in-room fax, cable TV, in-room VCRs, parking (fee), no-smoking rooms. AE, DC, MC, V. Tube: South Kensington.*

£££–££££ **The Cranley.** This small Victorian town house hotel in South Ken brings together traditional standards of service and the latest technology. High ceilings and huge windows make the bedrooms light, bright, and airy. The antique desks and four-poster or half-tester beds are in line with the period furnishings. Even the bathrooms have traditional Victorian fittings. Afternoon tea and evening canapés are complimentary. Some rooms are big enough for families. ✉ *10–12 Bina Gardens, South Kensington SW5 0LA,* ☎ *020/7373–0123, FAX 020/7373–9497, WEB www.thecranley.co.uk. 33 rooms, 2 suites, 1 apartment. Room service, in-room data ports, some kitchens, cable TV, Internet. AE, DC, MC, V. Tube: Gloucester Rd.*

£££–££££ **The Gore.** Just down the road from the Albert Hall, this very friendly hotel, run by the same people who run Hazlitt's, has a similarly eclectic selection of prints, etchings, and antiques—the lobby looks like a set from a Luchino Visconti film. Upstairs are spectacular follylike rooms—Room 101 is a Tudor fantasy with minstrel gallery, stained glass, and four poster bed, and Room 211, done in over-the-top Hollywood style, has a tiled mural of Greek goddesses in the bathroom. As with everything eccentric, this place is not for everyone. ✉ *189 Queens Gate, Kensington SW7 5EX,* ☎ *020/7584–6601, FAX 020/7589–8127, WEB www.gorehotel.com. 54 rooms. Restaurant, no air-conditioning, minibars, cable TV, in-room VCRs, no-smoking floors. AE, DC, MC, V. Tube: Gloucester Rd.*

Lodging in Kensington, Knightsbridge, Chelsea, Belgravia, Victoria, and Westminster

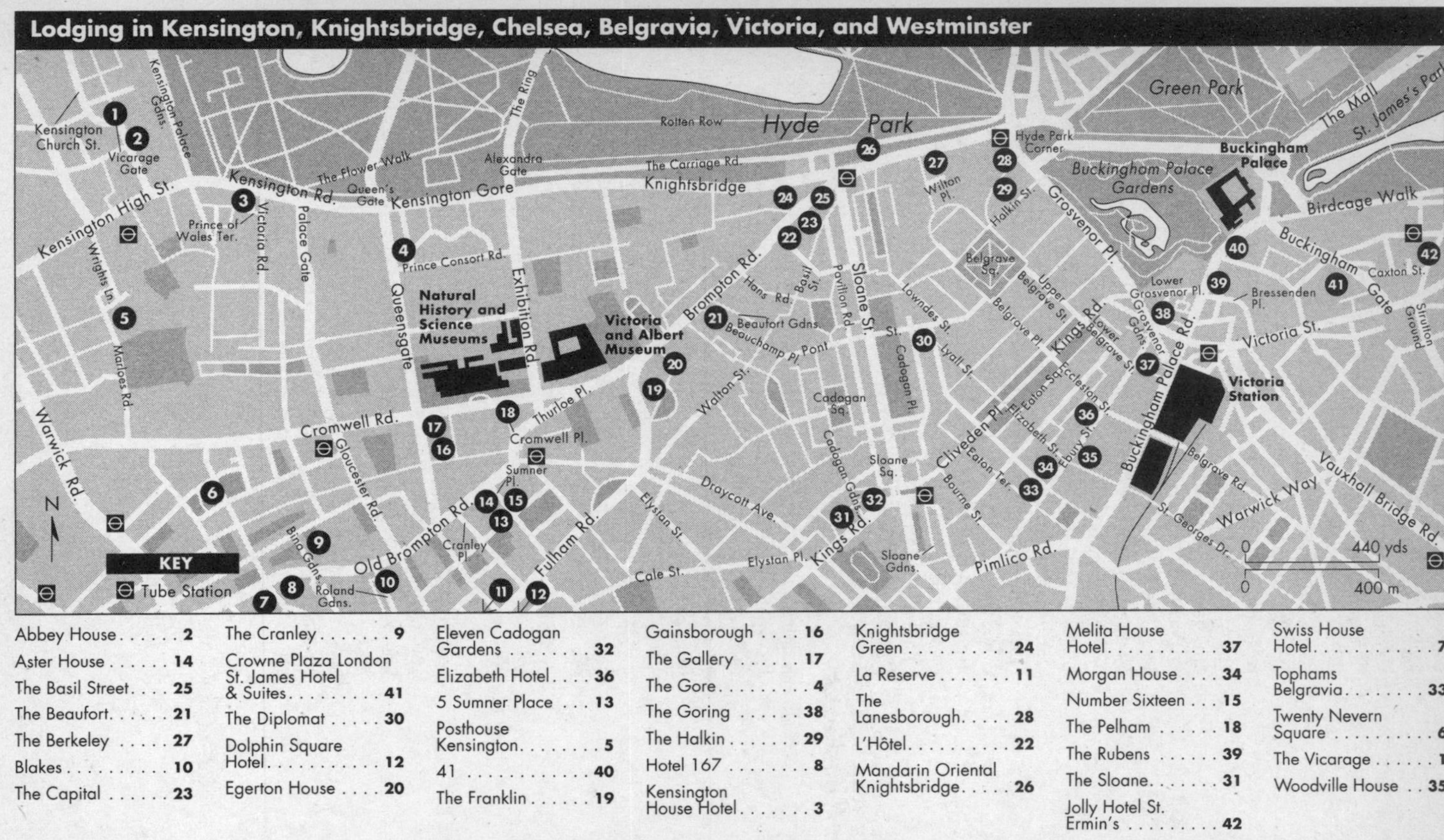

- Abbey House 2
- Aster House 14
- The Basil Street. . . . 25
- The Beaufort. 21
- The Berkeley 27
- Blakes 10
- The Capital 23
- The Cranley 9
- Crowne Plaza London St. James Hotel & Suites. 41
- The Diplomat 30
- Dolphin Square Hotel. 12
- Egerton House 20
- Eleven Cadogan Gardens 32
- Elizabeth Hotel 36
- 5 Sumner Place . . . 13
- Posthouse Kensington. 5
- 41 40
- The Franklin 19
- Gainsborough 16
- The Gallery 17
- The Gore. 4
- The Goring 38
- The Halkin 29
- Hotel 167 8
- Kensington House Hotel 3
- Knightsbridge Green 24
- La Reserve 11
- The Lanesborough. 28
- L'Hôtel. 22
- Mandarin Oriental Knightsbridge. 26
- Melita House Hotel. 37
- Morgan House 34
- Number Sixteen . . . 15
- The Pelham 18
- The Rubens 39
- The Sloane. 31
- Jolly Hotel St. Ermin's 42
- Swiss House Hotel. 7
- Tophams Belgravia. 33
- Twenty Nevern Square 6
- The Vicarage 1
- Woodville House . . 35

£££ **Number Sixteen.** A luxury bed-and-breakfast close to South Kensington tube and three blocks or so from the great museums, Number Sixteen stands in a white-portico row of Victorian houses, with no sign outside to identify it. There's no uniformity to the bedrooms except for their similar spaciousness and refitted bathrooms, but the style is not so much interior-designed as understated—new furniture and modern prints are juxtaposed with yellowed oils and antiques. There's an elevator and an enticing garden, with a conservatory and fountainette. ✉ *16 Sumner Pl., South Kensington SW7 3EG,* ☎ *020/7589–5232; 800/592–5387 in U.S.,* FAX *020/7584–8615,* WEB *www.numbersixteenhotel.co.uk. 36 rooms. Bar, in-room safe, in-room data ports, minibars. AE, DC, MC, V. CP. Tube: South Kensington.*

££–£££ **Aster House.** Rooms in this delightful guesthouse, in a residential area, are country casual. They include tea/coffeemakers. The owners are very friendly, and go out of their way to make you feel at home and answer questions. The conservatory where breakfast is served is an airy, light place, and the small garden at the back has a charming pond. Do note that there is no elevator, but there are five stories. The entire hotel is no-smoking. ✉ *3 Sumner Pl., South Kensington SW7 3EE,* ☎ *020/8400–9000,* FAX *020/7937–8289,* WEB *www.welcome2london.com/asterhouse. 14 rooms. Dining room, cable TV, in-room safe, tea/coffeemaker, no smoking. MC, V. BP. Tube: South Kensington.*

££–£££ **Gainsborough.** This hotel is a stone's throw from the Natural History Museum, the shops of South Kensington and Chelsea, and the once racy but now merely trendy King's Road. The style is one of a sumptuous (for this price range) English country home. Rooms have lovely period details and are very tasteful. The triple rooms are especially good for small families. ✉ *7–11 Queensberry Pl., Kensington SW7 2DL,* ☎ *020/7957–0000,* FAX *020/7957–0001,* WEB *www.eeh.co.uk. 45 rooms, 4 suites. Bar, room service, air-conditioning in some rooms, in-room safes, cable TV, business services. AE, DC, MC, V. Tube: South Kensington. BP.*

££–£££ **The Gallery.** Across the street from its sister property, the Gainsborough hotel, the Gallery offers an Arts-and-Crafts–style living room complete with a piano. There are lush carpets, cozy fires, and sturdy furniture. The rooms are a good size with solid comfortable beds. The bathrooms have London's ubiquitous polished granite. Included in the price is a full English breakfast—which will make lunching something of a challenge. Suites have a roof terrace, Jacuzzi bath, mini-bar, and CD and DVD players. ✉ *10 Queensberry Pl., Kensington SW7 2E8,* ☎ *020/7915–0000,* FAX *020/7915–4400,* WEB *www.eeh.co.uk. 34 rooms; 2 suites. Bar, room service, air-conditioning in some rooms, in-room data ports, in-room safe, cable TV, Internet, meeting room. AE, DC, MC, V. Tube: South Kensington. BP.*

££–£££ **Kensington House Hotel.** A refurbished 19th-century town house set just of Kensington High Street, the rooms here are modern and streamlined, thanks to large windows and the contemporary monotone furnishings. Rear rooms have views of trees and mews houses, and all rooms come with a bathrobe and tea/coffeemakers. ✉ *15–16 Prince of Wales Terr., Kensington W8 5PQ,* ☎ *020/7937–2345,* FAX *020/7368–6700,* WEB *www.kenhouse.com. 41 rooms. Restaurant, bar, room service, no air-conditioning, fans, cable TV, in-room data ports, in-room safes. AE, DC, MC, V. CP. Tube: High Street Kensington.*

££–£££ **Twenty Nevern Square.** The bedrooms of this 1880s' Victorian town house include carved wood furniture from Indonesia. Some have four-poster beds; others have sleigh beds. Some rooms have their own courtyard while another is split-level. The Pasha suite, which falls into the ££££ category, has wooden floors and its own balcony overlooking the garden square. Both the Chinese room and Rococo room display the hotel's use of silk and gold well. All of the rooms represent a European view of Asian decor—radiant colors reminiscent of jewels. The little touches like a CD player, robes, and free tea and coffee add to the decadence. If you need to work out, you can use the nearby gym. ✉ *20 Nevern Sq., Kensington SW5 9PD,* ☎ *020/7565–9555,* FAX *020/7565–9444,* WEB *www.twentynevernsquare.co.uk. 20 rooms. Restaurant, room service, in-room safe, in-room data ports, cable TV with movies, parking (fee). AE, DC, MC, V. BP. Tube: Earl's Court.*

££ **5 Sumner Place.** Once you've checked into this tall Victorian town house, you get your own key to the front door. If the weather is pleasant, you can enjoy the small, green garden. In the morning, take breakfast in the conservatory. Rooms are kitted out in Victoriana, the proprietors are gracious and welcoming, and the place has an elevator. It's an excellent budget choice. ✉ *5 Sumner Pl., South Kensington SW7 3EE,* ☎ *020/7584–7586,* FAX *020/7823–9962,* WEB *www.sumnerplace.com. 15 rooms. Room service, minibars, no air-conditioning, in-room data ports, some minibars, no-smoking floors, parking (fee). AE, MC, V. BP. Tube: South Kensington.*

££ **Posthouse Kensington.** This mammoth, fairly utilitarian hotel feels like a smaller one, and has a few extras you wouldn't expect for the rates, at the low end. It's in a good location—a quiet lane off Kensington High Street. The main attraction is the health club, with a swimming pool, two squash courts, a steam room, and a beauty salon; there's also a secluded little garden with a pond. Standard rooms are on the small side, with plain, chain-hotel built-in furniture. Some "executive" rooms are twice the size and are a particularly good value. ✉ *Wrights La., Kensington W8 5SP,* ☎ *020/8400–9000,* FAX *020/7937–8289,* WEB *www.posthouse-hotels.com. 543 rooms. 3 restaurants, 2 bars, cable TV, indoor swimming pool, health club, squash. AE, DC, MC, V. Tube: High Street Kensington.*

£ ★ **Abbey House.** Next door to the Vicarage, this pretty, white-stucco 1860 Victorian town house—once the home of a bishop and an MP before World War II—is in an excellent location close to trendy Notting Hill. You can spend the cash you save staying in the surrounding antiques shops. Rooms are spacious and have color TVs and washbasins, but every room shares a bath with another. An English breakfast is included in the rates, and a cuppa (cup of tea) is complimentary. ✉ *11 Vicarage Gate, Notting Hill W8 4AG,* ☎ *020/7727–2594,* WEB *www.abbeyhousekensington.com. 16 rooms without bath. No credit cards. BP. Tube: High Street Kensington.*

£ **Hotel 167.** Just a two-minute walk from the V&A is this white-stucco Victorian corner house. Rooms are pleasantly decorated with pine furniture and muted tones, and each has a minibar. The hallways and stairwells have seen better days, but the breakfast room/lounge has nice wrought iron furniture and sunny yellow walls. ✉ *167 Old Brompton Rd., South Kensington SW5 0AN,* ☎ *020/7373–0672,* FAX *020/7373–3360,* WEB *www.hotel167.com. 18 rooms. No air-conditioning, fans, cable TV. AE, DC, MC, V. CP. Tube: Gloucester Rd.*

£ **Swiss House Hotel.** With an ivy- and flower-bedecked entrance, this hotel is really a sweet little guesthouse with a friendly proprietor. Dried flower arrangements, pine furniture, and simple dark blue rugs and throws make the rooms welcoming and soothing. Ask for a back room for a garden view. Some single rooms do not have bathrooms. Families will appreciate the triple and quad rooms with more space and beds. ✉ *171 Old Brompton Rd., South Kensington SW5 OA,* ☎ *020/7373–2769,* FAX *020/7373–4983,* WEB *www.swiss-hh.demon.co.uk. 15 rooms. No air-conditioning, fans, in-room data ports, cable TV, no-smoking rooms. AE, DC, MC, V. Tube: Gloucester Rd.*

£ **The Vicarage.** Family-owned and set on a leaf-shaded street just off Kensington Church Street, the Vicarage occupies a large white Victorian house. Full of heavy and dark-stained wood furniture, patterned carpets, and brass pendant lights, the furnishings are old-fashioned. All in all, this still remains a charmer—but it is beginning to fray around the edges. All rooms share the bathroom, but a few doubles have their own showers. ✉ *10 Vicarage Gate, Notting Hill W8 4AG,* ☎ *020/7229–4030,* FAX *020/7792–5989,* WEB *www.londonvicaragehotel.com. 18 rooms, 13 without bath. No air-conditioning, no TV in some rooms. No credit cards. BP. Tube: High Street Kensington.*

Knightsbridge, Chelsea, Belgravia, Victoria, and Westminster

££££ **The Berkeley.** The Berkeley successfully mixes the old and the new—it's a luxurious, air-conditioned, double-glazed modern building with a splendid penthouse swimming pool. The bedrooms have swags of William Morris prints or are plain and masculine with little balconies. All have sitting areas and big bathrooms with bidets. For the ridiculously rich, there are spectacular suites, one with its own conservatory terrace, another with a sauna. Choose from two fine restaurants: the posh, European-style La Tante Claire or the thoroughly modern, Thai-French hybrid Vong. ✉ *Wilton Pl., Belgravia SW1X 7RL,* ☎ *020/7235–6000,* FAX *020/7235–4330,* WEB *www.savoy-group.co.uk. 160 rooms. 2 restaurants, in-room VCRs, in-room safe, indoor-outdoor swimming pool, hair salon, health club, cinema, meeting rooms. AE, DC, MC, V. Tube: Knightsbridge.*

££££ **The Capital.** Reserve well ahead if you want a room here—as you must for a table in the hotel's popular, top-quality French restaurant. This grand hotel decanted into a private house is the work of the Levin family, who also own nearby L'Hotel, and it exudes their irreproachable taste: fine-grained woods, original prints, and soothing country chic furnishings. Ask for a front-facing room to get more space; if you're going for a deluxe double ask for the L-shaped rooms in the atmospheric Edwardian wing, where each room has a desk. The staff is conscientious and friendly. ✉ *22–24 Basil St., Knightsbridge SW3 1AT,* ☎ *020/7589–5171,* FAX *020/7225–0011,* WEB *www.capitalhotel.co.uk. 48 rooms. Restaurant, bar, dining room, in-room safes, cable TV, meeting rooms. AE, DC, MC, V. Tube: Knightsbridge.*

££££ **Crowne Plaza London St. James Hotel & Suites.** You enter through a pair of enormous wrought-iron gates that once admitted carriages into what is now the towering reception. The pièce de résistance is the landscaped courtyard with its fountain and ceramic frieze of scenes from Shakespeare. As is to be expected in a chain hotel, the rooms here are plainly decorated in pallid shades. Be sure to ask for a large room, as the hotel prices its double rooms equally—regardless of the size. Unless you have business at Buckingham Palace, the location isn't central enough to warrant the rates. ✉ *45–51 Buckingham Gate, Westminster SW1E 6AF,* ☎ *020/7834–6655,* FAX *020/7630–7587,* WEB *www.london.crowneplaza.com. 356 rooms. 3 restaurants, 2 bars, in-room data ports, cable TV, health club, hot tub, sauna, steam room, business services, no-smoking rooms. AE, DC, MC, V. Tube: St. James's Park.*

££££ **41.** Unlike other hotels, everything you might want is included in the rate here—fine meals, minibar snacks and drinks, cocktails, wine, dry cleaning, laundry, and local and national calls. Rooms are filled with high-tech gadgets: printer, scanner, and fax. You'll even find business cards with your name on them. When you're not working, you can relax on the butter-soft leather sofa in front of the fireplace, recline on the exquisite bed linens and feather duvets, or luxuriate in the marble bath.

✉ *41 Buckingham Palace Rd., Victoria SW1W OPS,* ☎ *020/7300–0041,* FAX *020/7300–0141,* WEB *www.redcarnationhotels.com. 16 rooms, 4 suites. Lounge, in-room data ports, in-room fax, in-room safes, minibars, room service, dry cleaning, laundry service, business services, Internet, meeting rooms. AE, DC, MC, V. BP. Tube: Victoria.*

££££ **The Goring.** Readers love this hotel—where else would the concierge offer to pack up some bread crumbs for the ducks if you're heading for a stroll in Hyde Park? This hotel is ideal if you have to drop in at Buckingham Palace, just around the corner. (Visiting VIPs use it as a convenient, and suitably dignified, base for royal occasions.) The hotel, built by Mr. Goring in 1910 and now run by third-generation Gorings, retains an Edwardian style: bathrooms are marble-fitted, some bedrooms have brass bedsteads and original built-in closets, and many bedrooms have been opulently redecorated. ✉ *15 Beeston Pl., Grosvenor Gardens, Victoria SW1W 0JW,* ☎ *020/7396–9000,* FAX *020/7834–4393,* WEB *www.goringhotel.co.uk. 67 rooms, 7 suites. Restaurant, bar. AE, DC, MC, V. Tube: Victoria.*

££££ **The Halkin.** Escape the clutter and floral motifs of other hotels and chill out to the Milanese design here: the clean-cut white-marble lobby with its royal-blue-leather bucket chairs; the arresting, curved, charcoal-gray corridors; and the gray-on-gray bedrooms that light up when you insert your electronic key. The bathrooms are palaces of shiny chrome. Staying here might be like living in the Design Museum, except that this place employs some of the friendliest and well-dressed staff around. You may use of the Shambhala Health Club at the trendsetting Metropolitan Hotel. ✉ *5 Halkin St., Belgravia SW1X 7DJ,* ☎ *020/7333–1000,* FAX *020/7333–1100,* WEB *www.halkin.co.uk. 41 rooms. Restaurant, in-room data ports, in-room fax, in-room safes, cable TV, in-room VCRs, business services. AE, DC, MC, V. Tube: Hyde Park Corner.*

££££ ★ **The Lanesborough.** Royally proportioned public rooms lead one off the other in this multimillion-pound, American-run conversion of St. George's Hospital. Everything undulates with richness—moiré silks and fleurs-de-lys in the colors of precious stones; magnificent antiques and oil paintings; reproductions of more gilded splendor than the originals; handwoven £250-per-square-yard carpet—as if Liberace and Laura Ashley had collaborated. To check-in, sign the visitor's book, then retire to your room, where you are waited on by a personal butler. If you yearn for a bygone age and are very rich, this is certainly for you. ✉ *Hyde Park Corner, Belgravia SW1X 7TA,* ☎ *020/7259–5599; 800/999–1828 in U.S.,* FAX *020/7259–5606; 800/937–8278 in U.S.,* WEB *www.lanesborough.com. 95 rooms. 2 restaurants, bar, room service, minibars, in-room data ports, in-room fax, cable TV, Internet, no-smoking rooms, parking (fee). AE, DC, MC, V. Tube: Hyde Park Corner.*

££££ **Mandarin Oriental Knightsbridge.** Stay here and the three greats of Knightsbridge are right on your doorstep—Hyde Park, Harrods, and Harvey Nichols. The Mandarin Oriental, originally built in 1880, has had a major overhaul, making it one of the poshest places to stay in London. Bedrooms are traditional Victorian with hidden high-tech gadgets and luxurious touches—potted orchids, chocolates, and fruit. The service here is legendary and includes guest butlers on every floor to check you in and out, arrange cars, restaurants, and theater tickets. Rooms over the park have the only really good views. ✉ *66 Knightsbridge, Knightsbridge SW1X 7LA,* ☎ *020/7235–2000,* FAX *020/7235–4552,* WEB *www.mandarinoriental.com. 177 rooms, 23 suites. 2 restaurants, room service, minibars, in-room safe, some in-room fax, in-room data ports, cable TV, in-room VCRs, health club, spa, hot tub, massage, sauna, steam room, Internet, meeting rooms, no-smoking rooms. AE, DC, MC, V. Tube: Knightsbridge.*

££££ **The Rubens.** This hotel likes to say it treats you like royalty. In fact, you're only a stone's throw from the real thing, as Buckingham Palace is just across the road. The elegant Rubens, which looks out over the Royal Mews, provides the sort of deep comfort needed to soothe away a hard day's sightseeing, with cushy armchairs crying out for you to sink into them with a cup of Earl Grey. With decent-size rooms—not quite furnished like the ones at the palace, it must be said—and a location that could not be more truly central, this hotel remains a favorite for many travelers. ✉ *39 Buckingham Palace Rd., Westminster SW1W OPS,* ☎ *020/7834–6600,* FAX *020/7233–6037,* WEB *www.redcarnationhotels.com. 160 rooms, 13 suites. Restaurant, bar, room service, in-room data ports, some in-room fax, some minibars, cable TV with movies, business services, meeting rooms. AE, DC, MC, V. Tube: Victoria.*

£££–££££ **The Basil Street Hotel.** This gracious Edwardian hotel has been family-run for nearly a century, and it has always been popular with women travelers who get access to the women-only Parrot Club—a comfortable tea room and lounge. Though all the bedrooms are different, many are like Grandma's guest room, with fluffy duvets and a random selection of furniture. You can write letters home in the peaceful gallery, which has polished wood floors and fine Turkish carpets underneath a higgledy-piggledy wealth of antiques. Those with a taste for period charm favor this place. ✉ *Basil St., Knighstbridge SW3 1AH,* ☎ *020/7581–3311,* FAX *020/7581–3693,* WEB *www.thebasil.com. 80 rooms. Restaurant, cable TV. AE, DC, MC, V. Tube: Knightsbridge.*

£££–££££ **The Beaufort.** This elegant pair of Victorian houses includes a guest house where you can expect personal service in an informal, cozy environment. You get a front-door key, free run of the drinks cabinet in the drawing room, and an in-room CD player and radio. The high-ceilinged, contemporary styled rooms are decorated in muted, sophisticated shades. Rates include English cream tea and membership at a local health club. Junior suites include a free one-way airport transfer. Four of the rooms have pretty wrought-iron balconies. ✉ *33 Beaufort Gardens, Knighstbridge SW3 1PP,* ☎ *020/7584–5252,* FAX *020/7589–2834; 800/584–7764 in U.S.,* WEB *www.thebeaufort.co.uk. 28 rooms. Cable TV, in-room VCRs. AE, DC, MC, V. CP. Tube: Knightsbridge.*

£££–££££ **Egerton House.** This utterly peaceful small hotel was the first in the group that includes the Franklin and Dukes hotels, and it remains many people's favorite. The staff here is especially personable. Many chintzy, floral, or Regency-stripe bedrooms overlook the gorgeous gardens in back or the redbrick facades of the buildings in the area; some have quirky shapes, one has a four-poster bed, still others are bigger, with closet space. The two drawing rooms, decorated in high Victorian style, are good places to write letters or relax with a drink from the honesty bar. ✉ *17–19 Egerton Terr., Knightsbridge SW3 2BX,* ☎ *020/7589–2412; 800/473–9492 in U.S.,* FAX *020/7584–6540,* WEB *www.egertonhousehotel.co.uk. 30 rooms. Dining room, in-room data ports, in-room safes, minibars, cable TV. AE, DC, MC, V. Tube: Knightsbridge or South Kensington.*

£££–££££ **Eleven Cadogan Gardens.** This aristocratic, late-Victorian gabled town house is perfect if you want to be pampered. Fine period furniture and antiques, books and magazines on the tables, landscape paintings and portraits, coupled with some of that solid, no-nonsense furniture that *real* English country houses have in abundance make it seem like you're staying in a family home. The best rooms are at the back, overlooking a private garden. If you want to spare no expense and hire a chauffeur-driven car, there is one on standby. The complimentary freshly baked cake for afternoon tea, and sherry and canapés in the evening, are excellent. ✉ *11 Cadogan Gardens, Sloane Sq., South Kensington SW3 2RJ,* ☎ *020/7730–3426,* FAX *020/7730–5217,* WEB *www.number-eleven.co.uk. 62 rooms. Dining room, in-room safes, cable*

TV, exercise equipment, massage, meeting room. AE, MC, V. Tube: Sloane Sq.

£££–££££ **The Franklin.** It's hard to imagine, while taking tea in this pretty hotel overlooking a quiet lawn and garden, that you're an amble away from busy Brompton and Cromwell roads and the splendors of the V&A Museum. A few of the rooms are small, but the marble bathrooms—in which Floris toiletries and heated towel racks are standard issue—are not; the large garden rooms and suites (which fall into the ££££ category) are romantic indeed. Some rooms have four-poster beds; all have antique furnishings. Tea is served daily in the lounge, and there's also an honesty bar. The staff is friendly and accommodating. ✉ *28 Egerton Gardens, Knightsbridge SW3 2DB,* ☎ *020/7584–5533; 800/473–9487 in U.S.,* FAX *020/7584–5449; 800/473–9489 in U.S.,* WEB *www.franklinhotel.co.uk. 50 rooms. Dining room, in-room data ports, in-room safes, Internet, business services, parking (fee). AE, DC, MC, V. Tube: Knightsbridge or South Kensington.*

£££–££££ ★ **The Pelham.** The second of Tim and Kit Kemp's gorgeous hotels is run the same as the Dorset Square, except that this one looks more like the country house to end all country houses. There's 18th-century pine paneling in the drawing room, flowers galore, quite a bit of glazed chintz and antique-lace bed linen, and the occasional four-poster and bedroom fireplace. The first-floor (American second-floor) suites are extra spacious, with high ceilings and chandeliers; some of the top-floor rooms under the eaves have sloping ceilings and casement windows. ✉ *15 Cromwell Pl., South Kensington SW7 2LA,* ☎ *020/7589–8288,* FAX *020/7584–8444,* WEB *www.firmdale.com. 50 rooms. Restaurant, bar, room service, in-room data ports, minibars, cable TV, in-room VCRs and movies, business services, parking (fee). AE, MC, V. Tube: South Kensington.*

£££–££££ **Jolly Hotel St. Ermin's.** Smack in the middle of Westminster, the hotel is just a short stroll from Westminster Abbey and minutes from Buckingham Palace and the Houses of Parliament. An Edwardian anomaly in the shadow of modern skyscrapers, the hotel is set on a tiny cul-de-sac courtyard fronted with iron gates that have imaginary animals carved into them. The lobby is an extravaganza of Victorian Baroque—all cake-frosting stucco-work in shades of baby blue and creamy white. The Cloisters restaurant, an ornately carved 19th-century Jacobean-style salon, is one of the most magnificent rooms in which to dine in London. Guest rooms are tastefully decorated; some have snug dimensions. ✉ *2 Caxton St., Westminster SW1H 0QW,* ☎ *020/7222–7888,* FAX *020/7222–6914,* WEB *www.jollyhotels.it. 290 rooms, 8 suites. Restaurant, bar, minibars, room service, laundry service. AE, DC, MC, V. CP. Tube: St. James's Park.*

£££–££££ **The Sloane.** Many hotels use the word "unique" to describe their identical canopied beds or garden views, but the tiny Sloane really *is* unique. You can lie in your canopied bed, pick up the phone, and buy the bed. You could buy the phone, too, but it's the covetable antiques that you might actually want to take home. Nothing so tacky as a price tag besmirches the gorgeous decor—which doesn't stint on strong hues to show off the ever-changing collection of Regency armoires and Victorian desk lamps—instead, the staff maintains a book of price lists at the desk. Room service runs from about 7 AM–11 PM, but you can eat lunch and dinner on the roof terrace, which has upholstered garden furniture and a panoramic view of Chelsea. ✉ *29 Draycott Pl., Chelsea SW3 2SH,* ☎ *020/7581–5757,* FAX *020/7584–1348,* WEB *www.sloanehotel.com. 22 rooms. Dining room, in-room data ports, Internet, cable TV, in-room VCRs, parking (fee). AE, DC, MC, V. Tube: Sloane Sq.*

£££ **Dolphin Square Hotel.** Here you get an entire apartment for a good price, in an interesting if slightly out of town center location—on the outer edge of Westminster, near the Thames. The Dolphin Square Hotel is outfitted with contemporary, airy, bright, and comfortable one-, two-, and three-bedroom suites. The extensive gardens offer lots of green space. Another perk: celebrity chef Gary Rhodes owns one of the hotel's restaurants, Rhodes in the Square. The hotel offers total independence—they provide a kitchen and living room. There is, however, room service if you just can't be bothered. ✉ *Dolphin Sq., Chichester St., Westminster SW1V 3LX,* ☎ *020/7798–8890,* FAX *020/7798–8896,* WEB *www.dolphinsquarehotel.co.uk. 148 suites. 2 restaurants, bar, in-room data ports, in-room safes, kitchens, room service, tennis court, indoor swimming pool, exercise equipment, hair salon, massage, sauna, spa, steam rooms, croquet, squash, shops, business services, parking (fee), no-smoking rooms. AE, DC, MC, V. BP. Tube: Pimlico.*

£££ ★ **L'Hotel.** Rooms at this upscale B&B have an air of provincial France: white bedcovers, pine furniture, and beige color schemes in the rooms and delicious breakfast croissants and baguettes served in the Le Metro cellar wine bar. It's really like staying in a house—you're given your own front-door key, there's no elevator, and the staff leaves in the evening. Ask for a fireplace room, they're biggest. All rooms have tea/coffeemakers; some rooms only have hand-held showerheads. You have access to the restaurant and concierge services of the plush Capital hotel, run by the same family, a few doors down the street. ✉ *28 Basil St., Knightsbridge SW3 1AT,* ☎ *020/7589–6286,* FAX *020/7823–7826,* WEB *www.lhotel.co.uk. 12 rooms, 1 suite. Restaurant, bar, fans, cable TV, in-room VCRs. AE, V. CP. Tube: Knightsbridge.*

££–£££ **The Diplomat.** From its aristocratically elegant exterior, this hotel looks like a Cecil Beaton stage set: a Wedgwood-white "palazzo" terrace house built by the 19th-century architect Thomas Cubitt, flatiron shape (it stands at the confluence of two streets), and often decked out with hanging flowerpots of geraniums. It's the very picture of Belgravian chic. Inside, the reception area gives way to a circular staircase lit by a Regency-era chandelier and topped with a winter-garden dome. Rooms are pleasantly decorated, some with Victorian touches. ✉ *2 Chesham St., Belgravia SW1X 8DT,* ☎ *020/7235–1544,* FAX *020/7259–6153,* WEB *www.btinternet.com/~diplomat.hotel. 27 rooms. Business services. AE, DC, MC, V. BP. Tube: Sloane Sq. or Knightsbridge.*

££ **Knightsbridge Green.** For just £25 more than a double room, in a modernized Georgian building, the suites here are not overpriced—especially since they have sofa beds on which kids can sleep. All rooms have trouser presses and tea/coffeemakers. Be sure to ask for the newer rooms, which have double-glazed windows to muffle the sound of traffic on busy Knightsbridge Road. There's no restaurant, but there are plenty in the area; or if you ask, they'll send the porter out to find you a sandwich. The hotel is only a two-minute walk from Harrods. ✉ *159 Knightsbridge, Knightsbridge SW1X 7PD,* ☎ *020/7584–6274,* FAX *020/7225–1635,* WEB *www.theKGHotel.co.uk. 17 rooms, 11 suites. In-room safes, cable TV. Closed 3 days at Christmas. AE, MC, V. Tube: Knightsbridge.*

££ **La Reserve.** You'll find this unusual small hotel, at the top of its price category, in the lively, classy residential neighborhood of Fulham. The varnished floorboards, black Venetian blinds, works of art (for sale), and primary-color upholstery in the public areas are very 1980s. Bedrooms have minibars, hair dryers, trouser presses, and tea/coffeemakers. Fulham is not within walking distance of central London, but it is two minutes from the Fulham Broadway tube, and is near Chelsea Football (soccer) Grounds and plenty of restaurants; there's also an in-house brasserie. ✉ *422–428 Fulham Rd., Chelsea SW6 1DU,*

☎ *020/7385–8561,* FAX *020/7385–7662,* WEB *www.la-reservehotel.co.uk/. 43 rooms. Restaurant, bar, in-room data ports, cable TV, free parking. AE, DC, MC, V. BP. Tube: Fulham Broadway.*

££ **Tophams Belgravia.** Family-owned since 1937, this hotel comprises five Georgian houses linked together. Rooms tend toward the flowery style, and the hallways are narrow. The family extends a warm welcome, and has many loyal clientele who return to the higgledy-piggledy collection of bedrooms and public rooms. ✉ *28 Ebury St., Belgravia SW1W 0LU,* ☎ *020/7730–8147,* FAX *020/7823–5966,* WEB *www.tophams.co.uk. 39 rooms. Restaurant, bar, room service, in-room data ports, cable TV, meeting room, parking (fee). AE, DC, MC, V. Tube: Victoria.*

£ **Elizabeth Hotel.** Near Victoria Station and an attractive garden square, and once the private home of aristocrats (including relatives of Edward VII), the Elizabeth Hotel offers standard rooms with 1970s era furniture. Rooms come with a bath and/or shower, TV, and English breakfast. Shared-bath singles and doubles are also available. The hotel also offers luxury studio and two-bedroom apartments next door. ✉ *37 Eccleston Sq., Victoria SW1V 1PB,* ☎ *020/7828–6812,* FAX *020/7828–6814,* WEB *www.elizabethhotel.com. 38 rooms. No air-conditioning, fans, meeting room. MC, V. BP. Tube: Victoria.*

£ **Melita House Hotel.** The Gabriele family have run this small hotel for more than 30 years. It's on a quiet residential road, and the Tate Britain and Victoria Station are within walking distance. Each room includes a fridge, desk, hair dryer, safe, and direct phone line. The rate includes a full English breakfast. ✉ *35 Charlwood St., Victoria SW1V 2DU,* ☎ *020/7828–0471,* FAX *020/7932–0988,* WEB *www.melitahotel.com. 22 rooms. In-room data ports, in-room safes. AE, MC, V. BP. Tube: Victoria.*

£ **Morgan House.** Near Victoria Station in classy Belgravia, this charming Georgian B&B has flowery rooms with orthopedic mattresses, TVs, hair dryers, beautiful ornamental fireplaces, and tea- and coffee-making facilities. The house has one family room with bunk beds and a double bed. Ask for a room in the back if you're sensitive to street noise. ✉ *120 Ebury St., Belgravia SW1W 9QQ,* ☎ *020/7730–2384,* FAX *020/7730–8442,* WEB *www.morganhouse.co.uk. 11 rooms, 8 without bath. No air-conditioning. No credit cards. BP. Tube: Victoria.*

£ **Woodville House.** Owned by the same couple who own Morgan House, this Georgian hotel has flowery furnishings and a friendly welcome. It's better suited, however, to families; rooms accommodate up to five people. Bathrooms are communal, but rooms do have sinks and shaver points. Tea, coffee, ice, and a hearty English breakfast are included in the price. The patio is a nice place to relax with a drink. ✉ *107 Ebury St., Belgravia SW1W 9QU,* ☎ *020/7730–1048,* FAX *020/7730–2574,* WEB *www.woodvillehouse.co.uk. 12 rooms without bath. Air-conditioning in some rooms, some kitchenettes. MC, V. BP. Tube: Victoria.*

Mayfair to Regent's Park

££££ **Brown's.** Founded in 1837 by Lord Byron's "gentleman's gentleman," James Brown, the 11 Georgian town houses are patronized by many Anglophilic Americans—a habit that was established by the two Roosevelts (Teddy while on honeymoon). Bedrooms are thickly carpeted, and furnished with soft armchairs, brass chandeliers, and brocade wallpapers; rooms also have air-conditioning. The public rooms retain their cozy oak-paneled, chintz-laden, grandfather-clock-ticking-in-the-parlor sensibility. In the Drawing Room, one of London's best-known afternoon teas is served from 3 to 5:45 on weekdays, and from 2:30 on weekends. ✉ *34 Albemarle St., Mayfair W1X 4BT,* ☎ *020/7493–6020,* FAX *020/7493–9381,* WEB *www.brownshotel.com. 108 rooms, 10 suites.*

Lodging in Mayfair, Regent's Park, St. James's, Soho, Covent Garden, and The South Bank

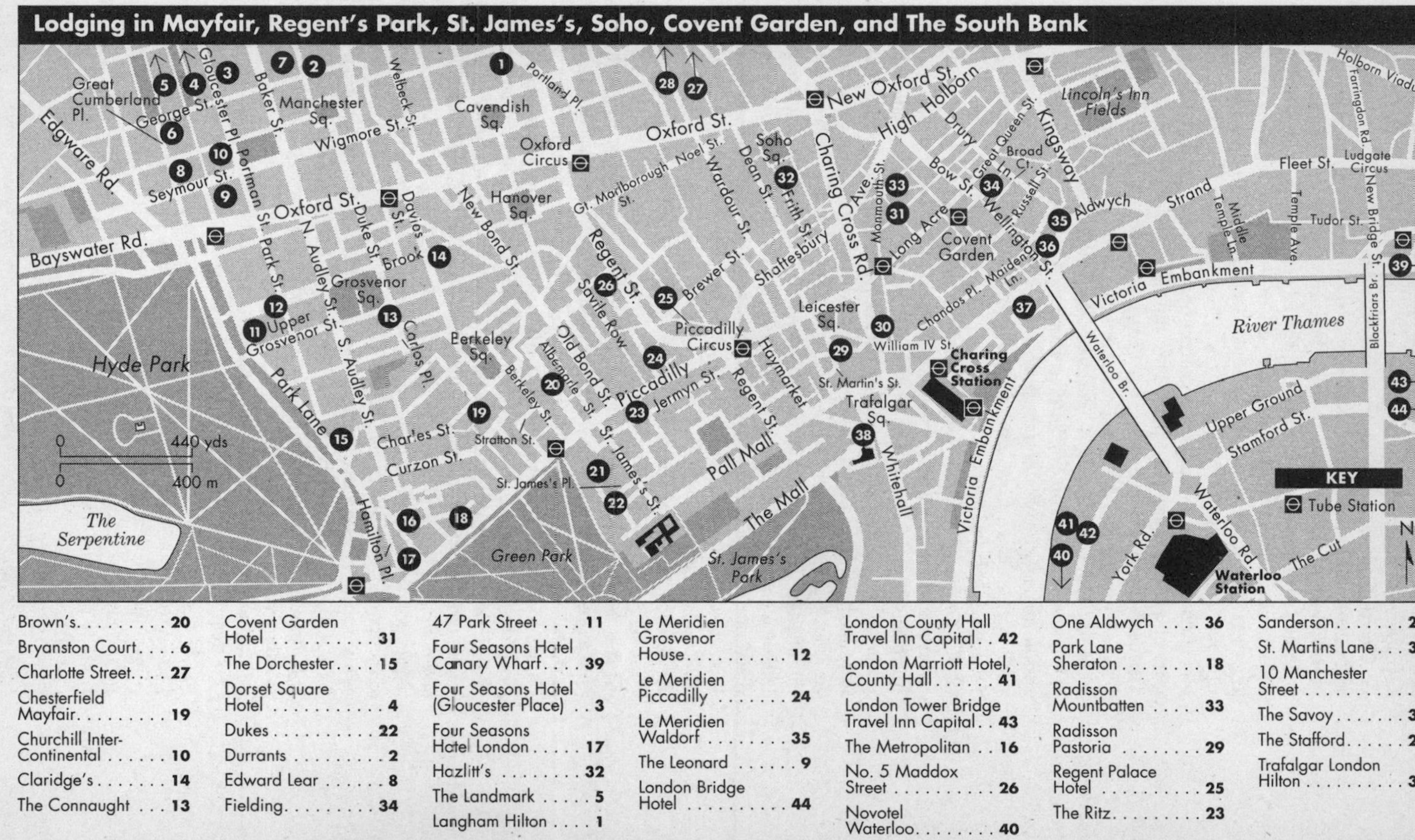

Brown's . . . 20	Covent Garden Hotel . . . 31	47 Park Street . . . 11	Le Meridien Grosvenor House . . . 12	London County Hall Travel Inn Capital . . 42	One Aldwych . . . 36	Sanderson . . . 28
Bryanston Court . . . 6	The Dorchester . . . 15	Four Seasons Hotel Canary Wharf . . . 39	Le Meridien Piccadilly . . . 24	London Marriott Hotel, County Hall . . . 41	Park Lane Sheraton . . . 18	St. Martins Lane . . . 30
Charlotte Street . . . 27	Dorset Square Hotel . . . 4	Four Seasons Hotel (Gloucester Place) . . 3	Le Meridien Waldorf . . . 35	London Tower Bridge Travel Inn Capital . . 43	Radisson Mountbatten . . . 33	10 Manchester Street . . . 7
Chesterfield Mayfair . . . 19	Dukes . . . 22	Four Seasons Hotel London . . . 17	The Leonard . . . 9	The Metropolitan . . 16	Radisson Pastoria . . . 29	The Savoy . . . 37
Churchill Inter-Continental . . . 10	Durrants . . . 2	Hazlitt's . . . 32	London Bridge Hotel . . . 44	No. 5 Maddox Street . . . 26	Regent Palace Hotel . . . 25	The Stafford . . . 21
Claridge's . . . 14	Edward Lear . . . 8	The Landmark . . . 5		Novotel Waterloo . . . 40	The Ritz . . . 23	Trafalgar London Hilton . . . 38
The Connaught . . . 13	Fielding . . . 34	Langham Hilton . . . 1				

Restaurant, bar, room service, exercise equipment, meeting room. AE, DC, MC, V. Tube: Green Park.

££££ **Churchill Inter-Continental London.** Modern Park Avenue luxury came to London when the Tisch family opened this homage to Winston Churchill in the 1970s. The lobby is opulent: it has a gilded ceiling and black marble columns, and the Regency-style notes continue throughout. The Terrace on Portman Square—the main restaurant, with the theme of an indoor garden terrace—serves a buffet and à la carte options, as well as afternoon tea. The Churchill Bar and Cigar Divan, a gleaming maple-wood nook, proffers private-label smokes, 75 varieties of whiskey, and grand-piano entertainment. Business travelers and visiting VIPs love this place and its Portman Square location, just two blocks from Marble Arch and the shops of Oxford Street. ✉ *30 Portman Sq., Mayfair W1A 4ZX,* ☎ *020/7486–5800,* FAX *020/7486–1255,* WEB *www.london-churchill.interconti.com. 405 rooms, 40 suites. 2 restaurants, bar, in-room data ports, in-room safes, minibars, tennis court, health club, hair salon, business services, meeting rooms. AE, DC, MC, V. Tube: Marble Arch.*

££££ ★ **The Connaught.** Make reservations well in advance for this very exclusive small hotel—it's the most understated of any of London's grand hostelries, and the London home-away-from-home for those who have inherited the habit of staying at the Connaught from their great-grandfathers. The bar and lounges have the air of an ambassadorial residence, an impression reinforced by the imposing oak staircase and dignified staff. Each bedroom has a foyer, antique furniture (if you don't like the desk, they'll change it), and fresh flowers. If you value privacy, discretion, and the kind of luxury that eschews new-money flashiness, this is the place for you. ✉ *Carlos Pl., Mayfair W1Y 6AL,* ☎ *020/7499–7070,* FAX *020/7495–3262,* WEB *www.savoy-group.co.uk. 90 rooms. Restaurant, bar, in-room data ports, in-room fax, exercise equipment, meeting room. MC. Tube: Bond St.*

££££ ★ **The Dorchester.** No other hotel this opulent manages to be this charming. The glamour level is off the scale: 1,500 square yards of gold leaf and 1,100 square yards of marble. Bedrooms (some not as spacious as you might imagine) have Irish linen sheets on canopied beds, brocades and velvets, and Italian marble and etched-glass bathrooms with Floris brand toiletries. Furnishings throughout are opulent English country-house style, with more than a hint of art deco—in keeping with the original 1930s building. You can take afternoon tea, drink, lounge, and pose in the catwalk-shape Promenade lounge. ✉ *Park La., Mayfair W1A 2HJ,* ☎ *020/7629–8888,* FAX *020/7409–0114,* WEB *www.dorchesterhotel.com. 195 rooms, 53 suites. 2 restaurants, 2 bars, cable TV with movies, in-room VCRs, health club, hair salon, spa, nightclub, business services, Internet, meeting room, parking (fee), no-smoking rooms. AE, DC, MC, V. Tube: Marble Arch.*

££££ **47 Park Street.** Back to back with the grand hotels of Park Lane, this dear (in every sense) little all-suite hotel has the best room service in town, with 24-hour food direct from the kitchen of their restaurant, Le Gavroche. Business services range from three personal phone lines to in-house translation facilities. Bathrooms are on the small side, but no other drawbacks are apparent in this fabulously discreet, conventionally decorated, quiet, relaxed, and homey haven—as long as you can afford it. ✉ *47 Park St., Mayfair W1K 7EB,* ☎ *020/7491–7282,* FAX *020/7491–7281,* WEB *www.47parkstreet.com. 52 suites. Restaurant, bar, dining room, in-room data ports, in-room safes, kitchen, cable TV, baby-sitting, business services, meeting room. AE, DC, MC, V. Tube: Marble Arch.*

££££ **Four Seasons Hotel London.** Business travelers swear by Four Seasons' standards of luxury and comfort. This hotel opened in the 1970s as Inn on the Park, yet it carries an historic air, with art deco touches (especially in the gorgeous, jewel-colored Lanes restaurant). Still, the discretion and élan of this place inspire greater-than-average loyalty in those who frequent it. The conservatory rooms are most popular because they have glass-enclosed sitting rooms and access to a deck. ✉ *Hamilton Pl., Park La., Mayfair W1A 1AZ,* ☎ *020/7499–0888,* FAX *020/7493–6629,* WEB *www.fourseasons.com. 220 rooms, 26 suites. Restaurant, cable TV with video games, in-room VCRs, in-room safes, Internet, health club, meeting rooms, free parking. AE, DC, MC, V. Tube: Hyde Park Corner.*

££££ **The Landmark.** A palm-filled, eight-story atrium Winter Garden forms the core, and odd-numbered rooms overlook this. If size matters to you, note that even standard rooms here are among the largest in London and have glamorous bathrooms in marble and chrome, outfitted with robes and hair dryers. Despite appearances, this is one of the only London grand hotels that doesn't force you to dress up; even jeans are okay, except in the elegant John Burton-Race restaurant, where jacket and tie are required. ✉ *222 Marylebone Rd., Marylebone NW1 6JQ,* ☎ *020/7631–8000,* FAX *020/7631–8080,* WEB *www.landmarklondon.co.uk. 299 rooms. 2 restaurants, bar, in-room data ports, cable TV with movies, indoor swimming pool, hot tub, steam room, massage, sauna, health club, Internet, business services, no-smoking floors. AE, DC, MC, V. Tube: Marylebone.*

££££ **Langham Hilton.** Opened in 1865 by the Prince of Wales and once London's center of Victorian chic, the Langham is still a great hotel. One floor is dedicated to lodging and catering to business travelers, and another three floors house a full-service health club, with an Elizabeth Arden salon/spa. Otherwise, things haven't changed much since Mark Twain used to visit. The exterior is solid Empire stuff (from the Edwardian era). At night, floodlighting casts on the pillars and porticos a massive chiaroscuro. Guest rooms are done in soothing Queen Mother pastels; many have marble bathrooms. ✉ *1C Portland Pl., Mayfair W1B 1JA,* ☎ *020/7636–1000,* FAX *020/7323–2340,* WEB *www.langham.hilton.com. 429 rooms. 2 restaurants, bar, cable TV with video games, indoor pool, sauna, gym, health club, hot tub, spa, Internet, meeting rooms. AE, DC, MC, V. Tube: Oxford Circus.*

££££ **Le Meridien Grosvenor House.** "The old lady of Park Lane" is not the kind of place that encourages hushed whispers or which frowns on trendy Alexander McQueen outfits, despite the marble floors and wood-paneled library, open fires, oils, and fine antiques (all inspired by the Earl of Grosvenor's residence, which occupied the site during the 18th century). The health club is one of the best around, thanks to its good-sized pool. Bedrooms are spacious, and most of the marble bathrooms have natural light. ✉ *Park La., Mayfair W1A 3AA,* ☎ *020/7499–6363,* FAX *020/7493–3341,* WEB *www.lemeridien-grosvenorhouse.com. 380 rooms, 70 suites, 136 apartments. 2 restaurants, 2 bars, indoor pool, health club, hair salon, sauna, meeting rooms. AE, DC, MC, V. Tube: Marble Arch.*

££££ **Le Meridien Piccadilly.** The massive 1908 building is fin-de-siècle elegant and has been updated while still keeping its exquisite period architectural features. The effect is very much one of clean, bright spaces with an art deco touch. Infamous bad-boy French chef Marco Pierre White serves fantastic, rich, and expensive food in the Oak Room restaurant, which is traditional in limed oak paneling and gilt. The Terrace restaurant, on the other hand, is an ode to modernity: straight lines and an unfussy style. Bedrooms vary in size; a few seventh-floor ones have balconies overlooking Piccadilly. Champneys, the health club, is luxurious and exclusive—open to members and hotel guests only. ✉ *21 Piccadilly, Mayfair W1J 0BH,* ☎ *020/7734–8000,* FAX *020/7437–*

3574, WEB *www.lemeridien-piccadilly.com. 232 rooms, 35 suites. 2 restaurants, 2 bars, in-room fax, in-room data ports, in-room safes, cable TV with movies and video games, indoor pool, aerobics, sauna, health club, squash, billiards, library, Internet, business services, meeting rooms, no-smoking rooms, parking (fee). AE, DC, MC, V. Tube: Piccadilly Circus.*

££££ ★ **The Metropolitan.** This supertrendy hotel is one of the only addresses for fashion, music, and media folk in London. Its Met bar is an exclusive guest-list and hotel resident-only bar, and the restaurant is the famed Nobu, leased by Japanese wonder chef Nobu Matsuhisa. The lobby is sleek and postmodern, as are the bedrooms, which have identical minimalist taupe-and-white furnishings. The best rooms overlook Hyde Park, but all have a groovy minibar hiding the latest alcoholic and health-boosting beverages, as well as an emergency kit with aspirin, condoms, and other necessities you'd rather not have to ask for in person. ✉ *Old Park La., Mayfair W1K 1LB,* ☎ *020/7447–1000; 800/337–4685 in U.S.,* FAX *020/7447–1100,* WEB *www.metropolitan.co.uk. 137 rooms, 18 suites. Restaurant, bar, in-room data ports, in-room fax, cable TV, massage, exercise equipment, business services, meeting room, no-smoking floors, parking (fee). AE, DC, MC, V. Tube: Hyde Park Corner.*

££££ **No. 5 Maddox Street.** At No. 5 Maddox you'll find suites with everything you need to set up residence. Deluxe suites have balconies and working fireplaces. Room service will cater to your every whim such as delivering groceries or lending you CDs, videos, or a bicycle. Bedrooms have an understated Asian minimalist aesthetic with white on beige on brown color schemes and lots of bamboo. In keeping with the unexpected, the minibars are stocked with everything from Ben & Jerry's to herbal tea. You have access to a nearby gym and "Jet Lag Clinic." (They massage you, give you a facial, and make you drink water and sit in a steam room.) The hotel is tucked away in busy central London, just off Regent Street. ✉ *5 Maddox St., Mayfair W1R 9LE,* ☎ *020/7647–0200,* FAX *020/7647–0300,* WEB *www.living-rooms.co.uk. 12 suites. Room service, minibars, in-room safe, in-room fax, in-room data ports, kitchen, cable TV, in-room VCRs, business services. AE, DC, MC, V. Tube: Oxford Circus.*

££££ **Park Lane Sheraton.** Walking in to the Park Lane Hotel via the decadent, Asian-inspired, art deco Palm Court tea room and bar is worth the price of admission. The choice of doubles here ranges from regular doubles with traditional-style furnishings to "smart" rooms, which include ergonomically designed chairs, extra outlets and lighting, in-room data ports, and a combination printer/copier/fax machine. Executive doubles have stunning views of Green Park, which is just across busy Piccadilly Street. The ballroom of *Golden Eye* and *End of the Affair* fame is an exquisite room used for various functions. ✉ *Piccadilly, Mayfair W1J BX,* ☎ *020/7499–6321,* FAX *020/7499–1965,* WEB *www.sheraton.com. 268 rooms, 39 suites. Restaurant, bar, some in-room data ports, some in-room fax, cable TV with movies, hair salon, exercise equipment, business services, meeting rooms, parking (fee), no-smoking rooms. AE, DC, MC, V. Tube: Hyde Park Corner.*

£££–££££ **Chesterfield Mayfair.** Set deep in the heart of Mayfair, this hotel is the former town house of the Earl of Chesterfield. The welcoming wood-and-leather public rooms match the snug bedrooms done up in burgundy and forest green with dark wood furnishings. Double rooms may be on the small side, but the service is warm and the hotel suitably upscale. ✉ *35 Charles St., Mayfair W12 SEB,* ☎ *020/7491–2622,* FAX *020/7491–4793,* WEB *www.redcarnationhotels.com. 110 rooms. Restaurant, room service, in-room data ports, cable TV with movies, bar, meeting rooms, no-smoking rooms. AE, DC, MC, V. Tube: Green Park.*

£££–££££ ★ **Dorset Square Hotel.** This special small hotel was the first of five London addresses for husband and wife Tim and Kit Kemp, hoteliers extraordinaire. They decanted the English country look into a fine pair of Regency town houses. Everywhere you look you'll see antiques, rich colors, and design ideas *House & Garden* subscribers would love. Every room is different: the first-floor balconied "Coronet" rooms are the largest. The marble-and-mahogany bathrooms have power showers; glossy magazines, a half bottle of claret, and boxes of vitamin C are complimentary. There's a reason for the ubiquitous cricket memorabilia: Dorset Square was the first Lord's grounds. If you rent a car here, you get a Bentley. The hotel is off Baker Street. ✉ *39–40 Dorset Sq., Marylebone NW1 6QN,* ☎ *020/7723–7874,* FAX *020/7724–3328,* WEB *www.firmdale.com. 38 rooms. Restaurant, bar, room service, minibars, cable TV, in-room VCRs. AE, MC, V. Tube: Baker St.*

£££–££££ **The Leonard.** Its four 18th-century buildings create a stunning, relaxed, and friendly boutique hotel. Shoppers will appreciate the location, just around the corner from Oxford Street. All suites are remarkably cozy, with sitting and bedroom areas set off by small foyers. Rooms are decorated with a judicious mix of lived-in antiques and comfortable reproductions. For more elbow room, try one of the aptly named grand suites, with their palatial sitting rooms and tall windows. The welcoming lobby area is stocked with complimentary newspapers to read by the fire. ✉ *15 Seymour St., Mayfair W1H 5AA,* ☎ *020/7935–2010,* FAX *020/7935–6700,* WEB *www.theleonard.com. 20 suites, 9 rooms. Bar, dining room, some kitchens, cable TV, in-room VCRs, in-room data ports, room service, exercise equipment, business services. AE, DC, MC, V. Tube: Marble Arch.*

££–£££ **Novotel Waterloo.** It looks just like 280 other hotels in 44 countries, but this French-owned, inexpensive chain hotel is reliable. Views vary, but basically you're looking at Lambeth Palace, the Houses of Parliament, or Big Ben. It's a chain hotel, with rules and regulations, so even though it has a beautiful and awe-inspiring location on the Thames, you can't fling open the window to catch the Thames breeze (on account of the guest-room climate-control system). ✉ *113–127 Lambeth Rd., The South Bank SE1 7LS,* ☎ *020/7793–1010,* FAX *020/7793–0202,* WEB *www.novotel.com. 187 rooms, 12 suites. Restaurant, bar, cable TV with movies, health club, Internet, meeting room. AE, DC, MC, V. Tube: Waterloo or Lambeth North.*

££ **Bryanston Court.** These three converted Georgian houses are decorated in a style that's traditional English—open fireplaces, comfortable leather armchairs, oil portraits. The bedrooms are small and modern, with pink furnishings, creaky floors, and tiny bathrooms. Rooms at the back are quieter and face east, so they're bright in the mornings; Room 77 is as big as a suite, but, typical of rooms in London houses, it's dark. This family-run hotel is an excellent value for the area—a few blocks north of Hyde Park and Park Lane. ✉ *56–60 Great Cumberland Pl., Mayfair W1H 7FD,* ☎ *020/7262–3141,* FAX *020/7262–7248,* WEB *www.bryanstonhotel.com. 60 rooms. Bar, no air-conditioning, cable TV. AE, DC, MC, V. BP. Tube: Marble Arch.*

££ **Durrants.** A hotel since the late 18th century, Durrants occupies a quiet corner almost next to the Wallace Collection, a stone's throw from Oxford Street and the smaller, posher shops of Marylebone High Street. It's a good value for the area, especially if you like the old-English wood-paneled, leather-armchair, dark-red patterned carpet style. ✉ *George St., Mayfair W1H 5BJ,* ☎ *020/7935–8131,* FAX *020/7487–3510,* WEB *www.durrantshotel.co.uk. 92 rooms, 85 with bath. Restaurant, bar, dining room, no air-conditioning in some rooms, in-room data ports, cable TV. AE, MC, V. Tube: Bond St.*

££ Four Seasons Hotel. This has nothing to do with the Four Seasons opposite Hyde Park or the Four Seasons Hotel Canary Wharf; there are no stunning views over the Thames, Philippe Starck basins, or soundless elevators here. The rooms are clean, however, and all come with hair dryers and a digital television. The breakfast room sports a glass roof. This is bare-bones stuff, but the hotel is close to Regent's Park and is reasonably priced. Families can be accommodated in the rooms that sleep four. ✉ *173 Gloucester Pl., Mayfair NW1 6DX,* ☎ *020/7724–3461,* FAX *020/7402–5594,* WEB *www.4seasonshotel.co.uk. 28 rooms. Lounge. AE, DC, MC, V. CP. Tube: Baker St.*

££ **10 Manchester Street.** Tucked away on a quiet street between bustling Oxford Street and posh Marylebone High Street, "number 10" claims to offer no frills, good value, and high quality—and they deliver on the promise. This early 20th-century town house has been refurbished to a high standard. Rooms have CD players with radios, trouser press, and tea/coffeemaker. The small doubles are just as they sound, but for the price and location these no-frills rooms are great; their counterpart regular doubles, at £30 more, are spacious. ✉ *10 Manchester St., Mayfair W1M 5PG,* ☎ *020/7486–6669,* FAX *020/7224–0348,* WEB *www.10manchesterstreet.com. 37 rooms, 9 suites. Cable TV. AE, DC, MC, V. CP. Tube: Bond St.*

£ **Edward Lear.** This family-run guest house, just a minute's walk from Oxford Street, is in a Georgian town house that was formerly the home of the master of nonsense verse, Edward Lear. The location is the biggest selling point for this place, as rooms tend to be small and the furnishings worn. The management is very proud of the English breakfasts—it uses the same butcher as the Queen. ✉ *28–30 Seymour St., Mayfair W1H 5WD,* ☎ *020/7402–5401,* FAX *020/7706–3766,* WEB *www.edlear.com. 31 rooms, 15 with shower (no toilet), 4 with full bath. Cable TV, Internet. MC, V. BP. Tube: Marble Arch.*

St. James's

££££ ★ **Claridge's.** Stay here, and you're staying at a hotel legend (founded in 1812), with one of the world's classiest guest lists. The liveried staff is friendly and not in the least condescending, and the rooms are never less than luxurious. Enjoy tea or coffee in the Foyer lounge (24 hours a day) or retreat to the stylish Claridge's bar for cocktails and canapés—or, better, to Gordon Ramsay's inimitable restaurant. The bathrooms are spacious (with enormous showerheads), as are the bedrooms (Victorian style or art deco), with bells (which still work) to summon either maid, waiter, or valet. The grand staircase and magnificent elevator complete with sofa and driver are equally glamorous. ✉ *Brook St., St. James's W1A 2JQ,* ☎ *020/7629–8860; 800/637–2869 in U.S.,* FAX *020/7499–2210,* WEB *www.claridges.co.uk. 200 rooms. Restaurant, bar, in-room data ports, in-room fax, cable TV with movies, in-room VCRs, hair salon, health club, meeting rooms. AE, DC, MC, V. BP. Tube: Bond St.*

££££ **Dukes.** This small, exclusive, Edwardian-style hotel, with a gas lantern-lit courtyard entrance, is central but still quiet—it's in its own discreet cul-de-sac, where the Stafford also lies. The hotel has character: it's filled with over-stuffed sofas, oil paintings of assorted dukes, and muted, rich colors, and is the home of the finest dry martinis in town. Its trump cards are that, for such a central location, it offers immense peace and quiet and very reasonable rates, personal service (they greet you by name every time), and an especially sweet suite on the top floor with views over St. James's Park. ✉ *35 St. James's Pl., St. James's SW1A 1NY,* ☎ *020/7491–4840; 800/381–4702 in U.S.,* FAX *020/7493–1264,* WEB *www.dukeshotel.co.uk. 80 rooms, 9 suites. Restaurant, bar, dining room, minibars, in-room data ports,* *cable TV, exercise equipment, Turkish bath, spa. AE, DC, MC, V. Tube: Green Park.*

££££ **The Ritz.** The name conjures the kind of luxury associated with thick swagged curtains, handwoven carpets, the smell of cigars, polish, and fresh lilies; it signifies a magical Edwardian opulence. The only thing that has been lost is a certain vein of moneyed naughtiness that someone like F. Scott Fitzgerald, at least, would have banked on. The bedrooms are bastions of pastel, Louis XVI style with gilded furniture and walls, crystal chandeliers, and floral prints. With a ratio of two staff to every bedroom, you're guaranteed personal service despite the massive size of the hotel. ✉ *150 Piccadilly, St. James's W1J 9BR,* ☎ *020/7493–8181,* FAX *020/7493–2687,* WEB *www.theritzhotel.co.uk. 133 rooms. 2 restaurants, bar, in-room data ports, hair salon, gym, business services, meeting rooms. AE, DC, MC, V. Tube: Piccadilly Circus.*

££££ **The Stafford.** This hotel is most famous for its utterly amazing American Bar, where a million ties, baseball caps, and toy planes hang from a ceiling modeled, presumably, on New York's "21" Club, but it is also prized for its 13 carriage-house rooms, installed in the 18th-century stable block. Relative bargains, each of these cute and private accommodations has its own cobbled mews entrance and gas-log fires, black-stained exposed beams, and CD players. One nice perk is that you get complimentary access to Champney's Piccadilly, one of London's top health clubs. ✉ *St. James's Pl., St. James's SW1A 1NJ,* ☎ *020/7493–0111,* FAX *020/7493–7121,* WEB *www.thestaffordhotel.co.uk. 81 rooms. Restaurant, bar, dining room, cable TV, in-room data ports. AE, DC, MC, V. Tube: Green Park.*

Soho and Covent Garden

££££ **Charlotte Street.** As the newest of Tim and Kit Kemp's five hotels, Charlotte Street doesn't disappoint. Set in a quiet street in North Soho, it fuses the modern and traditional. Bathrooms are lined with gleaming granite and oak, and there are walk-in showers and deep baths; and, since each bathroom has a mini flat-screen TV, you can catch up on the news while you soak. The restaurant, Oscar, is excellent. There is a public screening room, with Ferrari leather chairs, if you feel like watching a movie. If not, you might just want to read a paper by the fire. ✉ *15 Charlotte St., Soho W1P 1HB,* ☎ *020/7907–4000,* FAX *020/7806–2002,* WEB *www.charlottestreethotel.com. 52 rooms. Restaurant, room service, in-room data ports, cable TV, in-room VCRs, minibars, gym, cinema. AE, DC, MC, V. Tube: Goodge St.*

££££ ★ **Covent Garden Hotel.** A former 1880s' hospital in the midst of artsy and boisterous Covent Garden, this hotel is now the London home-away-from-home for a mélange of off-duty celebrities, actors, and style mavens. The public salons will keep even the most picky happy: wallowing in painted silks, style *anglais* ottomans, and 19th-century Romantic oils, they are perfect places to decompress over a glass of sherry. Guest rooms are *World of Interiors* stylish, each showcasing matching-but-mixed couture fabrics to stunning effect. ✉ *10 Monmouth St., Covent Garden WC2H 9HB,* ☎ *020/7806–1000,* FAX *020/7806–1100,* WEB *www.firmdale.com. 58 rooms, 3 suites. Restaurant, room service, minibars, cable TV, in-room VCRs, gym, laundry service, business services, meeting rooms, cinema. AE, MC, V. Tube: Covent Garden.*

££££ **Four Seasons Canary Wharf.** Magnificent, copper-roofed, reminding one faintly of George Orwell's Ministry of Truth, the Four Seasons sits on a vast pedestal above a wriggling mass of thruways, tunnels, and overpasses. The hotel is thoroughly modern: glass doors swish open, and islands of armchairs float on cool gray marble. Rooms are spacious and have colorful, sleek furnishings, but only the more expensive ones have the breathtaking views over the river. If you have business in the City or just want to be far away from the West End and its theaters, then stay here. ✉ *46 Westferry Circus, East End E14 8R,* ☎ *020/7510–1999,* FAX *020/7510–1990,* WEB *www.fourseasons.com. 142 rooms. Restaurant, bar, in-room data ports, in-room safes, room service, massage, gym, baby-sitting, dry cleaning, laundry service, business services. AE, D, DC, MC, V. Tube: Canary Wharf.*

££££ **Le Meridien Waldorf.** Close to the Aldwych theaters and Covent Garden, the Waldorf gleams in luscious Edwardiana, with polished marble floors, chandeliers, and cozy, comfortable period bedrooms. This is a booking challenge for the wealthy theatergoer—Waldorf or Savoy?! The Waldorf is in the same category as the Savoy. They are both close to the theaters and offer glamorous, luxurious accommodation. But only the Waldorf has the famous Palm Court tea dances. Still going strong every weekend after nearly 90 years, the tea dances offer high tea. Couples gather on the dance floor to dance to the tunes of the 1930s and 1940s played by a live band. The Palm Court was inspired by the ballroom on that famous luxury ship, the *Titanic,* and even doubled for it in the eponymous Hollywood movie. ✉ *Aldwych, Covent Garden WC2B 4DD,* ☎ *020/7836–2400,* FAX *020/7836–7244,* WEB *www.lemeridien-waldorf.com. 292 rooms. 2 restaurants, 2 bars, room service, in-room safe, cable TV with movies and video games, hair salon, no-smoking rooms. AE, DC, MC, V. Tube: Aldwych.*

££££ **One Aldwych.** If stuffy Victoriana and chintz are not your scene, then One Aldwych's understated blend of contemporary and classic might offer the modern luxe you seek. This flawlessly designed hotel with its coolly eclectic, artsy lobby, feather duvets, Italian linen sheets, and quirky touches—a TV in every bathroom—is the ultimate in twenty-first century style. Poised between the City and the West End (and overlooking a major traffic intersection), the hotel has stylish restaurants and bars, a swimming pool, holistic fitness trainers, and an espresso bar. ✉ *1 Aldwych, Covent Garden WC2 4BZ,* ☎ *020/7300–1000,* FAX *020/7300–1001,* WEB *www.onealdwych.co.uk. 105 rooms. 2 restaurants, 3 bars, in-room safe, in-room data ports, room service, cable TV with movies, indoor swimming pool, spa, massage, sauna, steam rooms, health club, business services, cinema, meeting room, parking (fee), no-smoking floors. AE, MC, V. Tube: Charing Cross or Covent Garden.*

££££ **Radisson Mountbatten.** Naming the hotel after the late Lord Mountbatten, last viceroy of India and favorite uncle of Prince Charles, is probably just an excuse to go overboard with the old British Raj theme. The interior reflects Mountbatten's life: photos of the estate where he lived, Indian furnishings, silks, inlaid tables, and screens. It has a good standard of service; bedrooms in various shades of red, with chintz drapes; and bathrooms of Italian marble. A pianist performs in the comfortable bar, and there are post-theater cabarets at the Ad Lib restaurant twice a week. ✉ *20 Monmouth St., Covent Garden WC2H 9HD,* ☎ *020/7836–4300,* FAX *020/7340–3540,* WEB *www.radissonedwardian.com. 128 rooms. Restaurant, bar, room service, minibars, cable TV, exercise equipment. AE, DC, MC, V. Tube: Covent Garden.*

££££ **Sanderson.** Sister to St. Martins Lane hotel, the Sanderson sits in the revamped box that was the Sanderson fabrics office building. An Ian Schrager hotel, it was the first "urban spa" in London. From the serene Japanese garden to the billowy cloth used to separate the bathrooms from the bedrooms, this hotel is definitely walking to the beat of its own drum (and is slightly whimsical). The lobby furniture is a mix of French Louis XV and industrial, and bedrooms have sleigh beds. Some might find Agua (the "holistic bath house"), the in-room massage and spa services, the special menus and health programs, and the indoor/outdoor fitness classes just what the doctor ordered. Gourmands can try the well-known and popular Spoon restaurant. ✉ *50 Berners St., Soho W1T 3NG,* ☎ *020/7300–1400,* FAX *020/7300–1401,* WEB *www.ianschragerhotels.com. 150 rooms. Restaurant, 2 bars, in-room data ports, cable TV, minibars, room service, in-room VCRs, massage, sauna, gym, dry cleaning, laundry service, concierge, business services, meeting room, parking (fee), no-smoking room. AE, DC, MC, V. Tube: Oxford Circus or Tottenham Court Rd.*

££££ **St. Martins Lane.** Philippe Starck designed Ian Schrager's hip hotel to be theatrical, and he has succeeded. In the foyer are a Victorian chaise lounge, a row of golden molars doubling as tables, some life-size chess pieces, and the odd bowler hat. Expect to play your part (along with the staff) as an actor here—on display as you sit at the ice trough in the fish bar, wield your chopsticks in Asia de Cuba, or lounge on leather armchairs in the brasserie. Guest rooms are small, expensive, cluttered, and homogeneous, but if you're a fan of Schrager's hotels you're likely to be pleased. ✉ *45 St. Martins La., Covent Garden WC2N 4HX,* ☎ *020/7300–5500,* FAX *020/7300–5501. 204 rooms. 2 restaurants, bar, brasserie, in-room data ports, in-room VCRs, cable TV, minibars, no-smoking room, room service, in-room VCRs, massage, sauna, gym, dry cleaning, laundry service, concierge, business services, meeting room, parking (fee), no-smoking floors. AE, MC, V. Tube: Leicester Sq.*

££££ ★ **The Savoy.** This grand hotel hosted Elizabeth Taylor's first honeymoon in one of its famous river-view rooms; and it poured one of Europe's first dry martinis in its equally famous American Bar—haunted by Hemingway, Fitzgerald, Gershwin, et al. Does it measure up to this high profile? Absolutely. The art deco rooms are especially fabulous, but all rooms are impeccably maintained, spacious, elegant, and comfortable. A room facing the Thames costs a fortune and requires an early booking, but it's worth it. Bathrooms have original fittings, with sunflower-size showerheads. ✉ *Strand, Covent Garden WC2R 0EU,* ☎ *020/7836–4343,* FAX *020/7240–6040,* WEB *www.savoy-group.co.uk. 224 rooms. 3 restaurants, 2 bars, in-room data ports, in-room fax, cable TV, in-rooms VCRs, indoor pool, hair salon, health club, theater, meeting rooms, parking (fee), no-smoking rooms. AE, DC, MC, V. Tube: Aldwych.*

££££ **Trafalgar London Hilton.** This fresh, contemporary hotel defies the Hilton's norm. The rooms here, either in sky blue or beige color schemes, keep many of the 19th-century office building's original features—some have floor-to-ceiling windows with expansive views of Trafalgar Square. Twenty-one rooms are split-level with upstairs space for chilling out with a CD or DVD, and sleeping space below. Bathrooms take the cake—they have deep baths, huge sinks, full-size toiletries, eye masks, and mini televisions. Go up to the roof garden for spectacular views of the Houses of Parliament, Westminster Abbey, and the London Eye (the big Ferris wheel on the Thames, built for the Millennium project). ✉ *2 Spring Gardens, Covent Garden SW1A 2TS,* ☎ *020/7870–2900,* FAX *020/7870–2911,* WEB *www.hilton.com. 129 rooms. Restaurant, bar, room service, minibars, in-room safe, in-room data ports, cable TV, meeting rooms. AE, DC, MC, V. Tube: Leicester Sq.*

£££–££££ ★ **Hazlitt's.** This Soho hotel is in three connected, early 18th-century houses, one of which was the last home of essayist William Hazlitt (1778–1830). It's a disarmingly friendly place, full of personality, but devoid of elevators. Robust antiques are everywhere, assorted prints crowd every wall, plants and stone sculptures appear in odd corners, and every room has a Victorian claw-foot tub in its bathroom. There are tiny sitting rooms, wooden staircases, and more restaurants within strolling distance than you could patronize in a year. This is *the* London address of antiques dealers and theater and literary types. ✉ *6 Frith St., Soho W1V*

5TZ, ☎ 020/7434–1771, FAX 020/7439–1524, WEB www.hazlittshotel.com. 23 rooms. Room service, cable TV, in-room VCRs, business services. AE, DC, MC, V. Tube: Piccadilly Circus.

£££–££££ **Radisson Pastoria.** A slightly less exorbitant choice for the theatergoer than the Waldorf and the rest, the Pastoria is just off Leicester Square. The building is about 70 years old, with a suitably modern style; bedrooms are done in limed oak with light pink walls and navy-blue carpets. There's a brasserie-style restaurant to dine in, but Soho, which is restaurant central, is only a few hundred yards away. ✉ *3–6 St. Martin's St., Covent Garden WC2H 7HL, ☎ 020/7930–8641, FAX 020/7925–0551, WEB www.radissonedwardian.com. 58 rooms. Restaurant, bar, coffee shop. AE, DC, MC, V. Tube: Leicester Sq.*

££ **Fielding.** On a quiet pedestrian alley by the world's first police station (now Bow St. Magistrates' Court), this small hotel is popular with people visiting London to take in an opera—the Royal Opera House Covent Garden is just down the street. This is the cheapest place to stay in the area, but for the money you could get more comfort elsewhere. There are no amenities save for the residents' bar and the tea/coffeemakers in each room. ✉ *4 Broad Ct., Bow St., Covent Garden WC2B 5QZ, ☎ 020/7836–8305, FAX 020/7497–0064. 24 rooms. Bar, no smoking. AE, DC, MC, V. Tube: Covent Garden.*

££ **Regent Palace Hotel.** If you're on a tight budget, are not too fussy, and need to be in the thick of it, this is the place for you. There are 920 rooms in this warren just off Piccadilly Circus; some rooms have a toilet and shower. In general, the entire place, including the rooms, is in need of an overhaul. The foyer is reminiscent of a small airport terminal. Nonetheless, service is friendly and efficient, and the concierge can help with theater tickets and tours. ✉ *Glass House St., Soho W1A 4BZ, ☎ 020/8400–8703, FAX 087/0400–8703, WEB www.forte-hotels.co.uk. 920 rooms. Bar, no air-conditioning, concierge. AE, DC, MC, V. Tube: Piccadilly Circus.*

The South Bank

££££ **London Marriott Hotel, County Hall.** This exceptionally grand hotel has what many want—a view of the Houses of Parliament across the Thames (which means, of course, that the hotel is not in Westminster but on the south side of the river). It's in the former home of the long-defunct local governing body—a mammoth, spectacular, pedimented and columned affair—and uses the old Members' entrance, with its bronze doors and marble lobby leading into the former Council Chamber. A Marriott is a reliable thing, and this one has all the expected deluxe accoutrements—from a modern, businesslike style to almost instantly arriving elevators to a fantastic 24-hour health and fitness spa. ✉ *County Hall, The South Bank SE1 7PB, ☎ 020/7928–5200, FAX 020/7928–5300, WEB www.marriotthotels.com. 200 rooms. 2 restaurants, 2 bars, room service, in-room safe, in-room data ports, cable TV with movies, indoor swimming pool, hair salon, health club. AE, DC, MC, V. Tube: Westminster.*

£££ **London Bridge Hotel.** Just steps away from the London Bridge rail and tube station, this thoroughly modern and stylish hotel is popular with business travelers. Most of the South Bank's attractions are within walking distance. Each sleek room, decorated in understated, contemporary style, has a trouser press, tea/coffeemaker, and minibar. Three spacious two-bedroom apartments in the ££££ range come complete with kitchen, living room, and dining room. Room service is around-the-clock. Foodies will definitely want to stop in at the delightful Borough Market on Fridays and Saturdays, just across the street, for a snack. ✉ *8–18 London Bridge St., The South Bank SE1 9SG, ☎ 020/7855–*

2200, FAX *020/7855–2233,* WEB *www.london-bridge-hotel.co.uk. 138 rooms. Restaurant, bar, cable TV, in-room data ports, in-room safe, gym, meeting rooms. AE, DC, MC, V. Tube: London Bridge.*

£ **London County Hall Travel Inn Capital.** Don't get too excited—this neighbor of the fancy Marriott lacks the river view (it's at the back of the grand former seat of local government). Still, you get an incredible value, with the standard facilities of the cookie-cutter rooms of this chain: TV, tea/coffeemaker, en suite bath/shower and—best of all for families on a budget—fold-out beds that let you accommodate two kids at no extra charge. *That's* a bargain. ✉ *Belvedere Rd., The South Bank SE1 7PB,* ☎ *087/0238–3300 (central reservation line),* FAX *020/7902–1619,* WEB *www.travelinn.co.uk. 312 rooms. Restaurant, bar, in-room data ports, no-smoking rooms. AE, DC, MC, V. Tube: Westminster.*

£ **London Tower Bridge Travel Inn Capital.** The name may not be snappy, but the price certainly is—it's practically unbeatable, especially for families. Not exactly central, the hotel is based in the Tower Hill area, which has good tube connections. Despite having been around for centuries, this is now one of London's trendy neighborhoods; it's popular with artists because of the area's warehouse space. ✉ *Tower Bridge Rd., The South Bank SE1 3LP,* ☎ *087/0238–3303 or 020/7940–3700,* FAX *020/7940–3719,* WEB *www.travelinn.co.uk. 196 rooms. Restaurant, bar, no-smoking rooms, parking (fee). AE, MC, V. Tube: Tower Bridge.*

Bed-and-Breakfast and Apartment Agencies

££ **Bulldog Club.** It promises luxe, chic, and delightful accommodations. In days of yore, you actually got to book rooms in some of London's poshest houses, where grown-up children's rooms were converted for guests. A three-year membership is around £25, with most properties available for around £100 a night. A full British breakfast, as well as other goodies, are often provided. Accommodations are generally available in Knightsbridge, Kensington, and Chelsea. ✉ *14 Dewhurst Rd., Kensington W14 0ET,* ☎ *020/7371–3202,* FAX *020/7371–2015,* WEB *www.bulldogclub.com. AE, MC, V.*

££ **Uptown Reservations.** As the name implies, this B&B booking service accepts only the more upscale addresses, and specializes in finding hosted homes or short-term apartments for Americans, often executives of small corporations. Nearly all the 85 homes on its register are in Knightsbridge, Belgravia, Kensington, and Chelsea, with a few farther west in Holland Park or to the north in Hampstead. The private homes vary, of course, but all are good-looking and have private bathrooms, plus a full Continental breakfast. ✉ *41 Paradise Walk, Chelsea SW3 4JL,* ☎ *020/7351–3445,* FAX *020/7351–9383,* WEB *www.uptownres.co.uk. Facilities vary. Payment by bank transfer or U.S. check or credit card; 20% deposit required. AE, MC, V.*

£–££ **At Home in London.** More than 70 private homes in central London locations, including Knightsbridge, Kensington, Mayfair, Chelsea, and West London are on their books. They're closed on weekends, so make sure to phone between 9:30 and 5:30 on a weekday. Breakfast is included in the rate. ✉ *70 Black Lion Ln., Hammersmith W6 9BE,* ☎ *020/8748–1943,* WEB *www.athomeinlondon.co.uk. MC, V.*

£–££ **Coach House London Vacation Rentals.** Stay in the properties of Londoners who are temporarily away. Apartments and houses are primarily in Notting Hill, Kensington, and Chelsea. The extra touches—airport pickup, complimentary breakfast provisions, and a welcome drink with a representative—make this service personal. Homes also come with a mini guide and a phone number to call for help in planning your stay. ✉ *2 Tunley Rd., Balham SW17 7QJ,* ☎ *020/8772–1939,* WEB *www.vacrent.cwc.net. MC, V.*

£–££ **London B&B.** This long-established family-run agency has some truly spectacular—and some more modest—London homes in practically all neighborhoods of the city. Check many of them out via its Web site before making a commitment. The staff here is most personable and helpful. ✉ *437 J St., Suite 210, San Diego, CA 92101,* ☎ *800/872–2632,* WEB *www.londonbandb.com. 30% deposit required.*

£ **Host & Guest Service.** A huge selection of B&Bs in London as well as the rest of the United Kingdom. The service has been in business for forty years. They also book stays on farms in rural Britain as well as conducting tourist services such as bus tours. ✉ *103 Dawes Rd., Chelsea SW6 7DU,* ☎ *020/7385–9922,* WEB *www.host-guest.co.uk. MC, V.*

£ **Primrose Hill B&B.** This is a small, friendly bed-and-breakfast agency genuinely "committed to the idea that traveling shouldn't be a rip-off." Expatriate American Gail O'Farrell has family homes (to which you get your own latchkey) in or near villagey Hampstead, and all are comfortable or more than comfortable. So far this has been one of those word-of-mouth secrets, but now that everyone knows, book well ahead. ✉ *14 Edis St., Regent's Park NW1 8LG,* ☎ *020/7722–6869. No credit cards.*

5 NIGHTLIFE AND THE ARTS

"Ladies and gentlemen, the curtain is about to rise" on London's artful pleasures: Damien Hirst at the Saatchi Gallery, Sylvie Guillem at the Royal Ballet, Domingo at the Royal Albert Hall, and the best theater in the world—perhaps Ralph Fiennes and Vanessa Redgrave doing star turns, a West End revival of *Chicago,* and unparalleled servings of Shakespeare. You can see, say, *The Winter's Tale* at the reconstructed Globe Theatre, where the interaction between player and audience often goes beyond polite applause. Finish off the night at a club sizzling with comedy, cabaret, or all that jazz.

Updated by Heather Elton

AFTER DARK, LONDON is a wonderful place to play. Shakespearean theater and Handel oratorios, the roof-rattling Proms concerts, Andrew Lloyd Webber–ish extravaganzas, magnificent opera and contemporary dance theater, opulent Russian vodka bars, and the latest UK garage dance music—if you're into the arts or the glamorous late-night scene, London will definitely fill your fancy.

Tony Blair's popular ad campaign Cool Britannia rule has encouraged a bit of a renaissance—shiny new buildings and renovated homes have given the performing arts and cultural groups many new homes. The Royal Ballet now has a permanent home inside the world-renowned Royal Opera House. The Donmar, Almeida, and Royal Court have all been renovated to reveal their stripped-down, intimate structures. And there are new studios and a renovated theater for contemporary dance at The Place. But the biggest story is south of the river. Architects Herzog and de Meuron's magnificent transformation of the Bankside Power Station into the Tate Modern has finally given London a flagship contemporary art gallery to rival other major cities. In 2003, London's vibrant cultural scene is in a better position that ever to play on the world stage.

NIGHTLIFE

London is the party capital of Europe. Despite the draconian liquor laws and the inconvenience that the tubes stop running around midnight, Londoners still go out every night. The restrictions to late-night drinking have relaxed in the past few years, however, and will likely become even more liberal in the future. Today, there is a staggering variety of places with late licenses where you can party after 11 PM when the fuzzy, friendly neighborhood pubs close their doors.

Not everyone likes a loud, smoky bar. Thankfully, nightlife in London is diverse enough that whatever your pleasure, there's always somewhere to go. If you prefer a romantic evening at the opera, wine-soaked experimental jazz, Camden's rough indie guitar sounds, raucous laughter in a comedy club, or a few cocktails in a sexy bar where the clientele look like they've walked off the catwalk, our listings provide a sampling of the best the capital has to offer. The gay listing is small but gives you all you need to find the thriving scene.

In one night, you can circle the West End (or some trendy district like Hoxton), drop into half a dozen bars and in each one find a completely unique world. There's everything from Moulin-rouge style lounge clubs, industrial microbreweries, velvet dripping drum 'n' bass clubs, to lavish Asian-themed cocktail bars. Bars go in and out of fashion with incredible speed here. Minimalist chic design was the rage last year, but has been replaced with the "extravagance" and "opulence" of traditional Asian design. The phenomenon of Absinthe, which has always intrigued drinkers by its 70%–200% proof mystique and ritual pouring, has now been eclipsed by the Russian decadence of vodka bars which offer flavor-infused varieties, everything from chocolate to chicken tikka.

If you want to savor the high life with the glitterati, you have to pay for the privilege of glamor. The price of a Bellini (with Dom Perignon, of course) in an ultra swank hotel bar will put you back £20. But then, that's London's West End. In trendier-than-thou East London, drinks aren't so expensive. Communities like Clerkenwell, Hoxton, and Shoreditch are hubs for artists, indie musicians, and fashion and media types. The raw culture of racially diverse Brixton, with its heady mix of art, poetry, and music on Coldharbour Lane, is like Harlem in the 1920s, while Leicester Square can be a bit Disney-fied like Times Square in New York.

Once 2 AM arrives, much of the bar scene has moved on to the clubs, where you can dance until 9 AM. Whether you're into twisted disco, deep house, jazzy breaks, or hip-hop, the multi-dance-floor clubs will have a room to suit your musical tastes, and whoever is behind the decks will be delivering the most cutting-edge sounds on the planet. The talent pool here is enormous; chances are whatever you're looking for you'll see it here first.

Bars

London bar culture is known for its innovative elixirs, its stylishness, and its fashionable people. Bars used to be the place to go post-pub or pre-club, but with the emergence of the "club bar," —which is essentially a swank bar with a more social sensibility than a club, DJs spinning cutting-edge sounds, and a late license that caters to a clubbing clientele—the boundaries between club and bar are fading, and many people stay until it's over. You can choose from expensive hotel bars (from the ultra chic postmodern kind to the stately Victorian), Cuban cigar lounges, swank vodka bars in the West End, industrial microbreweries, pool halls, and "chilled" hang-outs in trendier-than-thou Hoxton, or style clubs in Brixton.

American Bar. Festooned with a chin-dropping array of club ties, signed celebrity photographs, sporting mementos, and baseball caps, this sensational bar has won such accolades as "Best Martini in the World" and "Second Best Cocktail Bar in the World." ✉ *Stafford Hotel, 16–18 St. James's Pl., St. James's SW1A,* ☎ *020/7493–0111.* ⌚ *Weekdays 11:30 AM–midnight, Sat. 11:30 AM–3 PM and 5:30–midnight, Sun. noon–2:30 PM and 6:30–10:30. Tube: Green Park.*

Atlantic Bar. A huge marble staircase spirals dramatically into the glamorous art deco Atlantic Bar. The original furnishings are intact and the impeccable service, fantastic cocktails, and Oliver Peyton's excellent restaurant keep pulling in the crowds. ✉ *20 Glasshouse St., Soho W1,* ☎ *020/7734–4888.* ⌚ *Mon.–Fri. noon–3 AM, Sat. 5 PM–3 AM. Closed Sun. Tube: Piccadilly Circus.*

Beach Blanket Babylon. In Notting Hill, close to Portobello Market, this always-packed bar is distinguishable by its eclectic interior of indoor/outdoor spaces filled with Gaudi-esque curves and snuggly corners—like a fairy-tale grotto or a medieval dungeon, visited by the gargoyles of Notre-Dame. ✉ *45 Ledbury Rd., Notting Hill W11,* ☎ *020/7229–2907.* ⌚ *Daily noon–11 PM. Tube: Notting Hill Gate.*

Bug Bar. Inside the crypt of a church, this intimate vaulted bar with Gothic overtones is attached to the tasty Bar Humbug restaurant and the trendy dance club Mass. Brixton hipsters shake it up to quality DJing, and knock back "Bugtai" shooters at the bar. ✉ *Brixton Hill (under St. Matthew's Church), Brixton SW2,* ☎ *020/7738–3184.* ⌚ *Wed., Thurs., and Sun. 7 PM–2 AM, Fri. and Sat. 7 PM–3 AM. Tube: Brixton.*

Cadogan Hotel Bar. Once you've done Harrods, Harvey Nichols, Gucci, Chanel, and Armani, stop by this elegant hotel for afternoon tea, or a cocktail, in the bar that exudes comfort and surroundings still characteristic of the late Victorian age when it was built. Oscar Wilde was arrested in room 118. ✉ *Cadogan Hotel, 75 Sloane St., Knightsbridge SW1,* ☎ *020/7235–7141.* ⌚ *Daily 11–11. Tube: Sloane Sq.*

Cafe des Amis du Vin. This relaxed brasserie/wine bar near the Royal Opera House is the perfect pre- or post-theater spot—and a place you can go on your own. More than 30 wines are served by the glass. Opera buffs will enjoy the performance and production prints on the walls. ✉ *11–14 Hanover Pl., Covent Garden WC2,* ☎ *020/7379–3444.* ⏲ *Mon.–Sat. 11:30–11:30 PM. Tube: Covent Garden.*

Che. It's in a stylish former bank building with high ceilings, suede walls, leather banquettes, and a rare collection of Che Guevara portraits. The colorful backlit bar has the largest range of spirits in Europe. Cuba's finest are available in the subdued cigar lounge. ✉ *23 St. James's St., St. James's SW1,* ☎ *020/777–9380.* ⏲ *Mon.–Sat. 11 AM–11 PM. Tube: Green Park.*

Detroit. The subterranean bar is a bit like a sand dune, or a Moroccan cave, with mud-colored walls lit in luminous green, blue, and orange. Burrow into your own little nook, sip a Detropolitan, or one of 70 cocktails, including the more daring "overproofs." ✉ *35 Earlham St., Covent Garden WC2,* ☎ *020/7240–2662.* ⏲ *Mon.–Sat. noon–11, Sun. noon–10:30 PM. Tube: Covent Garden.*

Dogstar. The Brixton riots happened out front of this popular South London hangout frequented by local hipsters and counter-culture types. The vibe is unpretentious and gritty. Visual projections light up the interior and top-name DJs play cutting-edge sounds for free on weekdays. Follow on to the nearby dance club, Mass, and your sampling of local Brixton life will be complete. ✉ *389 Coldharbour La., Brixton SW9,* ☎ *020/7733–7515.* 🎟 *Free–£6.* ⏲ *Mon.–Thurs. noon–3 AM, Fri.–Sat. noon–4 AM. Tube: Brixton.*

Freedom Brewing Company. Watch the brewing process in this American-style microbrewery while sampling the five signature beers, including Freedom Organic lager, and some tasty bar snacks. Inside, it's minimalist with blonde wood tables and chairs and a large steel bar with pink neon. Media workers, trendy shoppers, and tourists pack it out. ✉ *41 Earlham St., Covent Garden WC2,* ☎ *020/7240–0606.* ⏲ *Mon.–Sat. noon–11, Sun. noon–10:30 PM. Tube: Covent Garden.*

Hoxton Square Bar & Kitchen. The rectangular concrete bar, reminiscent of a Swedish airport hanger, has long, comfortable sofas, a plate-glass window at the back, and tables overlooking leafy Hoxton Square. The vibe is less pretentious than neighboring bars, and creative types keep it packed. ✉ *2–4 Hoxton Sq., Hoxton E1,* ☎ *020/7613–0709.* ⏲ *Mon.–Sat. 11 AM–midnight, Sun. 11 AM–10:30 PM. Tube: Old Street.*

Library Bar. In this exquisite bar at the luxurious Lanesborough Hotel, bar manager Salvatore Calabrese offers a remarkable collection of vintage cognacs, some of which are more than 200 years old. A shot of liquid history can set you back £700. Enjoy the luxe surroundings and don't ask for a brandy Alexander. ✉ *1 Lanesborough Pl., Hyde Park Corner, Knightsbridge SW1,* ☎ *020/7259–5599.* ⏲ *Mon.–Sat. 11–11, Sun. noon–10:30. Tube: Hyde Park Corner.*

The Pool. The glass-fronted industrial-style bar attracts a hip beer-swilling crowd who play pool on three full-size tables, dance to some of London's most famous DJs, and chill out in the bean bag chairs. There is a modest menu and daily specials. ✉ *104 Curtain Rd., East End EC2,* ☎ *020/7739–9608.* ⏲ *Mon.–Tues. noon–11 PM, Wed.–Thurs. noon–1 AM, Fri.–Sat. noon–2 AM, Sun. noon–10:30 PM. Tube: Old Street.*

Opium. Fashionable young things sip exotic cocktails amidst the trappings of the Orient. Amber-colored light, delicate wooden carvings, and small alcoves dripping in velvet and gold take you back to French Colonial Vietnam. The cocktails are impressive and pricey, as is the nouvelle Vietnamese cuisine. ✉ *1 Dean St, Soho W1,* ☎ *020/7287–9608.* ⏲ *Mon.-Sat. 5 PM–3 AM. Tube: Tottenham Court Rd.*

Revolution. A smart vodka bar with obscure premium vodkas from Russia, Poland, and Finland, plus over 100 ways to enjoy the clear elixir.

Try it blended with melted chocolate, ice cold from the freezer, stirred in a martini, or in a three-pint pitcher for sharing with friends. ✉ *2 St. Anne's Court, Soho W1,* ☎ *020/7434–0330.* ⏲ *Weekdays 8:30* AM–*11* PM, *Sat. 8:30* AM–*midnight, Sun. 8:30* AM–*11* PM. *Tube: Tottenham Court Rd.*

Smiths of Smithfield. This loft-style megabar with exposed wood beams, steel columns, and huge windows overlooks the Victorian Smithfield's market. Have a beer in the airy ground-floor pub, a cocktail in the intimate champagne cocktail bar, or some fine British Modern cuisine in the restaurants. The 7 AM opening hour captures the fall-out from nearby superclub Fabric. ✉ *67–77 Charterhouse St., East End EC1,* ☎ *020/7236–6666.* ⏲ *Mon.–Sat. 7* AM–*midnight, Sun. 11* AM–*11* PM. *Tube: Farringdon.*

Comedy & Cabaret

Backyard Comedy Club. Owned by comic and TV performer Lee Hurst (who is the regular MC here), this 400-seat club in the East End hosts a strong line-up of stand-ups until 11:30 PM. There's a DJ and bar service until 2 AM. ✉ *231 Cambridge Heath Rd., East End E2,* ☎ *020/7739–3122.* ⏲ *Fri. and Sat. 8:30* PM–*2* AM. 🎟 *£11. Tube: Bethnal Green.*

Banana Cabaret. This pub is one of London's finest comedy venues. Well worth the trek, it's only a hundred yards from Balham station and there's a minicab office close by for those tempted to make a long night of it. ✉ *Bedford Pub, 77 Bedford Hill, Balham SW12,* ☎ *020/8673–8904.* 🎟 *£10.* ⏲ *Fri. and Sat. 7* PM–*2* AM. *Tube: Balham.*

Canal Café Theatre. You'll find famous comics and cabaret performers every night of the week in this intimate, picturesque canalside venue. NewsRevue, now in its 21st year, is a topical song and sketch show—it provides a witty take on current affairs. ✉ *Bridge House, Delamere Terr., Maida Vale W2,* ☎ *020/7289–6054.* 🎟 *£5–£10.* ⏲ *Mon.–Sat. 7:30* PM–*11* PM, *Sun. 7* PM–*10:30* PM. *Tube: Warwick Ave.*

Comedy Café. In addition to lots of stand-up comedy, this popular dive in trendy Hoxton has an open mike on Wednesdays and late-night disco on weekends. Tex-Mex cuisine is available and there's a late license. ✉ *66 Rivington St., Hoxton EC2,* ☎ *020/7739–5706.* 🎟 *Free–£12.* ⏲ *Wed.–Thurs. 7* PM–*midnight, Fri.–Sat. 7* PM–*1* AM. *Tube: Old St.*

Comedy Store. It's known as the birthplace of alternative comedy. The UK's funniest stand-ups have cut their teeth here before being launched onto prime-time TV. Comedy Store Players entertain audiences on Wednesdays and Sundays. The Cutting Edge team steps in every Tuesday; and weekends have up-and-coming comedians performing on the same stage as established talent. ✉ *1A Oxendon St., Soho SW1,* ☎ *020/7344–4444 or 020/7344–0234.* 🎟 *£12–£15.* ⏲ *Shows Tues.–Thurs. and Sun. 8* PM–*10:15* PM, *Fri. and Sat. 8* PM–*10:15* PM *and midnight–2:30* AM. *Tube: Piccadilly Circus or Leicester Sq.*

Jongleurs Camden Lock. Jongleurs was the first chain of comedy clubs in the country and this flagship venue, housed in an old stable in the Camden Lock, is popular because of its late-night bar and disco. The billing, sometimes featuring North American comics, is strong but not quite as tasty as at the Comedy Store. ✉ *Dingwalls Building, 36 Camden Lock Pl., Camden Market, Chalk Farm Rd., Camden Town NW1,* ☎ *0870/787–0707.* ⏲ *Fri. 7:15* PM–*2* AM, *Sat. 7:15* PM–*9:45* PM *and 11:30* PM–*3* AM. 🎟 *£12–£15. Tube: Camden Town.*

Casinos

The 1968 Gaming Act states that any person wishing to gamble must make a declaration of intent to gamble at the gaming house in question and must apply for membership in person. Membership takes 24 hours to process. Some clubs prefer that a member sponsor you as an applicant. Personal guests of existing members are always allowed in.

Crockford's. Established more than 150 years ago, this civilized club has none of the jostling for tables that mars many of the flashier clubs. It attracts a large international clientele and offers American roulette, Punto Banco, and blackjack. ✉ *30 Curzon St., Mayfair W1,* ☎ *020/7493–7771.* 🎫 *Membership £325 yearly.* ⏲ *Daily noon–6 AM. Jacket required. Tube: Green Park.*

50 St. James. Built in 1828, this magnificent London club in the Regency Baroque style combines opulent decor with an intimate environment. Done in crimson, gold, and white, with a grand staircase, domed ceiling, salles prives (private rooms), and art deco restaurant, reminiscent of ocean liners, it's the epitome of elegance. Average wager £5,000. ✉ *50 St. James's St., St. James's SW1,* ☎ *020/7629–7704.* 🎫 *Membership charge of £500 (complimentary off-peak membership is available).* ⏲ *Daily 2 PM–4 AM. Jacket required. Tube: Green Park.*

Golden Nugget. This large and friendly casino just off Piccadilly has a fast-moving, exciting pace. It has blackjack, roulette, Punto Banco, slot machines, and new gaming technology. ✉ *22–32 Shaftesbury Ave., Soho W1,* ☎ *020/7439–0099.* 🎫 *Life membership £10; free membership via the Internet.* ⏲ *Daily 2 PM–4 AM. Jacket required. Tube: Piccadilly Circus.*

Palm Beach Casino. An elegant club with palm trees, chandeliers, and deco styling—it used to be the famous ballroom of the Mayfair Hotel. A cosmopolitan crowd chooses from American roulette, blackjack, casino stub poker, slot machines, and Punto Banco. Average wager is £600. ✉ *30 Berkeley St., Mayfair W1,* ☎ *020/7493–6585.* 🎫 *Life membership £25; free membership via the Internet.* ⏲ *Daily 2 PM–4 AM. Smart casual with jacket after 7:30 PM. Tube: Green Park.*

Dance Clubs

If you are looking for the latest craze in dance music, you've come to the right place. Britain pioneered rave culture, and for the past decade, London DJs and club owners have been the style-makers of cool. As one of the most ethnically diverse cities in the world, Londoners "mix up" their music to create a fusion of sounds that has revolutionized dance. DJs are the gods of the dance world with a devoted following of punters who flock from club to club to dance to UK garage, drum 'n' bass, hip-hop, deep house, Latin house, Japanese bible, London Zok, Oriental eclectica, and the latest decknology. Clubs, like **Ministry of Sound** and **Fabric,** are housed in multi-level buildings with numerous dance floors, bars, and chill-out rooms—and devastatingly loud state-of-the-art sound systems—accommodate hundreds. But, Londoners maintain that the most cutting-edge sounds are heard in more intimate clubs, like **333** and **The Edge,** or the style bars like **Dogstar** in Brixton, where DJs play for free on week nights.

The club scene is in constant flux, especially the "club nights" that take place at particular clubs on the same night every week, or which shift locations, so keep an eye out for music fliers in the various style bars, or check the daily listings in *Time Out.*

Bagley's Studio. A film studio by day, this massive warehouse is reminiscent of the old raves. A diverse crowd dances to everything from uplifting anthems and UK garage to hard house, Nu-Latin, and Nu-Disco. After surfacing at King's Cross, walk north on York Way, and turn left on Goods Way. ✉ *Goods Yard, Euston N1,* ☎ *020/7278–2777.* 🎫 *£15–£20.* ⏲ *Sat. 10:30 PM–7 AM, with other raves usually scheduled Thurs. and Fri. Tube: King's Cross.*

Bar Rumba. Though nothing special to look at, this smallish West End venue has a reputation for good fun. The staff is friendly and the club is almost always heaving with serious clubbers grooving to different styles of music each night. Stop by weekdays for cheap cocktails during happy hour. ✉ *36 Shaftesbury Ave., Soho W1,* ☎ *020/7287–2715.* 🎫 *£3–£12.* ⏲ *Mon.–Fri. 6 PM–3 AM, Sat. 8 PM–3 AM, Sun. 8 PM–1:30 AM. Tube: Piccadilly Circus.*

Café de Paris. Open since 1924 and known as the "Bower of Love," this is one of London's most glamour-puss settings. Once a haunt of royals and consorts, the boîte brought in such stars as Noel Coward, Marlene Dietrich, Fred Astaire, and Frank Sinatra. These days, it pays host to the A-list—Kate Moss, Puff Daddy, and Madonna. ✉ *3–4 Coventry St., Soho W1V 7FL,* ☎ *020/7734–7700,* FAX *020/7434–0347.* 🎫 *£10–£15.* ⏲ *Weekdays 5 PM–4 AM. Tube: Piccadilly Circus.*

Camden Palace. Popular with the New Romantics post-punk music style (from Manchester's legendary Hacienda Club) in the 1980s, this Victorian theater with original plasterwork, and five levels of balconies, is one of London's most stunning venues. Excellent lights and the sounds of UK garage, live indie-rock, and hard house keeps the big dance floor heaving. ✉ *1A Camden High St., Camden Town NW1,* ☎ *090/6210–0200.* 🎫 *£5–£20.* ⏲ *Tues.–Thurs. 10 PM–2:30 AM, Fri.–Sat. 10 PM–6 AM. Tube: Mornington Crescent or Camden Town.*

Elbow Room. This innovative club designed in 60s pool hall chic has 11 tables, leather-booth seating, and a neon-lit bar. One of the best deals is the Sunday Jam when indie guitar bands play for free and owner, NY Electro pioneer Arthur Baker, spends time on the decks. ✉ *89–91 Chapel Market, Islington N1,* ☎ *020/7278–3244.* 🎫 *Free–£5.* ⏲ *Mon. 6 PM–1 AM, Tues.–Thurs. noon–2 AM, Fri.–Sat. noon–3 AM, Sun. noon–11 PM. Tube: Angel.*

The End. Owned by Mr. C (ex-Shamen MC), this intimate club was designed by clubbers for clubbers. Top-name DJs, state-of-the-art sound system, and minimalist steel and glass decor—clubbing doesn't get much better than this. Next door, the AKA Bar (owned by same) is a stylish split-level Manhattan-esque cocktail bar with excellent food and a cinema screen. ✉ *16A West Central St., Holborn WC1,* ☎ *020/7419–9199.* 🎫 *£5–£15.* ⏲ *Mon., Wed.–Thurs. 9 PM–3:30 AM, Fri. and Sat. 10 PM–6 AM. Tube: Tottenham Court Rd.*

Fabric. This sprawling subterranean club was *the* place to be the past few years. *Fabric Live* hosts hip-hop crews and live acts on Fridays, while international big-name DJs play slow sexy bass lines and cutting-edge music on Saturdays. The devastating sound system and bodysonic dance floor ensure that bass riffs vibrate through your entire body. Get there early to avoid a lengthy queue, and don't wear a suit. ✉ *77A Charterhouse St., East End EC1,* ☎ *020/7336–8898.* 🎫 *£12–£15.* ⏲ *Fri. and Sun. 10 PM–5 AM, Sat. 10 PM–7 AM. Tube: Farringdon.*

Hanover Grand. This former Masonic Hall is now an extravagant and opulent West End club, popular with the glamourous, glitzy crowd. There is a £100,000 light and sound show and a large dance floor. Glam disco and chart-bound house 'n' garage nights attract long lines, so dress up to impress the bouncers. ✉ *6 Hanover St., Oxford Circus W1,* ☎ *020/7499–7977.* 🎫 *£5–£15.* ⏲ *Wed. 10:30 PM–3:30 AM, Thurs.–Fri. 10:30 PM–4 AM, Sat. 10:30 PM–5 AM. Tube: Oxford Circus.*

Mass. In what was previously St. Matthew's Church, but is now an atmospheric club with Gothic overtones, winding stone steps lead to the main room where an extended balcony hangs over the dance floor. An unpretentious and friendly crowd dances, on rotating club nights, to hip-hop grooves and jazzy beats. ✉ *Brixton Hill, St. Matthew's Church, Brixton SW2,* ☎ *020/7733–7515 ext. 22.* 🎫 *£8–£20.* ⏲ *Fri. and Sat., 10 PM–6 AM. Tube: Brixton.*

Ministry of Sound. It's more of an industry than a club, with its own record label, on-line radio station, a magazine, and international DJs. The stripped down warehouse-style club has a super sound system and pulls in the world's most legendary names in dance. There are chill-out rooms, two bars, and three dance floors. ✉ *103 Gaunt St., The South Bank SE1,* ☎ *020/7378–6528.* 🎫 *£10–£15.* ⏲ *Fri. 10:30 PM–6 AM, Sat. 11:30–8 AM. Tube: Elephant and Castle.*

Notting Hill Arts Club. Rock stars like Liam Gallagher and Courtney Love have been seen at this small basement club-bar. An alternative crowd swills beer to an eclectic music policy that spans Asian underground, Latin-inspired funk, deep house, and jazzy grooves. What it lacks in looks it makes up for in mood. ✉ *21 Notting Hill Gate, Notting Hill W11,* ☎ *020/7460–4459.* 🎫 *£3–£5.* ⏲ *Mon.–Wed. 6 PM–1 AM, Sat. 6 PM–2 AM, Sun. 4 PM–1 AM. Tube: Notting Hill Gate.*

Sound. One of the best ways to experience this high-tech, futuristic, but cramped West End palace is Trevor Nelson (R 'n 'Bs biggest name in Europe) and the eighties disco music of Loveshank. There are gay nights on Sundays. The Pepsi chart show is filmed here and you can be part of the audience. ✉ *Swiss Center, Leicester Sq., Soho WC2,* ☎ *020/7287–1010.* 🎫 *Free– £12.* ⏲ *Sun.–Thurs 5 PM–3 AM, Fri.–Sat. 5 PM–4 AM. Tube: Leicester Sq.*

333. *The* last word in new dance music for the trendier-than-thou Shoreditch crowd. Fashionable bright young things dance to drum and bass, twisted disco, and underground dance genres. There are three floors. You can chill upstairs, on leather sofas, at the relaxed Mother Bar. ✉ *333 Old St., East End EC1,* ☎ *020/7739–5949.* 🎫 *£5–£10.* ⏲ *Fri.–Sat. 10 PM–5 AM, Sun. 10 PM–4 AM. Tube: Old Street.*

Eclectic Music

The Borderline. This important small venue has a solid reputation for booking everything from metal to country and beyond. Oasis, Pearl Jam, Blur, Sheryl Crow, PJ Harvey, Ben Harper, Jeff Buckley, and Counting Crows have all played live here. ✉ *Orange Yard off Manette St., Soho W1,* ☎ *020/7395–0777.* 🎫 *£6–£15.* ⏲ *Mon.–Sat. 8 PM–11 PM. Tube: Tottenham Court Rd.*

Brixton Academy. This legendary Brixton venue has seen it all—mods and rockers, hippies and punks. Despite a capacity of 4,000 people, this refurbished Victorian hall with original art deco fixtures retains a club-like charm; it has plenty of bars, and upstairs seating. ✉ *211 Stockwell Rd., Brixton SW9,* ☎ *020/7771–2000.* 🎫 *£10–£20. Tube: Brixton.*

Dingwalls. This mid-size venue in the Camden Lock warehouses caters to the full spectrum of musical tastes—country, jazz, blues, folk, indie, and world beat. (Note that on Fridays and Saturdays it becomes a comedy club, Jongleurs.) ✉ *Camden Lock off Camden High St., Camden Town NW1,* ☎ *020/7267–1577.* 🎫 *£7–£20.* ⏲ *Sun.–Thurs. 7:30 PM–midnight. Tube: Camden Town.*

Ocean. Bhangra to blues, classical to country, rock to reggae. This state-of-the-art building sports three venues and bars, an atrium, and a café-bar. On Decks Territory night there are three rooms of resident DJs on Saturdays. ✉ *270 Mare St., East End E8,* ☎ *020/8533–0111 or 020/8533–0111.* 🎫 *£6–£25. British Rail: Hackney Central.*

Shepherd's Bush Empire. Once a grand old theater and former BBC TV studio, this intimate venue with fine balcony views now hosts a great cross-section of mid-league UK and US bands. ✉ *Shepherd's Bush Green, Shepherd's Bush W12,* ☎ *020/7771–2000.* 🎫 *£12–£15. Tube: Shepherd's Bush.*

Spitz. In charming Spitalfields Market, where the City interfaces with the East End, this two-level venue has eclectic music that includes world-beat, folk, Americana, and electronic sounds. The downstairs bar and bistro has DJs and live jazz for free on Fridays. ✉ *109 Commercial St., East End E1,* ☎ *020/7392–9032.* 🎟 *£4–£8.* ⏲ *Mon.–Sat. 11 AM–11 PM; Sun. 11 AM–10 PM. Tube: Liverpool St.*

12 Bar Club. This rough-and-ready acoustic club hosts notable singer-songwriters. Four different acts of new folk and contemporary country perform each night in this intimate venue. They serve a good selection of bottled beer and gastro-pub food. ✉ *22–23 Denmark St., West End WC2,* ☎ *020/7916–6989.* 🎟 *£5–£10.* ⏲ *Daily 8 PM–1 AM. Cafe opens at noon. Tube: Tottenham Court Rd.*

Union Chapel. This beautiful old chapel has excellent acoustics and sublime architecture. The world fusion music program has hosted performances by Bjork, Talvin Singh, Trilock Gurtu, and Beth Orton. ✉ *Compton Ave., Islington N1,* ☎ *020/7226–1686 or 0870 1201349.* 🎟 *Free–£15. Tube: Highbury and Islington*

Jazz and Blues

Expect a highly individual scene of British-based musicians supplemented by top name visiting artists. The city hosts two major festivals: the *Soho Jazz Festival* (October) is traditional jazz and Dixieland, and the *London Jazz Festival* (November) promotes experimental jazz and top world-beat names. These festivals are held at venues throughout the capital.

Ain't Nothin' but Blues. The name sums up this bar that whips up a sweaty and smoky environment. Local musicians, as well as some notable names, squeeze onto the tiny stage. There's good bar food of the chili-and-gumbo variety. Most weekday nights there is no cover. ✉ *20 Kingly St., Soho W1,* ☎ *020/7287–0514.* 🎟 *Free–£6.* ⏲ *Mon.–Wed. 6 PM–1 AM, Thurs. 6 PM–2 AM, Fri.–Sat. 6 PM–3 AM, Sun. 7:30 PM–midnight. Tube: Oxford Circus.*

Bull's Head. Its pleasant location, right on the River Thames, and the big-name musicians who jam here regularly, make the excursion to Bull's Head worthwhile. It's open normal pub hours, and shows start nightly at 8:30 PM. ✉ *373 Lonsdale Rd., Barnes Bridge, Barnes SW13,* ☎ *020/8876–5241.* 🎟 *£4–£10. Tube: Hammersmith, then Bus 209 to Barnes Bridge.*

Jazz Café. A palace of high-tech cool in bohemian Camden—it remains an essential hangout for fans of both the mainstream end of the repertoire and hip-hop, funk, rap, and Latin fusion. Book ahead if you want a prime table overlooking the stage, in the balcony restaurant. ✉ *5 Parkway, Camden Town NW1,* ☎ *020/7916–6060 or 020/7344–0044.* 🎟 *£6–£20.* ⏲ *Mon.–Thurs. 7 PM–1 AM, Fri.–Sat. 7 PM–2 AM, Sun. 7 PM–midnight. Tube: Camden Town.*

100 Club. Since it opened in 1942, all the greats have played here, from Glen Miller and Louis Armstrong, on down to the best traditional jazz artists, British and American Blues, R&B, and punk. Little has changed in this cool, inexpensive club. You can still take jitterbug and jive lessons from the London Swing Dance Society. ✉ *100 Oxford St., Soho W1,* ☎ *020/7636–0933.* 🎟 *£6–£10.* ⏲ *Mon.–Thurs. 7:30–midnight, Fri.–Sat. 7:30 PM–2 AM, Sun. 7:30 PM–11:30 PM. Tube: Oxford Circus or Tottenham Court Rd.*

Pizza Express. The capital's best-loved pizza chain is also a principal jazz club. The darkly lit venue hosts top-quality international jazz acts every night except Mondays. The Italian-style thin-crust pizzas are delicious. Eight other branches also have live music. ✉ *10 Dean St., Soho W1,* ☎ *020/7437–9595 or 020/7439–8722.* 🎟 *£8–£20.* ⏲ *From 11:30 AM for food; music nightly 9 PM–midnight. Tube: Tottenham Court Rd.*

Pizza on the Park. This upscale restaurant across from Hyde Park has a spacious jazz club in the basement that hosts mainstream acts. They serve excellent pizzas. ✉ *11 Knightsbridge, Hyde Park Corner, Knightsbridge W1,* ☎ *020/7235–5273.* 🎟 *£10–£18.* ⏲ *From 8 AM for food; music nightly 9 PM–midnight. Tube: Hyde Park Corner*

Roadhouse. Roadhouse pays homage to the American dream of the open road, with a Harley behind the bar and much memorabilia. Music fits into the feel-good-but-middle-of-the-road end of the R&B-blues-rock-soul spectrum. ✉ *Jubilee Hall, 35 The Piazza, Covent Garden WC2,* ☎ *020/7240–6001.* 🎟 *Free–£10.* ⏲ *Mon.–Sat. 5:30 PM–3 AM, Sun. 5:30 PM–10:30 PM. Tube: Covent Garden.*

Ronnie Scott's. Since the '60s, this legendary jazz club has attracted big names. It's usually crowded and hot, the food isn't great, and service is slow—but the mood can't be beat, even since the sad departure of its eponymous founder and saxophonist. Reservations are recommended. ✉ *47 Frith St., Soho W1,* ☎ *020/7439–0747.* 🎟 *£15–£20 nonmembers, £5–£9 members, annual membership £50.* ⏲ *Mon.–Sat. 8:30 PM–3 AM, Sun. 7:30 PM–11:30 PM. Tube: Leicester Sq.*

606 Club. Expect a civilized Chelsea club that showcases mainstream and contemporary jazz by well-known British-based musicians. You must eat a meal in order to consume alcohol, so allow for an extra £8.50–£18. Booking is advisable. ✉ *90 Lots Rd., Chelsea SW10,* ☎ *020/7352–5953.* 🎟 *£5–£6 music charge is added to the bill.* ⏲ *Mon.–Wed. 7:30 PM–1:15 AM, Thurs.–Sat. 8 PM–2 AM, Sun. 8 PM–midnight. Tube: Earl's Court or Fulham Broadway.*

Rock

Since the '60s, London has had one of the best live music scenes in the world. Everyone of note (except Elvis Presley) has played here, and the city is an essential stop on any band's world tour.

A few years ago, headlining bands would kick off at 9 PM and it would all be over by 11 PM. Now that rock clubs have late licenses it's less likely you'll be thrown out onto the street with nowhere to go. Most shows sell out quickly, leaving fans at the mercy of scalpers; it's a good idea to buy tickets in advance. The "Gigs" page at www.nme.com, one of the most comprehensive search engines, lets you book tickets online.

The Astoria. A balconied theater, host to cutting-edge alternative bands (punk, metal, indie guitar). Shows start early; the building is often cleared, following gigs, for club events. ✉ *157 Charing Cross Rd., West End W1,* ☎ *020/7434–9592.* 🎟 *£8–£20.* ⏲ *Mon.–Sat. 7 PM–4 AM, Sun. 7 PM–midnight. Tube: Tottenham Court Rd.*

Barfly Club. At one of the finest small clubs in the capital, punk, indie guitar bands, and new metal rock attract a non-mainstream crowd. Weekend club nights at the club Monarch, upstairs, host DJs who rock the decks. ✉ *49 Chalk Farm Rd., Camden Town NW1,* ☎ *020/7691–4246.* 🎟 *£6.* ⏲ *Weekdays 7:30 PM–midnight, Fri.–Sat. 8 PM–2 AM, Sun. 7:30 PM – 11 PM. Tube: Camden Town or Chalk Farm.*

Forum. The best medium-to-big-name rock performers consistently play at the 2,000-capacity club. It's a converted 1920 art deco cinema, with a balcony overlooking the dance floor. Saturday club night "House of Fun" plays '70s and 80's nostalgia. ✉ *9–17 Highgate Rd., Kentish Town NW5,* ☎ *020/7284–1001.* 🎟 *£10–£15.* ⏲ *Most nights 7–11; Sat. until 2 AM. Tube: Kentish Town.*

The Garage. An intimate, two-stage club with a solid reputation for programming excellent indie and rock bands, including American bands. Club nights start after the gigs. ✉ *20 Highbury Corner, Islington N1,* ☎ *020/7607–1818.* 🎟 *£5–£8.* ⏲ *Mon.–Wed. 8 PM–11:30 PM, Thurs. 8 PM–2 AM, Fri. and Sat. 8 PM–3 AM. Tube: Highbury & Islington.*

Water Rats. This high-spirited pub hosted Bob Dylan on his 1963 tour, as well as the first Oasis gig. Anything from alt-country, hip-hop, to indie guitar bands thrash it out most nights of the week. Saturday night is club night with DJs and guest bands. ✉ *328 Gray's Inn Rd., Euston WC1,* ☎ *020/7436–7211 or 020/7284–0077.* 🎫 *£5–£7.* ⏲ *Mon.–Sat. 8 PM–11 PM. Tube: King's Cross.*

The Gay Scene

London's gay and lesbian scene is diverse and well established. Soho is the homo heart of London, though plenty of clubbers, restaurant patrons, and tourists are in evidence. Old Compton Street, in particular, is heaving with fashionable people. The clubs cater to every taste: besuited boyzy clubs, divey drag, tea dances, lesbian-only strip joints, and late-night queercore with butch leather, rubber, and uniform fetish nights. Whatever your preference, you can be guaranteed a steamy, cruisey, or sleazy night out in London. Lesbian chic is as trendy in London as it is in New York or Los Angeles, but while a few clubs have opened up in prime Soho spots, the scene is predominantly male.

There are two annual outdoor events—*Mardi Gras* (early July) and *Summer Rites* (early September). *Mardi Gras* is the largest pink party of the year; the colorful pageant winds through London before ending up in Finsbury Park for a ticketed party. Call 020/7494–2225 or check www.londonmardigras.com for details. *Summer Rites* is held in Brixton's Brockwell Park and has musical events, performances, and stalls.

Queer theater and other arts take place throughout the year, but there are several gay-oriented annual arts festivals. The National Film Board hosts the Gay and Lesbian film festival in March and the *Mardi Gras Arts Festival* precedes the festival in June.

Check the listings in *Time Out, Boyz, Gay Times, Attitude,* or the lesbian monthly, *Diva.* GAY to Z www.gaytoz.com offers a comprehensive on-line directory. www.rainbownetwork.com and www.dykesnow.com also have up-to-date listings and reviews of bars, clubs, and events.

Bars, Cafés, and Pubs

Café/bars (café by day, club bar by night) have emerged on the London scene, with DJs and a late license. Unless otherwise stated, hours for pubs and bars are the same as for all London pubs, with drinks available up to 11 PM.

Box. Modern and *très* chic, the Box has different DJs spinning every night. For peckish punters there's food before 5 PM daily. ✉ *32–34 Monmouth St., Soho WC2,* ☎ *020/7240–5828.* ⏲ *Mon.–Sat. 11 AM–11 PM, Sun. 11AM–10:30 PM. Tube: Leicester Sq.*

Candy Bar. The UK's first girl's bar is intimate and cruisey, with DJs mixing the latest sounds on three floors. Men are welcome as guests. ✉ *23–24 Bateman St., Soho W1,* ☎ *020/7437–1977.* 🎫 *£5 after 9 PM, Fri.–Sat.* ⏲ *Mon.–Thurs. 2 PM–1 AM, Fri.– Sat. 2 PM–3 AM, Sun. 5 PM–11 PM. Tube: Tottenham Court Rd.*

The Edge. *Poseurs* are welcome at this hip hangout. Straight groovers mingle with gay men over the four floors. In summer, sidewalk tables provide an enviable view of Soho's daily street theater. Risk the vodkas infused with candy. ✉ *11 Soho Sq., Soho W1,* ☎ *020/7439–1313.* ⏲ *Mon.–Sat. noon–1 AM, Sun. noon–10:30 PM. Tube: Oxford Circus.*

Rupert Street. For smart boyz, this gay chic among the sleaze has post-industrial touches and floor-to-ceiling windows. It's crowded and cruisey at night, civilized and café-like by day. ✉ *50 Rupert St., Soho*

W1, ☎ 020/7292–7141. ⏲ Mon.–Sat. noon–11 PM, Sun. noon–10:30 PM. Tube: Leicester Sq. or Piccadilly Circus.

Yard. An attractive bar, popular with the after work and pre-clubbing crowds, Yard has an outdoor courtyard with heater lamps in winter. It gets packed and smoky at night. Upstairs is more genteel, with sofas. ✉ *57 Rupert St., Soho W1, ☎ 020/7437–2652. ⏲ Mon.–Sat. noon–11 PM. Tube: Piccadilly Circus.*

Clubs

Some of the best gay dance clubs are held once a week in mixed clubs. Gay clubs, like **Heaven,** also offer straight nights. Most clubs are gay friendly, but if that's not your thing you can find ones more targeted to your taste. The following are well established and likely still to be going strong, but given the rate that clubs open and close in London, it's best to call first.

G.A.Y. London's largest gay and lesbian party is at the Astoria (Fridays and Saturdays) and at Mean Fiddler (formerly LA2), on Mondays and Thursdays. Saturday night hosts big-name talent; regular guests include Steps, Kylie Minogue, and Geri Halliwell. Buy advance tickets to avoid the long Saturday night queue. ✉ *157 & 165 Charing Cross Rd., Soho WC2, ☎ 020/7434–9592 or 020/7734–6963.* 🎟 *£5–£15. ⏲ Mon.–Thurs. 10:30 PM–3 AM at Mean Fiddler; Sat. 10:30 PM–4:30 PM at Astoria. Tube: Tottenham Court Road.*

Heaven. It has by far the best light show on any London dance floor, and it's unpretentious, loud, and huge, with a labyrinth of quiet rooms, bars, and live-music parlors. Friday is straight night. If you go to just one club, Heaven should be it. ✉ *The Arches, Villiers St., Covent Garden WC2, ☎ 020/7930–2020.* 🎟 *£1–£12. ⏲ Mon.–Wed. 10:30 PM–3 AM, Thurs.–Sat. 11 PM–7 AM. Tube: Charing Cross or Embankment.*

Love Muscle. Go-go dancers, big stage shows, and stunning lighting are part of this steaming, mixed-gender all-night party, held one Saturday a month at the fabulous Fridge Club. ✉ *The Fridge, Town Hall Parade, Brixton Hill, Brixton SW2, ☎ 020/7326–5100.* 🎟 *£13. ⏲ Sat. 10 PM–6 AM. Tube: Brixton.*

Original Sunday Tea Dance. A longtime fave with the girls, this is a very camp and very fun Sunday ballroom, line-dance, time-warp disco. Tea and sandwiches served up until 7 PM. ✉ *BJ's White Swan, 556 Commercial Rd., East End E14, ☎ 020/7780–9870.* 🎟 *£2. ⏲ Sun. 5:30–midnight. Tube: Aldgate East.*

Trade. This London institution among the hedonistic muscle boys is now over a decade old and begins when many clubs are closing. ✉ *Turnmills, 63 Clerkenwell Rd., East End EC1, ☎ 020/7250–3409.* 🎟 *£15. ⏲ 4 AM–1 PM. Tube: Farringdon.*

THE ARTS

Whether you fancy your art classical or modern, or as a contemporary twist on a time-honored classic, you'll find that London's arts scene pushes the boundaries. Watch a Hollywood star in a West End theater, or a gritty Irish drama. See a blockbuster contemporary art show at the Tate Modern, or a William Blake retrospective at the Tate Britain. There are international theater festivals, innovative music festivals, and obscure seasons of postmodern dance. Celebrity divas sing original-language librettos at the Royal Opera House, while the Almeida Opera is more daring with its radical productions of new opera and music theater. Shakespeare's plays are brought to life at the reconstructed Globe Theatre, while challenging new writing is produced at the Royal Court. Whether you feel like a light-hearted West End musical or the next shark-in-formaldehyde sculpture at the Saatchi Gallery, the choice is yours.

Theaters and Concert Halls

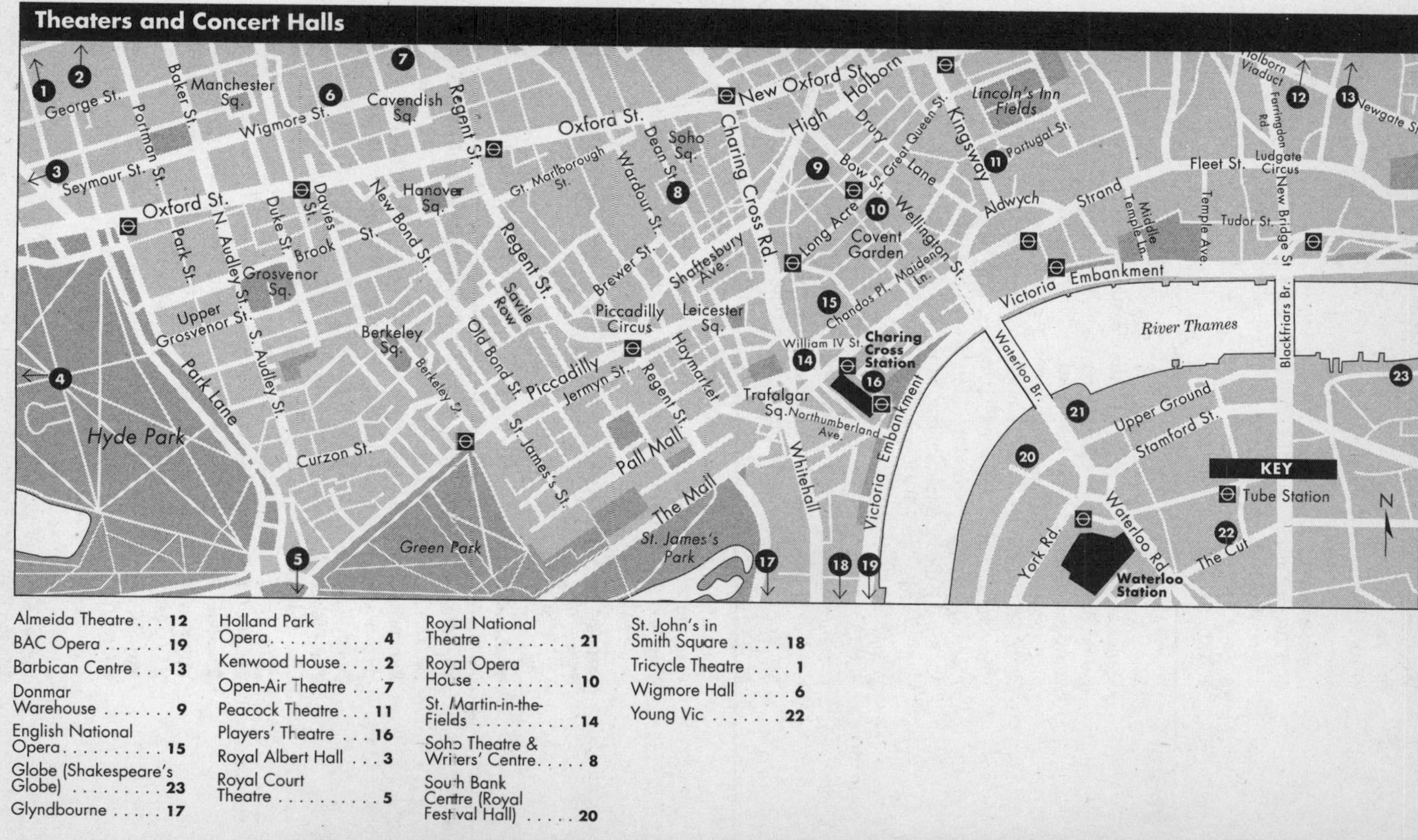

We've attempted a representative selection in the following listings, but to find out what's showing now, the weekly magazine *Time Out* (£2.20, issued every Wednesday) is invaluable. The *Evening Standard* also carries listings, especially in the supplement "Hot Tickets," which comes with the Thursday edition, as do the "quality" Sunday papers and the Saturday *Independent, Guardian,* and *Times.* You'll find leaflets and flyers in most cinema and theater foyers, too, and you can pick up the free fortnightly *London Theatre Guide* leaflet from hotels and tourist information centers.

Dance

Dance fans in London can enjoy the classicism of the world-renowned Royal Ballet, as well as innovative contemporary dance from several companies—Ballet Rambert, Matthew Bourne's Adventures in Motion Pictures, Random Dance Company, Michael Clark Dance Company, Richard Alston Dance Company, Wade McGregor, Russel Maliphant Company, Charles Lineham Company, DV8 Physical Theatre, and Akram Khan—and scores of independent choreographers. The English National Ballet and visiting international companies perform at the Coliseum. Sadler's Wells hosts various other ballet companies and regional and international modern dance troupes. The Royal Festival Hall has a seriously good contemporary dance program that hosts top international companies and important UK choreographers, as well multicultural offerings—from Japanese Butoh and Indian Kathak to hip-hop. The Place is where you'll find the most daring, cutting-edge performances.

The biggest annual event is *Dance Umbrella* (☎ 020/874–5881; WEB www.danceumbrella.co.uk), a six-week season in October/November that hosts international and British-based artists at various venues across the city.

Dance Box Offices

The following theaters are the key dance venues. Check weekly listings for current performances and fringe venues.

The London Coliseum. The English National Ballet performs in this Edwardian baroque theater (1904) with a magnificent auditorium and an illuminated globe. ✉ *St. Martin's La., Covent Garden WC2N 4ES,* ☎ *020/7632–8300. Tube: Leicester Sq.*

Peacock Theatre. This modernist theater near the University of London offers commercial dance as well as ballet. ✉ *Portugal St., Holborn WC2,* ☎ *020/7863–8222. Tube: Holborn.*

The Place. The Robin Howard Dance Theatre is London's only theatre dedicated to contemporary dance. Resolution! is the UK's biggest platform event for new choreographers. ✉ *17 Duke's Rd., Bloomsbury WC1,* ☎ *020/7380–1268. Tube: Euston.*

Riverside Studios. The two performance spaces are noted for postmodern movement styles and performance art. ✉ *Crisp Rd., Hammersmith W6 9RL,* ☎ *020/8237–1111. Tube: Hammersmith.*

Royal Opera House. The renowned Royal Ballet performs classical and contemporary repertoire in this spectacular state-of-the-art Victorian theater. ✉ *Bow St., Covent Garden WC2,* ☎ *020/7304–4000. Tube: Covent Garden.*

Sadler's Wells. Ballet Rambert and Random Dance Company have their home in this lovely modern theater, which produces an excellent season of ballet and contemporary dance. ✉ *Rosebery Ave., Islington EC1,* ☎ *020/7863–8000. Tube: Angel.*

South Bank Centre. A diverse and exciting season of international and British-based contemporary dance companies is presented in the Royal

Festival Hall, Queen Elizabeth Hall, and Purcell Room. ✉ *Belvedere Rd., The South Bank SE1,* ☎ *020/7960–4242. Tube: Waterloo or Embankment Station.*

Classical Music

Whether you want to hear cellist Yo-Yo Ma at the Barbican or a Mozart requiem by candlelight, it's possible to hear first-rank musicians in world-class venues almost every day of the year. The London Symphony Orchestra is in residence at the Barbican Centre, although other top orchestras—including the Philharmonia and the Royal Philharmonic—also perform here. The Barbican also hosts chamber music concerts with such celebrated orchestras as the City of London Sinfonia. Wigmore Hall, a lovely venue for chamber music, is renowned for its song recitals by up-and-coming young instrumentalists. The South Bank Centre has an impressive international music season, held in the Royal Festival Hall (one of the finest concert halls in Europe), the Queen Elizabeth Hall, and the small Purcell Room. Full houses are rare, so even at the biggest concert halls you should be able to get a ticket for £12. If you can't book in advance, arrive at the hall an hour before the performance for a chance at returns.

Lunchtime concerts take place all over the city in smaller concert halls, the big arts-center foyers, and churches; they usually cost less than £5 or are free, and will feature string quartets, singers, jazz ensembles, or gospel choirs. St. John's in Smith Square and St. Martin-in-the-Fields are popular locations. Performances usually begin about 1 PM and last one hour.

Classical music festivals range from the stimulating avant-garde Meltdown (WEB www.meltdown.co.uk) at the South Bank Centre in Juneto the more conservative Kenwood Lakeside Concerts (WEB www.picnicconcerts.com), at which you can listen to classical music outdoors. There are also church hall recitals at Spitalfields Festival (WEB www.spitalfieldsfestival.org.uk), venues around Covent Garden at the BBC Covent Garden Festival (WEB www.cgf.co.uk), and in livery stables and churches in and around the city during the month-long City of London Festival (WEB www.colf.org) in June/July.

A great British tradition, the Henry Wood Promenade Concerts (known to Brits as the "Proms") lasts eight weeks, from July to September, at the Royal Albert Hall. It's renowned for its last night, a madly jingoistic display of singing "Land of Hope and Glory," Union Jack waving, and general madness. Demand for tickets is so high you must enter a lottery. For regular Proms, tickets run £3–£30, with hundreds of standing tickets for £3, available at the hall on the night of the concert. The concerts are broadcast in Hyde Park on a jumbo-screen, but even here a seat on the grass requires a paid ticket.

Barbican Centre. Home to the London Symphony Orchestra and English Chamber Orchestra, the Barbican has an excellent season of big-name soloists and virtuostic musicians. ✉ *Silk St., East End EC2,* ☎ *020/7638–8891 or 020/7638–4141. Tube: Barbican.*

Kenwood House. Concerts are held in the grassy amphitheater in front of Kenwood House on Saturday evening from July to early September. ✉ *Hampstead Heath, Hampstead,* ☎ *020/7973–3427.*

Royal Albert Hall. Built in 1871, this splendid iron-and-glass domed auditorium hosts a varied music program, including Europe's most democratic music festival, the Henry Wood Promenade Concerts—the Proms. ✉ *Kensington Gore, Kensington SW7,* ☎ *020/7589–8212; 020/7589–8212 for information about Proms concerts. Tube: South Kensington.*

St. John's in Smith Square. This Baroque church behind Westminster Abbey offers chamber music and solo recitals. ✉ *Smith Square, Westminster W1,* ☎ *020/7222–1061. Tube: Westminster*

St. Martin-in-the-Fields. Free lunchtime concerts are held in this lovely 1726 church. ✉ *Trafalgar Sq., Covent Garden WC2,* ☎ *020/7839–1930. Tube: Charing Cross.*

South Bank Centre. The Royal Festival Hall hosts large-scale choral and orchestral works, the Queen Elizabeth Hall hosts chamber orchestras and A-team soloists, and the intimate Purcell Room has chamber music and solo recitals. ✉ *South Bank, The South Bank, SE1,* ☎ *020/7960–4242. Tube: Waterloo.*

Wigmore Hall. Hear chamber music and song recitals in this charming hall with near perfect acoustics. Don't miss the mid-morning Sunday concerts. ✉ *36 Wigmore St., Marylebone W1,* ☎ *020/7935–2141. Tube: Bond St.*

Film

There are many lovely cinemas in London and several that are committed to non-mainstream cinema, in particular, the National Film Theatre. Now in its 47th year, *Regus London Film Festival* brings hundreds of films made by masters of world cinema to London for 16 days each November, accompanied by often-sold-out events.

West End movie theaters continue to do good business. Most of the major houses (Odeon Leicester Square and UCI Empire, etc.) are in the Leicester Square–Piccadilly Circus area, where tickets average £8. Mondays and matinees are often cheaper, at around £5, and there are also fewer crowds.

Check out *Time Out* or the Guardian's *The Guide* section (free with the paper on Saturdays) for listings.

Barbican. In addition to Hollywood films, obscure classics and occasional film festivals with Screen Talks are programmed in the two cinemas here. Saturday Children's Cinema often has animation for the entire family. ✉ *Silk St., East End EC2,* ☎ *020/7382–7000. Tube: Barbican.*

BFI London IMAX Centre. The British Film Institute's glazed drum-shaped IMAX theater has the largest screen in Europe playing state-of-the-art 2D and 3D films. ✉ *South Bank, The South Bank SE1,* ☎ *020/7902–1234. Tube: Waterloo.*

Curzon Mayfair. This very comfortable cinema runs a program of mixed rep and mainstream films. ✉ *38 Curzon St., Mayfair W1,* ☎ *0871/871–0011. Tube: Hyde Park Corner or Green Park.*

The Electric Cinema. This refurbished Portobello Road art-house screens mainstream and international movies. ✉ *191 Portobello Rd., Notting Hill W11,* ☎ *020/7727–9958. Tube: Ladbroke Grove or Notting Hill.*

Everyman. London's oldest repertory theater is cozy and shows an excellent selection of classic, foreign, cutting-edge, and almost-new Hollywood titles. Many shows are double (even triple) features at no extra cost. ✉ *5 Hollybush Vale, Hampstead NW3,* ☎ *020/7431–1777. Tube: Hampstead.*

ICA Cinema. Underground and vintage movies are shown in the avant-garde Institute for Contemporary Art. ✉ *Nash House, The Mall, St. James's SW1,* ☎ *020/7930–3647. Tube: Piccadilly Circus or Charing Cross.*

National Film Theatre. The NFT's three cinemas show more than 2,000 titles each year, including foreign-language films, documentaries, director's seasons, cult Hollywood features, and animation. *Regus London Film Festival,* is based here; throughout the year there are mini-festivals, seminars, and guest speakers. Members (£16) get priority on bookings (useful for special events) and get £1 off each screening. ✉ *Belvedere Rd., South Bank Centre, The South Bank SE1,* ☎ *020/7928–3232. Tube: Waterloo.*

Riverside Studios Cinemas. The selection at this converted movie studio changes almost daily. Admission fees are very reasonable; £5.50 gets you entrance to a double bill. ✉ *Crisp Rd., Hammersmith W6,* ☎ *020/8237–1111. Tube: Hammersmith.*

Tricycle Theatre. Expect the best of new British, European, and World Cinema, as well as films from the U.S. There are annual Irish, Black, and Asian Film Festivals. ✉ *269 Kilburn High Rd., Kilburn NW6,* ☎ *020/7328–1000. Tube: Kilburn.*

Opera

The two key players in London's opera scene are the Royal Opera House (which ranks with the Metropolitan Opera House in New York), and the more innovative English National Opera, which presents English-language productions at the London Coliseum. Only the Theatre Royal, Drury Lane, has a longer theatrical history than the Royal Opera House, and the current theater—the third to be built on the site since 1858—underwent a monumental 16-year renovation in 1999. The new building has been very well received, especially the restored Victorian auditorium and the Floral Hall foyer, which beautifully integrates with the Covent Garden Piazza.

Like most opera houses, the Royal Opera House has been criticized for its elitism and outrageous ticket prices that escalate to £150. Since the renovation, it's made good on its promise to be more accessible—the cheapest tickets are just £2 (for a ballet matinee). Conditions of purchase vary; call for information. Prices for ENO are generally lower, ranging from £5 to £55. ENO sells same-day balcony seats for as little as £2.50.

Almeida Opera and BAC Opera produce opera festivals that showcase new opera and cutting-edge music theatre. During the summer months, Holland Park Opera presents the usual chestnuts in the open-air theater of leafy Holland Park. Bring a picnic and an umbrella. Serious opera fans should not miss the Glyndebourne Festival. It's the jewel in the crown of the country house opera circuit, and the greatest opera festival in the UK. Pavarotti made his debut here.

International touring companies often perform at Sadler's Wells, Barbican, South Bank Centre, and Wigmore Hall, so check the weekly listings for details.

Almeida Theatre. Now in its tenth year, the Almeida Opera Festival in July has an adventurous program of new opera and music theater. ✉ *Almeida St., Islington, N1,* ☎ *020/7359–4404. Tube: Angel or Highbury & Islington.*

BAC Opera. New opera is presented at the BAC Opera Festival each May. ✉ *Lavender Hill, Battersea, SW11,* ☎ *020/7223–2223. Tube: Clapham Junction.*

English National Opera. ENO tends to produce more ambitious and innovative opera for less expensive prices than the Royal Opera House. ✉ *Coliseum, St. Martin's La., Covent Garden WC2,* ☎ *020/7632–8300. Tube: Leicester Sq.*

Glyndebourne. Fifty-four miles south of London, Glyndebourne is one of the most famous opera houses in the world. Six operas are presented from mid-May to late-August. The best route by car is the M23 to Brighton, then the A27 towards Lewes. There are regular train services from London (Victoria) to Lewes with coach connections to and from Glyndebourne. ✉ *Lewes, BN8 5UU,* ☎ *Box Office 01273/813–813, information 01273/815–000. Tube: Covent Garden.*

Holland Park Opera. During the summer months, new productions and well-loved operas are presented against the remains of Holland House, one of the first great houses built in Kensington. Ticket prices range from £14–£28. ✉ *Holland Park, Kensington High Street, Kensington, W8,* ☎ *020/7602–7856. Tube: Covent Garden.*

Royal Opera House. Original-language productions are presented in this extravagant theater. If you can't afford £100 for a ticket, consider showing up at 8 AM to purchase a same-day seat, of which a small number are offered for £30. There is the odd free lunch-time recital and occasional summer concerts broadcast live to a large screen in Covent Garden Piazza. ✉ *Bow St., Covent Garden, WC2,* ☎ *020/7304–4000. Tube: Covent Garden.*

Theater

London's theatrical past goes back to the streets, marketplaces, and cathedrals. These were a backdrop for the medieval mystery plays—when London, indeed, was a stage. Theaters here, which are some of the finest theatrical gems in the world, embody this history.

The first permanent theater, The Theatre, was built by Richard Burbage in Shoreditch in 1576, and was soon followed by the Swan, Curtain, Rose Fortune, Hope and Shakespeare's Globe Theatre on the South Bank—where the Bard's plays were staged alongside brothels, bear-baiting, and cock-fighting pits. The Puritans put an end to the fun, and the next dramatic boom didn't happen until after the Restoration of 1660, with the building of the Theatre Royal, Drury Lane (1662), and the Royal Opera House (1732). Most of London's theaters were built toward the end of the Victorian era when Shaftesbury Avenue cut through the Soho slums, and theaters like the Shaftesbury (1886) and Aldwych (1905) became the center of London's theater scene. Covent Garden became host to frothy Edwardian theater facades along St. Martin's Lane and the Strand. The 1930s saw the emergence of jazzy art deco theaters until the outbreak of World War II, and the 1970s saw the first intervention of state funding and the concrete Brutalist-style architecture of the Barbican Centre and National Theatre. In more recent years, lottery funds have subsidized renovations of existing spaces like the Royal Court and the Almeida, as well as new construction, most of which has resulted in unremarkable, modernist structures. Sitting in an exquisite Edwardian theater, soaking up the intricate plasterwork and plush boxes, even ordering a drink at the classy bar during interval, is a big part of the theater-going experience.

But really, the play is the thing, and chances are good you can see Nicole Kidman in a Sam Mendes Off-West End production, the umpteenth production of *Les Misérables,* a Peter Brook deconstruction of Shakespeare, innovative physical theater from Complicité, the latest offering from Cirque du Soleil or Robert Lepage, or even a fringe production above a pub. While West End glitz and glamour continues to pull in the audiences, so do the more innovative players. Only in London will a Tuesday matinee of the Royal Shakespeare Company's *Henry IV* be sold out in a 1,200-seat-theater.

In London, the words "radical" and "quality," or "classical" and "experimental," are not mutually exclusive. The Royal Shakespeare Company and the Royal National Theatre Company often stage contemporary versions of the classics. The Almeida, Battersea Arts Centre (BAC), Donmar Warehouse, Royal Court Theatre, Soho Theatre, and the Young Vic attract famous actors and have excellent reputations for new writing and innovative theatrical languages. These are the places that shape the theater of the future, the venues where you'll see an original production before it becomes a hit in the West End. (And you'll see them at a fraction of the cost.)

Another unique thing about the London theater scene is that it doesn't shut down in the summer—it's business as usual for the Royal Shakespeare Company and Royal National Theatre. From mid-May through mid-September, you can see the Bard served up in his most spectacular manifestation—at the open-air reconstruction of Shakespeare's Globe Theatre. In addition, the Open Air Theatre presents a season of Shakespeare-under-the-stars, from the last week in May to the third week in September, in the lovely Regent's Park. B.I.T.E., the Barbican's International Theater Event, presents cutting-edge performance May–October. Some theater festivals like London Mime Festival (WEB www.mimefest.co.uk) and L.I.F.T. (WEB www.completelynaked.co.uk)take place throughout the year, so unlike other cities, there is always something good to see in London. Check *Time Out* for details.

Theater-going doesn't come cheap. Tickets under £10 are a rarity; in the West End you should expect to pay from £15 for a seat in the upper balcony to at least £25 for a good one in the stalls (orchestra) or dress circle (mezzanine). Tickets may be booked at the individual theater box offices or over the phone by credit card; most theaters still don't charge a fee for the latter. You can also book through ticket agents (see below) or go to the theater box office, as the vast majority of theaters have some tickets (returns and house seats) available on the night of performance. All the larger hotels offer theater bookings, but they tack on a hefty service charge.

Warning: Be *very* careful of scalpers and unscrupulous ticket agents outside theaters and working the line at *tkts* (a half-price ticket booth); they try to sell tickets at five times the price of the ticket at legitimate box offices; you might be charged £200 or more for a sought-after ticket (and you'll pay a stiff fine if caught buying a scalped ticket).

Ticketmaster (☎ 020/7344–0055; 800/775–2525 in the U.S., WEB www.ticketmaster.com) sells tickets to a number of different theaters, although they charge a booking fee. First Call (☎ 020/7420–0000, WEB www.firstcalltickets.com) sells theater tickets. You can book tickets in the U.S. through Keith Prowse (✉ 234 W. 44th St., Suite 1000, New York, NY 10036, ☎ 212/398–1430 or 800/669–8687). You can buy tickets at the New York office of Edwards & Edwards (✉ 1 Times Sq. Plaza, 12th floor, New York, NY 10036, ☎ 800/223–6108). For discount tickets, Society of London Theatre (☎ 020/7557–6700) operates *tkts,* the SOLT, half-price ticket booth (no phone) on the southwest corner of Leicester Square and sells the best available seats to performances at about 25 theaters. It's open Monday–Saturday 10–7, Sunday noon–3; there is a £2 service charge. All major credit cards are accepted. You might consider using one particular booking line that doubles the price of tickets: West End Cares (☎ 020/7833–3939) donates half of what it charges to AIDS charities.

Almeida. Hollywood stars often perform at this Off-West End venue that premieres excellent new plays and exciting twists on the classics. ✉ *Almeida St., Islington N1,* ☎ *020/7359–4404. Tube: Angel or Highbury & Islington.*

Barbican Centre. Built in 1982, The Barbican Center is the home of the Royal Shakespeare Company, whose productions are presented in the theater for six months of the year. During the rest of the year, you can see the Barbican's own **B.I.T.E.** (Barbican International Theatre Festival), with ground-breaking performance, dance, drama, and music theater from May–October. ✉ *Silk St., East End EC2,* ☎ *020/7638–8891. Tube: Barbican.*

BAC. Battersea Arts Centre has an excellent reputation for producing innovative new work. Check out Scratch, a night of low-tech cabaret theater by emerging artists, and the BAC October Festival of innovative performance. ✉ *176 Lavender Hill, Battersea SW11,* ☎ *020/7223–2223. British Rail: Clapham Junction.*

Donmar Warehouse. Hollywood stars often perform in diverse and daring new works, bold interpretations of the classics, and small-scale musicals. ✉ *41 Earlham St., Covent Garden WC2,* ☎ *020/7369–1732. Tube: Covent Garden.*

Shakespeare's Globe Theatre. This faithful reconstruction of the open-air playhouse where Shakespeare worked and wrote many of his greatest plays re-creates the 16th-century theater-going experience. Standing seats cost £5. The season runs May through September, with a winter season in the indoor Inigo Jones Theatre. ✉ *New Globe Walk, Bankside, The South Bank SE1,* ☎ *020/7401–9919. Tube: Southwark, Mansion House (walk across Southwark Bridge), or Blackfriars (walk across Blackfriars Bridge).*

Open Air Theatre. On a warm summer evening, classical theater in the pastoral, and royal, Regent's Park is hard to beat for magical adventure. Enjoy a supper before the performance and during the interval on the picnic lawn, and drinks in the spacious bar. ✉ *Inner Circle, Regent's Park NW1,* ☎ *020/7486–2431. Tube: Baker St., Regent's Park.*

Players' Theatre. This long-running Music Hall takes you back to the reign of Queen Victoria. It's quite a hoot—actors in period costume perform bawdy Victorian songs, and the audience joins in the choruses (lyrics are printed in the program). Dinner is served before and after performances in their own restaurant; there are also two bars. Closed Mondays. Sunday lunch and afternoon tea is also served. ✉ *The Arches, Villiers St., Strand, Covent Garden WC2,* ☎ *020/7839–1134,* FAX *020/7839–8067,* WEB *www.theplayerstheatre.co.uk. Tube: Charing Cross or Embankment.*

Royal Court Theatre. Britain's undisputed epicenter of new writing, the RCT has produced gritty British and international drama since the middle of the 20th century, much of which gets produced in the West End. Don't miss the best deal in town–£7.50 tickets on Mondays. ✉ *Sloane Sq., Chelsea SW1,* ☎ *020/7565–5000. Tube: Sloane Sq.*

Royal National Theatre. Opened in 1976, the RNT has three theaters: the 1,160-seat Olivier, the 890-seat Lyttelton, and the 400-seat Cottesloe. Musicals, classics, and new plays are in repertoire. It's closed Sundays. ✉ *South Bank Arts Centre, Belvedere Rd., The South Bank SE1,* ☎ *020/7452–3000. Tube: Waterloo.*

Soho Theatre + Writers' Centre. This sleek theater in the heart of Soho is devoted to new writing and work by emerging writers. ✉ *21 Dean St., Soho W1,* ☎ *020/7478–0100. Tube: Tottenham Court Rd.*

Tricycle Theatre. The Tricycle is committed to the best in Irish, African-Caribbean, Asian, and political drama, and the promotion of new plays. ✉ *269 Kilburn High Rd., Kilburn NW6 7JR,* ☎ *020/7328–1000. Tube: Kilburn.*

Young Vic. Big names perform in daring, innovative productions of classic plays. No one sits more than five rows from the stage in this unique theater-in-the-round auditorium. The seats are unreserved; each has a perfect view. ✉ *66 The Cut, The South Bank SE1,* ☎ *020/7928–6363. Tube: Waterloo.*

Contemporary Art

For centuries, Britain has accumulated extraordinary caches of art and housed them in national institutions like the National Gallery, National Portrait Gallery, Tate Britain, Tate Modern, and Victoria and Albert Museum. (See the Exploring chapter for these listings.) If you include the precious Courtauld and the Wallace Collection, London is a treasure trove of Western art.

No less high-profile is London's contemporary art scene, displayed in public-funded exhibition spaces like the Barbican Gallery, Hayward Gallery, Institute of Contemporary Arts, Serpentine Gallery, and Whitechapel. And with the arrival of the Tate Modern, that's even more the case; London now has a flagship modern art gallery on par with Bilbao's Guggenheim and the Museum of Modern Art in New York. In the past decade, the contemporary art scene here has exploded, and Young British Artists (YBA)—a.k.a. Damien Hirst, Tracey Emin, Gary Hume, Rachel Whiteread, Jake and Dinos Chapman, Sarah Lucas, Gavin Turk, Steve McQueen—have made London one of the most dynamic spots for contemporary art in the world.

British artists may complain about how the visual arts are severely underfunded and their rough ride in the media, but Damien Hirst is a household name in London, and where else would his six-meter-high bronze version of an anatomy model fetch £1 million? Hirst and his Goldsmith's College contemporaries took the art world by storm in the late 1980s, when they rented a disused Docklands warehouse to put on seminal shows, like *Freeze*. It coincided with a recession that saw West End galleries closing, and a property slump that enabled young artists to open trendy artist-run places in the East End.

West End dealers, and particularly the enigmatic advertising tycoon Charles Saatchi, championed these Young British Artists (YBA). Depending on who you talk to, the Saatchi Gallery is considered to be either the saviour of contemporary art or the wardrobe of the emperor's new clothes. Since 1992, Saatchi has shown several shows of YBA, including the decade's most memorable sculptures—Damien Hirst's shark in formaldehyde, *The Impossibility of Death in the Mind of the Living*, and Rachel Whiteread's plaster cast of room, *Ghost*. The 1997 show "Sensation" at the Royal Academy propelled the have-nots into the mainstream. Most of the Hirst generation are now represented by established West End galleries like Lisson and White Cube, but even Jay Joplin has opened a second gallery, White Cube 2, on Hoxton Square—which confirms that the East End has become the establishment. There are dozens of galleries in the fashionable spaces around Old Street, Vilma Goldbeing one of the more interesting.

YBA are now firmly planted in the public imagination and thanks to the annual Turner Prize, which always stirs up controversy in the media during month-long display of the work at Tate Britain, the next YBA will surely be the talk of the town.

In addition to the trendy, Arts Council–funded scene, there are hundreds of other small galleries all over London with interesting work by artists struggling for recognition. Check the weekly listings for details. Expect to pay around £7 for entry into the major galleries and exhibition spaces; most commercial galleries are free.

Barbican Centre. Innovative exhibitions of 20th-century and current art and design are shown in the Barbican Gallery and The Curve. Recent highlights have included the world-renowned photographers

Helmut Newton and Andres Serrano, and the British furniture and textile designers Robin and Lucienne Day. ✉ *Silk St., East End EC2,* ☎ *020/7638–8891.* 🎟 *£4–£7.* ⏲ *Mon.–Sat. 10 AM–6 PM, Wed. until 8 PM, Sun. noon–6 PM. Tube: Barbican.*

Hayward Gallery. This purpose built, modern art gallery is a classic example of 1960s Brutalist architecture, and is one of London's major venues for important touring exhibitions. ✉ *Belvedere Rd., South Bank Centre, The South Bank SE1,* ☎ *020/7960–5226.* 🎟 *£7.* ⏲ *Daily 10 AM–6 PM, Tues. and Wed. until 8 PM. Tube: Waterloo.*

Institute of Contemporary Arts. Housed in an elegant John Nash–designed Regency terrace, the ICA programs visual art, contemporary drama, film, new media, literature and photography. There's an arts bookstore, cafeteria, and bar. To visit you must be a member of the ICA; a day membership costs £1.50. ✉ *Nash House, The Mall St. James's SW1,* ☎ *020/7930–3647 or 020/7930–0493.* 🎟 *Mon.–Fri. £1.50, Sat. and Sun. £2.50.* ⏲ *Daily noon–7:30 PM. Tube: Charing Cross.*

Lisson. Arguably the most respected gallery in London, owner Nicholas Logsdai represents over 40 blue-chip artists, including minimalist Sol Lewitt and Dan Graham. The gallery is most associated with New Object sculptors like Anish Kapoor and Richard Deacon, many of whom have won the Turner Prize. ✉ *52–54 Bell St., Marylebone NW1,* ☎ *020/7724–2739.* 🎟 *Free.* ⏲ *Mon.–Fri. 10 AM–6 PM, Sat. 10 AM–5 PM. Tube: Edgware Rd.*

Photographer's Gallery. Britain's first photography gallery brought world-famous photographers like André Kertesz, Jacques-Henri Lartigue, and Irving Penn to the UK, and continues to program cutting-edge photography. Richard Billingham and Boris Mikhailov recently exhibited controversial work. There is a print sales room, bookstore, and a café. ✉ *5 & 8 Great Newport St., Covent Garden WC2,* ☎ *020/7831–1772.* 🎟 *Free.* ⏲ *Mon.–Sat. 11 AM–6 PM, Sun. noon–6 PM. Tube: Leicester Sq.*

Royal Academy. Housed in an aristocratic mansion and home to Britain's first art school founded in 1768, the Academy is best known for its major one-off exhibitions—like the record-breaking Monet—and occasional controversial shows by contemporary British artists. ✉ *Burlington House, Soho W1,* ☎ *020/7300–8000.* 🎟 *£6–£8.* ⏲ *Daily 10 AM–6 PM, Fri. until 10 PM. Tube: Piccadilly Circus.*

Saatchi Gallery. Charles Saatchi's ultra-modern gallery tends to grab headlines. If your taste is traditional, this is not the gallery for you. Damien Hirst's famously controversial shark in formaldehyde was first exhibited here. ✉ *98a Boundary Rd., St. John's Wood NW8,* ☎ *020/7624–8299.* 🎟 *£5.* ⏲ *Thur.–Sun. noon–6 PM. Tube: Swiss Cottage.*

Serpentine Gallery. In a classical 1934 tea pavilion in Kensington Gardens, the Serpentine has an international reputation for exhibitions of modern and contemporary art. Man Ray, Henry Moore, Andy Warhol, Bridget Riley, Damien Hirst, and Rachel Whiteread are a few of the artists who have exhibited here. ✉ *Kensington Gdns., South Kensington W2,* ☎ *020/7402–6075.* 🎟 *Donation.* ⏲ *Daily 10 AM–6 PM. Tube: South Kensington.*

Tate Modern. This converted power station is the largest modern art gallery in the world. The permanent collection, which includes work by all the major 20th-century artists, is organized thematically rather than chronologically, and alongside blockbuster touring shows and solo exhibitions of international artists. ✉ *Bankside, The South Bank SE1,* ☎ *020/7887–8008.* 🎟 *Free –£8.50.* ⏲ *Daily 10 AM–6 PM, Sat. and Sun. until 10 PM. Tube: Southwark.*

Vilma Gold. This serious commercial gallery in Hoxton shows outré work by international and British artists. ✉ *Rivington St., East End EC2,* ☎ *020/7613–1609.* 🎟 *Free.* ⏲ *Thur.–Sun. noon–6 PM. Tube: Old St.*

Whitechapel Art Gallery. Established in 1897, this independent East End gallery is one of London's most innovative. Jeff Wall, Bill Viola, Gary Hume, and Janet Cardiff have exhibited here. ✉ *80–82 Whitechapel High St., East End E1.* 🎫 *Free.* ⏲ *Tues.–Fri. 11 AM–5 PM, Wed. until 8 PM, Sat. and Sun. 11 AM–6 PM. Tube: Aldgate East.*

White Cube. This intimate white cube is arguably one of the most influential galleries of the past decade. Turner Prize artists—Hirst, Emin, Hume, et al—have exhibited here. ✉ *44 Duke St., St. James's SW1,* ☎ *020/7930–5373.* 🎫 *Free.* ⏲ *Tues.–Sat. 10 AM–6 PM. Tube: Green Park.*

White Cube 2. Jay Joplin's second gallery is housed in a 1920s light industrial building on Hoxton Square. Many of its now-famous artists live in the East End, which supposedly has the highest concentration of artists in Europe. ✉ *48 Hoxton Sq., Hoxton N1,* ☎ *020/7930–5357.* 🎫 *Free.* ⏲ *Tues.–Sat. 10 AM–6 PM. Tube: Old St.*

6 OUTDOOR ACTIVITIES AND SPORTS

Some days you win, some days you lose, and some days you get rained out. But that seldom dampens one of the liveliest sports calendars around. Tennis, of course, means Wimbledon (if the show courts are sold out, try for the outside courts). In summer, Her Majesty makes an appearance at Ascot, while the Test Matches, the world series of cricket, are played on the manicured grass of Lord's and the Oval. In cooler weather, football (which means soccer) takes over, and in any season you can enjoy anything from yoga to squash indoors and let it rain, rain, rain.

Updated by Julius Honnor

THERE ARE THE WIMBLEDON TENNIS CHAMPIONSHIPS, and there's cricket, and then there's football (soccer in the United States), and that's about it for the sports fan in London, right? Wrong. London is a great city for the weekend player of almost anything. It comes into its own in summer, when the parks sprout nets and goals and painted white lines, outdoor swimming pools open, and a season of spectator events gets under way. The listings below concentrate on facilities available in various sports, and on the more accessible or well-known spectator events. Bring your gear, and branch out from that hotel gym.

PARTICIPANT SPORTS AND FITNESS

If your sport is missing from those listed below, or if you need additional information, **Sportsline** (☎ 020/7222–8000), staffed weekdays 10–6, supplies details about London's clubs, events, and facilities. It's only the price of a local call, but is often busy.

Baseball and Softball

Join in a game on summer afternoons and evenings in Regent's Park or on the south edge of Hyde Park. If you're serious about joining a team contact **BaseballSoftballUK** (☎ 020/7453–7055).

Bicycling

London is becoming more cycle-friendly, with special lanes marked for bicycles on some major roads, but it isn't safe to ride without a helmet. If you plan to cycle much in the city, get the excellent London Cycling Campaign maps, with detailed cycling routes through the city. They're now available free from bike shops, major travel interchanges, or directly from the offices of **London Cycling Campaign** (☎ 020/7928–7220).

London Bicycle Tour Company offers three-hour bike tours of various London neighborhoods for £14.95. Reserve in advance by phone or on the Internet (WEB www.londonbicycle.com). You can also go it alone: bikes can be rented for £2.50 an hour or £12 per day (£6 for each subsequent day). You can also rent Rollerblades, tandems, and rickshaws. ✉ *1A Gabriel's Wharf, The South Bank SE1,* ☎ *020/7928–6838. Tube: Waterloo.*

You can rent anything you want at **Bikepark** from approximately March to November. Prices for mountain, hybrid, or road bikes start at £12 for the first day, £6 for the second, and £4 for each day thereafter, plus a returnable deposit of £200. All machines are new each spring and are issued with locks; accessories are available, too. ✉ *63 New Kings Rd., Chelsea W6,* ☎ *020/7731–7012. Tube: Parsons Green.*

Boating

If you feel inspired by the crews at the Henley Royal Regatta or the Oxford and Cambridge Boat Race, you can try your hand at the oars in London's parks. On the Serpentine, Hyde Park has pedalos (paddleboats), canoes, and rowboats holding up to seven people for £5 per hour. You can also spend a vigorous afternoon rowing about the large scenic lake in Regent's Park. Both parks have boats available March through September, daily from 9 to 6:30 PM or dusk, weather permitting. **Regent's Park Boating Lake** (☎ 020/7486–4759) rents rowboats that hold up to five adults at £4 per hour.

Gyms

As you'd expect from the Y, **Central YMCA** has every facility and sport, including a great 25-meter pool and a well-equipped gym. Weekly membership is £39, a "one-day taster" £15. ✉ *112 Great Russell St., Bloomsbury WC1,* ☎ *020/7637–8131. Tube: Tottenham Court Rd.*

The conveniently central **Oasis** sports center has a gym which costs £5.40 per session after completion of a one-off induction. ✉ *32 Endell St., Covent Garden WC2,* ☎ *020/7831–1804. Tube: Covent Garden.*

The day rate is £6.90 and the monthly rate £53 at **Jubilee Hall,** a very crowded but happening and super-well-equipped central gym. Many are addicted to the "Fatbuster" workouts here, but there are also classes in everything from body sculpting, spinning, and step to kick boxing and jazz dance. Classes cost £6. ✉ *30 The Piazza, Covent Garden, WC2,* ☎ *020/7379–0008. Tube: Covent Garden.*

In a prime Belsize Park location, **Spring Health Leisure** offers luxurious spa and beauty treatments, a pool, Jacuzzi, and gym. Day memberships, which include use of the gym, cost £25 or you can sweat for a whole week for £50. ✉ *81 Belsize Park Gardens, Belsize Park, Hampstead NW3,* ☎ *020/7722–8220. Tube: Belsize Park.*

The Peak is expensive but has top equipment, a pool, great ninth-floor views over Knightsbridge, and a sauna—with TV—in the full beauty spa. A day membership is relatively good value at £35. ✉ *Hyatt Carlton Tower Hotel, 2 Cadogan Pl., Belgravia SW1,* ☎ *020/7858–7008. Tube: Sloane Sq.*

AEROBICS

Porchester Centre has about eight daily classes, from beginner to pro; step, yoga, circuit training, and aquaerobics are included in the mix. All classes cost £4.65 for non-members. ✉ *Porchester Centre, Queensway, Bayswater W2,* ☎ *020/7792–2919. Tube: Bayswater.*

Portobello Green Fitness Club is under the Westway overpass, and you'll have to battle through flea-market shoppers on weekends to reach these popular classes. Membership is £11 for a day or £30 for a week. ✉ *3–5 Thorpe Close, Notting Hill W10,* ☎ *020/8960–2221. Tube: Ladbroke Grove.*

Horseback Riding

Hyde Park Riding Stables keeps horses for hacking the sand tracks. Rates are £32 per person per hour during the week, £35 at weekends. ✉ *63 Bathurst Mews, Bayswater W2,* ☎ *020/7723–2813. Tube: Lancaster Gate.*

Ice-Skating

London's most central ice-skating rink is the **Leisure Box,** where skating will cost you £6 per session, including skate rental. ✉ *17 Queensway, Bayswater W2,* ☎ *020/7229–0172. Tube: Queensway.*

Broadgate Ice Arena is the United Kingdom's only outdoor rink. Available to skaters of all abilities, it's usually open between October and early April, and costs £7 a session, including skate rental. Call for opening times. ✉ *Broadgate Arena, Eldon St., The City EC2,* ☎ *020/7505–4068. Tube: Liverpool St.*

Running

London is a delight for joggers. If you don't mind a crowd, popular spots include Green Park, which gets a stream of runners armed with maps from Piccadilly hotels, and—to a lesser extent—adjacent St. James's Park. Both can get perilous with deck chairs on summer days. You can run a 4-mi perimeter route around Hyde Park and Kensington Gardens or a 2½-mi route in Hyde Park alone if you start at Hyde Park Corner or Marble Arch and encircle the Serpentine. Most Park Lane hotels offer jogging maps for this, their local green space. Regent's

Park has the most populated track because it's a sporting kind of place; the Outer Circle loop measures about 2½ mi.

Away from the center, there are longer, scenic runs over more varied terrain at Hampstead Heath: highlights are Kenwood, and Parliament Hill, London's highest point, where you'll get a fabulous panoramic sweep over the entire city. Richmond Park is the biggest green space of all, but watch for deer during rutting season (October and November). Back in town, there's a rather traffic-heavy 1½-mi riverside run along Victoria Embankment from Westminster Bridge to the Embankment at Blackfriars Bridge, or a beautiful mile among the rowing clubs and ducks along the Malls—Upper, Lower, and Chiswick—from Hammersmith Bridge.

GROUP RUNS

If you don't want to run alone, call the **London Hash House Harriers** (☎ 020/8995–7879). They organize daily noncompetitive hour-long runs around interesting bits of town, with loops and checkpoints built in. The cost is £1.

Squash

There are four squash courts at **Finsbury Leisure Centre,** a popular sports center in the City frequented by execs who work nearby. You can book by phone without a membership, and you're more likely to get a court if you show up to play during Londoners' regular office hours, or possibly on weekends, when courts are less busy. A court costs £7.40 for non-members (£5 off-peak) and £5.90 for members (£4 off-peak). Annual membership is £36. ✉ *Norman St., Finsbury EC1,* ☎ *020/7253–2346. Tube: Old St.*

Swimming

INDOOR POOLS

Chelsea Sports Centre, with a renovated, turn-of-the-century 32- by 12-meter pool, is just off King's Road, so it's usually busy. It's packed with kids on weekends. Each swim costs £2.80. ✉ *Chelsea Manor St., Chelsea SW3,* ☎ *020/7352–6985. Tube: South Kensington.*

INDOOR/OUTDOOR POOLS

Oasis has a heated outdoor pool (open year-round) and a 32- by 12-meter pool indoors. Needless to say, both pools are packed in summer. A swim costs £2.90. ✉ *32 Endell St., Covent Garden WC2,* ☎ *020/7831–1804. Tube: Covent Garden.*

PARKS

Hampstead Ponds, three Elysian little lakes, are surrounded by grassy lounging areas. The women's one is particularly secluded (though crowded in summer) and is open all year, as is the men's. Opening times vary with sunrise and sunset. The Mixed Pond is open May through September, 7 AM to 7 PM. All have murky-looking but clean, fresh water, and all are free. Less murky is **Hampstead Lido,** open May through September. A swim here is free from 7 AM to 9:30 AM, £3.50 for the day after that. ✉ *E. Heath Rd., Hampstead NW3,* ☎ *020/7485–4491. Tube or British Rail: Hampstead Heath.*

Serpentine Lido is technically a beach on a lake, but a hot day in Hyde Park is surreally reminiscent of the seaside. There are changing facilities, and the swimming section is chlorinated. There's also a paddling pool, sandpit, and kids' entertainer in the afternoons. It's open daily from June through September 10–6; admission costs £2.50. ✉ *Hyde Park, Kensington W2,* ☎ *020/7706–3422. Tube: Knightsbridge.*

A Brixton suntrap, **Brockwell Lido,** open May through September, has a younger and more modern feel than its Hyde Park and Hampstead Heath alternatives. Entrance costs £2 for a morning, £4 for an afternoon. The easiest way to get here is to take British Rail to Herne Hill. ✉ *Brockwell Park, Brixton SE24,* ☎ *020/7274–3088. Tube: Brixton.*

SPA POOLS

There's a 36- by 14-meter pool for serious lap swimmers at **Porchester Baths,** costing £2.55 a swim, plus a 1920s Turkish bath, sauna, and spa of gorgeous (though slightly faded) grandeur that is more expensive, at £18.95. It has separate sessions for men and women. ✉ *Queensway, Bayswater W2,* ☎ *020/7792–2919. Tube: Queensway.*

Tennis

Many London parks have courts that are often cheap or even free: **Holland Park** is one of the prettiest places to play, with six hard courts available all year. The cost is here is £9.70 for annual membership and £4.80 per game. ✉ *Holland Park, W8,* ☎ *020/7602–2226. Tube: Holland Park.*

Islington Tennis Centre is about the only place where you don't need membership to play indoors year-round, but you need it to reserve by phone. There are two outdoor courts, too, and coaching is available. Prices range from £15.50 for the indoor courts to £7 for outdoors. ✉ *Market Rd., Islington N7,* ☎ *020/7700–1370. Tube: Caledonian Rd.*

A surprisingly large and busy green space, **Paddington Sports Club** has a set of 10 courts. Annual membership at this members-only club is £380 (£665 to also use the squash courts and multi-gym) with a £150 joining fee. Per-game charges only apply to floodlit games. ✉ *Castellain Rd., Maida Vale W9,* ☎ *020/7286–4515. Tube: Maida Vale.*

Walking

There are plenty of possibilities for rambling in the countryside around the city. Generally well-signposted footpaths offer attractive routes through rural southern England. The Chiltern Hills to the northwest, the South Downs to the south, and Kent to the southeast are probably the best areas to try, and are all reasonably well served by local trains. If you want to walk in a group, the Saturday Walkers' Club, based around the *Time Out Book of Country Walks* (£10.99, available from most bookshops), leaves from a London station every Saturday of the year.

Yoga

Life Centre, London's best yoga school, specializes in the dynamic, energetic Ashtanga Vinyasa technique. Beautiful premises enhance the experience. A huge variety of holistic health therapies is available upstairs. Classes cost from £8–£10 and run all day every day. ✉ *15 Edge St., Kensington W8,* ☎ *020/7221–4602. Tube: Notting Hill Gate.*

SPECTATOR SPORTS

Boating

One of London's most beloved sporting events (since 1845) is also the easiest to see, and it's free. The only problem with the late-March Oxford and Cambridge Boat Race is securing a good position among the crowds that line the Putney-to-Mortlake route (mostly at pubs along the Hammersmith Lower and Upper Malls, or on Putney Bridge). The Saturday start time varies from year to year according to the tides but is usually around 2:30 PM. The Head of the River Race is the professional version, only this time up to 420 crews of eight row the university course in the other direction. It usually happens the Saturday before the university race, beginning at 10 AM; the best view is from above Chiswick Bridge.

Cricket

Lord's has been hallowed turf for worshipers of England's summer game since 1811. Tickets can be hard to procure for the five-day Test Matches

Close-Up

A RUNDOWN OF CRICKET RULES

CRICKET IS PLAYED by two 11-member teams on a roughly circular grass pitch about 90 yards in diameter, surrounded by a rope boundary. Most of the action, however, takes place on a central rectangle, 22 yards long. The batting team places two batsmen (batters) at opposite sides of the rectangle; wickets (two bails balanced atop three stumps of wood) stand behind each batsman. The object of the batsman is twofold: to guard the wickets and to score runs. The fielding team's bowler (pitcher) at one end of the rectangle bowls a ball to the batsman at the opposite end, attempting to bowl them out by knocking the bails off the stumps. The ball is bowled overhand with a straight arm (bent elbows count as "throwing," accusations of which are taken very seriously) and is usually bounced off the pitch, which has been hardened by rollers.

The batsman attempts to hit the ball far enough that he and his batting partner can exchange places and score runs. Unlike in baseball, there are no foul lines, so the ball may go in any direction. If the ball crosses the boundary on the ground, the batsman scores four runs; if it crosses the boundary before touching the ground, six runs are scored. The batsman's wicket is taken (he's out) if the bails are knocked off the stumps by the bowler or while the batsmen are changing places, or if his ball is caught on the fly. The LBW (Leg Before Wicket) rule is complex, but essentially means that players can't defend their wickets with their legs or feet. Once a player's wicket is taken, he is replaced by the next batsman.

An over (six balls) is bowled from one end of the rectangle; then another bowler takes over from the other end and the fielders rotate accordingly. The batting team remains in bat until 10 wickets have been taken (the end of an innings) or until they declare (decide to stop batting and take the field). A team will declare because to win, they must not only score the most runs but also take all of the opposing side's wickets by the scheduled end of the game.

The length of a match varies widely: limited over matches have a set number of overs and are usually one-day events, other county matches last four days, and international test matches last up to five days. Rain and bad light frequently stop play, and draws (when time runs out without a result) are common.

(full internationals) and one-day internationals played here: obtain an application form and enter the ballot (lottery) to purchase tickets. Forms are sent out from early December. Standard Test Match tickets cost between £26 and £48. Countmatches can usually be seen by lining up on the day. ✉ *St. John's Wood Rd., St. John's Wood NW8,* ☎ *020/7432–1066. Tube: St John's Wood.*

The **Oval,** the home of Surrey County Cricket Club, is an easier place than Lord's to witness the *thwack* of leather on willow, with tickets for internationals sold on a first-come-first-served basis from late October. Though slightly less venerated than its illustrious cousin, the standard of cricket here is certainly no lower. ✉ *Kennington Oval, Brixton SE11,* ☎ *020/7582–6660. Tube: Oval.*

Equestrian Events

RACING

The main events of "the Season," as much social as sporting, occur just outside the city. Her Majesty attends **Royal Ascot** (✉ Grand Stand, Ascot, Berkshire, ☎ 01344/622211) in mid-June, driving from Windsor in an open carriage and processing before the plebs daily at 2. You'll need to book good seats far in advance for this event, although some tickets—far away from the Royal Enclosure and winning post—can usually be bought on the day of the race for £10–£15. Grandstand tickets, which must be bought well in advance, cost £40–£49. There are also Ascot Heath tickets available for a mere £3, but these only admit you to a picnic area in the middle of the race course. You'll be able to see the horses, of course, but that's not why people come to Ascot. The real spectacle is the crowd itself: enormous headgear is de rigueur on Ladies Day—usually the Thursday of the meet—and those who arrive dressed inappropriately (jeans, shorts, tank tops) will be turned away from their grandstand seats.

Derby Day (✉ The Grandstand, Epsom Downs, Surrey, ☎ 01372/470047), usually held on the first Saturday in June, is, after Ascot, the second biggest social event of the racing calendar; it's also one of the world's greatest races for three-year-olds.

SHOW JUMPING

The late September or early October **Horse of the Year Show** is the top international competition, with fun events held alongside the serious. Best of all are the Pony Club Games, where children perform gymnastics on horseback. ✉ *Wembley Arena, Wembley, Middlesex,* ☎ *020/8900–9282. Tube: Wembley Park.*

Marathon

Starting at 9:30 AM on a Sunday in April, some 30,000 runners in the huge **Flora London Marathon** (☎ 020/7620–4117) race from Blackheath or Greenwich to the Mall. Entry forms for the following year are available between August and October.

Rugby

This is somewhat similar to American football, but team members play unpadded. It raises the British and (especially) Welsh blood pressure enormously. To find out about top clubs playing Rugby Union in and around the capital during the September to May season, peruse *Time Out* magazine.

Twickenham hosts the Rugby Union Six–Nations tournament, where relative newcomer Italy joins old-timers England, France, Scotland, Wales, and Ireland. During this competition, held January through March, rugby can rival even football for the nation's sporting attentions, and tickets for these matches are more precious than gold. The domestic Pilkington Cup Final is fought out at Twickenham in early May. Harlequins and London Scottish are club teams that both play their rugby here. ✉ *Twickenham Rugby Football Ground, Whitton Rd., Twickenham TW2,* ☎ *020/8892–2000.*

Rugby League is played much more in the north of England than in the south, but you can, however, catch the local Super League team, the London Broncos, at the **Stoop Memorial Ground** (✉ Langhorn Dr., Twickenham TW2, ☎ 020/8410–5000).

Football

To refer to the national sport as "soccer" is to blaspheme. It is football, and its importance to the people and the culture of the country seems to grow inexorably. British football has had massive injections of money from television and sponsorship, creating millionaire players and high-profile foreign stars in the domestic game. The domestic season (August through May) culminates in the FA Cup Final, traditionally the biggest day in the sporting calendar, for which tickets are about as easy to get as they are for the Super Bowl. International matches are marginally easier to attend. Normally held at Wembley, these games will take place at the country's other top grounds until a new National Stadium is complete.

For a real sample of this British obsession, nothing beats a match at the home ground of one of the London clubs competing in the Premier League, and a taste of the electric atmosphere only a vast football crowd can generate. Try to book tickets (from about £25 upwards) in advance. You might also check out London's lower division games: though the standard of football in Division 3 may not match that of the Premiership, tickets are much cheaper and easier to get hold of, and the environment can be just as fervent. For more information on teams, games and prices, look in *Time Out* magazine.

PREMIER LEAGUE TEAMS

Arsenal is historically London's most successful team, though it still often fails to match the northern giants Liverpool and Manchester United. ✉ *Avenell Rd., Highbury, Islington N5,* ☎ *020/7413–3366. Tube: Arsenal.*

Charlton Athletic has more passion than money, and its main goal is to prolong its stay in the top division as long as possible. You can get here by taking British Rail to Charlton. ✉ *The Valley, Floyd Rd., Greenwich SE7,* ☎ *020/8333–4010.*

Chelsea, adored by the slightly more genteel west London fan, has become famous for its showy continental players and style of play, but also its inconsistent results. ✉ *Stamford Bridge, Fulham Rd., Fulham SW6,* ☎ *020/7386–7799. Tube: Fulham Broadway.*

Fulham has relatively new hopes of joining the big-time, but certainly possesses the money and the self-confidence to join the big boys. ✉ *Craven Cottage, Stevenage Rd., Fulham SW6,* ☎ *020/7893–8383. Tube: Putney Bridge.*

Tottenham Hotspur, or "Spurs," traditionally an exponent of attractive, positive football, has underperformed in recent years, but is showing some signs of a renaissance. Take British Rail to White Hart Lane to get here. ✉ *White Hart Lane, 748 High Rd., Tottenham N17,* ☎ *08700/112–222.*

West Ham United, historically the high achiever of east London, finds it harder these days to match the salaries or the results of Arsenal or

Chelsea. ✉ *Boleyn Ground, Green St., East End E13,* ☎ *020/8548–2700. Tube: Upton Park.*

Tennis

The **Wimbledon Lawn Tennis Championships**—Wimbledon is famous among fans for the green, green grass of Centre Court; for strawberries and cream; and for rain, which always falls, despite the last-week-of-June/first-week-of-July high-summer timing. This event is the most prestigious of the four Grand Slam events of the tennis year. Whether you can get grandstand tickets is literally down to the luck of the draw, because there's a ballot system (lottery) for advance purchase. To apply, send a self-addressed, stamped envelope between September 1 and December 31 to ✉ Ticket Office, All England Lawn Tennis & Croquet Club, PO Box 98, Church Rd., Wimbledon SW19 5AE, ☎ 020/8946–2244, and hope for the best.

There are other ways to see the tennis. A block of Centre and Number 1 Court tickets is kept back to sell each day and fanatics line up all night for these, especially in the first week. Each afternoon tickets collected from early-departing spectators are resold (profits go to charity). These can be excellent grandstand seats (with plenty to see—play continues until dusk). You can also buy entry to the grounds to roam matches on the outside courts, where even the top-seeded players compete early in the fortnight. Get to Southfields or Wimbledon tube station as early as possible and start queuing to be sure of getting one of these.

If you don't fancy the crowds and snaking queues of Wimbledon, you can watch many of the top names in men's tennis play in the pre-Wimbledon **Stella Artois Tournament.** Ticketmaster (☎ 020/7413–1444) sells tickets for this increasingly popular event. ✉ *Queen's Club, Palliser Rd., West Kensington W14,* ☎ *020/7385–3421. Tube: Barons Court.*

7 SHOPPING

Napoléon must have known what he was talking about when he called Britain a nation of shopkeepers. The finest emporiums are in London, still. You can shop like royalty at Her Majesty's glove maker, run down a leather-bound copy of *Wuthering Heights* at a Charing Cross bookseller, find antique Toby jugs on Portobello Road, or drop in on clothier Paul Smith—a fave of Sir Paul McCartney. Whether you're out for fun or for fashion, London can be the most rewarding of hunting grounds.

Updated by Jacqueline Brown

WHEN IT COMES TO LONDON, shopping can be a transforming experience. It's an open secret that Cary Grant was virtually "created" by a bespoke suit from Kilgour, French, Stanbury (the tailors extended the shoulders of his jackets 6½ inches to improve his form and draped the material to slim his hips). Then there was that other fashion plate, the Duchess of Windsor—for at-home style, she couldn't be beat, thanks in part to the soigné accessories she bought at Colefax & Fowler, still purveying the "country-house look" from its shop on Brook Street. Today, London's stores continue to create icons and make styles—as you can see from a visit to Harvey Nichols, shrine of the *Absolutely Fabulous* crowd.

As befits one of the great trading capitals of the world, London's shops have been known to boast, "You name it, we sell it." If you have a yen to keep up with the Windsors, look for the BY APPOINTMENT logo, which means that this particular emporium supplies Her Majesty the Queen, Prince Philip, or the Prince of Wales—check the small print and the insignia to find out which. More fashionable types will prefer to check out the ever-expanding Browns of South Molton Street (bliss, to label hunters) while the surrounding small stores there and along quaint St. Christopher's Place aren't bad either. The most ardent fashion victims will shoot to Notting Hill, London's prime fashion location and scene of *that* movie. London's emporiums have gifts in every price range. Head to Bond Street or Knightsbridge if you're looking for the sort of thing you would find in every Rockefeller's Christmas stocking; if you're bargain-hunting, try one of the street antiques fairs (it wasn't so long ago that a Wordsworth manuscript was discovered in Brick Lane Market for less than $50).

If you have only limited time, zoom in on one or two of the West End's grand department stores, where you'll find enough booty for your entire gift list. Marks & Spencer is one of Britain's largest, and most beloved, chain stores, legendary primarily for its women's lingerie, its men's knitwear, and its food, good enough to pass off as home-cooked. Selfridges, London's answer to Macy's in New York, is a splendid pile of '20s architecture that dominates the whole of one block toward Marble Arch and is increasingly fashion-conscious and up to date. Liberty is famous for its prints—multitudes of floral designs, which you can buy as fabric or have made into everything from book covers to dresses. It may be hokey, but Harrods is not to be missed; apart from anything else, it's one of the best free shows in the city. And though Harrods trumpets that it can supply anything to anyone anywhere in the world (once, a baby elephant to Ronald Reagan) and boasts that the Queen sometimes does her Christmas shopping here, you can just pick up one of its distinctive green-and-gold-logo totes—a perfect touch of class for your marketing back home.

Credit cards are accepted virtually everywhere, but to make sure that your Cirrus or Plus card (to cite just two of the leading names) works in European ATMs, have your bank reset it to use a four-digit PIN number before your departure. Apart from bankrupting yourself, the only problem you'll encounter is exhaustion, since London is a town of many far-flung shopping areas. The farthest—in fact on the outskirts of London, at Greenhithe in the county of Kent just by the Thames—is Europe's largest gift to shopaholics, the 240-acre Bluewater. The mega glass-and-steel pleasure palace (with cute Kentish oasthouse roofs) by the water was designed by American architect Eric Kuhne and contains every up-market, high-street, brand-name store, department store, and chain store (more than 320) a shopper could desire. Trains depart frequently from Charing Cross. Shuttle buses go directly to the center from the local rail station.

Quick Tours

These itineraries are organized by special interest; full addresses are given in the listings below.

SUPER SHOPPING TOUR

For those who can make their way across the map faster than Napoléon and only have a few hours to spare, here's a suggested plan of action. Just keep in mind that you will return to your hotel room weary and wiped out, and your bathroom scale will show you've become 3 pounds lighter! Let's start with a great London trademark: **Harrods.** Be there when the doors open—this is one-stop shopping at its best (and one of the city's great sights). If you're chic to the cuticles, then make a beeline for **Harvey Nichols,** just a block away. Harvey Nicks always has the best in modern Brit style, be it couture, menswear, or home furnishings. Want a more traditional gift that would please any Lord and Lady Fitzuppity? Head to the nearby **General Trading Co.** on Sloane Street for that lovely Staffordshire spaniel, or run down to Pimlico to see the objets d'art and furniture of **David Linley,** the most talented royal around. For still more decorative goodies, tube or cab it over to Regent Street—one of London's main consumer hubs—and **Liberty** (which actually helped create the Arts and Crafts style of the Edwardian era). High rollers should walk east several blocks to Bond Street, Old and New. Of course, there's nothing like a visit to **Asprey & Garrard** or the other upper-crust stores here to make you acutely aware of how poor you are. Fashionistas should then stroll up through Mayfair several blocks to the northwest and South Molton Street to find **Browns,** flooded with Kate Moss lookalikes, then head down Davies Street to the couture salon of **Vivienne Westwood.** On Davies Street you'll also find **Grays Antique Market** and **Grays in the Mews**—just the places to find a Charles II silver spoon. For gifts with gentler price tags, tube or cab it south to Piccadilly and **Hatchards**—bookseller to the royals, which still retains a trad atmosphere—or nearby **Fortnum & Mason,** the Queen's grocers, to buy some tea. Speaking of which, head upstairs and collapse for the high tea here, or make a last stop at **Floris,** a few blocks south on Jermyn Street—it's one of London's prettiest perfumeries. Opt for a scent once favored by Queen Victoria or—at almost pocket-money prices—a natural-bristle toothbrush. Oh, yes: if you want to add the very latest stores to this list, check out the suggestions in the monthly glossies, such as *Tatler* magazine's "I Can't Get Through the Month Without . . ." shopping pages or the *World of Interiors* "Antennae" section, or the glossy shopping sections in the Sunday newspapers. Whew! As you can see, for out-of-the-ordinary shopping, London can't be beat.

ANTIQUES

Start early morning around 8 AM (Saturday or Wednesday, when the dealers haggle) and head to **Camden Passage** in Islington, where you can browse through silverware, porcelain, prints, and old books. For under £30 you can often find pretty silver spoons. Take the tube from Highbury and Islington to Oxford Circus and the **Liberty** Antiques Department, whose top floor has top-scale antiques, the refurbished chairs with the distinctive Liberty print. If you fancy your chances at auction, just a few blocks south is **Sotheby's,** which has some classy pieces, from Impressionist paintings to country-house furnishings. You can stop for lunch at the Sotheby's Café, or stride on to **Grays Antiques**

Market on Davies Street for smaller, more affordable pieces, such as old jewelry, prints, and ceramics.

BARGAINS

In January and July, stores slash prices and armor-plating is a must-have when negotiating London's premier shopping mile, Oxford Street. Shifting street fashion fast is **Top Shop**'s speciality, but for higher quality and over-twenties, **John Lewis** professes to be never knowingly undersold. Whisk into the branch of **Accessorize** at 293 Oxford Street for the latest discount beads and baubles. **Debenhams** department store, a block west, has sale events throughout the year and runs the Jasper Conran diffusion line. Designer shoppers look sharp at **Browns**; check out Browns Labels for Less at No. 50 on nearby Molton Street for big labels at low prices. **Marks & Spencer** in Marble Arch has the largest selection of budget separates, year-round.

Shopping Districts

Camden Town

Crafts and vintage-clothing markets and shops clustered in and around picturesque but over-renovated canalside buildings have filled up every available space all the way up to the Roundhouse, Chalk Farm, in this frenetic locale for the world's youth. It's a good place for boots, T-shirts, inexpensive leather jackets, ethnic crafts, antiques, and recycled trendy wear. Things are quieter midweek.

Chelsea

Chelsea centers on King's Road, which is no longer synonymous with ultra fashion but still harbors some designer boutiques, plus antiques and home-furnishings emporiums. The fashionable section is more off-road Chelsea, toward Belgravia, where the hot young stars of fashion are creating a haven: Lulu Guinness, Erickson Beamon, and Philip Treacy line up on Elizabeth Street.

Covent Garden

The restored 19th-century market building—in a something-for-everyone neighborhood named for the market itself—houses mainly high-class clothing chains, plus good-quality crafts stalls. Neal Street and the surrounding alleys offer amazing gifts of every type—bikes, kites, tea, herbs, beads, hats . . . you name it. Floral Street and Long Acre have designer and chain-store fashion in equal measure, while Monmouth Street, Shorts Gardens, and the Thomas Neal's mall on Earlham Street offer trendy clothes for club kids. The area is good for people-watching, too.

Hampstead

For picturesque peace and quiet with your shopping, stroll around here midweek. Upscale clothing stores and representatives of the better chains share the half-dozen streets with cozy boutique-size shops catering to the home and stomach.

Kensington

Kensington Church Street has expensive antiques, plus a little fashion. The main drag, Kensington High Street, is a smaller, less crowded, and classier version of Oxford Street, with a selection of clothing chains and larger stores at the eastern end.

Knightsbridge

Harrods dominates Brompton Road, but there's plenty more, especially for the well-heeled and fashion-conscious. Harvey Nichols is the top clothes stop, with many expensive designers' showcases along Sloane Street. Walton Street and narrow Beauchamp (pronounced "Beecham")

Place offer more of the same, plus home furnishings and knickknacks; and Brompton Cross, at the start of Fulham Road, is the most design-conscious corner of London, with the Conran Shop and Joseph Ettudgui's store leading the field.

Marylebone

Behind the masses of Oxford Street lies this quiet backwater with Marylebone High Street as its main artery. Restaurants once coexisted peacefully along with delis and practical stores until the arrival of the Conran Shop and Orrery restaurant, which paved the way for a retinue of smart designer furniture stores. Satellite streets now have understated designer women's wear and menswear. Stride along a block or two to Great Portland Street and you'll arrive at the smart Villandry food emporium and the gateway to fashionable Fitzrovia.

Mayfair

Here is Bond Street, Old and New, with desirable dress designers, jewelers, plus fine art (old and new) on Old Bond Street and Cork Street. South Molton Street has high-priced, high-style fashion—especially at Browns—and the tailors of Savile Row are of worldwide renown.

Notting Hill

Branching off from the famous Portobello Road market are various enclaves of boutiques selling young designers' wares, antiques, and things for the home—now favored stops for trendsetters. Go westward and explore the Ledbury Road–Westbourne Grove axis, Clarendon Cross, and Kensington Park Road, for an eclectic mix of antiques and up-to-the-minute must-haves for body and lifestyle. Toward the more bohemian foot of Portobello are Ladbroke Grove and Golborne Road, where, in among the tatty stores, Portuguese cafés, and patisseries, you can bag a bargain. This is a hot treasure-trove area.

Oxford Street

Overcrowded Oxford Street is past its prime and is lined with tawdry discount shops at the Tottenham Court Road end, but many still flock here for some of London's great department stores in the run up to Marble Arch—particularly Selfridges, John Lewis, and Marks & Spencer—and the interesting boutiques secreted in little St. Christopher's Place and Gees Court.

Piccadilly

The actual number of shops is small for a street of its length (Green Park takes up a lot of space), but Piccadilly fits in several quintessential British emporiums. Fortnum & Mason is the star, and the historic Burlington Arcade is an elegant experience even for shop-phobics.

Regent Street

At right angles to Oxford Street, this wider, curvier version has several department stores, including the legendary Liberty. Hamleys is the capital's toy center; other shops tend to be stylish men's chain stores or airline offices, though there are also shops selling china and bolts of English tweed. "West Soho," around Carnaby Street, stocks designer youth paraphernalia, which these days is becoming more grown-up and desirable.

St. James's

Where the English gentleman shops, this district has some of the most elegant emporiums for hats, handmade shirts and shoes, and silver shaving kits and flasks. Doorways often bear royal warrants, and shops along Jermyn Street, like Floris, have museum-quality interiors and facades. Nothing is cheap, in any sense.

Shopping (Map A): Mayfair, Soho, and Covent Garden

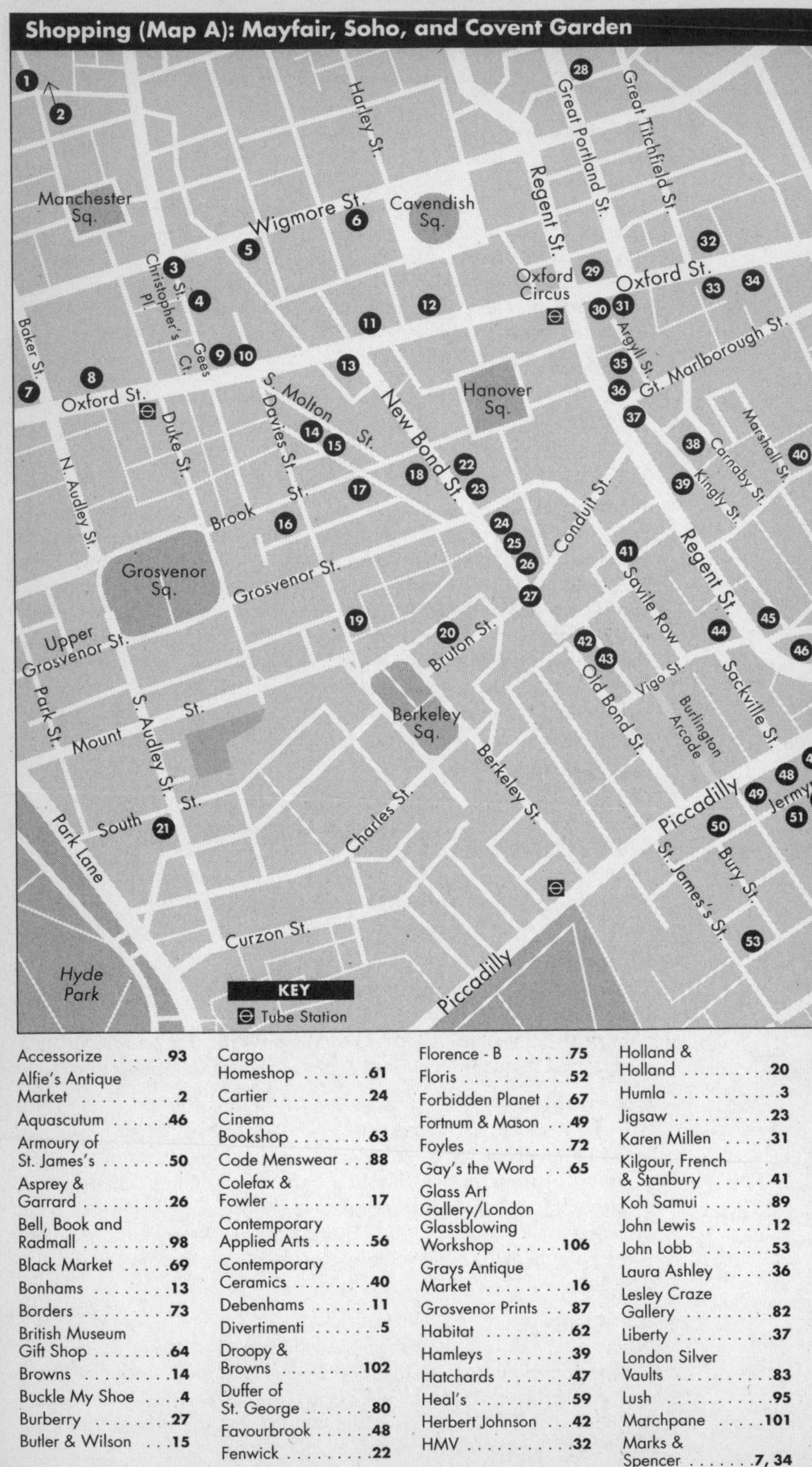

Accessorize 93
Alfie's Antique Market 2
Aquascutum 46
Armoury of St. James's 50
Asprey & Garrard 26
Bell, Book and Radmall 98
Black Market 69
Bonhams 13
Borders 73
British Museum Gift Shop 64
Browns 14
Buckle My Shoe 4
Burberry 27
Butler & Wilson . . .15
Cargo Homeshop 61
Cartier 24
Cinema Bookshop 63
Code Menswear . . .88
Colefax & Fowler 17
Contemporary Applied Arts 56
Contemporary Ceramics 40
Debenhams 11
Divertimenti 5
Droopy & Browns 102
Duffer of St. George 80
Favourbrook 48
Fenwick 22
Florence - B 75
Floris 52
Forbidden Planet . . .67
Fortnum & Mason . . .49
Foyles 72
Gay's the Word . . .65
Glass Art Gallery/London Glassblowing Workshop 106
Grays Antique Market 16
Grosvenor Prints . . .87
Habitat 62
Hamleys 39
Hatchards 47
Heal's 59
Herbert Johnson . . .42
HMV 32
Holland & Holland 20
Humla 3
Jigsaw 23
Karen Millen 31
Kilgour, French & Stanbury 41
Koh Samui 89
John Lewis 12
John Lobb 53
Laura Ashley 36
Lesley Craze Gallery 82
Liberty 37
London Silver Vaults 83
Lush 95
Marchpane 101
Marks & Spencer 7, 34

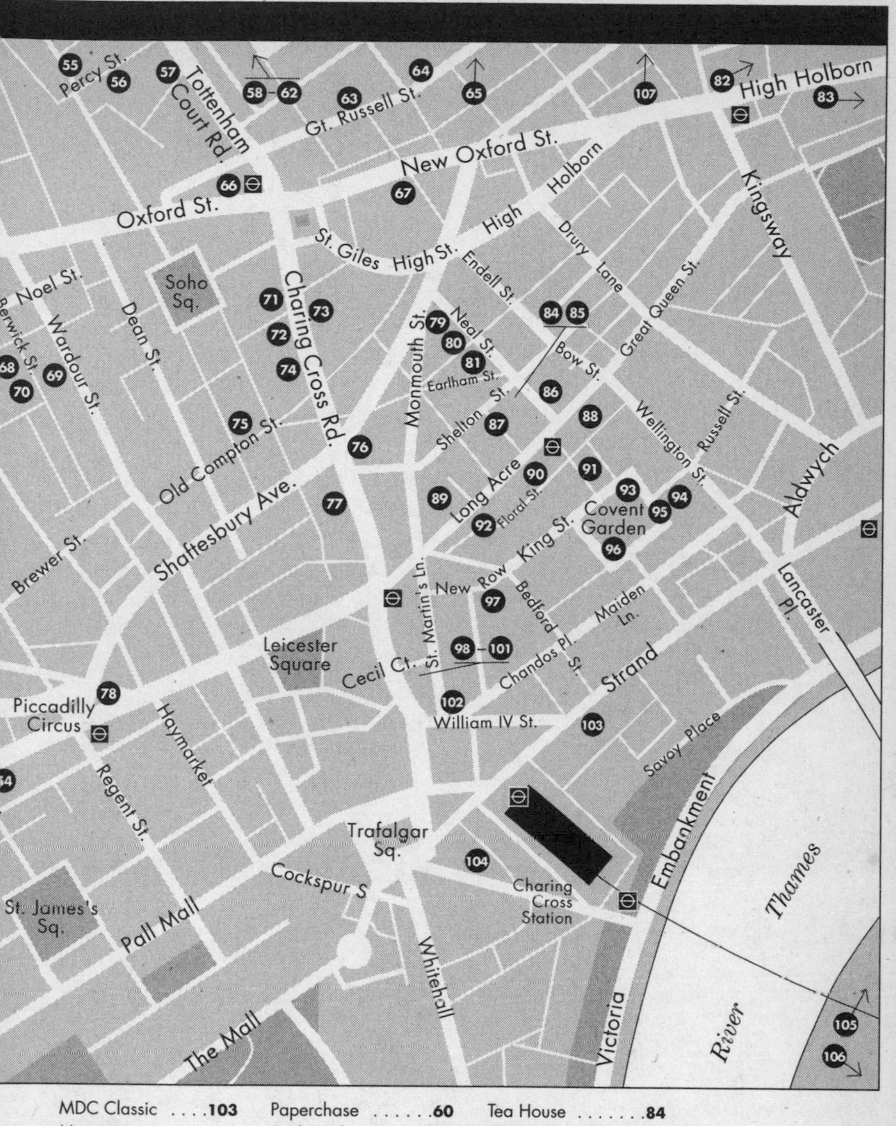
Percy St.
Tottenham Court Rd.
Gt. Russell St.
High Holborn
New Oxford St.
Oxford St.
Holborn
High
St. Giles High St.
Drury Lane
Kingsway
Endell St.
Great Queen St.
Noel St.
Soho Sq.
Berwick St.
Wardour St.
Dean St.
Charing Cross Rd.
Monmouth St.
Neal St.
Bow St.
Earlham St.
Shelton St.
Wellington St.
Russell St.
Old Compton St.
Long Acre
Floral St.
Covent Garden
Aldwych
Shaftesbury Ave.
Brewer St.
King St.
New Row
Bedford St.
Maiden Ln.
Lancaster Pl.
St. Martin's Ln.
Leicester Square
Cecil Ct.
Chandos Pl.
Strand
Piccadilly Circus
Haymarket
William IV St.
Savoy Place
Regent St.
Embankment
Trafalgar Sq.
Thames
Cockspur S
Charing Cross Station
St. James's Sq.
Pall Mall
Whitehall
Victoria
River
The Mall

Shopping (Map B): Kensington, Knightsbridge, and Chelsea

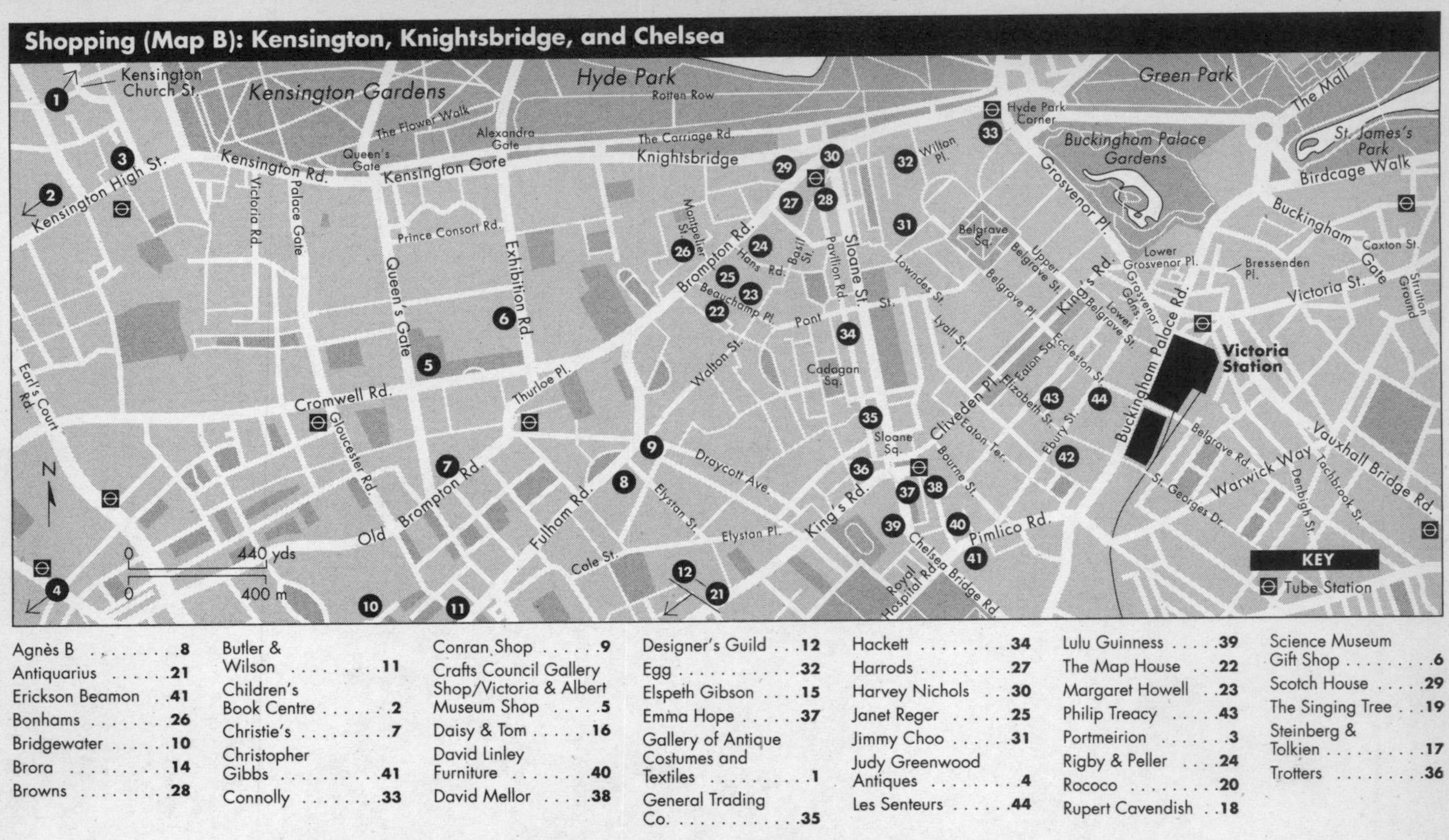

Agnès B 8
Antiquarius 21
Erickson Beamon . .41
Bonhams 26
Bridgewater 10
Brora 14
Browns 28
Butler & Wilson 11
Children's Book Centre 2
Christie's 7
Christopher Gibbs 41
Connolly 33
Conran Shop 9
Crafts Council Gallery Shop/Victoria & Albert Museum Shop 5
Daisy & Tom 16
David Linley Furniture 40
David Mellor 38
Designer's Guild . . .12
Egg 32
Elspeth Gibson 15
Emma Hope 37
Gallery of Antique Costumes and Textiles 1
General Trading Co. 35
Hackett 34
Harrods 27
Harvey Nichols . . .30
Janet Reger 25
Jimmy Choo 31
Judy Greenwood Antiques 4
Les Senteurs 44
Lulu Guinness 39
The Map House . . .22
Margaret Howell . .23
Philip Treacy 43
Portmeirion 3
Rigby & Peller 24
Rococo 20
Rupert Cavendish . .18
Science Museum Gift Shop 6
Scotch House 29
The Singing Tree . . .19
Steinberg & Tolkien 17
Trotters 36

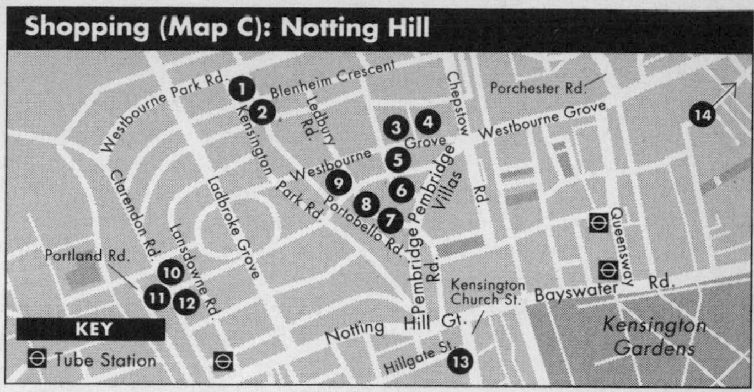

Department Stores

London's department stores range from Harrods—which every tourist is obliged to visit—through many serviceable middle-range stores devoted to the middle-of-the-road tastes of the middle class, to a few cheapjack ones that sell merchandise you would find at a better price back home. Most of the best and biggest department stores are grouped in the West End around Regent Street and Oxford Street, with two notable exceptions out in Knightsbridge.

Harrods. The only English department store classed among monuments and museums on every visitor's list, it hardly needs an introduction. It is swanky and plush and as deep-carpeted as ever; its spectacular food halls are alone worth the trip; and it stands out from the pack for fashion, too. You can forgive the store its immodest motto, *Omnia, omnibus, ubique* ("Everything, for everyone, everywhere"), because there are more than 230 departments, including a pet shop rumored to supply you with anything from aardvarks to zebras on request and a toy department—sorry, "kingdom"—which does the same with plush versions. During the pre-Christmas period and sales—the legendary one is during the last three weeks of January, but another storewide event, usually only one week, is held in mid-July—the entire store is a menagerie. ✉ *87 Brompton Rd., Knightsbridge SW1,* ☎ *020/7730–1234. Tube: Knightsbridge.* (☞ Map B)

Harvey Nichols. It's just a block away from Harrods, but it's not competing on the same turf, because its passion is fashion, all the way. There are nearly six floors of it, including departments for dressing homes and men, but the woman who invests in her wardrobe is the main target. Accessories are strong suits, especially jewelry, scarves, and makeup—England's first MAC counter here was 10 deep for months. The fourth floor now has a chic home-design department, featuring such names as Nina Campbell, Mulberry, Ralph Lauren, and Designer's Guild. A reservation at the Fifth Floor restaurant is coveted. ✉ *109 Knightsbridge, Knightsbridge SW1,* ☎ *020/7235–5000. Tube: Knightsbridge.* (☞ Map B)

John Lewis. This store's motto is "Never knowingly undersold," and for an all kinds of goods at sensible prices, John Lewis is hard to beat. The brother store, Peter Jones, in Sloane Square, has a place in Sloane Ranger history, and you will probably encounter more Barbour jackets, velvet hair bands, and pearls here than anywhere else in town—and that's just on the customers. If you're handy with the needle, John Lewis has a wonderful selection of dress and furnishing fabrics. Many's the American home with John Lewis drapes. ✉ *278 Oxford St., Mayfair W1,* ☎ *020/7629–7711. Tube: Oxford Circus.* (☞ Map A)

Liberty. With a wonderful black-and-white mock-Tudor facade, it's a peacock among pigeons in humdrum Regent Street. Inside, it is a labyrinthine building, full of nooks and crannies stuffed with goodies, like a dream of an Eastern bazaar. Famous principally for its fabrics, it also has an Oriental department, rich with color; menswear that tends toward the traditional; and women's wear that has lately been spiced up with extra designer ranges. It is a hard store to resist, as you may well find an original gift—especially one made from those classic Liberty prints. ✉ *200 Regent St., Mayfair W1,* ☎ *020/7734–1234. Tube: Oxford Circus.* (☞ Map A)

Selfridges. It's near the Marble Arch end of Oxford Street, where blocks are crowded in the middle of the day and at sale time. This giant, bustling store was started early in the 20th century by an American, though it's now British-owned. If this all-rounder has one outstanding department it has to be its Food Hall, or else its frenetic cosmetics department—one of the largest in Europe—which seems to perfume the air the whole length of Oxford Street. Selfridges has made a specialty of high-profile popular designer fashions and has spent a lot of money spurcing up to great result. There's a theater-ticket counter and British Airways travel shop in the basement. ✉ *400 Oxford St., Mayfair W1,* ☎ *020/7629–1234. Tube: Bond St.* (☞ Map A)

Specialty Stores

Antiques

Investment quality or lovable junk, London has lots. Try markets first—even for pedigree silver, the dealers at these places often have the best wares and the knowledge to match. Camden Passage and Bermondsey are the best; the Portobello market has become a bit of a tourist trap, but its side streets are filled with interesting shops that are open outside market hours (Westbourne Grove is fast becoming the most stylish section of this part of town). Kensington Church Street is *the* antiques-shopping street, with prices and quality both high. If you know your stuff (and your price limit) head out to Tower Bridge Road, south of the river, where there are mammoth antiques warehouses, some of which are open on Sunday. The Furniture Cave, at the corner of Lots Road, Chelsea, has one of the largest stocks around. Or you could try your luck at auction against the dealers. Summer is usually a quiet period, but at any other time, there are plenty of bargains to be had. Of the hundreds of stores, listed here is a selection to whet your appetite. Opening times vary: many places that are open on Saturday and Sunday will close Monday or Tuesday.

Alfie's Antique Market. A huge and exciting labyrinth on several floors, it has dealers specializing in anything and everything but particularly in textiles, Arts and Crafts furniture, and theater memorabilia. You won't be deliberately stiffed, but it's a caveat emptor kind of place, thanks to the amazing range of merchandise. ✉ *13–25 Church St., Regent's Park NW8,* ☎ *020/7723–6066. Closed Sun.–Mon. Tube: Edgware Rd.* (☞ Map A)

Antiquarius. At the Sloane Square end of King's Road is an indoor antiques market with more than 200 stalls offering collectibles, including things that won't bust your baggage allowance: art deco brooches, meerschaum pipes, silver salt cellars, and so on. ✉ *131–145 King's Rd., Chelsea SW3,* ☎ *020/7351–5353. Closed Sun. Tube: Sloane Sq.* (☞ Map B)

Christopher Gibbs. This shop attracts such leading London tastemakers as J. Paul Getty Jr. and Mick Jagger, who, the society columns note, will hardly make a move without the judgment of Mr. Gibbs's legendary eye. If you're in the market for large decorative items, such as marble busts, priceless Elizabethan embroidery, and truly one-of-a-kind antiques from all ages, this is the place to go and dream. ✉ *3 Dove Walk, Pimlico Rd., Belgravia SW1,* ☎ *020/7730–8200. Closed weekends. Tube: Sloane Sq.* (☞ Map B)

Colefax & Fowler. The virtual birthplace of the English country-house look, this is one of the most beautiful interior decorating shops in London. John Fowler, Lady Colefax, and, most importantly, Virginia-born Nancy Lancaster together created that cozy yet grand style, and their legacy is preserved here in wonderful wallpapers, pretty painted-wood flower holders, and assorted antique accents. If you want to make your apartment back home a mini-Chatsworth, be sure to stop in here, if only to soak up the style. ✉ *39 Brook St., Mayfair W1,* ☎ *020/7493–2231. Closed weekends. Tube: Bond St.* (☞ Map A)

Facade. It has one of the largest eclectic collections of French and Italian chandeliers, sconces, and table lamps. Most of them aren't wired and cleaned to shining bright, and this is reflected in the reasonable prices, particularly for such an up-and-coming area. ✉ *196 Westbourne Grove, Notting Hill W11,* ☎ *020/7727–2159. Closed Sun.–Mon. Tube: Notting Hill Gate.* (☞ Map C)

Gallery of Antique Costume and Textiles. Numerous movie directors come here to get the period just right, because everything on the premises, from bedspreads to bloomers, was stitched before 1930—except for the copycat brocade vests. Models and Hollywood actors find incredible (and expensive) clothes here, too. It lies off our maps, but it is easily found three blocks north of the Edgware Road tube stop. ✉ *2 Church St., Regent's Park/Lisson Grove NW8,* ☎ *020/7723–9981. Closed Sun. Tube: Edgware Rd.* (☞ Map B)

Grays Antique Market. Dealers specializing in everything from Sheffield plates to Chippendale furniture assemble here under one roof. Bargains are not impossible, and proper pedigrees are guaranteed. Also try Grays in the Mews around the corner—it has more inexpensive, downscale merchandise. ✉ *58 Davies St., Mayfair W1,* ☎ *020/7629–7034. Closed Sun.; closed Sat. Jan.–Nov. Tube: Bond St.* (☞ Map A); ✉ 1–7 Davies Mews, Mayfair W1, ☎ 020/7629–7034.

Hope and Glory. This is one of the many specialty stores in Kensington with commemorative china and glass from 1887 to the present; there are also affordable lesser pieces. The entrance is on Peel St. ✉ *131A Kensington Church St., Kensington W8,* ☎ *020/7727–8424. Closed Sun. Tube: Notting Hill Gate.* (☞ Map C)

Judy Greenwood Antiques. It beckons with its glowing red walls and a delightful selection of high-style antiques: Miss Havisham-y settees, vintage fabrics and textiles, gilded mirrors, and side tables. ✉ *657 Fulham Rd., Chelsea SW6,* ☎ *020/7736–6037. Closed Sun. Tube: Fulham Broadway.* (☞ Map B)

London Silver Vaults. A basement conglomeration of around 40 dealers, it's a great place for the average Joe. Some pieces are spectacular, of course, but you can also pick up a set of Victorian cake forks or a dented candelabrum for around £50. ✉ *Chancery House, 53–64 Chancery La., Holborn WC2,* ☎ *020/7242–3844. Closed Sat. after 1, Sun. Tube: Chancery Lane.* (☞ Map A)

Rupert Cavendish. This most elevated of dealers has the Biedermeier market cornered, with Empire and Deco bringing up the rear. The shop is a museum experience. ✉ *610 King's Rd., Chelsea SW6,* ☎ *020/7731–7041. Closed Sun. Tube: Sloane Sq.* (☞ Map B)

Auction Houses

The pointers on going to auction: you don't need bags of money; the catalog prices aren't written in stone; and if you are sure of what you want when you view the presale, then bid with confidence. Listed below are the main houses, which all deal in fine art and furniture. And if you find these are out of your budget, snoop around Lots Road in Chelsea, where you can find more budget-priced contemporary furniture that compares favorably with the price of new.

Bonhams. One of the more buyer-friendly places, it has many interesting collections. Along with antiques, Bonhams specializes in 20th-century design. There is scope for extra browsing at Bonhams' other branch (Chelsea Galleries, 65–69 Lots Rd., Chelsea SW10). ✉ *Montpelier St., Knightsbridge SW7,* ☎ *020/7393–3900. Tube: Knightsbridge.* (☞ Map B)

Christie's. You'll find some great English country-house furniture in varying states of repair, paintings, prints, carpets, lighting, plus all manner of bona fide treasures. It's amazing what can be classed as infinitely desirable with surprising price tags: the blue door from the film *Notting Hill* and the blue pinafore dress worn by Judy Garland in *Wizard of Oz* went for a record £5,750 and £199,500 respectively. ✉ *85 Old Brompton Rd., Knightsbridge SW7,* ☎ *020/7581–7611. Tube: South Kensington.* (☞ Map B)

Phillips. It conducts many specialist sales and occasionally has an Old Master painting sale that nearly rivals Christie's. ✉ *101 New Bond St., Mayfair W1,* ☎ *020/7629–6602. Tube: Bond St.* (☞ Map A)

Sotheby's. There's a well-publicized calendar of regular auctions for the more well heeled. But if you just want to look, ponder on possible purchases and break for lunch in the superb café. ✉ *34–35 New Bond St., Mayfair W1,* ☎ *020/7293–5000. Tube: Bond St.* (☞ Map A)

Books

Charing Cross Road is London's booksville, with a couple of dozen stores here or hereabout. The many antiquarian booksellers tend to look daunting (deceptively, as Helene Hanff found by correspondence with No. 84), but there are many mainstream bookshops, too.

GENERAL

Borders. You'll find way more than books at this buzzing, vibrant chain-store—you can also get CDs and videos, and attend author signings and talks, and children's storytime and music sessions on Sundays. There's also a café. And, of course, a vast selection of books (an equally large branch is on Oxford Street). ✉ *120 Charing Cross Rd., Soho WC2,* ☎ *020/7379–8877. Tube: Tottenham Court Rd.* (☞ Map A)

Foyles. This store is especially large—so enormous it can be confusing—but it is the place to come to find almost anything. ✉ *113–119 Charing Cross Rd., Soho WC2,* ☎ *020/7437–5660. Tottenham Court Rd.* (☞ Map A)

Hatchards. This is one of London's well-established bookshops that hasn't been swallowed up by the big players. You can revel in its old-fashioned charm while perusing the well-stocked shelves lining the winding stairs. The staff have retained old-fashioned helpfulness, too. ✉ *187 Piccadilly, St. James's W1,* ☎ *020/7439–9921. Tube: Piccadilly Circus.* (☞ Map A)

Waterstone's. Part of an admirable, and expanding, chain, it is open late (until 8 PM Mon.–Sat.) and has a program of author readings and signings. The latest monster outlet is the Waterstone's at the revamped old Simpsons store on Piccadilly. ✉ *121–125 Charing Cross Rd., Soho WC2,* ☎ *020/7434–4291. Tube: Tottenham Court Rd.* (☞ Map A)

SPECIALTY

Bell, Book and Radmall. It has quality antiquarian volumes and specializes in modern first editions. ✉ *4 Cecil Ct., Covent Garden WC2,* ☎ *020/7240–2161. Tube: Tottenham Court Rd.* (☞ Map A)

Books for Cooks. With just about every cuisine from around the globe between covers, as well as the complete line-up of celebrity chef editions, it's quite simply the last word in food and cooking. Occasional cookery demonstrations (call for details) offer tempting samples. ✉ *4 Blenheim Crescent, Notting Hill W11,* ☎ *020/7221–1992. Tube: Notting Hill Gate.* (☞ Map C)

Children's Book Centre. In addition to children's books, it carries cards and a mass of multi-media. And if that doesn't spark the imagination, there are toys in the basement. ✉ *237 Kensington High St., Kensington W8,* ☎ *020/7937–7497. Tube: High Street Kensington.* (☞ Map B)

Cinema Bookshop. It has the subject taped with a comprehensive selection of old and new books on film from every angle. ✉ *13 Great Russell St., Bloomsbury WC1,* ☎ *020/7637–0206. Tube: Tottenham Court Rd.* (☞ Map A)

Fisher & Sperr. It has some real finds—secondhand books that time forgot. ✉ *46 Highgate High St., Highgate N6,* ☎ *020/8340–7244. Tube: Highgate.* (☞ Map C)

Forbidden Planet. Sci-fi, fantasy, horror, and comic books are for sale here. ✉ *71 New Oxford St., Bloomsbury WC1,* ☎ *020/7836–4179. Tube: Tottenham Court Rd.* (☞ Map A)

Gay's the Word. In the heart of London's gay community is this hot spot for literary and leisure interests, with a good selection of new and old books, magazines, and videos. ✉ *66 Marchmont St., Bloomsbury WC1,* ☎ *020/7278–7654. Tube: Leicester Sq.* (☞ Map A)

Marchpane. It stocks covetable rare and antique illustrated children's books and first editions, from the 18th-century to Harry Potter. ✉ *16 Cecil Ct., Charing Cross Rd., Covent Garden WC2,* ☎ *020/7836–8661. Tube: Tottenham Court Rd.* (☞ Map A)

Murder One. This is a must for fans of traditional Agatha Christie novels and techno sci-fi stories; it has everything from crimes of passion to fiendish horror. ✉ *71–73 Charing Cross Rd., Soho WC2,* ☎ *020/7734–3485. Tube: Tottenham Court Rd.* (☞ Map A)

Pleasures of Past Times. You can indulge your nostalgia for Victoriana here. ✉ *11 Cecil Ct., Charing Cross Rd., Covent Garden WC2,* ☎ *020/7836–1142. Tube: Tottenham Court Rd.* (☞ Map A)

Sportspages. It's an excellent place to start your cricket library. ✉ *Caxton Walk, 94–96 Charing Cross Rd., Soho WC2,* ☎ *020/7240–9604. Tube: Tottenham Court Rd.* (☞ Map A)

Stanfords. The shop specializes in travel books and maps; there are several floors. ✉ *12 Long Acre, Covent Garden WC2,* ☎ *020/7836–1321. Tube: Covent Garden.* (☞ Map A)

Talking Bookshop. Just behind Oxford Street, it has the listening scene taped up, with a large selection of fiction, autobiography, and famous memoirs—in user-friendly spoken form—in a selection to suit both adults and children. ✉ *11 Wigmore St., Regent's Park W1,* ☎ *020/7491–4117. Tube: Oxford Circus.* (☞ Map A)

Travel Bookshop. A short journey from foodies' paradise, this store covers the world on its shelves. It's great for globetrotters and armchair travelers alike. ✉ *13 Blenheim Crescent, Notting Hill W11,* ☎ *020/7229–5260. Tube: Notting Hill Gate.* (☞ Map C)

Zwemmer. Just off Charing Cross Road, it sells books on cinema, photography, and design. ✉ *24 Litchfield St., Covent Garden WC2,* ☎ *020/7240–4158. Tube: Tottenham Court Rd.* (☞ Map A)

CDs and Records

London created the great megastores that have taken over the globe, but for cutting-edge music from the clubs, there are specialty stores galore.

Black Market. Indie, house, garage, world—you'll find the hottest club music around. ✉ *25 D'Arblay St., Soho W1,* ☎ *020/7437–0478. Tube: Tottenham Court Rd.* (☞ Map A)

HMV. Make a special trip to the HMV flagship store for the widest selection at top volume. There are lots of autograph sessions and free shows, too. ✉ *150 Oxford St., Soho W1,* ☎ *020/7631–3423. Tube: Oxford Circus.* (☞ Map A)

MDC Classic Music. The helpful staff will guide you without a blink to the best deals, from Callas to Sutherland, and tell you whether the diva was in form. There's some jazz, too. ✉ *437 Strand, Covent Garden WC2,* ☎ *020/7240–2157. Tube: Charing Cross.* (☞ Map A)

Mr. CD. This tiny shop stocks a wide selection for all possible tastes. You must delve to find the bargains, but your discovery will likely be worthwhile. ✉ *80 Berwick St., Soho W1,* ☎ *020/7439–1097. Tube: Oxford Circus.* (☞ Map A)

Music & Video Exchange. It's fast becoming a destination for seekers of unusual and mainstream chart music. Young aspiring DJs are to be seen rifling among the used discs and 12-in selection. ✉ *95 Berwick St., Soho W1,* ☎ *020/7434–2939.* (☞ Map A)

Tower Records. Despite the fact that it doesn't carry records, its specialty departments are some of the best in London. ✉ *1 Piccadilly Circus, Soho W1,* ☎ *020/7439–2500. Tube: Piccadilly Circus.* (☞ Map A)

Virgin Megastore. This is Richard Branson's pride and joy (though his New York City store is even bigger). It's nice to have it all under one roof, but be prepared for an ear-blasting experience on the massive ground floor, which is stacked with current chart music. Other areas, with jazz and classics, are slightly more relaxed. Computer games are in vast supply. ✉ *14–16 Oxford St., Soho W1,* ☎ *020/7631–1234. Tube: Tottenham Court Rd.* (☞ Map A)

China and Glass

English Wedgwood and Minton china are as collectible as they ever were, and most large department stores carry a selection, alongside lesser varieties with smaller price tags. Regent Street has several off-price purveyors, and, if you're in search of a bargain, Harrods' sale (usually held during the last three weeks of January) can't be beat—but sharpen your elbows first. And for the latest in sleek Italian, French, and Scandinavian china and glassware, check out the modern kitchenware shops, which stock the young designer trends—stores such as Conran shops, Bluebird, Habitat, and Heal's. For handmade, signature glassware, try the Glass Art Gallery.

Bridgewater. This is the home of all those fruit bowls, cream jugs, and cheese platters that grace every country-style designer kitchen in London and the fashionable burbs. In the neighboring Bridgewater Pottery Café, you can create some of your own designs to take home. ✉ *739 Fulham Rd., Chelsea SW6,* ☎ *020/7371–5264. Tube: Fulham Broadway.* (☞ Map B)

David Mellor. It has practical Dartington crystal along with more unusual porcelain and pottery pieces by British craftspeople. ✉ *4 Sloane Sq., Chelsea SW1,* ☎ *020/7730–4259. Tube: Sloane Sq.* (☞ Map B)

Divertimenti. The store sells beautiful kitchenware, unusual culinary gifts—such as spoons made from polished horn—and lovely French pottery from Provence. An equally large selection can be found in the ultra-chic quarter of stores for stylish homes at ✉ *45–47 Wigmore St., Regent's Park W1,* ☎ *020/7935–0689, Tube: Oxford Circus* (☞ *Map A);* ✉ *139 Fulham Rd., Chelsea SW10. Tube: South Kensington.*

Portmeirion. It's been around for 40 years in its tabletop form (the design inspiration for the signature china is the famed town in North Wales). If you want to delve further into your re-creation of a country kitchen, this is the place. ✉ *13 Kensington Church St., Kensington W8,* ☎ *020/7938–1891. Tube: Notting Hill Gate.* (☞ Map B)

Summerhill & Bishop. A little piece of French country kitchen right down to the ancient black bicycle with basket (which probably contains garlic strings), it supplies French embroidered linen, Portuguese and Tuscan stoneware, natural candles and soaps, and all manner of authentic designer culinary ware for sleek city kitchens. ✉ *100 Portland Rd., Notting Hill W11,* ☎ *020/7221–4566. Tube: Notting Hill Gate.* (☞ Map C)

Thomas Goode. One of the world's top shops for formal china and leaded crystal has on display dinner plates designed and made for Dame Nellie Melba, Edward VII, Queen Victoria, and the last viceroy of India. ✉ *19 S. Audley St., Mayfair W1,* ☎ *020/7499–2823. Tube: Notting Hill Gate.* (☞ Map A)

Clothing

London is one of the world's four fashion capitals (along with Paris, Milan, and New York), and every designer you've ever heard of is sold here somewhere. As well as hosting the top names, though, London retains a reputation for quirky street style, and many an exciting young designer has cut his or her teeth selling early collections at a London street market or on the borders of the central shopping streets—Notting Hill, Islington, East End. Don't just go by the label, and you could be the first to wear clothes by a future star. Traditional British men's outfitters are rather well known. From the Savile Row suit, handmade shirt, and custom shoes to the Harris-tweeds-and-Oxford-brogues English country look that Ralph Lauren purloined, England's indigenous garments make for real investment dressing.

ACCESSORIES

Accessorize. Shrewd shoppers head here for the latest high-fashion items at low prices. Beady bags, feathery jewels, devoré scarves—clever copies of each season's catwalk versions reach these stores fast. There are branches across town. ✉ *Unit 22, The Market, Covent Garden WC2,* ☎ *020/7240–2107. Tube: Covent Garden.* (☞ Map A)

Georgina von Etzdorf. Made with finely woven metallic threads and delicate clusters of trapped fibers, Etzdorf's scarves and stoles give any outfit a million-dollar shimmer through the night. Too way-out? Then drool over sumptuous deep-colored devoré velvets and crushed silks (there are irresistible silk ties for men, but they're very expensive). Phosphorescent designs stretch to bags, shoes, and the most gorgeous jackets. A branch is at 1–2 Burlington Arcade, Piccadilly, W1. ✉ *61 Ledbury Rd., Notting Hill W11,* ☎ *020/7409–7789. Tube: Notting Hill Gate.* (☞ Map C)

Herbert Johnson. This store is one of a handful of gentlemen's hatters who still know how to construct deerstalkers, bowlers, flat caps, and panamas—all the classic headgear, with some Ascot-worthy hats for women, too. ✉ *54 St. James's St., St. James's W1,* ☎ *020/7408–1174. Tube: Piccadilly Circus.* (☞ Map A)

Lulu Guinness. This shop struck a death blow to the industrial black nylon bag by bringing in bags of beads, colored silks, and the loveliest designs. Guinness's store is equally girlish and fun (*Vogue* covers adorn a see-through floor), with a downstairs salon where you can take tea while selecting. ✉ *3 Ellis St., Chelsea SW1,* ☎ *020/7823–4828. Tube: Sloane Sq.* (☞ Map B)

Mulberry. It outdoes Ralph Lauren in packaging the English look. This quintessentially British company makes covetable, top-quality leather bags, belts, wallets, and cases for all sorts of things (even a mobile phone case and a travel case for laptop or computer organizer). Separates in fine wools, fine cotton shirts, and silk scarves and ties have widened the range. Although it is still considered traditional, Mulberry has increasingly been pursuing a quietly modern, international style niche. ✉ *11–12 Gees Ct., St. Christopher's Pl., Mayfair W1,* ☏ *020/7493–2546. Tube: Bond St.* (☞ Map A)

Philip Treacy. This name tops every fashion maven's Santa Claus list. Treacy's magnificent hats regularly grace the pages of *Harper's Bazaar*; one-half Mad Hatter, one-half Cecil Beaton, Treacy's creations always guarantee Making an Entrance. Only the most serious fashion plates need apply, truly: the atelier is open by appointment only. Cheapskates can shoot along to Debenhams department store on Oxford Street, where Treacy has a diffusion line. ✉ *69 Elizabeth St., Belgravia SW1,* ☏ *020/7824–8787. Tube: Sloane Sq.* (☞ Map B)

Swaine Adeney. It's been selling practical supplies for country pursuits since 1750. Not just for the horsey set, it has golf umbrellas, walking sticks, and hip flasks, all beautifully crafted and ingenious. One shouldn't be without the umbrella, with slim tipple-holder flask secreted inside the stick, on a frosty morning. Herbert Johnson, hatter, is housed downstairs. ✉ *54 St. James's St., St. James's SW1,* ☏ *020/7409–7277. Tube: Piccadilly Circus.* (☞ Map A)

GENERAL

Aquascutum. Known for its classic raincoats, it also stocks the garments to wear underneath, for both men and women. Style keeps up with the times but is firmly on the safe side, making this a good bet for solvent professionals with an anti-fashion-victim attitude. ✉ *100 Regent St., Soho W1,* ☏ *020/7675–9050. Tube: Piccadilly Circus.* (☞ Map A)

Burberry. It tries to evoke an English Heritage feeling, with mahogany closets and stacks of neatly folded merchandise adorned with the trademark "Burberry Check" tartan. In addition to being seen on those famous raincoat linings, the tartan graces scarves, umbrellas, and even pots of passion-fruit curd and tins of shortbread. ✉ *21–23 New Bond St., Mayfair W1,* ☏ *020/7839–5222; Tube: Piccadilly Circus.* ✉ *165 Regent St., Soho W1,* ☏ *020/7734–4060. Tube: Piccadilly Circus.* (☞ Map A)

Connolly. The leather made by this elite company is the essence of Rolls-Royce elegance and the flash of Ferrari. Drivers leave their vehicles to be made over inside, but you can content yourself with the accessories: a pair of leather driving gloves or a leather driving helmet and goggles. Prices are on a prestige basis—high—although you could settle for a smaller-statement souvenir belt or cuff links. ✉ *32 Grosvenor Crescent Mews, Belgravia SW1,* ☏ *020/7235–3883. Tube: Hyde Park Corner.* (☞ Map B)

Debenhams. This is one of the large department stores lining Oxford Street that has moved up the fashion stakes. Years ago it wasn't on the hip shoppers' map, but with the arrival of the pretty, affordable, Jasper Conran collection, wise buying gals soon homed in, and the latest big name to join the store is Pearce Fionda (other creations, by in-house design, are becoming more desirable, too). ✉ *334–348 Oxford St., Mayfair W1,* ☏ *020/7580–3000. Tube: Oxford Circus.* (☞ Map A)

Favourbrook. It tailors exquisite handmade vests, jackets, and dresses, all crafted from silks and brocades, velvets and satins, embroidered linens and chenilles. For ties and cummerbunds as well, men should kit out at 55 Jermyn Street, but from both branches you can order your own *Four Weddings and a Funeral* outfit. ✉ *18 Piccadilly Arcade, St. James's W1,* ☏ *020/7491–2337. Tube: Piccadilly Circus.* (☞ Map A)

Holland & Holland. At this place for the hunting-and-shooting fraternity, bespoke is the byword. It has everything from guns (by appointment to the Duke of Edinburgh and the Prince of Wales) to clothing requirements for hunting, all with the Holland & Holland brand label.

Tailor-made travel wear (especially of the adventure variety) is also available. The company has been in business since 1830 (rifles have been made by the same London factory since 1835) but was bought out by Chanel—a reason for the brighter, trendy yet practical separates aimed at the younger country set. "Sloane rangers" have their own branch at 171–172 Sloane Street. ✉ *31–33 Bruton St., Mayfair W1,* ☎ *020/7499–4411. Tube: Bond St.* (☞ Map A)

Jigsaw. It's popular for its separates, which don't sacrifice quality to fashion, are reasonably priced, and suit women from their twenties to forties. There's a men's branch on Bruton Street, W1, and other branches are found across town. Juniors get in on the act, too, with their own line, Jigsaw Junior. ✉ *126–127 New Bond St., Mayfair W1,* ☎ *020/7491–4484. Tube: Bond St.* (☞ Map A)

Marks & Spencer. A major chain of stores that's an integral part of the British way of life, it sells sturdy practical clothes and basic accessories, all at moderate, though not bargain-basement, prices. "Marks and Sparks," as it is popularly known, has never been renowned for its high style, though that is changing as it continues to bring in (anonymously) big-name designers to spice up its lines. What it *is* renowned for is underwear; the English all buy theirs here. This holds true for knitwear as well. This Marble Arch branch has the highest stock turnover of any shop in the land. ✉ *458 Oxford St. (main store), Mayfair W1,* ☎ *020/7935–7954. Tube: Marble Arch.* (☞ Map A)

Muji. This exponent of no-frills lifestyle has functional white cotton T-shirts, simply cut underwear, pants in neutral and plain colors, and navy and black sweaters that are all so popular they walk out of the shop. The merchandise is in complete harmony: white earthenware tableware on minimal steel shelving; cream duvets on understated maple beds; gray towels and skin-care products in white recyclable containers—it's a lifestyle dream that defies the cumulative heaps in most mortals' homes. Branches are as follows: 187 Oxford St., W1; 135 Long Acre, Covent Garden, WC2; 157 Kensington High St., W8; 77 King's Rd., Chelsea, SW3. ✉ *Unit 5, 6–17 Tottenham Court Rd., Bloomsbury W1,* ☎ *020/7436–1779. Tube: Tottenham Court Rd.* (☞ Map A)

Next. This store carries clothing for men, women, and children that gives Gap a run for its money. In general, the styles are a little wilder and more fashionable, yet are reasonably priced. ✉ *203 Oxford St., Soho W1,* ☎ *020/74434–0477. Tube: Oxford Circus.* (☞ Map A)

Paul Smith. He's your man if you don't want to look outlandish but you're bored with plain pants and sober jackets. Smith's well-tailored suits have a subtle quirkiness (like an outrageous, witty flash of colorful lining); his shirts and ties have a sense of humor; and his jeans and sweats are cut well. Customers include Paul McCartney, Harrison Ford, and David Hockney. The boutique itself is worth seeing: it's re-created from a Victorian chemist's shop, and Smith's own collection of toiletries and jewelry (women are also catered to here) adorns the shelves. The sale shop for discontinued lines is at 23 Avery Row (W1), and the minimalist-style women's store is at 84–86 Sloane Avenue (SW3). But the latest Smith buzz is Westbourne House (122 Kensington Park Rd., W11): a shop in a house designed to feel like an actual London home where women's, men's, and children's clothes and accessories are arranged in homelike settings. ✉ *40–44 Floral St., Covent Garden WC2,* ☎ *020/7379–7133. Tube: Covent Garden.* (☞ Map A)

Scotch House. As you'd guess, this is the place to buy your kilts, tartan scarves, and argyle socks without going to Edinburgh. It's also well stocked with cashmere and accessories. ✉ *2 Brompton Rd., Knightsbridge SW1,* ☎ *020/7581–2151. Tube: Knightsbridge.* (☞ Map B)

Top Shop. One of London's niftiest megachains for young men and women, it's also the largest fashion store in the world. If you can circumnavigate round it and still keep your hearing intact, head for the faux-vintage "souled-out" section—the prices are as reasonable as at any market stall. Top-notch trendsetting designers are keeping the store one step ahead: Clements Ribeiro has produced a line for TS Design. ✉ *214 Oxford St., Soho W1,* ☎ *020/7636–7700. Tube: Oxford Circus.* (☞ Map A)

Zara. It has swept across Europe and the East (the price tags carry 25 flags and related prices) and has won a firm position in London. It's not hard to see why. The style is young and snappy; colors are great, with clothes sorted into color groupings for work and play; and the prices are unbelievably low. However, don't expect durability. These are fun, fashion pieces with a few basics. The whole spectrum is covered, including accessories: beady bags, wacky shoes and boots, moleskin mule slippers, jewelry. Menswear and a terrific line for kids each has its own floor. ✉ *118 Regent St., Soho W1,* ☎ *020/7534–9500. Tube: Piccadilly Circus.* (☞ Map A)

CHILDREN'S WEAR

Kids are making it big in retail fashion. While the chain stores, such as Marks & Spencer and Debenhams, produce sensible and fun collections, the fashion chains offer hipper versions and greater selection. Check out H&M, Jigsaw Junior, Next, and Zara, which rival Gap for variety. For ultra-expensive label gear, Harrods and Selfridges give plenty of choice. If you're on the lookout for lesser-known kidswear designers, check out one of the growing number of small boutiques especially for kids, such as those below; kids' clothes are increasingly found in shops for mom, too, such as Cath Kidston.

Daisy & Tom. This shop is for cool kids and smart parents, who know that a happy child is an entertained child. Sadly there is no designer gear for mom to try on while her child is busy on the carousel, cuddling soft toys, or having a haircut. On one dedicated floor there are high-fashion junior clothes (Kenzo, IKKS, and Polo), shoes aplenty (for newborns to 10-year-olds), a bookshop, and a soda fountain–café. What's more, it's all open on Sunday. ✉ *181–183 King's Rd., Chelsea SW3,* ☎ *020/7352–5000. Tube: Sloane Sq.* (☞ Map B)

Humla. It brought a colorful taste of Sweden to London before superstore IKEA steamrolled in. Mrs. Harris has been stocking beautifully made, quality children's clothes for 25 years and not so long ago used to make her own stripey handknits at the back of the shop. That originality is there still, although not her own work. Another branch is at 9 Flask Walk, Hampstead, where there is also a collection of nursery furniture and timeless wooden toys. ✉ *23 St. Christopher's Pl., Mayfair W1,* ☎ *020/7224–1773. Tube: Bond St.* (☞ Map A)

Trotters. The last word in the latest ranges for parents who want to dress their darlings in trad styles, and for cool young things who want to look just that. All the trendy labels can be found here, to cater from top to toe (a hairdressing service is offered, plus shoes with good fitting attendants) along with videos to keep tempers cool, toys, and books. Convenient for style-hunters at the Sloane end of King's Road, and open seven days. ✉ *34 King's Rd., Chelsea SW3,* ☎ *020/7259–9620. Tube: Sloane Sq.* (☞ Map B)

MEN'S WEAR

Most stores listed above under General Clothing stock excellent menswear. Try Aquascutum, Burberry, and Paul Smith. All the large department stores, too, carry men's clothing, Selfridges and Harrods especially. There is a stealthy revolt away from the bastion of traditional made-to-order suits as young careerists break away from fatherly City-gent tailors. Sharp suiters, such as Ozwald Boateng, are noticeably un–Savile Row in style and demeanor. Those with more flash than cash will hot foot to the trend-setting fashion chains: Top Man at Top Shop and Zara.

Code. The Moss Bros. suit group goes streetwise with a reinvention of the previous Blazer store. With shirts from £25, the redirection is toward a cool stance on classics, from denim to stripes. Other separates follow a similar fashion theme, offering stylish lines at affordable prices (even if the garment has a hand-tailored finish). Other branches are in Broadgate, the City, and King Street, just off Covent Garden's piazza. ✉ *117B Long Acre, Covent Garden WC2,* ☏ *020/7379–0456. Tube: Covent Garden.* (☞ Map A)

Duffer of St. George. In addition to having fashions by hip designers of street style, it sells its own label of sporty and dress-up lines for clubbing and posing with attitude. ✉ *29 Shorts Gardens, Covent Garden WC2,* ☏ *020/7379–4660. Tube: Covent Garden.* (☞ Map A)

Hackett. Started as a posh thrift shop, it once recycled cricket flannels, hunting pinks, Oxford brogues, and similar British wear. Now it makes its own attire, and it has become a genuine—and very good—gentlemen's outfitter, though polo shirts and faux sports gear are a strong theme. ✉ *137 Sloane St. (main store), Knightsbridge SW3,* ☏ *020/7730–3331. Tube: Knightsbridge.* (☞ Map B)

Kilgour, French & Stanbury. This classic and highly expensive tailor makes custom-cut suits and shirts (but note the cutters all go to lunch between 1:30 and 2:30 every afternoon). The 11th commandment here: you know a man looks like an English gentleman only when you do not notice that he is well dressed. ✉ *8 Savile Row, Mayfair W1,* ☏ *020/7734–6905. Tube: Piccadilly Circus.* (☞ Map A)

Mercer. It's been quietly cutting a dash in increasingly trendy Marylebone district. Before he got the top job, Tony Blair used to buy here, but he is more likely to be seen now in British tailored suits. Mercer's is filled with softly constructed menswear (casual weekend wear, trendy business suits, and a hint of formal evening attire) in more unusual fabrics sourced and made in Italy. The soft tones and styles don't scream fashion but show a quiet cut of confidence. The staff is delightfully helpful. ✉ *13–15 Chiltern St., Regent's Park W1,* ☏ *020/7487–4383. Tube: Baker St.* (☞ Map A)

Nick Ashley. This boutique in one of the coolest areas of shops and restaurants in London, just west of Portobello, is in the mold of big-outdoors-goes-urban-cool. Ashley calls it performance wear—whether you're streaking about on a motorbike, loafing about looking cool in the city, or just keeping warm in Egyptian cotton vests and thermal long johns. The laid-back formula of chunky boots, polar fleece, and leather lookalike fabrics brings in the pop stars and young politicos. ✉ *57 Ledbury Rd., Notting Hill W11,* ☏ *020/7221–1221. Tube: Notting Hill Gate.* (☞ Map C)

Ozwald Boateng. It's one of the breed of bespoke tailors, not on Savile Row but on the fringe. Boateng's made-to-measure suits are sought after (by rock luminaries George Michael, Mick Jagger and Bill Wyman, and even Lisa Stansfield) for their exclusive fabrics, fashionable detail, and shock-color lining as well as great classic cut. If custom tailoring is out of financial reach (around £1,000–£2,000), there is a ready-to-wear collection (from under £1,000), or the zappiest ties to be had in town (from £60). ✉ *9 Vigo St., Mayfair W1,* ☏ *020/7734–6868. Tube: Piccadilly Circus.* (☞ Map A)

Tom Gilbey. The exciting part of this custom-tailor outfitter is his exquisite vests—in silk or brocade or hand-embroidered, others marginally plainer. Gilbey has moved from the New Burlington Place address to space at Richard Branson's Virgin Bride store. (But to wear one of his pieces to bridal-only occasions would be far too singular.) ✉ *The Grand Buildings, Northumberland Ave., Covent Garden WC2,* ☎ *020/7930–8885. Tube: Charing Cross.* (☞ Map A)

Turnbull & Asser. This is *the* custom shirtmaker. Unfortunately for those of average means, the first order must be for a minimum of six shirts, from around £100 each. But you'll find less expensive, though still exquisite, ready-to-wear shirts, too. ✉ *72–73 Jermyn St., St. James's W1,* ☎ *020/7808–3000. Tube: Piccadilly Circus.* (☞ Map A)

WOMEN'S WEAR

Agnès B. It has pretty, understated French clothing: many items are timelessly perfect, like fine knitwear and feminine cotton tops. Prices are mid-range and worthy for the quality—Ms. B has been a stalwart of the fashion press for years. There are branches at 41 Marylebone High Street (W1), 58–62 Heath Street (NW3), and in Hampstead (NW3); 35–36 Floral Street (WC2) has elegant men's suits. ✉ *111 Fulham Rd., South Kensington SW3,* ☎ *020/7225–3477. Tube: South Kensington.* (☞ Map B)

Brora. You'll find the very latest in cashmere and *those* shawls (pashminas, of course) here. There are prettily dressed-up camisoles, jumpers and cardigans, practical pants, and non-cashmere items as well (picnic blankets and wash bags). Prices are surprisingly mid-range for such high-fashion products. ✉ *344 King's Rd., Chelsea SW3,* ☎ *020/7352–3697. Tube: Sloane Sq.* (☞ Map B)

Browns. It was the first notable store to populate the South Molton Street pedestrian mall, and it seems to sprout more offshoots every time you visit it. Well-established, collectible designers (Donna Karan, Romeo Gigli, Jasper Conran, Jil Sander, Yohji Yamamoto) rub shoulder pads here with younger, funkier names (Dries Van Noten, Clements Ribeiro, Anne Demeulemeester, Hussein Chalayan), and Browns also has its own label. Its July and January sales are famed. Menswear gets a corner, too. Bargain hunters should hotfoot it down to Browns Labels for Less at No. 50. ✉ *23–27 S. Molton St., Mayfair W1,* ☎ *020/7491–7833. Tube: Bond St.* ; ✉ *6C Sloane St., Knightsbridge SW1,* ☎ *020/7514–0040. Tube: Knightsbridge.* (☞ Maps A and B)

Cath Kidston. This store brings charming ginghams and flower-sprig cotton prints to housecoats (with matching bed linens, cushions, wallpaper, and bath wear) and nightshirts. In fact, Kidston has everything you could want for a girl's bedroom in an English country cottage. The sweaters are practical, cozy handknits; the Anonymous line includes skimpy lace-edged vest tops and cardigans, and skirts in flouncy wools. There is a delightful children's wear line in the same nostalgic vein. ✉ *8 Clarendon Cross, Notting Hill W11,* ☎ *020/7221–4000. Tube: Notting Hill Gate.* (☞ Map C)

Droopy & Browns. Beautifully constructed, extravagantly theatrical frocks and suits, made up in raw silks, fine linens, brocades, and velvets are to be found here. Colors are strong, tailoring is impeccable, and salespeople don't turn up their noses at larger ladies. ✉ *99 St. Martin's La., Covent Garden WC2,* ☎ *020/7379–4514. Tube: Leicester Sq.* (☞ Map A)

Egg. The loosely ethnic work wear in limited colors with minimal, almost-no-fashion details is a winner. Maureen Doherty (co-founder) worked for Issey Miyake, so you get the idea. The off-street address and locale add to the shop's interest factor: a former Victorian dairy tucked away in a Knightsbridge mews. ✉ *36 Kinnerton St., Belgravia SW1,* ☎ *020/7235–9315. Tube: Knightsbridge.* (☞ Map B)

Elspeth Gibson. It has been building up a steady following as the firm favorite of models and personalities in the glossy mags and Sunday supplements: these clothes are for the flaunty girlie in you. There are delicate beads on soft cardies; swirly, flirty, embroidered Tyrol-type skirts; and simply herds of cashmere. ✉ *7 Pont St., Knightsbridge SW1,* ☎ *020/7235–0601. Tube: Knightsbridge.* (☞ Map B)

Fenwick. Around for years in a prime fashion spot, this shop manages to be very competitive. At sale time, it's a bargain one-stop shop, with a vast selection of bags, gloves, scarves, and shoes, and with a good selection of designers on the upper floors: Ben de Lisi, Jean Muir, Christian Lacroix, and Katherine Hamnett to name a few. ✉ *63 New Bond St., Mayfair W1,* ☎ *020/7629–9161. Tube: Bond St.* (☞ Map A)

Ghost. This store can be found with regularity in the fashion press. The design team, led by Tania Sarne, has the feel of the moment, producing willowy dresses and skirts in silks, velvets, and the ubiquitous viscose, which sculpts into wonderful crinkly textures. Indispensable little cardigans in silky weaves have been the wardrobe essential for quite some time and show no signs of fading. Pretty puff-sleeve blouses are also a strong feature. It's also at 14 Hinde St., W1. ✉ *36 Ledbury Rd., Notting Hill W1,* ☎ *020/7229–1057. Tube: Notting Hill Gate.* (☞ Map C)

Janet Reger. It's queen of the silk teddy, having become synonymous with the ultimate in luxurious negligees and lingerie many years ago. ✉ *10 Beauchamp Pl., Knightsbridge SW3,* ☎ *020/7584–9360. Tube: Knightsbridge.* (☞ Map B)

Karen Millen. Striking a clever balance between functional working clothes with subtle fashion detailing (muted pastels and soft colors in separates), fun urban weekend wear (leather biker jackets and black-and-white ponyskin coats), and glam for evenings (little dresses with Japanese almond-sprig detail), Millen appeals to all from grown-up teens through women in their forties. Mid-range prices are also a draw. ✉ *262–264 Regent St., Soho W1,* ☎ *020/7287–6158. Tube: Oxford Circus.* (☞ Map A)

Koh Samui. It stocks the clothing and accessories—some still steaming off the catwalk—of around 40 young designers, most of them British, some exclusive to this store, and all on the cutting edge. There are small items for under a tenner (eclectic hair clips by Japanese designer Heesoo) and drop-dead dresses for thousands of pounds (an exquisite hand-beaded dress by Berardi for £4,500). KS is the place to discover the next wave before *Vogue* gets the story. ✉ *65 Monmouth St., Covent Garden WC2,* ☎ *020/7240–4280. Tube: Covent Garden.* (☞ Map A)

Laura Ashley. The country dresses, blouses, and skirts, plus wallpapers and fabrics in dateless patterns that rely heavily on flowers, fruit, leaves, or just plain stripes have captured the nostalgic imagination of the world. ✉ *256–258 Regent St. (main store), Soho W1,* ☎ *020/7437–9760. Tube: Oxford Circus.* (☞ Map A)

Margaret Howell. Along with Paul Smith, Margaret Howell is the top exponent of Britishness in the Far East. Think classic fabrics—wools, silks—and perfect detail. It's the ultimate in investment, one-stop shopping. ✉ *29 Beauchamp Pl., Knightsbridge SW3,* ☎ *020/7584–2462. Tube: Knightsbridge.* (☞ Map B)

Nicole Farhi. This is the place for the career woman who requires quality, cut, *and* style in a suit, plus weekend wear in summer linens and silks, or winter hand-knit woolens. Prices are on the high side, but there is some affordable wear as well, especially the sporty, casual Diversion label. Farhi offers an equally desirable men's line. The downstairs in-store restaurant, **Nicole's,** is not just somewhere to resuscitate between purchases; Ms. Farhi designed the space and the menu to her own taste, and it is an extension of the fashion statement, a hot spot for lunching fashionistas who like to be seen. It's wise to reserve ahead (☎ 020/7499–8408). Main stores: ✉ *158 New Bond St., Mayfair W1,* ☎ *020/7499–8368. Bond St.;* ✉ *27 Hampstead High St., Hampstead NW3,* ☎ *020/7435–0866. Tube: Hampstead.* (☞ Map A)

Oasis. Good interpretations of designer trends are the stock in trade here. The latest colors and fabrics—from neutrals and brights to heavy jacquards and microfibers, in fact, whatever's hot on the catwalk—are translated into pared-down versions that suit all pockets. ✉ *13 James St., Covent Garden WC2,* ☎ *020/7240–7445. Tube: Covent Garden.* (☞ Map A)

Rigby & Peller. It's for those who love pretty lingerie. Many of the luxurious makes are here: La Perla and Gottex, as well the corsetières' own line. But if the right fit eludes, have one made to measure. Most of the young royal and aristo ladies buy here, not just because the store holds the royal appointment but because the quality and service are excellent, and much friendlier than you might expect. There is also a branch at 22A Conduit Street, off New Bond Street, W1. ✉ *2 Hans Rd., Knightsbridge SW3,* ☎ *020/7589–9293. Tube: Knightsbridge.* (☞ Map B)

Shirtsmith. Custom-made and ready-made shirts, suits, and jackets for women, using fine cottons and Indian silks are the staple here. Some designs are classic and fitted; others are slightly outrageous. ✉ *2A Ledbury Mews North, Notting Hill W11,* ☎ *020/7229–3090. Tube: Notting Hill Gate.* (☞ Map C)

Vivienne Westwood. If you want to see where it all started, the Pompadour-punk ball gowns, Lady Hamilton vest coats, and foppish landmark getups are the core of Westwood's first boutique at 430 King's Road. The designer still represents the apex of high-style British couture, and the Davies Street boutique sells the Gold Label line of intoxicatingly glamorous creations: ready-to-wear or made-to-measure. At 44 Conduit Street, the story is the sharper Red Line: hot, pared-down catwalk versions; menswear is also on offer here—the Westwood influence is far-reaching. ✉ *6 Davies St., Mayfair W1,* ☎ *020/7629–3757. Tube: Bond St.* (☞ Map A)

Warehouse. It has practical, stylish, reasonably priced separates in easy fabrics and lots of fun colors. The finishing isn't so hot, but style, not substance, counts here, and the shop's youthful fans don't seem to mind. The stock changes very quickly, so it always presents a new face to the world. ✉ *19 Argyll St. (main store), Soho W1,* ☎ *020/7437–7101. Tube: Oxford Circus.* (☞ Map A)

Whistles. This small chain stocks its own high-fashion, mid-price label, plus several selected eclectic designers. Clothes are hung in color-coordinated groupings in shops that resemble designers' ateliers. ✉ *The Market, Covent Garden WC2,* ☎ *020/7379–7401. Tube: Covent Garden ;* ✉ *Heath St., Hampstead NW3,* ☎ *020/7431–2395. Tube: Hampstead.* (☞ Map A)

Design

There's been a tremendous resurgence of interest in objects not mass-produced. The burgeoning market areas such as Spitalfields, the state-of-the-art OXO Tower, and Lesley Craze have become the new, eclectic fashion suppliers of jewelry, clothes, and housewares, and often to personal order. These sites are not in a central place. If you can't stretch out to these areas, then a good starting point is the Crafts Council Gallery Shop within the Victoria & Albert Museum. But forget the outmoded word "crafts"—this work is often more modern than modems.

Contemporary Applied Arts. Expect to see quite a range of work by designers and craftspeople. Regular shows and exhibitions display anything from glassware and jewelry to furniture and lighting. ✉ *2 Percy St., Soho W1,* ☎ *020/7436–2344. Tube: Tottenham Court Rd.* (☞ Map A)

Contemporary Ceramics. Formed by some of the best British potters as a cooperative venture to market their wares, this modernized store carries a wide spectrum of pottery, from thoroughly practical pitchers, plates, and bowls to ceramic sculptures. It's possibly the best selection of ceramics to be found in central London (just behind Oxford Street), with each piece carrying its own potted biography. There are lots of books on the art as well. Prices range from the reasonable to way up. ✉ *7 Marshall St., Soho W1,* ☎ *020/7437–7605. Tube: Oxford Circus.* (☞ Map A)

Crafts Council Gallery Shop/Victoria & Albert Museum Shop. This is where you'll find a microcosmic selection of British craftspeople's work (jewelry, glass, ceramics, toys). Accompanying the exhibitions in the museum are more focused displays, such as the Summer Show showcase. The Crafts Council has a smaller shop at its base in Islington, where you can source information on craftspeople and browse in the showcase gallery. ✉ *Cromwell Rd., South Kensington SW7,* ☎ *020/7589–5070. Tube: South Kensington (☞ Map B);* ✉ *44A Pentonville Rd., Islington N1,* ☎ *020/7806–2500.*

David Linley Furniture. This outpost for Viscount Linley—the only gentleman in the kingdom who can call the queen "Auntie" and, more importantly, one of the finest furniture designers of today—has heirlooms of the future; the desks and chairs have one foot in the 18th century, another in the 21st. The large pieces are suitably expensive, but small desk accessories and objets d'art are also available. ✉ *60 Pimlico Rd., Chelsea SW1,* ☎ *020/7730–7300. Tube: Sloane Sq.* (☞ Map B)

Designers Guild. Tricia Guild shows her fabrics and accessories of fabulous, saturated colors here. Inspirational, many designers vouch; and she has now incorporated furniture, objets d'art, and linens. ✉ *267–271 and 275–277 King's Rd., Chelsea SW3,* ☎ *020/7351–5775. Tube: Sloane Sq.* (☞ Map B)

Glass Art Gallery/London Glassblowing Workshop. Glassblowers and designers make decorative and practical pieces on site. The artists are British-based and display their work in the gallery. If you visit on weekdays, you can see them at work, and buy or commission your own variation. Prices can go into the thousands, but there are Saturday sales in April, July, and November–December, when many pieces go for less than £30. In the Leathermarket, which is off our map, you can find other craftspeople as well, most notably a silversmith and papermaker. ✉ *7 The Leathermarket, Weston St., The South Bank SE1,* ☎ *020/7403–2800. Tube: London Bridge.* (☞ Map A)

Lesley Craze Gallery. This gallery is making quite a name for itself. Craze has cornered a design market in what is now a fashionable area. You'll find the most exquisite jewelry to drool over, by some 100 young British designers (fashion editors source upcoming talent here for their glossy spreads). The adjacent Craze 2 and C2+ specialize in nonprecious metals and sumptuous scarves and textiles. ✉ *33–35 Clerkenwell Green, East End EC1,* ☎ *020/7608–0393. Tube: Farringdon.* (☞ Map A)

OXO Tower. Many and varied artisans have to pass rigorous selection procedures to set up in the prime riverside workshops and make, display, and sell their work. The workshops are glass-walled, and you're invited in, even if you're just browsing. You can commission, too—anything from a cushion cover to custom-made jewelry, furniture, and sculpture. There are 23 studios in all, and a quick browse on the first floor reveals some very inviting items: hand-painted silk dresses by Nana Agyeman, handwoven textiles by Archipelago, multidiscipline design by Hive. The second floor has more of the same, including lamps, clothing, and jewelry. The very swish Harvey Nick's restaurant is on the eighth—top—floor, which has a fantastic view across the river to St. Paul's and Somerset House. You don't need to pay for the view, as there is a public terrace, but beware of the wind whipping along the Thames. You'll find more craftspeople at Gabriel's Wharf, next door. ✉ *Barge-*

house St., The South Bank SE1, ☎ *020/7401–2225. Tube: Southwark.* (☞ Map A)

Space. It has contemporary handmade furniture and other home-style designs, from beanbags and hand-embellished bed linens to sculpted candles. Owner Emma Oldham's theme focuses on mixing the affordable with the aspirational, and she has instigated an exhibition-selling space for individual artists. ✉ *214 Westbourne Grove, Notting Hill W11,* ☎ *020/7229–6533. Tube: Notting Hill Gate.* (☞ Map C)

Walter Castellazzo Design. Castellazzo has been getting lots of notice in the glossy interiors press with his very individual designs of modern-Gothic painted furniture. His signature style is the tall bookcase (which you'll love or hate) with its gently curving pointed apex. A similar theme is used for wall and corner cabinets and mirrors. Castellazzo's shelves are filled with other craft designers' work: silk purses, metallic cushions, jewelry. His latest direction (commissions undertaken) is toward space-capsule bunk beds in brushed silver with rocket chests of drawers—a must for young space cadets. The store is off our map, in the center of Georgian Highgate Village close to the Gothic Highgate Cemetery. ✉ *84 Highgate High St., Highgate N6,* ☎ *020/8340–3001. Tube: Archway or Highgate, then bus.*

Food Halls & Stores

London excels at posh nosh, and the place with the widest selection of all is Harrods' Food Halls. Even if you don't actually buy one of the beautifully packaged teas, chocolates, or biscuits (though it is hard to resist), you can salivate at the gorgeous displays, from freshly caught fish to furry and feathered game, which are as much akin to art as food. Selfridges is the other department store that comes in a close second; it's not as daunting, instead specializing in more streamlined self-service, with shelves filled with enough goodies to make a five-star dinner party—to which any of the following places would provide a delicious contribution.

Fortnum & Mason. Although it's the Queen's grocer, this store is, paradoxically, the most egalitarian of gift shops; it has plenty of irresistibly packaged luxury foods, stamped with the gold BY APPOINTMENT crest, for less than £5. Try the teas, preserves, blocks of chocolate, tins of pâté, or a box of Duchy Originals oatcakes—like Paul Newman, the Prince of Wales has gone into the retail food business. ✉ *181 Piccadilly, St. James's W1,* ☎ *020/7734–8040. Tube: Piccadilly Circus.* (☞ Map A)

Paxton & Whitfield. This is the most venerable of London's cheese shops, in business for over 200 years. The fabulous aromas come from some of the world's greatest cheeses stacked on the shelves—in rounds, in boxes, and on straw, but always ready to be tasted. Whichever cheese is in season and ripe for eating is on display for sampling, and the staff is ready to help you pick the best wine to serve with it. ✉ *93 Jermyn St., St. James's SW1,* ☎ *020/7930–0259. Tube: Piccadilly Circus.* (☞ Map A)

Rococo. It's run by Chantal Coady, who writes, eats, and lives for chocolate. Vegetable fats are forbidden words in this cocoa fantasyland, and there are interesting and off-beat additions to the main chocolate recipe, such as essence of Earl Grey. ✉ *321 King's Rd., Chelsea SW3,* ☎ *020/7352–5857. Tube: Sloane Sq.* (☞ Map B)

Thorntons. It may not be the classiest chocolatier, but that doesn't make one of Britain's most popular chocolate makers any the less desirable. Filled chocolates, chocolate bars, fudge, and toffee are their mainstays, but the truffles are to die for (and there's an extensive selection). Come at Easter-time, and the gift-wrapped eggs are rushing out the door. At this branch you can enjoy tea, coffee, and pastries—in addition to chocolate, of course. ✉ *254 Regent St., Soho W1,* ☎ *020/7434–2483. Tube: Oxford Circus.* (☞ Map A)

Close-Up

BY ROYAL APPOINTMENT

FROM SOFT DRINKS (Coca–Cola) and champagne (Moët & Chandon) to breakfast cereal (Weetabix) and household cleaning fluid (Jeyes), the royal family chooses the products it likes and hands their makers a warrant, a seal of satisfaction that honors the maker. Warrant holders can then adorn their packaging with a regal coat of arms, as well as the words "By Royal Appointment."

Only three royals can bestow warrants: the Queen, the Duke of Edinburgh, and Prince Charles. The warrants appear proudly on the facades of many an old and established London specialist shop; you'll find the stores are within a short carriage ride from the royal palaces. Fortnum & Mason is the royal grocer, but for British and Continental cheeses, Paxton & Whitfield holds the seal of approval. The glass cases at Floris, which have displayed classic perfumes since 1730, could be out of a Jane Austen novel. Penhaligon's is similarly well perfumed, and has products for the well-groomed gentleman and his lady.

All members of the royal family pursue sports with a passion. The outfitter for bridling is WH Gidden (⊠ 15 Clifford St., ☎ 020/7495–3670). Farlow's (⊠ 5 Pall Mall, ☎ 020/7839–2423) tackles other hardware (including fishing rods, reels, and shotguns), while Swaine Adeney has riding whips, saddles, and breeches in the best possible taste.

Villandry. Step inside the characterless building to a Provençal-style food store. Dark-wood shelves from floor to ceiling are laden with French and Belgian pâtés, French and Italian cheeses, pretty colored pastas, jars of fancy sauces, and other goodies galore. Bread baskets filled with rolls and pastries sit on heavy wood trestle tables. Behind the rustic calm of the food store are a café and dining room where you can indulge in some of the products. ⊠ *170 Great Portland St., Regent's Park W1,* ☎ *020/7631–3131. Tube: Great Portland St.* (☞ Map A)

Gifts

Of course, virtually anything from any shop in this chapter has gift potential, but these selections lean toward stores with a lot of choice, both in merchandise and price. Chances are you'll be wanting the recipients of your generous bounty to know how far you traveled to procure it for them, so these gift suggestions tend toward identifiable Britishness. You should also investigate the possibilities in the shops attached to the major museums, most of which offer far more than racks of souvenir postcards these days. Some of the best are at the British Museum and the V&A. For specialized gifts, the Royal Academy has great prints and cards and art paraphernalia; the London Transport Museum has transport models; the Natural History Museum has the largest selection of toy dinosaurs and real gemstones; and the London Aquarium is top-scale for all things undersea.

GENERAL

British Museum Gift Shop. Here you'll find stacks of Egyptiana, particularly cute scarabs in ceramic. You can be an archaeologist for an afternoon and buy your own ancient pottery pieces. The bookshop has a huge selection and is a mine of historical information for adults and children. ✉ *Great Russell St., Bloomsbury WC1,* ☎ *020/7323–8872. Tube: Tottenham Court Rd.* (☞ Map A)

Cross. It's an ultrachic cornucopia with something to suit everyone—even your pet pooch. The idea has been around in other London shops for years, but the Cross succeeds with its selection of hedonistic, beautiful things: silk scarves, brocade bags, embroidered chinoiserie, check housecoats, and fragrant candles and butterflies by Jade Jagger. Finally, the location: the Cross is right in the middle of Portobello–cum–Holland Park, London's trendy area. ✉ *141 Portland Rd., Notting Hill W11,* ☎ *020/7727–6760. Tube: Notting Hill Gate.* (☞ Map C)

General Trading Co. This place has just about every upper-class wedding gift list but also caters to slimmer pockets with merchandise shipped from farther shores (as the name suggests). ✉ *2 Symons St., Sloane Sq., Knightsbridge SW1,* ☎ *020/7730–0411. Tube: Sloane Sq.* (☞ Map B)

Neal Street East. While it isn't big on British stuff, this importer of Asian everything does carry stock with universal appeal. There are several floors of what you'd expect in the way of woks, chopsticks, bowls, books, kimonos, and toys, but there are also glorious lacquered boxes, woven baskets, amber and silver jewelry, silk flowers, Japanese kites, and loads of fun gifts for less than a fiver. ✉ *5 Neal St., Covent Garden WC2,* ☎ *020/7240–0135. Tube: Covent Garden.* (☞ Map A)

Soccer Scene. At this mammoth temple to the world's most popular sport you can grab any replica kit you care to mention. Beware of some high prices. ✉ *56–57 Carnaby St., Soho W1,* ☎ *020/7439–0778. Tube: Oxford Circus.* (☞ Map A)

Tea House. It purveys everything to do with the British national drink; you can dispatch your entire gift list here. Alongside the varieties of tea (including strange or rare brews like orchid, banana, Japanese Rice, and Russian Caravan) you'll find teapots in the shape of a British bobby or a London taxi, plus books, and what the shop terms "teaphernalia"—strainers, trivets, and infusers, and some gadgets that need explaining. ✉ *15A Neal St., Covent Garden WC2,* ☎ *020/7240–7539. Tube: Covent Garden.* (☞ Map A)

PERFUMES AND COSMETICS

Floris. One of the most beautiful shops in London, it has gleaming glass and Spanish mahogany showcases (acquired from the Great Exhibition of 1851). Gift possibilities include swan's-down powder puffs, cut-glass bottles, and the elegant ivory and faux tortoiseshell combs that the shop has sold since the place opened in 1730. Queen Victoria used to daub her favorite Floris fragrance on her lace handkerchief. ✉ *89 Jermyn St., St. James's W1,* ☎ *020/7930–2885. Tube: Piccadilly Circus.* (☞ Map A)

Lush. It's crammed with fresh, pure, very wacky, handmade cosmetics. 13 Rabbit is chocolate and spice soap for the shower; Angels on Bare Skin is divine lavender cleansing mush; Banana Moon, Dirty Boy, and Pineapple Grunt are soaps sliced off huge slabs like cheese and paper-wrapped as in an old-fashioned grocer's; Bath Bombs fizz furiously, then leave the water scattered with rosebuds or scented with honey and vanilla. It's all too irresistible. ✉ *Unit 11, The Piazza, Covent Garden, Covent Garden WC2,* ☎ *020/7240–4570. Tube: Covent Garden.* (☞ Map A)

Neal's Yard Remedies. This place has exquisitely fragranced bath oils, shampoos, massage lotions, soaps, and so on, plus some of the purest essential oils money can buy, complete with burners for scenting the air back home; all are packaged in the company's distinctive cobalt-blue apothecary bottles. ✉ *15 Neal's Yard, Covent Garden WC2,* ☎ *020/7379–7222. Tube: Covent Garden.* (☞ Map A)

Penhaligon's. William Penhaligon, court barber at the end of Queen Victoria's lengthy reign, established this shop. He blended perfumes and toilet waters and often created private blends for such customers as Lord Rothschild and Winston Churchill, using essential oils and natural, sometimes exotic ingredients. You can buy the very same formulations today, along with soaps, talcs, bath oils, and accessories, with the strong whiff of Victoriana both inside and outside the pretty bottles and boxes. Although constructed only a decade ago, the shop is sumptuously outfitted with 19th-century perfumer furnishings. Main branches: ✉ *41 Wellington St., Covent Garden WC2,* ☎ *020/7836–2150. Tube: Covent Garden ;* ✉ *16 Burlington Arcade, Mayfair W1,* ☎ *020/7629–1416. Tube: Piccadilly Circus.* (☞ Map A)

Les Senteurs. An intimate, unglossy perfumery run by a French family, it sells some of the lesser-known yet wonderfully timeless fragrances in town. Sample Creed, worn by Eugénie, wife of Emperor Napoléon III. ✉ *71 Elizabeth St., Belgravia SW1,* ☎ *020/7730–2322. Tube: Sloane Sq.* (☞ Map B)

Space NK Apothecary. This shop is rapidly acquiring cult status as the cutting-edge purveyor of makeup and cosmetics. The makeup artists' lines (MAC, Bobbi Brown, and Stila) lead the alternative trend to the giant names, and the upcoming niche lines here always have the newest, hottest colors. You'll also find everything else to complete your body pampering. ✉ *37 Earlham St., Covent Garden WC2,* ☎ *020/7379–7030. Tube: Covent Garden.* (☞ Map A)

STATIONERY

Ordning & Reda. It has the hottest colors of the moment for cool, sleek Swedish stationery and useful pieces to dress up the drabbest of desks. There are high-style rucksacks, too. ✉ *22 New Row, Covent Garden WC2,* ☎ *020/7240–8090. Tube: Covent Garden.* (☞ Map A)

Paperchase. The stationery superstore of London, it sells writing paper in every conceivable shade and in a dozen mediums. There are lovely cards, artists' materials, notebooks, and paperware. The three-floor store has a bookstore and café. ✉ *213 Tottenham Court Rd., Bloomsbury W1,* ☎ *020/7467–6200. Tube: Goodge St.* (☞ Map A)

TOYS AND MODELS

Armoury of St. James's. This shop stocks perfect playthings for kids of all ages in the form of some of the world's finest antique and newly painted lead soldiers (most wars with British involvement can be fought in miniature), plus medals, brass buttons, uniforms, painted drums, and military prints. ✉ *17 Piccadilly Arcade, St. James's SW1,* ☎ *020/7493–5082. Tube: Piccadilly Circus.* (☞ Map A)

Hamleys. The huge stock, including six floors of toys and games for children and adults, ranges from traditional teddy bears to computer games and all the latest technological gimmickry. Try to avoid it at Christmas, when police have to rope off a section of Regent Street for customers. ✉ *188–196 Regent St., Soho W1,* ☎ *020/8752–2278. Tube: Oxford Circus.* (☞ Map A)

Science Museum Gift Shop. It's best for imaginative toys and models, such as those darling little balsa-wood planes. The books and puzzles are extensive and will satisfy the most inquiring minds. ✉ *Exhibition Rd., South Kensington SW7,* ☎ *020/7942–4499. Tube: South Kensington.* (☞ Map B)

Singing Tree. A fantastic display of classic English dollhouses and accessories makes this store the leader in its field. The houses themselves might not fit in your hand baggage, but you can still treat yourself to one or two of the exquisite extras. ✉ *13 Harbledown Rd., Chelsea SW6,* ☎ *020/7736–4527. Tube: Fulham Broadway.* (☞ Map B)

Housewares

London's main department stores, such as John Lewis, Harrods, and Selfridges, have just about everything you would need in a home from day to night, but if you are looking for something that is a little more cutting edge, then stroll along Tottenham Court Road to the grandfather of them all—Heal's—which is now the grandee among a crop of modern imitators and innovators, including the first Terence Conran baby of the '60s, Habitat. Muji takes home style a step further by embracing clothes to match the furnishings. For handmade, eclectic designer pieces, you should explore farther afield to David Mellor, David Linley Furniture in Chelsea, and the wacky Walter Castellazzo Design in Highgate, North London.

Cargo Homeshop. It makes a virtue of light, bright, and funky: you'll find functional tables, chairs, and inexpensive sofas in the latest earthy and vibrant shades—many can be made to order in tempting fabrics from Italy and Spain. If you want to carry away a little something for under £10, try the colorful Indian rag rugs. There is another branch at 245–249 Brompton Rd., SW3. ✉ *209 Tottenham Court Rd., Bloomsbury W1,* ☎ *020/7580–2895. Tube: Goodge St.* (☞ Map A)

Conran Shop. This is the domain of Sir Terence Conran, who has been informing British middle-class taste since he opened Habitat in the '60s. Home enhancers from furniture to stemware, both handmade and mass-produced, famous-name and young-designer, are displayed in a suitably gorgeous building. The household articles are almost objets d'art in their own right. Bluebird on King's Road and the Conran Shop on Marylebone High Street are the latest offspring, with similarly beautiful wares. ✉ *Michelin House, 81 Fulham Rd., South Kensington SW3,* ☎ *020/7589–7401. Tube: South Kensington.* (☞ Map B)

Habitat. It has all the cool furnishings from global sources, colorful and shiny kitchen stuff, and linens in the latest ethnic and traditional themes by the store's own designers. Although most items are affordable, the workmanship is such that they may only last until the next decade's trend. The other central branch is in Chelsea (206 King's Rd., SW3). ✉ *196 Tottenham Court Rd., Bloomsbury W1,* ☎ *020/7631–3880. Tube: Goodge St.* (☞ Map A)

Heal's. The king of the furniture shops lining Tottenham Court Road, it has designs that combine modern style with classicism and are well made, particularly beds and seating. Prices are high, but the store makes for delightful browsing, and the kitchenware and decorative pieces are more affordable while still retaining good looks. At Christmas time, Heal's decorative baubles are gorgeous. There is another store at 234 King's Rd., SW3. ✉ *196 Tottenham Court Rd., Bloomsbury W1,* ☎ *020/7636–1666. Tube: Goodge St.* (☞ Map A)

Purves & Purves. It's a great place whether you've over £500 or only a £5 note to spend. Classic modern furniture and kitchenware designs by Phillipe Starck and cool Italian trendsetters are definitely upscale, but almost investment pieces. Inexpensive, colorful, and witty gift items, such as bubbly plastic napkin rings, toothbrushes, or silly soap dishes, abound. The store showcases many British designs. ✉ *220–224 Tottenham Court Rd., Bloomsbury W1,* ☎ *020/7580–8223. Tube: Goodge St.* (☞ Map A)

Jewelry

Jewelry—precious, semiprecious, and totally fake—can be had by just rubbing an Aladdin's lamp in London's West End. Of the department stores, Liberty and Harvey Nichols are particularly known for their fashion jewelry, but, in addition to viewing the more traditional baubles, bangles, and beads, check out the exceptionally creative kids on the jewelry block, such as Slim Barrett, whose designs are worn by supermodels, young aristos, and TV personalities. Seek out also the talent in the crafts and jewelry galleries, such as OXO Tower and Lesley Craze.

Asprey & Garrard. It offers exquisite jewelry and gifts, both antique and modern, and has been described as the "classiest and most luxurious shop in the world." If you're in the market for a six-branched Georgian candelabrum or a six-carat emerald-and-diamond brooch, you won't be disappointed. Garrard is the royal jeweler, in charge of the upkeep of the Crown Jewels. ✉ *165 New Bond St., Mayfair W1,* ☎ *020/7493–6767. Tube: Bond St.* (☞ Map A)

Butler & Wilson. Designed to set off its irresistible costume jewelry to the very best advantage—against a dramatic black background—this shop has some of the best displays in town; it keeps very busy marketing silver, diamanté, French gilt, and pearls by the truckload. ✉ *20 South Molton St., Mayfair W1,* ☎ *020/7409–2955. Tube: Bond St.;* ✉ *189 Fulham Rd., South Kensington SW3,* ☎ *020/7352–8255. Tube: South Kensington.* (☞ Maps A and B)

Cartier. It exudes an exclusivity that captures the very essence of Bond Street, combining royal connections—Cartier was granted its first royal warrant in 1902—with the last word in luxurious good taste. The store also sells glassware, leather goods, and stationery. ✉ *175 New Bond St., Mayfair W1,*☎ *020/7408–5700. Tube: Bond St.* (☞ Map A)

Dinny Hall. There's a very simple collection of designs in mainly gold and silver. Pared-down necklaces with a single drop feature, delicate gold spot-diamond earrings, and a simple choker with delicate curls are indicative of the styles on offer—a relief from the many other highly decorative jewels and baubles in fashion at the moment. There is another branch at 54 Fulham Road, SW3. ✉ *200 Westbourne Grove, Notting Hill W11,* ☎ *020/7792–3913. Tube: Notting Hill Gate.* (☞ Map C)

Erickson Beamon. Beamon's highly individual style of chokers, hair decorations, and brooches calls for plenty of colored fronds along with wool and other nonmetallic material woven intricately among the jewels. Designers Alexander McQueen and John Galliano have shown Beamon's bold work to his great advantage, and his dramatic Gothic style has spawned many imitators. Costume pieces start from around £40. ✉ *38 Elizabeth St., Belgravia SW1,* ☎ *020/7259–0202. Tube: Sloane Sq.* (☞ Map B)

Florence-B. Pieces from this shop are often to be found in the glossy fashion pages. This comes as no surprise, as this is a showcase for contemporary British designers. From cuff links to tiaras (from the abovementioned Slim Barrett) at a great price range, you'll find a bauble or two to tempt you. Other branches are at 25A Old Compton Street and 188A King's Road. ✉ *37A Neal St., Covent Garden WC2,* ☎ *020/7240–6332. Tube: Covent Garden.* (☞ Map A)

Steinberg & Tolkien. This shop has the last word in costume jewelry from the 1920s and onward. Chanel and Schiaparelli are just two of the famous designers that you might leap on here. And if you're lucky, you may find a piece that has been signed by its creator. These pieces are sometimes cheaper than those of the top-notch jewelers, and they may be of extra interest because you know who made them. ✉ *193 King's Rd., Chelsea SW3,* ☎ *020/7376–3660. Tube: Sloane Sq.* (☞ Map B)

Prints

London harbors loads of prints, and they make great gifts—for yourself, perhaps. You'll find, below, some West End stores, but should also try street markets (Camden Passage in Islington, particularly) and Cecil Court, just north of Trafalgar Square; the intriguing shops close to the British Museum; and the Royal Academy museum shop, which has a small selection. Auction houses, such as Christie's, South Kensington, and Phillips, New Bond Street, can often prove fun hunting grounds.

Grosvenor Prints. Antiquarian prints and 18th- and 19th-century portraits, with an emphasis on views and architecture of London—and dogs!—are for sale. It's an eccentric collection, and the prices range widely, but the stock is so odd that you are bound to find something interesting and unusual to meet both your budget and your taste. ✉ *28 Shelton St., Covent Garden WC2,* ☎ *020/7836–1979. Tube: Covent Garden.* (☞ Map A)

Map House. It has antique maps (that run from a few pounds to several thousand) and excellent reproductions of maps and prints, especially of botanical subjects, cityscapes, and *Punch* cartoons and prints. ✉ *54 Beauchamp Pl., Knightsbridge SW3,* ☎ *020/7589–4325. Tube: Knightsbridge.* (☞ Map B)

New Academy Gallery. You can browse through prints (including originals) with a traditional bent: landscapes and scenes of London. The partner gallery—the Curwen, at No. 4 (☎ 020/7636–1459)—has a wider selection of modern art prints. ✉ *34 Windmill St., Soho W1,* ☎ *020/7323–4700. Tube: Tottenham Court Rd.* (☞ Map A)

Shoes

Buckle My Shoe. A place for children who like to be well shod, this store has some of the most expensive makes and exciting styles in every shade imaginable. The little wellie-boots (galoshes) are delightful. ✉ *19 St. Christopher's Pl., Mayfair W1,* ☎ *020/7935–5589. Tube: Bond St.* (☞ Map A)

Emma Hope. This shop with handmade shoes first opened in Amwell St., Islington—handy if you are mooching around Islington and Camden Passage antiques stalls. But since custom footwear has had a mini-meteoric upturn, and the designer's pretty pumps in brocades and satins have been gliding down the catwalks of Nicole Farhi and Betty Jackson, Hope has opened a more upscale central branch in Sloane Square, Chelsea. ✉ *53 Sloane Sq., Chelsea SW1,* ☎ *020/7259–9566. Tube: Sloane Sq.* (☞ Map B)

Jimmy Choo. It's the name on every supermodel's and fashion editor's feet. Choo's exquisite, elegant designs are fantasy itself, and he's become a contender for Manolo Blahnik's crown. Obviously, these designs aren't cheap—nothing under £100—but the workmanship is out of this world. ✉ *20 Motcomb St., Knightsbridge SW1,* ☎ *020/7235–0242. Tube: Knightsbridge.* (☞ Map B)

John Lobb. If you are planning to visit for your first pair of handmade shoes (after which your wooden "last," or foot mold, is kept), take note: this shop has a waiting list of six months plus. As well as plenty of time, you will need to have plenty of money: around £1,500. But this buys a world of choice—from finest calf to exotic elk—and they will be your finest pair of shoes ever. ✉ *9 St. James's St., St. James's SW1,* ☎ *020/7930–3664. Tube: Piccadilly Circus.* (☞ Map A)

Shellys. It sells shoes for men and women, from city slickers to shoes for clubbing, at all prices and even at unimaginable platform heights. Also available are the de rigueur Dr. Marten shoes—Britain's answer to Timberland. ✉ *266–270 Regent St., Soho W1,* ☎ *020/7287–0939. Tube: Oxford Circus.* (☞ Map A)

Swear. This was the shoemaker for the movie *Star Wars,* which is an indicator of the style you can expect to encounter here: wild and wacky, larger-than-life platforms for daring wearers who have a head for the heights of fashion—around 4 inches and up. ✉ *61 Neal St., Covent Garden WC2,* ☎ *020/7240–7673. Tube: Covent Garden.* (☞ Map A)

Street Markets

London is as rich in street markets as it is in parks, and they contribute as much to the city's thriving culture. Practically every neighborhood has its own cluster of fruit-and-vegetable stalls, but listed here are the bigger, specialist sort of market, which provides not only a bargain (if you luck out) but also a great day out. A Sunday morning strolling the stalls of Brick Lane and breakfasting on the native bagels (smaller than New York's, but just as good) or a Saturday antiquing on Portobello Road, is a Londoners' pastime as much as it is a tourist activity, and markets are a great way to see the city from the inside out.

Bermondsey. Also known as the New Caledonian Market, it's London's best antiques market, one of the largest, and the one the dealers frequent. The Fridays-only market starts at the unearthly hour of 5 AM, and it's then that the really great buys will be snapped up. You should still be able to find a bargain or two if you turn up a bit later. ✉ *Tower Bridge Rd., The South Bank SE1.* ⏲ *Fri. 5 AM–noon. Bus 15 or 25 to Aldgate, then Bus 42 over Tower Bridge to Bermondsey Sq. Tube: London Bridge or Borough.*

Berwick Street. It's a relief from the frenzy of Oxford Street and its chain and department stores. The hub of the market is in Berwick Street, but there is an overspill through backstreet Soho, past Raymond's Revue Bar, and onto Rupert Street. Behind the bustling stalls there are pleasures galore: cafés, from greasy spoon to chic bar; fresh meat and game; Camembert on the edge of over-ripeness; giant slabs of chocolate; fresh fruits and vegetables; natty custom tailors; Borovik's fabrics; classy, risqué underwear to be found at Agent Provocateur (from Vivienne Westwood's son)—all provide a cosmopolitan, lively, delightfully brassy backdrop. ✉ *Soho W1.* ⏲ *Tues. 8–6, Sat. 9–4. Tube: Oxford Circus or Piccadilly Circus.*

Brick Lane. Not a showcase but more a collection of bric-a-brac, it's worth a visit for the bagels from the all-night bakery and a host of bargain Bengali curry houses. The old Truman Brewery (Black Eagle Brewery) has also become a trendy retail focus, with the Vibe Bar, a cybercafé, at its hub. Arty types hang out at the Atlantis Art Shop—and Whitechapel Art Gallery is just a block away. From here it is a stone's throw to Spitalfields, the burgeoning designer market, and the Columbia Road flower market, where the whole of London converges in late spring to buy trays of cheap flowers for window boxes and gardens. ✉ *East End E1.* ⏲ *Sun. 8–1. Bus 25 to Whitechapel Rd., or Bus 8 to Bethnal Green Rd. Tube: Aldgate East or Shoreditch.*

Camden Lock Market. This is the place to visit on a sunny August Sunday if you want your concept of a crowd redefined. Camden is actually several markets gathered around a pair of locks in the Regent's Canal, and it was once very pretty. Now that more stalls and a faux warehouse have been inserted into the surrounding brick railway buildings, the haphazard charm of the place is largely lost, although the variety of merchandise is mind-blowing: vintage and new clothes (design stars have been discovered here), antiques and junk, jewelry and scarves, candlesticks, ceramics, mirrors, and toys. Underneath it's really a date spot for hip teens. The neighborhood is bursting with shops, cafés, and other markets, and it's a whole lot calmer, if stall-free, at midweek. ✉ *Camden Town NW1.* ⏲ *Shops Tues.–Sun. 9:30–5:30, stalls weekends 8–6. Bus 24 or 29 to Camden Town. Tube: Camden Town.*

Camden Passage. Despite the name, it's not in Camden but a couple of miles away in Islington, a neighborhood first gentrified by media hippies in the '60s. Around 350 antiques dealers set up stalls here Saturdays and Wednesdays, with the surrounding antiques shops open Tuesday to Saturday 10–5 PM; even in the shops you can try your hand at price negotiation, although prices are generally fair. All in all, this remains a fruitful and picturesque hunting ground. ✉ *Islington, Islington N1.* ⏲ *Wed. and Sat. 8:30–3. Bus 19 or 38 to Angel. Tube: Angel.*

Greenwich Antiques Market. If you're planning to visit Greenwich, then combine your trip with a wander around this open-air market near St. Alfege Church. You'll find one of the best selections of secondhand and antique clothes in London—quality tweeds and overcoats can be had at amazing prices. ✉ *Greenwich High Rd., Greenwich SE10.* ⏲ *Antiques, crafts, and clothes weekends 9–5; fruit and vegetables weekdays 9–5. British Rail to New Gate Cross, then Bus 117; or bus direct to Greenwich.*

Leadenhall Market. The draw here is not so much what you can buy—plants and posh food, mainly—as the building itself. It's a handsome late-Victorian structure, ornate and elaborate. ✉ *Whittington Ave., The City EC3.* ⏲ *Weekdays 7–4. Tube to Bank or Monument.*

Petticoat Lane. Actually, Petticoat Lane doesn't exist; this Sunday clothing and fashion market, one of London's most entertaining diversions, centers on Middlesex Street, then sprawls in several directions, including northeast to Brick Lane and Spitalfields. Between them, the crammed streets turn up items of dubious parentage (CD players, bikes, car radios), alongside clothes (vintage, new, and just plain tired), jewelry, books, underwear, antiques, woodworking tools, bed linens, jars of pickles, and outright junk. ✉ *Middlesex St., Aldgate E1.* ⏲ *Sun. 9–2. Tube: Liverpool St., Aldgate, or Aldgate East.*

Portobello Market. London's most famous market still wins the prize for the all-round best. It sits in a most lively and multicultural part of town; the 1,500-odd antiques dealers don't rip you off (although you should haggle where you can); and it stretches over a mile, changing character completely as it goes. The top end (Notting Hill Gate) is antiquesland and more tourist-bound (with shops mid-week; don't miss antiquers David and Charles Wainwright [No. 251] and Trude Weaver [No. 71]); the middle is where locals buy fruit and vegetables and hang out in trendy restaurants; the section under the elevated highway called the Westway has the best flea market in town and then it tails off into a giant rummage sale among record stores, vintage-clothing boutiques, and art galleries. The bargains are to be found, here, in Golborne Road (W10) at the Ladbroke Grove end of Portobello. For original French country furniture and other pretty pieces, the market is hard to beat. For refreshment, pop into one of the many Portuguese patisseries and cafés. The western section of Portobello around the Westbourne Grove end is also worthy of exploration. ✉ *Portobello Rd., Notting Hill W11.* ⏲ *Fruit and vegetables Mon.–Wed. and Fri. 8–5, Thurs. 8–1; antiques Fri. 8–3; both food market and antiques Sat. 6–5. Bus 52 or Tube to Ladbroke Grove or Notting Hill Gate.*

Spitalfields. Trendsville has arrived in the form of creative crafts and design shops. The scene at this old 3-acre indoor fruit market, near Petticoat Lane, is now reminiscent of a more chic Camden Town, before the student crowds descended. At Spitalfields you'll find food, crafts, and clothes stalls; cafés; and performance and sports areas. On Sunday the place really comes alive, with stalls selling beautiful paper lampshades, antique clothing, handmade rugs, soap filled with flowers and fruits, homemade cakes, Portuguese deli foods, and cookware. The resident stores have more beautiful things for body and home (particularly Redhouse). In the center, racks of easels are filled with the cheapest (around £10) original artwork from the Alternative Art Market. For refreshment it's possible to eat from West to East, with Spanish tapas or Thai among the bars and food stalls. ✉ *Brushfield St., East End E1.* ⏲ *Organic market Fri. and Sun. 10–5; general market weekdays 11–3, Sun. 10–5. Tube to Liverpool St., Aldgate, or Aldgate East.*

8 SIDE TRIPS FROM LONDON

Sometimes you just need to get away from Old Smoke, and even if time is limited, a trip to the countryside is well worth your while. A train ride past hills dotted with sheep, a stroll through a preserved medieval town, or a history lesson at one of England's great castles will make you feel as though you added another week to your vacation.

Updated by Stephanie Adler

LONDONERS ARE UNDENIABLY LUCKY. Few urban populations enjoy such glorious—and easily accessible—options for day-tripping. This chapter presents seven of the most popular destinations: Bath, Brighton, Cambridge, Canterbury, Oxford, Stratford-upon-Avon, and Windsor Castle. Each can easily be done as a day trip but is also well worth considering for an overnight.

Pleasures and Pastimes

DINING

If you're dining outside London, stick to local specialties and produce whenever possible—get seafood in Brighton, for example. Don't forget that one of the best ways to experience any town is to pop into a good old-fashioned pub.

CATEGORY	COST*
££££	over £22
£££	£16–£22
££	£9–£15
£	under £9

**per person for a main course at dinner, excluding drinks, service, and VAT*

BATH

"I really believe I shall always be talking of Bath . . . I do like it so very much. Oh! who can ever be tired of Bath," wrote Jane Austen in *Northanger Abbey.* Today, thousands of visitors heartily concur. A remarkably unsullied Georgian city, Bath looks as if John Wood, its chief architect, "Beau" Nash, its principal dandy, and Jane Austen (1775–1817) might still be seen strolling on the promenade. Stepping out of the train station puts you right in the center, and Bath is compact enough to explore on foot. A single day is sufficient for you to take in the glorious yellow-stone buildings, tour the Roman baths, and stop for tea, though it will give only a brief hint of the cultural life that thrives in this vibrant town.

Exploring Bath

The Romans set about building the **Pump Room and Roman Baths** around the healing spring of the English goddess Aquae Sulis in AD 60, after wars with the Brits had laid the city to waste. The site became famous as a temple to Minerva, the Roman goddess of wisdom. Legend has it the first taker of these sacred waters was King Lear's leprous father, Prince Bladud, in the 9th century BC. (Yes, it's claimed he was cured.) Below the beautifully restored 18th-century Pump Room (oft-described in Austen's works) is a museum of quirky objects found during excavations. Last admission is an hour before closing, but allow at least 90 mins for the museum. ✉ *Abbey Churchyard,* ☎ *01225/477784,* WEB *www.romanbaths.co.uk.* 🎫 *£7.50, combined ticket with Assembly Rooms £9.50.* ⏲ *Mar.–June, Sept.–Oct., daily 9–6; July–Aug., daily 9–10; Nov.–Feb., daily 9:30–5:30.*

Bath Abbey was commissioned by God. Really. The design came to Bishop Oliver King in a dream, and was built during the 15th century. In the **Heritage Vaults** is a museum of archaeological finds, with a scale model of 13th-century Bath. Look up at the fan-vaulted ceilings in the nave and the carved angels on the restored West Front. *Abbey Churchyard,* ☎ *01225/422462,* WEB *www.bathabbey.org.* 🎫 *Abbey free (suggested donation £2), Heritage Vaults £2.* ⏲ *Abbey mid-Apr.–Oct., Mon.–Sat. 9–6; Nov.–mid-Apr., Mon.–Sat. 9–4:30. Heritage Vaults Mon.–Sat. 10–4. Call for Sun. hrs.*

NEED A BREAK? A thorough turn around Bath Abbey's many nooks and crannies will leave you ready to take succor in **Sally Lunn's Refreshment House & Museum** (✉ 4 North Parade Passage, ☎ 01225/461634). In Bath's oldest house (1482), this may be the world's only tearoom-museum. Try the eponymous Sally Lunn, invented here in the 17th century; these buns measure a foot across. The tearoom is open 10 to 10 Monday through Saturday and 11 to 6 on Sunday; the museum opens at the same time as the tearoom and closes daily at 6. Admission to the museum is free if you're eating, 30p if you're not.

One of the most famous landmarks of the city, **Pulteney Bridge** (✉ Off Bridge St. at the Grand Parade) was the great Georgian architect Robert Adam's sole contribution to Bath and is, in its way, as fine as the only other bridge in the world with shops lining either side: the Ponte Vecchio in Florence.

Among Bath's remarkable architectural achievements is **The Circus** (✉ Intersection of Brock, Gay, and Bennett Sts.), a perfectly circular ring of three-story stone houses designed by John Wood. The painter Thomas Gainsborough lived at number 17 from 1760 to 1774.

On the east side of Bath's Circus are more thrills for Austen readers: her much-mentioned **Assembly Rooms,** which now contain the **Museum of Costume,** which displays fashions from the 17th through 20th centuries. Last admission is 30 minutes before closing, but allow at least an hour to tour the museum. ✉ *Bennett St.,* ☎ *01225/477789,* WEB *www.museumofcostume.co.uk.* 🎫 *£4.20, combined ticket with Roman Baths £9.50.* ⏲ *Daily 10–5.*

The **Royal Crescent** is the most famous site in Bath, and you can't help but see why. Designed by John Wood the Younger, it's perfectly proportioned and beautifully sited, with sweeping views over parkland. A marvelous museum at **Number 1 Royal Crescent** shows life as Beau Nash would have lived it circa 1765. ✉ *1 Royal Crescent,* ☎ *01225/428126,* WEB *www.bath-preservation-trust.org.uk.* 🎫 *£4.* ⏲ *Mid-Feb.–Oct., Tues.–Sun. 10:30–5; Nov., Tues.–Sun. 10:30–4.*

Dining

££ ✕ **Number Five.** Just over the Pulteney Bridge from the center of town, this airy bistro, with its plants, framed posters, and cane-back chairs, is an ideal spot for a light lunch. The regularly changing menu includes tasty homemade soups, roast quail on wild rice, and char-grilled lamb loin. ✉ *5 Argyle St.,* ☎ *01225/444499. AE, DC, MC, V. Closed Sun. No lunch Mon.*

BRIGHTON

Ever since the Prince Regent first visited in 1783, Brighton has been England's most exciting seaside city, and today it's as eccentric and cosmopolitan as ever. With its rich cultural mix—Regency architecture, amusement pier, specialist shops, pavement cafés, lively arts, and, of course, the odd and exotic Royal Pavilion—Brighton is a truly extraordinary city by the sea. For most of the 20th century the city was known for its tarnished allure and its faded glamour, but recently a young, bustling spirit has breathed new life into this ever-popular destination.

Exploring Brighton

In the 1860s, Brighton featured the very first example of that peculiarly British institution, the amusement pier. The restored **Brighton Pier** follows the great tradition, with a crowded maze of arcade games, amusement-park rides, and chip shops. The decaying ghost of a Victorian structure down the beach from Brighton Pier is **West Pier** (☎ 01273/321499, WEB www.westpier.co.uk), which was damaged in World War II and has been closed since 1975. At press time, an extensive renovation program was under way to restore the pier to its former glory, complete with museum, performance area, and restaurants. Until renovations are complete, you can take a fascinating tour of the rusting Victorian relic. These tours are not for the faint of heart; participants don hard hats and walk on scaffolding (and must be age 16-plus). The tours cost £10 and are given daily mid-April through October, weekends October through mid-April; call for times. ✉ *Waterfront along Madeira Dr.,* ☎ *01273/609361,* WEB *www.brightonpier.co.uk.* 🎫 *Free, costs of rides vary.* ⏲ *June–Aug. daily 9 AM–2 AM; Sept.–May daily 10 AM–midnight.*

The heart of Brighton is the **Steine** (pronounced *steen*), a large open area close to the seafront. This was a river mouth until the Prince of Wales had it drained in 1793.

The most remarkable building on the Steine, perhaps in all Britain, is unquestionably the extravagant, fairy-tale **Royal Pavilion.** Built by architect Henry Holland in 1787 as a simple seaside villa, the Pavilion was transformed by John Nash between 1815 and 1823 for the Prince Regent (later George IV), who favored an exotic, eastern design with opulent Chinese interiors. When Queen Victoria came to the throne in 1837, she disapproved of the palace and planned to demolish it. Fortunately, the local government bought it from her, and after a lengthy process of restoration, the Pavilion looks much as it did in its Regency heyday. Take particular note of the spectacular Music Room, styled as a Chinese-style pavilion, and the Banqueting Room, with its enormous flying-dragon "gasolier," or gaslight chandelier, a revolutionary invention in the early 19th century. The gardens, too, have been restored to Regency splendor, following John Nash's uncommonly naturalistic design of 1826. ✉ *Old Steine,* ☎ *01273/290900,* WEB *www.royalpavilion.brighton.co.uk.* 🎫 *£5.20.* ⏲ *June–Sept., daily 10–6; Oct.–May, daily 10–5.*

The grounds of the Royal Pavilion contain the **Brighton Museum and Art Gallery,** whose buildings were designed as a stable block for the Price Regent's horses. A complete overhaul during much of 2001 resulted in new galleries that show the museum's collections to wonderful effect. These include theme-based permanent exhibitions focusing on concepts like fashion and style, the body, and performance. Of particular note here are the wonderful collections of Art Nouveau and Art Deco furniture, ceramics, and glass. ✉ *Church St.,* ☎ *01273/290900.* 🎫 *Free.* ⏲ *Mon., Tues., and Thurs.–Sat. 10–5, Sun. 2–5.*

The Lanes (✉ bordered by West, North, East, and Prince Albert Sts.), a maze of alleys and passageways, was where legions of fishermen and their families once lived. Now closed to vehicular traffic, the area's cobbled streets are filled with interesting restaurants, boutiques, and antiques shops. The heart of the Lanes is Market Street and Square, lined with fish and seafood restaurants.

Volk's Electric Railway, built by inventor Magnus Volk in 1883, was the first public electric railroad in Britain. It's among Brighton's quirkier delights; you might like to take the 1¼-mi trip along Marine Parade. ✉ *Marine Parade,* ☎ *01273/292718.* 🎫 *£1.20 one way, £2.20 round trip.* ⏲ *Mid-Apr.–Sept., weekdays 10:30–5, weekends 10:30–6.*

Below the boardwalk near Palace Pier, the enchanting **National Museum of Penny Slot Machines** fills a tiny room with Victorian-era Nickelodeons and fortune-telling machines. Buy a few Victorian pennies, drop them in the slots, and you'll agree: there's nothing like good old-fashioned fun. ✉ *250C King's Road Arches, Lower Esplanade (opposite the end of East St.),* ☎ *01273/608620.* 💳 *Free.* ⏲ *Mid-Apr.–June, weekends 11–6; July–Sept., daily 11–6; Oct.–mid-Apr., Sun. 11–6.*

Dining

££–£££ ★ ✕ **English's of Brighton.** Buried in the Lanes, this is one of the few old-fashioned seafood havens left in England. It has been a restaurant for more than 150 years and a family business for more than 50. You can eat succulent oysters and other seafood at the counter or take a table in the dining room. Daily specials and reasonable prices make it a worthwhile mealtime destination. ✉ *29–31 East St.,* ☎ *01273/327980. AE, DC, MC, V.*

££ ✕ **Havana.** The high ceilings, dark wood-and-leather furnishings, and sophisticated food at Havana will make you think you're still in London. Don't let that deter you, however—this place is a pleasure. Expect modern twists on British classics: Chicken pie, for example, actually includes a delectable mound of sautéed baby vegetables topped with an understated triangle of puff pastry. The bar/café area is a perfect place to rest your weary feet at the end of a long day. ✉ *32 Duke St.,* ☎ *01273/773388. AE, MC, V.*

£–££ ✕ **Terre à Terre.** Exploring the outer bounds of vegetarian cuisine, Terre à Terre consistently draws hordes of admirers to its bright, art-filled dining room. The menu might surprise first-timers, but fear not: inventive dishes like "Himmel und Erbe" (apple, potato, onion, and cheddar latkes) and an eclectic choice of salads (often with ingredients like smoked tofu, shoyu sauce, and various roasted seeds) will satisfy even the most devout carnivore. ✉ *71 East St.,* ☎ *01273/729051. AE, DC, MC, V. Reservations required. No lunch Mon.*

CAMBRIDGE

Having trouble distinguishing between Oxford and Cambridge? That's not surprising, because in the United Kingdom, the names of these two important educational institutions are often elided into the term "Oxbridge." Their histories, too, are inextricable: Cambridge was founded by Oxford students after a bloody 13th-century clash with Oxford townspeople. Today, a healthy rivalry persists between the two schools.

This university town may be one of the most beautiful cities in Britain, but it's no museum. Even when the students are on vacation, there's a strong cultural and intellectual buzz here. It's a preserved medieval city of some 100,000 souls and growing, dominated culturally and architecturally by its famous university and beautified by parks and gardens and the quietly flowing River Cam. Punting on the Cam (one occupant propels the narrow, square-ended, flat-bottom boat with a long pole, while another steers with a small paddle) is a quintessential Cambridge pursuit, followed by a stroll along the Backs, the quaintly named left bank of the Cam fringed by St. John's, Trinity, Clare, King's, and Queens' colleges, and Trinity Hall.

VISITING THE COLLEGES

College visits are certainly a highlight of a Cambridge tour, but remember that the colleges are private homes and workplaces, even when school isn't in session. Each is an independent entity within the university; some are closed to the public, while at others you can see the chapels, dining rooms (called halls), and sometimes the libraries, too. Some colleges charge a small fee for the privilege of nosing around. All are closed during exams, usually from mid-April to late June. For details about visiting specific colleges not listed here, you can contact **Cambridge University** (☎ 01223/337733, WEB www.cam.ac.uk).

By far the best way to gain access without annoying anyone is to join a walking tour led by an official Blue Badge guide—in fact, many areas are off-limits unless you do. The two-hour tours leave daily from the **Tourist Information Centre** (✉ The Old Library, Wheeler St., ☎ 01223/322640, WEB www.cambridge.gov.uk/leisure/tourism.htm).

Exploring Cambridge

Pembroke College (1347) has delightful gardens and bowling greens. Its chapel, completed in 1665, was Christopher Wren's first commission. ✉ *Pembroke St.,* ☎ *01223/338100,* WEB *www.pem.cam.ac.uk.* 🎫 *Free.* ⏲ *Daily dawn–dusk.*

Emmanuel College (1584) is the alma mater of one John Harvard, who gave his books and his name to the American university. A number of the Pilgrims were Emmanuel alumni; they named Cambridge, Massachusetts, after their alma mater. ✉ *Emmanuel and St. Andrew's Sts.,* ☎ *01223/334200,* WEB *www.emma.cam.ac.uk.* 🎫 *Free.* ⏲ *Daily 9–6.*

East Anglia's finest art gallery, the **Fitzwilliam Museum** houses outstanding collections of art, including several Constable paintings, oil sketches by Rubens, and antiquities from ancient Egypt, Greece, and Rome. ✉ *Trumpington St.,* ☎ *01223/332900,* WEB *www.fitzmuseum.cam.ac.uk.* 🎫 *Free.* ⏲ *Tues.–Sat. 10–5, Sun. 2:15–5.*

King's College (1441) is notable as the site of the world-famous Gothic-style **King's College Chapel** (built 1446–1547). Some deem its great fan-vaulted roof, supported by a delicate tracery of columns, the most glorious example of Perpendicular Gothic in Britain. It's the home of the famous choristers, and, to cap it all, Rubens's *Adoration of the Magi* is secreted behind the altar. ✉ *Kings Parade,* ☎ *01223/331212,* WEB *www.kings.cam.ac.uk.* 🎫 *£3.50.* ⏲ *Daily 9:30–3:30 (hrs vary with services; call to confirm before visiting).*

In 1284, the Bishop of Ely founded **Peterhouse College,** Cambridge's smallest and oldest college. Take a tranquil walk through its former deer park, by the riverside of its ivy-clad buildings. ✉ *Trumpington St.,* ☎ *01223/338200,* WEB *www.pet.cam.ac.uk.* 🎫 *Free.* ⏲ *Daily 1–5.*

Reached along the Backs, **Queens' College**—built around 1448, and named after Margaret, queen of Henry VI, and Elizabeth, queen of Edward IV—enjoys a reputation as one of Cambridge's most eye-catching colleges. Enter over the **Mathematical Bridge,** said to have been built by Isaac Newton without any binding save gravity, then dismantled by curious scholars anxious to learn Sir Isaac's secret. The college maintains, however, that the bridge wasn't actually put together until 1749, 22 years after Newton's death, thus debunking the popular myth. ✉ *Queen's La.,* ☎ *01223/335511,* WEB *www.quns.cam.ac.uk.* 🎫 *£1.20 Apr.–Sept., free Oct.–Mar.* ⏲ *Apr.–Sept., weekdays 11–3, weekends 10–4:30; Oct.–Mar., weekdays 1:45–4:30, weekends 10–4:30. Closed late May–late June.*

Along King's Parade is **Corpus Christi College.** If you visit only one quadrangle, make it the beautiful, serene, 14th-century Old Court here; it's the longest continuously inhabited college quadrangle in Cambridge. ✉ *King's Parade,* ☎ *01223/338000,* WEB *www.corpus.cam.ac.uk.* 🎫 *Free.* ⏲ *Daily dawn–dusk.*

St. John's College (1511), the university's second largest, has noted alumni (Wordsworth studied here) and two of the finest sights in town: the School of Pythagoras, the oldest house in Cambridge; and the Bridge of Sighs, whose only resemblance to its Venetian counterpart is its covering. (Unlike Venice's bridge, this one does not lead to a prison.) The windowed, covered stone bridge reaches across the Cam to the mock-Gothic New Court (1825–1831). The New Court's cupola, with its white crenellations, have earned it the nickname "the wedding cake." ✉ *St. John's and Bridge Sts.,* ☎ *01223/338600,* WEB *www.joh.cam.ac.uk.* 🎫 *£1.75 Mar.–Oct., free Nov.–Feb.* ⏲ *Mar.–Oct., daily 10–5; Nov.–Feb., daily dawn–dusk.*

Trinity College was founded by Henry VIII in 1546, and has the largest student population of all the colleges. It's also famous for being attended by Herbert, Dryden, Byron, Thackeray, Tennyson, Bertrand Russell, Nabokov, and Nehru, India's first prime minister. Many of Trinity's features reflect its status as the largest college, not least its 17th-century "great court" and the massive gatehouse that houses Great Tom, a giant clock that strikes each hour with high and low notes. Don't miss the wonderful library by Christopher Wren, where you can see a letter written by alumnus Isaac Newton with early notes on gravity, and Milne's hand-written manuscript of *The House at Pooh Corner.* ✉ *Trinity St.,* ☎ *01223/338400,* WEB *www.trin.cam.ac.uk.* 🎫 *£1.75 Mar.–Oct., free Nov.–Feb.* ⏲ *Mar.–Oct., daily 10–5; Nov.–Feb., daily 10–dusk.*

Dining

£££ ★ ✕ **Midsummer House.** In fine weather, the gray-brick Midsummer House's conservatory, beside the River Cam, makes for a memorable lunchtime jaunt. Choose from a selection of traditional European and Mediterranean dishes. You might get tender local lamb or the best from the daily fish market, adorned with inventively presented vegetables. ✉ *Midsummer Common,* ☎ *01223/369299. Reservations essential. AE, MC, V. Closed Mon. No lunch Sat., no dinner Sun.*

CANTERBURY

For many people, Geoffrey Chaucer's *The Canterbury Tales*, about a pilgrimage to Canterbury Cathedral, brings back memories of a sleepy high-school English class. But according to Chaucer, medieval Canterbury was as much a party for people on horses as it was a spiritual center, and it's still a lively place: rich in history and full of leaning Tudor buildings that make for fine photo opportunities.

The height of Canterbury's popularity came in the 12th century, when thousands of pilgrims flocked here see the shrine of the murdered Archbishop St. Thomas à Becket. (Buildings that served as pilgrims' inns still dominate the streets of Canterbury's pedestrian center.) But dig a little deeper, and you'll find that Canterbury's been a hive of activity since before the martyrdom—a town has occupied this site since the Romans arrived 2,000 years ago. Wherever you go in Canterbury, centuries of history literally lie just beneath your feet. Don't believe it? Ask the staff at Waterstone's Bookstore on St. Margaret's Street to show you what's behind the door in the cellar.

You can easily cover Canterbury in a day. The 90-minute journey south from London's Victoria Station leaves plenty of time for a tour of the cathedral, a museum visit or two, and (if the weather's right) a walk around the perimeter of the old walled town. To get your bearings, remember that Canterbury is bisected by a road running northwest, along which the major tourist sites cluster. Confusingly, this road begins as St. George's Street, then becomes High Street, and finally turns into St. Peter's Street.

On St. George's Street a lone church tower marks the site of **St. George's Church**—the rest of the building was destroyed in World War II—where playwright Christopher Marlowe was baptized in 1564.

The **Canterbury Roman Museum,** including its colorful mosaic Roman pavement, is below ground, at the level of the Roman town. Computer-generated reconstructions of Roman buildings and the marketplace re-create the ancient town. ✉ *Butchery La.,* ☎ *01227/785575,* WEB *www.canterbury-museum.co.uk.* 💷 *£2.50.* ⏲ *June–Oct., Mon.–Sat. 10–5, Sun. 1:30–5; Nov.–May, Mon.–Sat. 10–5; last entry at 4. Closed last wk in Dec.*

Mercery Lane, with its medieval-style cottages and massive, overhanging timber roofs, runs right off High Street and ends in the tiny **Buttermarket,** a market square that was known in the 15th century as the Bullstake: animals were tied here for baiting before slaughter.

The immense **Christchurch Gate,** built in 1517, leads into the cathedral close. As you pass through, look up at the sculpted heads of two young figures: Prince Arthur, elder brother of Henry VIII, and the young Catherine of Aragon, to whom he was betrothed. The gate was commissioned to celebrate the alliance, but Arthur died prematurely. Catherine ended up marrying his brother, Henry, whose eventual decision to divorce her created an irrevocable breach with the Catholic Church, and altered the course of English history.

★ **Canterbury Cathedral,** the focal point of the city, was the first of England's great Norman cathedrals. Still the heart of worldwide Anglicanism, the Cathedral Church of Christ Canterbury (its formal name) is a living textbook of medieval architecture.

The cathedral was only a century old, and still relatively small in size, when Thomas à Becket, the Archbishop of Canterbury, was murdered here in 1170. An uncompromising defender of ecclesiastical interests, Becket had angered his friend Henry II, who supposedly exclaimed, "Who will rid me of this troublesome priest?" Thinking they were carrying out the king's wishes, four knights burst in on Becket in one of the side chapels and killed him. Two years later Becket was canonized, and Henry II's subsequent penitence helped establish the cathedral as the undisputed center of English Christianity.

Becket's tomb, destroyed by Henry VIII in 1538 as part of his campaign to reduce the power of the Church and confiscate its treasures, was one of the most extravagant shrines in Christendom. In **Trinity Chapel,** near the tomb's original site, you can still see a series of 13th-century stained-glass windows illustrating Becket's miracles. The actual site of Becket's murder is down a flight of steps just to the left of the nave.

If time permits, be sure to explore the **Cloisters** and other small monastic buildings north of the cathedral. ✉ *Cathedral Precincts,* ☎ *01227/762862,* WEB *www.canterbury-cathedral.org.* 💷 *Precincts free, cathedral £3.50, free for services.* ⏲ *Precincts daily 7 AM–9 PM; cathedral Mon.–Sat. 9–5, Sun. 12:30–2:30 and 4:30–5:30 (open all day Sun. for worship). Restricted access during services.*

To make Canterbury's history come alive for you, spend some time at a vivid exhibition called **The Canterbury Tales,** an audio-visual (and occasionally olfactory) dramatization of 14th-century English life. Don't be surprised if one of the figures comes to life: an actor dressed in period costume often performs a charade as part of the scene. ✉ *St. Margaret's St.,* ☎ *01227/479227,* WEB *www.canterburytales.org.uk.* 💷 *£5.90.* ⏲ *Mar.–June and Sept.–Oct., daily 9:30–5:30; July–Aug., daily 9–5:30; Nov.–Feb., Sun.–Fri. 10–4:30, Sat. 9:30–5:30.*

The medieval Poor Priests' Hospital is now the site of the comprehensive and popular **Canterbury Heritage Museum.** The exhibits provide an excellent overview of the city's history and architecture from Roman times to World War II. Visit early in the day to avoid the crowds. ✉ *20 Stour St.,* ☎ *01227/452747,* WEB *www.canterbury-museum.co.uk.* 🎫 *£2.40.* ⏲ *June–Oct., Mon.–Sat. 10:30–5, Sun. 1:30–5; Nov.–May, Mon.–Sat. 10:30–5. Last entry at 4. Closed last wk Dec.*

The only survivor of the city's seven gatehouses, at one end of St. Peter's Street, contains the **West Gate Museum.** Inside are medieval bric-a-brac and armaments used by the city guard. The building became a jail in the 14th century; you can see prison cells. Climb to the roof for a panoramic view of the city spires. ☎ *01227/452747,* WEB *www.canterbury-museum.co.uk.* 🎫 *£1.* ⏲ *Mon.–Sat. 11–12:30 and 1:30–3:30.*

For an essential Canterbury experience, follow the circuit of the mainly 13th- and 14th-century **medieval city walls,** built on the line of the original Roman walls. Walls to the east survive intact, towering some 20 ft high and offering a panoramic view of the town. You can access these from a number of places, including Castle and Broad streets.

St. Augustine's Abbey, one of the oldest monastic sites in the country, is where Augustine, England's first Christian missionary, was buried in 597. The abbey was later seized by Henry VIII, who destroyed some of the buildings and converted others into a royal manor for his fourth wife, Anne of Cleves. An interactive audio tour vividly puts events into context. ✉ *Longport,* ☎ *01227/767345,* WEB *www.english-heritage.org.uk.* 🎫 *£2.60.* ⏲ *Apr.–Sept., daily 10–6; Oct., daily 10–5; Nov.–Mar., daily 10–4.*

The **Dane John Mound,** just opposite the Canterbury East train station, was originally part of the city defenses. Kids love the fantastic medieval maze here.

Dining

£–££ ✕ **Marlowe's.** For lunch or a late-afternoon snack, lively Marlowe's is a worthwhile alternative to the café franchises that populate Canterbury's pedestrian center. The staff is friendly and welcoming, as is the setting—walls are brightly colored and plastered with posters of old-time movie stars. The menu is eclectic: expect lunchtime standards (soup, sandwiches, baked potatoes), Tex-Mex dishes, and daily specials, such as lemon-dill chicken. ✉ *55 St. Peter's St.,* ☎ *01227/462194. AE, DC, MC, V.*

£–££ ✕ **Weavers.** In one of the Weavers' Houses on the River Stour, this popular restaurant in the center of town is an ideal place to revel in the Tudor surroundings and feast on generous portions of British comfort food, such as traditional pies, seafood, and pasta dishes. You'll find a good selection of wines. Ask for a table in the more sedate ground-floor dining area. ✉ *1 St. Peter's St.,* ☎ *01227/464660. AE, MC, V.*

OXFORD

To get Oxford fixed in your mind's eye, say the phrase "Dreaming Spires" over and over—all the tour guides do—and think *Brideshead Revisited,* Sebastian Flyte, and Evelyn Waugh, in general. Think Rhodes scholars—former President Clinton was one—and think J. R. R. Tolkien, Percy Bysshe Shelley, Oscar Wilde, W. H. Auden, and C. S. Lewis. Wanna-be wizards will want to visit Oxford for yet another reason: many of its most formidable buildings stood in for the Hogwarts School in the Harry Potter films.

Oxford University is older than its sibling to the east, dating from the 12th century, but the city is bigger and more cosmopolitan than Cambridge. Of course, here, too, there's no shortage of hushed quadrangles, chapels, and gardens. Bikes are propped against wrought-iron railings, and punting is popular along the Cherwell (rent a punt yourself, at the foot of Magdalen Bridge), but Oxford is also a major industrial center, with large car and steel plants based in its suburbs.

VISITING THE COLLEGES

The same concerns for people's work and privacy hold here as in Cambridge. Guided city walking tours leave the Oxford Information Centre several times a day. If you have limited time, get a detailed map from the tourist office and focus on selected sights. The Oxford University Web site (www.ox.ac.uk) is a great source of information if you're planning to go it alone.

Note that many of the colleges and university buildings are closed around Christmas (sometimes Easter, too) and on certain days from April to June for exams and degree ceremonies.

Exploring Oxford

Any Oxford visit should begin at its very center—a pleasant walk of 10 minutes or so east from the train station—with the splendid university church of **St. Mary the Virgin** (1280). Climb 127 steps to the top of its 14th-century tower for a panoramic view of the city. ✉ *High St.*, ☎ *01865/279111*, WEB *www.university-church.ox.ac.uk.* 🎫 *Church free, tower £1.60.* ⏲ *July–Aug. Mon.–Sat. 9–7, Sun. 12–7; Sept.–June Mon.–Sat. 9–5, Sun. 12–5.*

Among Oxford's most famous sights, the **Radcliffe Camera** (1737–1749) is one of the buildings that house the august Bodleian Library. Not many of the 2-million-plus volumes are on view to non-dons, but you can see part of the collection on a tour. (Harry Potter fans should know that the Bodleian Library's other buildings—Duke Humfrey's Library, the Old Schools Quadrangle, and the Clarendon Building—stood in for some of Hogwarts interiors). ✉ *Broad St.*, ☎ *01865/277224*, WEB *www.bodley.ox.ac.uk.* 🎫 *£3.50, extended tour £7 (call to pre-book).* ⏲ *Tours Mar.–Oct., weekdays 10:30, 11:30, 2, 3 and Sat. 10:30, 11:30; Nov.–Feb., weekdays 2, 3 and Sat. 10:30, 11:30.*

The **Sheldonian Theatre,** built between 1664 and 1668, was Sir Christopher Wren's first major work (the chapel at Pembroke College was his first commission). The theatre, which he modeled on a Roman amphitheater, made his reputation. It was built as a venue for the University's public ceremonies, and graduations are still held here, entirely in Latin, as befits the building's spirit. Outside is one of Oxford's most striking sights—a metal fence topped with stone busts of 18 Roman emperors (modern reproductions of the originals, which were eaten away by pollution). ✉ *Broad St.*, ☎ *01865/277299*, WEB *www.sheldon.ox.ac.uk.* 🎫 *£1.50.* ⏲ *Mon.–Sat. 10–12:30 and 2–4:30. Closed Sun. and occasionally for university events.*

Brush up on local history at the **Oxford Story.** Take your place at a medieval student's desk as it trundles, Disney-style, through 800 years of Oxford history. In just 20 minutes, you can see Edmund Halley discover his comet, and watch the Scholastica's Day Riot of 1355. There's commentary tailored for kids, too. ✉ *6 Broad St.*, ☎ *01865/728822*, WEB *www.oxfordstory.co.uk.* 🎫 *£6.10.* ⏲ *Apr.–Oct., daily 9:30–5; Nov.–Mar., weekdays 10–4:30, weekends 10–5.*

Outside the "new" (that is, Victorian) college gates of prestigious **Balliol College** (1263), a cobblestone cross in the sidewalk marks the spot where Archbishop Cranmer and Bishops Latimer and Ridley were burnt, in 1555, for their Protestant beliefs. The original college gates (rumored to have existed at the time of the scorching) hang in the library passage, between the inner and outer quadrangles. ✉ *St. Giles St.,* ☎ *01865/277777,* WEB *www.balliol.ox.ac.uk.* 🎫 *£1.* ⏲ *Daily 2–5 (or dusk, if earlier).*

The **chapel** of Trinity College (1555) is an architectural gem, with some superb wood carvings by Grinling Gibbons, a 17th-century master carver whose work can be seen in Hampton Court Palace and St. Paul's Cathedral, and who inspired Thomas Chippendale. ✉ *Broad St.,* ☎ *01865/279900,* WEB *www.trinity.ox.ac.uk.* 🎫 *£2.* ⏲ *Daily 10–noon and 2–4 (or dusk, if earlier).*

The **Ashmolean Museum,** founded in 1683, is Britain's oldest public museum. Some of the world's most precious art objects are stashed here—Egyptian, Greek, and Roman artifacts; drawings by Michelangelo and Raphael; European silverware and ceramics; and a world-class numismatic collection. All of the objects are the property of the university. The café upstairs, with delightful sandwiches and tasty cakes, makes a good rest stop. ✉ *Beaumont St.,* ☎ *01865/278000,* WEB *www.ashmol.ox.ac.uk.* 🎫 *Free.* ⏲ *Jun.–Oct., Tues.–Wed. and Fri.–Sat. 10–5, Thurs. 10–7, Sun. 12–5; Nov.–May, Tues.–Sat. 10–5, Sun. 2–5. Closed Mon.*

St. John's College, founded in 1555, is worth a stop for its very lovely gardens and its library, where you can view some of Jane Austen's letters, and the William Caxton's illustrated 1482 edition of *The Canterbury Tales.* ✉ *St. Giles St.,* ☎ *01865/277300,* WEB *www.sjc.ox.ac.uk.* 🎫 *Free.* ⏲ *Daily 1–5 (or dusk, if earlier).*

Tom Tower, designed by Christopher Wren, marks the entrance to the leading college of the southern half of Oxford: **Christ Church College.** Called "the House" by its modest members, Christ Church has the largest quadrangle in town, named Tom Quad, after the over-6-ton bell in the tower. Christ Church is where Charles Dodgson, better known as Lewis Carroll, was a math don; a shop opposite the meadows in St. Aldate's was the inspiration for the shop in *Through the Looking Glass.* Don't miss the 800-year-old chapel, or the medieval dining hall, with its portraits of former students—John Wesley, William Penn, and 14 prime ministers. The dining hall should look familiar to fans of a certain young wizard: it appeared as the Hogwarts School dining hall in *Harry Potter.* ✉ *St. Aldate's,* ☎ *01865/276150,* WEB *www.chch.ox.ac.uk.* 🎫 *£4.* ⏲ *Mon.–Sat. 9–5:30, Sun. 12–5:30.*

Dining

££–£££ ✕ **Le Petit Blanc.** Raymond Blanc's Conran-designed brasserie is sophisticated even by London standards. The top British chef populates his menu with modern European and regional French dishes: you might see a goats' cheese soufflé with hazelnut dressing, or fresh salmon trout with lemon sabayon. At £12.50 for two courses or £15 for three, the prix-fixe lunch is an incredible value, and well worth the short walk north of town. ✉ *71–72 Walton St.,* ☎ *01865/510999. Reservations essential. AE, DC, MC, V.*

STRATFORD-UPON-AVON

Stratford-upon-Avon has become adept at accommodating the hordes of people who come for a glimpse of William Shakespeare's world. Punctuated with distinctive Tudor half-timber buildings that have survived from its 16th-century heyday as a crafts and trading center, Stratford is a handsome town. But it can feel, at times, like a literary amusement park, so if you're not a fan of Bill, you'd probably do better to explore some other quaint English village.

That said, how best to maximize your immersion in the Bard's works? It's difficult to avoid feeling like a herd animal as you board the Shakespeare bus, but tours like **Stratford and the Shakespeare Story** (✉ 14 Rother St., ☎ 01789/294466, WEB www.guidefriday.com, 🎫 £8.50), with a hop-on/hop-off route around the five Shakespeare Birthplace Trust properties—two of which are out of town—can make a visit infinitely easier if you don't have a car.

Exploring Stratford-upon-Avon

Most who visit Stratford start at **Shakespeare's Birthplace Museum.** The half-timber building in which Shakespeare grew up has been a national memorial since 1847, and it is now split in half: one part is a re-creation of a typical home of the time, while the other contains an intelligent biographical exhibit about Shakespeare, and a history of the house itself. ✉ *Henley St.,* ☎ *01789/204016,* WEB *www.shakespeare.org.uk.* 🎫 *£6; combined ticket with Shakespeare Birthplace Trust properties (Nash's House; Hall's Croft; Anne Hathaway's Cottage; Mary Arden's House; allow at least 4 hrs, but ticket is valid for one year) £12; 3 in-town properties (not including Anne Hathaway's Cottage and Mary Arden's House) £8.50.* ⏲ *Late Mar.–late Oct., Mon.–Sat. 9–5, Sun. 9:30–5; late Oct.–late Mar., Mon.–Sat. 9:30–4, Sun. 10–4.*

Nash's House, which belonged to Thomas Nash, first husband of Shakespeare's granddaughter Elizabeth Hall, now houses an exhibit charting the history of Stratford, against a backdrop of period furniture and tapestries. On the grounds of Nash's House is **New Place,** the home where the Bard spent his last years and died in 1616. An Elizabethan knot garden is set around the remaining foundation of the house, which was destroyed in 1759 by its last owner, Reverend Francis Gastrell, in an attempt to stop the tide of visitors. ✉ *Chapel St.,* ☎ *01789/292325,* WEB *www.shakespeare.org.uk.* 🎫 *£3.50, combined ticket with Shakespeare's Birthplace Trust properties £12, 3 in-town properties £8.50.* ⏲ *Late Mar.–late Oct., Mon.–Sat. 9:30–5, Sun. 10–5; late Oct.–late Mar., Mon.–Sat. 10–4, Sun. 10:30–4.*

Hall's Croft is Stratford's most beautiful Tudor town house. This was—almost definitely—the home of Shakespeare's daughter, Susanna, and her husband, Dr. John Hall. It's outfitted with furniture of the period and the doctor's dispensary, and the walled garden is delightful. ✉ *Old Town St.,* ☎ *01789/292107,* WEB *www.shakespeare.org.uk.* 🎫 *£3.50, combined ticket with Shakespeare's Birthplace Trust properties £12, 3 in-town properties £8.50.* ⏲ *Late Mar.–late Oct., Mon.–Sat. 9:30–5, Sun. 10–5; late Oct.–late Mar., Mon.–Sat. 10–4, Sun. 10:30–4.*

"Shakespeare's church," the 13th-century **Holy Trinity,** is fronted by a beautiful avenue of lime trees. Shakespeare is buried here, in the chancel. The bust of Shakespeare is thought to be an authentic likeness, executed a few years after his death. Last admission is 20 minutes before closing. ✉ *Trinity St.,* ☎ *01789/266316.* 🎫 *Church free, chancel £1.* ⏲ *Mar.–Oct., Mon.–Sat. 8:30–6, Sun. 2–5; Nov.–Feb., Mon.–Sat. 9–4, Sun. 2–5.*

On the bank of the Avon is the **Royal Shakespeare Theatre,** where the Royal Shakespeare Company performs in Stratford; they mount several productions each season. The design of the smaller **Swan Theatre,** in the same building, is based on the original Elizabethan Globe. It's best to book in advance, but day-of-performance tickets are nearly always available. Backstage tours take place around performances, so call ahead. ✉ *Waterside,* ☎ *01789/403403 box office, 01789/403405 tours,* WEB *www.rsc.org.uk.* 🎫 *Tours £4.* ⏲ *Tours weekdays 1:30, 5:30; Sun. hourly noon–3; matinee days (usually Thurs., Sat.) 11:30, 5:30.*

STRATFORD ENVIRONS

The two remaining stops on the Shakespeare trail are just outside Stratford. **Anne Hathaway's Cottage,** the early home of the playwright's wife, is possibly the most picturesque abode in Britain—a rather substantial thatched cottage, it has been restored to reflect the comfortable middle-class Hathaway life. You can walk—it's just over a mile from downtown Stratford. ✉ *Cottage Lane, Shottery,* ☎ *01789/292100,* WEB *www.shakespeare.org.uk.* 🎫 *£4.50, combined ticket with Shakespeare's Birthplace Trust properties £12.* ⏲ *Late Mar.–late Oct., Mon.–Sat. 9–5, Sun. 9:30–5; late Oct.–late Mar., Mon.–Sat. 9:30–4, Sun. 10–4.*

The **Shakespeare Countryside Museum,** with displays that illustrate life in the English countryside from Shakespeare's time to the present day, is the main attraction at **Palmer's Farm,** the site of a recent and radical Shakespearean revelation. In late 2000, research findings based on newly discovered real-estate records revealed that the property, which had been referred to since the 18th century as Mary Arden's House, was not in fact the house in which the Bard's mother grew up. The real **Mary Arden's House,** hitherto known as Glebe Farm, was actually nearby and (thankfully) already owned by the Shakespeare Birthplace Trust. ✉ *Wilmcote,* ☎ *01789/293455,* WEB *www.shakespeare.org.uk.* 🎫 *£5.50, combined ticket with Shakespeare's Birthplace Trust properties £12.* ⏲ *Late Mar.–late Oct., Mon.–Sat. 9:30–5, Sun. 10–5; late Oct.–late Mar., Mon.–Sat. 10–4, Sun. 10:30–4.*

Some 8 mi out of Stratford in the medieval town of Warwick, **Warwick Castle** fulfills anyone's most clichéd Camelot daydreams. This medieval, fortified, much-restored, castellated, moated, landscaped (by Capability Brown) castle, now managed by the experts at Madame Tussaud's, is a true period museum—complete with dungeons and a torture chamber, state rooms, and the occasional battle reenactment. ✉ *Off Mill St., Warwick,* ☎ *01926/495421; 08704/422000 24-hr information line,* WEB *www.warwick-castle.co.uk.* 🎫 *£10.25.* ⏲ *Apr.–Sept., daily 10–6; Oct.–Mar., daily 10–5.*

Dining

£–££ ✕ **Black Swan.** Known locally as the Dirty Duck, this is one of Stratford's most celebrated pubs—it has attracted actors since Garrick's days. A little veranda overlooks the theaters and the river here. Along with a pint of bitter, it's a fine place to enjoy English grill specialties, as well as braised oxtail and honey-roasted duck. You can also choose from an assortment of bar meals. ✉ *Waterside,* ☎ *01789/297312. AE, DC, MC, V. No dinner Sun.*

WINDSOR CASTLE

Windsor Castle, the largest inhabited castle in the world, is the star sight of Windsor, a quiet Berkshire town. Windsor Great Park, however, shouldn't be forgotten; Eton College, England's most famous public school, with its Old Village, is a lovely walk across the Thames from Windsor; and there's also the kid's paradise of Legoland.

Windsor is the only royal residence to have been in continuous royal use since the days of William the Conqueror, who chose this site to build a timber stockade soon after his conquest of Britain in 1066. It was Edward III in the 1300s who really founded the castle, building the Norman gateway, the great round tower, and the State Apartments. Charles II restored the State Apartments during the 1600s and, during the 1820s, George IV—with his mania for building—converted what was still essentially a medieval castle into the palace you see today. The queen uses Windsor a lot, spending most weekends here, often joined by family and friends. She's here when the Royal Standard is flown above the Round Tower but not when you see the Union Jack. Arrive early at the main entrance, as lines can be long.

Exploring Windsor Castle

The massive citadel occupies 13 acres, but the first part you notice on entering is the **Round Tower,** on top of which the Standard is flown and at the base of which is the 11th-century Moat Garden. Passing under the portcullis at the Norman Gate, you reach the **Upper Ward,** the quadrangle containing the State Apartments—which you may tour when the queen is out—and the sovereign's Private Apartments. Processions for foreign heads of state and other ceremonies take place here, as does the Changing of the Guard when the queen is in. A short walk takes you to the Lower Ward, where the high point is the magnificent **St. George's Chapel,** symbolic and actual guardian of the Order of the Garter, the highest chivalric order in the land, founded in 1348 by Edward III. Ten sovereigns are buried in the chapel—a fantastic Perpendicular Gothic vision 230 ft long, complete with gargoyles, buttresses, banners, swords, and choir stalls. This is also where royal weddings usually take place, the most recent having been that of Prince Edward and Sophie Rhys-Jones in June 1999.

The **State Apartments** are grander than Buckingham Palace's and have the added attraction of a few gems from the queen's vast art collection: choice canvases by Rubens, Rembrandt, Van Dyck, Gainsborough, Canaletto, and Holbein; da Vinci drawings; Gobelin tapestries; and limewood carvings by Grinling Gibbons. The entrance is through a grand hall holding cases crammed with precious china—some still used for royal banquets. Don't miss the outsize suit of armor in the armory, made for Henry VIII. Make sure you take in the magnificent views across to Windsor Great Park, the remains of a former royal hunting forest. One unmissable treat—and not only for children—is **Queen Mary's Dolls' House,** a 12:1 scale, seven-story palace with electricity, running water, and working elevators, designed in 1924 by Sir Edwin Lutyens. The detail is incredible—some of the miniature books in the library are by Kipling, Conan Doyle, Thomas Hardy, and G. K. Chesterton, written by the great authors in their own hand. The diminutive wine bottles hold the real thing, too.

In 1992, a fire that started in the queen's private chapel gutted some of the State Apartments. A swift rescue effort meant that, miraculously, hardly any works of art were lost, and a £37 million effort has restored the Grand Reception Room, the Green and Crimson drawing rooms, and the State and Octagonal dining rooms to their former, if not greater, glory. ✉ *Windsor Castle,* ☎ *01753/869898,* WEB *www.royalresidences.com.* 🎟 *£11, £8.50 Sun., £5.50 when State Apartments are closed.* ⏲ *Mar.–Oct., daily 9:45–5:15 (last admission at 4); Nov.–Feb., daily 9:45–4:15 (last admission at 3). St. George's Chapel closed Sun. except to worshipers.*

SIDE TRIPS A TO Z

To research prices, get advice from other travelers, and book travel arrangements, visit www.fodors.com.

BUS TRAVEL

National Express coach lines runs buses from Victoria Coach Station to six of the towns in this chapter. Coaches depart for Bath (3 hrs, 15 mins) every 90 minutes; for Brighton (2 hrs) hourly; for Cambridge (about 2 hrs) hourly; for Canterbury (1 hr, 50 mins) hourly; for Oxford (1 hr, 40 mins) about every half hour; and for Stratford-upon-Avon (3 hrs) about three times daily.

Take the Green Line bus to Windsor. It leaves from Stop 1 in front of the Colonnades Shopping Centre on Buckingham Palace Road, *not* from Victoria Coach Station. The fast direct service takes around 1 hour and runs hourly; the stopping services take up to 1 ½ hours or more.

FARES AND SCHEDULES

➤ BUS INFORMATION: **Green Line** (☎ 0870/608–7261, WEB www.greenline.co.uk). **National Express** (☎ 0870/580–8080, WEB www.nationalexpress.co.uk). **Victoria Coach Station** (✉ Buckingham Palace Rd. SW1).

TRAIN TRAVEL

Trains run from Paddington Station to Bath (90 mins, hourly departures), Oxford (55 mins, half-hourly departures), and Windsor (45 mins, departs half-hourly and requires one change). Direct trains leave Paddington for Stratford-upon-Avon (2 hrs, 20 mins) each morning; other routes depart from Marylebone (2½ hrs) and Euston (2½ hrs) stations and require a change at Leamington Spa. Direct trains for Windsor (50 mins, departs every 30 mins) depart hourly from Waterloo Station. Trains depart King's Cross Station hourly for Cambridge (1 hr). Victoria Station is the point of departure for rail service to Brighton (50 mins, hourly) and Canterbury (85 mins, half-hourly). There is also service to Brighton (1 hr, departures every 15 mins) and Canterbury (90 mins, half-hourly) from London Bridge Station.

FARES AND SCHEDULES

➤ TRAIN INFORMATION: **Railtrack** (☎ 0870/580–8080, WEB www.railtrack.co.uk).

TRANSPORTATION AROUND THE COUNTRYSIDE

Normally, the seven towns covered in this chapter are best reached by train. Bus travel costs less, but can take twice as long. However, train routes throughout Britain are often subject to delays as a result of engineering work being carried out on the national rail system. Wherever you're going, be sure to plan ahead for any day trip: check the latest timetables before you set off, and try to get an early start.

VISITOR INFORMATION

➤ TOURIST INFORMATION: **Bath Tourist Information Centre** (✉ Abbey Church Yard, ☎ 01225/477101, WEB www.visitbath.co.uk). **Brighton Tourist Information Centre** (✉ 10 Bartholomew Sq., ☎ 08457/573512, WEB www.tourism.brighton.co.uk). **Cambridge Tourist Information Centre** (✉ The Old Library, Wheeler St., ☎ 01223/322640, WEB www.cambridge.gov.uk/leisure/tourism.htm). **Canterbury Visitor Information Centre** (✉ 34 St. Margaret's St., ☎ 01227/766567, WEB www.canterbury.co.uk). **Oxford Information Centre** (✉ The Old School, Gloucester Green, ☎ 01865/726871, WEB www.oxford.gov.uk/tourism). The **Royal Windsor Information Centre** (✉ 24 High St., ☎ 01753/743900, WEB www.windsor.gov.uk). **Stratford Tourist Information Centre** (✉ Bridgefoot, ☎ 01789/293127, WEB www.shakespeare-country.co.uk).

9 PORTRAIT OF LONDON

VORACIOUS LONDON: A LITTLE DRINK OR TWO

Verlaine (1873) considered Londoners to be "noisy as ducks, eternally drunk," while Dostoevsky (1862) noted that "everyone is in a hurry to drink himself into insensibility." A German journalist, Max Schlesinger (1853), saw the inhabitants of a public house "standing, staggering, crouching, or lying down, groaning, and cursing, drink and forget." An observer closer to home, Charles Booth, noticed that drinking among women in the 1890s had materially increased. "One drunken woman in a street will set all the women in it drinking," he quotes one male inhabitant of the East End as saying. Nearly all women "get drunk of Monday. They say "we have our fling; we like to have a little fuddle on Monday.' " All classes of London women seem to have been drinking, largely because it was no longer considered wrong for a female to enter a public house for a "nip." In the evening, children of the poorer classes were sent around to the local public house to have a jug filled with ale; as Booth reported, "it was constant come and go, one moment to go in and get the jug filled, and out again the next; none of the children waited to talk or play with one another, but at once hurried home."

Gentlemen drank as deeply and freely as the poor. Thackeray noted those "who glory in drinking bouts" with "bottlenoses" and "pimpled faces." "I was so cut last night" is one of the phrases he recalled.

In each year of the nineteenth century, approximately 25,000 people were arrested for drunkenness in the streets. Yet the con ditions of life often drove poorer Londoners into their condition. One of them, a collector of "pure" (dog excrement) told Mayhew that he had often been drunk "for three months together"—he had "bent his head down to his cup to drink, being utterly incapable of raising it to his lips."

So even though the gin fever had subsided, and its shops closed down, its spirit—we might say—was continued in the "gin palaces" of the nineteenth century. These large establishments, clad in shining plate-glass windows with stucco rosettes and gilt cornices, were resplendent with advertisements lit by gas-lamps announcing "the only real brandy in London" or "the famous cordial, medicated gin, which is so strongly recommended by the faculty." The fine lettering reveals the attractions of "The Out and Out!," "The No Mistake," "The Good for Mixing" and "The real Knock-me-down." Yet the exterior brightness was generally deceptive; the scene within these "palaces" was a dismal one, almost reminiscent of the old gin-shops. There was characteristically a long bar of mahogany, behind which were casks painted green and gold, with the customers standing-or sitting on old barrels-along a narrow and dirty area beside it. It might be noted here, too, that social observers believed drink to be "at the root of all the poverty and distress with which they came into contact." Again the emphasis is upon the unhappy conditions of the city itself, literally driving men and women to drink with its relentless speed, urgency and oppression. Of the skeletons investigated in St. Bride's Lower Churchyard, "just under 10 per cent had at least one fracture." It is also revealed, in the fascinating London Bodies compiled by Alex Werner, that "almost half of these were rib fractures, commonly caused by stumbling or brawling."

In the same period the breweries had become one of the wonders of London, one of the sights to which foreign visitors were directed. By the 1830s there were twelve principal brewers, producing, according to Charles Knight's London, "two barrels, or 76 gallons, of beer per annum for every inhabitant of the metropolis-man, woman and child." Who would not want to observe all this industry and enterprise? One German visitor was impressed by the "vast establishment" of Whitbread's brewery in Chiswell Street, with its buildings "higher than a church" and its horses "the giants of their breed." In similar fashion, in the summer of 1827, a German prince "turned my 'cab' to Barclay's brewery, in Park Street, Southwark, which the vastness of its dimensions renders almost romantic." He observed that steam engines drove the machinery which manufactured from twelve to fifteen thousand barrels a day;

ninety-nine of the larger barrels, each one "as high as a house," are kept in "gigantic sheds"; 150 horses "like elephants" transport the beer. His awareness of the size and immensity of London are here reflected in its capacity for beer and, in a final parallel, he notes that from the roof of the brewery "you have a very fine panoramic view of London."

That emblematic significance was recognised by painters as well as visitors, and by the beginning of the nineteenth century there was established what London art historians have termed "the brewery genre." Ten years after the prince's visit, for example, Barclay's brewery was painted by an anonymous hand; the entrance is depicted, together with the thriving life of London all around it. To the right is the great brewhouse, with a suspension bridge connecting to the other side of the street. In the foreground a butcher's boy, in the blue apron typical of his trade, stands with another customer beside a baked-potato van; barrels of beer on sleds are being drawn by horses into the yard, passing a dray which is just leaving. In the street, to the right, a hansom cab is bringing in more visitors. It is a picture of appetite, with the meat carried on the shoulders of the butcher's boy as an apt token of the London diet, as well as of immense energy and industry.

But there are other ways of conveying the immensity of the city's drinking. Blanchard Jerrold and Gustave Doré visited the same premises for their London: a Pilgrimage—"the town of Malt and Hops" as Jerrold called it in 1871—in order to see the brewing of the beer named Entire which assuaged "Thirsty London." Jerrold noted that against the great towers and barrels the working men "look like flies," and indeed in Doré's engravings these dark anonymous shapes tend to their beer-mashing and beer-making duties like votaries; all is in shadow and chiaroscuro, with fitful gleams illuminating the activities of these small figures in vast enclosed spaces. Here again the life of the city is like that within some great decaying prison, with the metal pipes and cylinders as its bars and gates. Jerrold, like the German visitor before him, looked over London "with St. Paul's dominating the view from the north," and apostrophises beer as the city's sacred drink. "We are," he remarked, "upon classic ground."

The gin palace was supplanted by the public house which was the direct descendant of the tavern and the alehouse. Of course taverns survived in the older parts of London, known to their adherents for privacy and quiet, to their detractors for gloom and silence. Public houses continued the tradition of segregation, with saloon, lounge and private bars being distinguished from public bars and jug and bottle departments. Many pubs were not salubrious, with plain and dirty interiors and a long "zinc-topped" counter where men sat solemnly drinking—"You enter by a heavy door that is held ajar by a thick leather strap . . . striking you in the back as you go in and often knocking off your hat." Instead of the gin palace's long bar, the public house bar was characteristically in the shape of a horseshoe with the variously coloured bottles rising up within its interior space. The furniture was plain enough, with chairs and benches, tables and spittoons, upon a sawdusted floor. By 1870 there were some 20,000 public houses and beer-shops in the metropolis, catering to half a million customers each day, reminiscent of "dusty, miry, smoky, beery, brewery London."

A stranger asking directions in 1854, according to The Little World of London, was likely to be told "Straight on till you come to the Three Turks, then to turn to the right and cross over at the Dog and Duck, and go on again till you come to the Bear and the Bottle, then to turn the corner at the Jolly Old Cocks, and after passing the Veteran, the Guy Fawkes, the Iron Duke, to take the first turn to the right which will bring you to it." In this period there were seventy King's Heads and ninety King's Arms, fifty Queen's Heads and seventy Crowns, fifty Roses and twenty-five Royal Oaks, thirty Bricklayers Arms and fifteen Watermen's Arms, sixteen Black Bulls and twenty Cocks, thirty Foxes and thirty Swans. A favoured colour in pubs' names was red, no doubt complementing the analogy in London between drink and fire, while London's favourite number seemed to be three: the Three Hats, the Three Herrings, the Three Pigeons, and so on. There were also more mysterious signs such as the Grave Maurice, the Cat and Salutation and the Ham and Windmill.

The variety and plentitude of the nineteenth-century pubs continued well into the twentieth century, with the basic shape and nature changing very little, ranging from the munificent West End establishment to the sawdusted corner pub in Poplar or in Peckham. Then, in one of those paradoxes of London life, public houses became more mixed and lively places during the Second World War. The beer may have run out before the close of proceedings, and glasses may have been in short supply, but Philip Ziegler suggests in *London at War* that "they were the only places in wartime London where one could entertain and be entertained cheaply, and find the companionship badly needed during the war." There was an odd superstition that pubs were more likely to be hit by bombs, but this did not seem to affect their popularity; in fact, during the forced absence of men, women once again began to use pubs. A report of 1943 recorded that "they were often to be seen there with other women or even on their own." "Never had the London pubs been more stimulating," John Lehmann recalled, "never has one been able to hear more extraordinary revelations, never witness more unlikely encounters."

By the end of that war in 1945 there were still some four thousand pubs in the capital, and peace brought a new resurgence of interest. Novels and films have conveyed the atmosphere of pubs in the late 1940s and early 1950s, from the East End, where the men still wore caps and scarves and the girls danced "holding cigarettes in their fingers," to local saloons where what Orwell described as the "warm fog of smoke and beer" surrounded the "regulars."

— By Peter Akroyd

In *London: The Biography,* Peter Akroyd engagingly traces the growth of London, from the time of the Druids to the beginning of the 21st century. He evokes the city's history, habits, and idiosyncrasies through anecdotes and the voices of its citizens. The result is darkly funny and alarming, insightful and entertaining.

BOOKS & VIDEOS

London has been the focus of countless books and essays. For sonorous eloquence, you still must reach back more than half a century to Henry James's *English Hours* and Virginia Woolf's *The London Scene.* Today, most suggested reading lists begin with V. S. Pritchett's *London Perceived* and H. V. Morton's *In Search of London,* both decades old. Three more up-to-date books with a general compass are: Peter Ackroyd's anecdotal *London: The Biography,* which traces the city's growth from the Druids to the 21st century (☞ see the excerpt at the beginning of this chapter), John Russell's *London,* a sumptuously illustrated art book, and Christopher Hibbert's *In London: The Biography of a City.* Piet Schreuders's *The Beatles' London* follows the footsteps of the Fab Four.

That noted, there are books galore on the various facets of the city. *The Art and Architecture of London* by Ann Saunders is fairly comprehensive. *Inside London: Discovering the Classic Interiors of London,* by Joe Friedman and Peter Aprahamian, has magnificent color photographs of hidden and overlooked shops, clubs, and town houses. For a wonderful take on the golden age of the city's regal mansions, see Christopher Simon Sykes's *Private Palaces: Life in the Great London Houses.* For various other aspects of the city, consult Mervyn Blatch's helpful *A Guide to London's Churches,* Andrew Crowe's *The Parks and Woodlands of London,* Sheila Fairfield's *The Streets of London,* Ann Saunders' *Regent's Park,* Ian Norrie's *Hampstead, Highgate Village, and Kenwood,* and Suzanne Ebel's *A Guide to London's Riverside: Hampton Court to Greenwich.* For the last word on just about every subject, see *The London Encyclopaedia,* edited by Ben Weinreb and Christopher Hibbert.

Of course, the history and spirit of the city are also to be found in celebrations of great authors, British heroes, and architects. Peter Ackroyd's massive *Dickens* elucidates how the great author shaped today's view of the city; Martin Gilbert's magisterial, multivolume *Churchill* traces the city through some of its greatest trials; J. Mansbridge's *John Nash* details the London buildings of this great architect.

Nineteenth-century London—the city of Queen Victoria, Tennyson, and Dickens—comes alive through *Mayhew's London,* a massive study of the London poor, and Gustave Doré's *London,* an unforgettable series of engravings of the city (often reprinted in modern editions) that detail its horrifying slums and grand avenues. When it comes to fiction, of course, Dickens's immortal works top the list. Stay-at-home detectives have long walked the streets of London, thanks to great mysteries with London settings by Sir Arthur Conan Doyle, Dorothy L. Sayers, Agatha Christie, Ngaio Marsh, and Antonia Fraser. For a little-known fictional account of London's most deadly villain, Jack the Ripper, read Marie Belloc-Lowndes's *The Lodger.*

There are any number of films—from *Waterloo Bridge* and *Georgy Girl* to *Secrets and Lies* and *Notting Hill*—that have used London as their setting. But always near the top of anyone's list are four films that rank among the greatest musicals of all time: Walt Disney's *Mary Poppins,* George Cukor's *My Fair Lady,* Sir Carol Reed's *Oliver!,* and the Beatles' *A Hard Day's Night.*

LONDON AT A GLANCE: A CHRONOLOGY

Note that the dates given for British kings and queens are those of their reigns, not of their lives.

ca. 400 BC Early Iron Age hamlet built at Heathrow

54 BC Julius Caesar arrives with short-lived expedition

AD 43 Romans conquer Britain, led by the emperor Claudius

AD 50 First London Bridge built

AD 60 Boudicca, queen of the Iceni, razes the first Roman Londinium

ca. 100 The Romans make Londinium center of their British activities, though their capital remains at Camulodunum (now Colchester)

410 Roman rule of Britain ends

604 London's first bishop, Melitus, builds a cathedral in the name of St. Paul

700–800 Saxon trading town of Lundenwic (London) develops on the present site of Covent Garden and the Strand

886 Alfred the Great (871–99), king of the West Saxons, retakes the city; he is said to have "restored London and made it habitable"

1042 Edward the Confessor (1042–66) builds an abbey and palace at Westminster, and moves his court out of the City (London's original "square mile," now the financial district)

1066 William the Conqueror (1066–87), Duke of Normandy, wins the Battle of Hastings and is crowned William I

1067 William grants London a charter confirming its rights and privileges

1078 Tower of London construction begins with the building of the White Tower

1176–1209 After fire destroys the first London Bridge, a stone version is built by Peter de Colechurch

1191 First mayor of London elected

1265 First Parliament held in Westminster Abbey Chapter House

1314 Original St. Paul's Cathedral completed

1348–58 The Black Death kills one-third of London's population; 30,000 residents remain

1382 The Peasants' Revolt destroys part of the city

1476 In Westminster, William Caxton (1422–91) introduces printing to England

1529 Hampton Court given by Cardinal Wolsey to Henry VIII (1509–47); it becomes a favorite royal residence

1533 The Reformation: monasteries close and land goes to wealthy merchant families, creating new gentry

1558 Queen Elizabeth I (1558–1603) crowned

1568 Royal Exchange founded

1599 James Burbage (d.1619) opens the Globe Theatre on the South Bank

1605 Unsuccessful Gunpowder Plot to blow up the Houses of Parliament

1637 Hyde Park opens to the public

1649 Charles I (1625–49) beheaded outside the Banqueting House on Whitehall

1660 The Restoration: Charles II (1649–85) restored to the throne after years of exile in Europe

1665 The Great Plague: deaths reach approximately 100,000

1666 The Great Fire: London burns for three days; its medieval center is destroyed

1675 Sir Christopher Wren (1632–1723) begins work on the new St. Paul's Cathedral

1694 The Bank of England founded

1712 Georg Friedrich Handel (1685–1759) settles in London

1732 No. 10 Downing Street becomes the prime minister's official residence

1739 London's second bridge is built at Westminster

1755 Trooping the Colour (parade to celebrate the monarch's birthday) first performed for George II

1759 The British Museum opens to the public

1762 George III (1760–1820) makes Buckingham Palace a royal residence

1785 *The Times* newspaper is first published, as the *Daily Universal Register*

1801 First census records 1,117,290 people living in London

1802 First gaslights on London streets

1829–41 Trafalgar Square laid out

1834 The Houses of Parliament gutted by fire (the present Westminster Palace built 1840–52)

1836 The University of London established

1837 Victoria (1837–1901) assumes the throne. London Bridge rail station opens

1849 Harrods opens as a small grocery store

1851 The Great Exhibition, Prince Albert's brainchild, held in the Crystal Palace, Hyde Park

1863 Birth of the "Tube": First underground railway runs between Farringdon and Paddington stations

1869 Albert Embankment completed, first stage in containing the Thames's floodwaters

1877 First Wimbledon tennis tournament

1888 "Jack the Ripper" strikes Whitechapel

1897 Queen Victoria celebrates her Diamond Jubilee

1901 Victoria dies. London's population reaches about 4,500,000

1909 Selfridges department store opens

1914–18 World War I: London bombed (1915) by German zeppelins (670 killed, 1,962 injured)

1936 The BBC begins television broadcasting in north London

1939–45 World War II: during the Blitz (1940–41 and 1944–45), 45–50,000 bombs are dropped on London.

1946 Heathrow Airport opens

1951 The Festival of Britain lifts postwar morale

1952 Coronation of Queen Elizabeth II (born 1926)

1956 Clean Air Act abolishes open fires and makes London's "pea soup" fogs a romantic memory

1960–68 The Beatles, Twiggy, Mary Quant: "Swinging London" dominates the international music and fashion scenes

1965 Sir Winston Churchill's funeral, a great public pageant. Greater London Council established. First Notting Hill Carnival (now the biggest street fair in Europe)

1974 Covent Garden fruit-and-vegetable market moves across the Thames; the original buildings open in 1981 as a shopping and entertainment complex

1976 Royal National Theatre opens on the South Bank

1977 Queen Elizabeth II celebrates her Silver Jubilee

1981 Prince Charles marries Lady Diana Spencer in St. Paul's Cathedral

1982 July bombings in Hyde and Regent's Parks bring IRA violence to London

1983 The first woman Lord Mayor takes office

1984 The Thames Barrier, designed to prevent flooding in central London, is inaugurated

1986 The Greater London Council abolished by Parliament; London's population almost 7 million

1991 One Canada Square, Britain's tallest building, opens at Canary Wharf

1994 The Channel Tunnel opens a direct rail link between Britain and Europe

1996 The Prince and Princess of Wales receive a precedent-setting divorce. The reconstructed Shakespeare's Globe Theatre opens

1997 "New Labour" comes to power, with Tony Blair as Prime Minister. Princess Diana dies in car crash at age 36 in Paris.

2000 The Tate Modern opens to much fanfare in the former Bankside Power Station. The Queen Mum, Queen Elizabeth's mother, turns 100. London welcomes the 21st century with the Millennium Dome

2001 The Millennium Dome closes, its future uncertain. Prime Minister Tony Blair is elected to a second term

2002 Princess Margaret, the queen's sister, dies Feb. 9 at the age of 71; Queen Mum dies Mar. 30 at age 101; Queen Elizabeth II celebrates her Golden Jubilee

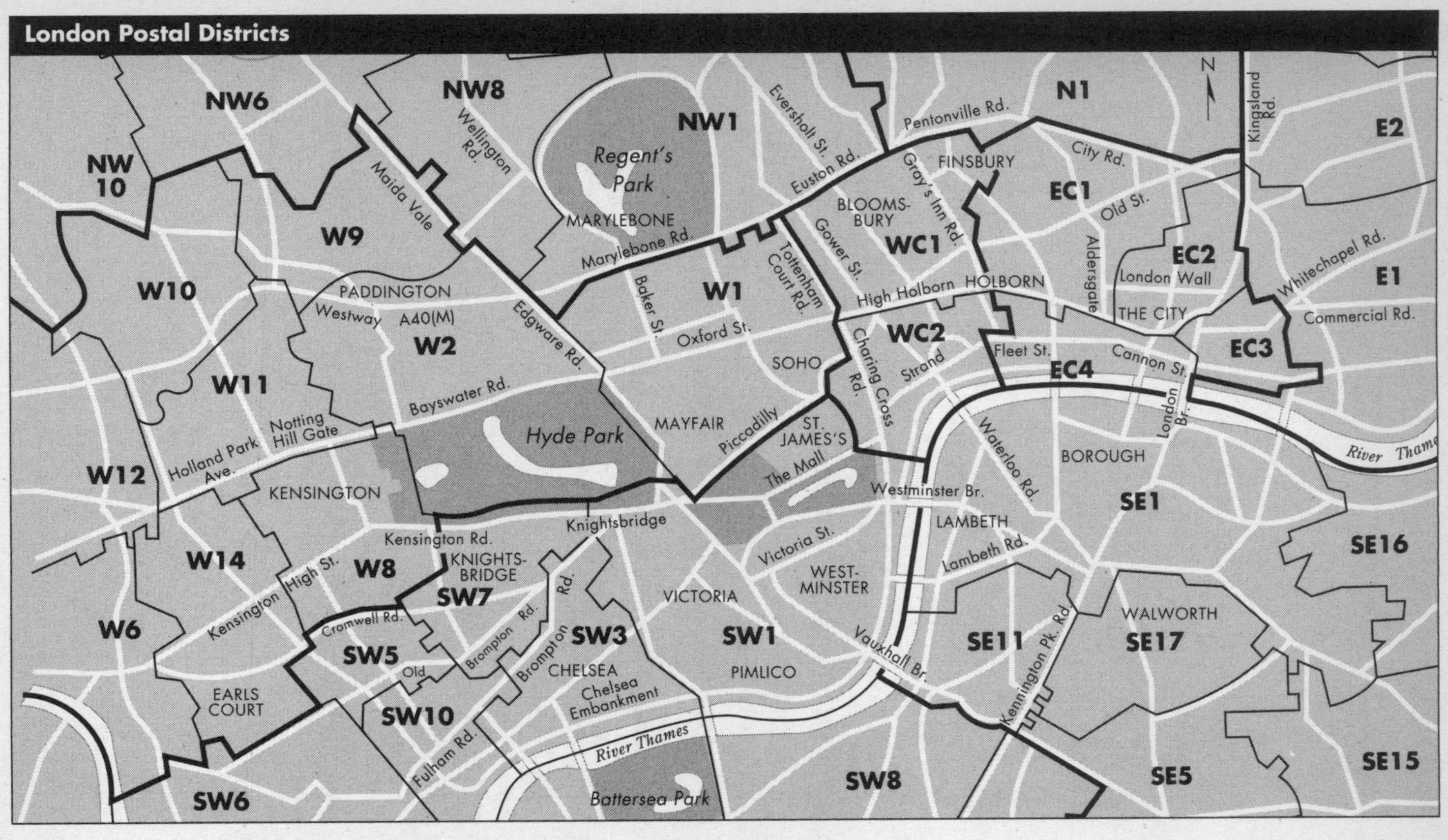
London Postal Districts
N
NW6
NW8
NW1
NW
10
N1
E2
E1
EC1
EC2
EC3
EC4
WC1
WC2
W1
W2
W6
W8
W9
W10
W11
W12
W14
SW1
SW3
SW5
SW6
SW7
SW8
SW10
SE1
SE5
SE11
SE15
SE16
SE17
Regent's Park
Hyde Park
Battersea Park
River Thames
MARYLEBONE
PADDINGTON
KENSINGTON
KNIGHTS-
BRIDGE
CHELSEA
EARLS
COURT
VICTORIA
PIMLICO
WEST-
MINSTER
LAMBETH
BOROUGH
WALWORTH
MAYFAIR
SOHO
ST.
JAMES'S
BLOOMS-
BURY
FINSBURY
HOLBORN
THE CITY
Wellington Rd.
Maida Vale
Marylebone Rd.
Eversholt St.
Euston Rd.
Pentonville Rd.
City Rd.
Old St.
Kingsland Rd.
Whitechapel Rd.
Commercial Rd.
London Wall
Aldersgate
Gray's Inn Rd.
Gower St.
Tottenham Court Rd.
High Holborn
Baker St.
Oxford St.
Edgware Rd.
Westway
A40(M)
Bayswater Rd.
Notting Hill Gate
Holland Park Ave.
Piccadilly
Charing Cross Rd.
Strand
Fleet St.
Cannon St.
London Br.
Waterloo Rd.
Westminster Br.
The Mall
Knightsbridge
Kensington Rd.
Kensington High St.
Cromwell Rd.
Brompton Rd.
Old Brompton Rd.
Fulham Rd.
Chelsea Embankment
Victoria St.
Vauxhall Br.
Lambeth Rd.
Kennington Pk. Rd.

INDEX

Icons and Symbols

★ Our special recommendations
✕ Restaurant
🏨 Lodging establishment
✕🏨 Lodging establishment whose restaurant warrants a special trip
🦆 Good for kids (rubber duck)
☞ Sends you to another section of the guide for more information
✉ Address
☎ Telephone number
🕒 Opening and closing times
🎟 Admission prices

Numbers in white and black circles ③ ❸ that appear on the maps, in the margins, and within the tours correspond to one another.

A

B

T

NOTES

NOTES

Fodor's Key to the Guides

America's guidebook leader publishes guides for every kind of traveler. Check out our many series and find your perfect match.

Fodor's Gold Guides
America's favorite travel-guide series offers the most detailed insider reviews of hotels, restaurants, and attractions in all price ranges, plus great background information, smart tips, and useful maps.

Fodor's Road Guide USA
Big guides for a big country—the most comprehensive guides to America's roads, packed with places to stay, eat, and play across the U.S.A. Just right for road warriors, family vacationers, and cross-country trekkers.

COMPASS AMERICAN GUIDES
Stunning guides from top local writers and photographers, with gorgeous photos, literary excerpts, and colorful anecdotes. A must-have for culture mavens, history buffs, and new residents.

Fodor's CITYPACKS
Concise city coverage with a foldout map. The right choice for urban travelers who want everything under one cover.

Fodor's EXPLORING GUIDES
Hundreds of color photos bring your destination to life. Lively stories lend insight into the culture, history, and people.

Fodor's POCKET GUIDES
For travelers who need only the essentials. The best of Fodor's in pocket-size packages for just $9.95.

Fodor's To Go
Credit-card–size, magnetized color microguides that fit in the palm of your hand—perfect for "stealth" travelers or as gifts.

Fodor's FLASHMAPS
Every resident's map guide. 60 easy-to-follow maps of public transit, parks, museums, zip codes, and more.

Fodor's CITYGUIDES
Sourcebooks for living in the city: Thousands of in-the-know listings for restaurants, shops, sports, nightlife, and other city resources.

Fodor's AROUND THE CITY WITH KIDS
68 great ideas for family days, recommended by resident parents. Perfect for exploring in your own backyard or on the road.

Fodor's ESCAPES
Fill your trip with once-in-a-lifetime experiences, from ballooning in Chianti to overnighting in the Moroccan desert. These full-color dream books point the way.

Fodor's FYI
Get tips from the pros on planning the perfect trip. Learn how to pack, fly hassle-free, plan a honeymoon or cruise, stay healthy on the road, and travel with your baby.

Fodor's Languages for Travelers
Practice the local language before hitting the road. Available in phrase books, cassette sets, and CD sets.

Karen Brown's Guides
Engaging guides to the most charming inns and B&Bs in the U.S.A. and Europe, with easy-to-follow inn-to-inn itineraries.

***Baedeker's* Guides**
Comprehensive guides, trusted since 1829, packed with A–Z reviews and star ratings.

At bookstores everywhere. www.fodors.com/books